BASIC PROCESSES IN
HELPING RELATIONSHIPS

BASIC PROCESSES IN HELPING RELATIONSHIPS

Edited by

Thomas Ashby Wills

Mahoney Institute for Health Maintenance
American Health Foundation
New York, New York

 1982

ACADEMIC PRESS

A Subsidiary of Harcourt Brace Jovanovich, Publishers

New York   London
Paris   San Diego   San Francisco   São Paulo   Sydney   Tokyo   Toronto

ACADEMIC PRESS, INC.
111 Fifth Avenue, New York, New York 10003

United Kingdom Edition published by
ACADEMIC PRESS, INC. (LONDON) LTD.
24/28 Oval Road, London NW1 7DX

Library of Congress Cataloging in Publication
Main entry under title:

Basic processes in helping relationships.

    Bibliography: p.
    Includes index.
    1. Helping behavior. 2. Counseling. 3. Psychotherapy.
4. Psychotherapist and patient. I. Wills, Thomas Ashby.
[DNLM: 1. Counseling. 2. Psychotherapy.
3. Interpersonal relations. 4. Professional relationships. 5. Professional-patient relations. 6. Helping
behavior. WM 55 B311]
BF637.H4B38   1982   616.89'14   82-8877
ISBN 0-12-757680-0   AACR2

To Joan, Joanne, and Rosemary

Contents

chapter 1

The Study of Helping Relationships 1

THOMAS ASHBY WILLS

PART I

DECISION PROCESSES 9

chapter 5

Personalistic Attributions and Client Perspectives in Child Welfare Cases: Implications for Service Delivery

81

LEROY H. PELTON

PART II

SOCIAL-PSYCHOLOGICAL PROCESSES

103

chapter 6

Attributions of Responsibility by Helpers and Recipients

107

JURGIS KARUZA, JR., MICHAEL A. ZEVON,
VITA C. RABINOWITZ, and PHILIP BRICKMAN

PART IV

PROCESSES IN THERAPEUTIC RELATIONSHIPS   281

chapter 13

The Role of Feedback in Help Seeking and the Therapeutic Relationship   287

C. R. SNYDER, RICK E. INGRAM, and CHERYL L. NEWBURG

chapter 14

Communication, Interpersonal Influence, and Resistance to Medical Treatment   307

D. DANTE DiNICOLA and M. ROBIN DiMATTEO

chapter 15

The Empirical Analysis of Help-Intended Communications: Conceptual Framework and Recent Research   333

ROBERT ELLIOTT, WILLIAM B. STILES, SAUL SHIFFMAN,
CHRISTOPHER B. BARKER, BONNIE BURSTEIN, and
GERALD GOODMAN

chapter 16

Similarity between Clinician and Client: Its Influence on the Helping Relationship   357

STEPHEN I. ABRAMOWITZ, ALLEN BERGER, and GIFFORD WEARY

chapter 17

Nonspecific Factors in Helping Relationships   381

THOMAS ASHBY WILLS

chapter 18

**Environmental Factors in Dependency among
Nursing Home Residents: A Social Ecology Analysis**   405

MARGRET M. BALTES

PART V

PROCESSES IN STRESS ON THE HELPER   427

chapter 19

The Organizational Context of Helping Relationships   431

RICK CRANDALL and RICHARD D. ALLEN

chapter 20

Helpers' Motivation and the Burnout Syndrome   453

AYALA PINES

PART VI

SUMMARY AND DISCUSSION   477

chapter 21

Directions for Research on Helping Relationships   479

THOMAS ASHBY WILLS

Contributors

Numbers in parentheses indicate the pages on which the authors' contributions begin.

Stephen I. Abramowitz (357), Department of Psychiatry, University of California, Davis, and Sacramento Medical Center, 2315 Stockton Boulevard, Sacramento, California 95817

Richard D. Allen (431), Counseling Center, University of San Francisco, San Francisco, California 94117

Toni C. Antonucci (233), Institute for Social Research and Department of Family Practice, University of Michigan, Ann Arbor, Michigan 48106

Margret M. Baltes (405), Department of Gerontopsychiatry, Free University of Berlin, University Clinic Charlottenburg, 1 Berlin 19, Ulmenallee 32, Federal Republic of Germany

Christopher B. Barker (333), Department of Educational Enquiry, The University of Aston in Birmingham, Birmingham B4 7ET, England

C. Daniel Batson (59), Department of Psychology, University of Kansas, Lawrence, Kansas 66045

Allen Berger (357), Department of Psychiatry, University of California, Davis, and Sacramento Medical Center, 2315 Stockton Boulevard, Sacramento, California 95817

Philip Brickman[1] (107, 187), Institute for Social Research, University of Michigan, Ann Arbor, Michigan 48106

[1] Deceased.

Fred B. Bryant (187), Institute for Social Research, University of Michigan, Ann Arbor, Michigan 48106

Bonnie Burstein (333), Department of Psychology, University of California, Los Angeles, Los Angeles, California 90024

Rick Crandall[2] (431), Department of Psychology, University of San Francisco, San Francisco, California 94117

Robyn M. Dawes (37), Department of Psychology, University of Oregon, Eugene, Oregon 97403 and Center for Advanced Study in the Behavioral Sciences, 202 Junipero Serra Boulevard, Stanford, California 94305

Bella M. DePaulo (255), Department of Psychology, University of Virginia, Charlottesville, Virginia 22901

Charlene E. Depner (233), Survey Research Center, Institute for Social Research, University of Michigan, Ann Arbor, Michigan 48106

M. Robin DiMatteo (307), Department of Psychology, University of California, Riverside, Riverside, California 92521

D. Dante DiNicola (307), School of Medicine, University of California, Los Angeles, Los Angeles, California 90024

Robert Elliott (333), Department of Psychology, The University of Toledo, Toledo, Ohio 43606

Peter A. Fehrenbach (13), Department of Psychiatry and Behavioral Sciences, GI-80, University of Washington, Seattle, Washington 98109

Jeffrey D. Fisher (131), Department of Psychology, University of Connecticut, Storrs, Connecticut 06268

Gerald Goodman (333), Department of Psychology, University of California, Los Angeles, Los Angeles, California 90024

Rick E. Ingram (287), Graduate Training Program in Clinical Psychology, Department of Psychology, University of Kansas, Lawrence, Kansas 66045

Jurgis Karuza, Jr. (107), Department of Psychology, State University College at Buffalo, 1300 Elmwood Avenue, Buffalo, New York 14222

Jeanne Parr Lemkau (187), Departments of Family Practice and Psychiatry, Wright State University School of Medicine, 601 Miami Boulevard West, Dayton, Ohio 45408

Roger E. Mitchell (213), Social Ecology Laboratory, Department of Psychiatry and Behavioral Sciences, Stanford University School of Medicine and Veterans Administration Medical Center, Palo Alto, California 94305

Rudolf H. Moos (213), Social Ecology Laboratory, Department of Psychiatry and Behavioral Sciences, Stanford University School of Medicine, and Veterans Administration Medical Center, Palo Alto, California 94305

Arie Nadler (131), Department of Psychology, School of Social Work, Tel-Aviv University, 69978 Ramat-Aviv, Israel

Cheryl L. Newburg (287), Graduate Training Program in Clinical Psychology, Department of Psychology, University of Kansas, Lawrence, Kansas 66045

[2]*Present address:* Crandall Associates, 5093 Paradise Drive, Tiburon, California 94920

Michael R. O'Leary[3] (13), Department of Psychiatry and Behavioral Sciences, University of Washington School of Medicine and Veterans Administration Medical Center, Seattle, Washington 98108

Karen O'Quin (59), Department of Psychology, University of Kansas, Lawrence, Kansas 66045

Leroy H. Pelton[4] (81), New Jersey Division of Youth and Family Services, 1 South Montgomery Street, Trenton, New Jersey 08625

Ayala Pines (453), Department of Psychology, University of California, Berkeley, Berkeley, California 94720

Virginia Pych (59), Department of Psychology, University of Kansas, Lawrence, Kansas 66045

Vita C. Rabinowitz (107), Psychology Department, Hunter College, New York, New York 10021

Judith Rodin (155), Department of Psychology, Yale University, New Haven, Connecticut 06520

Dennis Schorr (155), Department of Psychology, Yale University, New Haven, Connecticut 06520

Saul Shiffman (333), Department of Psychology, University of South Florida, Tampa, Florida 33620

C. R. Snyder (287), Graduate Training Program in Clinical Psychology, Department of Psychology, University of Kansas, Lawrence, Kansas 66045

William B. Stiles (333), Department of Psychology, Miami University, Oxford, Ohio 45056

Gifford Weary (357), Department of Psychology, The Ohio State University, 164 West 19th Avenue, Columbus, Ohio 43210

Thomas Ashby Wills (1, 381, 479), Mahoney Institute for Health Maintenance, American Health Foundation, 320 East 43rd Street, New York, New York 10017

Michael A. Zevon (107), Department of Psychology, State University College at Buffalo, 1300 Elmwood Avenue, Buffalo, New York 14222

[3]*Present address:* Kitsap Psychiatric Associates, 2500 Cherry Avenue, Bremerton, Washington 98310

[4]*Present address:* Plainsboro, New Jersey 08536

Preface

In recent years there has been considerable research on helping, and particularly on the effects of formal psychotherapy. The quality of outcome research conducted in clinical settings has been high and the results have been generally consistent. These results, however, have raised more questions than they have answered. We now know that helping interventions have a significant impact on the participants; but it is not at all clear what processes are involved in an effective helping relationship. We need a better understanding of the psychological processes involved in the development of a productive interpersonal relationship between a helper and a recipient.

This volume began with my interest in how the helper's and recipient's perceptions of each other are influenced by participation in a helping relationship. A consideration of evidence from both traditional psychotherapy and other types of professional helping relationships indicated some basic conclusions about the consequences of helping. At the same time, other programs of research on helping processes by clinical and social psychologists were beginning, and the results suggested new perspectives on the nature of helping relationships. This work has important implications for the way in which helping relationships are construed, as well as for the design and evaluation of helping interventions.

The purpose of this volume is to integrate current research on basic psychological processes in helping relationships. Rather than concentrating on therapy outcome research, this book focuses on the processes that are involved in helping interactions, both from the helper's viewpoint and the client's viewpoint. The chapters report new and important findings from research programs that have taken directions differing somewhat from traditional investigations of helping. Topics covered include decision and attribution processes, psychological processes in help seeking, clients' perceptions of the helping relationship and their reactions to receiving help, the development of commitment (versus resistance) to the helping relationship, processes that define the nature of a therapeutic relationship, and organizational influences on helper–client interaction. The work reported here has been conducted in a variety of settings: psychological laboratories, inpatient hospitals, outpatient clinics, public schools, social work agencies, drug treatment centers, and gerontology settings. In each case the contributors discuss their findings to show the implications for helping relationships in general.

This book will be of interest to researchers and practitioners in various helping professions. The contributors suggest creative ideas about, and approaches to, basic research on helping relationships; their proposals will stimulate discussion and further research by academic faculty, graduate students in psychology or related disciplines, and clinician researchers. The chapters also present specific suggestions on how to increase the effectiveness of helping interventions. Practitioners will find here many approaches that apply to their direct work with clients and will deepen their understanding of therapeutic interaction.

The book is organized into five sections that provide a comprehensive perspective on helping relationships. Part I covers basic decision processes, discussing several ways in which biasing factors may affect clinical judgment. Part II presents recent work on social-psychological processes in helping relationships: attribution, self-esteem maintenance, perceived control, and commitment. In Part III the importance of informal social support networks and help seeking from nonprofessionals is considered. Part IV discusses therapeutic relationships and environments, delineating the factors that contribute to (or interfere with) effective therapeutic interaction. The final section introduces recent research showing ways in which the process of helping produces stress on the helpers themselves.

Acknowledgments

I would like to express my gratitude to the contributors to this volume, who combine theoretical creativity with practical perseverance in the conduct of research. This volume also owes much to the efforts of social and clinical psychologists who provided the empirical findings that represent the point of departure for this work. Clinicians often feel (with some justification) that outsiders do not appreciate the complexity of therapeutic interaction and the challenge of designing research that reflects the reality of clinical settings. At the same time, social psychologists feel—again with justification—that their efforts are underappreciated by clinical professionals, who may think that any study done in a laboratory is, ipso facto, devoid of generality or clinical significance. At present, both clinical researchers and social-psychological researchers have a good deal to show for their efforts. I hope that the present volume will continue this work and lead to a more complete understanding of helping relationships.

I would also like to thank the staff of Academic Press for their careful attention to this volume. I appreciate the professionalism that these individuals showed in dealing capably and cheerfully with both the lofty issues and the specific details of scientific publication.

Finally, I wish to note that the contribution of Philip Brickman to this book was considerable. Phil was involved in the volume in many ways: through the conceptual formulation he originated on attributional models of helping and his nurturing of a generation of innovative researchers, by suggesting possible contributors during the early stages of the volume, by working actively as a co-author for several of the chapters, through comments about words, titles, commas, and other marks of the attention to detail that is shown by a dedicated scholar. This book owes a great deal to Phil's ideas and energy—as one of the authors (Jeanne Parr Lemkau) put it, "He was in the vanguard of the movement to build conceptual bridges and collegial networks to bring the clinical and social-psychological worlds closer together"—and numerous concepts in this volume are, directly or indirectly, the fruits of Philip Brickman's work and influence. The death of this brilliant and likable man was a tragedy in all senses of the word and a terrible loss to the profession and the world.

chapter 1

The Study of Helping Relationships

THOMAS ASHBY WILLS

Introduction

When one person sits down and tries to help another, what ensues? What processes are involved in a relationship between a helper and a recipient? These are the questions addressed by this volume. The goal is to arrive at a better understanding of how a helping relationship works. Like other human relationships, a helping relationship is a complex social interaction, involving several types of processes at different levels of analysis. In order to understand what actually occurs in helping, we should have sound knowledge of the basic processes involved. The purpose of this book is to provide a comprehensive picture of current research on the psychological processes that are funda-mental aspects of a helping relationship.

Past research on formal helping relationships has resolved several issues, but has also raised a number of important questions. For example, a quantitative review of psychotherapy outcome studies by Smith, Glass, and Miller (1980) provided compelling evidence that therapy produces beneficial effects for clients. This review also showed, however, that there was essentially comparable effectiveness for different therapies varying widely in theoretical background and treatment approach. Why such radically different therapies

1

are all effective to the same extent is a question that deserves an answer. Also, a review by Durlak (1979) showed that there was no overall difference in effectiveness between highly trained professional helpers and untrained laypersons. How untrained helpers achieve such effective results is not known at the present time. These findings, and other evidence from the clinical literature, indicate a need for more basic research on the helping relationship itself.

Other findings have raised profound questions about how a helping relationship develops. It usually has been assumed that extended therapeutic interaction is necessary for personality change to occur, yet the evidence shows that a therapeutic relationship develops quite rapidly. Smith *et al.* (1980) found no correlation between duration of therapy and outcome effect size; for all practical purposes, the observed benefit from a few sessions of therapy is equivalent to that from 10, 20, or more sessions. Several studies of psychotherapy (Bishop, Sharf, & Adkins, 1975; Brown, 1970; Meehl, 1960) have shown that therapists' perceptions of outpatient clients crystallize rapidly, typically within one or two sessions; similar results also have been found for hospital staff perceptions of inpatients (Rosenzweig & Harford, 1972; Shader, Kellam, & Durell, 1967). With regard to the interpersonal relationship between helper and client, studies of psychotherapy and behavior therapy (Ford, 1978; Saltzman, Luetgert, Roth, Creaser, & Howard, 1976) show that liking between therapist and client—which itself strongly determines the subsequent therapeutic outcome—is essentially established within the first two or three sessions of therapy. Findings such as these do not fit easily into existing formulations of psychotherapy, and suggest that more needs to be known about how the basic relationship between helper and client is established.

It was traditionally assumed that client improvement in therapy depended on the application of specific technical skills, derived from a theoretical system of psychotherapy and implemented by a trained professional. However, the evidence just considered makes this seem unlikely. Here it is taken as a given that therapeutic gain, broadly construed (namely increased self-esteem, self-control, and ability to deal effectively with social situations), is based on a significant relationship with another person, characterized by feelings of mutual respect, acceptance, and liking or positive regard.[1] This has been shown consistently in studies of clients' perceptions of therapy (e.g., Ford, 1978; Saltzman *et al.*, 1976), as well as by all other evidence on the subject (see, e.g., Strupp, 1977). How this actually occurs is the question that needs an answer: how the interpersonal perceptions of helper and client can develop so rapidly; how the interpersonal relationship between helper and client

---

[1]This is not to argue that the interpersonal relationship by itself is entirely responsible for a successful therapy outcome. Several different factors are involved in the initiation and maintenance of client improvement (for further discussion see Chapter 17, by Wills, in this volume).

develops or dissolves; how the interpersonal relationship is related to the client's self-perceptions, expectations for improvement, or general sense of self-efficacy and perceived control. These are the issues addressed in this volume.

Formulation of the Helping Relationship

The approach taken in this book is to consider a helping relationship (whether by a professional therapist or a nonprofessional) in the same terms as other social relationships.[2] This leads to consideration of a number of processes traditionally examined in social-psychological studies of interpersonal relationships, for example, the liking between the participants, their perceptions and attributions about each other, and the role of perceived choice and commitment processes. This formulation tends to deemphasize the distinction between professional therapists and other helpers; approximately equal weight is given to treatment by highly trained professionals, to consultation with nonprofessional helpers, and to social support and informal help seeking involving friends and family members. At the same time, this approach leads to greater emphasis on situational factors in helping relationships and the effect that the context of the relationship has on the interaction between the participants. Thus, specific attention is given to the role of situational (compared with personality) factors in clients' problems, and to the way in which organizational aspects of helping institutions affect the helper's orientation toward the client. Such influences may be expected to affect not only the helper–client interaction but also the therapist's own attitudes and psychological well-being.

The present formulation of a helping relationship draws more attention to client variables: how clients perceive their own problems, the helper, and the therapeutic relationship. Although research on clients' perceptions of therapy has been sparse, the results have been remarkably consistent, showing that client ratings are as good—if not better—predictors of therapy outcome than ratings by therapists (e.g., Lambert, DeJulio, & Stein, 1978). In this volume, extensive consideration is given to the attributional models with which clients view their problems, how clients react to receiving help, and how their perceptions change over the course of therapy. Not least, specific attention is given to the client's decision to seek help in the first place, a decision that surely has important consequences for the client's self-image and perception of self-efficacy, as well as for the helping relationship itself.

The emphasis on client perceptions leads to a focus on the reciprocal,

[2]Indeed, there is evidence that what are usually construed as therapeutic conditions in psychotherapy are found with comparable frequency outside of professional relationships (e.g., Armstrong, 1969; Shapiro, Krauss, & Truax, 1969).

interactive nature of a helping relationship; an interpersonal relationship is, by its very nature, an interaction between two parties who react to each others' behavior. The clinical evidence, although again somewhat sparse, provides compelling support for this formulation. Studies of variance components in ratings of psychotherapy sessions have shown consistently that most of the variance is accounted for not by therapist or patient main effects but by the interaction between therapist, patient, and session in therapy (Houts, MacIntosh, & Moos, 1969; Howard, Orlinsky, & Perilstein, 1976; Moos & Clemes, 1967; Moos & MacIntosh, 1970; van der Veen, 1965). Thus, considerable attention is given to exploring how the outcome of a helping relationship develops from the initial perceptions of therapist and client, their respective reactions to giving and receiving help, and the subsequent development of a therapeutic alliance.

Following from the emphasis on reciprocal aspects of helping is a formulation of a helping relationship as an influence process, an approach that has notable precedents in the clinical literature (e.g., Haley, 1963; Strupp, 1976). This leads to a detailed consideration of the processes of perceived freedom and psychological reactance (e.g., Brehm & Brehm, 1981), discussing how clients may react against the influence emanating from the helper, how clients maintain a sense of perceived control and self-guidance while simultaneously accepting assistance from another person, and how the client makes attributions about the causal basis for his or her own behavior change. Although these issues have been examined in the literature at one time or another, the research reported in this book is beginning to provide a systematic examination of these processes in clinical settings.

Overview of Processes in Helping Relationships

To summarize the types of processes considered in this volume, a conceptual model of helping relationships is presented in Figure 1.1. As a background to initial help seeking, problems develop because of situational, interpersonal, or personality factors, or more probably a complex interaction of all three factors. Subjective distress leads initially to support seeking from informal networks—a process that is only beginning to be clarified in current research. Persistence of distress, it is posited, ultimately leads a person to a crucial decision: to seek help from a formal helping agency. The act of making this decision undoubtedly represents a profound turning point in a person's life.[3] Once formal help seeking has been initiated, a treatment decision is made by the therapist based on a (rapid) assessment of the nature of the

[3] Epidemiological studies have shown that even at the highest levels of subjective distress, only 50% (at most) of persons in the community ever seek professional psychological help (see Wills, in press).

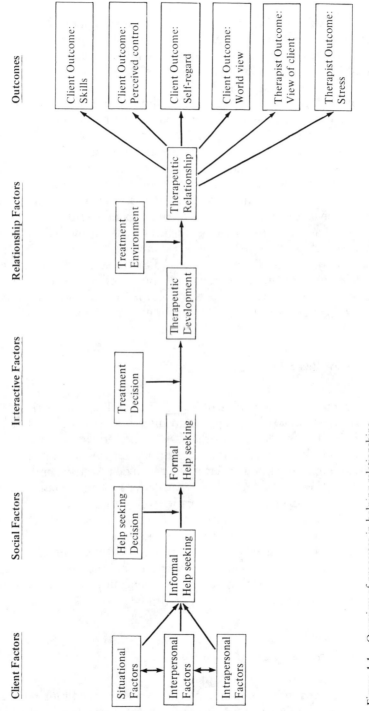

Client Factors   **Social Factors**   **Interactive Factors**   **Relationship Factors**   **Outcomes**

Figure 1.1.   Overview of processes in helping relationships.

client's problem, suitability for therapy, and compatibility with the therapist. Another rapid occurrence is early development of the relationship between therapist and client, elaboration of their views and expectations about therapy, and establishment of commitment to therapeutic effort (versus dropout from treatment). Given that this initial stage is passed, from the second or third session of therapy there follows (in traditional inpatient or outpatient treatment) an extended therapeutic relationship, with more extensive work on the client's problems. At this stage of helping, factors in the treatment environment may act to influence the interaction between helper and client, and perhaps the ultimate outcome of helping. It is posited that a helping relationship ultimately produces a range of outcomes, including changes not only in the client's overt symptomatology but also in specific social skills, in sense of perceived control, and in the client's general world view. In addition, it is evident that a helping relationship has effects on the helper. Observed consequences of professional helping experience are a shift toward a less positive view of clients (Fehrenbach & O'Leary, Chapter 2 in this volume; Wills, 1978) and an increased level of perceived stress on the helpers themselves. The work reported in this volume provides several suggestions about how these shifts in helpers' perceptions may occur.

Generality of Basic Processes

In the context of the approach I have outlined, a central thesis of this volume is that a basic process applies to many different varieties of helping relationships. If a psychological process is identified that is truly basic to a helping relationship, then it should be important for helping situations in general (although the particular setting in which help is given, and the specific training and approach of the helper, may differ in some details). Thus, this volume considers evidence from a variety of settings, including not only formal psychotherapy but also inpatient alcoholism treatment, child welfare interventions, peer counseling, social work intervention for the elderly, primary medical care, nursing homes, and drug treatment clinics. I think that the results presented in this book show that the processes in question apply to many settings in which helping occurs. The generality of the effects suggests that basic processes have in fact been identified.

Overview of the Chapters

The chapters that follow report empirical research on helping relationships and discuss the implications of the findings for research and practice. The content and approach of the individual chapters reflect the current state of research. Some chapters are more conceptually oriented, presenting a framework that provides a productive way of viewing the helping process. Some chapters report original research on helping relationships that is currently under way; others review and integrate extensive research programs. Throughout the volume, an attempt is made to derive clinical applications from the empirical findings. The aim of the contributors is to provide creative ideas and approaches that will lead to new developments in basic research and, ultimately, to improvements in clinical practice.

References

Armstrong, J. C. Perceived intimate friendship as a quasi-therapeutic agent. *Journal of Counseling Psychology*, 1969, *16*, 137–141.

Bishop, J. B., Sharf, R. S., & Adkins, D. M. Counselor intake judgments, client characteristics, and number of sessions at a university counseling center. *Journal of Counseling Psychology*, 1975, *22*, 557–559.

Brehm, S. S., & Brehm, J. W. *Psychological reactance: A theory of freedom and control.* New York: Academic Press, 1981.

Brown, R. D. Experienced and inexperienced counselors' first impressions of clients and case outcomes: Are first impressions lasting? *Journal of Counseling Psychology*, 1970, *17*, 550–558.

Durlak, J. A. Comparative effectiveness of paraprofessional and professional helpers. *Psychological Bulletin*, 1979, *86*, 80–92.

Ford, J. D. Therapeutic relationship in behavior therapy: An empirical analysis. *Journal of Consulting and Clinical Psychology*, 1978, *46*, 1302–1314.

Haley, J. *Strategies of psychotherapy.* New York: Grune & Stratton, 1963.

Houts, D. B., MacIntosh, S., & Moos, R. H. Patient–therapist interdependence: Cognitive and behavioral. *Journal of Consulting and Clinical Psychology*, 1969, *33*, 40–45.

Howard, K. I., Orlinsky, D. E., & Perilstein, J. Contribution of therapists to patients' experiences in psychotherapy: A components of variance model for analyzing process data. *Journal of Consulting and Clinical Psychology*, 1976, *44*, 520–526.

Lambert, M. J., DeJulio, S. S., & Stein, D. M. Therapist interpersonal skills: Process, outcome, methodological considerations, and recommendations for future research. *Psychological Bulletin*, 1978, *85*, 467–489.

Meehl, P. E. The cognitive activity of the clinician. *American Psychologist*, 1960, *15*, 19–27.

Moos, R. H., & Clemes, S. R. Multivariate study of the patient–therapist system. *Journal of Consulting and Clinical Psychology*, 1967, *31*, 119–130.

Moos, R. H., & MacIntosh, S. Multivariate study of the patient–therapist system: A replication and extension. *Journal of Consulting and Clinical Psychology*, 1970, *35*, 298–307.

Rosenzweig, S. P., & Harford, T. Correlates of therapists' initial impressions of patients in a psychiatric day center. *Psychotherapy: Theory, Research and Practice*, 1972, *9*, 126–129.

Saltzman, C., Luetgert, M. J., Roth, C. H., Creaser, J., & Howard, L. Formation of a therapeutic relationship: Experiences during the initial phase of psychotherapy as predictors of treatment duration and outcome. *Journal of Consulting and Clinical Psychology*, 1976, *44*, 546–555.

Shader, R. I., Kellam, S. G., & Durell, J. Social field events during the first-week of hospitalization as predictors of treatment outcome for psychotic patients. *Journal of Nervous and Mental Disease*, 1967, *145*, 142–153.

Shapiro, J. G., Krauss, H. H., & Truax, C. B. Therapeutic conditions and disclosure beyond the therapeutic encounter. *Journal of Counseling Psychology*, 1969, *16*, 290–294.

Smith, M. L., Glass, G. V., & Miller, T. I. *The benefits of psychotherapy.* Baltimore: Johns Hopkins Univ. Press, 1980.

Strupp, H. H. The nature of the therapeutic influence and its basic ingredients. In A. Burton (Ed.), *What makes behavior change possible?* New York: Brunner/Mazel, 1976.

Strupp, H. H. A reformulation of the dynamics of the therapist's contribution. In A. S. Gurman & A. M. Razin (Eds.), *Effective psychotherapy: A handbook of research.* New York: Pergamon, 1977.

van der Veen, F. Effects of the therapist and the patient on each other's therapeutic behavior. *Journal of Consulting Psychology,* 1965, *29,* 19–26.

Wills, T. A. Perceptions of clients by professional helpers. *Psychological Bulletin,* 1978, *85,* 968–1000.

Wills, T. A. Social comparison and help-seeking. In B. M. DePaulo, A. Nadler, & J. D. Fisher (Eds.), *New directions in helping* (Vol. 2): *Help-seeking.* New York: Academic Press, in press.

PART I

DECISION PROCESSES

One of the fundamental aspects of a helping relationship is the judgments and decisions that a helper makes about a client. These include decisions about prognosis, acceptance for treatment, judgments about the nature of the client's problem, and (if there is much latitude about the services available) assignment to a treatment method. Such decisions obviously have important implications for the client's well-being and the outcome of the helping relationship.

Early work in this area assumed that an informal, intuitive, or "clinical" approach to judgment processes was preferable to other approaches. This notion was soon questioned, however, by evidence showing that clinical judgments made from extensive psychological test results were no more accurate than judgments made from simple demographic information (see Megargee, 1966), and that predictions made through simple mathematical procedures were consistently superior to predictions made through informal judgment (Goldberg, 1970). Subsequent research has confirmed the validity of these findings; in the entire literature there is no study that has shown informal judgment procedures to be superior to predictions made from a simple linear statistical model.

Against this background, recent research has moved to examine the

9

dimensions actually used in clinical judgments and the processes that might, in various ways, represent biasing factors in the judgment process. One such factor is the therapist's personal liking versus disliking for the client. In Chapter 2 Fehrenbach and O'Leary report an extensive research program, conducted in both inpatient and outpatient settings, showing that clinical judgments are influenced to a significant extent by interpersonal attraction. The investigators have replicated their basic findings across a number of different studies and clinical contexts. The results of this work indicate that clinicians' basic judgments about clients are formed quite rapidly and that therapist liking for a client is related to treatment decisions. These studies also confirm a formulation based on previous findings suggesting that professional helping experience produces a negative tendency in perceptions of clients (Wills, 1978). The authors discuss several processes that may account for this tendency among clinicians in the settings they studied.

Chapter 3, by Dawes, discusses evidence on the superiority of explicit decision processes over informal judgments and shows why formal decision procedures are consistently superior. The mathematical and empirical basis for this approach is compelling, yet as Meehl (1973) noted there is resistance among practitioners to the use of formal decision procedures. Dawes also discusses several tendencies that have been demonstrated to produce bias in informal judgments. These processes are not unique to clinicians, for they all have been demonstrated in the general population. Yet there is presumptive evidence that these biasing factors are operative in clinical judgments made in applied settings. One striking aspect in Dawes's chapter is his demonstration that the biasing factors all operate so as to produce overestimates of pathology. This is in fact what the evidence on helpers' perceptions of clients shows (see Wills, 1978). Dawes also suggests a simple procedure for countering judgment bias: Just keep a record of the input to your decisions and the eventual outcomes.

Another aspect of clinical decision making is the basic attributional judgment that the helper makes about the nature of the client's problem. Every time that a therapist confronts a new client, a basic judgment must be made about the extent to which the client's distress is caused by a personality problem, by a situational difficulty, or by some kind of interaction between personality and situation. (For an excellent discussion of this judgment process, see Kanfer & Goldstein, 1980, pp. 7–8.) Research on person perception had previously shown a general tendency for people to attribute others' behavior to personality factors, but to attribute their own behavior more to situational factors. The questions soon arose as to whether helpers' judgments of clients' problems have a comparable tendency toward personalistic attributions and whether this tendency is accentuated by clinical training and experience. In Chapter 4 Batson, O'Quin, and Pych provide a comprehensive, logical examination of this issue. Their conclusion is a cautious one; although the available evidence consistently shows that trained helpers (compared with other sources) are more likely to make personalistic attributions about clients,

Batson *et al.* suggest that this does not, prima facie, prove bias. They note some of the methodological difficulties for obtaining valid measurements of attributions about clients' problems—particularly attributions as the *client*, rather than the investigator, views them—and make some valuable suggestions about further research that would provide a more conclusive answer to the hypothesis of attributional bias among helpers. In addition, Batson *et al.* report some laboratory research showing how the available helping resources may shape the helper's treatment decisions.

The possibility of attributional bias is an important issue for professional helpers. Traditional diagnostic systems were almost exclusively concerned with intrapsychic (intrapersonal) factors, with little attention to interpersonal or situational factors, and many treatment approaches were designed with an intrapsychic focus. Recent research has suggested, however, that situational variables (particularly economic factors) and interpersonal variables are related to psychological well-being or psychological disorder (see, e.g., Dooley & Catalano, 1980; McLemore & Benjamin, 1979). Chapter 5, by Pelton, examines these issues in the context of child welfare interventions by social work agencies. Pelton's consideration of evidence from social work settings indicates that, as do helpers in other settings, social workers show a marked tendency to view clients' problems as being caused by personality deficiencies. In contrast, the studies show that social work clients view their own problems as being attributable more to situational factors, specifically the difficulties posed by living in poverty conditions. Although clients' judgments cannot necessarily be accepted as an absolute standard, since there is a tendency for persons to emphasize situational determinants of their own behavior (e.g., Jones & Nisbett, 1971), Pelton discusses some other evidence from social work research that indicates there may be substantial validity to the clients' focus on economic factors. In combination with evidence on the validity of clients' perceptions of psychotherapy relationships (noted in Chapter 1, Introduction), this suggests that serious attention should be given to the client's viewpoint. Pelton also observes that, consistent with the research of Batson *et al.* (Chapter 4), the helping resources available in social work agencies are predominantly oriented toward intrapersonal treatment (i.e., counseling and psychotherapy), in contrast to the clients' expressed needs for material assistance for dealing with situational problems. Chapters 4 and 5 together raise a basic issue about considerations involved in the design of helping resources.

References

Dooley, D., & Catalano, R. Economic change as a cause of behavioral disorder. *Psychological Bulletin*, 1980, *87*, 450–458.

Goldberg, L. R. Man versus model of man: A rationale, plus some evidence, for a method of improving on clinical inferences. *Psychological Bulletin*, 1970, *73*, 422–432.

Jones, E. E., & Nisbett, R. E. The actor and the observer: Divergent perceptions of the causes of behavior. In E. E. Jones, D. E. Kanouse, H. H. Kelley, R. E. Nisbett, S. Valins, & B. Weiner (Eds.), *Attribution: Perceiving the causes of behavior*. Morristown, N.J.: General Learning Press, 1971.

Kanfer, F. H., & Goldstein, A. P. Introduction. In F. H. Kanfer & A. P. Goldstein (Eds.), *Helping people change* (2nd ed.). New York: Pergamon, 1980.

McLemore, C. W., & Benjamin, L. S. Whatever happened to interpersonal diagnosis? A psychosocial alternative to DSM-III. *American Psychologist*, 1979, *34*, 17–34.

Meehl, P. E. Why I do not attend case conferences. In P. E. Meehl (Ed.), *Psychodiagnosis: Selected papers*. Minneapolis: Univ. of Minnesota Press, 1973.

Megargee, E. M. (Ed.), *Research in clinical assessment*. New York: Harper & Row, 1966.

chapter 2

Interpersonal Attraction and Treatment Decisions in Inpatient and Outpatient Psychiatric Settings

PETER A. FEHRENBACH
MICHAEL R. O'LEARY

Introduction

Despite the obvious importance of clinical judgments and decisions in helping relationships, the basic processes involved in clinical decision making are not completely understood. Furthermore, recent evidence has suggested that a number of psychological processes, such as interpersonal attraction, can influence clinical judgments (e.g., Wills, 1978). If important clinical decisions are being biased in part by helpers' reactions to clients, then there is a need to elucidate the bases of these perceptions, and the process by which they influence clinical decisions, before corrective action can take place. In our research program we have examined the role of helpers' perceptions of clients in the clinical decision-making process.

An assumption made in our research, first articulated by Garfield (1971) with respect to the psychotherapeutic process but clearly applicable to many helping relationships, is that any conceptualization of basic processes in helping relationships must take into account the characteristics of the client and of the helper, as well as the resulting interaction of the two individuals. Thus, we have examined the nature of helper perceptions of clients, the relative impact of client and clinician characteristics upon helper perceptions

13

Basic Processes in Helping Relationships

of clients, and the extent to which helper perceptions actually have an effect on important decisions regarding client treatment.

Client and helper variables and their interactions appear to have potential influence at three stages in the helping relationship: (1) the entry "boundary" that marks the acceptance or rejection of applicants for treatment or help, (2) assignment to different therapeutic modalities or programs within the service delivery system, and (3) the continuation or termination of the helping relationship (Garfield, 1971). We have attempted to examine the impact of client and helper characteristics on a variety of clinical decisions at each of these stages, and with several client and helper groups. From these studies has emerged a consistent pattern of findings about interpersonal evaluations and clinical decisions, which will be summarized in this chapter. First, a brief review of research that formed the background for our program will be presented.

Review of Research

SOCIAL CLASS AND CLINICAL JUDGMENT

A number of therapist and client variables have been examined with respect to their impact on clinical judgment. Among the client variables, social class has been the most intensively studied. In general, social class has been defined in terms of one or more of the following: occupational status, income, and educational achievement. Early epidemiological studies (Dohrenwend & Dohrenwend, 1969; Hollingshead & Redlich, 1958) showed an association between lower socioeconomic status and increased psychological problems. In addition, data were presented showing an overrepresentation of lower-class individuals among mental hospital patients. Lower social class has been shown to be related to ratings of lower acceptability for treatment, fewer inpatient visits, treatment by pharmacotherapy rather than psychotherapy, and less perceived similarity to admitting residents (Lowinger & Dobie, 1968). In a review of the literature on the effects of client characteristics on psychotherapy process, Garfield (1971) concluded that social class variables are more predictive of both acceptance into psychotherapy and duration of treatment than are personality variables.

Abramowitz and Dokecki (1977), in examining the research on client and clinician characteristics that have been implicated as contributing to evaluative prejudice against clients, found social class designation to be systematically related to psychological appraisals in 9 of 14 analogue studies. Consistent with correlational research, these experimental analogues in general showed that less-favorable clinical judgments were given to lower-class as compared to middle-class clients. However, Abramowitz and Dokecki warned that, due to methodological and experimental design shortcomings, inferring from these studies that clinicians' judgments are biased against lower-class persons may be premature. As an alternative explanation, they suggested that clinicians may be effectively utilizing social class designation as a cue that evokes certain expectations about a given client. Similar conclusions have been reached by other investigators. For example, Stern (1977) noted that the effects of social class operate indirectly, with its effects being mediated by the evocation of certain stereotyped expectations about lower-class clients. In general treatment personnel may believe that lower-class clients do not possess the necessary attitudes and skills to effectively utilize and benefit from psychotherapy. Another study (Dowds, Fontana, Russakoff, & Harris, 1977) showed that certain patient cognitive variables (i.e., psychological differentiation and locus of control orientation) serve as mediators between patients' social class and therapists' differential evaluations of patients' suitability for psychotherapy.[1]

INTERPERSONAL ATTRACTION AND CLINICAL JUDGMENT

Other factors involved in the helper–client relationship may have an important impact on clinical decisions. In particular, helpers' liking of or attraction toward the client seems to significantly influence clinical judgments. In reviewing the earlier literature on interpersonal attraction and helper–client relationships, Doherty (1971) concluded that therapeutic effort is not impartially distributed, in that clients who are liked more by helpers may receive more help. In addition, there appears to be a general tendency on the part of helpers to prefer clients who are perceived to have a better prognosis. Often this preference is associated with a lower level of pathology in the client. For example, in two related studies (Strupp & Wallach, 1973, Strupp & Williams, 1973) interviewers' liking for the patient as a person was shown to be positively related to judgments about the client's emotional maturity, motivation for treatment, and expected level of improvement in psychotherapy. In addition, the more-liked clients were seen as having higher levels of ego strength, were given less-severe diagnostic labels, and were more likely to be recommended for insight-oriented psychotherapy. Conversely, decreased liking was associated with higher ratings of clients' hostility, defensiveness, and degree of disturbance. Among hospitalized psychiatric patients, Brown, Wooldridge, and VanBruggen (1973) found that, of the variables studied, the degree of pathology in the patient exerted the greatest influence on social attractiveness on the ward. Less-disturbed patients were generally more preferred than more-disturbed patients. Finally, more favorable judgments of clinical prognosis have been shown to be correlated with psychiatrists' ratings of personal attraction toward clients presented in written case histories (Schwartz & Abramowitz, 1975).

[1]When client and therapist variables such as sex, race, and social–political values have been studied experimentally, the evidence for evaluative prejudices has been marginal (Abramowitz & Dokecki, 1977).

PERCEPTION OF ALCOHOLIC CLIENTS

It has been suggested that client characteristics influence the treatment of alcoholics in similar ways to that occurring with psychiatric patients (Blane, 1977). For example, Smart, Schmidt, and Moos (1969) observed that, aside from personality and disease process, social class of an alcoholic was most likely to influence the type of clinical services received. Also as in psychotherapy research, social class and social stability are related to acceptance into alcoholism treatment, to the form of treatment received, and to outcome of alcoholism treatment (e.g., Baekeland, Lundwall, & Kissin, 1974; Bateman & Peterson, 1971; Trice, Roman, & Belasco, 1969).

Little research has been conducted on the effects of therapist characteristics, or client–therapist interactions, at the three stages of the treatment process with problem drinkers. Several potential therapist variables that may have an impact on the alcoholism treatment process have been suggested (Blane, 1977). Background factors such as the age, sex, and experience of the therapist may be important. In addition, the extent to which the therapist finds the client interpersonally attractive can potentially influence clinical decisions. In fact, alcoholics are frequently perceived by therapists as unattractive, poorly motivated, lacking a sense of morality, and highly intractable (Baekeland & Lundwall, 1977). How then do clinicians' perceptions of their clients, in addition to client background and personality variables, affect clinical decisions in alcoholism treatment?

Study 1: Decisions Regarding Continuation in Treatment

The first study in this series (O'Leary, Donovan, Chaney, & O'Leary, 1979) attempted to answer the preceding question by examining factors associated with the decision to continue inpatient alcoholism treatment following a 2-week evaluation period. This decision can be conceptualized as taking place at the second and third stages of the treatment process (i.e., a decision to assign to a certain treatment modality and a decision regarding continuation of the therapeutic relationship, respectively).

The study was conducted at the Alcohol Dependence Treatment Program (ADTP) at the Seattle Veterans Administration Medical Center. The staff of the ADTP is interdisciplinary, consisting of a psychiatrist, clinical psychologist, social workers, a vocational rehabilitation specialist, nurses, and alcoholism counselors. The treatment approach involves alcohol education using lecture, film, and discussion formats, small group therapy with a process orientation (Yalom, 1975), and interpersonal skills training (Chaney, O'Leary, & Marlatt, 1978), all within the overall context of a therapeutic community. At the time of the study, all patients were involved in a 2-week evaluation period following admission and detoxification, if necessary. Following the 2-week evaluation period, the staff came to a consensual decision about offering the patient continued treatment in the ADTP. The continued treatment involved 3 more weeks of inpatient treatment followed by 1 month of day treatment and 9 months of weekly aftercare groups.

The subjects were 50 male patients who were consecutively admitted to the program. All subjects carried the primary diagnosis of alcohol addiction.[2] Their mean age was 45.08 years ($SD = 10.57$) and their mean education level was 12.60 years ($SD = 2.66$).

In order to assess client variables that may affect the treatment decision, a variety of demographic factors were surveyed and several measures of personality and cognitive functioning were obtained approximately 10 days following admission. Client age, education level, and social status were the primary demographic variables employed. Social status was based on procedures developed by Hollingshead and Redlich (1958) and yielded two variables. The first was a two-factor index of social position based on the sum of weighted scores for occupational and educational levels. The second variable represented the conversion of the social position index into one of five levels of social class. Higher scores on both variables indicate lower social status.

PERSONALITY MEASURES

A number of questionnaire measures of personality traits were administered to clients as part of the intake procedure.

MMPI. The Minnesota Multiphasic Personality Inventory (MMPI) was used as a generalized measure of psychopathology. The three validity scales, the 10 clinical scales, and the Manifest Anxiety, Ego Strength, Social Desirability, and Dependency scales were employed.

FIRO-B. The FIRO-B (Schutz, 1966) was used to assess the clients' orientation toward interpersonal relationships. This scale provides scores for wanted and expressed attitudes toward interpersonal relationships along three basic dimensions: inclusion, control, and affection (Ryan, 1970). Inclusion assesses the degree to which a person associates with others. Control measures the extent to which the individual assumes responsibility and dominates people. Affection assesses the degree to which a person becomes emotionally involved with others.

---

[2]In all studies involving alcoholic patients, subjects were screened for gross evidence of serious physical illness, severe thought disorder, psychosis, and organic brain syndrome. Applicants were not included in the study if they showed any of these conditions.

Internal–External Locus of Control Scale. This scale (Rotter, 1966) was included as a measure of the extent to which individuals assume responsibility for their behavior. An internal locus of control, reflected in a low score on the scale, has been associated with individuals' perceptions that significant events and outcomes in their lives are contingent upon their own initiative and thus under their personal control.

Drinking-Related Locus of Control Scale (DRIE). The degree to which individuals perceive themselves as having control over drinking behavior is assessed by this scale. Greater levels of physical, psychological, and social impairment due to problem drinking have been associated with an external score on this scale (Donovan & O'Leary, 1978).

MEASURES OF INTELLECTUAL AND COGNITIVE FUNCTIONING

Intellectual and cognitive functioning were assessed using the Shipley–Hartford Scale (Shipley, 1940) and the Trail Making Test (Reitan, 1958). The Shipley–Hartford Scale yields scores for verbal ability, abstracting ability, cognitive impairment (Conceptual Quotient), and general intelligence (IQ), with higher scores on all scales reflecting higher levels of functioning.

MEASURES OF WARD ATMOSPHERE

Ward Atmosphere Scale. This scale (WAS; Moos, 1974a, 1974b) assesses clients' perceptions of ward atmosphere. The WAS was administered to the subject on the day the staff decided about the client's continuation in treatment. The WAS measures 10 dimensions of ward atmosphere within three broad categories: (1) staff and client relationship (includes subscales for involvement, support, and spontaneity), (2) personal development and the program's treatment orientation (subscales for autonomy, practical orientation, personal problem orientation, and anger and aggression), and (3) system maintenance (subscales for order and organization, program clarity, and staff control).

CLINICIAN VARIABLES

The major clinician variables under study were the interpersonal judgments made of the subject. The Interpersonal Judgment Scale (IJS; Byrne, 1974) was completed by each of the six primary staff members prior to discussion of a particular client's case and the decision regarding continuation in treatment. The IJS involves the use of 7-point rating scales in evaluating the client on six dimensions: intelligence, knowledge of current events, morality, adjustment, personal feelings of likability, and desire to work in a group with the person. The last two subscales reflect general interpersonal attractiveness, and a subject's total interpersonal attractiveness score was defined as the mean of these two ratings. The mean ratings of the six primary staff members were used for each of the six subscales and the total interpersonal attractiveness score.

DETERMINANTS OF CONTINUATION

Of the 50 subjects, the staff decided to offer continued treatment to 28 (56%) and not to offer continued treatment to 22 (44%). The accepted and rejected clients were then compared on all of the client and staff measures using an analysis of variance. The results indicated that client variables played only a minimal role in the decision. Of the 40 client variables, only 4 showed a significant difference between accepted and rejected clients. Accepted clients were better educated ($p<.05$), had higher FIRO-B Want Affection scores ($p < .01$), reflecting a greater need for others to initiate close relationships with them, and were higher on the MMPI scales of Ego Strength ($p<.05$) and K ($p<.05$), the latter reflecting a higher level of functional defensiveness. No differences on any of the other measures of personality and cognitive functioning were obtained, and no differences in demographic features, including social class, resulted.

In marked contrast to the client measures, significant differences were obtained at the .05 level or better for the clinician ratings of clients on the IJS. Accepted clients were seen as more intelligent, having a better knowledge of current events, more moral, better adjusted, more personally likable, and more desirable for work in a group. The accepted clients were significantly more interpersonally attractive to the clinicians.

In order to see which combination of client and clinician variables was most powerful in terms of differentiating the two groups, a stepwise multivariate discriminant function analysis was conducted. The 9 most discriminating variables, as determined from the original analysis of variance, plus the social position index were entered into the analysis. Three of the 10 variables entered showed significant contributions to the discrimination. These were total interpersonal attractiveness ($p < .001$), wanted affection ($p < .002$), and ego strength ($p < .02$).

DISCUSSION

The failure to show a relationship between social class and the decision to continue clients in treatment was in contrast to much of the previous research indicating that such clinical decisions are influenced by the social status of clients (e.g., Abramowitz & Dokecki, 1977; Hollingshead & Redlich, 1958).

One possible explanation for our findings is that our sample was drawn from a relatively low and restricted range of social class found in the Veterans Administration system. However, examination of the social position index shows that although the sample mean fell within Class IV (a mean of 52.5 out of a possible range of 11–77), the sample was also characterized by a high degree of variability ($SD = 12.3$).

As state previously, it has been suggested that therapists' expectations are that lower-class clients hold attitudes and beliefs about therapy that are both different from middle-class clients' and likely to interfere with effective utilization of treatment. However, a recent study (Frank, Eisenthal, & Lazare, 1978) has found that client conceptions about therapy are quite similar across social classes. Furthermore, Stern (1977) found that client social status was not related to acceptance to treatment, assignment to different forms of treatment, or number of therapeutic sessions provided. These authors (Frank *et al.*, 1978; Stern, 1977) argue that the discrepancy in findings between early research conducted in the 1950s and 1960s and more recent studies may reflect both some fairly widespread changes in attitudes toward mental illness and the increased availability of psychological services for all social classes.

That client measures in general did not differentiate the accepted and rejected clients is consistent with the conclusions of Garfield (1971) about the relative noncontributory nature of client personality measures in determining psychotherapy outcome. However, staff perceptions of clients on inter-personal dimensions seemed to make a major contribution to the decision to continue clients in treatment. Of all the variables examined, ratings of interpersonal attractiveness, based on personal likability and willingness to work with the client in a group, were most predictive of acceptance.

The literature on clinical judgment and interpersonal attraction may help in interpreting these findings. Factor-analytic studies consistently have iso-lated at least three factors reflecting perceptual dimensions upon which helpers evaluate their clients (Wills, 1978). These dimensions have been labeled manageability, treatability, and likability/attractiveness. However, these various dimensions may simply represent different perceptions of the clients' treatability (i.e., the helper's instrumental concerns in providing treatment to clients). In making the decision to continue a particular client in their treatment program, the ADTP staff were likely to have been employing such an "implicit" treatability criterion in their evaluations. How then is rated attractiveness related to the treatment decision? It seems that staff rate as most likable and attractive those clients whom they view as most likely to benefit from the type of treatment they see themselves as capable of providing. According to Byrne's (1974) attraction paradigm, we are most attracted to those who interpersonally reward or reinforce us. In the clinicians' experience, working with certain clients has been more "rewarding" than working with others; that is, some clients have reinforced the clinician's personal sense of clinical effectiveness by making therapeutic gains. It follows then that these clients with whom it is reinforcing to work would be judged as more interpersonally attractive.

Perhaps the two client variables (Ego Strength, Want Affection) that were shown to be most contributory to the decision to continue treatment can shed some light on which clients clinicians perceive as more potentially rewarding and likely to benefit from their treatment program. The Ego Strength scale has been shown to be predictive of prognosis in psychotherapy in early studies (Barron, 1953), but more recent research has not completely replicated this finding (Garfield, 1978). Clients high in Wanted Affection, because of their desire for others to initiate close or intimate relationships with them, have developed an essentially dependent interpersonal style that elicits affectional responses from others, including clinicians. This speculation is consistent with other research that has found that therapists' personal feeling of comfort and attitudes and behaviors toward clients are significantly more favorable with dependent as compared to assertive or uncooperative clients (e.g., Palisi & Ruzicka, 1974; Parsons & Parker, 1968; Schuldt, 1966). The idea that clinicians prefer clients who are more dependent will be discussed in a later section.

Study 2: Effects of Client Background and Clinician Experience on Treatment Decisions

The second study in this series (O'Leary, Speltz, Donovan, & Walker, 1979) examined the effects of client and clinician variables at an even earlier stage in the treatment process—the preadmission screening interview. We reasoned that much less information about the client would be available to the clinician in such an interview, compared with a 2-week evaluation, and the clinician would have much less time to develop evaluative opinions. However, it has been reported that helper perceptions of clients crystallize rapidly and that initial ratings of clients by counselors are significantly related to measures obtained at termination of treatment (Bishop, Sharf, & Adkins, 1975; Brown, 1970); if so, we thought that our findings from the 2-week evaluation study might be replicated.

Another hypothesis was that less favorable interpersonal evaluations of clients, and perhaps less favorable admissions decisions, would be associated with more professional experience. Wills (1978) has considered evidence suggesting that helpers' perceptions of clients tend to become more negative during the first few years of clinical experience. There is a tendency for more experienced clinicians to emphasize negative aspects of the clients' characters, perceiving greater maladjustment and less client motivation for change. We wanted to see whether this was true for more and less experienced clinicians in our study.

The subjects were 156 male veterans who consecutively agreed to participate in a preadmission screening interview at the Alcohol Dependence Treatment Program. They had a mean age of 46.21 years ($SD = 11.56$) and a mean number of years of education of 11.70 ($SD = 3.05$). The screening interview with one of six staff members took place after an hour-long orientation meeting in which the program was described to applicants for admission. During this screening interview demographic information was collected, and the staff screened applicants on the basis of explicit criteria (see Footnote 2). Immediately following the interview, the staff members were asked to complete the IJS and to indicate their decisions regarding admission.

DETERMINANTS OF TREATMENT ACCEPTANCE

Of the 156 applicants, 79 (50.6%) were accepted for treatment, and 77 (49.4%) were rejected. Those applicants for admission who were accepted and those who were rejected were compared using t-tests on the continuous variables and chi-square analyses on the dichotomous variables. The client variables that we examined this time were educational level and current occupational level (based on Hollingshead & Redlich's [1958] two-factor index of social position), age, job history (regular or irregular employment), marital relationship (stable or unstable), source of referral (court referred or not court referred), presence or absence of previous alcoholism treatment, and VA eligibility status (service-connected or not service-connected illness).

Results of these analyses showed that, as in the first study, accepted and rejected applicants differed very little in the demographic and background variables surveyed. The exceptions were that accepted applicants were younger ($M = 43.6$ years) than rejected applicants ($M = 48.8$ years), and the accepted group had more court-referred applicants (72%) than the rejected group (28%).

Staff members' ratings of applicants on the IJS again showed significant differences between the two groups of applicants on three of the subscales. Accepted applicants were judged to be more intelligent, more personally likable, and more desirable for working together in a group. Accepted subjects also received higher total attractiveness ratings than rejected subjects. These results for interpersonal attraction are remarkably similar to our first study and suggest that clinicians' perceptions do crystallize quite rapidly.

A breakdown of the staff members into three groups based on years of experience indicated that the most experienced staff (7 or more years of experience) rated applicants as significantly less moral, less adjusted, and less likable than clinicians with less experience. It was also found that staff members with more experience tended more often to reject applicants for treatment than their less-experienced colleagues. Although these data are based on a sample of only six clinicians, the results support Wills's (1978) observation of a negative tendency in clinical judgments among more experienced clinicians.

As in the previous study we wanted to determine the measures that in combination best discriminated between rejected and accepted clients. Those variables that had yielded significant ($p < .05$) differences between groups on the previous analyses (age, referral source, years of staff experience, IJS ratings of intelligence, likability, and working together in a group), and the social position index were entered into a stepwise multivariate discriminant function analysis. The four variables that proved to be most significantly discriminating between rejected and accepted clients were (in rank order): ability to work in a group (one of the attraction measures) ($p < .001$), years of staff members' experience ($p < .05$), age of applicant ($p < .05$), and applicant referral source ($p < .05$).

DISCUSSION

The results of this study are quite similar to those of the previous one. This is especially noteworthy considering the fact that in this study the clinicians' judgments and decisions were based on a single, brief screening interview as compared to the 2-week evaluation period of the first study. The results also are consistent with the notion that clinicians go beyond "explicit" or standard criteria in evaluating clients and employ less formally developed "implicit" criteria in judging the suitability of clients for their treatment program.

The observation that younger and court-referred applicants were more likely to be accepted can be accounted for by the notion of a treatability criterion. Younger alcoholics may be seen by clinicians as having less ingrained patterns and shorter histories of problem drinking, and thus as more changeable. Although anecdotal evidence from the staff implied that court-referred clients are sometimes thought of as "less self-motivated" by clinicians, they, in fact, are subject to the external contingencies imposed by the courts. For this reason court-ordered clients may be accepted because they are more likely to complete the inpatient phase of treatment and to comply with posttreatment recommendations.

The IJS has given us some notion as to the basis of the implicit criteria used by clinicians in judging clients' treatability. Perceived intelligence, likability, and estimated ability to work well within a group (with the latter two combining to form a single measure of perceived interpersonal attractiveness) are dimensions upon which clinicians, in our setting at least, base important clinical decisions. The dimensions of intelligence and desirability for work in a group appear to be related to qualities assumed to be necessary for successful engagement in our treatment program, which emphasizes verbal participation in numerous therapy and discussion groups. That clinicians choose to accept applicants for alcoholism treatment who they believe are most treatable by their methods is further evidenced by findings of Pattison, Coe, and Doerr (1973) of congruence in philosophies and methods between alcoholism treatment program populations and the staff of the facility to which they are admitted.

Study 3: Clinical Decisions in a Walk-in Crisis Clinic

To determine the generality of our initial findings about alcohol treatment, additional studies were undertaken to extend the investigation of clinicians' perceptions of clients to the setting of a walk-in mental health crisis clinic. As in the alcoholism treatment studies, the influence exerted by various client and clinician variables was examined in the entry boundary of acceptance versus rejection of applicants into the service delivery system and in the assignment of clients to different therapeutic modalities within this system. These studies were conducted at the Behavioral Sciences Clinic (BSC) at the Seattle Veterans Administration Medical Center (SVAMC). The BSC is a walk-in crisis clinic in which all veterans seeking mental health services through the medical center are first evaluated before referral dispositions are made. The staff consists of an interdisciplinary team of psychiatrists, psychologists, social workers, psychiatric nurses, and professional students in training. Clients are seen for evaluation on a first-come–first-served basis (except in cases of extreme emergency) and are assigned to clinicians for interviewing on a rotating basis, regardless of presenting complaint. Dispositions are made generally on the same day as the evaluation.

In this study (Chaney, O'Leary, Donovan, Castle, & Speltz, 1980), the subjects were 157 male veterans who presented at the BSC over a 3-week period. They had a mean age of 38.6 years ($SD = 14.28$) and a mean education level of 12.9 years ($SD = 3.68$). Demographic and background information on the client was collected in the interview and from the client's medical records. Following the initial evaluation interview with the subject, the staff member completed the IJS. In addition, a referral to a specific mental health service was completed. Three categories of dispositions were considered for purposes of this study: (1) The client was either accepted or rejected for treatment within the SVAMC system, (2) the client was referred to an inpatient or an outpatient treatment facility, and (3) the client was provided with either short-term follow-up treatment beyond the initial interview by members of the BSC staff or was referred to some other service for treatment.

The results of this study, consistent with our previous research in alcoholism treatment, showed that clinicians' subjective evaluations of clients on a number of interpersonal dimensions, and the amount of clinicians' experience, significantly contributed to clinical decisions concerning referrals; in contrast, client background characteristics did not influence decisions. No significant differences were found in the pattern of referral dispositions as a function of such client background variables as age, education, and race. Table 2.1 summarizes the findings that staff experience and staff IJS ratings of clients were significantly related to clinical decisions. Clinicians with more experience in the crisis clinic were more likely than less-experienced clinicians to accept clients into the system and to recommend that clients continue short-term contacts with them. Three IJS rating dimensions also emerged as significantly related to referral decisions. Higher ratings of clients on knowledge of current events were associated with the decision to accept the client into the VA system, assignment to outpatient treatment, and follow-up appointments at the BSC. Similarly, higher ratings in morality were obtained for clients referred to outpatient treatment and to follow-up BSC appointments. Finally, outpatient referrals were rated higher on adjustment than inpatient referrals.

Although ratings of personal likability previously have been found to be related to clinical decisions, the dimensions of overall interpersonal attractiveness did not emerge as a significant factor in this study. On the other hand, the dimensions of knowledge of current events, morality, and adjustment contributed most consistently to the referral decisions. In another study (O'Leary, Donovan, Chaney, & Speltz, 1979), these three dimensions of the IJS were found to be related to a variety of personality traits implicitly associated with a perception of enhanced treatability and manageability. For example, knowledge of current events was related to a tendency to assume responsibility and to greater ego strength. Higher ratings of morality were associated with the minimization of psychological problems and the appearance of social extraversion and interpersonal independence on the MMPI. High ratings on adjustment were related to a tendency to endorse "normal" items on the MMPI and to deny bizarre thoughts and behaviors. These correlates suggest that patients who are referred to outpatient treatment are likely to be exhibiting behaviors in the interview that create the impression that they have a better prognosis and would be more manageable and treatable on an outpatient basis. Interpersonal attractiveness may be a less salient dimension than treatability and manageability in the context of a walk-in crisis clinic, where rapid evaluations and immediate referral decisions are frequently necessary.

The results on clinical experience are somewhat mixed with respect to its effects on clinical judgments and decisions. Interviewers with longer BSC experience (more than 4 months), compared to less-experienced interviewers, tended to rate clients as having lower levels of intelligence and morality, and were more likely to accept clients into the VA system. However, experienced clinicians were more willing to make follow-up interviews with their clients. One explanation for our findings has to do with the specialized nature of the crisis clinic in which clients are typically seen once and then referred. It may be that experienced clinicians in the crisis clinic were more willing to engage a client in follow-up treatment, despite some negative perceptions, because of the relative novelty of an ongoing treatment relationship.

Table 2.1
Means and t Values for Staff Experience Variables and IJS Ratings as a Function of Client Referral Dispositions[a]

| | Acceptance | | | Referral dispositions | | | | | | |
| | | | | Treatment type | | | Follow-up type | | |
Staff variables	VA	Non-VA	t	Inpatient	Outpatient	t	BSC	Non-BSC	t
Years in mental health	9.00	7.30	1.02	8.22	8.72	−0.30	9.76	8.27	0.95
Months in BSC	11.26	3.61	5.25**	8.44	9.80	−0.50	13.18	6.43	3.00**
IJS scales									
Intelligence	4.59	4.35	1.07	4.43	4.56	−0.64	4.56	4.49	0.33
Current Events	3.96	3.24	3.07**	3.29	3.94	−2.74**	4.10	3.55	2.82**
Morality	4.20	4.03	1.11	3.97	4.22	−2.26**	4.38	3.99	2.92**
Adjustment	2.90	3.15	−1.09	2.43	3.11	−3.13**	3.15	2.80	1.92
Likability	4.55	4.56	−0.04	4.77	4.49	1.17	4.71	4.41	1.48
Group Member	4.45	4.36	0.35	4.54	4.40	0.58	4.51	4.36	0.76
Total Attractiveness	9.00	8.79	0.46	9.31	8.85	1.04	9.22	8.72	1.36

[a]From Chaney, O'Leary, Donovan, Castle, and Speltz (1980). Reprinted with permission of Pergamon Press. Ltd.
*$p < .05$.
**$p < .01$.

Study 4: Client Symptomatology, Clinician Characteristics, and Referral Decisions

Our second study in the BSC (O'Leary, Fehrenbach, Johnson, Castle, Kaplan, & Williams, in press) was designed to extend the previous research by examining the influence of a wider range of client and clinician variables on clinical decisions. In addition, clinicians' evaluations of clients were assessed on a number of dimensions other than those represented on the IJS. The procedures were otherwise essentially the same as in Study 3. The client variables assessed were age, sex, marital status, income, years of education, social position, employment status, legal problems, VA eligibility, prior psychiatric treatment, history of suicide attempts or ideation, and history of violence. In addition, the client's diagnosis was determined and categorized into one of four groups: (1) psychoses including schizophrenia, (2) affective disorders, (3) anxiety disorders, and (4) personality disorders and substance abuse. The clinician's age, sex, professional status (student or staff), years experience in mental health services, and months experience in the BSC were examined. Clinicians rated the clients on seven dimensions of personal and interpersonal functioning using 7-point anchored ratings scales: grooming (1 = well groomed, 7 = poorly groomed), conventionality (1 = conventional, 7 = bizarre), rationality (1 = rational, 7 = irrational), calmness (1 = calm, 7 = agitated), cooperativeness (1 = cooperative, 7 = uncooperative), friendliness (1 = friendly, 7 = belligerent), and overall symptom severity (1 = mild symptoms, 7 = severe symptoms).

The dispositions the clinician made on each of the 256 clients were examined in three ways. First, it was determined if the subject was referred within (73% of the sample) or outside (27%) the VA system. Second, it was determined if the subject was referred to a unit or service that involved low therapist contact (e.g., outpatient clinic) (67.4%) or high therapist contact (e.g., inpatient psychiatry, alcoholism treatment, day hospital) (32.6%). Finally, it was determined to which of six specific treatment programs the client was referred.

As in previous research, only a few of the client variables affected the disposition decisions. Unemployed clients and clients with a prior history of psychiatric treatment were more likely to be referred into the VA system. This probably represents a dimension of chronicity in these clients. Clients referred to high-therapist-contact programs were more likely to have a history of suicidal ideation or attempts or of violence, or to have been diagnosed as having a personality disorder or alcohol addiction. In addition, clients with histories of suicide attempts and violence were more likely to be referred to acute psychiatric care programs. Since violent and suicidal patients pose considerable management problems for professional staff, it is likely they are viewed by interviewing clinicians as less treatable in anything other than intensive treatment programs.

None of the staff measures appeared to affect dispositions with the exception of professional status. Staff clinicians were more likely than student clinicians to accept clients into the VA system. This result is similar to that obtained in Study 3. A comparison of student and staff clinician ratings of clients also revealed that staff clinicians tended to rate subjects as significantly less calm and less friendly than did student clinicians. These results are quite similar to those obtained by Brown (1970).

The major finding with respect to clinician ratings of clients was that perceived severity of symptoms influenced every disposition measure. Clients who were rated as exhibiting more overall severe symptoms were more likely to be referred into the VA system, to high-therapist-contact programs, and specifically to acute psychiatric care units (day hospital, inpatient psychiatry). Examination of Table 2.2 shows that in general more negative interpersonal evaluations of clients were associated with referrals to high-therapist-contact programs. A further analysis of the data indicated that subjects referred to acute psychiatric treatment were perceived to be less well groomed than outpatient subjects, less rational than alcoholism treatment subjects, and less conventional and exhibiting more severe symptoms than all other subject groups, who did not differ among themselves. Finally, lower socioeconomic status of subjects was associated with less-favorable ratings on grooming, conventionality, and rationality.

In summary, the two studies in the BSC provide evidence consistent with our findings on the alcoholism unit that client and clinician demographic variables only minimally affect referral dispositions. However, two previously unexamined background variables, history of suicidal behavior and violent

Table 2.2
Differences on Clinician Ratings between Subjects Referred to Low-Therapist-Contact Programs and High-Therapist-Contact Programs[a]

| | Therapist contact | | | | | |
| | Low | | High | | | |
Rating dimension[b]	M	SD	M	SD	t	p
Grooming	2.24	1.26	3.00	1.73	4.04	<.0001
Conventionality	2.60	1.41	3.35	1.69	3.83	<.0001
Rationality	2.43	1.36	2.74	1.60	1.64	<.101
Calmness	2.73	1.66	2.89	1.53	0.77	ns
Cooperativeness	2.01	1.36	2.15	1.28	0.80	ns
Friendliness	1.93	1.24	2.25	1.35	1.90	<.06
Symptom severity	3.01	1.34	3.76	1.49	4.11	<.0001

[a] From O'Leary, Fehrenbach, Johnson, Castle, Kaplan, and Williams (in press). Reprinted with permission of Pergamon Press, Ltd.

[b] Higher ratings reflect less favorable impressions on each dimension.

behavior, did appear to influence dispositions such that clients with significant histories generally were considered to require more intensive treatment efforts. This is not surprising when one considers the potentially harmful consequences for society of such behaviors; hence clinicians are more likely to hospitalize such clients.

The two studies provide further evidence that interpersonal evaluations are related to clinical decisions. It appears that disposition decisions are mediated by clinicians' interpersonal evaluations of clients apart from diagnosis. The most salient dimension affecting decisions in the second study was the clinicians' evaluation of the overall severity of the clients' symptoms, with related but secondary dimensions being grooming, rationality of thinking, and friendliness. Such dimensions seem to form the bases for evaluation of the treatability and manageability of clients in different treatment modalities.

Study 5: Client Helplessness and Clinician Perceptions

Other factors related to social role components of the client–helper relationship also may be operative in determining clinician perceptions. For example, helpers are called upon by people in need to play the role of a facilitator of behavioral change. The client in this relationship enacts the role of one who is helped. In this context, a mutually satisfying and reinforcing relationship is one in which the client conveys the message of a need for help (behaves helplessly) and the clinician in turn responds with help-giving behavior. To the extent that clinicians see themselves as helpful and are rewarded for their efforts by providing an effective means of changing "helpless" client behaviors or reducing personal distress, then they will be more attracted toward such helpless clients. If clients exhibit behavior that are consistent with those expected of "good" treatment candidates, then they are similarly likely to be rated higher in perceived attractiveness.

Data from one recent study (O'Leary, Speltz, & Walker, 1980) support some of these contentions about client helplessness. Fifty-one male veterans participating in the ADTP were given the H25, a 24-item self-report measure designed to assess subjective helplessness (Glass, Note 1). The items describe a variety of activities and events that, when engaged in, provide a source of response-contingent reinforcement (e.g., "getting a good job"). Subjects are asked to rate the extent to which they are able to influence or control the initiation and outcome of each event along an 11-point scale. Higher scores reflect higher levels of subjective helplessness. In addition, the treatment staff completed the IJS for each subject during treatment planning.

Subjects were categorized into two groups, high and low helplessness, based on a median split of the H25. Initial analyses showed no differences between groups with respect to demographic variables and severity of alcohol abuse.

Marginally significant ($p < .09$) differences in rated morality and adjustment were obtained between groups. Significant ($p < .02$) differences between groups were found for rated likability and desirability to work in a group with the client. High-helplessness clients were judged as less moral, but better adjusted, more likable, and more desirable to work with in a group. Although these data support the notion that clients prefer more helpless clients, future research should include observational measures of overt behaviors associated with high and low levels of subjective helplessness as well as measures of clinician behavior during interactions with clients exhibiting varying degrees of helplessness.

Summary

CLIENT VARIABLES

The research discussed in this chapter has found relatively few client variables that are directly related to clinical decisions in the populations and settings studied. In particular, the social class of the client, contrary to much previous research, generally did not successfully differentiate clients who received more favorable clinical decisions from those who did not. In a similar manner, personality variables, as assessed by standard psychometric instruments, did not prove to be particularly good discriminators of clients who were, for example, accepted or rejected for inpatient alcoholism treatment. Those personality and demographic factors that did seem to be related to clinical decisions included education, age, desire for affection, ego strength, and functional level of defensiveness. In general, younger, better educated clients, with higher levels of ego strength and defensiveness, were given more opportunity for help.

Whereas client personality and demographic measures were found to have minimal impact on clinical decisions, helpers' interpersonal evaluations of clients seemed to have a significant effect upon clinical decisions in several of our studies. In particular, more favorable ratings of interpersonal attractiveness and likability of clients by helpers were significantly related to decisions to accept and to continue clients in alcoholism treatment. In addition, positive ratings of clients' knowledge of current events, morality, and adjustment were associated with decisions to continue clients in alcoholism treatment and with a variety of decisions about acceptance into treatment and type of treatment in a walk-in crisis clinic. It was also found that clients who were rated as having the most severe symptoms were given the most negative interpersonal evaluations and that clients' moods are related to interpersonal judgments by helpers. For example, it was noted that helpless clients are given the most favorable interpersonal evaluations.

In summary, our research supports the notion that there is a strong tendency by clinicians to prefer clients who appear to have a better prognosis, who have less severe perceived symptoms, and who are dependent and in need of affection. Furthermore, clients who are liked more by helpers are likely to receive more help than their less attractive counterparts. As suggested by Doherty (1971), these effects of client attractiveness lead to the conclusion that therapeutic effort is not always impartially distributed.

CLINICIAN VARIABLES

The primary clinician variable we have studied has been clinician experience. In discussing the literature on perceptions of clients by helpers, Wills (1978) concluded that more negative perceptions were associated with increased experience. Our data in general have been supportive of the hypothesis of a negative tendency in clinicians' judgments of clients on a number of dimensions.

Clinicians with more years experience in mental health (7 or more years) tended to rate alcoholics during a preadmission screening interview as less moral, less well-adjusted, and less likable than did clinicians with fewer years experience (O'Leary, Speltz, Donovan, & Walker, 1979). Lower ratings of perceived intelligence, knowledge of current events, and moral standards were attributed by more-experienced clinicians (compared with less-experienced clinicians) to clients in a walk-in crisis clinic (Chaney *et al.*, 1980). These same experienced clinicians were more likely to recommend treatment (i.e., they saw clients as more maladjusted) than inexperienced clinicians. In comparing student and staff clinicians in the same walk-in clinic, it was observed that staff clinicians tended to rate clients as less calm and less friendly than student clinicians (O'Leary, Fehrenbach, Johnson, Castle, Kaplan, & Williams, in press). In addition, older clinicians tended to rate these same clients as more poorly groomed than younger clinicians.

Conclusions

The research program we have described has attempted to elucidate some of the imporant helper and client variables that affect clinical decisions. In general, the results of our studies suggest the important mediating role of helpers' perceptions of clients in determining clinical decisions. Client personality and background variables have an impact upon clinical decisions to the extent to which they are relevant to the clinicians' estimation of a client's "treatability" in a given clinical context. Such an implicit treatability criterion is construed broadly and encompasses evaluations of the clients' manageability and likability as well. The significant finding of enhanced perceived attractiveness among clients receiving "favorable" treatment decisions (e.g., acceptance to treatment, continuation in treatment) has been explained in terms of similarity between client behavior and helper expectations of "treatable" clients in the helper's therapeutic modality. Furthermore, client behaviors that are consistent with the role of one who is in need of help (helpless, dependent) and client behaviors that are likely to reinforce the clinician's role as a helper (through compliance with treatment expectations and behavior change) are likely to result in increased perceptions of interpersonal attractiveness. However, these perceptions may become more negative with increased helper experience.

Wills (1978) has suggested that changes in helpers' perceptions of clients are most likely to occur during the first years of professional experience, during which time there develops a greater emphasis on negative characteristics of clients, especially an increased perception of maladjustment, and more negative views of clients' motivation for change. In general, our research is quite consistent with these hypotheses. These findings of more negative perceptions by helpers of clients associated with helper experience warrant explanation. During training and early in one's professional career, most helpers are still rather optimistic about their potential for effecting changes in their clients, and probably try to approach all new cases equally. However, with increased experience, such admirable attitudes may become subverted by a variety of psychological processes associated with helping relationships. For example, there is the principle of similarity and attraction, according to which we are most attracted to persons whom we view as similar to ourselves; when increased disparity among helpers and clients becomes apparent, a tendency toward more negative attitudes toward clients should be expected. With increased experience as a helper, there is a greater likelihood of encountering clients resistant to influence by the helper. Such resistance is likely to increase dislike for the "ungrateful" client by the helper. Finally, there is a tendency for helpers to focus on negative aspects of clients' behavior, perhaps because time constraints do not permit adequate sampling of behavior, or because there is a temptation to focus on negative aspects in formulating causal hypotheses about behavior.

How might these tendencies in judgments about clients by helpers be counteracted? Clearly, there is a need to continue to educate students (and experienced professionals as well) in the importance of minimizing personal biases regarding clients. Beyond this educative process, however, a number of things may help reduce the influence of interpersonal attraction on clinical judgments. For example, it may be useful to encourage helpers working with clients that they apparently dislike to make explicit those characteristics of the client that are similar to the helpers', rather than focusing on their differences. Focusing on clients' personal strengths, as well as weaknesses, in reports and case presentations may help overcome the tendency to select negative aspects of clients' behaviors. It may also be useful to have helpers explicitly examine those aspects of the client's situation that may contribute to his or her current problems, in addition to simply looking to personalistic attributions. Finally, there may be a great deal of usefulness in educating helpers in the apparently natural tendency of individuals to resist influence attempts, despite the fact that they, paradoxically, may be seeking help to change their behavior. Such psychological reactance to influence attempts may be an inherent part of the structure of many therapeutic relationships. Increased awareness of this process may help professionals to better understand, and perhaps react less negatively to, their clients' apparently resistive behavior.

Our research has implications for a number of additional areas of research and practice. For example, it may be detrimental to clients who are higher in subjective helplessness to be seen as more likable and attractive by clinicians. There is the possibility that clinicians in their relationships with clients inadvertently reinforce some ineffective and problem behaviors, such as passive and dependent responses. Similarly, clinicians may ignore or even discourage behaviors correlated with positive treatment outcomes, for example, active, self-initiated, and environment-manipulating responses. Furthermore, it has been suggested that the emotional exhaustion syndrome of "burnout," in which helpers seem to lose feeling and concern for clients and treat them in a detached manner, is partially in response to a passive–dependent stance frequently encountered in clients (Maslach, 1978). A passive–dependent stance in clients makes them more manageable and, as noted earlier, may even serve to validate helpers' feelings of competence by demonstrating how needed they are. But, passive–dependent clients are also likely to place more responsibility on clinicians to help them, and this can eventually lead to considerable resentment and detachment by helpers.

Another implication of our findings has to do with clinical research in general. One of the major concerns of clinical research is the extent to which the sample of subjects under study is representative of the population of individuals experiencing the particular problem or receiving a given treatment. If we obtain a biased or unrepresentative sample of subjects, then the generalizability of our findings to the population is significantly undermined. Alcoholism treatment outcome studies have been criticized for their lack of attention to variables that potentially bias samples of alcoholic patients studied (Baekeland & Lundwall, 1977; Miller, Pokorny, Valles, & Cleveland, 1970). One variable that may be particularly biasing is the acceptance or rejection of clients to programs at initial screening. The data indicate that many programs may accept only about half their applicants (e.g., Miller *et al.*, 1970; O'Leary, Donovan, Chaney, & O'Leary, 1979). Accepted clients may certainly differ from rejected clients on the basis of explicit or standard screening criteria, such as the absence of organic brain disease or serious physical illnesses. But our data suggest that there are differences in clients accepted and rejected for admission to treatment that are the result of the usage of implicit, informal admission criteria in screening. Similar criteria appeared to be employed in the walk-in psychiatric clinic. It is likely then that research conducted on clients in any treatment facility in which preadmission screening takes place are subject to potentially biasing influences.

A number of issues should be raised about the nature of the research reviewed here, and suggestions for future research need to be presented. First, the results of these studies are based on essentially correlational data. Thus, statements about causative "effects" and "determinants" are used rather loosely. Future studies should attempt to improve the methodologies so far employed so that more definitive statements can be made. Second, the data have been obtained primarily from self-report measures of clients and clinicians. This has provided much useful data, but the need for objective measures of behaviors in client–clinician interactions are also necessary at this time. For example, what specifically are the behavioral correlates of clients' moods that seem to influence clinicians' perceptions of them? Similarly, measures of clinicians' behavior during interactions with clients of varying degrees of helplessness may be useful in testing our hypotheses about the respective effects of client helplessness on helper–client relationships. The assessment of clinician perceptions of clients' moods also may be useful in this regard. Third, our data are limited to a male Veterans Administration client population. Further research and replication with females as well as males in different treatment settings would be needed to insure the generalizability of our findings. Larger samples of clinicians, representing differing professional and experience backgrounds, are needed. Fourth, a continuing effort needs to be made to determine the client and clinician variables that affect clinical judgments. Such research might now be more profitable if the selection of variables is guided by theoretical notions about the nature of clinical decisions, and the specific processes that may work against favorable perceptions of clients. Future research might explore how these processes work to influence clinical decisions.

Reference Note

1. Glass, D. R. *Measures of helplessness in research in depression*. Paper presented at the meeting of the Western Psychological Association, Seattle, April 1977.

References

Abramowitz, C. V., & Dokecki, P. R. The politics of clinical judgement: Early empirical returns. *Psychological Bulletin*, 1977, *84*, 460–476.

Baekeland, F., & Lundwall, L. K. Engaging the alcoholic in treatment and keeping him there. In B. Kissin & H. Begleiter (Eds.), *The biology of alcoholism* (Vol. 5). New York: Plenum, 1977.

Baekeland, F., Lundwall, L., & Kissin, B. Methods for the treatment of chronic alcoholism: A critical appraisal. In Y. Israel (Ed.), *Research advances in alcohol and drug problems* (Vol. 2). New York: Wiley, 1974.

Barron, F. An ego strength scale which predicts response to psychotherapy. *Journal of Consulting Psychology*, 1953, *17*, 327–333.

Bateman, N. I., & Peterson, D. M. Variables related to outcome of treatment for hospitalized alcoholics. *Journal of Addiction*, 1971, *6*, 215–244.

Bishop, J. B., Sharf, R. S., & Adkins, D. M. Counselor intake judgements, client characteristics, and number of sessions at a university counseling center. *Journal of Counseling Psychology*, 1975, *22*, 557–559.

Blane, H. T. Issues in the evaluation of alcoholism treatment. *Professional Psychology*, 1977, *8*, 593–608.

Brown, J. S., Wooldridge, P. J., & VanBruggen, Y. Interpersonal relations among psychiatric patients: The determinants of social attractiveness. *Journal of Health and Social Behavior*, 1973, *14*, 51–60.

Brown, R. D. Experienced and inexperienced counselors' first impressions of clients and case outcomes: Are first impressions lasting? *Journal of Counseling Psychology*, 1970, *17*, 550–558.

Byrne, D. *An introduction to personality: Research theory and applications* (2nd ed.). Englewood Cliffs, N.J.: Prentice-Hall, 1974.

Chaney, E. F., O'Leary, M. R., Donovan, D. M., Castle, A., & Speltz, M. L. Interpersonal evaluations and referral decisions in a psychiatric walk-in crisis clinic. *Journal of Psychiatric Treatment and Evaluation*, 1980, *2*, 245–250.

Chaney, E. F., O'Leary, M. R., & Marlatt, G. A. Skill training with alcoholics. *Journal of Consulting and Clinical Psychology*, 1978, *46*, 1092–1104.

Doherty, E. G. Social attraction and choice among psychiatric patients and staff: A review. *Journal of Health and Social Behavior*, 1971, *12*, 279–290.

Dohrenwend, B. P., & Dohrenwend, B. S. *Social status and psychological disorder*. New York: Wiley, 1969.

Donovan, D. M., & O'Leary, M. R. The drinking related locus of control scale (DRIE): Reliability, factor structure and validity. *Journal of Studies in Alcohol*, 1978, *39*, 759–784.

Dowds, B. N., Fontana, A. F., Russakoff, L. M., & Harris, M. Cognitive mediators between patients' social class and therapists' evaluations. *Archives of General Psychology*, 1977, *34*, 917–920.

Frank, A., Eisenthal, S., & Lazare, A. Are there social class differences in patients' treatment conceptions? Myths and facts. *Archives of General Psychiatry*, 1978, *35*, 61–69.

Garfield, S. L. Research on client variables in psychotherapy. In A. E. Bergin & S. L. Garfield (Eds.), *Handbook of psychotherapy and behavior change*. New York: Wiley, 1971.

Garfield, S. L. Reseach on client variables in psychotherapy. In S. L. Garfield & A. E. Bergin (Eds.), *Handbook of psychotherapy and behavior change* (2nd ed.). New York: Wiley, 1978.

Hollingshead, A. B., & Redlich, F. C. *Social class and mental illness*. New York: Wiley, 1958.

Lowinger, P., & Dobie, S. The attitudes of the psychiatrist about his patient. *Comprehensive Psychiatry*, 1968, *9*, 627–632.

Maslach, C. The client role in staff burn-out. *Journal of Social Issues*, 1978, *34* (4), 111–124.

Miller, B. A., Pokorny, A. D., Valles, J., & Cleveland, S. E. Biased sampling in alcoholism treatment research. *Quarterly Journal of Studies on Alcohol*, 1970, *31*, 97–107.

Moos, R. H. *Evaluating treatment environments*. New York: Wiley, 1974. (a)

Moos, R. H. *Ward Atmosphere Scale manual*. Palo Alto, Calif: Consulting Psychologists Press, 1974. (b)

O'Leary, M. R., Donovan, D. M., Chaney, E. F., & O'Leary, D. E. Interpersonal attractiveness and clinical decisions in alcoholism treatment. *American Journal of Psychiatry*, 1979, *136*, 618–622.

O'Leary, M. R., Donovan, D. M., Chaney, E. F., & Speltz, M. L. Correlates of clinicians' perceptions of patients in alcoholism treatment. *Journal of Clinical Psychiatry*, 1979, *40*, 344–347.

O'Leary, M. R., Fehrenbach, P. A., Johnson, M. H., Castle, A. F., Kaplan, B. M., & Williams, P. W. Interpersonal judgement and clinical decisions in psychiatric triage. *Journal of Psychiatric Treatment and Evaluation*, in press.

O'Leary, M. R., Speltz, M. L., Donovan, D. M., & Walker, R. D. Implicit preadmission screening criteria in an alcoholism treatment program. *American Journal of Psychiatry*, 1979, *136*, 1190–1193.

O'Leary, M. R., Speltz, M. L., & Walker, R. D. Influence of reported helplessness on client–clinician relationships in an alcoholism program. *Hospital and Community Psychiatry*, 1980, *31*, 783–784.

Palisi, A. T., & Ruzicka, M. F. Practicum students' verbal responses to different clients. *Journal of Counseling Psychology*, 1974, *21*, 87–91.

Parsons, L. B., & Parker, G. V. C. Personal attitudes, clinical appraisals, and verbal behavior of trained and untrained therapists. *Journal of Consulting and Clinical Psychology*, 1968, *32*, 64–71.

Pattison, E. M., Coe, B. S., & Doerr, H. O. Population variation among alcoholism treatment facilities. *International Journal of the Addictions*, 1973, *8*, 199–229.

Reitan, R. M. The validity of the Trail Making Tests as an indicator of organic brain damage. *Perceptual and Motor Skills*, 1958, *8*, 271–276.

Rotter, J. B. Generalized expectancies for internal versus external control of reinforcement. *Psychological Monographs*, 1966, *80* (Whole No. 609).

Ryan, L. R. *Clinical interpretations of the FIRO-B.* Palo Alto, Calif.: Consulting Psychologists Press, 1970.

Schuldt, W. J. Psychotherapists' approach–avoidance responses and clients' expressions of dependency. *Journal of Counseling Psychology*, 1966, *13*, 178–183.

Schutz, W. C. *The interpersonal underworld.* Palo Alto, Calif.: Science and Behavior Books, 1966.

Schwartz, J. M., & Abramowitz, S. I. Value-related effects on psychiatric judgment. *Archives of General Psychiatry*, 1975, *32*, 1525–1529.

Shipley, W. C. *Shipley-Hartford Retreat Scale: Manual and scoring key.* Hartford, Conn.: Hartford Retreat, 1940.

Smart, R. B., Schmidt, W., & Moss, M. K. Social class as a determinant of the type and duration of therapy received by alcoholics. *International Journal of the Addictions*, 1969, *4*, 543–556.

Stern, M. S. Social class and psychiatric treatment of adults in the mental health center. *Journal of Health and Social Behavior*, 1977, *18*, 317–325.

Strupp, H. H., & Wallach, M. S. Psychotherapists' clinical judgements and attitudes toward patients. In H. H. Strupp (Ed.), *Psychotherapy: Clinical, research, and theoretical issues.* New York: Aronson, 1973.

Strupp, H. H., & Williams, J. V. Some determinants of clinical evaluations. In H. H. Strupp (Ed.), *Psychotherapy: Clinical, research, and theoretical issues.* New York: Aronson, 1973.

Trice, H. M., Roman, P. M., & Belasco, J. A. Selection for treatment: A predictive evaluation of an alcoholism treatment regimen. *International Journal of the Addictions*, 1969, *4*, 303–317.

Wills, T. A. Perceptions of clients by professional helpers. *Psychological Bulletin*, 1978, *85*, 968–1000.

Yalom, I. D. *The theory and practice of group psychotherapy* (2nd ed.). New York: Basic Books, 1975.

chapter 3

The Value of Being Explicit
When Making Clinical Decisions[1]

ROBYN M. DAWES

Introduction

Decision making is central to helping. When a psychiatrist or psychologist recommends whether or not to hospitalize a patient, a social worker decides whether or not to place a child in foster care, or a physician opts for one diagnosis and course of treatment rather than another, the decision has important consequences for people's lives. Such decisions have become the object of considerable research over the past 25 years. The research results have suggested that the essential form of the decision-making process is similar across many different types of judgments. Although the particular information with which decision makers deal varies—it may be about psychiatric outpatients, stock performance, medical data, or graduate school applicants—decision makers' judgments follow (statistically) predictable patterns, some good, some bad. We consequently know the general way in which many types of clinical decisions are made, and how they might be

[1]This chapter was written while the author was a Fellow at the Center for Advanced Study in the Behavioral Sciences, 1980–1981. Support was derived from National Science Foundation Grant #BNS–76 22943.

37

improved. My purpose in writing this chapter is to share knowledge of the decision-making process, with a focus on suggesting how that knowledge may be used to make better decisions. I am writing "ex cathedra," as it were, because I myself am not a clinician (although I have done some clinical work). But it is precisely in the findings independent of content that the value of the research lies. And anything that improves decisions helps clients.

The central thesis of this chapter is that clinical judgment can be aided by systematic statistical thinking. For although decisions are made about an individual client, they are best made—and hence the client given the best *chance* of recovery, improvement, or learning to live with a condition—when each case is treated as if it were a guide for repeated decisions in the same circumstance. No single outcome is certain, but when the helper attends consistently to important predictive information, and applies rational decision-making procedures, then the *probability* of a good decision is increased. Moreover, by analyzing a given decision across many different clients (not just one who springs to mind), we can find which aspects are important for successful prediction, and how predictions can best be made.

Another finding in recent work is that people often eschew formal decision-making procedures and statistics, even when they understand their logic and value. Many people (including some psychologists) find numbers and statistics pallid, lifeless, and unmemorable; in contrast, people are quite willing to make decisions on the basis of a single *human* case study, even when they know that the case has been chosen in a biased manner, or know that the statistical information ignored in its favor is highly valid (Borgida & Nisbett, 1977; Nisbett & Borgida, 1975). For example, subjects presented with a videotape interview of a single punitive or mellow prison guard are prone to conclude that most guards are punitive or mellow—even when they are told that the guard interviewed was statistically unrepresentative of prison guards in general (Hamill, Wilson, & Nisbett, 1980). Judgments based on vividness, memorability, or "humanized understanding" of a particular case are compelling, even though they do not work and therefore (inadvertently) inhumane in some settings. Moreover, belief that experience is the best teacher is compelling—even though it is a good teacher only when it provides feedback.

Clinicians are not immune to these human tendencies, and because clinical experience is primarily with individual clients and case studies, there is ample reason to become highly involved in the circumstances and characteristics of a particular client. Yet this involvement may lead the clinician to give less emphasis to important statistical information that could lead to better decisions. The clinician Paul Meehl has described his frustration in attending case conferences at which the participants demonstrate repeated failure to understand probability logic as applied to the single case. The statement he often encountered is: "We aren't dealing with groups, we are dealing with this individual case." (Equivalently, "statistics don't apply to the individual.")

Meehl (1973) argues that denying the relevance of statistics is not helpful to clients:

> He who wishes to reform his thinking in case conferences must constantly reiterate the elementary truth that if you depart in your clinical decision making from a well-established (or even moderately supported) empirical frequency—whether it is based upon psychometrics, life-history material, rating scales, or whatever—your departure may save a particular case from being misclassified predictively or therapeutically; but that such departures are, prima facie, counterinductive, so that a decision *policy* of this kind is almost certain to have a cost that exceeds its benefits [p. 234].[2]

The research evidence does suggest that using a simple formal procedure for decision making will, in the long run, result in more correct decisions. And that also means that such use is the best bet in the "short run." Demonstrating the efficacy of the formal approach is my purpose in writing this chapter.

Recent research has also shown several kinds of bias in human judgment. When predictions or inferences are made inexplicitly and intuitively, that is, without the aid of explicit statistical reasoning, they will be biased in the direction of judging too much pathology to be present, or predicting too much about the future. Such biases—to be discussed in this chapter—have nothing to do with the character of the clinician and do not reflect maliciousness. My purpose here is to describe what the biases are, and to suggest ways in which they can be countered.[3]

In this chapter I hope to give the reader an appreciation of the beauty and usefulness of statistics. Are they lifeless? Perhaps, except when they must be used to help a person decide whether to have operation A or operation B, to apply treatment X or treatment Y, or to hold patients in a hospital or to discharge them—which is all the time. Are statistics dull and unmemorable? I hope not.[4]

---

[2]This point is still misunderstood by psychologists. For example, Gabinet (1981) writes: "In the first place, statistical prediction of abuse is not a predictor in the individual case [Meehl, 1954]."

[3]Plato, Aristotle, the Catholic Church, and Freud all held the "depth psychology" view that cognitive dysfunction is due primarily to interference from noncognitive sources, ranging from animal spirits to unconscious desires. Dawes (1964, 1976) has presented the "shallow psychology" view that most cognitive distortions—even those underlying such horrors as Nazism and the Vietnam War— are due primarily to limitations and biases intrinsic to the cognitive process itself, limitations and biases that can be demonstrated in the laboratory. Not surprisingly, the theses to be presented in this chapter are compatible with the latter view.

[4]But as they are often taught, they are. In my view, one big defect in our educational system— beginning with a demand that children memorize multiplication tables ($8 \times 7 = 56$)—is that we are taught mathematical techniques, rather than reasoning ($8 \times 7 = [10 \times 7] - [2 \times 7] = 70 - 14 = [70 - 10] - 4 = 56$). Thus, mathematics and statistics come to be viewed as the manipulation of symbols, rather than the discovery of structure ("mathematical form"). And who could care less? It is very difficult with such a background to appreciate the importance of mathematics (except for knowing that in some vague way it is essential to all our technology), let alone its beauty. Enough said. This chapter will concentrate entirely on statistical reasoning, not technique.

In the following sections I discuss two substantive issues. First, I discuss statistical considerations in making a clinical judgment, and the bias that may result if these considerations are ignored. Second, I discuss predictions based on multiple inputs, and the superiority of predictions based on simple weighted averages of such input compared to judgments based on human intuition.

Symptom-Disease Relationships

Let us be fanciful for a moment. Suppose that being a psychologist is a disease and that having a Ph.D. is a symptom of that disease. In order to help our clients who may be suffering from this disease, we wish to understand the relationship between it and the symptom. How do we do so?

One way is through anecdote, for example, "I have never yet met a psychologist who didn't claim to have a Ph.D." (In attempting to establish a strong relationship between alcoholism and obsessive–compulsive character, a famous psychologist claimed that he had never yet met an alcoholic who was not an obsessive–compulsive when sober. Maybe the others avoided him.)

Eschewing the obvious vagaries of evidence through anecdote, we may turn to the literature that compares psychologists with normals, or psychologists with people suffering from some other brand of psychopathology. We may, for example, read or hear about a study comparing the frequency of the Ph.D. symptom found in 100 psychologists and 100 normal controls. The results would look something like those in Figure 3.1. (These are *hypothetical* data.)

It is hard to overstate how striking these results would be: a phi value of .98, a chi-square of 192.08. We can conclude that there is a *very strong* relationship between having a Ph.D. and being a psychologist, and if we do not think beyond that verbal association, we are apt to accuse the next person we meet who has a Ph.D. of being a psychologist.

The problem with that accusation is that only 7.56% of people with Ph.D.'s are psychologists (U.S. Bureau of the Census, 1978). Having a Ph.D. may be typical of being a psychologist, but being a psychologist is not typical of holding a Ph.D. (Compare, however, to: "He made a typical schizophrenic response; therefore, he must be schizophrenic.")

What is wrong? Was sampling biased in such a way that the results were incompatible with our knowledge that only 7.56% of Ph.D.'s are psychologists? No, the table simply shows that almost all psychologists have Ph.D.'s and almost everyone else does not; that is not incompatible with the fact that the overwhelming majority of Ph.D. holders are not psychologists.

Irrational conclusions about the Ph.D.–psychologist contingency lie not in any mistake in the technique of assessing it, but in a failure to understand the basic logic of statistical inference (see Dawes, 1962; Meehl & Rosen, 1955). And as will be documented shortly, this failure is widespread.

Ph.D.

	Yes	No
Psychologists	99	1
Normals	1	99

Figure 3.1. Hypothetical sample.

The way to understand the statistical logic in this example is simplicity itself: *Systematically elaborate all possible combinations of symptom and disease and consider the frequencies in all these combinations.* That is a mental act that Piaget claims we all engage in once we reach adolescence, although others (e.g., Dawes, 1975; Wason, 1968, 1969) suggest that although systematic elaboration and consideration of possibilities is a capacity (potential) most of us have, we do not use it routinely (or much).

In the Ph.D.—psychologist example, we note that the combination of being a psychologist and not having a Ph.D. has an extremely low frequency in the general population. (Because people who call themselves psychologists are supposed to have a Ph.D., according to the ethics of their profession, it is unlikely that we will find a psychologist who does not at least claim to have one.) The frequency of the combination Ph.D.–psychologist is much larger, the frequency of the combination Ph.D.–nonpsychologist is about 12 times as large as that, and the frequency of the non-Ph.D.–nonpsychologist combination is huge compared to any of the others. Thus, the study findings—which compare the relative frequencies of the first and second categories to the relative frequencies of the third and fourth—are quite correct, but it is still true that someone who has a Ph.D. is more likely to be an aberrant normal than a

	No Ph.D.	Ph.D.
Psychologists	Cell 1 minuscule	Cell 2 N
Nonpsychologists	Cell 4 huge	Cell 3 $12N$

Figure 3.2. Rough relative frequencies.

normal aberrant (i.e., psychologist). The reason is that the latter inference involves comparing the relative frequencies of the first and third combination to the relative frequencies of the second and fourth. These inferences are illustrated in Figure 3.2.

(Unfortunately, I do not know what N is, and hence the example remains approximate. Government and education handbooks are full of information about how many Ph.D.'s were granted in a given year, and how many were granted in psychology—hence the 7.56% figure. But not even the Census Bureau seems to know how many living people in the United States have Ph.D.'s, let alone Ph.D.'s in psychology.)

Conditional Probabilities

> "Not all Democrats are horse thieves, but all horse thieves are Democrats."
> —Old Western saying

Figure 3.1 yields an estimate of *conditional probabilities*. A conditional probability is of the form: the probability of this given that (e.g., the probability of getting lung cancer given one has smoked heavily for 20 years). Figure 3.2 yields estimates of *compound probabilities*. A compound probability is of the form: *the probability of this **and** that* (e.g., the probability of not getting lung cancer and being a heavy smoker for over 20 years). Finally, *simple probabilities* involve no *givens* or *ands*. Conditional probabilities are usually written with a vertical bar between the subject of the probability and the event given, compound probabilities with a comma, and simple probabilities with no particular markings at all. For example, in our context, $P(S|D)$ refers to the probability of the symptom given the disease, $P(S,D)$ refers to the probability of the joint combination of the symptom and disease (S and D may be written in either order), and $P(S)$ refers to the probability of the symptom. The negation of D and S are symbolized $\bar{D}$ (read "not D") and $\bar{S}$ respectively. For the purpose of making rational judgments, there are only four things necessary to know about simple, compound, and conditional probabilities.

1. For most events or conditions A and B, $P(A|B) \neq P(B|A)$. In fact, the two conditional probabilities may be wildly asymmetric. For example, the probability of being a chronic smoker if you develop lung cancer is approximately .995; nonsmokers do not often get lung cancer, unless they are exposed to industrial pollutants (which can be as subtle as living along a road traveled by trucks carrying asbestos). On the other hand, the probability of developing lung cancer if you are a chronic smoker is .10. You probably will not get lung cancer; you will probably die of something else first.

2. $P(A|B) = P(A,B)/P(B)$. For example, the probability of being addicted to heroin (A) given one smokes pot (B) is equal to the probability of both being addicted and smoking pot (A,B) divided by the probability of smoking

pot. It is decidedly *not* equal to P(A,B)/P(A)—the probability of both smoking pot and being addicted divided by the probability of being addicted; hence the fact that most heroin addicts (A) also smoke pot (A,B) is an irrational justification for draconian marijuana laws.

It follows from Principle 2 that all conditional probabilities may be inferred from compound and simple probabilities. Principle 3 goes one step further.

3. $P(A) = P(A, B) + P(A, \bar{B})$. For example, the probability of a symptom S is equal to the compound probability of the symptom and the disease plus the compound probability of the symptom without the disease: $P(S) = P(S, D) + P(S, \bar{D})$. For example, the probability of seeing dragonflies on the Rorschach (S) is equal to the probability of seeing dragonflies and being schizophrenic (S, D) plus the probability of seeing dragonflies and not being schizophrenic (S, $\bar{D}$). If the latter term (symptom without disease) is quite high, $P(D|S)$ may be quite low, even though $P(S|D)$ is high. The reason is that Principles 2 and 3 may be combined to yield:

4. $$P(A \mid B) = \frac{P(A,B)}{P(A, B) + P(\bar{A},B)} ,$$

and conversely

$$P(B \mid A) = \frac{P(A,B)}{P(A,B) + P(A,\bar{B})}$$

Note than when we substitute Principle 3 in the denominators, the equations reduce to Principle 2 [e.g., because $P(A,B) + P(\bar{A}, B) = P(B)$].

For example, even if a file search revealed that every patient labeled schizophrenic in a clinic saw dragonflies, and that only 10% of the remaining patients did so, then if 95% of the patients were *not* schizophrenic, the probability that one who saw dragonflies would be is

$$\frac{.05}{.05 + .095} = .35,$$

because

$$P(S,D) = P(S \mid D)P(D) = 1.00 \times .05 = .05,$$

and

$$P(S,\bar{D}) = P(S \mid \bar{D})P(\bar{D}) = .10 \times .95 = .095.$$

This example could also be worked out using a 2 × 2 table that would show that $P(S|D)$ and $P(S|\bar{D})$ involved column comparisons, whereas $P(D|S)$ and $P(D|\bar{S})$ involve row comparisons (assuming the rows correspond to schizophrenic versus other).

An extremely important principle follows from these four: *Simple, and hence conditional, probabilities can be inferred from compound probabilities, but not vice versa*. But compound probabilities can be inferred—via Principle 2—only when both conditional and simple probabilities are known. If just simple or just conditional probabilities are known, however, no other type of probability can be inferred. For example, if data of the type presented in Figure 3.1 are collected to estimate $P(S|D)$, one cannot go beyond that without additional information to make inferences about $P(S)$, $P(D)$, $P(D|S)$, $P(S,D)$, or any similar terms involving negations of S and D. To continue the previous hypothetical example, if we knew only that all schizophrenic patients saw dragonflies on the Rorschach in our clinic and that only 10% of our nonschizophrenic patients did—but we did *not* know what proportion of the patients were schizophrenic—then we would have *no* way of assessing the probability that a patient who saw dragonflies was schizophrenic. Consider, for example, the possibility that there was only one schizophrenic patient out of thousands, and he saw dragonflies. That is perfectly compatible with the above figures but the probability that someone who saw dragonflies is schizophrenic would be minuscule. At the other extreme, if all but 10 of thousands were schizophrenic, then this probability would approach one.

Unfortunately, data of the type in Figure 3.1 are those most frequently gathered for assessing symptom–disease contingency, and they are often interpreted without reference to the other necessary probabilities. For example, Gabinet (1981) writes: "Yet in working with high-risk families, the Parenting Program staff has almost always known when parents were at the breaking point. Physical abuse has occurred only in those cases in which neither the parents nor the child protection authorities were willing to remove the child from the home [p. 321]." (In other words, abuse in the home occurs only when the child is in the home; therefore, the Parenting Program staff's judgment is confirmed.) This statement is remarkable. We do not know either the overall rate of abuse *or* the rate of abuse when *no* recommendation is made to remove the child. The method of interpretation is simple: confuse $P(S|D)$ with $P(D|S)$.

POSSIBLE BIASES IN JUDGMENT

The confusion just described will result in a bias to overestimate pathology. In general, $P(S) > P(D)$ because symptoms are common to many diseases, or forms of distress. It follows that $P(S,D)/P(D) > P(S,D)/P(S)$; that is, $P(S|D) > P(D|S)$. Hence the bias toward pathology when confusing the two.

Throughout the previous section, I have been assuming that there is a problem—that confusion in fact exists. The skeptical reader will rightly demand an illustration. The one I have chosen is not from the mental health field, but from medicine—because the issue is so clear. It involves the relationship between mammography results and the presence or absence of breast cancer. My analysis draws heavily from a paper by Eddy (1982). The data are drawn from two published reports by Shapiro (1971, 1977), one unpublished one by Beahrs (Note 1), and appendices to that report supplied to me by Thompson (Note 2). These people are not, however, responsible for the conclusions, which are my own.

EXAMPLE FROM MEDICAL SCREENING

Roughly 1 in 13 women will develop breast cancer at some time in her life, and 1 in 20 will die from its spread. Once a particular growth is suspected of being cancerous, a biopsy can confirm whether or not it is malignant. Because early detection is important, however, and because even biopsies are not without risk (as of 1977 they had a 2% rate of infection or drainage and a .02% death rate), the recently developed X-ray technique of mammography is coming into increasing use for screening for breast cancer. It is based on the fact that components of malignant cells absorb X-rays differently than do components of nonmalignant cells; this differential absorption can be spotted by a radiologist "reading" the X-ray of an area where there is a suspected tumor. Recent refinements in the techniques have reduced the number of rads in most mammography examinations to below 1, an acceptable dosage (the experts think) for an annual examination for women over 50.

There have been two large studies evaluating the mammography reading as an indicator of the disease. (To be consistent with the previous development, we will call a positive result a *symptom*.) Beginning in late 1963, the Health Insurance Plan (HIP) of Greater New York sponsored a study in which 31,000 randomly selected women were offered a free mammography and physical breast examination, and three additional examinations at annual intervals. In addition, 31,000 randomly selected women who continued to receive their usual medical care constituted a control group. These women ranged in age from 40 to 64 at the beginning of the study; their health status was evaluated until December 31, 1975.

The point of the study—which came to be known as the HIP project—was to evaluate the efficacy of such annual mammography and physical examinations in toto in reducing breast cancer deaths, and deaths in general. It worked. Ninety-one women from the group offered screening died of breast cancer, compared to 128 from the control group. There was no compensating increase in deaths due to other causes. This difference occurred despite the fact the 35% of the women in the group offered screening declined it.

Of the 20,200 women who agreed to screening, 1087 had biopsies recommended—either on the basis of mammography readings, physical examinations, or both. Six hundred twenty-four women actually had biopsies, and 127 cancers were found.

For the purposes of this chapter, we will look only at the relationship between the mammography results alone and disease. Estimated *joint frequencies* for mammography results and cancer are given in Figure 3.3. The figure in the lower right cell is approximate because it is necessary to assume that there are no cancers among those women for whom biopsy was not recommended, or rather a trivial number. Although it is not possible to know with certainty that a cancer *is not* present, we can make the approximate assumption that very, very few escape both mammography and physical examination. Moreover, it was necessary to estimate the number in the lower right cell in light of the fact that 42.6% of the women for whom biopsy was recommended refused.

From this joint frequency table, it is possible to estimate conditional probabilities. First, the estimated conditional probability of the symptom—a positive mammography result—given the disease is more than .50 (56%). That is termed the probability of a *detection* in the medical literature. In contrast, the estimated probability of the disease (cancer) given the symptom (a positive mammography result) is less than .50 (37%). That is termed the *true positive* rate.

Note also that there is 98.5% agreement between mammography results and the presence or absence of cancer only because there are so many women who have neither cancer nor a positive reading. One could obtain similar high agreement between ratings of whether children are schizophrenic and whether their mothers are—even if the ratings are not contaminated. Most mothers are not schizophrenic (although a friend of mine in psychiatric social work once estimated the frequency of schizophrenia in the general adult population to be 29%) and most children are not schizophrenic either.

I cannot give joint figures from the later Beahrs report, because—concentrating wholly on the detection rate—it completely omitted the lower right cell. However, it is possible to estimate conditional probabilities from its appendix (courtesy of Donovan Thompson, Note 2). The probability of a positive result given the presence of cancer, $P(S|D)$, has increased to approximately .80, with a corresponding lowering of the probability of cancer given a positive reading, $P(D|S)$, to approximately .20. This test has become more "sensitive," at some expense in "specificity."[5]

MISINTERPRETATIONS OF CONDITIONAL PROBABILITIES

People do confuse these conditional probabilities (e.g., believe the .20 probability of cancer given a positive reading to be the .80 probability of a positive reading given cancer). And they confuse agreement with accuracy.

[5] Incidentally, you could have a perfect detection rate by simply asserting that *all* the women tested had cancer. You could even develop something of a reputation as a diagnostician, because your colleagues would remember that you diagnosed several cancers no one else suspected. Of course, you would soon be shown up in the medical field as a bunco artist, because there would be clear evidence that you were misdiagnosing a number of people who were free of pathology. On

Cancer

Present   Absent

Positive   71   121

Mammography
Reading

Negative   56   11,453

Figure 3.3. Estimated number of cases.

The following are quotes from medical journals and newsletters taken from Eddy's (in press) paper.

"The accuracy of mammography is 90%."

"The results show 79.2% of malignant lesions were correctly diagnosed and 90.4% of benign lesions were correctly diagnosed for an overall accuracy of 87%."

"Asch found a 90% correlation [*sic*] of mammography with the pathologic findings of 500 patients."

What are these writers doing? They are averaging $P(S|D)$ and $P(\bar{S}|\bar{D})$. That does not tell us much about the validity of the readings. Consider, again, the psychologist Ph.D. example:

"The results showed that 99% of psychologists were correctly diagnosed on the basis of having a Ph.D. and 99% of nonpsychologists were correctly diagnosed on the basis of not having a Ph.D., for a 99% correlation of doctorates with the pathologic finding."

The problem is, of course, that those conditional probabilities do not involve *diagnosis*. What does is $P(D|S)$.

Finally, the most blatant error of all:

"In women with proven carcinoma of the breast, in whom mammograms are performed, there is no X-ray evidence of malignant disease in approximately one out of five patients examined. If then on the basis of a negative mammogram, we are to defer biopsy for a solid lesion of the breast, then

the other hand, in the mental health field—where it is never really clear that someone is not "sick"—you might benefit greatly by seeing pathology everywhere. In fact, I know someone who has done so primarily through a profligate and nontechnical use of the term *pseudoneurotic schizophrenic* ("I can tell that this person is sicker than you believed him to be, and since he is a pseudoneurotic, there is nothing he can do to prove me wrong").

there is a one in five chance that we are deferring biopsy on a malignant lesion."

This is wrong. The first sentence refers to the probability of a negative result given cancer is present, whereas the second refers to the probability that cancer is present given a negative result. The former is approximately .20, as stated. The latter, however, is extremely small (see Figure 3.3). To appreciate the logic of this confusion, *suppose* that only 5 women had cancer out of 20,000 with solid lesions on whom both mammography and a biopsy were performed. If one cancer were missed by mammography, then 20% of cancers would have, in fact, been missed. That would not be incompatible with the finding that *all* other women had negative results on mammography and hence there is 1 chance in 19,996 (not 5) that on the basis of a negative mammography result "we are deferring biopsy on a malignant lesion." (Remember, these figures are hypothetical.) (Incidentally, if we followed the writer's advice, we would perform biopsies on *all* women with any sort of lesion or growth—hardly a rational use of mammography.)

Dispersed quotes are easy to come by. Is there a general trend to confuse $P(S|D)$ with $P(D|S)$? Eddy (1982) informally polled 100 medical colleagues. He found that, "unfortunately, most physicians (approximately 95 out of 100 in an informal sample by the author) misinterpret the statements about the accuracy of the test and estimate $P(ca|pos)$ to be about 75% [p. 11]."

How do these results affect patients? Too many biopsies. The fact is that a negative mammography result is *extremely* diagnostic, and yet people are urged to ignore it due to the confused interpretation of the .20 value of $P(\bar{S}|D)$. Moreover, a positive result is much *less* diagnostic than it is believed to be.[6]

SUMMARY

Those are the types of diagnostic confusion that are commonly found—all biased toward overestimating pathology—when careful counts of instances have been made. My recommendation for avoiding these biases is to estimate conditional probabilities *explicitly*, perhaps using Principles 1 and 4 mechanically until thoroughly familiar with the logic. One may feel like a "mere clerk" for doing so, but the patient may benefit. For example, Shulman, Elstein, and Sprafka (1978) have found that medical diagnosticians who use explicit search and test procedures are superior to those who do not.

[6]Medical people who perform unnecessary operations and order unnecessary tests are often accused of doing so out of greed. The "shallow psychology" approach of this chapter leads to the conclusion that confused probabilistic thinking alone will lead to these practices. Also, Shulman, Elstein, and Sprafka (1978) demonstrate a cognitive bias among physicians to seek potentially confirming information when they should seek potentially disconfirming information. That too leads to too much testing.

Intuitive Estimation

When frequencies (or relative frequencies) are estimated intuitively, or on the basis of memory, the bias problem is even worse, and in the same direction. Here, I will first review some studies in which instances of disease–symptom combinations are presented and the subjects are asked to estimate relationships, then studies in which relationships are estimated on ideas and instances that "come to mind" from memory or training, or from anchors or question frames that direct thinking.

ILLUSORY CORRELATION

Chapman and Chapman (1967, 1969), noting that certain "obvious" signs of psychopathology in Rorschach responses are in fact unrelated to actual diagnosis (as is almost everything else on the Rorschach), decided to test whether there was an illusory relationship. For example, there is no relation between male homosexuality and a tendency to see rear parts of the human anatomy (i.e., buttocks), or anal parts. Chapman and Chapman found that clinical psychologists believe there to be such a relationship. They then presented naive subjects with a series of Rorschach responses paired with diagnoses in such a way that there was no statistical relationship between these obvious (but invalid) signs and homosexuality. Nevertheless, their subjects judged the signs to be related to that diagnosis. In addition, Chapman and Chapman ran a study in which they created a statistical relationship between the diagnosis and a nonobvious but possibly true sign (for males, seeing large monsters), while maintaining the obvious but incorrect sign unrelated to the diagnosis. (There is some evidence that male homosexuality is, or was, related to seeing such monsters—perhaps an unconscious characterization of one's mother.) Here again, the subjects believed there to be a relationship between the diagnosis and the obvious sign, but not between the diagnosis and the sign that was both correct and statistically paired with it. The prior bias of the subjects created an illusory correlation that overwhelmed the data. (Of course, it is always possible that the subjects were responding to their theories of what *should* be seen, that their theories were correct, and that the previous finding of no relationship was what was incorrect, for example, because the wrong patients had been used.)[7]

Rothbart, Evans, and Fulero (1979) showed the same type of illusory

---

[7] The subjects in all these experiments, unless otherwise characterized, were college students; aside from capitalizing on their availability, the use of students is based on the assumption that their cognitive biases and limitations are similar to everyone else's, including experts'. This assumption has yet to be challenged empirically.

correlation when the expected relationship was not based on subjects' prior beliefs, but instead was supplied by the experimenters. They asked subjects to recall 50 behaviors, 17 of which were friendly (but previously judged neither intelligent nor unintelligent), 17 of which were intelligent (but previously judged neither friendly nor unfriendly), 3 of which were unfriendly, 3 of which were unintelligent, and 10 of which were neutral with regard to friendliness and intelligence. The experimenters attempted to create a *stereotype* by explaining that all these behaviors had been engaged in by a group of people known to be particularly (*a*) friendly or (*b*) intelligent. This attempt at stereotype formation was successful: Subjects estimated there were more congruent behaviors (e.g., intelligent ones) than unrelated ones (e.g., friendly). (But there was no effect for incongruent behaviors related to the stereotype as opposed to the other negative behaviors.) And subjects recalled more congruent behaviors.

Smedslund (1963) asked nurses to estimate the contingency between a symptom and a disease on the basis of instances presented from the four logically possible combinations (symptom present versus absent crossed by disease present versus absent).

Smedslund found that the estimates were systematically related *only* to the frequency with which the symptom *and* the disease occurred, and that the frequencies of the other three possibilities were ignored. That is, the subjects responded only to the frequencies in Cell 1 ("I've known several people who were short of breath one day and who had a heart attack the next; therefore . . . "). The disease was hypothetical; hence there was no prior idea that the symptom and the disease should be associated.

Hamilton and Gifford (1976) as well showed that it is possible to create an illusory correlation in a situation in which subjects have no prior bias. These investigators presented subjects with instances of positive and negative behaviors (69% versus 31%) attributed to members of Group A or Group B. Two-thirds of each type of behavior was attributed to Group A and one-third to Group B. Although there was no relationship between type of behavior and group membership, Hamilton and Gifford argued that since both undesirable behaviors and membership in Group B were in a minority, they would become associated in the subjects' mind, due to their distinctiveness. In fact, when presented with the undesirable behaviors, subjects attributed 52% (rather than the correct 33%) to members of Group B. In contrast, only 35% (close to the correct 33%) of desirable behaviors were attributed to members of Group B. Does mere minority satus (e.g., being a criminal and being a minority group member) create an illusory correlation? Hamilton and Gifford reversed their procedure by presenting behaviors two-thirds of which were negative, and then they found an illusory correlation between Group B membership and *positive* behaviors.

JUDGMENTAL HEURISTICS: REPRESENTATIVENESS AND AVAILABILITY

Tversky and Kahneman (1974) have reviewed heuristics by which people establish statistical contingencies in the absence of any systematically presented instances. One such heuristic is *representativeness*: If the instance about which we have no information is representative of a category, then it probably belongs to it. And to the degree to which representative information is compelling, this judgment is made without reference to the known or estimated frequencies (base rates) of the category in question (Ginosar & Trope, 1980). For example, a young man is said to be of high intelligence, although lacking in true creativity. He is said to have a need for order and clarity, and for neat and tidy systems (Kahneman & Tversky, 1973, p. 238). Ninety-five percent of subjects presented with this description judged that the man would be more likely to major in computer science in graduate school than in humanities or education, even though these same subjects judged there to be almost three times as many majors in the latter fields. Moreover, subjects persisted in such judgments even when they were told that the personality sketch was written 5 years earlier by an unknown psychologist on the basis of projective tests— despite the fact that these subjects estimated that projective tests would yield only a 23% hit rate for predicting graduate majors 5 years later! Moreover, Tversky and Kahneman have found that such judgments remained unaltered when base rates were experimentally manipulated. Ignoring base rates—when they are presented in an abstract manner—is the most replicable finding in this field. Yet, as has been argued in this paper, these base rates (e.g., the simple probabilities of D or $\bar{D}$ unrelated to the evidence) are absolutely essential for reaching logically correct decisions (Dawes, 1962; Meehl & Rosen, 1955).

Another heuristic is termed *availability*. Briefly, instances are judged by the ease with which they come to mind. For example, in order to determine whether a suicide threat should be taken seriously, a clinician may attempt to think of other suicide threats he or she has heard in the past. Naturally, the instances that come readily to mind are those in which the person who threatened actually committed suicide. The estimate based on mental availability will then be quite discrepant from an estimate based on counting (e.g., going back over prospective notes).

Anchoring, yet another heuristic, can best be explained by an example. Suppose you are asked to estimate (Slovic & Lichtenstein, 1971) the percentage of African nations in the United Nations (U.N.), *but* you are first asked to answer one of two questions: (1) Are over 10% in it? or (2) Are over 65% in it? Naturally, which question you are asked has no bearing on the percentage of African nations in the U.N., and consequently should have no effect on your second answer. But it does. The median estimate of people asked the 10%

question first was 25%, whereas that of the people asked the 65% question first was 45%. The first question, even though it is arbitrary, provides an anchor that directs thinking.

Finally, the way in which questions are framed can be an obvious source of bias—so obvious that it is often overlooked. For example, when we ask: "Why is Mr. Jones so sick?" we are eliciting information about pathology, not strength. We could ask: "Why is Mr. Jones not sicker?" ("With his background and stresses, why has he managed to function outside a hospital so many years?") And we thereby elicit information about strength. We can ask not why someone gets drunk so often, by why he stays sober so often. These different questions can elicit evaluatively different information, from the same source. In fact, Tversky and Kahneman (1981) have shown that even when the *same* information is elicited from questions framed in different ways, the decision may be different. For example, when Tversky and Kahneman's subjects were asked whether they would prefer to save for certain 200 of 400 people threatened by an epidemic or take a 50–50 chance on saving all 400 or none, most chose to save the 200. But when subjects were asked whether they would prefer to let 200 die for certain or take a 50–50 chance that none or all would die, most preferred the 50–50 chance.

SUMMARY

So much for intuitive estimation of frequency. But does it lead to a systematic bias in the direction of overestimating pathology from symptoms? Only if the answer to any of the following questions is yes. Do clinicians have a prior idea that the symptom should be associated with the diagnosis? Will clinicians over time have more and more experience with the joint occurrence of the symptom and disease? Are both symptoms and disease low-frequency events? Are the people with the symptoms who most readily spring to mind those with the disease also? Will the disease possibly serve as an anchor? Do clinicians ask why people are so sick?

I do not have good advice on how to avoid these biases. Experimental psychologists have been able to change some sorts of biases sometimes—but it is not clear that their subjects' thinking outside the laboratory is affected. Subjects are compliant, and if they are told that their answers are wrong, they will change them. In some contexts (see, for example, Lichtenstein, Slovic, Fischhoff, Layman, & Combs, 1978), even that is not possible.

All I can recommend is to *think sideways*—that is, to look at the decision or inference from perspectives that are not those normally adopted. Do it deliberately but playfully at the same time, if possible. Realize that a serious commitment to a patient or client is in no way incompatible with the entertainment of all logical possibilities. The solution to a problem—no matter how humanly crucial—does, in the end analysis, require problem-solving skills.

Making Better Multivariate Predictions

Multivariate prediction refers to the prediction of a criterion variable from many predictors. Typical criterion variables of interest to psychologists and others involved in the helping professions are psychiatric diagnosis (after extensive testing), prognosis, recidivism, death, and the potential success of applicants to graduate school in health-related professions. Typical predictor variables are psychological test scores, interview impressions, characteristics of physical tests such as biopsies, letters of recommendation, and self-ratings on relevant dimensions. The criterion variables to be reviewed here are crude psychiatric diagnosis (psychotic versus neurotic), college success, graduate school success, parole violation, elementary training school success of GIs, longevity of patients with Hodgkin's disease (before it could be arrested), and (even) business bankruptcies. The predictor variables are the "obvious" ones suited to each problem, that is, those that people who have studied the problem believe (correctly) will predict, and which are therefore obvious to *them*.

How is the prediction best made? One way is through *clinical integration* of the predictor information. The clinical expert simply looks at the predictors and makes an estimate of the criterion value: for example, yes or no (this prisoner will or will not violate parole), a check on a 6-point scale indicating how good a psychologist the applicant would probably be, a categorization of the severity of Hodgkin's disease, or a probability estimate that a firm will go bankrupt within the next 3 years. The predictor information may or may not be coded numerically, or categorically. The clinical integration may be done one case at a time or with all the information displayed in front of the clinical judge. With the exception of standardized medical tests, most multivariate predictions are made in this manner, that is, done by a single individual recognized as an expert (e.g., psychiatrist, psychologist) or by a group of people recognized as experts (e.g., an admissions committee, a parole board).

Another method of prediction is through the *statistical integration* of the predictor information. Each criterion variable is numerically coded in a manner compatible with its meaning (e.g., 1 for psychotic and 0 for neurotic, 1–5 for increasingly favorable categories of faculty evaluations of former graduate students). Then each predictor is coded in such a way that higher values on the predictor are believed to be associated with higher values on the criterion. This coding is done prior to the statistical analysis relating predictors to criterion. For example, GPAs (grade point averages) and GRE (graduate record examination) scores are coded so that high numbers predict higher probability of success. Then, the final prediction is made on the basis of a multiple regressional analysis, which finds the best *linear combination* (i.e., weighted average) for predicting the criterion.

COMPARISONS OF INTUITIVE AND EXPLICIT DECISIONS

Meehl (1954) and Sawyer (1966) have compared the two means of prediction, reviewing over 60 studies. Most of these studies involved a comparison of statistical versus clinical prediction based on exactly identical inputs, where the statistic of comparison was the correlation coefficient— between the actual and predicted values for the clinical method, and the *cross-validated correlation* for the statistical method.[8]

In all the studies reviewed, statistical (linear) prediction did at least as well as or better than intuitive prediction. In addition, in those studies in which there were differences in the amount of predictor information, the clinical judge had more; in some cases the clinical experts had access to interview information or letters of recommendation that were not used in the regression equation (Bloom & Brundage, 1947; Dawes, 1971). Still intuitive judgment did not do as well. And note that the superiority of statistical integration occurred despite the greater flexibility of clinical integration; the clinician is not constrained by a prior choice of how to code the predictor variables and is not required to use a linear weighting system. Incidentally, the finding that interviews were worthless in this situation is consistent with the review conclusion of Kelly (1954), who maintained that they are good in predictive situations only to the extent that they are standardized (i.e., approach tests).

Two examples can be found in Einhorn (1972) and in Deacon (1972) and Libby (1976). In Einhorn's study, expert doctors coded biopsies of patients with Hodgkin's disease and then made an overall rating of the severity of the process. The overall ratings of severity did not predict the survival times of 193 patients, all of whom died. The variables that the doctors coded did, however, predict survival time when used in a multiple regression model. Deacon and Libby were concerned with predicting which 30 of 60 financially shaky firms would go bankrupt within 3 years. (Rather, they were concerned with "postdictions" from people and statistical models who had no knowledge of which 30 firms went under.) The predictor variables were business ratios chosen by bank loan officers and other financial experts. Deacon found that a linear model would predict with 78% accuracy on cross-validation, and Libby found that 16 loan officers from large banks could predict with 74% success.

---

[8]The multiple regression analysis yields optimal weights for combining the predictors in a linear way in order to maximize the correlation with the criterion values; these weights are then applied to a new sample of data. Because in this sample of data they do not optimize anything, these weights form a linear combination of the predictors that is directly comparable to the clinical prediction.

That is almost a tie, but when you consider the potential amount of money involved . . . .

It is my contention that if there is only *one* patient involved, it is ethically advisable to use the prediction method that has been found to be superior, or to invent a new one that can withstand the ravages of scientific skepticism. For although this or that study may be imperfect (e.g., Einhorn's doctors were trying to predict severity, not longevity), there has yet to be a single study whose results go in the opposite direction. The studies favoring statistical integration should be rejected only if they can be shown to have systematic flaws.

Why does statistical prediction work? The two studies just outlined provide a clue. In both, the experts *chose* the variables, and in the Einhorn study they *coded* them as well. If people are better at choosing and coding information than at integrating it, then a system that makes use of peoples' selection and coding abilities, while removing the integration problem from them, may be optimal. In fact, cognitive psychologists have found that people are much worse at integrating information than they naively believe themselves to be— especially information from intrinsically incomparable dimensions (Dawes, 1979). Statistical prediction solves this problem by having the integration of data done automatically. (This explanation hinges on the assumption that the thinking processes of experts are no different from those of the rest of us, an assumption stated earlier.)

But building a regression model requires a numerical criterion. What if none is available? Or what if the sample is so small that the weights in the linear composite cannot be estimated with acceptable accuracy? Is there nothing to do other than fall back on clinical integration?

A number of us became interested in this problem after noting that regression analyses could be performed using a clinical judge's estimate of the criterion values in place of the true values, and that such models out-performed the judges themselves when these true criterion values were later available. We termed such a procedure *bootstrapping*, and thought it was due to the weights of the linear models distilling the essence of the judges' expertise while simultaneously removing random and situational variability— or some such Pythagorean nonsense (Dawes, 1971).

What this interpretation implied, however, was that the linear composites derived from the judges' behavior should be superior to other linear composites, and that turned out not to be true. Weights determined ad hoc do almost as well—and just as well as the weights obtained from analyzing the judges. What Corrigan and I (Dawes & Corrigan, 1974) did was to construct *random linear models* consisting of weights whose directions (positive or negative) were determined a priori but whose magnitude was determined at random. They did as well as the weights determined from the judges, and better than the judgment of the clinicians, in the data sets available to us. For mathematical reasons beyond the scope of this chapter, unit weights (each being the average of all possible random weights) did better yet. For example, when predicting (reliable) faculty ratings of students who had been in graduate school in psychology at the University of Oregon from 2 to 5 years, the unit-weighted average of the (standardized) variables available in the admissions files at entrance correlated .48 with the criterion. In contrast, the average judgment of the members of the admissions committee for 1 year correlated only .19 with the criterion. (Because the admissions form changed from year to year, only the ratings of the committee evaluating the largest number of accepted applicants could be examined.)

Why are such random or unit models superior to clinical judgment? First, the problems associated with informal integration of information are, as has been noted, severe. Second, the problems of forming a weighted average with approximate weights are not severe, provided that (*a*) all the weights are in the right direction and (*b*) the predictors are not negatively related to (correlated with) each other. It was over 40 years ago that Wilks (1938) noted that linear composites satisfying these conditions do, in fact, correlate highly with each other, and Corrigan and I essentially rediscovered this with our random linear models. But the Wilks article was largely ignored except for weighting items in a test equally. Now, with the understanding that it applied to a vast body of prediction and decision-making problems, this finding has been expanded upon (Wainer, 1976), occasionally challenged, but not found wanting. (One can always *hypothesize* situations with unknown direction or negative correlations and show that it will not work, but none has been found—just as no instance of superiority of clinical judgment to multiple regression has been discovered.) As Dawes and Corrigan (1974) concluded: "The whole trick is to know what variables to look at and then to know how to add [p. 105]."

Conclusion

Diagnosis and classification are best done by explicitly counting, considering all logical possibilities, noting or estimating as best one can the frequency of each, and then keeping in mind the distinctions between simple, compound, and conditional probabilities. It is especially important not to confuse different conditional probabilities. That may not be as much fun as making a diagnosis or classification on the basis of a burst of intuition, unless one enjoys logical puzzles, but its results are better, and, if these activities are of any value to clients, it serves them better as well. In particular, *all the confusion and intuitive estimation procedures described earlier in this paper systematically lead to an overestimation of pathology*.

Prediction, as well, is best done by taking thought, not about the specific cases, alternatives, or people about whom the prediction is to be made, but about the variables by which it is best made. Then perform a multiple regression analysis, if one is possible, or pick weights that you have reason to believe are close to the best possible weights, or simply standardize and add. Again, this may not sound like much fun, but it works.

Reference Notes

1. Beahrs, O. H. *Summary report of the group to review NCJ/ACS breast cancer detection projects.* Mimeograph, September 6, 1977.
2. Thompson, D. Personal communication, February 18, 1979.

References

Bloom, R. F., & Brundage, E. G. Prediction of success in elementary schools for enlisted personnel. In D. B. Smith (Ed.), *Personnel research and test development in the Bureau of Naval Personnel.* Princeton, N.J.: Princeton Univ Press, 1947.

Borgida, E., & Nisbett, R. E. The differential impact of abstract vs. concrete information on decisions. *Journal of Applied Social Psychology*, 1977, 7, 258–271.

Chapman, L. J. Illusory correlation in observational reports. *Journal of Verbal Learning and Verbal Behavior*, 1967, 6, 151–155.

Chapman, L. J., & Chapman, J. P. Illusory correlation as an obstacle to the use of valid diagnostic signs. *Journal of Abnormal Psychology*, 1969, 74, 271–280.

Dawes, R. M. A note on base rates and psychometric efficiency. *Journal of Consulting Psychology*, 1962, 36, 422–434.

Dawes, R. M. Cognitive distortion. *Psychological Reports Monograph Supplement*, 1964, 14, 443–459.

Dawes, R. M. A case study of graduate admissions: Applications of three principles of human decision making. *American Psychologist*, 1971, 26, 180–188.

Dawes, R. M. The mind, the model, and the task. In F. Restle, R. M. Shiffroy, N. J. Castellan, H. R. Lindman, & D. P. Pisoni (Eds.), *Cognitive theory* (Vol. 1). Hillsdale, N. J.: Erlbaum, 1975.

Dawes, R. M. Shallow psychology. In J Carroll & J. Payne (Eds.), *Cognition and social behavior.* Hillsdale, N.J.: Erlbaum, 1976.

Dawes, R. M. The robust beauty of improper linear models in decision making. *American Psychologist*, 1979, 34, 571–582.

Dawes, R. M., & Corrigan, B. Linear models in decision making. *Psychological Bulletin*, 1974, 81, 95–106.

Deacon, E. B. A discriminant analysis of the predictors of business failure. *Journal of Accounting Research*, 1972, 10, 167–179.

Eddy, D. M. Probabilistic reasoning in clinical medicine: Problems and opportunities. In D. Kahneman, P. Slovic, & A. Tversky (Eds.), *Judgment under uncertainty: Heuristics and biases.* Cambridge: Cambridge Univ. Press, 1982.

Einhorn, H. J. Expert measurement and mechanical combination. *Organizational Behavior and Human Performance*, 1972, 7, 86–106.

Gabinet, L. Comment on Jay Belsky. *American Psychologist*, 1981, 36, 320–322.

Ginosar, Z., & Trope, Y. The effects of base rates and individuating information on judgments about another person. *Journal of Experimental Social Psychology*, 1980, 16, 228–242.

Hamill, R., Wilson, T. D., & Nisbett, R. E. Insensitivity to sample bias: Generalizing from atypical cases. *Journal of Personality and Social Psychology*, 1980, 38, 889–906.

Hamilton, D. L., & Gifford, R. K. Illusory correlation in interpersonal perceptions: A cognitive basis of stereotype judgments. *Journal of Experimental Social Psychology*, 1976, 12, 392–407.

Kahneman, D., & Tversky, A. On the psychology of prediction. *Psychological Review*, 1973, *80*, 237–252.

Kelly, E. L. Evaluation of the interview as a selection technique. In *Proceedings of the 1953 Conference on Testing Problems*. Princeton, N.J.: Educational Testing Service, 1954.

Libby, R. Man versus model of man: Some conflicting evidence. *Organizational Behavior and Human Performance*, 1976, *16*, 1–12.

Lichtenstein, S., Slovic, P., Fischhoff, B., Layman, M., & Combs, B. Judged frequency of lethal events. *Journal of Experimental Psychology: Human Learning and Memory*. 1978, *11*, 551–578.

Meehl, P. E. *Clinical versus statistical prediction: A theoretical analysis and a review of the evidence*. Minneapolis: Univ. of Minnesota Press, 1954.

Meehl, P. E.(Ed.). *Psychodiagnosis: Selected papers*. Minneapolis: Univ. of Minnesota Press, 1973.

Meehl, P. E., & Rosen, A. Antecedent probability and the efficiency of psychometric signs, patterns, or cutting scores. *Psychological Bulletin*, 1955, *52*, 194–216.

Nisbett, R. E., & Borgida, E. Attribution and the psychology of prediction. *Journal of Personality and Social Psychology*, 1975, *32*, 932–943.

Rothbart, M., Evans, M., & Fulero, S. Recall for continuing events, memory processes and the maintenance of social stereotypes. *Journal of Experimental Social Psychology*, 1979, *15*, 343–355.

Sawyer, J. Measurement and prediction, clinical *and* statistical. *Psychological Bulletin*, 1966, *66*, 178–200.

Shapiro, S. Periodic breast cancer screening in reducing mortality from breast cancer. *Journal of the American Medical Association*, 1971, *215*, 1780.

Shapiro, S. Evidence on screening for breast cancer from a randomized trial. *Cancer*, 1977, *39*, 2772–2782.

Shulman, L. S., Elstein, A. S., & Sprafka, S. *Medical problem solving: An analysis of clinical reasoning*. Cambridge, Mass.: Harvard Univ. Press, 1978.

Slovic, P., & Lichtenstein, S. Comparison of Bayesian and regression approaches to the study of information processing in judgment. *Organizational Behavioral Human Performance*, 1971, *6*, 649–744.

Smedslund, J. The concept of correlation in adults. *Scandinavian Journal of Psychology*, 1963, *4*, 163–173.

Tversky, A., & Kahneman, D. Judgment under uncertainty: Heuristics and biases. *Science*, 1974, *185*, 1124–1130.

Tversky, A., & Kahneman, D. The framing of decisions and the psychology of choice. *Science*, 1981, *211*, 453–458.

U.S. Bureau of the Census. *Statistical abstracts of the United States: 1978*. Washington, D.C.: Government Printing Office, 1978.

Wainer, H. Estimating coefficients in linear models: It don't make no nevermind. *Psychological Bulletin*, 1976, *41*, 9–34.

Wason, P. C. Reasoning about a rule. *Quarterly Journal of Experimental Psychology*, 1968, *20*, 273–281.

Wason, P. C. Regression in reasoning? *British Journal of Psychology*, 1969, *60*, 471–480.

Wilks, S. S. Weighting systems for linear functions of correlated variables when there is no dependent variable. *Psychometrika*, 1938, *8*, 23–40.

chapter 4

An Attribution Theory Analysis of Trained Helpers' Inferences about Clients' Needs

C. DANIEL BATSON
KAREN O'QUIN
VIRGINIA PYCH

Introduction

Typically, the first step in the delivery of professional help is to locate the problem. For the trained helper—whether doctor, therapist, counselor, social worker, or minister—the initial question is: "What seems to be the problem?" Although a clear answer to this question may not be immediately forthcoming, the helper must arrive at some answer. And that answer, whether well founded or not, will almost certainly affect the subsequent helping process, and hence the client's well-being.

The importance of the helper's answer to this question becomes clear when the answer is wrong. Consider, for example, the case of a young newlywed who complained of abdominal pains at bedtime. Her therapist inferred that the pains were due to sexual fears, and told her so. Based on this diagnosis, the young woman began to make disparaging inferences about her own psychological health. Over time, her anxiety increased, providing fuel for further self-deprecation. She continued to get worse, until she happened to visit an old-fashioned doctor. He suggested that her pains might not be a sign of sexual fears but an allergic reaction. Tests proved that she was, indeed, allergic to

Basic Processes in Helping Relationships

tomatoes. The young woman stopped eating tomatoes, and her "sexual fears" disappeared (Valins & Nisbett, 1972).

Admittedly, this is an extreme example. We present it not to suggest that blatant errors of this kind are common, but to suggest, first, the importance of the inferences that trained helpers make about a client's need and, second, that making such inferences about the nature of problems can be extremely difficult. Often, the helper cannot observe the problem directly, only its consequences, and these may form a complex and even inconsistent pattern. Errors in helpers' inferences about clients' needs, although lamentable, seem inevitable.

But here we encounter a cause for added concern. A number of researchers (Batson, 1975; Caplan & Nelson, 1973; Goffman, 1961; Halleck, 1971; Langer & Abelson, 1974; Rosenhan, 1973) have suggested that we must expect more than inevitable, chance errors; these researchers suggest that there is a systematic bias in the way trained helpers make inferences about clients' needs.

THE CHARGE OF DISPOSITIONAL BIAS IN HELPERS' INFERENCES

These researchers claim that trained helpers have a *dispositional bias*, that they are likely to infer that a client's problem lies with the client as a person even when it is really due to some aspect of the client's situation. Trained helpers, it is said, are too quick to infer personal problems (e.g., an inability to deal with authority figures) from the disturbed, upset actions of a person attempting to cope with a problematic situation (e.g., an unreasonably demanding boss). Moreover, these researchers claim to have evidence of this kind of bias, and not only on the part of helpers trained in the person-oriented model of depth psychology but also on the part of clinicians, counselors, social workers, and ministers trained in situation-oriented and interactive models.

To illustrate this dispositional bias, Goffman (1961) presented dramatic anecdotes of the inferences of psychiatrists in mental hospitals. For example:

> I have seen a therapist deal with a Negro patient's complaints about race relations in a partially segregated hospital by telling the patient that he must ask himself why he, among all the other Negroes present, chose this particular moment to express this feeling, and what this expression could mean about him as a person, apart from the state of race relations in the hospital at the time [pp. 376–377].

Szasz (1961, 1963), Laing (1967), Halleck (1971), and Rosenhan (1973, 1975) have presented similar anecdotes. But anecdotes are not enough.

To accuse trained helpers of bias in their inferences about clients' problems is a serious charge. If true, it raises questions about the appropriateness of a wide range of institutional helping services; if false, it could inappropriately undermine public confidence in these services, keeping needy individuals from valuable sources of help. Thus, it seems essential to resist jumping to a verdict, whether pro or con. Instead, we need to consider seriously and carefully whether such bias exists.

As a first step toward this goal, it is necessary to gain some conceptual understanding of how a dispositional bias might arise. Attribution theory (Heider, 1958; Jones & Davis, 1965; Kelley, 1967) has proved quite useful in providing a conceptual framework for identifying and studying potential sources of inferential bias. So we have tried to understand helpers' inferences from the perspective of attribution theory.

THE INFERENCE PROCESS FROM THE PERSPECTIVE OF ATTRIBUTION THEORY

Think about the case of a student who comes for help to a university counseling service. He complains that his residence hall has been extremely noisy and that his parents have been pressuring him, so that he cannot concentrate. As a result, he has been unable to prepare for a final exam to be given the next day, and he wants the counselor to help by getting him permission to take the exam late. Has the counselor been handed a fabricated excuse by a student who is irresponsible in his studies and is now trying to escape the consequences? If so, to comply with his request would not help the student with his real problem; it would only reinforce irresponsibility. But if the student is telling the truth, to refuse his request would not only be failing to help in the immediate situation; it might also make it less likely that the student would ever seek a counselor's help again.

How will the counselor decide what the student's problem really is? In thinking about the inference process from the perspective of attribution theory, we need to be clear first on the type of attribution at issue. Attribution theory has tended to focus on causal attributions, but as leading attribution theorists have long been aware (cf. Heider, 1958; Jones & Davis, 1965), not all inferences concern causes. Indeed, the most important attribution made about a client's problem by a helper seems to be a *locus attribution* rather than a causal one. A helper is less concerned to know what caused the problem than to know where the problem lies.

The distinction between causal and locus attributions becomes clear if we think in terms of an analogy proposed by Erving Goffman (1961). He suggests a parallel between repairing automobiles and helping people; both involve tinkering with a complex system to get it to work better. So think first about causal versus locus attributions in auto repair. If your car is not running well because a fender is rubbing against a tire, you will make little progress toward getting the car to run better by knowing that a recent minor collision *caused* the problem. You need to know the *location* of the rub if you are to fix it. Now apply the distinction between causal and locus attributions to our example of the student who wants to have his exam postponed. Even if the counselor were able to ascertain with confidence that the student was irresponsible because of his parents' inconsistent child-rearing practices (a situational cause), it would not change the fact that the problem requiring attention is the irresponsibility that had become a characteristic of him as a person (a dispositional locus).

As this example also implies, at the most general level, the counselor's locus attribution involves a dichotomous choice: dispositional versus situational. Locus attributions do not seem to be made on two independent dimensions, one dispositional and one situational. This kind of multidimensionality is often found for causal attributions (cf. House, Note 1), but it makes less sense for locus attributions, because it is hard to imagine something being in two different locations at once. One can, of course, imagine a helper deciding that there are problems lying both with the client and with his or her situation, although such cases are probably best conceived as ones in which there are multiple problems.

For a given problem, then, the helper's most basic attribution is to decide whether the problem lies within the client (a dispositional attribution) or with the client's physical and social environment (a situational attribution). Actually, there is a third possibility as well, that the problem lies with the client being in this situation (an interactional attribution). Even though interactional attributions are possible, and indeed are often advocated in theory, they seem to be relatively rare in practice. Perhaps this is because they require a more complex view of the need situation or because the helping reponse most often implied by an interactional attribution, removing the person from the situation, is seldom a viable alternative. Although we recognize the possibility of an interactional attribution, we shall focus our attention on the dichotomous choice between dispositional and situational attributions. A dispositional attribution should lead to a helping response directed toward changing something about the client; a situational attribution either to acting directly to change something about the client's situation or to helping the client act to change it.

Given this basic choice between a dispositional and a situational locus attribution, let us return to the question of how the counselor in our example will go about deciding where the student's problem lies. Generalizing from Kelley's (1967) analysis of causal attributions, we may expect the counselor to follow the logic of analysis of variance in making a locus attribution. If this student has made similar complaints before every final exam, the counselor may attribute the problem to the student and not believe that the problem lies with his social situation. On the other hand, if this student has never made such a request before and his residence hall is widely known to be rowdy, the counselor's attribution is more likely to be situational. In the former case, the student as a person covaries with the complaints; in the latter case, his situation does.

Although this method of covariation seems an eminently rational way to infer where the problem lies, a closer look at the attribution process suggests a way that a dispositional bias may creep into such inferences. Jones and Nisbett (1972) suggested that whereas a person acting in a situation is likely to attribute any difficulties to characteristics of the situation, an observer of the situation is more likely to attribute these difficulties to dispositional characteristics of the actor. Applying this actor–observer difference to the helping situation, we would expect the student seeking help to emphasize the situational determinants of the problem, making a situational attribution. But the counselor, as an observer, should instead focus upon the student as the source of the trouble, making a dispositional attribution. This observer-role predilection toward dispositional attributions, if strong enough, could override a logical inference based on Kelley's (1967) analysis of variance model.

An observer-role bias is not the only reason to suggest a dispositional bias in trained helpers' attributions. As we shall see, the specific role of helper also brings pressures to bear that could encourage dispositional attributions. In all, we have been able to identify seven potential sources of a dispositional bias in trained helpers' attributions, four due to the helpers being in the role of *observer*, and three to their being in the specific role of *helper*.

Seven Potential Sources of Dispositional Bias in Helpers' Attributions

In Figure 4.1 we have presented a schematic model that lists these seven possible sources of dispositional bias. The list is not intended to be exhaustive, but these seven sources are the ones most frequently considered by attribution researchers.

The model in Figure 4.1 places these seven factors in the context of the overall inference process, in which the helper collects information and uses it to reach decisions about, first, where the client's problem lies and, second, the appropriate helping response. Information comes from three basic sources: (*a*) *Third parties* such as a referral agent or psychometrician may provide preliminary diagnostic information, psychological test scores, or a record of the client's prior treatment history; (*b*) the *client* provides his or her description and explanation of the problem; and (*c*) the helper makes *direct observation* of the client's verbal and nonverbal behavior during the initial interview(s), and possibly also observation of the client's environment and even of the client in that environment.

In the model, the road is wide that leads to a dispositional attribution and helping response; the road to a situational or interactional attribution and response is narrow. This is because seven characteristics of the helper's information-processing perspective may introduce dispositional bias into the decisions made on the basis of the three types of information. Let us consider how each characteristic might introduce bias.

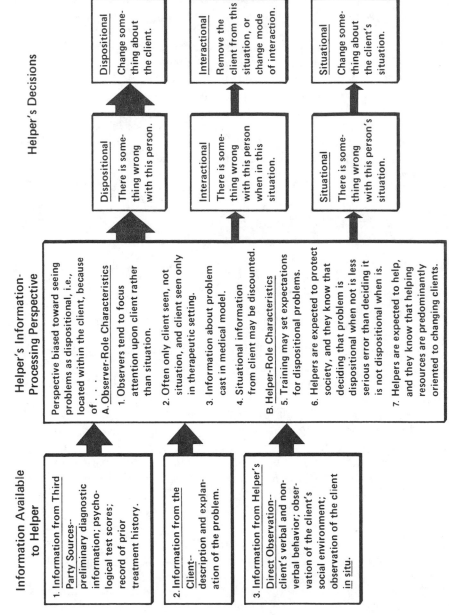

Figure 4.1. Attributional analysis of helper's inferential process.

OBSERVER-ROLE CHARACTERISTICS

1. *As an observer, the helper's attention is focused on the client rather than the situation.* A client comes in for an initial interview. The helper, trying to learn as much as possible about this person and problem, focuses carefully on the client. Already, a perceptual orientation is forming, an orientation in which, to use terms from gestalt psychology, the client is the *figure* and his or her physical and social situation is the *ground*. Jones and Nisbett (1972) suggest that this person-as-figure, situation-as-ground perceptual orientation, in which the person is the most salient element, is a major contributor to the tendency for observers to make relatively dispositional attributions.

Consistent with this view, Storms (1973) found a shift toward fewer situational attributions among individuals shown a video playback of themselves engaged in a conversation with another person. Presumably, seeing themselves in this way placed these individuals in the role of observer of their own behavior; it directed their attention away from the person they had been talking to and toward themselves. Focusing upon themselves as figure and no longer upon the social situation, they made fewer situational attributions for their behavior. Storms also found that when observers who originally watched one of the participants in the conversation were shown a replay shot from that participant's point of view, these observers made more situational attributions. Thus, whether individuals were actually actors in or observers of the original conversation, if they viewed the conversation from an observer's perspective they made relatively more dispositional attributions for the actor's behavior.

Applying this actor–observer role difference to the helping process, Snyder, Shenkel, and Schmidt (1976) asked undergraduates to listen to an audiotape of a peer counseling session. Some of the students were instructed to take the role of the client, and some to take the role of the peer counselor. The client on the tape presented her problem as lying with her situation. Students instructed to take the client's role tended to view the problem as situational, whereas those instructed to take the counselor's role were significantly more likely to view it as dispositional. This difference was especially strong among students who were also told that this was not the first time that this client had come for counseling. These results are quite consistent with the suggestion that people who identify with the helper role are prone to adopt an observer set and, as a result, to make more dispositional attributions.

2. *Information about the problem is selective: Helpers often see only the client, and only in the therapeutic setting.* Trained helpers can easily become "office bound." There are important exceptions of course, such as social workers and some ministers, but many trained helpers—doctors, psychiatrists, psychologists, and counselors—wait in their offices for clients to come to them. As a result, they get little direct information about the client's physical and social environment compared with the amount of information they get about the

client. This asymmetry of available information could increase the likelihood that the office-bound helper will make dispositional attributions for clients' problems, since the helper is apt to know more about clients' personal difficulties than about difficulties in clients' situations.

Indeed, the information available to the office-bound helper may be even more restricted than suggested so far. Imagine a client who, in each of the first three therapy sessions, is nervous, fidgety, and confused. The logical inference on the part of the therapist would seem to be that this is a nervous, fidgety, and confused person; after all, these behaviors covary with the client across time. But such an inference ignores the possibility that the client's behavior is a reaction to this specific situation—to the unsettling process of seeking help, or perhaps even to the intimidating behavior of the therapist. Heider (1958) quotes from Ichheiser's essay, "Misunderstandings in Human Relations," to make the point that a false impression of consistency in the behavior of another can result from our seeing that person in only one situation (e.g., a teacher seeing a pupil only at school) or from seeing that person react to us: "It is our own presence which either evokes or suppresses the manifestations of certain personality aspects of other people [p. 55]."

Of course, even social workers and other helpers who visit clients in their homes see only a small segment of the client's total environment. So they too may get a distorted sample. A welfare mother's behavior may take on a very atypical character when the caseworker comes to visit; she may seem consistently withdrawn, aloof, and suspicious. Lacking the opportunity to see this woman in other social settings under other circumstances, the caseworker may interpret this behavior as evidence of stable dispositional qualities of the client.

3. *Information about the problem is cast in the medical model.* Except for the information coming from direct observation, information that the helper receives about the problem comes prepackaged in language. The most readily available language in our society for talking about problems is what has been called the *medical model* (Goffman, 1961); we speak of mental "illness" and a "sick" society, much as we would talk of someone having the flu. Given the predominance of this medical metaphor for speaking of problems, it will likely be employed not only by third-party sources but also by clients as they relay information about the need situation. And although there may have been no intent to do so, use of this metaphor may introduce a dispositional bias into the information that the helper receives. For, as Goffman has noted, implicit in the medical model is the assumption that some part of an organic system is defective or diseased and in need of change. This assumption is, of course, far more readily applicable to people than to situations, so it naturally directs the helper's attention toward trying to detect the sickness within the

client and toward reviewing the client's personal history to uncover evidence of developing disease (Wills, 1978).[1]

Consistent with this reasoning, Langer and Abelson (1974) have presented evidence that applying the medical model label *patient* to a client increases the likelihood that at least some helpers will make a dispositional attribution for the client's problem. Langer and Abelson showed a videotaped interview to psychodynamically and behaviorally oriented therapists. They found that when the interviewee was described as a job applicant, both groups perceived him to be relatively well adjusted and his problems to be situational (Snyder, 1977). When the interviewee was described as a patient, however, the psychodynamically oriented therapists viewed him as significantly more maladjusted and his problems as more dispositional (Snyder, 1977). Langer and Abelson (1974) concluded that the label *patient* elicited a dispositional bias on the part of the psychodynamically oriented therapists.

4. *Situational information provided by the client may be discounted.* One might think that the client would be the best source of information about the problem; after all, the client probably knows most about his or her own behavior, dispositions, and situation. But the helper may be inclined to doubt information coming from the client, especially information suggesting that the problem is situational. There are at least three possible reasons for this. First, the helper may be aware that, as Jones and Nisbett (1972) suggested and Storms (1973) demonstrated, there is a tendency for actors to make situational attributions for their behavior. Knowing this, the helper may feel a need to correct—in a dispositional direction—the presumed situational bias of the client.

Second, the client's credibility may be undercut by a preliminary dispositional diagnosis, however tentative, formed either by the helper or suggested by third-party information. If, for example, one suspects that the client may be psychopathic or involved in illegal or socially inappropriate behaviors, one is not likely to take what he or she says very seriously. Consistent with this possibility, Batson (1975) found that the attributions of trained helpers (ministerial students) as well as untrained individuals (undergraduates) were heavily influenced by third-party information about the

---

[1] The medical model does have one virtue; patients are usually not held responsible for being sick. So the medical model may reduce the tendency to blame clients for their problems (see Chapter 6, by Karuza, Zevon, Rabinowitz, & Brickman, in this volume). Still, it clearly implies that the problem lies with the client and it is the client who is in need of change. Moreover, a second type of language, trait language, often occurs in conjunction with language cast in the medical model. Trait language assumes that personal characteristics (e.g., "He's smart," "He's compulsive") have the same stability as physical characteristics like weight or height. As Goldberg (1981) has shown, the English language is heavily loaded with trait-descriptive words, and trait language is common in everyday conversation.

client's credibility. When helpers learned that a client (who presented evidence that his problem was situational) had scored low on a psychological test of self-awareness and high on a test of interpersonal manipulation, they made substantially fewer situational attributions.

Third, trained helpers know that a situational attribution is probably less damaging to the client's self-esteem. This seemingly innocent fact may also cause the client's situational view of the problem to be discounted. Walster, Aronson, and Abrahams (1966) presented evidence that when people argue in a way that is consistent with their self-interest, we are much less likely to be persuaded than if they present an argument against their self-interest. Even when people arguing against their self-interest have low credibility, we are likely to believe them. Applying these findings to the attribution process, helpers should be more likely to be persuaded by clients who make dispositional attributions for their problems than by clients who make situational attributions. It even seems likely that if a client presents a mixture of information, some suggesting a dispositional attribution and some a situational attribution, the helper will tend to overemphasize the former and underemphasize the latter.

HELPER-ROLE CHARACTERISTICS

5. *Training as a helper may set expectations for dispositional problems.* When helpers are being trained, one thing they are taught is the kinds of problems that they can expect to see in their clients. Knowing this is essential if the helpers are to be prepared. However, if they are led to expect that their clients will have problems of a particular kind, namely, dispositional problems, then this expectation could easily become a self-fulfilling prophecy. The helpers may see what they are expecting to see, and so make dispositional attributions for their clients' problems.

Two lines of empirical research lend support to this reasoning. First, Snyder's (1977) further analysis of Langer and Abelson's (1974) data revealed a difference in attributions between psychodynamically and behaviorally oriented therapists. As noted above, in that study some therapists watched an interview with a young man described as a patient. Then these therapists were asked to indicate where the young man's problems lay. Judges' ratings of the therapists' responses indicated that the psychodynamically oriented therapists perceived his problems to be significantly more dispositional than did behaviorally oriented therapists. Presumably, this was because the focus on depth analysis in psychodynamic training led the psychodynamically oriented therapists to expect a patient to have dispositional problems. There were no reliable differences in attributions between the two types of therapists when the young man was described as a job applicant.

Second, our research group (Batson, 1972; 1975; Batson & Marz, 1979) has found consistently that trained helpers are more likely to make dispositional attributions for clients' problems than are untrained individuals (e.g., undergraduates). Moreover, we have found this difference for several different types of trained helpers (clinical psychologists who were behaviorally as well as psychodynamically trained, ministers, and social welfare caseworkers). The differences we found suggest a more pervasive bias than did the difference found by Langer and Abelson (1974). These differences suggest that although there may be a difference in degree of dispositional bias as a result of different types of training, there is also a pervasive tendency for trained helpers, however trained, to perceive clients' problems as more dispositional than do people without training.[2]

6. *Helpers are expected to protect society, and they know that deciding a problem is dispositional when it is not is a less serious error than deciding it is not dispositional when it is.* Rosenhan (1973) suggested that physicians recognize two basic types of error in their diagnoses. Since these errors are analogous to the statistical errors of rejecting a true hypothesis as false and accepting a false hypothesis as true, Rosenhan termed them Type 1 and Type 2 errors, respectively. His Type 1 error involves inferring that a patient who really is sick is healthy; his Type 2 error involves inferring that a patient who really is healthy is sick.

Rosenhan argued that physicians, including psychiatrists, quickly learn that calling a healthy person sick (a Type 2 error) is a less serious mistake than calling a sick person healthy (a Type 1 error). We would suggest that Rosenhan's reasoning can easily be extended to the inferences made by a wide range of trained helpers who deal with disturbed individuals. One aspect of the helping role of therapists, counselors, social workers, and ministers is to protect the rest of society from individuals who are so disturbed that they are dangerous. Given this role demand, these helpers know that incorrectly diagnosing a problem as dispositional, and having the client committed to an institution, when the problem is really situational (a Type 2 error) is a less serious mistake than incorrectly inferring that the problem is *not* dispositional when it really is (a Type 1 error).

[2]A note of caution is in order here. We have implied that the more dispositional attributions of trained helpers were due to expectations set by the training received, that trained helpers were *socialized* to see problems dispositionally. But it may be that the observed difference was a product of *selection* rather than socialization. In the studies mentioned, the trained helpers themselves had always chosen that role; they were not randomly assigned. So it is possible that the difference between trained helpers and untrained individuals was due to a dispositional orientation among those who chose to go into helping professions rather than something that they were taught during training. Longitudinal research would be needed to tease apart the effects of helper-role selection and socialization (see Chapter 15, by Elliott, Stiles, Shiffman, Barker, Burstein, & Goodman, in this volume for an analogous point concerning the effects of self-selection on helping responses).

To illustrate, consider a social worker confronted with a mother who has severely beaten her infant child for crying. Imagine that the social worker decides that the problem lies with the situation: The mother was under unusual stress because her husband had been laid off that day and she had just learned that she was pregnant again. Based on this attribution, the social worker tries to help by reassuring the mother and sending her home with arrangements for an abortion. But what if the social worker has made a Type 1 error, and the mother's problem is really dispositional? What if the mother is a child abuser? The consequences of this error could be serious indeed; the next time the mother abuses her baby, the child may not survive. Now imagine instead that the social worker decides that the mother's problem is dispositional—that she is a child abuser and should be separated from her baby until she undergoes a treatment program—when the problem is really situational. This Type 2 error is apt to cause the mother some unnecessary embarrassment and grief, but it is not likely to produce the dramatic negative consequences that a Type 1 error could.

To our knowledge there is no clear empirical evidence for or against the proposition that trained helpers are more concerned to avoid Type 1 than Type 2 errors; there is only Rosenhan's (1973) anecdotal evidence. Still, it seems likely that such a concern exists. And if it does, then as the emphasis on accountability on the part of trained helpers increases, as it has in recent years, we may expect the concern to avoid Type 1 errors to increase. In this regard, the move toward greater accountability may backfire. Intended to insure more accurate assessment and treatment, it may instead increase the pressure toward a dispositional bias.

7. *Helpers are expected to help, and they know that the available resources are predominantly oriented to changing the client.* It may seem obvious and trivial to observe that helpers feel obliged to help, but this aspect of their role definition may introduce additional pressure to view clients' problems dispositionally. Kelley (1972) has suggested that helpers may be aware that they are more likely to succeed in changing the client than the client's situation. If a helper knows this, and also feels some desire or obligation to help, then it is easy to understand why he or she would want to find that a client's problem is dispositional rather than situational. If the problem is dispositional, then the helper may anticipate some success in alleviating it, for the appropriate response to a dispositional problem is to effect some change in the client. But if the problem is situational, then the helper cannot be as confident of success. And given a desire to help, the helper wants to succeed.

This reasoning is predicated on the assumption that helpers hold a general belief that they are better able to help with a dispositional problem than with a situational problem. What could be the reason for such a belief? We can think of three reasons. First, as we have already noted, helpers typically have more immediate access to the client than to the client's situation. Second, most helpers know that situations are harder to change than individuals; to change a "sick" situation may involve legal or political action affecting many people and costing much time and money. (Although, in Chapter 5 of this volume, Pelton suggests some approaches for relatively inexpensive situational interventions.) Third, the helping resources in our society are designed to deal with personal rather than situational problems. Goffman (1961), Caplan and Nelson (1973), Halleck (1971), and Katz (1974) have all noted that the majority of our society's resources are directed toward helping individuals adapt to their social environments; far fewer are directed toward changing the social environments that breed poverty, crime, depression, and despair.

Batson, Jones, and Cochran (1979) reported a series of three experiments providing evidence that helpers' attributions for clients' needs are affected by the type of helping resources available. In each experiment, undergraduates served as referral agents in a simulated referral agency. Referral resources for some of the agents were oriented toward dealing with dispositional problems; these included a mental hospital, a residential treatment center, a mental health clinic, group therapy, and a family counseling service. Resources for other agents were oriented toward dealing with situational problems; these included a career information center, a sounding board, an ombudsman, an action agent, and a community coalition. In each of the three experiments the agents with the dispositionally oriented resources were more likely to perceive clients' problems to be dispositional than were the agents with situationally oriented resources. Linking these results with the observation that helping resources in our society are predominantly dispositional, trained helpers may be under subtle pressure to view their clients' problems as dispositional. Moreover, since the backward inference from resources to needs is predicated on a desire or obligation to help, we expect that those who most want to help would feel this pressure the most.

Now consider the long-term effect of a backward inference from resources to needs. Over time, it may lead to a vicious circle. If it is true that (a) our society's helping resources are heavily oriented toward changing clients rather than their social situations and (b) resources influence perceptions of clients' needs, then it is not surprising that when questions arise about what problems exist and what additional helping resources are needed, the answer seems clear. Dispositional problems exist, so we need even more resources to deal with dispositional problems. And once these resources are available, it is not surprising that an even greater number of dispositional problems are found. The circle is closed, each revolution leading to greater pressure to perceive clients' problems in line with society's dispositionally oriented resources. Borrowing a phrase from Jacques Brel, we are on a carousel.

Do Trained Helpers Really Have a Dispositional Bias?

After reviewing these seven biasing factors, as well as the supporting empirical research, the answer to the question of whether trained helpers have a dispositional bias may seem obvious. Certainly most researchers interested in the possibility of a dispositional bias have thought the answer was obvious, for they claim to have provided evidence of bias (see, for example, Batson, 1975; Goffman, 1961; Halleck, 1971; Langer & Abelson, 1974; Rosenhan, 1973; Snyder, Shenkel, & Schmidt, 1976). We believe, however, that these claims are premature. On careful examination of the evidence, none of these researchers, nor any others to our knowledge, has clearly demonstrated a dispositional bias on the part of trained helpers.

This assertion flies in the face of the conclusions of many researchers, one of the authors (CDB) among them. We have not made it lightly, however. As we agreed at the outset, the charge of a dispositional bias in trained helpers' inferences is a serious one and therefore should be examined carefully. Before we conclude that trained helpers are biased, we need to think carefully about what the charge implies.

To charge that trained helpers have a dispositional bias when making attributions about the locus of clients' problems seems to imply two things. First, it implies an attributional *difference*. The person who is biased sees the world differently from the person who is not. Attributional differences between trained helpers and untrained individuals have in fact been observed frequently (Batson, 1972, 1975; Batson & Marz, 1979; Benlifer & Kiesler, 1972; Brown, 1974; Carkhuff & Truax, 1965; Durlak, 1973). Trained helpers do, it seems, make more dispositional attributions for clients' problems than do untrained individuals.

But the existence of a systematic difference is not all that is implied by a charge of bias. The charge also implies an attributional *error*. The person who is biased sees what is not there or does not see what is there. Thus, to prove the charge of bias, one must not only demonstrate that trained helpers are more dispositional in their attributions, but also that their more dispositional attributions are wrong.[3] And to demonstrate error requires that one have a standard for veridical perception. If one is to recognize error, one must first know truth.

Four different approaches have been used to provide a standard of truth with which to compare trained helpers' attributions. Yet, in our judgment, none provides clear evidence that trained helpers are guilty of a dispositional bias.

---

[3] Harvey, Town, and Yarkin (1981) have recently made a similar point with regard to the general proposition of a dispositional bias in observers' attributions.

EVIDENCE USING CLIENTS WHO ARE "NORMAL PLUS..."

A "normal plus" standard was employed by Rosenhan (1973) and Langer and Abelson (1974). People who had no severe problems assumed the role of clients and then some problem-related information was added—that this person showed up at a mental hospital claiming to hear voices (Rosenhan) or was a patient (Langer & Abelson). This information led at least some therapists to make more dispositional attributions, which was taken as evidence of a dispositional bias.

A little reflection reveals that this inference is probably unfounded, because the normal plus standard is ambiguous. It is impossible to determine whether the additional information was relatively trivial and should not have led to more dispositional attributions or whether the additional information was sufficient and the attributions justified (cf. Spitzer, 1975). One can argue that failure to adjust one's perception in light of added information is evidence of an attributional error as easily as one can argue the opposite.

EVIDENCE USING PROBLEMS THAT CONFORM TO
A PREDETERMINED STANDARD

Batson (1975) used a second approach to establish the true locus of the problem. Relying upon Kelley's (1967) principle of covariation, Batson constructed audiotapes in which supposed clients stated that they had not experienced difficulties in similar situations and that other people had experienced similar problems when in the client's situation. According to the covariation principle, this information should logically lead to a situational rather than dispositional attribution for the locus of the client's problem. Consistent with this assumption, independent judges perceived each of the clients to be saying that the problem was situational. When trained helpers made their attributions, however, they perceived the problems to be predominantly dispositional. Further, they were significantly more dispositional in their attributions than were untrained individuals.

Batson (1975) interpreted these results as evidence that trained helpers' attributions not only differ from those of untrained individuals but are in error. After all, the trained helpers made relatively dispositional attributions for problems that were constructed to be situational. These results are not conclusive, however, for one cannot be certain where on a situational–dispositional dimension the problems that the clients presented actually lay. The intended situational orientation of the problems was checked by judges' ratings. But the judges rated where the clients *said* their problems lay (with themselves or with their social situations), not where, on the basis of the information presented, the judges themselves thought the problems lay. Thus, the operational standard for veridical perception in this experiment was actually the clients' own perceptions of the nature of their problems, as interpreted by judges. And as we shall see in the next section, there is reason to doubt the value of this standard.

Batson and Marz (1979) improved on Batson's (1975) research in two ways. First, they had trained helpers (advanced graduate students in clinical psychology, all with considerable experience providing therapy) and untrained individuals (undergraduates) conduct face-to-face interviews with persons whom the interviewers thought were real clients. Second, the persons interviewed were carefully trained to present their problems in each of two ways. Half of the time they presented information that on the basis of Kelley's (1967) covariation principle should lead to a situational attribution, and half the time they presented information that should lead to a dispositional attribution. Batson and Marz reasoned that one type of error implied by the charge of dispositional bias is that trained helpers are insensitive to the difference between situational and dispositional problems; they make dispositional attributions for the former as well as the latter.

The results of this experiment showed a clear difference in the attributions of the trained helpers and the untrained individuals; consistent with the results of previous research, attributions of the trained helpers were significantly more dispositional. But there was no clear evidence that the trained helpers were less sensitive than the undergraduates to differences between situational and dispositional problems; each group made significantly more situational attributions for situational problems. Batson and Marz concluded that, to the degree that the charge of bias implies a failure to be sensitive to differences in the information provided, their results provided no evidence of a dispositional bias on the part of trained helpers.

EVIDENCE COMPARING HELPERS' ATTRIBUTIONS
WITH CLIENTS' ATTRIBUTIONS

One might suggest that the most reasonable standard of truth as to where a client's problem lies would be the client's own perception. Indeed, this standard has often been used by researchers, not only by Batson (1975) through his judges' ratings but also by others (e.g., Goffman, 1961; Halleck, 1971; Hornstein, Houston, & Holmes, 1973; Rubenstein & Bloch, 1978; Snyder, Shenkel, & Schmidt, 1976). Once again, however, careful examination of research using this standard does not support the charge of bias, for two reasons. First, as pointed out earlier, the clients may be biased in the way they view the problem. Not only is there the possibility that, as actors, the clients' attention will be narrowly focused on situational pressures (Jones & Nisbett, 1972; Storms, 1973), but there is also the possibility that the clients' emotional involvement will lead them to blame the situation rather than the self. Thus, clients' attributions cannot simply be taken at face value; they may be unduly situational.

Given this possibility, the second reason for concluding that using clients' attributions as a standard provides no evidence of a dispositional bias on the part of trained helpers becomes all the more striking. The evidence from the only three studies we know of in which systematic empirical data were collected from actual clients suggests that clients often make dispositional attributions for their own problems—as dispositional as those of trained helpers. Calhoun, Dawes, and Lewis (1972) reported that of the 36 adult outpatients at the University of Georgia Psychology Clinic during a 3-month period, 33 said that their problem was dispositional. Sherrard and Batson (1979) found that among the 42 new clients who entered the Counseling Center at Kansas State University during three 2-week periods in the spring, summer, and fall of 1975, the mean rating of the locus of their problem was 3.81 on an 8-point scale (1 = exclusively personal; 8 = exclusively situational). This mean was more dispositional although not significantly so, than the mean attribution rating for the problems made by the clients' counselors, 3.96.

In a study of 50 cases of care for unwed mothers, Rubenstein and Bloch (1978) reported results that seem to suggest that the helpers made more dispositional attributions than clients. They reported that the caseworkers placed more emphasis than the unwed mothers on the mother's intrapersonal and interpersonal difficulties relative to her lack of resources and tangible goods and services. But Rubenstein and Bloch reported no statistical tests, and our analysis of their data does not fully support their conclusion.[4] Moreover, Rubenstein and Bloch (1978) offered a plausible reason for caseworkers being more likely than clients to report intrapersonal and interpersonal problems.[5]

In sum, in therapeutic settings we have been able to find no empirical evidence that trained helpers are more dispositional in their attributions than are the clients themselves, even though one might expect clients' attributions to be less dispositional than they should be. Only among social workers is there evidence of a tendency for trained helpers to report more dispositional problems than do clients, and this tendency may be a result of the greater insight of the social workers.

[4]When compared with the clients, caseworkers did report more intrapersonal and interpersonal difficulties relative to difficulties with resources (p's $< .001$). But there was no statistically reliable evidence of more disagreement between clients and caseworkers over the existence of intrapersonal or interpersonal problems than over resource problems [$\chi^2(1) = 2.35$, $p > .10$ for intrapersonal, $\chi^2(1) = .66$, $p > .30$ for interpersonal]. And log-linear analyses (Bishop, Fienberg, & Holland, 1975) of the patterns of agreement and disagreement failed to produce significant Problem Type × Caseworker Perception × Client Perception interactions.

[5]The unwed mothers were often young, poorly educated, and relatively inexperienced; the more knowledgeable and experienced caseworkers may have been better able than these clients to recognize the signs of present or future problems.

EVIDENCE EXAMINING SPECIFIC BIASING FACTORS

The fourth approach to detecting error in attributions of clients' needs is to vary systematically the presence of one or another biasing factor (e.g., resources) to determine whether that factor affects attributions as predicted. This was presumably the logic behind Langer and Abelson's (1974) comparison of the inferences of psychodynamically and behaviorally oriented therapists. But as we have noted, their use of the "normal plus" technique to implement this logic rendered their results ambiguous. The observed difference in inferences suggests that some bias exists, but it remains unclear which group of therapists (perhaps both) was in error.

A less ambiguous application of this technique is found in the three experiments reported by Batson, Jones, and Cochran (1979). They assessed the impact on attributions of having resources that were oriented either toward changing clients or changing clients' situations. Logically, attributions of the locus of clients' problems should be independent of treatment options, but they were not. Relative to a more balanced set of resources, availability of dispositional resources led to more dispositional attributions.

To our knowledge this set of experiments is the only research that provides clear evidence to support the error component of the charge of bias in helpers' attributions for clients' needs. It is important to note, however, that the helpers in these three experiments were not trained professionals; they were undergraduates. Thus, the only clear evidence of attributional bias we have been able to find—of both difference and error—is not on the part of trained helpers but of untrained individuals.

Summary and Conclusion

The first question to be answered on the way to effective helping is: "What is the problem?" Typically, the helper's answer to this question determines the helping response, and hence the client's welfare. But it has been charged that trained helpers are prone to a dispositional bias in their assessment of clients' needs, that they are likely to perceive the problem to lie with the client as an individual, even when the client is actually reacting to a problematic situation. If such a bias exists, it could lead to inappropriate and ineffective helping whenever a client's problem is situational.

Exploring the possibility of bias, we examined helpers' inferences about the locus of clients' problems from the perspective of attribution theory. We suggested seven characteristics that might contribute to a dispositional bias on the part of trained helpers. Four were a result of the helper being in the role of an observer when processing information about the client's need; the other three were a result of the helper being in the specific role of a trained helper.

Even though one can make a plausible argument for the biasing impact of each of these seven factors, and often can provide at least some empirical support, we concluded that the charge of a dispositional bias in trained helpers' inferences has not been proved. There is considerable evidence that trained helpers are more dispositional in their attributions than untrained individuals, but there is as yet no clear evidence that these more dispositional attributions are in error. And the charge of bias implies more than a difference; it implies error as well.

Where does this conclusion leave us? Can we simply dismiss the charge of bias and assume that the seven biasing characteristics, however plausible, can be ignored? No, we cannot. The possibility of a dispositional bias on the part of trained helpers remains, even if it has not yet been proved. The observed differences in attributions for clients' needs suggests that *someone* is in error, although we need additional evidence before we can say who. It may be untrained individuals; it may be trained helpers; it may be both.

Moreover, our review of the strategies used to demonstrate bias provides a basis for suggesting which research strategy may be the most fruitful source of the needed additional evidence. The "normal plus" strategy seems least fruitful, since it contains an inherent ambiguity. The second strategy, presenting helpers with problems constructed to be situational or dispositional, would seem to be of some value, since it can detect one type of error, the error of failing to adjust one's inference to different information. The third strategy, using clients' own attributions as the standard for the true locus of the problem, seems problematic, since clients' attributions may themselves be biased. Still, clients' own attributions should not be ignored; the finding that clients often tend to make dispositional attributions for their own problems raises a number of questions that deserve attention. Do clients really perceive their problems dispositionally, or do they only say they do because that is the response they think the helper wants to hear, or because our language emphasizes personalistic descriptions of problems? If real, is this perception limited to people who come for help, or does it apply to the problem perception of the person in the street? Could the very term *problem* evoke dispositional attributions? If so, a dispositional bias may exist at a far more fundamental level than so far suspected. Rather than just a bias on the part of trained helpers, it may pervade our entire culture's way of thinking about people in need.

We believe that the fourth approach to studying bias is potentially the most fruitful. This approach involves a shift of attention away from *personnel*— trained helpers versus untrained individuals, psychodynamically versus behaviorally oriented therapists, etc.—toward *process*. Instead of asking who is biased, this approach asks what situational factors (the seven we have proposed or others) can produce bias, and under what conditions. A start toward answering this question has been made by research examining the effect on helper's attributions of having helping resources of a particular type, but far more could be done.

Two consequences follow from recommending the last strategy as the best, one consequence for practitioners and one for researchers. For practitioners, it suggests a shift from concern over whether they or someone else is biased toward a concern to identify and be aware of the array of potentially biasing situational pressures impinging on them as they try to decide what a given client's problem may be. The seven sources of bias that we have discussed provide at least a start in identifying such pressures. Three of these sources of bias are already well known to most practitioners: (a) seeing only the client, not the situation, and the client only in the therapeutic setting, (b) having information about the problem cast in the medical model, and (c) expecting dispositional problems as a result of particular training. But the other four are not as well known: (d) viewing the problem from the perspective of an observer, (e) discounting situational information presented by the client, (f) wanting to protect society and so being especially concerned that no dispositional problems slip by, and (g) wanting to help and knowing that it is easier to help with dispositional problems. We would encourage practitioners to think carefully about the impact on their inferences of each of these last four potential sources of bias.

For researchers, recommending the last strategy raises the possibility that they themselves have shown a dispositional bias in the way they have approached the issue of bias in trained helpers' attributions. In making the charge of dispositional bias we researchers have made a dispositional attribution, that the problem of bias lies with the helpers rather than with the helpers' situation. And just as we have cautioned practitioners to resist a premature dispositional attribution for their clients' problems, so we may need to caution ourselves to resist premature dispositional attributions for the problem of bias. Whatever bias exists may lie more with situational pressures impinging on trained helpers than with the helpers themselves.

Reference Note

1. House, W. C. *Correlates of outpatients' attributions of their psychological problems*. Paper presented at the meeting of the American Psychological Association, Montreal, September 1980.

References

Batson, C. D. *"I'm here to help you": Variables affecting the implementation of helping behavior*. Unpublished doctoral dissertation, Princeton University, 1972.

Batson, C. D. Attribution as a mediator of bias in helping. *Journal of Personality and Social Psychology*, 1975, *72*, 455–466.

Batson, C. D., Jones, C. H., & Cochran, P. J. Attributional bias in counselors' diagnoses: The effect of resources on perception of need. *Journal of Applied Social Psychology*, 1979, *9*, 377–393.

Batson, C. D., & Marz, B. Dispositional bias in trained therapists' diagnoses: Does it exist? *Journal of Applied Social Psychology*, 1979, *5*, 476–489.

Benlifer, V. E., & Kiesler, S. B. Psychotherapists' perceptions of adjustment and attraction toward children described as in therapy. *Journal of Experimental Research in Personality*, 1972, *6*, 169–177.

Bishop, Y. M. M., Fienberg, S. E., & Holland, P. W. *Discrete multivariate analysis: Theory and practice*. Cambridge, Mass.: MIT Press, 1975.

Brown, W. F. Effectiveness of paraprofessionals: The evidence. *Personnel and Guidance Journal*, 1974, *53*, 257–263.

Calhoun, L. G., Dawes, A. S., & Lewis, P. M. Correlates of attitudes toward help seeking in out-patients. *Journal of Consulting and Clinical Psychology*, 1972, *38*, 153.

Caplan, W., & Nelson, S. On being useful: The nature and consequence of psychological research on social problems. *American Psychologist*, 1973, *28*, 199–211.

Carkhuff, R. R., & Truax, C. B. Lay mental health counseling: The effects of lay group counseling. *Journal of Consulting Psychology*, 1965, *29*, 426–431.

Durlak, J. A. Myths concerning the nonprofessional therapist. *Professional Psychology*, 1973, *4*, 300–304.

Goffman, E. *Asylums: Essays on the social situation of mental patients and other inmates*. Garden City, N.Y.: Doubleday, 1961.

Goldberg, L. R. Language and individual differences: Seeking universals in personality lexicons. In L. Wheeler (Ed.), *Review of personality and social psychology* (Vol. 2). Beverly Hills, Calif.: Sage, 1981.

Halleck, S. L. *The politics of therapy*. New York: Harper, 1971.

Harvey, J. H., Town, J. P., & Yarkin, K. L. How fundamental is "the fundamental attribution error"? *Journal of Personality and Social Psychology*, 1981, *40*, 346–349.

Heider, F. *The psychology of interpersonal relations*. New York: Wiley, 1958.

Hornstein, D., Houston, B. K., & Holmes, D. S. Clients', therapists', and judges' evaluations of psychotherapy. *Journal of Counseling Psychology*, 1973, *20*, 149–153.

Jones, E. E., & Davis, K. E. From acts to dispositions: The attribution process in person perception. In L. Berkowitz (Ed.), *Advances in experimental social psychology* (Vol. 2). New York: Academic Press, 1965.

Jones, E. E., & Nisbett, R. E. The actor and the observer: Divergent perceptions of the causes of behavior. In E. E. Jones, D. E. Kanouse, H. H. Kelley, R. E. Nisbett, S. Valins, & B. Weiner (Eds.), *Attribution: Perceiving the causes of behavior*. Morristown, N. J.: General Learning Press, 1972.

Katz, D. Factors affecting social change: A social-psychological interpretation. *Journal of Social Issues*, 1974, *30*(3), 159–180.

Kelley, H. H. Attribution theory in social psychology. In D. Levine (Ed.), *Nebraska Symposium on Motivation* (Vol. 15). Lincoln: Univ. of Nebraska Press, 1967.

Kelley, H. H. Attribution in social interaction. In E. E. Jones, D. E. Kanouse, H. H. Kelley, R. E. Nisbett, S. Valins, & B. Weiner (Eds.), *Attribution: Perceiving the causes of behavior*. Morristown, N. J.: General Learning Press, 1972.

Laing, R. D. *The politics of experience*. London: Penguin, 1967.

Langer, E. J., & Abelson, R. P. A patient by any other name . . . : Clinician group differences in labeling bias. *Journal of Consulting and Clinical Psychology*, 1974, *42*, 4–9.

Rosenhan, D. L. On being sane in insane places. *Science*, 1973, *179*, 250–258.

Rosenhan, D. L. The contextual nature of psychiatric diagnosis. *Journal of Abnormal Psychology*, 1975, *84*, 462–474.

Rubenstein, H., & Bloch, M. H. Helping clients who are poor: Worker and client perceptions of problems, activities, and outcomes. *Social Service Review*, 1978, *52*, 69–84.

Sherrard, P. A. D., & Batson, C. D. Client and counselor perception of the client's problem: An analysis of initial assessment based on attribution theory. *Journal of College Student Personnel*, 1979, *20*, 14–23.

Snyder, C. R. "A patient by any other name" revisited: Maladjustment or attributional locus of problem? *Journal of Consulting and Clinical Psychology*, 1977, *45*, 101–103.

Snyder, C. R., Shenkel, R. J., & Schmidt, A. Effects of role perspective and client psychiatric history on locus of problem. *Journal of Consulting and Clinical Psychology*, 1976, *44*, 467–472.

Spitzer, R. L. On pseudoscience in science, logic in remission, and psychiatric diagnosis: A critique of Rosenhan's "On being sane in insane places." *Journal of Abnormal Psychology*, 1975, *84*, 442–452.

Storms, M. Video-tape and attribution process: Reversing actors' and observers' points of view. *Journal of Personality and Social Psychology*, 1973, *27*, 165–174.

Szasz, T. S. *The myth of mental illness: Foundations of a theory of personal conduct*. New York: Harper, 1961.

Szasz, T. S. *Law, liberty, and psychiatry: An inquiry into the social uses of mental health practices*. New York: Collier, 1963.

Valins, S., & Nisbett, R. E. Attribution process in the development and treatment of emotional disorders. In E. E. Jones, D. E. Kanouse, H. H. Kelley, R. E. Nisbett, S. Valins, & B. Weiner (Eds.), *Attribution: Perceiving the causes of behavior*. Morristown, N.J.: General Learning Press, 1972.

Walster, E., Aronson, E., & Abrahams, D. On increasing the persuasiveness of a low prestige communicator. *Journal of Experimental Social Psychology*, 1966, *2*, 325–342.

Wills, T. A. Perceptions of clients by professional helpers. *Psychological Bulletin*, 1978, *85*, 968–1000.

Personalistic Attributions and Client Perspectives in Child Welfare Cases: Implications for Service Delivery

LEROY H. PELTON

Introduction

There are at least two perspectives in any helping relationship: the helper's and the client's. Each perspective is a subjective reality, grounded in interests, motives, values, prior beliefs, and inferences from facts, as well as in facts. If the perspectives are significantly discrepant, this suggests that they embody different understandings of the client's problems and different implications for service delivery. Yet in social work research, the perspective of the client has been given relatively little attention.

The paucity of information on clients' perspectives available in the social work research literature has been noted by several writers (Giordano, 1977; Maluccio, 1979; Mayer & Timms, 1969, 1970; LeBailly, Note 1). These commentators have noted that even when research attempts have been made to ascertain the clients' opinions about their interactions with social service agencies, usually only global ratings of client satisfaction have been elicited (Maluccio, 1979; Mayer & Timms, 1969).

One possible reason for this inattention to the subjective reality of the client who, after all, is the central participant in any helping interaction (cf. Bush & Gordon, 1978), is that in striving for objectivity and status as scientists, social

Basic Processes in Helping Relationships

science researchers have had a history of emulating the research methodologies of the physical sciences. But there is growing recognition that knowledge of the cognitive constructions of the subjects themselves is especially important for understanding situations that entail social interaction, particularly if they entail some degree of conflict between the involved parties (Pelton, 1974). Other explanations for the dearth of research on clients' perspectives are specific to the field of social work itself. Social work has long been under the influence of psychodynamic theories of human behavior. Although this influence has begun to wane in recent years because of developments such as the ecological perspective (Germain, 1973) and task-centered casework (Reid & Epstein, 1972), psychodynamic concepts continue to pervade the field of social work and the social work literature. Ignoring to a considerable extent developments in psychology, such as the rise of social psychology, the field of social work has tuned in on *personality* theories of human behavior to an inordinate degree, and even more narrowly, on psychodynamic theories.

Some basic assumptions of the psychodynamic model are that (*a*) unconscious processes underlie and largely direct human behavior, (*b*) the direct expression of such processes in conscious experience is often blocked or distorted by psychodynamic defense mechanisms (e.g., repression, projection, and displacement), and (*c*) irrational forces within the individual pervade and determine human behavior. Given these assumptions, one is tempted to conclude that there is little point in soliciting the views of clients, save as symptoms that, if properly analyzed and interpreted, might yield clues about the nature of the "real" underlying problems. As Mayer and Timms (1970) noted: "The client's appraisal of the services offered (especially if negative) and his reasons for feeling as he does are apt to be viewed [by social workers] as epiphenomena, as derivations of his underlying problem and the manner in which he has related to the worker [p. 14]."

THE CONTEXT OF CLIENT–AGENCY INTERACTION

This chapter is concerned with research relevant to client perspectives in child welfare cases, or more precisely, child protection cases of the type reported to public child welfare agencies. Such cases often involve alleged child abuse and/or neglect but also include cases in which, for various other reasons, the children are considered at risk of being harmed in the home and thereby face the possibility of being removed from their parents and placed in foster care. Most reports of alleged child abuse and neglect come from neighbors, friends, and relatives, followed by reports from law enforcement agencies, schools, and medical personnel; very few come from the parents themselves (American Humane Association, 1978). When a public child welfare agency receives such reports, it is required by law to investigate the complaints. Thus, in child protection cases, there exists a situation in which parents are brought into a nonvoluntary relationship with a social service agency in regard to problems alleged and defined by others. In this relationship, moreover, the agency (and hence the caseworker) has a dual role: a helping, service-oriented, treatment function combined with a coercive, regulatory, investigative function.

Given the coercive context of this helping relationship, the suspicions that initiate the relationship, the implicit threat to the parents that their children may be removed from them, and the emotional nature of the issue, we might anticipate considerable differences between the agency's and parent's perspectives in that relationship. Yet a number of factors mitigate against the parents' views being given a hearing in research or in social work practice.

MEDICAL MODEL FORMULATION OF CHILD ABUSE

Since the reports of the "battered child syndrome" by Denver pediatrician C. Henry Kempe and his associates in the early 1960s, a psychodynamic orientation toward child abuse and neglect, within the context of a medical model of disease, treatment, and cure, has become the dominant viewpoint within the field (Antler, 1981). It has been presumed that there are certain personality deficits that distinguish most abusing and neglecting parents from all other people and that explain the phenomena. In the context of this approach, the parent–client is regarded as a patient, whose "illness" involves his or her entire personality and who is an object of treatment. The psychodynamic medical orientation has led researchers to be more concerned with psychological defects thought to characterize such parents than with their subjective realities. Interviews, when conducted, take the form of clinical interviews to find out more *about* the parents, rather than conversational interviews designed to ascertain their own cognitive constructions of reality. After all, the parents cannot be expected to know anything about their own illness, just as we do not look to cancer patients for explanations of their illness.

The specific character defects reported in the research literature further discourage the idea that the parents' views would be of any value. The parents have been characterized as childlike, hostile, manipulative, and deceitful (e.g., Polansky, DeSaix & Sharlin, 1972; Young, 1964). One might therefore conclude that there is little reason to give any credence to their remarks. What the parents say may be regarded with suspicion, as not being what they really mean, and as one more manifestation of their illness, a symptom to be analyzed and interpreted.

Yet the validity of the specific personality traits that have been attributed to parents in abuse and neglect cases is highly questionable. Gelles (1973) has gleaned from the literature a partial catalogue of the plethora of personality deficits said to describe abusing parents, ranging from pervasive anger, poor emotional control, and immaturity, to sadomasochism, narcissism, and "transference psychosis," and has identified several problems with the validity of these trait attributions. There is little agreement among studies in regard to the traits identified; most of the discussions are inconsistent and contradictory as to the nature and presence of various personality deficits. Most studies do not test the assumptions they make: Attributions are made simply on the basis of the abusing behavior, and are then offered as explanations. Finally, inadequate sampling procedures are used (e.g., subjects are selected from hospital emergency room admissions, which represent extreme cases), and comparable control groups of nonabusers are lacking. Thus we have no way of knowing whether the proposed attributions can be generalized to all child abusers, or whether they differentiate abusers from nonabusers.

RATIONALE FOR STUDYING THE CLIENT PERSPECTIVE

The need to study the client perspective arises from a very different conception of human experience and behavior (Pelton, 1974, Chapter 2). According to this conception, the objective facts of behavior lend themselves to multiple—even discrepant—interpretations. In social interaction, two parties can come to hold discrepant views of the situation, and yet both views of the situation can be in accordance with the facts, with each view rationally developed from those facts. The very process of the interpretation of facts (of the cognitive construction of reality) necessitates inference, which can take the form of the attribution of motives and characteristics. When the facts pertain to social interaction, each of the parties to that interaction will interpret the facts in accordance with his or her own particular belief system. Moreover, knowledge of what each party to the interaction believes to be the case is indispensable for understanding the interaction and dealing effectively with the parties. There are many perspectives on reality, and to understand social phenomena one must study the perspectives of all parties involved.

Perspectives are determined by prior individual learning experiences, beliefs, motives, and self-interests, which may be a function of one's particular role within the larger society and within the particular social interaction itself. Since research is performed by middle-class professionals, most of whom have had no experience of living in poverty, whereas child welfare cases, as we shall see, typically involve families from the lowest socioeconomic classes, the client perspective is all the more likely to be discrepant from that of the professionals and there is all the more reason to study it.

In considering the conflict dynamics of parent–agency interaction in child welfare cases, one must note that the relationship involves a tremendous imbalance of power. The agency has on its side the police, the law, and public opinion. The social worker has emergency power to remove a child from the home on the spot. When the agency goes to court, it has an abundance of reports containing interpretations according to its own lights, the product of considerable investigatory resources. The case record (which is often the researcher's source of information) is embellished with opinions freely expressed by the caseworker, school officials, psychologists, and representatives of other agencies. It contains the results of psychological tests and medical examinations, not to mention the allegations of neighbors. No one collects evidence on the parents' behalf, presents their side of the story, presents the results of psychological tests commissioned by them rather than the government, or bears witness on their behalf.

In order to understand the clients' problems and the phenomena in question, in order to learn how best to help clients, and in order to generate greater empathy for their perspective, we must learn their views. Research must be partially geared toward helping agencies to deal more effectively with their clients, in terms of the influence attempts the agencies make and the services they offer. The design of effective persuasive attempts requires an understanding of the subjective reality of those we wish to persuade. Moreover, to determine what services would be most attractive and acceptable to the clients, we would have to ask them. Their perceptions of what services they want and need are important because services that are not attractive are not likely to be effective, especially if they require the active participation and willing cooperation of the client. At the very least, the clients' views of their problems can offer alternative hypotheses about their problems that could be tested in further research.

Evidence on Client Perspectives

Here I shall review research evidence on client perspectives in child welfare cases in regard to the clients' views of their problems, their interactions with child welfare agencies, and the services they need. I will also consider social workers' attributions about the nature of clients' problems. We shall see that the evidence reveals a wide discrepancy between client and professional perspectives.[1] We shall also see that the methodology of some of the studies

[1] In regard to the issue of foster care, this review will be limited to conceptions of why children entered foster care. It will not go beyond that point to evidence on client views of the foster care placement situation itself (e.g., Bush, 1980; Bush, Gordon, & LeBailly, 1977; Jenkins & Norman, 1975; Pelton, 1981).

reviewed here leaves much to be desired; some of the methodological problems will be discussed later.

Although the Mayer and Timms (1969, 1970) study of client perspectives dealt with clients who voluntarily sought help from a nongovernmental family service agency for interpersonal problems (such as marital discord) or economic problems, its findings are relevant to the concerns of this chapter. The clients in that study, like the parents in child protection cases referred to public child welfare agencies, were of low socioeconomic status and were not well educated.

Open-ended interviews were conducted with 61 former clients in their own homes by trained interviewers not associated with the agency. The selection process insured that about half of the clients interviewed had been satisfied with the services received, and about half dissatisfied. Nine social workers, about a third of those who had been involved in these cases, were also interviewed. The reported findings were entirely qualitative in nature.

The study showed that the clients seemed to have a present-oriented, environmental perspective on their problems. They sought concrete advice about and intervention (directed at the "offending" party) for their current interpersonal problems, and material assistance with their economic problems. They became confused, frustrated, and dissatisfied when confronted by workers who took a psychological, personalistic, and more specifically, psychodynamic approach to their problems and who were rather inattentive to their material needs. These social workers focused on the intrapersonal problems of the clients, attempted psychotherapy, listened rather than advised, and delved into the clients' personal histories and childhoods. The clients attributed the causes of their problems to other people or to environmental circumstances, whereas the workers attributed the causes to the clients themselves, and more particularly, to underlying psychodynamic conflicts within the clients. To the clients, the presenting problems were indeed the problems; to the workers, they were merely symptoms of unconscious conflicts that required "insight" to resolve.

But by no means did all of the workers employ this psychodynamic approach. Those who took a supportive–directive counseling approach were more in tune with the clients' own perspective, and their clients tended to be satisfied with their social work experiences. These clients received guidance, advice, and emotional relief and support from their workers, who were also more likely to recognize and deal with their clients' material problems. Thus, the results of this study suggest that clients tend to view their problems as interpersonal and socioeconomic, and are dissatisfied when met by workers who view their problems as intrapsychic.

In another study of worker and client perspectives in a voluntary family service agency, the clients were unmarried mothers who were poor and relatively young and uneducated (Rubenstein & Bloch, 1978). Data on client problems (and agency services) were collected in individual interviews with 50 clients and four agency staff members, conducted by researchers using an interview schedule not described in the report. It was found that workers tended to view the clients' problems as more psychological in nature than did the clients, who tended to emphasize their lack of resources and tangible goods. Workers identified more interpersonal problems than did the clients, although the clients viewed more of their problems as interpersonal than intrapersonal. Workers identified intrapersonal or emotional problems in 39 of the 50 cases (78%), whereas clients identified themselves as having such problems in only 21 cases (42%). Although no statistical analyses were reported, this discrepancy is statistically significant [χ^2 (1) = 12.04, $p < .01$].

RESOURCES AND PERCEIVED NEEDS

Turning to research on client perspectives in child abuse and neglect cases, a study of more than 900 families known to child protection systems in four California counties (Giovannoni & Becerra, 1979) includes some interesting findings regarding the issue of resources and perceived needs. The research instrument consisted of a lengthy questionnaire to be filled out by the workers handling these cases. One item on the questionnaire consisted of a checklist of resources. For each case, the worker was asked to check the resources that he or she would ideally recommend, to indicate whether they were available, and if available, whether, in the worker's opinion, they would be acceptable to the client.

It was found that the resources that were most often available—they were available in over 90% of the cases for which they were recommended—were the ones *least* likely to be acceptable to the clients. These were resources of a therapeutic and educative nature: mental health services, parent education, instruction in money management, and Parents Anonymous. On the other hand, many of the resources that were judged to be most often acceptable to the clients were least frequently available. These included increased income, housing, employment, and homemaker services. These resources were also among the least frequently recommended by caseworkers. Mental health and parent education were among the most frequently recommended resources, even though they were judged to be among the least frequently acceptable to the clients. Day care and babysitting services were far less frequently recommended than mental health and parent education, even though the former were relatively frequently available and were judged to be highly acceptable to the clients.

Thus, the following pattern emerges. The most abstract services, of a psychotherapeutic and educative nature, designed to change the person in some way, tend to be the ones the agencies most frequently want to offer (in terms of both availability and recommendations). These services, however, tend to be the ones least acceptable to the clients. The most concrete and supportive services, directed at altering the client's situation, are the ones the agencies are least frequently willing to offer, even though they are the services most acceptable to the clients.

This pattern is confirmed, to a greater or lesser extent, by other studies. Shapiro (1979) studied 171 families who were involved in child abuse and neglect cases drawn from six public child protection agencies located in various parts of the country. Parent interview schedules and protocols for extracting information from case records were developed, and the data were collected by workers hired from the agencies (although they were not assigned to cases on their own case loads). The data were analyzed by two coders using a pretested code book. It was found that mental hygiene was one of the most frequently recommended services and was the most frequently available of recommended services. Yet, along with parent groups, it was the service most frequently refused by parents. Evidence from the interviews tended to indicate that parents were little interested in services aimed at psychological change and were far more interested in material help. It must be added that in this study, however, homemaker service was the one most likely to be suggested by the caseworker and was frequently available, but had a relatively high client refusal rate. (Some clients may fear that homemakers might provide negative information about them to the agency.)

Clients interviewed in 172 child protection cases (selected by their case-workers) from 23 Texas counties most frequently indicated clothing, basic subsistence, housing, and general health services as their service needs (Texas Department of Human Resources, Note 2). All of the protective service workers in those counties plus seven other counties were surveyed by questionnaire, and they most frequently listed day care and counseling as the greatest needs of the clients. Through a mail survey questionnaire that elicited more than 1000 responses in these 30 counties from community organizations providing human services, community and political leaders, and leaders of voluntary service-oriented organizations, it was found that these organizations and individuals saw counseling and parent education as the most important service needs of clients in abuse and neglect cases.

In an assessment of a demonstration project designed to reduce foster care placement, Jones, Neuman, and Shyne (1976) studied a sample of 549 families in New York State who were identified as being at risk for placement of their child. Collecting information through forms filled out by the caseworkers on individual cases, they found that, aside from casework counseling, parents most often requested financial assistance, day care, and homemaker service. The caseworkers indicated on these forms that, if the cases were to be assigned to the experimental program, they most expected to provide (aside from counseling) psychological evaluation and treatment, family life education, education in home management, and help with housing.

In the Rubenstein and Bloch (1978) study cited earlier, the investigators concluded from the reports of both workers and clients that, although the workers tended to view their clients' problems as psychological, there was in fact a high level of worker activity directed at providing concrete services. There are other indications that the workers may end up providing supportive or concrete services more often than they say they would when asked beforehand what they would recommend or offer. This might be partly a function of the high client refusal rate of the services that the workers prefer to offer, such as psychiatric services, as seen in the Shapiro (1979) study. In the Jones *et al.* (1976) study, it turned out that the workers provided financial assistance more frequently than they thought they would. However, they provided day care less frequently than they thought they would.

Undoubtedly, worker perspectives are not the exclusive determinant of services offered or used. Such factors as client acceptability of services (which might have a greater influence in voluntary service agencies, such as the one studied by Rubenstein and Bloch, than in nonvoluntary child protection relationships) and of course, availability of resources, are also partial determinants. But the resources that the agency makes available must be ultimately determined by *someone's* perspective on the clients' problems, and we have seen that it is usually not the clients' perspective. To the extent that the perspective that determines resources differs from the clients' perspective, services will be offered that are inconsistent with the clients' perceived needs.

The effects that resources may have on workers' perceptions were illustrated in a study of an experimentally simulated referral agency situation (Batson, Jones, & Cochran, 1979). College students who served as lay referral counselors and who had only person-oriented helping resources available to them made more dispositional (personalistic) diagnoses than those who had only situation-oriented resources available to them. (For further discussion, see Chapter 4, by Batson, O'Quin, & Pych, in this volume.) Furthermore subjects having person-oriented resources were more likely to perceive their role as involving helping people with personal problems, and those who perceived their role as such were more likely to make dispositional diagnoses. The authors suggested that if an agency's resources are heavily oriented toward changing people rather than social situations, then its workers will tend to perceive their roles as personalistically oriented and will tend to make personalistic diagnostic attributions. The preponderance of these diagnoses will then inspire the agency to acquire even more person-oriented resources to meet the expanding "need."

PERCEIVED LOCUS OF THE PRIMARY PROBLEM

In the Jones *et al.* (1976) study, caseworkers were asked to check, on a problem list, the families' problems (that had created the need for service) as seen from the perspective of the workers and as the workers thought the parents saw them. Whereas the workers identified problems in the parents' functioning far more often than they thought the parents would, they perceived environmental or situational problems (concerning inadequate housing and financial need) in as many cases as they thought the parents perceived them. However, when asked to select the *most important problem* in each case, the workers identified a problem in parents' functioning far more often than they assumed the parents would, and identified an environmental or situational problem, or poor functioning of the children, as the most important problem far *less* often than they assumed the parents would. These findings indicate that even though the workers are by no means insensitive to the clients' situational needs, there is a marked difference in emphasis between worker and client perspectives.

The authors of this study also summarized the results of four major foster care studies in regard to the locus of the *primary reason for placement* as determined by caseworkers. In these studies, the percentage of cases in which the locus of the problem was judged to reside within the parent ranged from 79% to 86% (although this category included physical illness of the parent). The percentage of cases in which the locus of the problem was judged to be environmental or situational ranged from 0% to 5%. Clearly caseworkers do not believe, or do not like to admit, that in this day and age children are separated from parents for poverty-related reasons.

In one foster care study in which 425 clients were interviewed by a staff of trained social workers and social scientists, only 4% of the respondents were classified as having said "housing" was the main reason for placement, although this was higher than the mere 1% of families in which the trained social workers, based on review of the case records as well as the client interviews, judged housing to be the main reason (Jenkins & Sauber, 1966). However, there are indications throughout the report that financial need had been emphasized as a reason for placement by many of the clients, but that the investigators, in their selection of categories for quantification of their findings, had masked this fact. For example, many of the respondents whose answers had been categorized as "unwilling or unable to continue care" might have been unable to do so, according to their own reports, because of financial distress.

In another foster care study, in which interviews could be obtained with only 27% of the parents, the parents were asked by research staff what they thought was the reason for placement (Gruber, 1978). Although the table summarizing the findings indicates many parent problems, it does not contain any category referring to situational factors, although the "other" category includes 26.5% of the cases (Gruber, 1978). Elsewhere in the report we learn that 25% of the parents had said that financial problems had made foster care placement necessary (p. 183).

This chapter focuses on the perspective of the parents as clients in child welfare cases, since it is the parents against whom complaints are made.

However, it is interesting to note the results of a study that compared *children's* perspectives on the reasons for their placement with those of their case-workers (LeBailly, Note 1). Children who had been placed outside of their homes by a state child welfare agency cited "not enough money" more often than any other reason why they had to leave home, whereas the caseworkers cited the mental health of the caretaker more often than any other. Since both the transcripts of the children's interviews and the case files in the 370 cases contained multiple reasons, research judges were asked to assess from these documents the primary focus of the reasons in each case. (Unfortunately, the children had not been asked directly for the primary reason.) From the child's perspective, the focus was determined to be on problems of the parents (a category that included the death and physical illness of the caretaker) in 40.5% of the cases, compared with 68.1% of the cases as viewed by caseworkers. The focus was on money or outside forces in 10.5% of the cases from the child's perspective, compared with 1.1% from the caseworker's perspective. Thus, although parent problems are seen as the most frequent primary reason from both perspectives, they are far more often seen as the primary reason by case-workers. Conversely, money and outside forces are far more often the primary reason from the children's perspective, and hardly ever from the caseworker's perspective.

Why Do Worker and Client Perspectives Differ?

The research evidence on client perspectives indicates that, despite some overlap, the client and the professional perspectives are significantly different from each other. This difference prompts the questions: Why do the per-spectives differ from each other? Which perspective is more valid?

There is ample research evidence to show that there is a pervasive tendency among people in general to attribute the causes of others' behavior to personality characteristics more than to situational factors (see reviews by Ross, 1977; Wills, 1978). The influence of the psychodynamic medical model in child welfare has no doubt tremendously encouraged the already present tendency to emphasize the role of personality factors in child welfare problems, while minimizing the importance of the socioeconomic context in which these problems arise.

In contrast to the personalistic tendency in observers' perceptions, research evidence indicates that there is a general tendency among people to attribute their own behavior more to situational factors (Wills, 1978). This tendency has been seen in studies on the client's perspective; it is particularly evident in cases of alleged abuse and neglect. In two foster care studies, it was found that the most frequent discrepancy between social worker and parent judgments regarding the main reason for placement was in cases in which the social worker judged abuse or neglect to be the main reason (Jenkins & Norman,

1972; Jenkins & Sauber, 1966). The parents in these cases often attributed the need for placement to the child's behavior, or otherwise denied personal responsibility. In a parent interview and case record study of 60 child abuse and neglect cases (in 33 of which I was able to obtain interviews with the parents) in Mercer County, New Jersey, I found that some parents in abuse cases had denied that physical abuse had taken place (Pelton, 1981). In neglect cases, which are far more frequent than abuse and which most often involve children being left alone, several mothers told me that they had delegated responsibility to other persons who proved negligent. Thus in child abuse–neglect cases, the process of actor versus observer effects on attributions, combined with the emphasis in the social work field on personalistic theories, may account for the difference between clients' and professionals' perspectives.

Another process influencing the personality traits attributed to parents in abuse and neglect cases derives from the fact that the attributions are based on observations of parents made while they are involved in a *conflict situation* with a child welfare agency. The behaviors observed might well be situationally rather than dispositionally determined (Pelton, 1976). The conflict arises from the fact that the will of the parents to keep their child is in opposition to the potential threat represented by the agency through its responsibility to investigate suspected child abuse and neglect and its power to obtain the removal of children from their homes. Claims in the literature that the parents are deceptive and manipulative might not reflect personality characteristics of the parents, as that same literature implies, but responses to a conflict situation by the least powerful party to that conflict. Overlooking the context of action, or the nature of the parent–agency interaction, can lead to false inferences. When we take into account the parents' subjective reality, part of which is the threat and fear that they feel, we understand why they might react with hostility and suspicion, and we recognize that such reactions may be situation-specific and not indicative of pervasive personality characteristics. Behaviors cannot be fully understood until we consider the situational context in which they occur.

Which Perspective Is More Valid?

There is considerable evidence that the great majority of families in child abuse and neglect cases live in poverty or near-poverty circumstances (see Pelton, 1978, for a review of this evidence; see also American Humane Association, 1979; Giovannoni & Becerra, 1979; Shapiro, 1979; Burgdorf, Note 3). Moreover, poverty is the single most prevalent characteristic of these families, who tend to be the *poorest* of the poor (Pelton, 1981; Wolock &

Horowitz, 1979). It is also a well-documented fact that the children who enter foster care are predominantly from poor families (e.g., Gruber, 1978; Jenkins & Norman, 1972).

In light of these facts, the conclusion that problems of poverty might be partial determinants of child abuse and neglect and foster care placement is inescapable. Indeed, it has been theorized that the problems of poverty may generate stressful experiences that become precipitating factors in child abuse and neglect (Gil, 1970; Pelton, 1978). In leading to neglect, these stresses may produce the mediating factor of despair (rather than anger, as in abuse) when, for example, a single parent attempts to raise a large family in cramped and unsafe living quarters with no help and little money.

I have pointed out that poverty may also act in a more direct way in causing harm to neglected children, by providing the hazardous environment that makes neglect so dangerous (Pelton, 1978). A middle-class parent's inadequate supervision will not put the children in as great danger as will that of the impoverished parent, because the middle-class home is not as drastically beset with health and safety hazards. Moreover, on a tight welfare budget, any indiscretion with money on the part of an impoverished parent might cause her children to go hungry during the last few days of the month. Thus, poor people have very little margin for lapses in responsibility or mismanagement of either time or money.

Furthermore, I have suggested that some mothers in cases in which neglect is alleged were forced to gamble with their children's safety because of impoverished living conditions and lack of child care supports (Pelton, 1978). A welfare mother with many children cannot easily obtain or pay for a babysitter every time she must leave the house to do her chores; in addition, she may find it more difficult to get around to do her shopping than would a middle-class mother. If she leaves her children alone, she is gambling with their safety; if she stays with them, she may be unable to provide proper food or other necessities. Thus, she may be caught up in a difficult situation that has less to do with her adequacy and responsibility as a parent than with the hard circumstances of her life.

Some of the case illustrations of alleged abuse and neglect presented in the Jenkins and Sauber (1966) foster care study indicate that other factors were involved, such as the mother having a job to go to and not being able to pay for child care. Also, impoverished living conditions may have been mistakenly attributed to neglect. My own experience with case records has led me to suspect that in some cases there is a tendency to "justify" a decision to remove a child on the grounds of child abuse and neglect when in fact other reasons were involved. Lack of adequate housing, for example, is not a socially acceptable reason for separating families. We would rather believe that we have come further than this as a caring society, and the social worker who has to separate families for this reason might prefer to believe that the parents are to blame for the need for separation. Thus "evidence" may be sought to locate the problems in the parents rather than in living conditions over which they have no control.

On the other hand, only a small proportion of poor people maltreat their children, and not all poor children wind up in foster care. As Jenkins and Norman (1972) state in regard to foster care: "For most households poverty is a necessary but not a sufficient condition for placement. It is the marginal family, whose characteristics and social circumstances are such that it cannot sustain further stress, which utilizes the placement system as a last resort when its own fragile supports break down [p. 19]." The most reasonable conclusion that can be drawn from the nature of the relationship between poverty, on the one hand, and child abuse and neglect and foster care placement, on the other, is that poverty is often a contributing factor, a partial determinant, and that there must be other *mediating* factors between poverty and these resultants. These mediators might well include parent-centered, personal, and psychological problems and characteristics, although just what characteristics these might be is unclear. They might be of a quite different nature than those suggested by the professionals.

There is a pervasive tendency in the literature on child abuse and neglect, as indeed among laypersons, to assume that people are what they do, that their actions in a particular situation necessarily betray corresponding personality characteristics. Behind cruel or violent acts, it is supposed, we will invariably find cruel or violent people. In someone who has allegedly abused or neglected a child, we are prepared to find traits of pervasive anger, sadomasochism, or lack of conscience. But the doubts cast upon the validity of the personality characteristics implied in the literature, together with the strong relationship found between poverty and child maltreatment, lead one to suspect that if any personality traits are characteristic of parents in abuse and negelct cases, they are ones that have more to do with the ability to cope with poverty and its stresses than anything else.

We have found sufficient reason why the client and professional perspectives would differ. Both professional and client are motivated to focus upon different aspects of the overall situation. The professional is not unaware of the inadequate housing of his or her clients, but tends to focus on personal problems. The client is not unaware of personal problems, and in many cases the client's judgment of a personal problem as the reason for placement is the same as the professional's. However, there is an apparent tendency for clients to emphasize situational factors more than professionals do. Although there is some question as to the validity of the specific personalistic attributions that professionals have made, it is likely that both economic and personal factors contribute to child maltreatment and foster care placement. In this sense, both client and professional perspectives are valid in that they both reflect aspects of reality. The difference between the two perspectives, at least in their broad dimensions, is one of emphasis. But this difference in emphasis is extremely important and has far-reaching implications for practice. While the professional perspective has led toward decisions to provide psychological and educative services, the clients tend to prefer concrete and supportive services.

Implications for Service Delivery

If, as we have seen, poverty has not constituted a "sufficient reason" for placement, neither have the reasons cited by professionals in the foster care studies. For example, "physical illness" of the mother or "confinement of the mother for a current pregnancy" (Jenkins & Sauber, 1966) cannot be sufficient reason for child placement since there are many mothers similarly indisposed whose children are *not* placed. Even child abuse or neglect is not sufficient reason for placement, since many children who might have been abused or neglected in the past can be served and protected in their own homes. Thus, in terms of practice, it would be far more fruitful to ask what services could have prevented placement rather than what are the reasons for placement. Put another way, the true reason for placement is very often that the family, often due to poverty, does not have the resources to offset the impact of situational or personal problems, which themselves are often caused by poverty, *and the agencies have failed to provide the needed supports.* If we were to go through the classifications of so-called reasons for placement listed in the foster care studies, and more surely, if we were to go through the actual placement cases on a case-by-case basis, we would find in many instances that the services most frequently requested by the clients—babysitting, homemaker, day care, financial assistance, housing assistance—are the ones that best and most logically fit the situational deficits, and the personal deficits and problems, that prompted placement.

I am not proposing that child welfare agencies prevent placement by raising families out of poverty, because this they cannot do. But they can, more frequently than they do now, plug the poverty-related gaps that precipitate placement. Even the provision of emergency financial assistance is not beyond the ability of child welfare agencies. For example, the New Jersey Division of Youth and Family Services has set up a statewide emergency fund that is being used by caseworkers to overcome some of the poverty-related crises that might otherwise result in placement (Pelton & Fuccello, 1978).

In regard to the treatment of child abuse, Gelles (1973) observed that psychotherapy has had limited effectiveness (possibly because the supposed personality deficits it has been directed at are nonexistent in many cases). Psychotherapeutic intervention failing, the only alternative, in the absence of other resources, is to remove the child. Sudia (1981) has concluded that research and evaluation indicate that recent efforts to treat child abuse and neglect have not been very effective. After reviewing some of the same client perspective research cited in this chapter, and other evaluation research, she also concluded that the failure of agencies to take into account the perceptions and needs of the problem families, and to provide concrete services, has impeded the effort to deal more effectively with child abuse and neglect.

Problems in Ascertaining What the Parent Wants

In light of the failure of agencies to provide the concrete and supportive services that the clients want and need, I have difficulties with findings suggesting that families want their children removed. In the Jenkins and Norman (1972) foster care study, for example, it was found that parents in approximately 36% of the cases said that they were the initiators of placement. When mothers in 297 cases were asked how necessary they thought the placement was, in only 24% of the cases did they indicate that it was not necessary at all. Such findings lead me to question whether parents are fully aware of the options that should be available to them.

Poor people may have rather low expectations of what government can, or even should, provide to families to help keep them together. There are many cases in which a mother, because of inadequate housing, perhaps compounded by physical illness or emotional strain, is urged by caseworkers to "temporarily" place her children in foster care. In some cases, the mother may look upon such an offer as a favor, since she knows that she is unable at the moment to care for her children without help. Gratefulness for such assistance, however, may only occur in the subjective context of not expecting the agency to offer housing assistance, emergency financial assistance, and in-home supportive services such as babysitting. In other words, the mother may perceive a limited range of options for gaining help for her family, and in that context may indeed be grateful for any assistance offered. To be sure, we have seen that agencies in general have been more interested in offering, aside from foster care itself, psychological and educative services rather than concrete and supportive services. Thus the agencies have shaped and reinforced the parents' limited expectations. The agencies themselves may have restricted the range of clients' response options to such questions as whether or not they want their children removed (see also Bush & Gordon, 1978, for a discussion of client choice).

Moreover, the client perspective has been unintentionally slighted by the research itself. In assessing the attitudes toward the agencies of parents who had children in foster care, Jenkins and Norman (1972) developed a scale of nine statements. Three of the statements depicted the agencies as being facilitators of child care, helping families in time of need; three as usurpers of parental rights; and three as surrogates for parents, fulfilling a socially appropriate role. For each statement, the parent was allowed only two options: to agree or disagree. It was found that the parents saw the agencies much more as "facilitators" than as "usurpers" or "surrogates." However, when I examined the statements, I found that their construction could have biased the outcome. All three usurper items and all three surrogate items were written in overgeneralized, stereotyped, all-or-none terms. For example, one usurper statement was: "Agencies act like parents have no rights at all—they think they own the children." One of the surrogate items was: "When you come right down to it, the children belong to the government, so why shouldn't they take care of them?" On the other hand, all of the facilitator items expressed reasonable, nonstereotypic, particularized items, such as: "It's a good thing there are institutions and foster mothers to do the job when a real mother is not able to take care of her child."

Nevertheless, it was found that many parents did view the agencies as usurpers of parental rights. Whereas 92% of the mothers agreed with the above-mentioned facilitator statement, as many as 27% agreed with the above usurper item. In another foster care study, 21% of the mothers were thought by the workers to view the agency as a usurper of their rights to care for their children, and this percentage apparently increased over time (Shapiro, 1976).

The fact that at least a sizable minority of the parents of children in foster care view the agencies as usurpers of parental rights is not surprising in light of certain findings in the Mercer County study. I found that although most placements in child abuse and neglect cases had been made without court order, 38% of the interviewed parents who had signed so-called voluntary agreements told me that they had been against placement at the time (Pelton, 1981). They perceived themselves to have been threatened, or at least frightened, into signing the agreements.

It should be said, however, that most parents interviewed in child abuse and neglect cases indicated positive attitudes toward the caseworkers themselves (Pelton, 1981). In the Mercer County study, I found that the parents tended to perceive the workers as nonaccusatory, polite, respectful, and sincerely interested in helping. Moreover, there was some indication that the parents tended to distinguish the workers from the agency in their attitudes, sometimes being positive toward the former and negative toward the latter. Indeed, the sum total of the information collected in the Mercer County study led me to conclude that the occasional transgressions of parents' rights by caseworkers were mostly due to their being given the difficult assignment of protecting children from harm and few resources with which to do it. The information presented in this chapter leads to the conclusion that the greatest problem in child welfare might be, ultimately, the failure of child welfare agencies to make available the services that the clients want and need. The implication is that agencies should shift their resources, in the main, from those of a mental health and educative nature to those of a concrete and supportive nature.

Methodological Improvements for Further Research

Although, as we have seen, the research on client perspectives has been, on the whole, adequate enough to reveal broad trends in client perspectives, and broad discrepancies between client and professional perspectives, much of it has been deficient in some ways, and several pitfalls that should be avoided in future research have become obvious. Research that wrongly concludes that "this is what the parents want" can serve as justification for business as usual or misguided changes. The erroneous assessment of the parents' perspective would be a disservice to the parents and their children.

The deficiencies stem from the fundamental difficulty that the researchers are the allies of the agencies in many ways. The researchers must depend upon the agencies for their access to the clients and may be viewed with fear and suspicion by the clients they interview. Their first glimpse at the clients has come through the case records and conversations with the agency employees, and so their views may have been shaped before they met the clients. Socioeconomic class is another important commonality between researcher and agency professional that puts a considerable social distance between both of them and the lower-class client.

These factors perhaps cannot be altered, but they at least point to certain precautions that should be taken in the research. We must beware of too much structuring of questions that might limit, and thereby distort, the clients' responses. A perspective, after all, is a structure itself, and it cannot be properly assessed by forcing the client merely to select one of several responses generated by the researcher. We must not restrict the clients' response options by presenting fixed-alternative questions and statements. Open-ended questions that give the client a wide latitude for response, in conjunction with follow-up probing questions that draw out a more detailed response, are preferable.

Needless to say, asking caseworkers to tell us what they think the client's view might be is not entirely adequate, even though this approach did yield valuable information, some of which was presented in this chapter. We would not, for example, try to understand the caseworkers' perspective by asking clients to tell us what they think it is. I am sure that these researchers would agree that their findings, although instructive, especially in light of the general paucity of client-oriented research, should be succeeded by research that goes directly to the clients for their views. It also should be noted that caseworkers should not be employed as the interviewers, especially not in the cases they have handled, for the caseworker is party to the conflict dynamics described previously.

In many of the studies cited in this chapter, the researchers were unable to obtain interviews with all of the clients in their original samples. This difficulty raises the problem that the views of the parents not interviewed might differ systematically from those of the parents who were interviewed. In particular, the parents who could not be contacted or interviewed are likely to be those who, for other reasons, are often dubbed "uncooperative" by social workers, and we could expect that their views might be more discrepant from the workers' perspective than parents with whom research interviews could be obtained. The best that researchers can and should do is to go to as great lengths as possible in trying to contact the parents and, short of outright refusal by the parents or violation of their right to privacy, to make several attempts before giving up on obtaining an interview.

Future research should be aimed at providing us with a far more articulated representation of client perspectives than we now have. We must better understand the client's subjective reality in regard to child welfare problems. One of the most important tasks currently facing child welfare researchers is to ascertain the *mediators* between poverty, on one hand, and child abuse and neglect and child placement, on the other. What causes some poor families to maltreat their children, or to face the possible need for child placement? A full understanding of these mediators cannot be gained without consulting the client, for it is the subjective reality to which the client is responding. Moreover, researchers should interview nonclient parents who have demonstrated the ability to cope with poverty in a superior manner, in order to learn how they do it and what characteristics allow them to do so.

Conclusion

Many human acts are determined more by situations than by dispositions, and by the limited number of alternatives available to the actor. Actions often betray the situation that one is in rather than enduring personality characteristics. Abnormal responses may often be responses to extraordinary situations rather than symptoms of abnormal personalities. But to ascertain whether we are dealing with the former rather than the latter, we would have to study the situational context of the actions. Certain facts about this context can be gained without going to the individuals themselves. For example, we can study the economic status of the clients and the physical aspects of their environment. However, the clients' own perceptions are a crucial part of this context, and must be studied if we are to understand the clients' actions. Individuals respond not to the objective context per se but to the situation as it appears to them, to the subjective context.

We have seen that clients present an entirely reasonable and in many ways valid perspective on their problems and the services they need. The study of this perspective yields valuable insights that cannot be gained in any other way. The clients' perspective may not be wholly valid or the only valid one, but in this chapter I believe I have shown why it should not be ignored.

Reference Notes

1. LeBailly, R. *Patterns of disagreement between multiple perspectives*. Center for Urban Affairs, Northwestern University, April 9, 1978.
2. Texas Department of Human Resources. *Child abuse and neglect resources demonstration project* (Final report, U.S. Department of Health, Education, and Welfare, 90–C–411). August 31, 1978.
3. Burgdorf, K. *Recognition and reporting of child maltreatment: Summary findings from the national study of the incidence and severity of child abuse and neglect* (draft). Prepared for the National Center on Child Abuse and Neglect, U.S. Department of Health and Human Services, by Westat, Inc., in affiliation with Development Associates, Inc., October 14, 1980.

References

American Humane Association. *National analysis of official child neglect and abuse reporting (1976)*. Denver: author, 1978.

American Humane Association. *National analysis of official child abuse and neglect reporting (1977)*. Washington, D.C.: National Center on Child Abuse and Neglect, U.S. Department of Health, Education, and Welfare, 1979.

Antler, S. The rediscovery of child abuse. In L. H. Pelton (Ed.), *The social context of child abuse and neglect*. New York: Human Sciences Press, 1981.

Batson, C. D., Jones, C. H., & Cochran, P. J. Attributional bias in counselors' diagnoses: The effect of resources. *Journal of Applied Social Psychology*, 1979, 9, 377–393.

Bush, M. Institutions for dependent and neglected children: Therapeutic option of choice or last resort? *American Journal of Orthopsychiatry*, 1980, 50, 239–255.

Bush, M., & Gordon, A. C. Client choice and bureaucratic accountability: Possibilities for responsiveness in a social welfare bureaucracy. *Journal of Social Issues*, 1978, 34 (4), 22–43.

Bush, M., Gordon, A. C., & LeBailly, R. Evaluating child welfare services: A contribution from the clients. *Social Service Review*, 1977, 51, 491–501.

Gelles, R. J. Child abuse as psychopathology: A sociological critique and reformulation. *American Journal of Orthopsychiatry*, 1973, 43, 611–621.

Germain, C. B. An ecological perspective in casework practice. *Social Casework*, 1973, 54, 323–330.

Gil, D. G. *Violence against children*. Cambridge, Mass.: Harvard Univ. Press, 1970.

Giordano, P. C. The client's perspective in agency evaluation. *Social Work*, 1977, 22, 34–39.

Giovannoni, J. M., & Becerra, R. M. *Defining child abuse*. New York: Free Press, 1979.

Gruber, A. R. *Children in foster care: Destitute, neglected, betrayed*. New York: Human Sciences Press, 1978.

Jenkins, S., & Norman, E. *Filial deprivation and foster care*. New York: Columbia Univ. Press, 1972.

Jenkins, S., & Norman, E. *Beyond placement: Mothers view foster care*. New York: Columbia Univ. Press, 1975.

Jenkins, S., & Sauber, M. *Paths to child placement: Family situations prior to foster care*. New York: Community Council of Greater New York, 1966.

Jones, M. A., Neuman, R., & Shyne, A. W. *A second chance for families: Evaluation of a program to reduce foster care*. New York: Child Welfare League of America, 1976.

Maluccio, A. N. *Learning from clients: Interpersonal helping as viewed by clients and social workers*. New York: Free Press, 1979.

Mayer, J. E., & Timms, N. Clash in perspective between worker and client. *Social Casework*, 1969, 50, 32–40.

Mayer, J. E., & Timms, N. *The client speaks: Working class impressions of casework*. New York: Atherton, 1970.

Pelton, L. H. *The psychology of nonviolence*. New York: Pergamon, 1974.

Pelton, L. H. The conflict dynamics of parent–agency interaction in child abuse and neglect cases. Trenton, N. J.: Bureau of Research, New Jersey Division of Youth and Family Services, 1976.

Pelton, L. H. Child abuse and neglect: The myth of classlessness. *American Journal of Orthopsychiatry*, 1978, *48*, 608 –617. (Reprinted in L. H. Pelton (Ed.), *The social context of child abuse and neglect*. New York: Human Sciences Press, 1981.)

Pelton, L. H. Child abuse and neglect and protective intervention in Mercer County, New Jersey. In L. H. Pelton (Ed.), *The social context of child abuse and neglect.* New York: Human Sciences Press, 1981.

Pelton, L. H., & Fuccello, E. An evaluation of the use of an emergency cash fund in child protective services. Trenton, N.J.: Bureau of Research, New Jersey Division of Youth and Family Services, 1978.

Polansky, N. A., DeSaix, C., & Sharlin, S. A. *Child neglect: Understanding and reaching the parent*. New York: Child Welfare League of America, 1972.

Reid, W. J., & Epstein, L. *Task-centered casework*. New York: Columbia Univ. Press, 1972.

Ross, L. The intuitive psychologist and his shortcomings: Distortions in the attribution process. In L. Berkowitz (Ed.), *Advances in experimental social psychology* (Vol. 10). New York: Academic Press, 1977.

Rubenstein, H., & Bloch, M. H. Helping clients who are poor: Worker and client perceptions of problems, activities, and outcomes. *Social Service Review*, 1978, *52*, 69–84.

Shapiro, D. *Agencies and foster children*. New York: Columbia Univ. Press, 1976.

Shapiro, D. *Parents and protectors: A study in child abuse and neglect*. New York: Child Welfare League of America, 1979.

Sudia, C. E. What services do abusive and neglecting families need? In L. H. Pelton (Ed.), *The social context of child abuse and neglect*. New York: Human Sciences Press, 1981.

Wills, T. A. Perceptions of clients by professional helpers. *Psychological Bulletin*, 1978, *85*, 968–1000.

Wolock, I., & Horowitz, B. Child maltreatment and material deprivation among AFDC-recipient families. *Social Service Review*, 1979, *53*, 175–194.

Young, L. *Wednesday's children*. New York: McGraw-Hill, 1964.

PART II

SOCIAL-PSYCHOLOGICAL PROCESSES

The chapters in the following section consider four processes that have been of central importance in social-psychological research: attribution, self-esteem maintenance, perceived control, and commitment. Although these have been previously examined in laboratory research, the authors of the chapters provide new perspectives through a careful investigation of how these basic processes are involved in actual helping situations. Their conclusions suggest that these processes are important factors in several different helping settings.

In Chapter 6 Karuza, Zevon, Rabinowitz, and Brickman report a systematic investigation of the types of attributions that helpers and clients make about problems. The authors have developed a conceptual framework that distinguishes between perceived responsibility for the *problem* and perceived responsibility for the *solution* to the problem; this framework defines four distinct models of helping based on the attributions made for the problem and solution dimensions, respectively. Karuza and colleagues report results from several studies conducted with young adults and elderly recipients of social work services. Their results show that clients' perceptions of responsibility for solutions to problems are related to psychological well-being. The findings raise several questions about the extent to which helping agents encourage client responsibility and the manner in which clients are socialized

Basic Processes in Helping Relationships

to adopt a medical model orientation to helping rather than a more responsibility-oriented model. The authors' framework also provides a theoretical basis for more rigorous investigation of the matching between helpers' and clients' expectations about treatment, an area that has generally been characterized by contradictory and noncumulative studies (see Berzins, 1977; Duckro, Beal, & George, 1979).

Fisher and Nadler, in Chapter 7, report findings from an extensive research program on recipients' reactions to help. Considering helping from the recipient's viewpoint, these investigators have found that self-esteem maintenance is an important aspect of a helping relationship. Receiving help is not a straightforward, one-sided transaction in which a client presents a problem and receives a solution; rather, the helping relationship involves a mixture of elements that are either *self-supportive* or *self-threatening* for the recipient. The client's subsequent reaction and the ultimate outcome of the relationship are strongly determined by the extent to which one or the other of these elements is dominant in the client's perceptions. Another significant aspect of this work is the question of the extent to which a helping relationship tends to foster self-help versus dependency on the part of the recipient; the findings suggest that certain factors may act to increase dependency, a finding that (in combination with Fehrenbach and O'Leary's finding that therapists show a preference for clients higher in helplessness; see Chapter 2, this volume) suggests that more attention should be given to this issue. In other work Fisher has investigated the influence of *medical model* versus *social learning* views about the nature of psychological problems. Replicated findings from this research show that some perceptions of problems encourage personal responsibility and self-help, whereas others seem to encourage passivity and dependence by recipients. The implications of these findings for the helping professions warrant serious consideration.

The process of perceived control is clearly important for helping relationships. Psychological well-being is strongly determined by perception of control over the self and the environment (see Garber & Seligman, 1980), and persons typically seek psychological help because of feelings that they are losing control over their behavior or life situation. Yet when a client enters a helping relationship he or she typically must accept overall control of the relationship by the therapist, who is in a position of greater power and status relative to the client. How clients' feelings of control are restored while they are accepting direction from another person is a paradoxical, yet central, aspect of helping. Chapter 8, by Schorr and Rodin, provides a rigorous examination of the construct of control and an extended discussion of the mechanisms through which a client's sense of self-efficacy can be enhanced or restored. The presentation is addressed to common aspects of primary medical care and psychotherapy relationships, settings in which the client often has little or no choice about the method or conduct of treatment. Efficacy-enhancing mechanisms include giving clients greater choice and information about treatment, providing feedback about therapeutic progress, identifying clients' beliefs about treatment approaches, and encouraging them to discuss any dissatisfactions they may have with the treatment. Schorr and Rodin propose a helping process where social influence is explicit and discrepancies between helper and client views are discussed and negotiated, rather than being left as implicit (and possibly hindering) factors in the relationship. There is no single "magic bullet" to enhance perceived control, so the authors discuss a number of approaches that will increase clients' understanding of the rationale, costs, and benefits of treatment, their skills in coping with difficulties both within and outside of the treatment setting, and their motivation to adhere to difficult treatment regimens. The authors point out that encouraging greater control by the client does not detract from the helper's effectiveness, and in fact probably serves to increase the helper's satisfaction with the relationship.

The ambivalence with which persons approach help seeking, and the process through which initial ambivalence develops into clients' commitment to a therapeutic alliance, is clarified by Lemkau, Bryant, and Brickman in Chapter 9. These authors provide a thoughtful examination of the construct of commitment and a theoretical formulation of the stages of therapy, which is not a static process but a reciprocal, developing, interpersonal relationship and appears to involve principles similar to those occurring in the development of other social relationships. The authors' formulation is successful in accounting for many existing findings on psychotherapy and suggests a number of specific approaches that can serve to enhance clients' commitment to the helping relationship; these procedures operate largely through increasing clients' assumption of personal responsibility for therapeutic progress. This formulation leads in some unexpected and interesting directions. It draws attention to the conceptualization of therapy, as well as general world view, shared by helper and client, a process that is clearly involved in the phenomenon of *convergence effects* in psychotherapy (considered in more detail in Chapter 16 of this volume, by Abramowitz, Berger, & Weary). The analysis by Lemkau and colleagues also considers the role of clients' expectations about treatment, another factor that is relevant to therapy outcome, and proposes some theory-based guidelines for helper-client matching. Finally, in common with work by several other authors in this volume, the commitment formulation places emphasis on clients' attributions of personal responsibility for therapeutic change. The ramifications of this theoretical approach suggest that it will be productive for further research on psychotherapy.

References

Berzins, J. I. Therapist–patient matching. In A. S. Gurman & A. M. Razin (Eds.), *Effective psychotherapy: A handbook of research*. New York: Pergamon, 1977.

Duckro, P., Beal, D., & George, C. Research on the effects of disconfirmed client role expectations in psychotherapy: A critical review. *Psychological Bulletin*, 1979, 86, 260–275.

Garber, J., & Seligman, M. E. P. *Human helplessness: Theory and applications*. New York: Academic Press, 1980.

chapter 6

Attribution of Responsibility by Helpers and Recipients

JURGIS KARUZA, JR.
MICHAEL A. ZEVON
VITA C. RABINOWITZ
PHILIP BRICKMAN

Introduction

Society today provides much of its assistance to those in need through a network of formal, institutionalized, and often socially mandated programs. In programs designed for the elderly, the handicapped, the delinquent, the victims of abuse, and many other special populations, trained professionals develop and implement specific interventions that address the problems of their clients. The purpose of this chapter is to consider the implicit pyschological dynamics that determine the form and outcomes of these helping interventions. Our analysis is built on the theoretical framework developed by Brickman, Rabinowitz, Karuza, Coates, Cohn, and Kidder (1982), which classifies helping approaches according to their assumptions about the cause of, and solution to, the client's problems. In addition, we review empirical research that demonstrates the impact of these assumptions

---

This chapter and Chapter 9 are dedicated to the memory of our friend and co-author Philip Brickman, whose tragic death occurred after the completion of the chapters. Phil's special intellect, energy, and human kindness deeply touched our lives and our work. We will miss him.

Basic Processes in Helping Relationships

on the efficacy of applied interventions for the elderly and other at-risk populations.

The existing literature on helping in social and clinical psychology is weak in a number of ways. Most studies concentrate on whether or not people help or how much help they will give—ignoring what we regard as the crucial question, namely, what *kind* of help people will see as appropriate. This, in our view, is determined by what helpers (and recipients) believe are the causes of problems and what must be done to solve them. These beliefs and the helping strategies they dictate are in turn crucial determinants of whether or not clients actually benefit from these helping interventions. It has often been assumed that helping is good and beneficial in all cases. However, recent evaluations of established social programs (e.g., McCord, 1978), as well as empirical studies of institutional environments (e.g., Rodin & Langer, 1977) suggest that even well-intentioned interventions may go astray. It should be a key goal of analysis and research to understand why certain interventions are successful and others are not.

Basic Assumptions about Helping

In seeking assistance from a helping professional, clients concede that they suffer from problems that impede their adaptive functioning and acknowledge that they are unable to deal with these problems alone. Helping can be conceptualized as an interaction between helper and client that has the specific aim of resolving the client's presenting problem.

Our contention is that for both client and helper, the helping interaction is justified and shaped by answers to two basic questions: (1) Who is to blame for the problem, that is, who is responsible for the cause or origin of the problem? and (2) Who is to have control over the problem, that is, who or what is responsible for the solution to the problem (cf. Brickman *et al.*, 1982; Feinberg, 1970)? These judgments define the meaning and purpose of the intervention. They reflect a set of assumptions and expectations about the client, the helper, and in many instances human nature as well, and often imply a unique helping strategy.

We posit that from the very beginning of the interaction, both client and helper have in mind a set of assumptions about the nature of the problem and also about what should be done to solve the problem. On one level, these assumptions determine the helper's explicit choice of a therapeutic approach in dealing with the client's problem. The instrumental functions and activities such as the diagnosis of the problem, the choice of treatment, and the setting of the goals of the intervention are, in part, selected according to the underlying orientation of the helper (see Rabinowitz, Zevon, & Karuza, in press). Further, the verbal and nonverbal behaviors of the helper and client, as well as the atmosphere in which the help is given, can be affected by the assumptions of this adopted helping orientation (Friedman, 1979).

The explicit rationale of an intervention is always to ameliorate the client's problem, but an intervention may have implicit functions that are quite different, such as caring or social control (see Kaswan, 1981). A helping orientation may express both explicit and implicit aspects of helping. In either case, it does so by socializing clients into accepting views about their problems, potentials, and proper role in the intervention (Rodin & Janis, 1979). From this perspective, clients may disagree with helpers about what form of help is more appropriate to the nature of their problem. Thus, to develop and implement a successful intervention, the helper must deal with the fact that his or her professional diagnosis of the problem and expectations for its resolution may, or may not, coincide with the assumptions the client is making.

Models of Helping

Central to the derivation of helping orientations is the realization that all clients and their problems are not identical, and that all treatments cannot be subsumed under a single rubric. In the analysis that follows, we note that attributions of responsibility for the cause of and solution to the client's problem define four internally consistent and unique helping orientations. In theory, a client can be perceived as having either high or low responsibility for the *cause* of the problem, and at the same time be expected to have high or low

Table 6.1

Consequences of Attribution of Responsibility in Four Models of Helping and Coping[a]

Attribution to self of responsibility for problem	Attribution to self of responsibility for solution	
	High	Low
High	Moral model	Enlightenment model
Perception of self	Lazy	Guilty
Actions expected of self	Striving	Submission
Others besides self who must act	Peers	Authorities
Actions expected of others	Exhortation	Discipline
Implicit view of human nature	Strong	Bad
Pathology	Loneliness	Fanaticism
Low	Compensatory model	Medical model
Perception of self	Deprived	Ill
Actions expected of self	Assertion	Acceptance
Others besides self who must act	Subordinates	Experts
Actions expected of others	Mobilization	Treatment
Implicit view of human nature	Good	Weak
Pathology	Alienation	Dependency

[a]From P. Brickman, V. C. Rabinowitz, J. Karuza, D. Coates, E. Cohn, & L. Kidder. Models of helping and coping. *American Psychologist*, 1982, 37, 368–384. Copyright 1982 by American Psychological Association.

responsibility for the *solution* to the problem. Crossing these two attributional dimensions yields the four models of helping that are summarized in Table 6.1. Traditionally, responsibility for the cause of the problem and responsibility for the solution to the problem were assumed to be correlated (e.g., "You got yourself into this, now get yourself out" or "It's my fault, let me fix it"). Although responsibility for the problem's cause and solution may often covary, in many cases it is incorrect to think that knowing the solution to the problem implies knowing the cause, or that once the cause of the problem has been isolated, the solution to the problem has been found (Brickman *et al.*, 1982). For many clients, the cause of the problem may be attributed to one set of conditions, whereas the solution to the problem is contingent on a different set entirely. In the following section, we describe the nature and implications of the four helping models.

MEDICAL MODEL

The helping model in which clients are not held responsible for either the cause of the problem or its solution is called the *medical model*, since the practice and orientation of modern medicine most clearly exemplify these attributional assumptions. In this model, clients see themselves, or are seen by others, as ill or as victims of social forces that were and will be beyond their control. Neither the "illness" nor the treatment is regarded as being the client's responsibility. Implicit in this model, according to Brickman *et al.* (1982), is a view of the client and of human nature as essentially passive. Clients are expected to accept this view, which frees them from ordinary social obligations but at the same time requires them to acquiesce to the ministrations of the professional helper. The helper is seen as the primary agent of change. Expert others (e.g., doctors, social workers, nurses) are expected to take responsibility for the problems' solutions, applying their professional training in order to recognize the problem and provide the necessary service or treatment. The treatment may be aimed directly at the source of the problem (e.g., drugs, surgery, psychoanalysis), or it may attempt to provide needed resources unavailable to the client (e.g., rent subsidy, home-delivered meals, homemaker services). Ultimately, the responsibility for prescribing the solution and judging its effectiveness rests with the professional, not the client.

The foremost advantage of this model is that it allows clients to seek and accept help without being blamed for their weakness and relieves them of the anxiety associated with finding a solution to their problems. In addition, since the treatment requires a passive client and is aimed at a specific cause, it allows the helper to treat large numbers of clients within a short period of time (Rabinowitz, Zevon, & Karuza, in press).

One potential drawback of this model is that it may foster needless and dysfunctional dependency. Clients may be taught to become overly passive as a result of the role expectations implicit in the intervention (Taylor, 1979) or may be dissuaded from questioning the diagnosis or adequacy of the treatment because of the authority associated with the helper (Rodin & Janis, 1979). Other examples of the potential dangers of the medical model can be found in the analysis of learned helplessness effects in institutional settings (e.g., Rodin & Langer, 1977; Wack & Rodin, 1978). These studies demonstrate that psychological and physical deterioration may result from institutional and medical procedures that constrain the freedom and self-determination of the client.

COMPENSATORY MODEL

The helping model in which clients are not held responsible for the cause of their problems but are still held responsible for finding a solution is called the *compensatory model* by Brickman *et al.* (1982) The term reflects the underlying rationale of the model, namely that clients see themselves, or are seen by others, as having to personally compensate for their handicaps or the environmental constraints imposed on them. Clients are assumed to be deprived individuals who were not given the opportunities or allowed to develop the skills necessary to deal with their environment in an adaptive manner.

Although the cause of the problem is seen as beyond the control of the client, the ultimate responsibility for its solution is regarded as within the client's grasp. Implicit in this model is a particularly optimistic view of the client's potential and a belief in the inherent goodness of human nature (i.e., if given the opportunity, all individuals can achieve an adaptive fit with the environment). Clients are expected to adopt a problem-solving orientation in overcoming the difficulties they face. It is assumed that clients will take charge and find a solution to the problem by developing their potentials, learning new skills, and assertively compelling others to yield the resources, training, and opportunities required to effect the necessary changes. The essential agent of change is the client; the professional helper, therefore, assumes a subordinate role. In the compensatory model, the helper adopts a cooperative stance vis à vis the client. At the onset of the intervention, the helper may work to redefine the problem in such a way as to allow the client to feel a sense of control over the situation (Meichenbaum & Genest, 1980). As the intervention progresses, the helper works with the client by mobilizing resources, providing training, and creating needed opportunities. Examples of compensatory models of helping can be found in many community action programs (e.g., Project Head Start and Jesse Jackson's Project Excel) and various cognitive behavior modification psychotherapies (Meichenbaum & Genest, 1980; Rabinowitz, Zevon, & Karuza, in press).

The advantage of this model is that it permits clients to become actively involved in finding a solution, thus combining the resources of both the client and helper. At the same time, the model allows clients to discount past failures, and in so doing, feelings of guilt or incompetence are relieved.

Further, the model permits clients to maintain their self-respect, since they are not blamed for the problem and are given credit for developing an adaptive solution, if one emerges. The potential disadvantage of this model is that clients may feel pressured into continually solving problems, and, in the long run, feel alienated or bitter when their efforts are unsuccessful (Karuza, Zevon, & Rabinowitz, Note 1).

MORAL MODEL

The model in which clients are held responsible for both the cause of the problem and its solution is called the *moral model*. This term springs from the notion that individuals' problems are of their own making and that it is their moral duty to help themselves (e.g., the belief in rugged individualism). In this model, according to Brickman *et al.* (1982), clients see themselves, or are seen by others, as creating problems for themselves as a result of their stubbornness, laziness, or misdirected efforts. In addition, only clients can find a solution to their problems. Implicit in this model is the view that clients, despite their misdirection or laziness, are basically strong and have the potential to reorient themselves and solve their problems. Clients are expected to pull themselves up by their bootstraps and strive to better themselves. The essential agent of change is the client, for it is assumed that no one else should (or can) effect a change. The activity of the professional helper in this model is limited to reminding clients of their responsibility for causing their problems and for finding a solution to them, and to exhorting clients, by coercion or praise, to change themselves. Examples of the moral model of helping can be found in the popular self-help movement (Hill & Stone, 1975). Self-help treatments such as Erhard Seminar Training (Brewer, 1975) and rational–emotive and existential psychotherapies also exemplify this helping approach. In each of these cases, clients are urged to see themselves as active causal agents who are responsible for both creating and resolving the problem.

The primary advantage of this model is that clients are able to assume total responsibility for their lives and thereby are motivated to work harder, longer, and more effectively in dealing with their problems (Brickman, Linsenmeir, & McCareins, 1976; Janoff-Bulman & Brickman, 1982). In addition, by taking responsibility for causes and solutions, clients may avoid the dependency and passivity associated with the medical model. The danger of this model is that clients may begin to adopt a view of the world in which everything is contingent on their own behavior, and problems are personally caused and solved only by the client's force of will. Under these circumstances, clients may feel alone and separate from others, since the key to success and happiness lies only within themselves. Further, when problems are truly beyond the client's control, an unrealistic notion of self-sufficiency may preclude the client from drawing upon more appropriate forms of help.

ENLIGHTENMENT MODEL

The model in which clients are held responsible for their problems, but not responsible for finding a solution, is called by Brickman *et al.* (1982), the *enlightenment model*. This term reflects the belief that clients must be enlightened about the true nature of their problem and the difficult course of action that will be needed to deal with it. In this model, clients are seen as guilty, sinful, or at least culpable for their problems and suffering. Their willful lack of impulse control is the cause of the problem, and the flawed nature of the client makes self-control of these impulses impossible. Implicit in this model is the view of clients as out of control and unable to come to grips with their problems or their lives. Clients are expected to accept their guilt and submit to the strength, support, and discipline of legitimate authority. The authority, viewed as the essential agent of change, can be represented by an individual (e.g., a parole officer), or be embodied by a larger community (e.g., Alcoholics Anonymous). This submission to authority constitutes the solution to the clients' impulse control problems. Helpers structure the lives of clients, offering understanding and sympathy, as well as discipline, in order to assist clients in controlling their wayward impulses. Since the solution to the problem lies outside the clients, control over the problem requires clients to maintain a close tie to external authority.

Examples of the enlightenment model approach to helping can be found in therapeutic communities that deal with a variety of problems, such as alcoholism (Alcoholics Anonymous), drug addiction (Daytop Village), obesity (Weight Watchers), gambling (Gamblers Anonymous), and old age and institutionalization (see Gartner, 1976). The advantage of the enlightenment model lies in the clients' admission that the solution is beyond their control. Coincident with this admission is a sense of relief based on relaxation of the clients' often fruitless striving and expectations for change. Further, the support and structure that are offered by helpers or the therapeutic community may engender in clients feelings of comfort and the knowledge that control of the problem is possible. On the other hand, there is a danger of the enlightenment model leading clients to overidentification with the authority figures, with a resultant restructuring of the clients' entire life around the source of authority (see Cummings, 1979).

Research on Models of Helping

In the sections that follow, we review previous literature and present some original research that begins to test propositions concerning the existence and consequences of these models of helping. We arrive at an apparent paradox that exists in helping the elderly, and then consider a number of implications of this analysis for planning future interventions.

DEMONSTRATION OF THE EXISTENCE OF THE MODELS

It would be helpful, to begin with, to demonstrate that each of the models posited by Brickman *et al.* (1982) actually exists in various natural settings. Rabinowitz (1978) undertook such a direct test by interviewing respondents from four organized groups whose orientation and ideology were predicted to represent each of the helping models in relatively pure form. Thus, the moral model was operationalized by est (Erhard Seminar Training), the compensatory model by a job training program under CETA (Comprehensive Education and Training Act), the medical model by a college infirmary, and the enlightenment model by a national evangelical group (the Campus Crusade for Christ). Twelve participants in each group were interviewed in order to determine their beliefs, assumptions, and expectations about the nature of the help offered by their organizations and the actions required by helpers and recipients. Subjects completed a Help Orientation Test, which contained a total of 40 closed-ended questions, with 10 questions assessing the assumptions of each of the four helping models. In addition, separate closed-ended questions were asked concerning the subjects' perceived responsibility for the cause of and solution to their problems. The responses of each participant were recorded on 7-point scales.

Separate one-way analyses of variance were performed for each attribution dimension. The results indicated significant differences across groups in perceived responsibility for problem, $F(3, 44) = 10.44, p < .01$, and perceived responsibility for solution, $F(3, 44) = 7.76$, $p < .01$. Consistent with the assumptions of each model, est participants (moral model) and Campus Crusade for Christ participants (enlightenment model) rated themselves as more responsible for their problems and past lives than CETA participants (compensatory model) or infirmary patients (medical model). CETA and est participants rated themselves as more responsible for finding solutions to their problems than Campus Crusade for Christ participants and infirmary patients.

For each Help Orientation Test question, a Newman-Keuls analysis was performed, comparing the item endorsement of each group relative to the others. Overall, the participants of each group endorsed those assumptions of the helping model that their group was predicted to embody significantly more than did members of other groups ($p < .01$). Specifically, est participants saw themselves as stubborn individuals and the essential agents of change. CETA participants saw themselves as deprived individuals who needed someone in the role of a tutor to assist them for a short period of time. Infirmary patients saw themselves as sick and needing the help of skilled professionals. Campus Crusade for Christ participants saw themselves as self-destructive individuals who required guidance from others who had "been there" and subsequently had come to grips with their problem.

In summary, the results indicated strong support for our primary hypothesis, namely that helping approaches can be categorized in terms of their attributions of responsibility. The results further indicate that, at least in the settings sampled, approaches to helping exist that embody the orientation and assumptions of each of the four helping models.

HELPER STEREOTYPES AS A DETERMINANT OF THE CHOICE OF MODELS

At the most general level, we hypothesize that different helping models are chosen by helpers and clients to maximize their chances of influencing each other in what they believe to be desirable ways. One factor that is likely to affect this choice is what helpers believe about the characteristics and resources possessed by recipient populations, or their stereotype of these populations. Karuza and Firestone (Notes 2, 3) have carried out some preliminary research on what models helpers report using with different target populations. The first study examined the impact of general age-related stereotypes on the selection of helping models. The second study built upon the first by considering the moderating effect of helper–recipient intimacy on models applied to different-aged targets.

The attitude literature (e.g., Collette-Pratt, 1976) reveals that the elderly population is generally stereotyped as passive, sickly, and dependent compared to younger age groups. Based on this stereotype, it was assumed that young adult helpers would employ a medical model in approaching elderly recipients, since the assumptions of the medical model parallel the stereotypic view of the elderly. In the first study, 195 young adults responded to a questionnaire that asked their "general opinions" of how children, other young adults, or the elderly should be helped. The helping models were operationalized in terms of general helping strategies: motivating and encouraging recipients (moral model); training recipients to develop their skills and abilities so they can take care of themselves (compensatory model); giving them goods and services they cannot provide for themselves (medical model); and comforting and consoling them (enlightenment model).[1] Subjects were asked to rate how desirable and effective each of these strategies would be in helping the targeted age group. The questions relevant to each helping model were summed to create a preference index for that model.

---

[1]Although these models are more general than this, it should be noted that there is a striking correspondence between the helping strategies they imply and the four forms of social support recently elaborated by House (1981): appraisal support, which we would see as moral model support; emotional support, which we would see as enlightenment model support; information support, which we would see as congruent with the assumptions of the compensatory model; instrumental support, which we would see as being implied by the medical model. For further discussion of social support see Moos and Mitchell (Chapter 10 in this volume) and Antonucci and Depner (Chapter 11 in this volume).

When viewing children, subjects equally preferred the strategies associated with each helping model. When viewing young adults, subjects preferred strategies associated with the moral and compensatory models significantly more than those associated with the medical and enlightenment models. When viewing the elderly, subjects preferred the strategy associated with the medical model over all others. The results of the first study suggested that, all other factors being equal, stereotypes about old age may indeed predispose helpers to adopt medical model orientations in helping elderly recipients.

In the second study, 142 young adults were asked to describe their approaches to helping specific individuals they actually knew, using the scales from the first study. Subjects were randomly assigned to one of eight conditions. For each condition, subjects were instructed to choose a recipient whom they had recently helped who was either another young adult or an elderly individual, and who was either very intimate, moderately intimate, not too close, or a stranger to the helper. It was assumed that intimacy would increase the subjects' concern for the recipient's welfare (Levinger & Snoek, 1972) and dilute age-related stereotypes, thus resulting in a more varied choice of helping strategies.

The results indicated no significant intimacy effects on the preference for helping strategies. Paralleling the results from Study I, the subjects used moral and compensatory model helping strategies to a significantly greater extent than medical or enlightenment model strategies when helping other young adults. When helping elderly recipients, subjects used the medical model strategy to a significantly greater degree than the others. This was the case despite the fact that subjects rated the elderly recipients' problems as no more serious or debilitating than the problems of young adults.[2]

Together the two studies indicate that age stereotypes can affect the preference for, and choice of, helping models. Further, the results suggest that this bias may generalize across different levels of intimacy. It should be noted that these results were not based on the reactions of professional helpers, and to that extent, the conclusions may be limited in their generalizability. There is, however, other evidence that the bias toward the medical model in helping the elderly occurs among professional helpers and in institutional settings (Wack & Rodin, 1978). The potential impact of personally held biases on the design and implementation of interventions is clearly an important topic for future research. If these stereotypes are inaccurate, helpers may develop treatments that conflict with clients' views of themselves, and may, in the

---

[2]Although the seriousness of the recipients' problems was perceived to be equal, the question remains whether the *types* of problems were identical for both age groups. It may very well have been that the preference for using specific helping models was influenced by the special problems facing young adults and elderly adults. This suggests interesting avenues of investigation: the extent to which the selection of helping models is determined by the type of problems facing recipients, and whether particular helping models are more effective than others for certain types of problems.

process of helping, socialize clients into accepting potentially dysfunctional views of themselves and their problems.

RECIPIENT WELL-BEING AS A CORRELATE OF THE CHOICE OF MODELS

There is ample evidence from past research that individuals who believe that they are responsible for their outcomes perform and cope with stress better than individuals who do not believe that they have such control (e.g., Brickman *et al.*, 1976; Janoff-Bulman & Brickman, 1982). Most compelling is the research that has been done in applied settings, such as Rodin and Langer (1977) and Schulz (1976). Interventions that made nursing home residents feel that their environments were more predictable or controllable resulted in higher activity levels and more favorable health status than was found in groups not receiving such treatments. Other studies have found similarly positive effects for teaching medical patients to take a more active part in their recovery and/or providing them with more complete information about their treatments (Egbert, Battit, Welch, & Bartlett, 1964; Johnson & Leventhal, 1974; Langer, Janis, & Wolfer, 1975). In a pyschotherapeutic vein, Saltzman, Luetgert, Roth, Creaser, and Howard (1976) found that in the eyes of both clients and therapists, successful resolution of the clients' presenting problem was correlated with clients' assuming responsibility for the problem. Further, Bulman and Wortman (1977) found that paraplegics who assumed responsibility for their paralysis, in the sense of seeing it as the outcome of an activity that they freely chose (e.g., diving), were rated by nurses as coping more effectively than those who saw themselves as victims of circumstances (e.g., those injured in car accidents).

None of this past research, however, draws a distinction between attribution of responsibility for problems and attribution of responsibility for solutions, a distinction that is critical for specifying which of our helping models will apply. Our general hypothesis (see Brickman *et al.*, 1982) is that attribution of responsibility for solutions is more important for future coping and well-being than attribution of responsibility for problems. Some clues to this question can be derived from a comparison of studies that have looked at the effects of attributing the source of symptoms to external causes with studies that have looked at the effects of attributing progress or improvement to external causes (cf. Valins & Nisbett, 1971). The evidence on symptom attribution or attribution of responsibility for problems is equivocal. Some studies (e.g., Rodin & Langer, 1980; Ross, Rodin, & Zimbardo, 1969; Storms & Nisbett, 1970) have found therapeutic gains when subjects are induced to believe that their symptoms (e.g., physical decline, anxiety, insomnia) have external rather than internal causes. Other studies have found that highlighting possible external causes for symptoms has no effect or negative effects (e.g., Bootzin, Herman, & Nicassio, 1976; Singerman, Borkovec, & Baron, 1976). These contradictory results may be due to the fact that mentioning an external cause for symptoms may also have led subjects to attribute any improvement they experienced merely to a change in this external cause.

On the other hand, the evidence is quite clear that benefits result from making internal rather than external causes salient in the attribution of responsibility for improvement (to use the causal language employed in past studies). In a study of smoking reduction that found no effects resulting from what subjects were told about the causes of their symptoms (e.g., irritability), Chambliss and Murray (1979) found that informing subjects that their gains (reduced smoking) were due to their own efforts, rather than a drug, helped subjects reduce their smoking. Earlier, Davison and Valins (1969) found that subjects who believed that the improvement in their ability to tolerate painful shocks was attributable to themselves, rather than to a pill they had taken, were better able to endure shocks in the future. Working with psychiatric outpatients, Liberman (1978) found that a group induced to attribute their improvement to medication (actually a placebo) was significantly less likely to maintain these changes 3 months later than a group induced to attribute improvement to their own efforts.

Responses of a General Sample of Elderly Subjects

Several studies that illuminate the connection between attributions of responsibility, helping models, and recipient well-being among the elderly have been conducted by Gleason, Karuza, and Zevon (Note 4), Zevon, Karuza, and Nash (Note 5), and Karuza, Zevon, and McArdle (Note 6). The first of these studies sampled 106 young adult and elderly subjects to examine the relationship between the adoption of each of the helping models and the subjects' sense of well-being. Elderly subjects were recruited from a local senior citizen center and the younger subjects were recruited from under-graduate psychology classes.

The extent to which the individuals accepted the assumptions underlying each helping model was determined by a series of 20 closed-ended questions. Subjects were presented with five statements reflecting the assumptions underlying each model, that is, their view of what caused the problem, their implicit view of human nature, what they felt they needed to do to solve their problem, what they felt others had to do to solve the problem, and the basic orientation they adopted towards the help given by others. Acceptance of each assumption was measured by 7-point scales. Items were summed in order to create indices of the four helping models. In addition, six questions were asked concerning the individuals' perceived general responsibility for the cause of and solution to their problems. Each helping index was analyzed separately by means of a one-way analysis of variance with age as the between-subjects factor.

Affective well-being was measured by a 20-item checklist. The checklist was composed of adjectives that served as markers of two independent affect dimensions, positive and negative affect (Tellegen, Note 7; Zevon & Tellegen, 1982). Individuals were asked to indicate by means of a 7-point scale the extent to which each adjective was descriptive, in general, of their feelings about themselves. The relevant items were then summed to form an index of positive affect and an index of negative affect.

The results showed that elderly subjects adopted medical model assumptions, $F(1, 103) = 38.28, p < .01$, and enlightenment model assumptions, $F(1, 103) = 37.25, p < .01$, significantly more often than young adult subjects. No differences were found in the adoption of moral or compensatory model assumptions. Elderly subjects also saw themselves as less responsible for both the causes of [$F(1, 104) = 5.73, p < .02$] and solutions to [$F(1, 103) = 4.68, p < .05$] their problems than young adults. This pattern paralleled the elderly subjects' preference for the medical model, which assumes low responsibility for both the cause of and solution to problems, and the enlightenment model, which assumes low responsibility for the solution to problems (see Footnote 2).

Next, Pearson product–moment correlations were computed between indices of the independent positive and negative affect dimensions and: (*a*) the measure of the subjects' perceived responsibility for the cause of and solution to problems and (*b*) the adoption of each helping model. The results in this case dramatically support our hypothesis that attribution of responsibility for problems is quite different in its psychological correlates from attribution of responsibility for solutions.[3] Among elderly subjects, assuming responsibility for the causes of problems was related to greater negative affect ($r = .41$), whereas assuming responsibility for solutions to problems was related to increased positive affect ($r = .47$). Greater negative affect was also related to endorsement of either the moral, medical, or enlightenment model (r's ranged from .23 to .54). Only the adoption of compensatory model assumptions was related to increased positive affect ($r = .38$). The results for young adults were essentially similar. All models except the compensatory model were associated with greater negative affect and, for the medical and enlightenment model, reduced positive affect. However, the correlation between attribution of responsibility for the causes of problems and negative affect was not significant in the young adult sample.

Responses of Elderly Participants in Community Based Programs

In the second study, Zevon *et al.* (Note 5) evaluated the impact of clients' attributions on the effectiveness of the services provided by a home-delivered meals program.[4] In addition to the meal service, the program provides social work services and nutritional counseling, and acts as a referral and information source to approximately 600 elderly people residing at home. The

---

[3]All correlation coefficients reported in the text are significant ($p < .05$ or better).
[4]We are grateful to Richard Gehring for his cooperation in the evaluation.

organization of the program is essentially three-tiered, consisting of the program participants who receive the service, a group of volunteers who deliver the services (i.e., the meals), and a paid professional staff charged with the supervision and administration of the program. The volunteers are usually unpaid or receive minimal compensation, and work part-time. A total of 50 on-service program participants were randomly selected for participation in the evaluation. Each participant was interviewed at home by a trained interviewer using a standardized questionnaire. Attributions of responsibility and preference for helping models were indexed by questions similar to those used in the previous studies by our research group. In addition, dependent measures included program participants' reports on their social and self-care activity (Katz, Downs, Cash, & Grotz, 1970), life satisfaction (Neugarten, Havighurst, & Tobin, 1961), overall health, and ability to cope with the demands of daily living.

As in the previous study, retention of a sense of responsibility for the solution to problems was significantly related to positive elements: overall life satisfaction ($r = .24$); self-ratings of overall health ($r = .34$); increased activity level ($r = .29$); and increased ability to cope with the demands of daily living ($r = .53$). Unlike the previous study, however, retention of responsibility for the origin of problems was also positively related to several of these indicators, in particular, to self-ratings of health ($r = .24$) and ability to cope with the demands of daily living ($r = .30$). With regard to the individual models, endorsement of the enlightenment model was associated with decreased life satisfaction and lower ratings of overall health. On the other hand, despite the positive correlates of their own endorsement of responsibility for both problems and solutions, the elderly in this sample expressed a preference for receiving help that was based on the medical model, $F(3, 177) = 9.70, p < .01$. Goods, services, and support were the preferred forms of assistance. The positive effects associated with retention of responsibility seem, therefore, to have operated on an implicit level or without client awareness.

At the moment, we have only speculative explanations for why attribution of responsibility for the cause of problems was related to negative affect in the previous study and to positively valenced ratings in the present study. First, the dependent measures were different. It is possible that self-blame can be associated with negative affect while nonetheless being associated with a more active sense of coping with the demands of daily living and a sense of better health. Intuitively speaking, a sense of self-blame could result in a person's feeling bad and be "good for" a person. Alternatively, the difference may reflect variations between the populations of the two studies. The fact that the elderly in the second study were actively engaged in trying to make use of the services of a community-based program may have made self-attribution of responsibility for problems more useful to them than such attributions might have been for the more general sample of elderly in the first study. These ideas, of course, need to be tested in future research that will give both affective and coping measures to populations that differ in the extent to which their situations demand action. Meanwhile, the overall pattern of results in these studies is quite in accord with the expectations derived from the Brickman *et al.* (1982) review of the literature. Actors' self-attributions of responsibility for solutions were uniformly related to positive outcomes. Actors' self-attributions of responsibility for problems were inconsistently related to positive outcomes.

Responses of Volunteers in Community-Based Programs

In a complementary study, Karuza *et al.* (Note 6) focused on the program's volunteers. A total of 56 randomly selected volunteers completed a questionnaire that investigated, among other factors, their perceptions of the program participants. A correlational analysis of the volunteer data showed that an association existed between the volunteers' perceptions of the clients as not responsible for the cause of their problems and the volunteers' satisfaction with their roles and the program. To be specific, the less the volunteers viewed the clients as responsible for the cause of their problems, the more they enjoyed their volunteer activities, the greater their satisfaction with client contacts, the greater their belief in the program's effectiveness, and the more responsible they felt for the client's welfare. This pattern echoes the findings that helpers are more willing to help when recipients' problems are seen as caused by external factors (for a review, see Berkowitz, 1972). Further, the volunteers preferred to supply help to the elderly that was based on enlightenment and medical model assumptions, $F(3, 132) = 21.16, p < .01$. It would seem that volunteers, by feeling more comfortable when viewing clients as not responsible for causes, and by preferring to help in ways that do not hold clients as responsible for solutions, may in effect train or socialize the elderly to expect and prefer the medical model of helping. This is a crucial issue because the volunteers constituted the component of the program that had the most direct and sustained interaction with the elderly, and as such, the volunteers may have been operating as a conduit for these socialization effects. Thus, a program that has as its aim the maintenance of the elderly in the community on an independent living basis may be exerting an influence contrary to that goal. The identification and specification of the scope of these implicit effects are areas that require further and more intensive investigation.

A PARADOX IN HELPING THE ELDERLY

The foregoing set of studies by Karuza, Zevon, and their colleagues define an emerging paradox in helping the elderly. Two of these studies (Karuza & Firestone, Notes 2 and 3; Karuza *et al.*, Note 6) found, as expected, that young adults and community volunteers tend to apply the medical model in their efforts to help the elderly. Further, the studies by Gleason *et al.* (Note 4) and Zevon *et al.* (Note 5) found that the elderly tend to apply the medical model to themselves and that the elderly prefer the kind of help implied by the medical model. However, these last two studies (i.e., Gleason *et al.* and Zevon *et al.*) also found that attribution of responsibility by the elderly to themselves (especially attribution of responsibility for solutions) is correlated with a variety of favorable outcomes—in much the manner we would expect from past research.

This leaves an obvious agenda for future research: (*a*) to account for helpers' and recipients' preferences for the medical model, which may conceivably be based on quite different considerations in the two groups; (*b*) to explain the increased adaptive effectiveness of certain helping models over others, especially given the preference of elderly recipients and their helpers for the medical model; and (*c*) to explore strategies that may better bring into line actors' preferences for models with what appear to be the actual correlates of these models. At this point, for example, it is hard to tell to what extent the assumptions the elderly make about themselves represent the results of prior socialization, the results of current pressures from populations of helpers (either professional or nonprofessional), a calculation of what form of help is in their own best interest, or a response to what they feel are changes in their mental and physical state.

Implications for Research and Practice

MATCHING OF HELPING MODELS TO CLIENTS

Given the effect of attributions about responsibility on the helping process, an important factor in the success of interventions is the proper matching of the helping models preferred by helper and clients. Misapplication of models in which assumptions inadequately map the perception of the client's problem and potential may lead to ineffective treatment. Further, in some cases the implicit effects of the intervention may socialize both clients and helpers into adopting dysfunctional roles and views of themselves.

In ideal terms, the selection of the appropriate helping model would be made in accordance with a specific rational appraisal of the problem's etiology, the client's potential, and the possibly reactive effects of the helping models themselves. In the real world, however, the selection of models is often constrained by a number of factors. Institutional problems, such as unwieldy staff–client ratios and limited resources, may reduce staff contact with clients and lead to attributions that form the bases of expedient, rather than crafted, interventions. Legislative guidelines governing institutional settings, by adopting a "lowest common denominator" approach (i.e., protecting the most infirm), may reduce flexibility in the choice of helping models and result in the overutilization of medical model treatments, which may be counterproductive for clients who are more competent.

The formal training of the helper may foster expertise in an overly narrow range of treatment and predispose helpers to look for and understand problems in limited ways. For example, Snyder (1977) found some evidence suggesting that behaviorally trained therapists were more likely to view problems as situationally caused, whereas psychodynamically trained therapists were more likely to view problems as personally caused. Helping orientations may thus be adopted because of the helpers' clinical training, and treatments employed by virtue of their familiarity rather than their relevance to the client (Rabinowitz, Zevon, & Karuza, in press).

Finally, helpers' personal experiences may influence their views of the clients' problems. As Wills (1978) noted, helpers show a tendency to make personalistic attributions about clients, partially as a result of their training, which often emphasizes attending to the negative aspects of the client's behavior. Further, a history of treating clients who are unwilling or unable to change may result in helper "burnout" (Maslach, 1978; Pines, Chapter 20 in this volume). In the face of frequent failure, the helper may adopt a moral model orientation in dealing with clients, blaming them for their problems rather than helping them, a phenomenon extensively dealt with by research on the Just World hypothesis (Lerner & Miller, 1978).

If the helping model of the client does not mesh with that of the helper, a great deal of time and effort in the intervention may revolve around the resolution of this strain, thus detracting from the energy available to work on the original problem. We hypothesize that, in general, the resolution of conflict between models depends on the relative power of the client and helper. Clients who are perceived as more powerful or of higher status may sway the intervention's direction to fit their views of themselves. For example, males and young adults are given less psychotropic medication than females and the elderly (e.g., Rodin & Langer, 1980), and upper-class patients are less likely than lower-class patients to be involuntarily committed or diagnosed as psychotic (Rushing, 1969). Often, however, the power rests with the helpers because of their status and prestige and the relative insecurity of the client (Snyder & Clair, 1977; Snyder, Shenkel, & Lowery, 1977). Clients may uncritically accept the orientation of the helper, and, in situations where improper helping models are applied, be socialized into accepting maladaptive views of themselves. If clients resist these implicit socialization effects, they may be labeled as uncooperative, difficult, or unappreciative. Helpers may respond with more intensive socialization efforts, or may even start to avoid clients (Taylor, 1979), thereby creating new problems and setting the stage for iatrogenic disorders.

In a related vein, we can ask whether "matching" of the helping models held by client and helper leads to greater therapeutic effectiveness. Several studies suggest matching is related to enhanced outcomes. For example, Wallston, Wallston, Kaplan, and Maides (1976) found that women, enrolled in a weight reduction program consistent with their locus of control beliefs, were more satisfied with their treatment than those whose beliefs were not matched. Beutler, Pollack, and Jobe (1978) found that, in a psychotherapy setting, client improvement was related to their adopting the values and beliefs of their therapist. In the final analysis, however, it is perhaps best to treat the advantages of matching as an open issue. Although having client and therapist share their values and beliefs may lead to a less stressful interaction, it may not necessarily result in greater therapeutic effectiveness. Further, the matching of helping models should not be confused with the holding of identical models. In some cases, it may be more effective if clients were teamed with helpers who held different or complementary models than with helpers who shared identical views (cf. Abramowitz, Berger, & Weary, Chapter 16 in this volume).

In resolving the above issues, we recommend using the Brickman *et al*. (1982) models as the basis for a formal assessment of client assumptions about the nature, origins, and likely future of their symptoms. This will have several advantages for clinical practice. First, it will enable therapists and other helping agents to tailor their interventions, insofar as possible, so as to take into account client assumptions. Second, it will enable practitioners to anticipate instances of attributional conflict—cases in which their own model of the client's difficulty conflicts with the client's model—and to understand with some precision exactly where the areas of potential conflict lie. Thus, helpers can be prepared for misinterpretations and resistance on the part of the client, or on the other hand, unexpected areas of strength in the client that they would otherwise fail to make use of. Such a procedure will also have important advantages for clinical research. Most forms of treatment are at times successful and at other times unsuccessful, but relatively little is known about why certain forms of treatment are successful with some clients and not with others. Much of this unexplained variance may be explained by whether or not treatments are embedded in the context of one helping model or another, and whether or not the implicit models involved are acceptable to both helper and recipient. We can increase our knowledge in this domain only through the use of formal procedures to assess helper and client assumptions about the helping process. Work on the development of a diagnostic tool based on the Brickman *et al*. (1982) models is now in progress.

THE DYNAMICS OF INTERVENTION

While the initial matching of helping models to clients is important for the ultimate success of the intervention, one must not lose sight of the intervention's inherent dynamic quality. Initial assumptions and expectations regarding the cause of and solution to the client's problem may define only the first stage of the intervention. Changes brought about by the intervention's explicit and implicit processes may cause the client, helper, or both, to reevaluate or shift the assumptions and expectations with which the intervention began. Thus, there may be consistent, systematic shifts in the helping model involved at various stages of therapy.

Ironically, even if the model is properly matched to the client, the initial success of the intervention may create psychological dynamics that can threaten its continued success, a notion termed the *hedonic trap of helping* (Karuza, Zevon, & Rabinowitz, Note 1). In the short term, interventions—by addressing the client's presenting complaint—lead to more adaptive functioning and a heightened satisfaction on the client's part. Given the tendency of individuals to become habituated to their current level of satisfaction (Brickman & Campbell, 1971), clients may subsequently use their improved state to judge their future satisfaction with themselves, the help, and its outcomes. As a result of this hedonic adaptation, the initial satisfaction may fade and give way to new levels of indifference or dissatisfaction. In addition, as the attributional literature suggests, a competence adaptation can occur, since clients' patterns of success or failure become the baseline from which they determine future striving and expectations for success (e.g., Janoff-Bulman & Brickman, 1982). In time, a history of failure in dealing with the problem may produce feelings of helplessness and dependency, whereas as history of personally caused success may goad the client into seeking greater, and perhaps, unrealistic, levels of control. This habituation to the intervention by clients may cause them to expect, depending on the helping model in use, increasing levels of service, competence, adjustment, or happiness.

Given the role of attributional dynamics, helping professionals should be sensitive to the changes in the client's orientation throughout the intervention, as well as their own. These changes and their implications may alternatively facilitate the goal of the intervention or create impediments and problems for the client. One way of capitalizing on the differential effectiveness of interventions may be by adopting a "cyclical view" of helping (Rabinowitz, Zevon, & Karuza, in press). In the implementation of an intervention, the helper can shift models in accordance with shifts in the client's perception of the problem. Applying this adaptive procedure, rather than relying on a single helping model, may avoid some of the problems associated with helping. Alternatively, helpers may specify attempts to change clients' attributional assumptions as an overt goal of the intervention (Ross et al., 1969). Helpers may make use of the tendency of clients to accept interpretations from helpers (i.e., the "Barnum effect"; see Snyder et al., 1977, see also Synder, Ingram, & Newburg, Chapter 13 in this volume) to redirect the clients' views of their problems and themselves in a way that alleviates clients' feelings of guilt, dependency, hopelessness, or anger and makes the intervention more effective.

In all of this, issues of timing are crucial. Following the work of Coates and

7. Tellegen, A., *The structure of mood states.* Unpublished manuscript, University of Minnesota,

Wortman (1980) and Janoff-Bulman (1979), Brickman *et al.* (1982) have outlined a process whereby a kind of "secondary victimization" of the client can occur. When clients initially seek to reestablish a sense of control over their own lives, even at the price of blaming themselves for their misfortunes, they may be confronted by friends or helpers who find this course of action inexplicable and push the client to use a medical model orientation. By the time friends and professionals are finally ready to stop helping and have the erstwhile victim again take over responsibility for his or her life, the client may not feel able to do so. Clients may become so disoriented by this attributional conflict and the confusing messages sent by their friends and their therapist, that they themselves may begin to embrace the medical model. This in turn sets into motion a new and sometimes permanent form of attributional conflict between clients and their ostensibly supportive environments. All of this could conceivably be avoided if would-be helpers could encourage clients to take responsibility when the clients themselves are eager to do so, rather than when helpers deem it necessary.

There is an additional warning for practitioners. In some cases, the help that people are most inclined to seek may not be the help that is best for them. In helping the elderly, for example, professionals may have to choose between interventions that enhance this group's sense of responsibility and interventions that coincide with the group's own expectations, assumptions, and preferences. One possible resolution of this difficulty may be discovering alternative ways of presenting the same services, thus perhaps allowing clients to receive some of the material aid they need while at the same time imbuing them with a strong sense of responsibility for fully employing and assessing this aid. This amounts, in part, to asking whether some form of the compensatory model could be combined with some form of the medical model, or whether there might not be alternative versions of each model, some of which would be more useful with particular populations than others. If this is not possible, then professionals may have to forego the advantages of applying a model that is convenient for them and that matches the expectations of clients and incur the costs of applying a model over client resistance. But such a strategy raises some very serious practical and ethical difficulties. It would be better, we would think, to first acquaint clients with the known costs and benefits of different models, and then encourage them to select the model that would in fact be most helpful to their own future well-being.

In order to gain sensitivity to the changes in the adoption of helping models by clients and flexibility in the models they themselves use, helpers may need new types of training and new forms of institutional support. Currently, as discussed by Brickman *et al.* (1982) and Rabinowitz, Zevon, and Karuza (in press), most forms of clinical training instill in helpers a single dominant helping orientation. In a related vein, helpers may be further seduced into overrelying on a single helping model by their initial experience with some successful therapy cases based on that model. This may result in their overlooking the (apparently inexplicable) problems they encounter with other types of cases, and the changes, either optimistic or pessimistic, in clients' self-attributions. Here, as in the study of the matching of models, progress depends on our ability to assess exactly what models helpers and recipients are applying, and to identify characteristic patterns of change in different settings and circumstances. This is surely a worthy agenda for future research—with the ultimate goal of designing interventions likely to have the most therapeutic effect.

Reference Notes

1. Karuza, J., Jr., Zevon, M. A., & Rabinowitz, V. C. *The dangers of helping: Implications for community psychology*. Paper presented at the meeting of the American Psychological Association, Montreal, September 1980.
2. Karuza, J., Jr., & Firestone, I. J. Choice of helping strategies: Effects of recipient age and intimacy. In J. D. Fisher (Chair), *Factors affecting helping*. Symposium presented at the meeting of the American Psychological Association, New York, September 1979.
3. Karuza, J., Jr., & Firestone, I. J. *Preferred ways of helping across generations*. Paper presented at the meeting of the Gerontological Society, Washington, D.C., November 1979.
4. Gleason, T., Karuza, J., Jr., & Zevon, M. A. *Personal responsibility in coping*. Paper presented at the meeting of the Gerontological Society, Toronto, November 1981.
5. Zevon, M. A., Karuza, J., Jr., & Nash, L. *The role of client responsibility in community based agencies*. Paper presented at the meeting of the American Psychological Association, Los Angeles, August 1981.
6. Karuza, J., Jr., Zevon, M. A., & McArdle J. *Motivation and satisfaction of staff and volunteers working with elderly*. Paper presented at the meeting of the American Psychological Association, Los Angeles, August 1981.
7. Tellegan, A., *The structure of mood states*. Unpublished manuscript, University of Minnesota, 1981.

References

Berkowitz, L. Social norms, feelings and other factors affecting helping and altruism. In L. Berkowitz (Ed.), *Advances in experimental social psychology*, New York: Academic Press, 1972.
Beutler, L. E., Pollack, S., & Jobe, A. "Acceptance," values and therapeutic change. *Journal of Consulting and Clinical Psychology*, 1978, *46*, 198–199.
Bootzin, R., Herman, C. P., & Nicassio, P. The power of suggestion: Another examination of misattribution and insomnia. *Journal of Personality and Social Psychology*, 1976, *34*, 673–679.
Brewer, M. Erhard training seminars: We're going to tear you down and put you back together. *Psychology Today*, August 1975, pp. 35–40; 82–89.
Brickman, P., & Campbell, D. T. Hedonic relativism and planning the good society. In M. H. Appley (Ed.), *Adaptation-level theory: A symposium*. New York: Academic Press, 1971.
Brickman, P., Linsenmeir, J. A. W., & McCareins, D. Performance enhancement by relevant success and irrelevant failure. *Journal of Personality and Social Psychology*, 1976, *33*, 149–160.

Brickman, P., Rabinowitz, V. C., Karuza, J., Jr., Coates, D., Cohn, E., & Kidder, L. Models of helping and coping. *American Psychologist*, 1982, *37*, 368–384.

Bulman, R. J., & Wortman, C. Attributions of blame and coping in the "real world": Severe accident victims react to their lot. *Journal of Personality and Social Psychology*, 1977, *35*, 351–363.

Chambliss, C., & Murray, E. J. Cognitive procedures for smoking reduction: Symptom attribution versus efficacy attribution. *Cognitive Therapy and Research*, 1979, *3*, 91–95.

Coates, D., & Wortman, C. B. Depression maintenance and interpersonal control. In A. Baum & J. Singer (Eds.), *Advances in environmental psychology* (Vol. 2). Hillsdale, N.J.: Erlbaum, 1980.

Collette-Pratt, C. Attitudinal predictors of devaluation of old age in a multigenerational sample. *Journal of Gerontology*, 1976, *31*, 193–197.

Cummings, N. A. Turning bread into stones: Our modern antimiracle. *American Psychologist*, 1979, *34*, 1119–1129.

Davison, G. C., & Valins, S. Maintenance of self-attributed and drug-attributed behavior change. *Journal of Personality and Social Psychology*, 1969, *11*, 25–33.

Egbert, L. D., Battit, G. E., Welch, C. E., & Bartlett, M. K. Reduction of postoperative pain by encouragement and instruction of patients. *New England Journal of Medicine*, 1964, *270*, 825–827.

Feinberg, J. *Doing and deserving: Essays in the theory of responsibility.* Princeton, N. J.: Princeton Univ. Press, 1970.

Friedman, H. S. Nonverbal communication between patients and medical practitioners. *Journal of Social Issues*, 1979, *35*(1), 82–99.

Gartner, A. Self-help and mental health. *Social Policy*, 1976, *7*, 28–40.

Hill, N., & Stone, W. C. *Success through positive mental attitude.* New York: Wiley, 1975.

House, J. S. *Work stress and social support.* Reading, Mass.: Addison-Wesley, 1981.

Janoff-Bulman, R. Characterological versus behavioral self-blame: Inquiries into depression and rape. *Journal of Personality and Social Psychology*, 1979, *37*, 1798–1809.

Janoff-Bulman, R., & Brickman, P. Expectations and what people learn from failure. In N. T. Feather (Ed.), *Expectations and actions*. Hillsdale, N.J.: Erlbaum, 1982.

Johnson, J. E., & Leventhal, H. Effects of accurate expectations and behavioral instructions on reactions during a noxious medical examination. *Journal of Personality and Social Psychology*, 1974, *29*, 710–718.

Kaswan, J. Manifest and latent functions of psychological services. *American Psychologist*, 1981, *36*, 290–299.

Katz, S., Downs, T. D., Cash, H. R., & Grotz, R. C. Progress in development of the index of ADL. *The Gerontologist*, 1970, *10*, 20–30.

Langer, E. J., Janis, I. L., & Wolfer, J. A. Reduction of psychological stress in surgical patients. *Journal of Experimental Social Psychology*, 1975, *11*, 155–165.

Lerner, M. J., & Miller, D. T. Just world research and the attribution process: Looking back and ahead. *Psychological Bulletin*, 1978, *85*, 1030–1051.

Levinger, G., & Snoek, J. D. *Attraction in relationship: A new look at interpersonal attraction.* Morristown, N.J.: General Learning Press, 1972.

Liberman, B. L. The role of mastery in psychotherapy: Maintenance of improvement and prescriptive change. In J. D. Frank, R. Hoehn-Saric, D. D. Imber, B. L. Liberman, & A. R. Stone (Eds.), *The effective ingredients of successful psychotherapy.* New York: Brunner/Mazel, 1978.

Maslach, C. The client role in staff burnout. *Journal of Social Issues*, 1978, *34*(4), 111–124.

McCord, J. A thirty-year follow-up study of treatment effects. *American Psychologist*, 1978, *33*, 284–289.

Meichenbaum, D., & Genest, M. Cognitive behavior modification: An integration of cognitive and behavioral methods. In F. H. Kanfer & A. P. Goldstein (Eds.), *Helping people change*. Oxford: Pergamon, 1980.

Neugarten, B. L., Havighurst, R. J., & Tobin, S. S. The measurement of life satisfaction. *Journal of Gerontology*, 1961, *16*, 134–143.

Rabinowitz, V. C. *Orientations to help in four natural settings*. Unpublished doctoral dissertation, Northwestern University, 1978.

Rabinowitz, V. C., Zevon, M. A., & Karuza, J., Jr. Psychotherapy as help: An attributional analysis. In L. Abramson (Ed.), *Attributional processes in clinical psychology*. New York: Guilford Press, in press.

Rodin, J., & Janis, I. L. The social power of health-care practitioners as agents of change. *Journal of Social Issues*, 1979, *35*(1), 60–81.

Rodin, J., & Langer, E. J. Long-term effects of a control relevant intervention with the institutionalized aged. *Journal of Personality and Social Psychology*, 1977, *35*, 897–902. *Erratum* to Rodin & Langer. *Journal of Personality and Social Psychology*, 1978, *36*, 462.

Rodin, J., & Langer, E. Aging labels: The decline of control and the fall of self-esteem. *Journal of Social Issues*, 1980, *36*(2), 12–29.

Ross, L., Rodin, J., & Zimbardo, P. G. Toward an attribution therapy: The reduction of fear through induced cognitive–emotional misattribution. *Journal of Personality and Social Psychology*, 1969, *12*, 279–288.

Rushing, W. Two patterns in the relationship between social class and mental hospitalization. *American Sociological Review*, 1969, *34*, 533–541.

Saltzman, C., Luetgert, M. J., Roth, C. H., Creaser, J., & Howard, L. Formation of a therapeutic relationship: Experiences during the initial phase of psychotherapy as predictors of treatment duration and outcome. *Journal of Consulting and Clinical Psychology*, 1976, *44*, 546–555.

Schulz, R. Effects of control and predictability on the physical and psychological well-being of the institutionalized aged. *Journal of Personality and Social Psychology*, 1976, *33*, 563–573.

Singerman, K. J., Borkovec, T. D., & Baron, R. S. Failure of a "misattribution therapy" manipulation with a clinically relevant target behavior. *Behavior Therapy*, 1976, *7*, 306–313.

Storms, M. D., & Nisbett, R. E. Insomnia and the attribution process. *Journal of Personality and Social Psychology*, 1970, *16*, 319–328.

Snyder, C. R. "A patient by any other name" revisited: Maladjustment or attributional locus of problem. *Journal of Consulting and Clinical Psychology*, 1977, *45*, 101–103.

Snyder, C. R., & Clair, M. S. Does insecurity breed acceptance?: Effects of trait and situational insecurity on acceptance of positive and negative diagnostic feedback. *Journal of Consulting and Clinical Psychology*, 1977, *45*, 843–850.

Snyder, C. R., Shenkel, R. J., & Lowery, C. R. Acceptance of personality interpretations: The "Barnum effect" and beyond. *Journal of Consulting and Clinical Psychology*, 1977, *45*, 104–114.

Taylor, S. E. Hospital patient behavior: Reactance, helplessness or control? *Journal of Social Issues*, 1979, *35*(1), 156–184.

Valins, S., & Nisbett, R. E. *Attribution processes in the development and treatment of emotional disorders*. Morristown, N.J.: General Learning Press, 1971.

Wack, J., & Rodin, J. Nursing homes for the aged: The human consequences of legislation-shaped environments. *Journal of Social Issues*, 1978, *34*(4), 6–21.

Wallston, B. S., Wallston, K. A., Kaplan, G. D., & Maides, S. A. Development and validation of the health locus of control (HLC) scale. *Journal of Consulting and Clinical Psychology*, 1976, *44*, 580–585.

Wills, T. A. Perceptions of clients by professional helpers. *Psychological Bulletin*, 1978, *85*, 968–1000.

Zevon, M. A., & Tellegen, A. The structure of mood change: An idiographic/nomothetic analysis. *Journal of Personality and Social Psychology*, 1982, *43*, 111–122.

chapter 7

Determinants of Recipient Reactions to Aid: Donor–Recipient Similarity and Perceived Dimensions of Problems[1]

JEFFREY D. FISHER
ARIE NADLER

Introduction

An Indian proverb states, "Why do you hate me—I've never helped you." And at one time or another, all of us have probably had experience with recipients who "bite the hand that feeds them." Although the notion that helpers sometimes elicit negative reactions in recipients may at first seem counterintuitive, closer scrutiny suggests that this probably does occur in clinical relationships, when governments give aid to citizens (e.g., the welfare system), and in everyday helping situations. There is anecdotal evidence supporting this conclusion in the clinical psychology and social work literature (e.g., Ladieu, Hanfman, & Dembo, 1947), in writings about foreign aid programs (e.g., Gergen & Gergen, 1974), in the gerontology literature (e.g., Kalish, 1967; Lipman & Sterne, 1962), and in other areas as well. For example, in interviews with injured servicemen Ladieu *et al.* (1947) elicited the

[1]Work on this chapter was greatly facilitated by a grant from the United States–Israel Binational Science Foundation to both authors. Some of the research described herein was supported by grants from the University of Connecticut Research Foundation to Jeffrey D. Fisher, and from the Israeli Academy of Sciences to Arie Nadler.

131

following responses, among others: "When I was on crutches I would rather do things myself than be pawed at, pushed, and shoved [p. 175]." "Offers of help get me down unless I am in a real jam [p. 176]." Such reactions often draw negative responses from donors, who expect recipients to be duly appreciative. For example, note the following account by an injured serviceman: "We were walking on the sidewalk and there was some ice. So we were going slow. A fellow comes along and takes my hand and says, 'I will help you, soldier.' I said, 'Unhand me, Mack.' He got mad. He said, 'You guys don't appreciate somebody wanting to help' [Ladieu *et al.*, 1947, p. 181]." At the anecdotal level it seems clear that both needy individuals *and* well-intentioned helpers are sometimes hurt by the helping process.

Recipient reactions to aid have not been subject to experimental scrutiny until recent years. Initial work by Gergen and his associates provided laboratory evidence that help could lead to positive or negative evaluations of the donor and the aid, depending on situational conditions (Morse & Gergen, 1971). Subsequent research by others has focused on the effects of a variety of situational conditions associated with aid (i.e., characteristics of the donor, the help, the recipient, and the helping context) on diverse recipient responses. The latter have included donor and aid evaluations, self-perceptions, and postaid behavior (e.g., self-help versus future dependency). Here we shall summarize important findings from this body of literature (for detailed reviews, see Fisher, DePaulo, & Nadler, 1981; Fisher, Nadler, & Whitcher-Alagna, 1982; Gross, Wallston, & Piliavin, 1979).

There are some consistent relationships between conditions associated with aid and recipient reactions. People generally respond better to help when *donor characteristics* are positive (e.g., the donor is an ally, someone they like and respect) than when help is offered by those with negative qualities. The former type of donor tends to elicit more favorable evaluations of the donor and the aid, greater feelings of obligation, and increased reciprocity.[2] Positive reactions also occur when *aid characteristics* are favorable (e.g., it represents a large amount of help, is of high quality, or is appropriate to one's needs). When aid characteristics make help costly for the recipient (e.g., when it restricts important behavioral freedoms, or decreases one's rewards for successful outcomes), more negative responses occur. *Characteristics of the recipients* themselves also affect responses to help. For example, high self-esteem and high need state seem to predispose recipients to respond more negatively to assistance. Finally, *context characteristics* surrounding the aid transaction (e.g., whether there is an opportunity to reciprocate help, whether the recipient can remain anonymous) have important effects on how recipients react. For example, when help can be reciprocated or allows the recipient to remain anonymous, it elicits better reactions than when help giving is public or

[2]An important qualification to this occurs when the donor is a social comparison other. In much research, social comparability is operationally defined as similarity in terms of background, attitudes, skills, etc. Similar acquaintances are often liked (Byrne, 1971), but for reasons we will discuss later, tend to elicit negative reactions when they give aid.

cannot be reciprocated. From this summary, it is clear that aid-related conditions exert important influences on recipient reactions, which run the gamut from highly favorable to quite unfavorable.

Conceptual Frameworks for Studying Recipient Reactions

In past research, several approaches have been used to conceptualize the effects of aid on those who receive it, although many studies have been atheoretical. Most of these conceptual frameworks have been borrowed from other areas of social psychology and adapted by researchers to the present context. We will discuss each of these approaches briefly (see also Fisher *et al.*, 1982; Gross *et al.*, 1979). A careful consideration of the evidence suggests to us that a model based on perceived threat to the recipient's self-esteem is best (see Fisher *et al.*, 1982), and this model is presented in more detail.

Equity theories (Greenberg, 1980; Greenberg & Westcott, in press; Hatfield & Sprecher, in press) posit that the crucial variable determining reactions to help is recipients' perceptions of the amount of inequity between themselves and the donor. Inequity is an aversive state, experienced when one party in a relationship has a more favorable ratio of outcomes to inputs than the other. Perceived inequity (or indebtedness) associated with help is a function of both the objective value of aid and other situational conditions associated with it (e.g., whether help is accidental or intentional, or represents a high or low cost to the donor). For example, when a unit of help is intentional rather than accidental, or is costly for the donor to convey, perceived indebtedness is greater since the donor is viewed as having made more of a sacrifice (Walster, Berscheid, & Walster, 1973). Recipients may alleviate uncomfortable feelings of inequity by reciprocating to the donor in equal measure—a restoration of actual equity. If this is not possible, they try to restore psychological equity, often by derogating the donor and/or the aid.

Reactance theory (Brehm, 1966; Brehm & Brehm, 1981) suggests that responses to help are determined primarily by how much recipients feel their freedoms have been restricted by it. People prefer to maximize their freedom of choice, and any reduction arouses a motivational state (reactance) characterized by negative feelings, and directed toward reestablishing the lost freedoms. For example, to the extent that help limits the recipient's present or future actions (e.g., because they will have to act kindly toward the bene-factor), it will arouse reactance. Recipients can reduce their negative feelings by acting as though their behavior has *not* been restricted by help (e.g., by avoiding any actions based on perceived obligation toward the donor and/or by derogating the source of the threat).

Other studies have employed *attribution theories* (Jones & Davis, 1965; Kelley, 1967) to conceptualize reactions to help. These may be used to predict when recipients will (*a*) make attributions of the donor's motives for giving help and (*b*) make internal or external attributions about their own need for aid. The preconditions necessary for making attributions according to these theories are described in detail elsewhere (e.g., Jones & Davis, 1965; Kelley, 1967). Beyond predicting when attributions will be made for a prosocial act, the theories provide no explicit conceptual links between these and other recipient responses. However, based on past research it seems that people respond more favorably to help when they make positive attributions about the donor's motivation or can attribute their own problem to external factors, rather than to their own personality deficiencies.

A final set of studies have employed *threat to self-esteem* models (e.g., Fisher *et al.*, 1982; Gergen & Gergen, 1974) for prediction. Unlike equity, reactance, and attribution theories, these posit that the self-related consequences of aid (i.e., the effects of receiving help on self-concept) are critical in determining how the recipient responds to help. Threat to self-esteem models assume that aid potentially contains a mixture of *self-supportive elements* (e.g., instrumental value, evidence of caring and concern), and *self-threatening* ones (e.g., evidence of failure, inferiority, and dependency). The self-threat potential in aid is believed to arise from "Protestant ethic" values that suggest that independence is the greatest good and dependency an evil, and because implicit in any aid there is an inferiority–superiority relationship between donor and recipient.

As depicted in Figure 7.1, these models posit that specific aspects of the helping situation (i.e., the extent to which it highlights the supportive or threatening elements in aid) determine whether help is primarily a supportive or threatening experience for the recipient. To the extent that aid is perceived as self-supportive, a cluster of essentially positive responses (e.g., favorable evaluations of the donor and the aid, high acceptance of help) occur. However, to the extent that help is perceived as threatening to the recipient's self-esteem, a cluster of essentially negative reactions (e.g., unfavorable donor and aid evaluations, high refusal of aid) is observed. High self-help (as an alternative to continued dependency) occurs when aid is perceived as threatening, whereas help perceived as supportive tends to foster greater long-term dependency.

The work we will report here has been done in the theoretical context of the threat to self-esteem model and has focused in two areas: the effects of donor–recipient similarity on reactions to help and how one's beliefs about the nature of a problem affect his or her help-related behaviors. We shall discuss each of these in turn.

Donor–Recipient Similarity and Reactions to Help

At the time we ran our initial study (Fisher & Nadler, 1974), there was anecdotal evidence (but as yet no hard experimental data) suggesting that aid could be a threatening experience for the recipient. We took it as our first task

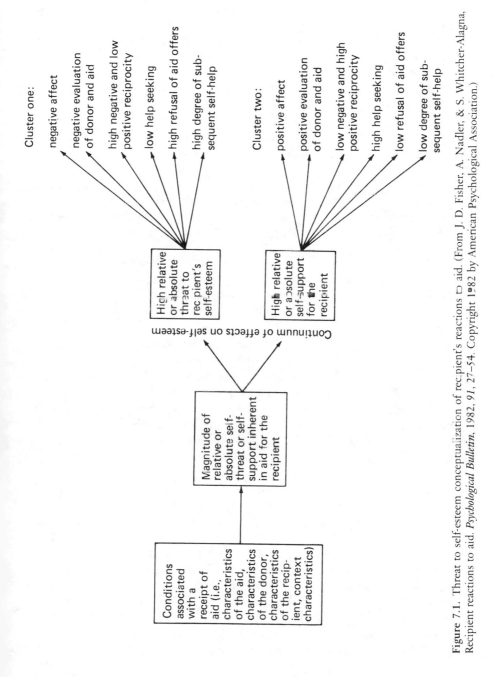

Figure 7.1. Threat to self-esteem conceptualization of recipient's reactions to aid. (From J. D. Fisher, A. Nadler, & S. Whitcher-Alagna, Recipient reactions to aid. *Psychological Bulletin*, 1982, *91*, 27–54. Copyright 1982 by American Psychological Association.)

to establish that, in some circumstances, receiving aid could be more threatening than a no-aid control condition, even though people receiving aid have an instrumental benefit not available to those without it. We searched for an easily manipulable social-psychological variable that for sound conceptual reasons could be expected to make aid a threatening experience. Donor–recipient social comparability seemed to be a good prospect. Social comparison theory suggests that we derive important information about ourselves through comparisons with others. The theory also assumes that comparisons with social comparison (e.g., similar) others are especially psychologically salient and meaningful (Festinger, 1954). Thus, we predicted that failing at a task and subsequently receiving aid from a more successful social comparison other should stress one's relative inferiority and dependency and generally be a threatening experience. On the other hand, failing and then receiving aid from a non-social-comparison other would not highlight one's relative inferiority and dependency to the same degree, and the positive, instrumental aspects of aid should be more apparent to the recipient. Receiving help in such conditions should, then, be a favorable experience.

Our initial operationalization of donor–recipient social comparability was attitude similarity,[3] although we have since used different ones (which have comparable effects). We measured the effects of donor–recipient attitude similarity on measures of the recipient's situational self-esteem, perceived intelligence, and self-confidence after receiving help.

To study reactions to aid in a laboratory requires that one create a meaningful failure experience and a credible donor and administer aid that has instrumental value to the recipient. Our early studies accomplished this through a highly involving stock market simulation in which subjects invested real money or poker chips (given to them by us). They studied information in a stock market guide to decide which companies to invest in, and could supposedly accumulate large amounts of money (or chips) if they did so wisely. Further, during the initial investment periods of the simulation, subjects invested alone but believed they would later make joint investments with a partner. The partner (actually the experimenter) was made salient in the instructions, and subjects were given an opportunity to exchange information about themselves with him. Through this means, we accomplished our manipulation of attitude similarity. In addition, there was a provision for sending and receiving messages between partners, and in this way the aid manipulation (in this case, money) was incorporated. Conditions were arranged so that all subjects did poorly and were in danger of being unable to make subsequent investments due to their low level of resources, so that receiving financial help from one's partner had definite instrumental value. The subjects' supposed partner was portrayed as performing much better than they had, and was thus in a position to give aid.

[3] Researchers in other contexts (e.g., Smith, Smythe, & Lien, 1972; Castore & De Ninno, 1977) had successfully used attitudinal similarity to manipulate social comparability.

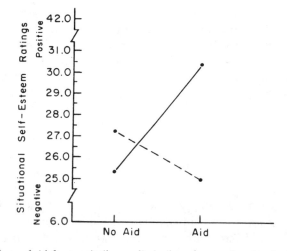

Figure 7.2. Effects of aid from a similar or dissimilar other on situational self-esteem. (Broken line represents similar other; solid line represents dissimilar other.) (From J.D. Fisher & A. Nadler, The effect of similarity between donor and recipient on recipient reactions to aid. *Journal of Applied Social Psychology*, 1974, *4*, 230–243. Reprinted by permission of V.H. Winston & Sons.)

Our initial study employed a 2 (aid versus no aid) × 2 (attitudinally similar versus dissimilar partner) factorial design. As can be seen in Figure 7.2, aid from a similar donor was more self-threatening, compared with a similar-partner–no-aid control condition, and help from a dissimilar partner was more self-supportive, compared with a dissimilar-partner–no-aid control. Also, aid from a similar partner was more threatening than help from a dissimilar one. This provided the first experimental demonstration that aid could be threatening. At a conceptual level, it implied that social comparison theory might be useful in predicting responses to aid as a function of characteristics of the donor and the recipient (e.g., their similarity). It also suggested some interesting practical implications. Research on help giving indicates that, in everyday interactions, we are more likely to *receive* aid from similar than dissimilar others (e.g., Baron, 1971). Our data imply that such help may often be costly for the recipient's self-concept. If this is the case, peer tutoring programs, for example, might be quite threatening to the recipient's self-esteem, an assumption that we tested in later research.[4]

---

[4]There are some important boundary conditions to the generalizability of the donor–recipient similarity studies we have done. First, they involve the effects of equivalent aid from similar and dissimilar others. When similar others can give more or better aid (e.g., as rape counselors), these effects are not expected to hold. Second, our findings apply to similar others who are not close friends, family members, or those with whom one has a long-term association. In such *communal* relationships (Clark & Mills, 1979) different types of norms operate that would probably ameliorate any threat associated with a similar donor. For a discussion of this type of helping relationship, see Chapter 12 by DePaulo in this volume.

Our second study (Nadler, Fisher, & Streufert, 1976) was an attempt to replicate and extend the Fisher and Nadler (1974) findings. In it we employed multiple measures of the self-related consequences of aid and assessed attributional patterns following help from similar and dissimilar donors. It was expected that aid from a social comparison other would elicit an internal attribution of failure (which is threatening to self-esteem), whereas help from a non-social-comparison other would allow an external attribution (which is not self-threatening). When we receive aid from a non-social-comparison other we can attribute their success, and our failure, to external factors (e.g., they had greater training or experience). In contrast, donor–recipient similarity makes the salience of the comparison greater, renders face-saving attributions more difficult, and internal attributions for failure more likely. We also tested the generalizability of donor–recipient similarity effects to both high- and low-self-esteem individuals. This will become more important later when we see that self-threat inherent in aid predicts a number of recipient reactions (cf. Fisher *et al.*, 1982). Two contrasting predictions can be made regarding the effects of one's persistent self-esteem on reactions to threatening aid.

A *cognitive consistency* formulation (Bramel, 1968) asserts that negative information about oneself is disturbing only when it is inconsistent with one's self-concept. This predicts that if aid from a similar other is threatening, it is more intensely negative for high- than low-self-esteem individuals. In contrast, a *vulnerability* prediction (cf. Tessler & Schwartz, 1972) suggests that since people with low self-esteem have few positive self-cognitions, they will be more disturbed by threatening information than those with high self-esteem. This would propose that aid from a similar other should be more threatening for low than high-self-esteem people.

Our results for the effects of aid on situational self-esteem replicated the similarity-by-aid interaction we observed previously, with lower self-esteem when aid was received from a similar other. The attribution findings were also as expected: Aid from a similar other led to an internal attribution for failure, whereas help from a dissimilar other permitted more of an external attribution. This suggests an explanation for *why* we obtained differential effects for aid as a function of donor–recipient similarity: because an internal attribution for failure produces greater perceived threat to the self. Finally, when persistent self-esteem is added as a factor, we obtained a triple interaction [see Figure 7.3 (a) and (b)], which supported the consistency interpretation spelled out above. Only high self-esteem individuals experienced aid from similar others as threatening and help from dissimilar others as supportive. Those with low self-esteem were not threatened by aid.

That persistent self-esteem affects responses to help in this way can be taken as corroborative of the threat to self-esteem model described earlier. This model views elements of support versus threat in aid as the intervening variables between the aid situation and recipient self-perception (as well as

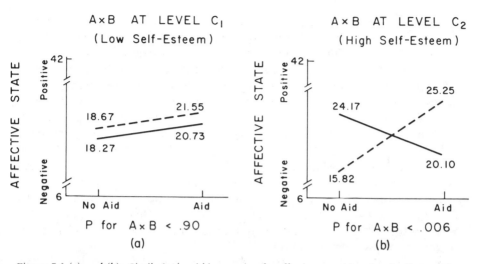

Figure 7.3 (a) and (b). Similarity by aid interaction for affective state (situational self-esteem) at each level of persistent self-esteem (Solid line represents similar other [A_1]; broken line represents dissimilar other [A_2].) (From A. Nadler, J. D. Fisher, & S. Streufert, When helping hurts: Effects of donor–recipient similarity and recipient self-esteem on reactions to aid. *Journal of Personality*, 1976, *44*, 392–409. Reprinted by permission. Copyright 1976, Duke University Press.)

other reactions). Underwood (1975) proposed an approach by which such hypothesized intervening variables can be substantiated. Specifically, an intervening construct is corroborated if people who differ on a relevant personality dimension (persistent self-esteem in this case) respond (*a*) differentially and (*b*) consistently with extant theory to the manipulation in question. This is exactly what occurred, and further suggests that self-related cues transmitted by aid may be an important determinant of diverse responses to it.

Our finding that people who think favorably about themselves react more negatively to help has been replicated in research using state rather than trait operationalizations of self-esteem (Nadler, Altman, & Fisher, 1979). Taken together, these studies and others (e.g., Tessler & Schwartz, 1972) make an interesting suggestion that is in accord with consistency theories: Receiving help, with its potentially negative implications, may be threatening only when inconsistent with one's view of self. In other words, high-self-esteem individuals, who generally view themselves as able and competent, are disturbed by aid because these positive self-cognitions do not accord well with evidence of failure and dependency implicit in help. There is no inconsistency between the self-view of low-self-esteem individuals and the failure cues contained in aid, so for these people help is not experienced as aversive. These findings take on added significance, since in later studies we have found that assistance that is threatening elicits independence, whereas supportive aid begets dependency.

One study that established this relationship between self-threat and self-help tested a boundary condition to donor–recipient similarity effects (Nadler & Fisher, Note 1). Our reasoning was that if it is threat to self-esteem that causes the negative effects of aid from similar others, then these should not occur on noncentral tasks (i.e., tasks that are unrelated to self-concept, such as games of chance). To test this possibility, we carried out an experiment in which high school students worked on a complex problem-solving task with no clear-cut solution. Half were told peformance was related to intelligence and creativity (i.e., were given a central task), and the others were informed that no such relationship existed (i.e., performed a noncentral task). All subjects were made to fail and they either received or did not receive aid from a similar or dissimilar other. In line with our conceptual analysis, the results showed that donor–recipient similarity effects like those observed previously occurred for central but not noncentral tasks. In fact, aid from similar others on *noncentral* tasks was supportive.

In the same study we assessed the relationship between the self-consequences of help and how much self-help behavior recipients engaged in after the helping experience. Our hypothesis was based on our threat to self-esteem model, as well as self-esteem theories (e.g., Coopersmith, 1967; Wylie, 1974). The latter suggest that people are generally motivated to maintain favorable self-attitudes, so that negative self-information inherent in aid should precipitate attempts to maintain or restore self-concept (e.g., self-help efforts).[5] However, we felt that self-threat should lead to self-help only up to point: Aid that is extremely threatening would probably be debilitating and cause helplessness. In contrast to the self-help-motivating properties of threatening aid, help that is supportive should lead to fewer efforts to avoid the need for future aid. In fact, such help may be viewed as reinforcing dependency (Skinner, 1976).

What did we find? Aid from a similar other on a noncentral task (which is supportive) elicited less self-help than a no-aid control. Aid from a similar other on a central task (which is threatening) elicited more self-help than a no-aid control. We have replicated our finding that self-help is facilitated by threatening aid, and inhibited by supportive help, in other research (Fisher & Nadler, 1976). For ethical reasons, we have been unable to test the assumption that extremely threatening aid becomes debilitating and fosters dependency. Interestingly, anecdotal studies in the social work literature also suggest the relationship we found in our research. For example, Weiss (1969) reported that welfare recipients feel more stigmatized, and get off the welfare rolls sooner, when they have similar rather than dissimilar caseworkers.

Given the pattern of our findings to this point we became more and more

[5] Based on consistency theories, one could alternatively predict that aid would be threatening, and thus lead to self-help only among those with high self-esteem. We view this as a reasonable hypothesis and plan to test it in the future. Unfortunately, the way in which the present study was done made this impossible.

interested in experimentally approximating real-world settings where parallel effects might occur. Peer tutoring seemed to be a natural case of aid from a similar other on a central task—something that should be fairly aversive. We first got this impression when we were graduate students at Purdue University where there were peer as well as nonpeer tutors (i.e., graduate students) available to undergraduates taking the introductory psychology course. The peer tutors were well qualified (they had received an A or A+ in the course the preceding semester) and were quite willing to help. The graduate students were obviously qualified but quite busy with other work, and gave the impression of being less than totally willing to help. Yet students were extremely hesitant to to seek help from peers, and hardly ever used them, perhaps because the thought of aid from a peer was too threatening. If peer tutoring has negative effects for recipient self-concept, this could be quite damaging, since such programs are becoming more and more popular each year. We began our research in this area with a laboratory study designed to approximate "real life" peer tutoring situations as closely as possible. We then moved into a school and did an initial study on the effects of peer tutoring there. Subsequent research on peer tutoring in Israeli schools is going on at this time.

In the laboratory at the University of Connecticut (Fisher, Harrison, & Nadler, 1978), we designed a study in which students received aid from a peer or nonpeer on an intellectual task that involved completing numerical patterns. Operationally, a peer was presented as having the same amount of previous experience relevant to the experimental task (i.e., courses in mathematics and logic) as the subject. This was analogous to another student in one's class serving as a peer tutor. The nonpeer was described as having many more courses in mathematics and logic than the subject, similar to a teacher's level of experience. The design was a 2 (aid versus no aid) × 2 (peer versus nonpeer) factorial, in which subjects failed at the numerical identifications and received or did not receive aid from a peer or a nonpeer partner. We found that aid from a peer led to lower self-ratings of intelligence and self-confidence compared with a no-aid control; aid from a nonpeer led to more favorable self-ratings than a no-aid control.

With these data in hand, we moved to an Israeli elementary school to test our hypotheses (Nadler, Fisher, & Klein, Note 2). Fifth-grade children who failed arithmetic were tutored by either another child from their own class who had received a very high grade (peer tutoring condition), or by a seventh grader. Both groups of tutors seemed to be competent to help the tutees with the work in question, although one group were peers and the other were not.[6] The tutoring sessions were held weekly for 4 weeks and lasted 20 minutes each, and interactions between tutor and tutee were standardized to a great degree. The tutors presented the tutees with a list of practice problems and

[6]In the studies in progress, degree of overall competence between the peer and nonpeer tutors is more closely controlled.

explained each problem to the tutee. After the tutee finished working on it, the tutor provided the correct answer. Instructions given in both groups limited tutor–tutee interaction to questions relating to the problem. In this setting, results showed that children tutored by a peer had lower affect scores, expressed less liking toward the tutor, and evaluated the tutoring sessions more negatively than those tutored by a nonpeer. We are currently studying self-help as a function of aid from a peer or nonpeer tutor. In addition to expecting more self-help in the peer than the nonpeer condition (because of our previous findings for the self-threat–self-help relationship), there is another reason. A peer tutor provides a similar role model and suggests that someone like the recipient *could* succeed if they would try.

In another study (Nadler & Fisher, Note 1) we tested our intuitive belief that students somehow sense the threat involved in help from a peer, and avoid seeking such aid whenever possible. We varied donor–recipient similarity and task centrality, and measured how much help subjects sought from someone else. It was found that the lowest degree of help seeking occurred when the donor was similar and the task was central, conditions that parallel those in peer-tutoring situations. Also, as we would expect on the basis of earlier findings and a consistency formulation about the effects of threatening information on behavior (cf. Bramel, 1968), the inhibiting effects of a similar other on help-seeking on central tasks are most pronounced for high-self-esteem subjects.

What conclusions can be drawn from our studies on donor–recipient similarity? At this point in our program of research, we have found that:

1. Effects of donor–recipient similarity on recipient's self-evaluation constitute a stable phenomenon across (*a*) different experimental contexts, (*b*) different cultures (i.e., the United States and Israel), and (*c*) different operationalizations of similarity.
2. Donor–recipient similarity moderates the elements of self-threat or support inherent in aid, which in turn affects (*a*) recipient self-evaluations and affective state and (*b*) behaviors that serve to enhance self-image (e.g., self-help efforts) *or* maintain a positive self-image (e.g., refraining from seeking help).
3. The effects of donor–recipient similarity are dependent on the type of person and type of aid. Specifically, the data indicate that in line with a consistency prediction, aid from a similar other is threatening only for recipients who are high in self-esteem. Furthermore, aid from a similar other is self-threatening only when it reflects inferiority on a *central quality*.

Moving to an applied perspective on the data, we can draw a number of conclusions, many of which may have significance for both institutional and person-to-person helping interactions. For any helping interaction to occur, one must first seek aid. Unfortunately, if help is needed on a central task, help seeking may be inhibited if the recipient perceives the donor as similar to himself or herself. This suggests that help seeking could be encouraged by (*a*) offering the recipient a choice of helpers varying in apparent similarity, (*b*) deemphasizing donor–recipient similarity, and (*c*) stressing the special expertise of the helper and the benefits the recipient would derive (e.g., only someone like you can understand your problems). Another avenue to decreasing the threat anticipated from dependency on a similar other could be to imply that although the giver is similar, he or she occupies the helping role primarily because of additional training not available to the recipient through no fault of his or her own. Finally, the therapist could attempt to begin helping on noncentral tasks as well as on major presenting problems.

Once the client has made contact with the helping facility, our research suggests that special cautions may be needed if the donor and recipient are similar. Under conditions of similarity, recipients may be apt to find aid to be uncomfortable, at least in the early stages. Practitioners should try to be especially sensitive to the recipient's feelings and attempt to allay any threat so that a comfortable relationship can emerge. Also, recipients in therapy relationships or even those receiving peer tutoring could be hesitant to express non-socially-desirable feelings, behaviors, or problems, due to the uncomfortable social comparison process that could result. This, too, would require vigilance on the part of the therapist to detect and also to disarm.

Once an effective working relationship has been established, donor–recipient similarity could become a blessing rather than a burden. Often, for example, similar helpers can have special insight into clients' problems that is not available to therapists who are dissimilar to the client. Also, since similar others are more effective models than dissimilar others (Bandura, 1971), they have an advantage here as well. This could result in greater learning of relevant skills by recipients, since they may be more likely to believe that they too could succeed and assume the donors' status. And, as we discussed earlier, any lingering self-threat from a similar donor could elicit greater efforts to *avoid* future dependency. Finally, aid from a similar donor may have consequences for how well recipients perform on subsequent tasks. Whether it facilitates or inhibits performance will probably depend, among other things, on task complexity (DePaulo, Brown, Ishii, & Fisher, 1981).

The foregoing discussion of our donor–recipient similarity studies may suggest the (erroneous) conclusion that we did the experiments consecutively and in a logical order. However a close look at the dates associated with the various studies would betray this: Like many research endeavors, ours was not entirely systematic. Although we have managed to concentrate our efforts rather intensively in several areas in an attempt to more fully understand a phenomenon and answer nagging questions, we have often "returned to pick up the pieces" in a particular domain, and we have also done studies in different areas more or less simultaneously. When we were doing our work on donor–recipient social comparability, we pursued related research interests, some with each other (e.g., our studies on the effects of donor resources), and others separately. (One of us [A.N.] has been heavily involved in studying various factors affecting help seeking; the other [J.D.F.] with understanding how individuals' views about the nature of their problem affect their help-related behaviors.) We shall now discuss this latter body of research.[7]

Effects of Views about the Nature of the Problem

Another factor in reactions to help is the view individuals have about the nature of their problem. The major point of the subsequent discussion is as follows: Often people are uncertain about the cause and the nature of their problem, and any information they receive about the type of problem they have can have profound effects on their attempts to cope with it. Such information can affect whether they try to help themselves or whether they become dependent on a therapist. Alternatively, information about the problem can influence *how* they attempt to cope, what type of external help they believe will be useful, and many other important reactions. The research reviewed here focuses on how beliefs about the nature of mental health problems affect help-related actions, though the findings may also apply to other types of problems.

People get information about the nature of mental disorders through a variety of sources (e.g., the media, socialization agents). One central set of beliefs falls along a *medical model* versus *social learning* continuum. At the medical model end, emotional disorders are viewed as diseases like any other (e.g., diabetes). Individuals are not seen as responsible for their problems, and inherent in this view is the assumption that powerful agents play an important role in any cure for the condition. At the other end of the continuum, mental disorder is believed to be due to social learning and the environment: Those who have not learned appropriate ways to cope with stress, and individuals in highly demanding environments, have difficulties that result in emotional disorders.

Our research suggests that what persons believe about the cause of emotional distress affects their self-help attempts. In several early studies (reported in Farina, Fisher, Getter, & Fischer, 1978), we administered medical model or social learning belief inductions randomly to 405 subjects. This was done by supplying subjects with authoritative (though selective) information about the nature of mental disorders. It was easy to change subjects' beliefs in the direction of the message. In addition, a variety of secondary beliefs also changed in a corresponding way, and these have very important implications

---

[7]For a complete review of the former, see the chapter by Nadler in DePaulo, Nadler, and Fisher (in press).

for self-help efforts. For example, subjects who were informed that mental disorders are manifestations of social learning problems thought they had more control over the difficulties than those who were led to believe that psychiatric disorders are illnesses. This finding, depicted in Table 7.1, was also replicated in several other studies (Farina *et al.*, 1978; Fisher & Farina, 1979).

We reasoned that belief that a problem was under personal control should lead to parallel efforts to exert control (i.e., to self-help efforts to alleviate one's problem). In a third study reported in Farina *et al.* (1978), we gave either medical model or social learning information to subjects who reported to a psychotherapy orientation session. This was provided in the booklets shown in Figures 7.4 and 7.5. Subjects who read the information then interacted with a clinical psychology graduate student therapist who was unaware of their experimental condition and was trained to interact with subjects about their current problems in a standard way. Following the therapy session, subjects were asked to keep a journal for the next week and to make an entry in it every time they thought about a problem and made some attempt to master it (i.e., when they engaged in self-help). As could be anticipated based on their lower expectations of control, subjects in medical model conditions made fewer entries than those in social learning conditions. Thus, medical model beliefs about the nature of a problem may lead to less self-help and to more dependency on practitioners than social learning views.

Another study (Fisher & Farina, 1979) further explored the self-help implications of beliefs about the nature of mental disorders in a field setting. The research was done with two classes of undergraduate students enrolled in an abnormal psychology course. One class was taught by an instructor with a strong social learning view; the other by a professor who imputed a much greater role to genetic factors and to the relationship between somatic states and behavior. There were no differences in beliefs between the two classes at the start of the semester. However, important differences emerged in both beliefs and behaviors at the end. Subjects in the medical model class (a) tended to view helping oneself as less valuable; (b) were more likely to feel that

Table 7.1
Belief Expressed by Subjects about the Degree of Personal Control over the Disorder[a,b]

	Social learning	Illness	$p<$
Farina *et al.* (1978)			
Study 1	3.25	2.76	.02
Study 2	3.51	3.15	.02
Fisher and Farina			
(1979)	3.98	3.43	.02

[a]Adapted from Farina, Fisher, Getter, and Fischer, 1978 and Fisher and Farina, 1979.

[b]The higher the number, the greater the extent of control believed to exist.

THE NATIONAL PSYCHIATRIC ASSOCIATION (NPA), a
branch of the American Medical Association, is generally recognized as the
professional group most knowledgeable regarding mental disorder and its
treatment. The essence of their view is given in the following position
statement which was adopted at the October, 1975 N.P.A. meeting in
Chicago, Illinois, and released to the press:

"Mental disorders can vary enormously, ranging from mild
and benign to totally disabling. In all cases, however, the person has
experienced problems in dealing with the environment and other people
which have been too much for him to handle. The Association believes that
people differ greatly in how they handle problems, no matter what the degree
of complexity or seriousness of the problem. However, much of what we view
clinically as abnormal behavior or emotional disturbance may be more
usefully construed as the result of environmental and interpersonal events
which are experienced by the person as overwhelming. This produces negative
consequences, such as anxiety, depression, and the creation of secondary
problems.

The Association no longer endorses the belief that behavioral problems represent mental illnesses associated with the organism's
biological or physiological structures. The evidence provided by clinical
observation and systematic research strongly supports the assertion that
emotional problems reflect environmental and interpersonal difficulties rather
than representing medical diseases. A number of recent studies strongly
indicate that symptoms such as anxiety and depression are a result of
environmental and interpersonal stress, and have very little to do with bodily
dysfunctions. Well-known studies which bear on this have to do with the
reactions of soldiers under combat conditions. Soldiers who experience lower
degrees of environmentally induced stress were less likely to develop neurotic
reactions. The same pattern of results was observed for reactions of college
students to college life. Of course, there are great differences among people as
to how well or poorly they deal with stressful events. And it seems clear now
that the family's role is crucial. Some people go through childhood without
learning to deal with people and environmental problems in an adequate
fashion.

Concerning the treatment of emotional problems, we
believe the mental health professions can play an important role by
encouraging the client to control environmental and interpersonal pressures.
Very significant progress has already been made. Therapeutic techniques now
help more individuals with mental problems than was conceivable twenty
years ago. Further advances will entail diligent observation and systematic
research which the Association strongly advocates."

Figure 7.4. A social learning view of mental disorders. (See Farina *et al.*, 1978.)

THE NATIONAL PSYCHIATRIC ASSOCIATION (NPA), a branch of the American Medical Association, is generally recognized as the professional group most knowledgeable regarding mental disorder and its treatment. The essence of their view is given in the following position statement which was adopted at the October, 1975 N.P.A. meeting in Chicago, and released to the press:

"Psychiatric disorders can vary enormously, ranging from mild afflictions of the personality to totally disabling mental conditions. In all cases, however, there is a basic underlying biochemical-physiological problem responsible for the condition. In this sense there is a strong similarity between a mental disease such as schizophrenia and somatic illnesses such as pneumonia and tuberculosis. The position advocated by the National Psychiatric Association is that the psychiatric patient should no more be blamed or held responsible for his condition than a patient suffering from a disease with physical symptoms. Nor should his parents, family, or others be held accountable for his state.

The association strongly and unequivocally advocates this view of mental patients and believes it is an enlightened and humanitarian one. But the view is dictated by more than desire to exonerate those stricken by mental illness or their families. The evidence provided by clinical observation and systematic research makes this conclusion virtually inescapable. As long ago as 1906 it was discovered that patients suffering from the mental illness *dementia paralytica* had an organism, *Treponema pallidum,* a spirochete, in their brain tissues. The common experience of anxiety, which in the exaggerated form of an anxiety neurosis can totally destroy normal functioning, is now known to be directly due to lactic acid in the blood. Experiments by Pitts, Ferris and others have shown that feelings of anxiety are accompanied by elevated proportions of lactic acid in the bloodstream. Moreover, severe anxiety can be induced by injection of lactic acid, and an anxiety state can be relieved by the administration of medicines which decrease the production of lactic acid in the blood. Even the harmonal imbalances produced by the menstrual cycle lead to feelings of tension and depression.

The most recent findings regarding the role of genes in mental illness make the biochemical bases of these conditions very clear even if the specific chemical reactions remain unknown. Rosenthal, Heston, and Denny, for example, have shown that children of schizophrenic mothers, separated from the mothers prior to the age of three days, are much more likely to develop schizophrenia than comparably treated children whose mothers had been mentally healthy. Thus mental illness, like diabetes or hypertension, is in part determined by the genes which play a causative role by influencing biochemical-physiological processes.

As to helping sufferers, we believe the mental health professional can play an important role through providing the patient with an understanding of his condition and reducing his fear and anxiety. And we believe the fundamental help, the cure, must come through appropriate medical and psychotherapeutic intervention. Very significant progress has already been made. Tranquilizers now help more sufferers from mental problems than was conceivable twenty years ago. Further advances will entail diligent observation and systematic research which the Association strongly advocates."

Figure 7.5. A medical model view of mental disorders. (See Farina *et al.,* 1978.)

more effective drugs were needed to cure mental disorders; (c) were less likely to believe it was important to attempt to identify the causes and solutions for their emotional problems; and (d) were more likely to endorse greater sales of over-the-counter drugs to relieve emotional disorders. An especially interesting difference between the two classes involved behavior: Those in the medical model class were more apt to take drugs and/or alcohol during the semester to relieve emotional difficulties. These individuals seemed to be prescribing medical cures to themselves as a form of self-help, whereas students in the social learning classes relied more on making changes in their behavior or environment.

Implications for Treatment Programs

We think that our findings related to emotional disorders could generalize to coping in many other types of situations. The general assumption behind the work—that views about the *nature* of a problem affect one's basic approach to helping and coping strategies—could be applicable in many domains. We will briefly suggest how our orienting assumption could apply to treatments for alcoholism, drug abuse, maladjustment in old age, and programs to help people lose weight and stop smoking. The discussion that follows is highly speculative, but, we feel, may lay out some avenues for future research.

ALCOHOLISM

The National Institute on Alcohol Abuse, an arm of the Federal Government, has mounted a campaign with the theme that "Alcoholism is a disease." Similarly, aspects of the Alcoholics Anonymous philosophy imply a medical orientation toward alcoholism. Although such a view may facilitate help seeking (e.g., Fisher *et al.*, 1982), it may contribute to alcoholism by making those with emerging problems perceive that they have no control over them and hence cope ineffectively. A medical model orientation may also lead to problems in therapy, because clients with this view of problems may passively accept their fate, become overly dependent on clinical practitioners, and expect a medical cure that does not yet exist. Even after treatment, clients with a medical orientation may have more recurrent problems.[8] They probably believe they have learned few coping skills for dealing with their difficulty, and often this may be true. Alcoholics with medical beliefs who

---

[8]Data relating medical or social learning orientations to recurrence of other problems (e.g., cigarette smoking) support this view (Colleti & Kopel, 1979; Coletti & Stern, 1980).

have one drink probably are more likely to be "lost," rather than able to remove themselves from the situation. Medically oriented treatments, such as Antabuse®, may also lead to less effective help-related behaviors. Use of this substance may contribute to a medical view of alcoholism and cause individuals to attribute success to the drug rather than their coping abilities, opening them to problems when it is withdrawn. In contrast, a social learning view of alcoholism might function to prevent people from becoming alcoholics in the first place and enable them to control problem drinking more effectively once it occurs. The tenability of a social learning formulation of alcoholism is suggested in the work of Marlatt and his colleagues (e.g., Marlatt, Demming, & Reid, 1973).

APPLICATION IN OTHER SITUATIONS

The preceding line of reasoning may hold in other settings as well (e.g., problems with drug abuse, adjustment in old age, programs to stop people from smoking, and weight loss programs). In each case, the belief that the problem is medical in origin may cause those afflicted to perceive that they have less control over the condition, to exercise less control, and to assume a more dependent role in therapy (cf. Cummings, 1979). They may employ and/or learn fewer coping skills and be more likely to have recurrent problems than people with a social learning orientation. When medical treatments (e.g., methadone for drug abuse) are used, this could tend to cause people to attribute treatment success to medical causes, thus contributing to a medical model orientation and its side effects (cf. Davison, Tsujimoto, & Glaros, 1973; Davison & Valins, 1969). We even feel that medical model beliefs may partially *cause* initial problems with drug abuse, adjustment in old age, and difficulties with smoking cessation and weight loss. This is because such beliefs make individuals feel they cannot exert personal efforts to control these problems, and to stop them from being difficulties in the first place.

Although admittedly speculative, the above patterns of effects, if they are supported by research, suggest some important considerations. Any information people receive about the nature of various problems may affect their coping strategies (if they have the difficulty themselves), or their dealings with others who have it. This indicates that there may often be important side effects of many such messages given to the public by practitioners, media, and socialization agents. Also, medical treatments that are prescribed may contain information for the client beyond that anticipated (e.g., prescribing tranquilizers communicates medical model information). All of these should be considered as potentially important influences on the helping process.

Many believe that a medical model orientation to various types of problems (e.g., mental disorder, alcoholism) represents an "enlightened" view, since it releases the individual, the family, and others from any responsibility for the difficulty. Whether it makes these disorders less stigmatizing remains a debated question; in fact, we have some data (Farina *et al.*, 1978; Fisher & Farina, 1979) that do *not* support that assumption. Another advantage claimed for medical model views is that they increase help seeking because the public and private admission that one has a medical problem is less threatening than an admission that one has been unable to learn appropriate skills or cope successfully with his or her environment. Although there is some support for this viewpoint (e.g., Tessler & Schwartz, 1972), this also remains somewhat of an open question.

Juxtaposed with these uncertain virtues of a medical model orientation there may be some real disadvantages, as we have suggested previously. Perhaps a strategy that could incorporate the favorable aspects of medical model views and social learning orientations would come from an expanded conceptualization to include both the locus of causality *and* the locus of a solution for various difficulties. This is similar to a framework developed by Brickman, Rabinowitz, Karuza, Coates, Cohn, and Kidder (1982) and discussed elsewhere in this volume (see Chapter 6, by Karuza, Zevon, Rabinowitz, & Brickman). Specifically, we could envision a 2 (medical versus social learning cause) × 2 (medical versus social learning cure) matrix. Here, it would be possible for medically caused problems to have social learning cures, for social learning problems to have medical cures, etc. This probably reflects more accurately the current state of the world. In addition to more closely approximating reality, it would then be possible, when appropriate, to give people information that would simultaneously make their disorder seem acceptable to them and encourage their taking an active role in dealing with it. Although more research is needed to fully understand the help-related effects of various combinations of beliefs about a problem, the available research suggests that such an approach could have important consequences.

Conclusion

In this chapter we have reviewed two lines of research performed within a social-psychological tradition that, we think, may have applications in various helping settings. Although the specific studies themselves may provide useful information to those with either an academic or practical interest in helping relationships, we think it is the *process* they exemplify that is most important. In Western culture we have for too long assumed that help is a good thing that should be encouraged, without further looking into matters. Our findings show that receiving help is a mixed blessing, and that aid may sometimes hurt rather than assist.

We strongly suggest considering carefully the various costs and benefits associated with particular types and models of aid, and attempting to specify when and where help is really in the recipient's best interests. Such cost–benefit analyses should be performed not only by practitioners, but also by a better informed body of recipients. However, before this can be done, we need more data. We can, and should, gather it in diverse ways: from laboratory studies, field research, and evaluations of intact helping programs. Becoming involved in this mission would provide not only important data regarding the conditions under which it is advisable to give aid, but also information about how to improve present and future helping programs so that they can more often accomplish what they set out to do.

Reference Notes

1. Nadler, A.,& Fisher, J. D. *Donor–recipient similarity and recipient reactions to aid.* Paper presented at the International Conference on the Development and Maintenance of Prosocial Behavior, Jablonna, Poland, June 1980.
2. Nadler, A., Fisher, J. D., & Klein, Y. *Is peer tutoring helping? Pupils' reactions to a peer tutoring program as affected by tutor–tutee similarity.* Unpublished manuscript, Tel Aviv University, 1980.

References

Bandura, A. *Psychological modeling.* Chicago: Aldine-Atherton, 1971.

Baron, R. A. Behavioral effects of interpersonal attraction: Compliance with requests from liked and disliked others. *Psychonomic Science,* 1971, *25,* 325–326.

Bramel, D. Dissonance, expectation and the self. In R. Abelson, E. Aronson, T. M. Newcomb, W. J. McGuire, M. J. Rosenberg, & P. H. Tannenbaum (Eds.), *Source book of cognitive consistency.* New York: Rand McNally, 1968.

Brehm, J. W. *A theory of psychological reactance.* New York: Academic Press, 1966.

Brehm, S. S., & Brehm, J. W. *Psychological reactance: A theory of freedom and control.* New York: Academic Press, 1981.

Brickman, P., Rabinowitz, V. C., Karuza, J., Jr., Coates, D., Cohn, E., & Kidder, L. Models of helping and coping. *American Psychologist,* 1982, *37,* 368–384.

Byrne, D. *The attraction paradigm.* New York: Academic Press, 1971.

Castore, C., & DeNinno, J. A. Investigations in the social comparison of attitudes. In J. M. Suls & R. L. Miller (Eds.), *Social comparison processes: Theoretical and empirical approaches.* Washington, D.C.: Halstead, 1977.

Clark, M. S., & Mills, J. Interpersonal attraction in exchange and communal relationships. *Journal of Personality and Social Psychology,* 1979, *34,* 12–24.

Colleti, G., & Kopel, S. A. Maintaining behavior change: An investigation of three maintenance strategies and the relationship of self-attribution to the long-term reduction of cigarette smoking. *Journal of Consulting and Clinical Psychology,* 1979, *47,* 614–617.

Colleti, G., & Stern, L. Two year follow-up of nonaversive treatment for cigarette smoking. *Journal of Consulting and Clinical Psychology,* 1980, *48,* 292–293.

Coopersmith, S. *The antecedents of self-esteem.* San Francisco: Freeman, 1967.

Cummings, N. Turning bread into stones. *American Psychologist,* 1979, *34,* 1119–1129.

Davison, G. L., Tsujimoto, R. N., & Glaros, A. G. Attribution and maintenance of behavior change in falling asleep. *Journal of Abnormal Psychology,* 1973, *82,* 124–133.

Davison, G. L., & Valins, S. Maintenance of self-attributed and drug-attributed behavior change. *Journal of Personality and Social Psychology*, 1969, *11*, 25–33.

DePaulo, B. M., Brown, P. L., Ishii, S., & Fisher, J. D. Help that works: The effects of aid on subsequent task performance. *Journal of Personality and Social Psychology*, 1981, *41*, 478–487.

DePaulo, B. M., Nadler, A., & Fisher, J. D. (Eds.). *New directions in helping* (Vol. 2): *Help-seeking.* New York: Academic Press, in press.

Farina, A., Fisher, J. D., Getter, H., & Fischer, E. Some consequences of changing people's views regarding the nature of mental illness. *Journal of Abnormal Psychology*, 1978, *87*, 272–279.

Festinger, L. A theory of social comparison processes. *Human Relations*, 1954, *1*, 117–140.

Fisher, J. D., DePaulo, B. M., & Nadler, A. Extending altruism beyond the altruistic act: The mixed effects of aid on the help recipient. In J. P. Rushton & R. M. Sorrentino (Eds.), *Altruism and helping behavior.* Hillsdale, N. J.: Erlbaum, 1981.

Fisher, J. D., & Farina, A. Consequences of beliefs about the nature of mental disorders. *Journal of Abormal Psychology*, 1979, *88*, 320–327.

Fisher, J. D., Harrison, C., & Nadler, A. Exploring the generalizability of donor-recipient similarity effects. *Personality and Social Psychology Bulletin*, 1978, *4*, 627–630.

Fisher, J. D., & Nadler, A. Effect of donor resources on recipient self-esteem and self-help. *Journal of Experimental Social Psychology*, 1976, *12*, 139–150.

Fisher, J. D., Nadler, A., & Whitcher-Alagna, S. Recipient reactions to aid: A conceptual review. *Psychological Bulletin*, 1982, *91*, 27–54.

Gergen, K. J., & Gergen, M. Understanding foreign assistance through public opinion. *1974 Yearbook of World Affairs* (Vol. 27). London: Institute of World Affairs, 1974.

Greenberg, M. S. A theory of indebtedness. In K. J. Gergen, M. S. Greenberg, & R. H. Willis (Eds.), *Social exchange: Advances in theory and research.* New York: Plenum, 1980.

Greenberg, M., & Westcott, D. Indebtedness as a mediator of reactions to aid. In J. D. Fisher, A. Nadler, & B. M. DePaulo (Eds.), *New directions in helping* (Vol. 1): *Recipient reactions to aid.* New York: Academic Press, in press.

Gross, A. E., Wallston, B. S., & Piliavin, I. M. Reactance, attribution, equity and the help recipient. *Journal of Applied Social Psychology*, 1979, *9*, 297–313.

Hatfield, E., & Sprecher, S. Equity theory and recipient reactions to aid. In J. D. Fisher, A. Nadler, & B. M. DePaulo (Eds.), *New directions in helping* (Vol. 1): *Recipient reactions to aid.* New York: Academic Press, in press.

Jones, E. E., & Davis, K. E. From acts to dispositions: The attribution process in person perception. In L. Berkowitz (Ed.), *Advances in experimental social psychology* (Vol. 2). New York: Academic Press, 1965.

Kalish, R. A. Of children and grandfathers: A speculative essay on dependency. *The Gerontologist*, 1967, *7*, 65–69.

Kelley, H. H. Attribution theory in social psychology. In D. Levine (Ed.), *Nebraska Symposium on Motivation* (Vol. 15). Lincoln: University of Nebraska Press, 1967. Pp. 192–240.

Ladieu, G., Hanfman, E., & Dembo, T. Studies in adjustment to visible injuries: Evaluation of help by the injured. *Journal of Abnormal and Social Psychology*, 1947, *42*, 169–192.

Lipman, A., & Sterne, R. Aging in the United States: Ascription of a terminal sick role. *Sociology and Social Research*, 1962, *53*, 194–203.

Marlatt, G. A., Demming, B., & Reid, J. B. Loss of control drinking in alcoholics: An experimental analogue. *Journal of Abnormal Psychology*, 1973, *81*, 233–241.

Morse, S., & Gergen, K. Material aid and social attraction. *Journal of Applied Social Psychology*, 1971, *1*, 150–162.

Nadler, A., Altman, A., & Fisher, J. D. Helping is not enough: Recipient's reactions to aid as a function of positive and negative self-regard. *Journal of Personality*, 1979, *47*, 615–628.

Nadler, A., Fisher, J. D., & Streufert, S. When helping hurts: The effects of donor–recipient similarity and recipient self-esteem on reactions to aid. *Journal of Personality*, 1976, *44*, 392–409.

Skinner, B. F. The ethics of helping people. *The Humanist*, January/February 1976, 7–11.

Smith, R., Smythe, L., & Lien, D. Inhibition of helping behavior by a similar or dissimilar nonreactive fellow bystander. *Journal of Personality and Social Psychology.* 1972, *23*, 414–419.

Tessler, R. C., & Schwartz, S. H. Help-seeking, self-esteem, and achievement motivation: An attribution analysis. *Journal of Personality and Social Psychology*, 1972, *21*, 318–326.

Underwood, B. J. Individual differences as a crucible in theory construction. *American Psychologist*, 1975, *30*, 128–134.

Walster, E., Berscheid, E., & Walster, G. W. New directions in equity theory. *Journal of Personality and Social Psychology*, 1973, *25*, 151–176.

Weiss, C. H. Validity of welfare mothers' responses. *Public Opinion Quarterly*, 1969, *32*, 622–633.

Wylie, R. C. *The self-concept*. Lincoln: Univ. of Nebraska Press, 1974.

chapter 8

The Role of Perceived Control in Practitioner–Patient Relationships

DENNIS SCHORR
JUDITH RODIN

Introduction

People typically enter the health care system only when they are sick and in need of help, and they tend to be viewed as relatively passive participants in their relationships with practitioners. The emergence of approaches to intervention that stress prevention of illness and regard patients as active participants may change this situation, but at present the predominant model is one that characterizes patients as passive recipients of care. This chapter examines the implications of different types of interaction for medical patients' and psychotherapy clients' feelings of control and discusses the consequences of different perceptions of control that may arise from health care relationships.

Since people generally see a health care professional only when they are ill, the difficulties and symptoms that lead them to seek professional help may diminish their feelings of control. The sensations and experiences they encounter may be unfamiliar and frightening, and they may be confused about how to make sense out of them or cope with them (Janis & Rodin, 1979). When people are confronted with physical illnesses, their ability to regulate their physiological processes may be threatened (Brody, 1980). When

155

they are faced with psychological or psychiatric concerns, they may feel a lowered sense of efficacy in their ability to deal with their environments (e.g., Bandura, Adams, Hardy, & Howells, 1980). In both cases, they may be having difficulties meeting the normal demands of daily living, such as holding a regular job and maintaining satisfactory interpersonal relationships. When people are well and not experiencing difficulties, they are less likely to be attuned to judging their degree of control in these domains. However, when they are ill and confronted with problems, vulnerable feelings centered around their personal efficacy and autonomy are likely to become more salient.

In addition to being threatened by the difficulties and symptoms that problems pose, individuals' feelings of control are likely to be threatened by the relationship with a practitioner itself. When they seek professional help, people are conveying the message that they do not have the competence to deal with their difficulties on their own. Furthermore, health care practitioners have many sources of power over patients (Rodin & Janis, 1979); for example, they possess information, skills, and expertise in health care that patients do not have, and they can and do exercise power on that basis. Thus, patients and clients are likely to feel in a "one-down" position in relation to the professional (Barofsky, 1978; Brody, 1980).

In their relationships with health care practitioners, patients and clients typically see few areas in which they have control (Barofsky, 1978; Tagliacozzo & Mauksch, 1972). Parsons's (1951) classic conception of the doctor–patient relationship presents a model of patient behavior in which the patient assumes a passive, dependent role in regard to the doctor, who has most of the control over the interaction. In this model, patients are expected to seek and trust professional help and to cooperate undoubtingly with the prescriptions the professional makes. This type of relationship characterizes the traditional way in which health-care-practitioner–patient interactions are viewed (e.g., Brody, 1980; Hayes-Bautista, 1976; Stimson, 1974).

In the psychotherapeutic relationship, clients are typically more active participants in that they are likely to do more talking and initiate more topics of conversation during a session. However, they usually have little input into the methods, goals, and decisions of treatment (Coyne & Widiger, 1978; Morrison, 1979). In addition, psychological–psychiatric symptoms are frequently less objectively definable and measurable than physical symptoms; thus, it is harder for clients to gauge progress in therapy.

Although patients and clients have little control in the typical helping transaction, there are many formulations enumerating a variety of possible types of relationships between patients or clients and health care practitioners. We believe that these can be best understood by analyzing the extent to which they afford patients and clients varying degrees of control in the interaction (e.g., Barofsky, 1978; Coyne & Widiger, 1978; Eisenthal, Emery, Lazare, &

Udin, 1979; Morrison, 1979; Szasz & Hollender, 1956). They range from total passivity on the part of patients, through mutual participation in goal formulation and treatment planning, to self-help.

Consequences of Different Levels of Perceived Control

What are the consequences of variations in perceptions of control on psychological and physiological functioning? The literature indicates that greater feelings of control have a positive impact on psychological well-being and physical health and conversely, that a diminished sense of control has undesirable consequences. A number of laboratory studies have demonstrated that the perceptions of having control over aversive stimuli, such as shock, loud noise, or taking intelligence tests, reduces the stressfulness of that event in the period preceding exposure to the stimulus; on the other hand, diminished feelings of control induce stress and anxiety (e.g., Bowers, 1968; Gatchel & Proctor, 1976; Geer, Davison, & Gatchel, 1970; Stotland & Blumenthal, 1964). These results hold both when stress is measured by indices of physiological arousal (such as galvanic skin response and heart rate) and when it is gauged by subjective report. In addition, perceptions of control lead to greater endurance of aversive stimuli (e.g., Bowers, 1968; Kanfer & Seidner, 1973; Staub, Tursky, & Schwartz, 1971). The crucial variable in these studies is the individual's *perception* of control, because even when control is not actually exercised or the objective level of control and exposure to the noxious stimulus are identical, those who believe they have more control exhibit reduced distress (e.g., Geer *et al.*, 1970).

Furthermore, greater feelings of control have been shown to enhance satisfaction (e.g., Liem, 1975) and performance (e.g., Glass & Singer, 1972; Perlmuter & Monty, 1977; Stotland & Blumenthal, 1964) in a variety of situations, whereas uncontrollable situations lead to performance decrements (e.g., Glass & Singer, 1972; Hiroto & Seligman, 1975; Seligman, 1975). In addition, exposure to a situation over which individuals have little control may result in greater reporting of physiological symptoms afterwards (Pennebaker, Burnam, Schaeffer, & Harper, 1977).

Being in an uncontrollable situation has been shown to lead to one of two negative states. The initial response to the loss of control is psychological reactance, a state characterized by increased arousal and anxiety during which the individual attempts to reexert control (Brehm, 1966; Wortman & Brehm, 1975). Enduring uncontrollable events, however, can lead to helplessness, a deficit distinguished by decreased attempts at mastery even when subsequent situations are controllable (Hiroto & Seligman, 1975; Seligman, 1975; Wortman & Brehm, 1975).

PERCEIVED CONTROL IN HEALTH CARE SITUATIONS

Since many health conditions and treatment procedures tend to be aversive, the literature just reviewed suggests that greater feelings of control in these situations should lead to less anxiety and a greater ability to cope. Applying the control construct to health care, studies have indicated that giving surgical patients techniques to increase their sense of control (e.g., means of focusing attention away from painful stimuli) lowers pulse rate under anesthesia (Pranulis, Dabbs, & Johnson, 1975), lowers preoperative stress, and reduces the need for sedatives and pain relievers after surgery (Langer, Janis, & Wolfer, 1975). Taylor and Levin (1976) have compared a two-stage surgical procedure for breast cancer treatment, in which biopsy to determine if cancer is present and mastectomy if cancer is discovered take place on separate occasions, to a one-stage procedure. The two-stage procedure seems to lead to a better outcome, as measured by rate of recovery from surgery. Taylor and Levin argue that the two-stage procedure is superior because it gives the patient a chance to prepare for the mastectomy and engage in decision making relevant to the operation. In addition, in psychotherapeutic situations, studies have suggested that when clients are allowed to choose between different types of therapy approaches, they show greater adherence to treatment (Eisenthal *et al.*, 1979) and better outcomes (Gordon, 1976; Kanfer & Grimm, 1978).

Hospital settings, in particular, have been characterized as places where patients experience a severe loss of control (Taylor, 1979). Taylor (1979) suggests that patients react to the uncontrollable situation of the hospital with either reactance or helplessness; the former is associated with "bad patient behavior" and the latter with "good patient behavior." Both states are expected to have negative consequences on psychological and physiological well-being.

PERCEIVED CONTROL, PHYSIOLOGICAL PROCESSES, AND ILLNESS

Many studies have shown that loss of control leads to physiological disorder. Of necessity, many of those using direct manipulations of the withdrawal of control have been performed with animals. For example, animals that are able to avoid or escape from aversive situations show lower rates of stomach ulceration (Weiss, 1968) and less elevation of plasma corticosterone (Davis, Porter, Livingstone, Herrmann, MacFadden, & Levine, 1977) and plasma cortisol levels (Hanson, Larson, & Snowdon, 1976) than animals receiving the same amount of aversive stimulation that was unavoidable or inescapable.

Similar results are now being demonstrated for humans as well. Lack of control-relevant behaviors generally activates both the pituitary adrenal system (e.g., Sachar, 1975) and the sympathetic–adrenal system (e.g.,

Frankenhaeuser, 1975). For example, subjects who were able to choose the intensity of aversive noise to which they were exposed secreted significantly less cortisol than no-choice subjects who were exposed to the same intensity noise for the same amount of time (Lundberg & Frankenhaeuser, 1978). In addition, novice parachute jumpers showed a marked rise in hormone levels at the time of their first jump from a mock training tower, but the amount that these levels decreased in subsequent jumps was correlated with skill at mastering this task (Ursin, Baade, & Levine, 1978). Furthermore, it has been shown that the amount of hydrocortisone produced by women awaiting breast tumor biopsy is correlated with their adequacy of coping with the situation (Katz, Weiner, Gallagher, & Hellman, 1970).

Corticosteroids may be implicated in disease processes since elevated levels may reduce immune system functioning (Gabrielsen & Good, 1967; Gisler, 1974). In healthy individuals, there are usually homeostatic regulatory mechanisms effectively counteracting the suppressive properties of corticosteroids (Northey, 1965; St. Rose & Sabiston, 1971; Solomon, 1969). However, in individuals who are ill, homeostatic regulatory mechanisms may be less effective (Timiras, 1972). Thus, it can be hypothesized that feelings of diminished control in medical patients may lead to elevated corticosteroid levels, which may weaken the individual's immunological system, thereby effecting relapse and the development of other problem conditions.

Consistent with these findings, feelings of helplessness and an ability to control one's environment have been implicated in the etiology of disease, such as uterine cervical cancer (Schmale & Iker, 1966) and coronary heart disease (Glass, 1977). It has been argued that psychological disorders, especially depression, also arise from feelings of helplessness (e.g., Seligman, 1975). Most dramatically, cases of sudden death have been thought to occur after severe feelings of uncontrollability over a stressful situation (Seligman, 1975).

On the other hand, induction of greater feelings of control in institutionalized older people has been shown to have dramatic positive effects on psychological and physical health. In one study, residents of a nursing home were given either a talk that emphasized their responsibility for themselves or one stressing the staff's responsibility for them (Langer & Rodin, 1976; Rodin & Langer, 1977). In addition, the former group was given more opportunities to make choices and take responsibility for aspects of their environment. Subsequently, residents in the responsibility induction group exhibited significantly more alertness, sociability, active participation, and general well-being, and these differences were shown to be maintained 18 months later. Furthermore, the responsibility induction group showed an increase in general health that was significantly greater than that of the other residents. In fact, residents who did not receive the responsibility induction intervention showed decreases in general health. Most strikingly, the mortality rate in the group that received the responsibility induction was half that of the other group. Other studies (Schulz & Hanusa, 1980) have suggested that the long-term benefits of control depend on the explanations older individuals have for the source of their control-relevant opportunities. Finally, Rodin (in press) has shown that direct instruction in self-regulation skills in older ill people greatly increases feelings of control, which are strongly correlated with decreased corticosteroid levels and improvements in a variety of health-relevant indicators such as change in use of medications and overall morbidity.

IMPLICATIONS OF PERCEIVED CONTROL FOR
THE HEALTH CARE RELATIONSHIP

The studies reviewed thus far suggest that if practitioners could bolster a patient's or client's perceptions of control, positive consequences would be likely to result.[1] Certain aspects of the clinician–patient relationship that threaten a person's feelings of control are inherently unchangeable features of any treatment situation, for example, the fact that the patient is seeking help for difficulties or potential difficulties for which the professional has greater skills or expertise than the patient. If practitioners are sensitive to these features and their potential implications, however, ways of dealing with them could be implemented. Furthermore, it is possible to identify aspects of the relationship in which perceptions of control can be bolstered. This chapter examines medical and psychotherapeutic health care relationships, identifies areas in which threats to a patient's feelings of control may be an issue, and highlights ways, based on prescriptions following from current empirical evidence, in which patients' feelings of control can be increased in a manner that is likely to benefit health care interactions and health outcomes. Testable hypotheses are formulated throughout to pinpoint areas in which additional research is needed.

Theoretical Refinements of the Construct of Control

Before identifying ways in which perceptions of control can be increased in the health-care-practitioner–patient relationship, it is necessary to elaborate some refinements that have been made in understanding the construct of control. *Control* is most easily defined as the ability to have an impact on an outcome. Outcomes can be influenced behaviorally, decisionally, or cognitively, leading to a distinction between three types of control (Averill, 1973). Behavioral control is the existence of a contingency between one's behavior

---

[1]Henceforth the term *patient* will be used to refer to both patients and clients, although the term *client* will be retained when speaking solely of psychotherapy clients.

and an outcome. One is said to have behavioral control if one's behavior can modify, influence, or obtain a given outcome. Decisional control refers to the opportunity to choose among various courses of action or outcomes. Cognitive control designates the ability to influence the impact of an event or situation by appraising it in different ways or engaging in some cognitive strategy. For instance, stressful situations have been shown to lead to different levels of distress depending on how an event is viewed (e.g., Klemp & Rodin, 1976; Langer *et al.*, 1975).

PREDICTABILITY

Closely tied to the concept of control is the notion of predictability. In most studies, and in most naturally occurring situations, control is confounded with predictability. For example, if one has control over bringing about an outcome by one's own action, one is usually able to predict that outcome. In studies where predictability has been examined without varying perceived control, it has been shown that more predictability has some of the same positive consequences as greater control and less predictability has some of the same negative consequences as less control, both psychologically and physiologically (e.g., Klemp & Rodin, 1976; Levine & Coover, 1976; Weiss, 1970). However, the few studies that have been able to independently vary controllability and predictability have shown that controllability reduces stress even when the amount of predictability in controllable and uncontrollable situations is held constant (e.g., Geer *et al.*, 1970; Geer & Maisel, 1972; Glass, Singer, Leonard, Krantz, Cohen, & Cummings, 1973). Thus, although predictability has beneficial effects and is closely associated with controllability, it appears that controllability has positive consequences that cannot be accounted for solely by the level of predictability present.

CONDITIONS AFFECTING THE BENEFITS
AND DESIRABILITY OF PERCEIVED CONTROL

Even though most studies have indicated that perceived control has positive effects, some studies have found that having control can be stress inducing and is not always desirable (Averill, 1973; Thompson, 1981). As a result, it is necessary to specify the conditions under which perceived control is desirable and has a beneficial impact and the circumstances under which it might not. Averill (1973) concluded that the meaning of the control response for the individual, influenced largely by the context in which it is embedded, determines whether or not personal control will be stress reducing. Miller (1980) and Thompson (1981) proposed that the beneficial effects of control arise because control may change the meaning of an event from one that is potentially unendurable to one that is within the limits of one's endurance.

From this prediction, it can be hypothesized that controllability will not lower stress if it is not seen as guaranteeing an acceptable upper limit of danger.

Conditions such as felt responsibility, information, and individual dispositional traits may also influence the desirability of control. Having control over a situation is likely to raise a person's perception of responsibility for the outcome. If the amount of felt responsibility is raised too high, having control may be seen as an undesirable result (Rodin, Rennert, & Solomon, 1980).

The presence of information enabling one to exercise control over an outcome more effectively has also been proposed as a condition that affects the desirability of control (Rodin *et al.*, 1980). Without sufficient information, control may be stressful. In medical settings, people who are asked to make choices between options about which they have little or no knowledge may find this decision aversive. However, if patients are informed about the options and given some comprehensible criteria for deciding among them, we hypothesize that they may desire to participate in the decision and show more positive outcomes from increased decisional control. Furthermore, relevant feedback indicating that a controlling response has been effective is another type of information that has been shown to affect the consequences of having control (Weiss, 1971).

Individual differences between people, such as locus of control (Rotter, 1966), have been associated with the desire for control. People with an internal locus of control are characterized as believing that reinforcements in their lives are contingent upon their behaviors. Those with an external locus of control tend to believe that reinforcements are not under their control. Therefore, it might be reasonably hypothesized that people with an internal locus of control are more likely to respond positively to having control than those with an external locus of control (e.g., Houston, 1972).

Perceptions of Self-Efficacy

Most importantly, it is necessary to distinguish between the belief that one has the opportunity to exercise control in a given situation and the perception of having the skills necessary to exercise that control effectively. On one hand, the opportunity to exercise control may exist in a given situation, but the person may feel that he or she does not have the competence to take advantage of that opportunity. On the other hand, a person may feel that he or she has the skills to exercise control in a given situation but the situation does not allow for the exercise of control.

The expectation of self-efficacy refers to the belief that one has the skills to be able to cope with a given situation, that is, to effectively exercise control in that situation (Bandura, 1977). An outcome expectancy is the estimate that a given behavior will lead to certain outcomes. This distinction coincides with the distinction between the competence to exercise control and the opportunity to perform a control-relevant response. Although similar distinctions have been made occasionally (Abramson, Seligman, & Teasdale,

1978), the literature on control has typically confounded beliefs about the *available* opportunity for control and beliefs about *self-efficacy*.

Feelings of self-efficacy may be one of the factors that determine whether greater control is desirable or not. It has been demonstrated that feelings of self-efficacy in relationship to threatening, aversive, or obstacle-laden situations are excellent predictors of the level of coping exhibited in that situation (e.g., Bandura *et al.*, 1980). Self-efficacy theory argues that this relationship is mediated by the amount of effort expended in coping with stressful conditions, with greater feelings of self-efficacy leading to greater efforts at coping. Thus, people who feel more self-efficacious seem to be more highly motivated to be in control of their situation. In addition, feelings of self-efficacy predict the amount of fear experienced in threatening situations, with greater feelings of self-efficacy leading to lower levels of fear (e.g., Bandura *et al.*, 1980). From these findings, it might be extrapolated that people may find situations aversive when they perceive that the opportunity for control exists but do not feel efficacious in exercising that control. Thus, feelings of self-efficacy may be needed for control opportunities to have beneficial effects.

Feelings of self-efficacy may be mediated by the other variables proposed to account for the conditions under which control is desirable. The type of meaning that is given to an event may influence feelings of self-efficacy. For example, if an event is interpreted as more endurable when the person has greater opportunity for control, then it is likely that feelings of self-efficacy will be higher. Likewise, people with an external locus of control are likely to have lower feelings of self-efficacy than those with an internal locus of control. In addition, it is conceivable that increased feelings of responsibility may focus attention to the possibility that one might not be able to exercise control effectively, and thus lower feelings of self-efficacy. Finally, although not all types of information are expected to have a positive effect on perceived control (Thompson, 1981), we hypothesize that information that increases feelings of self-efficacy should raise the desirability of perceived control. For example, perceived self-efficacy may be raised when information provides the skills necessary to exercise control effectively or when it provides an effective basis for deciding between different available options.

Perceived Control in Health Care Relationships

On the basis of the current literature, control is hypothesized to have a major impact on health care by raising adherence levels (e.g., Brody, 1980; Hayes-Bautista, 1976; Janis & Mann, 1977), in addition to having a direct effect on health and morbidity. For example, hypertensive patients who perceived the treatment process as allowing them to be active participants showed better adherence and were more likely to have their blood pressure within normal limits (Schulman, 1979). Furthermore, it has been argued that patients whose feelings of control are threatened (e.g., by being given recommendations in an authoritarian manner) are likely not to adhere to treatment as a way of reexerting their control in the situation (Hayes-Bautista, 1976). The literature on reactance predicts the same results (Brehm, 1966; Wortman & Brehm, 1975). Patients' satisfaction with treatment has also been shown to be associated with better adherence (Francis, Korsch, & Morris, 1969; Haynes, 1976). Since perceived control has been shown to increase satisfaction (e.g., Liem, 1975), enhanced control in medical settings may increase adherence as a result of its effects on satisfaction. However, it also seems that greater control leads directly to adherence without satisfaction as a mediating variable (Eisenthal *et al.*, 1979).

Recently it has been advocated that patients be encouraged to be more active participants and decision makers in the practitioner–patient relationship and be given more control in that setting (e.g., Brody, 1980; Coyne & Widiger, 1978; Deeds, Bernheimer, McCombs, McKenney, Richardson, & Fink, 1979; Eisenthal *et al.*, 1979). However, these proposals have not been based upon a solid theoretical framework. The theoretical and empirical literature on the construct of control provides such a foundation. On this basis, in the following sections we attempt to specify the conditions under which greater perceptions of control should be beneficial for the health care transaction. The health care relationship can be divided into a series of phases (e.g., Stone, 1979), and the role of perceived control will be examined in each of them.

DECIDING TO COME TO A HEALTH CARE PRACTITIONER

Prior to making contact with a health care professional, people generally go through the process of deciding whether or not to seek help and whom to see to obtain help. Feelings of control during this phase may have a significant impact on their subsequent interaction with a practitioner. Sometimes, patients may have been coerced to see a health care practitioner by friends, family members, employers, the legal system, or other health care providers. We expect that in such situations, they may be especially prone to feel a loss of control upon entering treatment. They may respond to the loss of control with reactance and try to sabotage the therapy in order to reexert their control (Cameron, 1978). On the other hand, if they are resigned to the loss of control, the resultant feelings of helplessness may interfere with their ability to adhere to the recommendations of therapy. Thus, in these cases, it is especially urgent that health care professionals be attuned to issues of control and that patients' perceptions of control be bolstered. In order to enhance feelings of control, the practitioner can ask these patients during a preliminary session to think about whether they want to commence therapy (Cameron, 1978). The social pressures to enter therapy are still present, but, in this way, feelings of decisional control are likely to be raised.

Even if patients freely decide to enter the health care setting, the process of finding a practitioner may leave them with diminished feelings of control. In searching for a health care professional, they may not have sufficient information about available practitioners to feel confident in deciding among them. This confusion is especially evident in finding a psychotherapist, since people tend to be less familiar with mental health professionals than with nonpsychiatric physicians (Kadushin, 1969). In such situations, the practitioner who is first seen can offer to recommend other professionals or other modes of treatment if the patient does not prefer the relationship that is being established. Most people probably would not accept this offer, but their feelings of control would be enhanced because they have had to choose explicitly the practitioner they are seeing. Sometimes, patients may be assigned to clinicians and have little or no input into the decision, for instance, in many clinic settings. In addition to the threat to one's sense of control that may arise in such situations, the therapeutic process may be hindered when patients are assigned to a therapist with characteristics that they do not prefer (e.g., Ziemelis, 1974).

More generally, in order to foster feelings of control in regard to entering therapy, people can be encouraged to interpret coming to a practitioner as a positive attempt at coping with their concerns. The current movement toward early screening, prevention, and wellness programs should enhance patients' feelings of control because, in such programs, people enter health care relationships without being threatened by the symptoms of illness.

DEFINING PROBLEMS, FORMULATING GOALS, AND DECIDING ON A GENERAL COURSE OF ACTION

In the next phases of the health care transaction, under conditions of optimal decision making, problems are defined, goals are formulated, ways of attaining these goals are considered, and a general course of action is decided upon (adapted from Janis & Mann, 1977; Stone, 1979).

The Patient's Perspective

In most health care transactions, patients are viewed as passive participants who are expected to adopt the professional's definition of their problems, goals for the interaction, and prescriptions for intervention (e.g., Brody, 1980; Coyne & Widiger, 1978; Morrison, 1979; Stimson, 1974). In actuality, though, patients typically enter the health care situation with their own perspective on their health care (e.g., Eisenthal *et al.*, 1979; Kasl, 1975;

Kleinman, Eisenberg, & Good, 1978; Stimson, 1974) and thus are far from passive recipients of the clinician's perspective.

Before seeking professional services, people usually try to deal with their problems on their own (Kleinman *et al.*, 1978). We live in a culture in which people receive considerable information about illness and health care (Stimson, 1974). Through past learning experiences, such as previous personal illnesses, contact with other people with illness, and exposure to the media, people are able to develop some conceptualization of what their problem is and how they should go about treating it. In addition, they are likely to turn to friends and relatives for help and advice about how to make sense of and deal with their difficulties (Kleinman *et al.*, 1978; Suchman, 1972). As a result, by the time patients see a practitioner, they often have developed a definition of their areas of concern, expectations of and goals for the health care interaction, and some ideas about how their difficulties should be handled (e.g., Eisenthal *et al.*, 1979, Francis *et al.*, 1969; Kleinman *et al.*, 1978; Stimson, 1974). Thus, they are likely to evaluate the practitioner–patient interaction in light of their own perspectives.

Often clinicians are inattentive to the patient's perspective (Kasl, 1975; Korsch, Gozzi, & Francis, 1968). If the patient's point of view is not adequately addressed in the health care interaction, satisfaction, adherence, and health care outcomes may be jeopardized (Benarde & Mayerson, 1978; Eisenthal *et al.*, 1979; Hayes-Bautista, 1976; Kasl, 1975; Kleinman *et al.*, 1978). For example, in pediatric settings, mothers who thought that the physician did not understand their concern over their child's illness were likely to show lowered adherence to treatment (Francis *et al.*, 1969).

The patient's point of view consists of different types of cognitions. On one hand, the patient may have expectancies about what *will* take place in the practitioner–patient interaction (Duckro, Beal, & George, 1979). On the other hand, the patient may have opinions and preferences about what *should* take place in the transaction (Duckro *et al.*, 1979). There are also other types of attitudes and beliefs that the patient may bring into the health care interaction, for example, attitudes about medications or the significance of one's symptoms. In most of the literature that has addressed the patient's perspective, the differentiation between types of cognitions is not made explicit. However, these distinctions may have important implications, which will be discussed below, for understanding why a disregard of the patient's point of view may have negative consequences for the health care relationship.

Expectancies about what will take place in treatment. Expectancies that patients have about what will take place in treatment are likely to provide them with a sense of predictability about the health care interaction. It follows from the literature reviewed earlier that when these expectancies are not met or aspects of the situation arise that were not anticipated, the resultant feelings of unpredictability may have a negative effect on the practitioner–patient relationship. When patients enter the health care interaction without a clear idea about what will take place, this sense of confusion may also lead to low feelings of predictability.

Closely tied in with expectancies about what will take place in the interaction are beliefs about how patients are expected to behave in the health care relationship (i.e., the role they are expected to adopt). If patients have correct beliefs in this domain, they are more likely to be able to modify their behavior to interact smoothly in the health care transaction. They may not be able to cope effectively with the transaction if they do not realize how one is expected to act.

The problem of unclear and inaccurate expectancies about what will take place and how one is expected to behave is especially prominent in psychotherapy. People are much less likely to have had previous personal experience with psychotherapy than with medical treatment. In addition, members of one's informal social support network are less likely to have had experiences with psychotherapy, and if they have been in therapy, they may be less likely to talk about it because of the stigma involved. A number of studies have indicated that people very often do not have accurate information about psychotherapy (Heitler, 1976).

The literature on control and predictability supports the hypothesis that unclear and inaccurate expectancies may in part be responsible for a high dropout rate and other negative effects in psychotherapy, although much more empirical investigation on this subject is still needed (Duckro *et al.*, 1979). On the other hand, some research suggests that when the start of psychotherapy is preceded by a session in which clients are given correct information about what will happen in therapy and what is expected of them, they are more likely to remain in therapy and benefit from it (Hoehn-Saric, Frank, Imber, Nash, Stone, & Battle, 1964; Sloane, Cristol, Pepernik, & Staples, 1970; Strupp & Bloxom, 1973). In medical treatments as well, it has been advocated that as a first step patients should be provided with a clear statement about what they can expect from the practitioner and what is expected of them (Deeds *et al.*, 1979).

Beliefs about what should take place in treatment. Patients' views about what should take place in treatment may not be changed sufficiently by the procedures just described because these procedures are based upon a one-sided communication of information, without consideration of the patient's perspective. As a result, patients may feel a loss of control. If patients feel that the interaction is unresponsive to their point of view, negative attitudes towards the interaction may develop, feelings of reactance may be engendered, and adherence may be lowered.

It is proposed that patients be given the opportunity to express their point of view in the health care transaction, for example, their goals for the interaction and opinions about the nature of their problem and how it should be handled (e.g., Brody, 1980; Eisenthal *et al.*, 1979; Kasl, 1975; Kleinman *et al.*, 1978). We hypothesize that patients' feelings of control would thus be enhanced. However, patients may not spontaneously express their opinions because the typical health care interaction does not address the patient's perspective and they may feel that it is inappropriate to do so or that the practitioner does not value their point of view. Nevertheless, such information will probably be obtained if the clinician encourages patients by showing them that their viewpoint is a valued part of the interaction and by eliciting their point of view with direct questions (Brody, 1980; Eisenthal & Lazare, 1976; Kleinman *et al.*, 1978). If patients believe that their opinion is valued and worthwhile, we predict that they may feel more efficacious. In addition, eliciting the patient's point of view may provide the practitioner with important information related to the person's difficulties that would not have been obtained otherwise (Lazare, Eisenthal, & Wasserman, 1975).

Other attitudes and beliefs. Many additional beliefs can affect how patients interpret the clinician's recommendations, and, as a result, have a profound impact on adherence and the subsequent course of the health care transaction (Stimson, 1974). For instance, patients who believe that drugs are only to be used for identifiable symptoms may interpret incorrectly the physician's prescription about the length of time they should continue to take an antibiotic. If these patients' attitudes are not addressed and changed, they are likely to terminate taking the antibiotic prematurely, with detrimental health consequences.

The Health Care Practitioner's Perspective

While health care professionals attend to the patient's perspective, they can present their own view of the situation (e.g., their definition of the problem, goals for treatment, and ways of handling the problem). As a result of having heard the patient's point of view, practitioners may be able to tailor the presentation of their recommendations accordingly. Also, it is important that professionals provide feedback to the patient about the perspective that the patient has expressed. Although some patients may not have a clearly formulated viewpoint upon entering treatment, they may have strong reactions to the practitioner's suggestions, and these reactions need to be elicited.

It is not being argued that the clinician should acquiesce to the patient's point of view. However, it is being proposed that the practitioner be aware of it and explicitly deal with it in the health care transaction. In cases in which patients have unrealistic, inaccurate, or medically counterproductive beliefs and opinions, the professional can provide them with convincing information indicating why the professional's view is more appropriate than their own (Lazare *et al.*, 1975); otherwise, they may leave the interaction without having seen why the clinician's perspective is more desirable.

The recommendations that the clinician makes to the patient can be presented in different ways, with various implications for feelings of control. The choice of words and tone of voice used to present the recommendations can create the impression of different levels of choice. For example, if the practitioner uses words like *must* or *should*, the patient's sense of control may be threatened (Brehm, 1976).

On the other hand, the practitioner may present alternative ways of dealing with the difficulty (including the patient's own view of how it should be handled, if one exists), present the pros and cons of each alternative, and then provide information indicating why a given choice is recommended over the others. This type of decision making is claimed to lead a greater adherence to the chosen course of action (Janis & Mann, 1977). Based on the line of reasoning we have been developing, it can be expected that the patient's sense of perceived choice may be enhanced because the patient is able to go through the decision making process of considering and weighing alternatives, and this enhanced sense of decisional control may foster adherence.

Negotiation of Discrepancies in the Patient's and Practitioner's Perspectives

When the patient and practitioner have different viewpoints about how the problem should be handled, they may negotiate a common position somewhere between each of theirs that is satisfactory to both parties (e.g., Brody, 1980; Eisenthal *et al.*, 1979; Kleinman *et al.*, 1978; Levinson, Merrifield, & Berg, 1967). The practitioner must identify areas in which negotiation is more and less feasible. In instances in which compromise would have negative medical outcomes, it is clearly undesirable; however, in many areas it is possible without disadvantageous medical results. In fact, health outcomes should be enhanced as a result of the patient's greater feelings of control.

It has been argued that negotiation in the professional–patient interaction leads to better satisfaction and adherence (e.g., Benarde & Mayerson, 1978; Kleinman *et al.*, 1978). If patients leave the health care situation feeling that the treatment is not entirely appropriate because their beliefs have not been included, then they may modify the treatment, for example, by combining the professional's recommendations with folk remedies (Hayes-Bautista, 1976). It is preferable that the practitioner negotiate with the patient a treatment that is acceptable to both parties, rather than the patient unilaterally modify the treatment. Evidence indicating the positive consequences of a negotiation approach has begun to accumulate (e.g., Eisenthal *et al.*, 1979; Hefferin, 1979).

The negotiation approach gains increased feasibility when it is remembered that most medical decisions are not unambiguous and different physicians will often prescribe different treatments for the same condition (Brody, 1980; Eisenberg, 1979). Thus, there is often room for flexibility in a practitioner's recommendations. Moreover, many medical decisions involve value judgments (e.g., Drucker, 1974; Levine, 1978; McNeil & Pauker, 1979). Practitioners and patients may place different values on the benefits and drawbacks that accompany different courses of action in dealing with a problem. For example, surgery sometimes entails a decision between continuation of one's life with certain handicaps if the person decides not to have the surgery and the possibility of lessening the handicap if surgery is elected, with a higher chance of death or greater distress in the short run (Levine, 1978). These judgments are highly subjective. Prevention and treatment of many conditions (such as coronary heart disease) frequently require life-style changes, such as the regulation of food intake, increases in exercise, and decreases in exposure to stressful situations. Since these types of changes require value judgments and major restructurings of a person's life, the patient must assume a role in these decisions.

In summary, there is great reason to involve patients in these decisions and to negotiate an acceptable compromise between patients' and practitioners' points of view. In offering patients the opportunity for greater decisional control, it is important that they feel efficacious in exercising that control. The information, perspective, and advice that clinicians have as a result of expertise in health care should be communicated in a way that is understandable to patients so as to facilitate their feelings of efficacy in participating in these decisions (see the section on information later in this chapter). In addition, patients should not feel entirely responsible for decisions since they are making them in conjunction with the practitioner.

In psychotherapy, decision making is even more ambiguous. It is more difficult to identify in an objective manner problem areas and goals for treatment for psychological–psychiatric difficulties than for typical medical conditions; thus, there is flexibility for giving clients a greater role in this process. For the vast majority of psychological–psychiatric problems, the current research literature does not provide a basis for choosing one type of therapy over another; the different types of psychotherapy that rest upon a reasonable empirical base seem to be equally effective for most problems (Bergin & Lambert, 1978). As a result, the opportunity for client involvement in these decisions is great.

Since most patients and practitioners have been socialized in a health care system that does not use a negotiation model, patients are not likely to anticipate this type of transaction. Thus, the expectancy of this type of relationship should be induced in the patient early in the interaction. Feelings of self-efficacy in playing a more active role should be maintained by the practitioner's sharing of information about the choices and advocacy of his or her own recommendations and rationale for them. We hypothesize that once this process is finished the patient is more likely to internalize the recommendations because he or she played an active role in choosing them.

When the process of negotiation has been completed, the point of view that has been agreed upon should be made explicit so that both parties have a clear set of accurate expectancies about the nature of their relationship. Negotiated contracts may serve the function of highlighting the patient's role in the decision-making process and make explicit the approach to health care that has been agreed upon; in addition, commitment to carrying through with the agreed-upon behavior may be enhanced (e.g., Champlin & Karoly, 1975). In order to further involve the patient in decision making and increase commitment to the agreed-upon course of action, the pros and cons of carrying through with the course of action can be listed and considered (Hoyt & Janis, 1982; Janis & Mann, 1977).

IMPLEMENTATION OF THE TREATMENT PLAN

The next stage of the health care process calls for implementation of the course of treatment. For some health care problems, implementation of the treatment plan rests primarily in the hands of the professional (e.g., in performing surgery). But, at some point in the process, even these patients must begin to assume more responsibility for implementation of health care decisions. For many health care concerns, implementation of health care decisions rests primarily with the patient (e.g., in the management of chronic illnesses such as diabetes). For control over treatment implementation to have beneficial effects, patients must believe that a given course of action will lead to desirable health outcomes (i.e., that a response-outcome contingency exists) and that they personally have the skills to exercise the course of action effectively (i.e., that they have self-efficacy). We will argue that both beliefs must be enhanced in the practitioner–patient relationship in order for adherence to be increased.

Beliefs in the Effectiveness of Treatment

It has been shown that when patients or mothers of pediatric patients do not believe in the effectiveness of a treatment plan, adherence is lowered (e.g., Becker, Drachman, & Kirscht, 1972; Geertsen, Gray, & Ward, 1973; Kirscht & Rosenstock, 1977). Prior experience with a course of action seems likely to influence beliefs about the effectiveness of a therapeutic intervention. For instance, mothers of pediatric patients were more likely to administer the prescribed medications if they believed that medicines obtained previously from the clinic were useful (Becker *et al.*, 1972). In addition, people often develop negative expectancies about the effectiveness of treatment for persistent and difficult-to-treat problems, such as weight control, because they have tried so many techniques that did not work.

Most medical and psychological treatments have both benefits and drawbacks. The timing of their occurrence may affect beliefs in the effectiveness of therapy. In many medical treatments, the drawbacks are experienced before health gains become evident, for example, painful surgical procedures may have to be endured before the person feels better. Likewise, in psychotherapy, difficult personal changes and distressing confrontations with difficult feelings may have to take place before improvement is seen. In some disorders, even the long-term advantages are much less perceptible than the drawbacks. For example, in therapy for high blood pressure, major life-style changes are often called for; however, the benefits, that is, lower blood pressure and lower risks of other diseases, are not even noticeable to the patient in the form of symptom relief. Thus, the practitioner must increase the salience of the benefits of the course of action that has been decided upon and perhaps also work to create some more short-term gains. As a result, beliefs in the effectiveness of the therapy might be raised and adherence would be enhanced.

In order to accomplish this goal, patients might be trained to change the things they say to themselves about the negative consequences of adherence. If people were trained to interpret the unpleasant experiences as an indication that gains will result afterwards, the salience of the benefits would be increased. Thus, techniques that increase cognitive control over a situation may be beneficial. For example, patients who were taught prior to surgery to focus on the positive and compensatory aspects of undergoing surgery showed less preoperative stress and less postoperative use of pain relievers and sedatives than those who did not receive this intervention (Langer *et al.*, 1975). In addition, Rodin (1978) reported increased adherence to weight loss plans when clients learn to label hunger as a "sign that the body is attacking the fat stores for energy," and therefore reinterpret it as a positive outcome rather than an unpleasant one.

Furthermore, if patients have correct expectancies about the course of illness, then they might have greater confidence in the effectiveness of their treatments. For example, it has been argued that patients should always be given a time frame about when changes should be expected (Cameron, 1978). If the positive results of a given course of action are delayed, patients may begin to doubt the effectiveness of the treatment; however, if patients are aware that the benefits will take place after a certain amount of time, they are less likely to get discouraged. Enumerating the pros and cons of treatment options may also decrease a sense of uncertainty and demoralization by highlighting what can be expected in one's attempts to deal with illness. Nevertheless, often patients are not given correct expectancies about the course of illness and treatment (e.g., Suchman, 1972; Svarstad, 1976). It is hypothesized that such uncertainty decreases adherence because it can lead to a sense of discouragement with a given course of action. One consequence of these feelings may be perceptions of diminished control.

Feelings of Self-Efficacy in Carrying Out Treatment

Even if patients believe that a given course of action is effective in leading to positive health outcomes, they may still feel out of control because they may perceive themselves as not having skills that are necessary to carry out the required treatment. Because low feelings of self-efficacy seem to lead to diminished persistence in coping with stressful situations (e.g., Bandura *et al.*, 1980), we predict that people who believe that they may not be efficacious in carrying out a course of therapy are less likely to adhere. Thus, in order for a person's sense of control to be enhanced, with benefits for health outcomes, it is necessary for practitioners to bolster *both* beliefs in the effectiveness of the treatment decided upon and feelings that one has the skills to carry out the treatment.

Explicating the specifics of implementation of a treatment plan. Since health care practitioners often do not discuss the specific details of implementation in a thorough enough manner (e.g., Svarstad, 1976), feelings of low self-efficacy in carrying out a treatment plan may arise. Identifying these specifics in advance has been implicated in increasing adherence (e.g., Janis & Mann, 1977; Leventhal, Watts, & Pagano, 1967). However, if the practitioner dictates the specifics of implementation in an authoritarian way, patients may feel a loss of control as a result of not participating in the decisions. In order to overcome these problems, the practitioner and patient should arrive at these decisions in collaboration with each other and tailor the implementation as much as possible to the patient's everyday habits, through the process of decision making and negotiation discussed earlier In psychotherapy, changes made in sessions may be more likely to generalize to everyday situations if therapists and clients jointly work out the details of implementing these changes in daily living. We hypothesize that involving patients in elaborating the specific details of a treatment plan will lead to greater adherence by raising feelings of self-efficacy and control.

Likewise, when a treatment regimen requires special skills, it is important that the practitioner ascertain that the patient has those skills before leaving the practitioner's office. If new skills must be developed, these can be rehearsed in the practitioner's office (e.g., by actually using the skill, by role playing, or through imagery). Thus, feelings of self-efficacy may be bolstered with resultant enhancement of adherence.

Establishing hierarchies of health care behaviors. Many treatment regimens are quite difficult to carry out (e.g., some call for unfamiliar, complex, and/or unwanted behaviors). When faced with a difficult treatment regimen, patients may become demoralized and feel a sense of discouragement in their ability to carry out the required behaviors. In order to build up feelings of self-efficacy, the treatment regimen can be broken up into a series of steps (Cameron, 1978; Matthews & Hingson, 1977). Patients can first be allowed to implement and master the behaviors called for in the least complex step before moving onto the next one. This kind of approach, known as the use of a hierarchy of behavior, has been widely used in behavioral and cognitive–behavioral approaches to psychotherapy (e.g., in systematic desensitization). In addition, it has been advocated that this type of procedure be used in helping patients to implement the treatment regimen for hypertension (Deeds *et al.*, 1979). Similarly, breaking down overall health care goals into more easily attainable subgoals should bolster feelings of self-efficacy (Bandura, 1980).

Stress inoculation for dealing with difficulties, discomforts, and setbacks. Patients typically encounter difficulties in implementing the agreed upon course of action, such as unpleasant side effects, absence of support from family members, and the need to sacrifice activities that they enjoy and engage in behaviors that may be stressful. As a result, patients may become demoralized with treatment, and adherence may be threatened.

A procedure called stress inoculation has been developed to counter this possibility. In this procedure, practitioners assist patients to identify in advance the difficulties, discomforts, and setbacks that are likely to occur and to develop strategies for being able to deal with them (Janis & Mann, 1982; Meichenbaum, 1977). Stress inoculation strategies have been shown to reduce distress and increase coping in patients undergoing stressful medical procedures (e.g., Egbert, Battit, Welch, & Bartlett, 1964; Johnson & Leventhal, 1974). From the perspective of the control literature, it is hypothesized that stress inoculation serves to enhance one's feelings of competence in dealing with difficulties, discomforts, and setbacks (Rodin, 1978). Since greater feelings of self-efficacy seem to lead one to make more persistent efforts in trying to deal with stressful situations, it can be argued that enhanced feelings of self-efficacy arising from stress inoculation procedures should lead to greater adherence to treatment regimens.

Cognitive reappraisal. Before encountering stressful aspects of implementation of a treatment regimen, patients can be taught cognitive strategies, a form of cognitive control, that can be used in order to lessen the distress of these unpleasant features. For instance, difficulties and setbacks encountered in implementing a therapeutic regimen can be interpreted in different ways. Adherence is likely to decrease if discomforts are appraised as evidence that one does not have the competence to follow the treatment regimen, but not if they are seen as a necessary step on the road to positive health outcomes. We believe that the former interpretation lowers adherence as a result of diminishing feelings of self-efficacy. Likewise, momentary failures to follow the therapeutic regimen can be viewed in various ways. On one hand, they can be attributed to stable, dispositional factors, that is, seen as evidence that one is generally incompetent to follow the treatment regimen. On the other hand, they can be attributed to unstable, situational factors, that is, interpreted as resulting from momentary temptations that are not generally present. Dispositional attributions should lead to lowered adherence because they have negative implications for one's feelings of self-efficacy (Rodin, 1978). The implications of different types of cognitive appraisals for perceived self-efficacy and adherence is an area that is ripe for further investigation.

EVALUATING THE TREATMENT

The Influence of Friends, Family Members, and Other Sources of Information

Once they leave the health care setting, people typically continue to evaluate the treatment regimen. Patients frequently discuss their treatment with relatives and friends (Stimson, 1974) and obtain new information relevant to their health care from books, magazine articles, and other health professionals (Matthews & Hingson, 1977). It has been argued that the information or misinformation obtained in this way can have as much or more influence on adherence than the explanations of the practitioner (Matthews & Hingson, 1977). As a result, a patient's beliefs in the appropriateness and effectiveness of the treatment may be lowered. In addition, friends and relatives and other sources of information may lower a patient's feelings of self-efficacy by casting doubts on the person's ability to follow through with the recommendations. For example, they may point out that the patient has been unsuccessful in similar efforts in the past. Finally, friends and family members may actually apply subtle and not-so-subtle pressure on the patient not to adhere, especially if the changes called for in a treatment are likely to pose difficulties for them.

Using stress inoculation procedures, health care practitioners can alert patients to the possibility that friends, family members, and other sources of information might undermine the therapy and help them develop ways of coping with these situations. In addition, it may be desirable to identify ways of enlisting friends' and family members' participation in the treatment process in a way that does not threaten patients' feelings of control and self-efficacy.

Dissatisfactions

In the course of implementing treatment, patients may develop dissatisfactions with the therapeutic regimen. Unforseen problems and setbacks may arise. Patients may develop new attitudes and beliefs about the goals of treatment and how their problems should be handled. In addition, the treatment may not be as effective as the patient had expected. We hypothesize that dissatisfactions would be minimized if the recommendations that have been discussed earlier, such as stress inoculation procedures, were utilized. Nevertheless, when dissatisfactions arise, they can be handled in various ways with differing implications for perceptions of control.

The literature on the construct of control indicates that if practitioners do not pay adequate attention to these dissatisfactions, then feelings of control will be diminished since patients may feel that their concerns do not have a real influence on the health care interaction. For instance, if patients are simply told that they need to try harder to implement the regimen, then they are likely to feel that their concerns have not been adequately addressed.

Ignoring patients' complaints and demanding compliance have been observed to lead to a breakdown in practitioner–patient communication, errors in clinical judgment, and lowered adherence (Svarstad, 1976). In psychotherapy, client dissatisfactions are sometimes attributed to resistance or to distortions that arise as a result of the client's psychological problems; as a result of not directly dealing with the dissatisfactions, feelings of control may be lowered.

A practitioner can respond to patients' dissatisfactions in different ways without endangering feelings of control. When the dissatisfactions are such that the current course of treatment needs to be modified, the same procedures should be applied for developing the new course of action as those discussed in the preceding sections. However, if, after considering the patient's dissatisfactions, the professional still concludes that the original treatment regimen is best, additional coping strategies for dealing with problems and setbacks can be developed with the patient. The patient's attitudes with regard to treatment efficacy should also be explicitly reconsidered and bolstered. In addition, some modifications of the treatment may be negotiated.

Gauging Improvement

As treatment proceeds, patients evaluate the progress that is being made. If overt symptoms disappear, then improvement is easily gauged. However, in many conditions improvement is not easily discernible to the patient and feedback from the professional (e.g., laboratory tests) is necessary in order to judge progress. High blood pressure is an example of a disorder in which improvements are usually not readily perceivable by patients. When this occurs, feelings of control may be threatened because patients may not be able to judge the effectiveness of their efforts at dealing with their condition. When objective measures are available to the practitioner (e.g., in blood pressure measurement), feedback about progress can be provided often or patients can be taught to gauge their own progress (Deeds *et al.*, 1979). In some conditions, unambiguous measures of improvement are not available to either professionals or patients. In this case, the best that can be done is to try to break down improvement into a set of explicit, narrowly focused dimensions that can be measured with some degree of reliability and validity and to aid patients to use these dimensions to judge their improvement.

In psychotherapy, the problem of evaluating progress is especially pronounced. Concerns that bring people into psychotherapy are typically much less easy to measure objectively than are medical conditions, and even professionals find it difficult to agree on criteria for evaluating what constitutes improvement (Bergin & Lambert, 1978). Because progress is difficult to gauge, lowered feelings of control may be a significant problem. Behavioral and cognitive–behavioral therapists have advocated that the therapist and client develop a set of specific goals for evaluating improvement. If these goals are made clear near the beginning of therapy, then progress can be gauged more easily. We expect that as a result feelings of efficacy would be enhanced.

INTERNALIZATION OF HEALTH CARE ATTITUDES AND BELIEFS

In order for adherence to be maintained over a sustained period of time, it is necessary that patients internalize beliefs about the health care program that the practitioner and patient have worked out (Rodin & Janis, 1979). If internalization occurs, the health care behaviors become an integral part of the person's life and the attitudes and beliefs underlying the program are incorporated into his or her belief system. Once internalization occurs, external inducements for adhering to the program are no longer required; as a result, feelings of control may be further enhanced. Internalization is especially important to ensure that health care behaviors continue, if necessary, after the relationship with the health care practitioner is terminated or reduced in frequency.

In order to enhance maintenance of the changes brought about in treatment, practitioners should foster two types of cognitions (Cameron, 1978), each of which we hypothesize will promote feelings of control. First, patients should see themselves as having learned new coping skills for dealing with their health or psychological concerns, which cannot be taken away when contact with the professional is made less frequent or terminated. Second, patients should attribute the changes they have experienced to themselves as opposed to external factors (Rodin, 1978). For example, patients who have brought their hypertension under control should be encouraged to attribute the improvement to their own efforts to cope with the disorder (e.g., by making changes in one's life, including remembering to take medications, exercising, and changing dietary habits).

Through stress inoculation procedures discussed earlier, patients should be prepared to handle difficulties and setbacks that arise once treatment is terminated or made less frequent. For example, patients should be prepared to handle backsliding (Marlatt, 1978). If temporary failure to maintain the health changes is seen as evidence that all their health care gains are lost, then adherence will be threatened. However, if patients are taught to see backsliding as a signal to reexert control by reactivating the coping skills they have learned, then health care gains are likely to be maintained.

It is hypothesized that enhanced feelings of self-efficacy may be a key factor in promoting the internalization of health care changes. Fostering attributions about one's own efforts and skills may lead to greater feelings of self-efficacy. These feelings, in turn, may be necessary for maintenance of gains that have been achieved. In addition, people have been shown to be more likely to internalize attitudes and behaviors when external inducements are not present (e.g., Lepper, Greene, & Nisbett, 1973). We predict that patients' perceptions of external inducements for changes will be reduced when they have greater feelings of control in the health care interaction.

The Role of Information in the Practitioner–Patient Relationship

CONSEQUENCES OF SHARING INFORMATION WITH PATIENTS

Exchange of information is a major component of the health care relationship and may have a significant impact on patients' feelings of control. It has been well established that the communication process between clinicians and patients is frequently defective (e.g., Coyne & Widiger, 1978; Golden & Johnston, 1970; McIntosh, 1974; Skipper, Tagliacozzo, & Mauksch, 1964; Svarstad, 1976). Clinicians may often be reluctant to share information with their patients because they feel that it would confuse and worry them, increase fear and anxiety, and threaten health outcomes (Brody, 1980; Skipper *et al.*, 1964). However, it seems that telling patients about their condition does not lead to greater distress than keeping them uninformed (Brody, 1980; McIntosh, 1974; Skipper *et al.*, 1964). In fact, the uncertainty associated with not being informed may actually increase anxiety (McIntosh, 1974) and feelings of uncontrollability. The literature on predictability also indicates that this would be the case.

In contrast to the hesitancy of health care practitioners to share information, patients generally seem to desire to be informed about their condition and treatment (e.g., Houston & Pasanen, 1972; McIntosh, 1974; Suchman, 1972). Patients' requests for information can be met in different ways. If they are not answered in a straightforward way, feelings of control may be jeopardized because the individual's behavior (i.e., the request) does not produce the intended outcome (i.e., a satisfactory answer from the practitioner).

Better communication of information and instructions from practitioners to patients has been linked to greater adherence (e.g., Becker *et al.*, 1972; Hulka, Cassel, Kupper, & Burdette, 1976; Svarstad, 1976) and satisfaction (e.g., Freemon, Negrete, Davis, & Korsch, 1971; Houston & Pasanen, 1972; Svarstad, 1976). However, the beneficial effects of information have not been consistently demonstrated (e.g., Gordis, Markowitz, & Lilienfeld, 1969; Sackett, Haynes, Gibson, Hackett, Taylor, Roberts, & Johnson, 1975). This lack of consistency in the effects of information may arise because different types of information have differential consequences (Kirscht & Rosenstock, 1979). Whereas it has been shown that information about the sensations that are likely to be experienced in stressful medical procedures is beneficial, the same set of studies indicates that descriptive information about the procedures that are to be administered does not have positive effects (Johnson, 1975). In addition, although information fostering correct expectations and coping strategies has been demonstrated to lead to desirable consequences in unpleasant medical procedures, such as surgery (e.g., Egbert *et al.*, 1964; Johnson & Leventhal, 1974), information conveying correct expectancies without fostering coping techniques may not lead to enhanced results (e.g., Langer *et al.*, 1975).

INFORMATION AND FEELINGS OF CONTROL AND SELF-EFFICACY

We hypothesize that the beneficial impact of certain types of information (and not others) can be attributed to the extent to which the information increases patients' feelings of control and self-efficacy. Information that increases feelings of self-efficacy may have positive health-relevant consequences, whereas information that does not increase these feelings may not. Studies that failed to show gains resulting from greater information have typically increased general knowledge about the illness and its treatment without providing information about the specifics of implementing ways of coping with the situation; thus, feelings of efficacy were probably not raised.

On the other hand, stress inoculation procedures provide explicit information about how patients can deal with difficulties that arise in the course of illness and its treatment, as well as practice in doing so. Therefore, feelings of self-efficacy are likely to be raised. Some types of preparatory information are beneficial even when skills for coping are not explicitly taught. Such information is hypothesized to have a beneficial effect because it reassures patients that they will be able to cope and encourages them to develop their own ways of coping (Janis & Mann, 1982); thus, feelings of self-efficacy would probably be enhanced. For example, sensation information may have positive effects when it allows patients to plan in advance ways of dealing with the negative sensations. In contrast, being informed about procedures that will be administered to them may not lead to feelings of greater self-efficacy because such procedures are less under the patient's control. The relationship between different types of information, the development of coping skills, feelings of self-efficacy, and consequences for the individual is an area in which much research is needed.

The line of reasoning developed here indicates that information promoting the belief that one is able to deal successfully with illness and treatment in order to obtain positive health outcomes may have a beneficial impact on the health care transaction. We hypothesize that information should foster both the belief that a given course of action is effective, thus raising perceptions of the opportunity for control, and the skills for dealing with the illness and carrying out the treatment plan, thus raising feelings of self-efficacy.

Conclusion

Patients' feelings of control can be enhanced in many aspects of the professional–patient interaction. This greater perception of control is expected to improve the treatment relationship, health care behaviors, and actual health outcomes. However, certain conditions must be established before perceptions of greater opportunities for control are raised; for example, adequate information about how to exercise that control must be provided and feelings of responsibility must not be made too great. Most importantly, feelings of self-efficacy must be bolstered when perceptions of greater opportunities for control are raised.

Increasing feelings of control when the situation is actually not controllable may have detrimental effects in the long run (Janis & Rodin, 1979). In such a situation, the person may make futile attempts to exert control, leading eventually to learned helplessness with its accompanying negative behavioral, cognitive, motivational, and physiological reactions. In addition, trust in practitioner–patient relationships may be severely damaged. Most aspects of the health care situation are actually controllable if practitioners and settings extend to patients the opportunities for control. In the nursing home study by Langer and Rodin (1976), the facility was willing to extend to residents the opportunity for greater control. Thus, when feelings of self-efficacy were raised, the environment provided options for a greater exercise of control. In other situations, it may be necessary to change the environment to allow the opportunity for greater control before people's feelings of control are bolstered.

The hypotheses and proposals that have been set forth throughout this chapter are derived from the separate literatures on the construct of control and the health care relationship. Rarely has the role of control and self-efficacy in the practitioner–patient relationship been empirically investigated. Many exciting avenues of research are open in this area. In addition, the conditions that affect the desirability of greater perceptions of control and the precise ways in which these variables are related to one another need to be further investigated. Moreover, the distinction between the opportunity for control and self-efficacy, and especially disparities between them, need to be addressed in future research. Furthermore, distinctions between different types of information and their effects on feelings of control need to be studied more. The clinician–patient interaction provides an important arena in which to investigate these issues.

The enhancement of greater feelings of control in patients should have important benefits for health care professionals as well. Because patients may be more likely to adhere and have better health outcomes when these feelings are promoted, practitioners will feel more successful and be more satisfied with the health care relationship. The amount of control available in the health care relationship is not a zero-sum situation: Increasing feelings of control in patients does not have to diminish the professional's feelings of control. In fact, practitioners' feelings of control and efficacy may actually be enhanced because of better outcomes. Clinicians may be concerned that a relationship in which patients' feelings of control are bolstered may be too time-consuming. However, the additional time that may be needed initially to enhance feelings of control should be more than compensated for later on when the practitioner may not have to spend as much time dealing with patient demoralization, nonadherence, and dissatisfactions.

Recently, there has been a movement toward models of the practitioner–patient relationship in which patients are more active participants, responsibility and decision making are shared with the patient, and the power differential between practitioner and patient is diminished. However, these models do not rest upon a comprehensive theoretical framework but rather on a growing movement of consumer advocacy. The literature on the construct of control provides a theoretical foundation for a new model of practitioner–patient relationships. In addition, the construct of control, with its components of self-efficacy and opportunity for control, seems to have considerable explanatory power in integrating many of the findings pertaining to the practitioner–patient interaction. Finally, this theoretical foundation suggests many exciting avenues for research.

References

Abramson, L. Y., Seligman, M. E. P., & Teasdale, J. Learned helplessness in humans: Critique and reformulation. *Journal of Abnormal Psychology*, 1978, *87*, 49–74.

Averill, J. R. Personal control over aversive stimuli and its relationship to stress. *Psychological Bulletin*, 1973, *80*, 286–303.

Bandura, A. Self-efficacy: Toward a unifying theory of behavioral change. *Psychological Review*, 1977, *84*, 191–215.

Bandura, A. The self and mechanisms of agency. In J. Suls (Ed.), *Social psychological perspectives on the self*. Hillsdale, N.J.: Erlbaum, 1980.

Bandura, A., Adams, N. E., Hardy, A. B., & Howells, G. N. Tests of the generality of self-efficacy theory. *Cognitive Therapy and Research*, 1980, *4*, 39–66.

Barofsky, I. Compliance, adherence and the therapeutic alliance: Steps in the development of self-care. *Social Science and Medicine*, 1978, *12*, 369–376.

Becker, M. H., Drachman, R. H., & Kirscht, J. P. Predicting mothers' compliance with pediatric medical regimens. *Journal of Pediatrics*, 1972, *81*, 843–854.

Benarde, M. A., & Mayerson, E. W. Patient–physician negotiation. *Journal of the American Medical Association*, 1978, *239*, 1413–1415.

Bergin, A. E., & Lambert, M. J. The evaluation of therapeutic outcomes. In S. L. Garfield & A. E. Bergin (Eds.), *Handbook of psychotherapy and behavior change; An empirical analysis* (2nd ed.). New York: Wiley, 1978.

Bowers, K. S. Pain, anxiety, and perceived control. *Journal of Consulting and Clinical Psychology*, 1968, *32*, 596–602.

Brehm, J. W. *A theory of psychological reactance*. New York: Academic Press, 1966.

Brehm, S. *The application of social psychology to clinical practice.* Washington, D.C.: Hemisphere, 1976.

Brody, D. S. The patient's role in clinical decision-making. *Annals of Internal Medicine,* 1980, *93,* 718–722.

Cameron, R. The clinical implementation of behavior change techniques: A cognitively oriented conceptualization of therapeutic "compliance" and "resistance." In J. P. Foreyt & D. P. Rathjen (Eds.), *Cognitive behavior therapy: Research and application.* New York: Plenum, 1978.

Champlin, S. M., & Karoly, P. Role of contract negotiation in self-management of study time: A preliminary investigation. *Psychological Reports,* 1975, *37,* 724–726.

Coyne, J. C., & Widiger, T. A. Toward a participatory model of psychotherapy. *Professional Psychology,* 1978, *9,* 700–710.

Davis, H., Porter, J. W., Livingstone, J., Herrmann, T., MacFadden, L., & Levine, S. Pituitary–adrenal activity and leverpress shock escape behavior. *Physiological Psychology,* 1977, *5,* 280–284.

Deeds, S. G., Bernheimer, E., McCombs, N. J., McKenney, J. M., Richardson, D. W., & Fink, J. W. Patient behavior for blood pressure control: Guidelines for professionals. *Journal of the American Medical Association,* 1979, *241,* 2534–2537.

Drucker, E. Hidden values and health care. *Medical Care,* 1974, *12,* 266–273.

Duckro, P., Beal, D., & George, C. Research on the effects of disconfirmed client role expectations in psychotherapy: A critical review. *Psychological Bulletin,* 1979, *86,* 260–275.

Egbert, L. D., Battit, G. E., Welch, C. E., & Bartlett, M. K. Reduction of postoperative pain by encouragement and instruction of patients. *New England Journal of Medicine,* 1964, *270,* 825–827.

Eisenberg, J. M. Sociologic influences on decision-making by clinicians. *Annals of Internal Medicine,* 1979, *90,* 957–964.

Eisenthal, S., Emery, R., Lazare, A., & Udin, H. "Adherence" and the negotiated approach to patienthood. *Archives of General Psychiatry,* 1979, *36,* 393–398.

Eisenthal, S., & Lazare, A. Specificity of patients' requests in the initial interview. *Psychological Reports,* 1976, *38,* 739–748.

Francis, V., Korsch, B. M., & Morris, M. J. Gaps in doctor–patient communication: Patients' response to medical advice. *New England Journal of Medicine,* 1969, *280,* 535–540.

Frankenhaeuser, M. Sympathetic adrenomedullary activity, behavior and the psychosocial environment. In P. H. Venables & M. J. Christie (Eds.), *Research in psychophysiology.* New York: Wiley, 1975.

Freemon, B., Negrete, V. F., Davis, M., & Korsch, B. M. Gaps in doctor–patient communication: Doctor–patient interaction analysis. *Pediatric Research,* 1971, *5,* 298–311.

Gabrielsen, A. E., & Good, R. A. Chemical suppression of adaptive immunity. In F. J. Dixon, Jr., & J. H. Humphrey (Eds.), *Advances in immunology* (Vol. 6). New York: Academic Press, 1967.

Gatchel, R. J., & Proctor, J. D. Physiological correlates of learned helplessness in man. *Journal of Abnormal Psychology,* 1976, *85,* 27–34.

Geer, J. H., Davison, G. C., & Gatchel, R. J. Reduction of stress in humans through nonveridical perceived control of aversive stimulation. *Journal of Personality and Social Psychology,* 1970, *16,* 731–738.

Geer, J. H., & Maisel, E. Evaluating the effects of the prediction–control confound. *Journal of Personality and Social Psychology,* 1972, *23,* 314–319.

Geertsen, H. R., Gray, R. M., & Ward, J. R. Patient non-compliance within the context of seeking medical care for arthritis. *Journal of Chronic Disease,* 1973, *26,* 689–698.

Gisler, R. H. Stress and the hormonal regulation of the immune response in mice. *Psychotherapy and Psychosomatics,* 1974, *23,* 197–208.

Glass, D. C. *Behavior patterns, stress, and coronary disease.* Hillsdale, N.J.: Erlbaum, 1977.

Glass, D. C., & Singer, J. E. *Urban stress: Experiments on noise and social stressors.* New York: Academic Press, 1972.

Glass, D. C., Singer, J. E., Leonard, H. S., Krantz, D., Cohen, S., & Cummings, H. Perceived control of aversive stimulation and the reduction of stress responses. *Journal of Personality*, 1973, *41*, 577–595.

Golden, J. S., & Johnston, G. D. Problems of distortion in doctor–patient communications. *Psychiatry in Medicine*, 1970, *1*, 127–149.

Gordis, L., Markowitz, M., & Lilienfeld, A. M. Why patients don't follow medical advice: A study of children on long-term antistreptococcal prophylaxis. *Journal of Pediatrics*, 1969, *75*, 957–968.

Gordon, R. M. Effects of volunteering and responsibility on the perceived value and effectiveness of a clinical treatment. *Journal of Consulting and Clinical Psychology*, 1976, *44*, 799–801.

Hanson, J. D., Larson, M. E., & Snowdon, C. T. The effects of control over high intensity noise on plasma cortisol levels in rhesus monkeys. *Behavioral Biology*, 1976, *16*, 333–340.

Hayes-Bautista, D. E. Modifying the treatment: Patient compliance, patient control and medical care. *Social Science and Medicine*, 1976, *10*, 233–238.

Haynes, R. B. A critical review of the "determinants" of patient compliance with therapeutic regimens. In D. L. Sackett & R. B. Haynes (Eds.), *Compliance with therapeutic regimens*. Baltimore: John Hopkins Press, 1976.

Hefferin, E. A. Health goal setting: Patient–nurse collaboration at Veterans Administration facilities. *Military Medicine*, 1979, *144*, 814–822.

Heitler, J. B. Preparatory techniques in initiating expressive psychotherapy with lower-class unsophisticated patients. *Psychological Bulletin*, 1976, *83*, 339–352.

Hiroto, D. S., & Seligman, M. E. P. Generality of learned helplessness in man. *Journal of Personality and Social Psychology*, 1975, *31*, 311–327.

Hoehn-Saric, R., Frank, J. D., Imber, S. D., Nash, E. H., Stone, A. R., & Battle, C. C. Systematic preparation of patients for psychotherapy: I. Effects on therapy behavior and outcome. *Journal of Psychiatric Research*, 1964, *2*, 267–281.

Houston, B. K. Control over stress, locus of control, and response to stress. *Journal of Personality and Social Psychology*, 1972, *21*, 249–255.

Houston, C. S., & Pasanen, W. E. Patients' perceptions of hospital care. *Hospitals*, 1972, *46*, 70–74.

Hoyt, M. F., & Janis, I. L. Increasing adherence to a stressful decision via the balance-sheet procedure: A field experiment on attendance at an exercise class. In I. L. Janis (Ed.), *Counseling on personal decisions: Theory and research on short-term helping relationships*. New Haven, Conn.: Yale Univ. Press, 1982.

Hulka, B. S., Cassel, J. C., Kupper, L. L., & Burdette, J. A. Communication, compliance, and concordance between physicians and patients with prescribed medications. *American Journal of Public Health*, 1976, *66*, 847–853.

Janis, I. L., & Mann, L. *Decision making: A psychological analysis of conflict, choice, and commitment*. New York: Free Press, 1977.

Janis, I. L., & Mann, L. A theoretical framework for decision counseling. In I. L. Janis (Ed.), *Counseling on personal decisions: Theory and research on short-term helping relationships*. New Haven, Conn.: Yale Univ. Press, 1982.

Janis, I. L., & Rodin, J. Attribution, control, and decision making: Social psychology and health care. In G. C. Stone, F. Cohen, & N. E. Adler (Eds.), *Health psychology: A handbook*. San Francisco: Jossey-Bass, 1979.

Johnson, J. E. Stress reduction through sensation information. In I. G. Sarason & C. D. Spielberger (Eds.), *Stress and anxiety* (Vol. 2). New York: Wiley, 1975.

Johnson, J. E., & Leventhal, H. Effects of accurate expectations and behavioral instructions on reactions during a noxious medical examination. *Journal of Personality and Social Psychology*, 1974, *29*, 710–718.

Kadushin, C. *Why people go to psychiatrists*. New York: Atherton, 1969.

Kanfer, F. H., & Grimm, L. G. Freedom of choice and behavioral change. *Journal of Consulting and Clinical Psychology*, 1978, *46*, 873–878.

Kanfer, F. H., & Seidner, M. L. Self-control: Factors enhancing tolerance of noxious stimulation. *Journal of Personality and Social Psychology*, 1973, *25*, 381–389.

Kasl, S. V. Issues in patient adherence to health care regimens. *Journal of Human Stress*, 1975, *1*, 5–17.

Katz, J. L., Weiner, H., Gallagher, T. F., & Hellman, L. Stress, distress, and ego defenses: Psychoendocrine response to impending breast tumor biopsy. *Archives of General Psychiatry*, 1970, *23*, 131–142.

Kirscht, J. P., & Rosenstock, I. M. Patient adherence to antihypertensive medical regimens. *Journal of Community Health*, 1977, *3*, 115–124.

Kirscht, J. P., & Rosenstock, I. M. Patients' problems in following recommendations of health experts. In G. C. Stone, F. Cohen, & N. E. Adler (Eds.), *Health psychology: A handbook*. San Francisco: Jossey-Bass, 1979.

Kleinman, A., Eisenberg, L., & Good, B. Culture, illness, and care: Clinical lessons from anthropologic and cross-cultural research. *Annals of Internal Medicine*, 1978, *88*, 251–258.

Klemp, G. O., & Rodin, J. Effects of uncertainty, delay, and focus of attention on reactions to an aversive situation. *Journal of Experimental Social Psychology*, 1976, *12*, 416–421.

Korsch, B. M., Gozzi, E. K., & Francis, V. Gaps in doctor–patient communication: I. Doctor–patient interaction and patient satisfaction. *Pediatrics*, 1968, *42*, 855–871.

Langer, E. J., Janis, I. L., & Wolfer, J. A. Reduction of psychological stress in surgical patients. *Journal of Experimental Social Psychology*, 1975, *11*, 155–165.

Langer, E. J., & Rodin, J. The effects of choice and enhanced personal responsibility for the aged: A field experiment in an institutional setting. *Journal of Personality and Social Psychology*, 1976, *34*, 191–198.

Lazare, A., Eisenthal, S., & Wasserman, L. The customer approach to patienthood: Attending to patient requests in a walk-in clinic. *Archives of General Psychiatry*, 1975, *32*, 553–558.

Lepper, M. R., Greene, D., & Nisbett, R. E. Undermining children's intrinsic interest with extrinsic reward: A test of the over-justification hypothesis. *Journal of Personality and Social Psychology*, 1973, *28*, 129–137.

Leventhal, H., Watts, J. C., & Pagano, F. Effects of fear and instructions on how to cope with danger. *Journal of Personality and Social Psychology*, 1967, *6*, 313–321.

Levine, C. Dialysis or transplant: Values and choices. *Hastings Center Report*, 1978, *8*, 8–10.

Levine, S., & Coover, G. D. Environmental control of suppression of the pituitary–adrenal system. *Physiology and Behavior*, 1976, *17*, 35–37.

Levinson, D. J., Merrifield, J., & Berg, K. Becoming a patient. *Archives of General Psychiatry*, 1967, *17*, 385–406.

Liem, G. R. Performance and satisfaction as affected by personal control over salient decisions. *Journal of Personality and Social Psychology*, 1975, *31*, 232–240.

Lundberg, U., & Frankenhaeuser, M. Psychophysiological reactions to noise as modified by personal control over noise intensity. *Biological Psychology*, 1978, *6*, 51–59.

Marlatt, G. A. Craving for alcohol, loss of control, and relapse: A cognitive–behavioral analysis. In P. E. Nathan, G. A. Marlatt, & T. Loberg (Eds.), *Alcoholism: New directions in behavioral research and treatment*. New York: Plenum, 1978.

Matthews, D., & Hingson, R. Improving patient compliance: A guide for physicians. *Medical Clinics of North America*, 1977, *61*, 879–889.

McIntosh, J. Processes of communication, information seeking and control associated with cancer: A selective review of the literature. *Social Science and Medicine*, 1974, *8*, 167–187.

McNeil, B. J., & Pauker, S. G. The patient's role in assessing the value of diagnostic tests. *Radiology*, 1979, *132*, 605–610.

Meichenbaum, D. *Cognitive-behavior modification: An integrative approach*. New York: Plenum, 1977.

Miller, S. M. Why having control reduces stress: If I can stop the roller coaster, I don't want to get off. In J. Garber & M. E. P. Seligman (Eds.), *Human helplessness: Theory and applications*. New York: Academic Press, 1980.

Morrison, J. K. A consumer-oriented approach to psychotherapy. *Psychotherapy: Theory, Research and Practice*, 1979, *16*, 381–384.

Northey, W. T. Studies on the interrelationship of cold environment, immunity and resistance to infection: I. Qualitative and quantitative studies on the immune response. *Journal of Immunology*, 1965, *94*, 649–657.

Parsons, T. *The social system*. New York: Free Press, 1951.

Pennebaker, J. W., Burnam, M. A., Schaeffer, M. A., & Harper, D. C. Lack of control as a determinant of perceived physical symptoms. *Journal of Personality and Social Psychology*, 1977, *35*, 167–174.

Perlmuter, L. C., & Monty, R. A. The importance of perceived control: Fact or fantasy? *American Scientist*, 1977, *65*, 759–765.

Pranulis, M. F., Dabbs, J. M., & Johnson, J. E. General anesthesia and the patient's attempts at control. *Social Behavior and Personality*, 1975, *3*, 49–54.

Rodin, J. Cognitive behavior therapy for obesity. In D. Meichenbaum (Ed.), *Cognitive behavior therapy: Applications and issues*. New York: BMA Audio Cassette Publications, 1978.

Rodin, J. Behavioral medicine: Beneficial effects of self-control training in aging. *Revue Internationale de Psychologie Appliquee*, in press.

Rodin, J., & Janis, I. L. The social power of health-care practitioners as agents of change. *Journal of Social Issues*, 1979, *35*(1), 60–81.

Rodin, J., & Langer, E. J. Long-term effects of a control-relevant intervention with the institutionalized aged. *Journal of Personality and Social Psychology*, 1977, *35*, 897–902.

Rodin, J., Rennert, K., & Solomon, S. K. Intrinsic motivation for control: Fact or fiction. In A. Baum & J. E. Singer (Eds.), *Advances in environmental psychology* (Vol. 2). Hillsdale, N.J.: Erlbaum, 1980.

Rotter, J. B. Generalized expectancies for internal versus external control of reinforcement. *Psychological Monographs*, 1966, *80*(1, Whole No. 609).

Sachar, E. J. Neuroendocrine abnormalities in depressive illness. In E. J. Sachar (Ed.), *Topics in psychoendocrinology*. New York: Grune & Stratton, 1975.

Sackett, D. L., Haynes, R. B., Gibson, E. S., Hackett, B. C., Taylor, D. W., Roberts, R. S., & Johnson, A. L. Randomised clinical trial of strategies for improving medication compliance in primary hypertension. *Lancet*, 1975, *1*, 1205–1207.

St. Rose, J. E. M., & Sabiston, B. H. Effect of cold exposure on the immunologic response of rabbits to human serum albumin. *Journal of Immunology*, 1971, *107*, 339–343.

Schmale, A., & Iker, H. The psychological setting of uterine cervical cancer. *Annals of the New York Academy of Sciences*, 1966, *125*, 807–813.

Schulman, B. A. Active patient orientation and outcomes in hypertensive treatment: Application of a socio-organizational perspective. *Medical Care*, 1979, *17*, 267–280.

Schulz, R., & Hanusa, B. H. Experimental social gerontology: A social psychological perspective. *Journal of Social Issues*, 1980, *36*(2), 30–46.

Seligman, M. E. P. *Helplessness: On depression, development, and death*. San Francisco: Freeman, 1975.

Skipper, J. K., Jr., Tagliacozzo, D. L., & Mauksch, H. O. Some possible consequences of limited communication between patients and hospital functionaries. *Journal of Health and Human Behavior*, 1964, *5*, 34–39.

Sloane, R. B., Cristol, A. H., Pepernik, M. C., & Staples, F. R. Role preparation and expectation of improvement in psychotherapy. *Journal of Nervous and Mental Disease*, 1970, *150*, 18–26.

Solomon, G. F. Stress and antibody response in rats. *International Archives of Allergy and Applied Immunology*, 1969, *35*, 97–104.

Staub, E., Tursky, B., & Schwartz, G. E. Self-control and predictability: Their effects on reactions to aversive stimulation. *Journal of Personality and Social Psychology*, 1971, *18*, 157–162.

Stimson, G. V. Obeying doctor's orders: A view from the other side. *Social Science and Medicine*, 1974, *8*, 97–104.

Stone, G. C. Patient compliance and the role of the expert. *Journal of Social Issues*, 1979, *35*(1), 34–59.

Stotland, E., & Blumenthal, A. L. The reduction of anxiety as a result of the expectation of making a choice. *Canadian Journal of Psychology*, 1964, *18*, 139–145.

Strupp, H. H., & Bloxom, A. L. Preparing lower-class patients for group psychotherapy: Development and evaluation of a role-induction film. *Journal of Consulting and Clinical Psychology*, 1973, *41*, 373–384.

Suchman, E. A. Stages of illness and medical care. In E. G. Jaco (Ed.), *Patients, physicians and illness: A sourcebook in behavioral science and health* (2nd ed.). New York: Free Press, 1972.

Svarstad, B. L. Physician–patient communication and patient conformity with medical advice. In D. Mechanic (Ed.), *The growth of bureaucratic medicine: An inquiry into the dynamics of patient behavior and the organization of medical care*. New York: Wiley, 1976.

Szasz, T. S., & Hollender, M. H. A contribution to the philosophy of medicine: The basic models of the doctor–patient relationship. *Archives of Internal Medicine*, 1956, *97*, 585–592.

Tagliacozzo, D. L., & Mauksch, H. O. The patient's view of the patient's role. In E. G. Jaco (Ed.), *Patients, physicians and illness: A sourcebook in behavioral science and health* (2nd ed.). New York: Free Press, 1972.

Taylor, S. E. Hospital patient behavior: Reactance, helplessness, or control? *Journal of Social Issues*, 1979, *35*(1), 156–184.

Taylor, S. E., & Levin, S. *The psychological impact of breast cancer: Theory and research*. San Francisco: West Coast Cancer Foundation, 1976.

Thompson, S. C. Will it hurt less if I can control it? A complex answer to a simple question. *Psychological Bulletin*, 1981, *90*, 89–101.

Timiras, P. S. *Developmental physiology and aging*. New York: Macmillan, 1972.

Ursin, H., Baade, E., & Levine, S. *Psychobiology of stress*. New York: Academic Press, 1978.

Weiss, J. M. Effects of coping responses on stress. *Journal of Comparative and Physiological Psychology*, 1968, *65*, 251–260.

Weiss, J. M. Somatic effects of predictable and unpredictable shock. *Psychosomatic Medicine*, 1970, *32*, 397–408.

Weiss, J. M. Effects of coping behavior with and without a feedback signal on stress pathology in rats. *Journal of Comparative and Physiological Psychology*, 1971, *77*, 22–30.

Wortman, C. B., & Brehm, J. W. Responses to uncontrollable outcomes: An integration of reactance theory and the learned helplessness model. In L. Berkowitz (Ed.), *Advances in experimental social psychology* (Vol. 8). New York: Academic Press, 1975.

Ziemelis, A. Effects of client preference and expectancy upon the initial interview. *Journal of Counseling Psychology*, 1974, *21*, 23–30.

chapter 9

Client Commitment to the Helping Relationship

JEANNE PARR LEMKAU
FRED B. BRYANT
PHILIP BRICKMAN

Introduction

Prospective clients approach psychotherapy with ambivalence. Only when the pain, embarrassment, or incapacitation of their symptoms is great enough to overshadow their apprehensions do they turn to a professional helper. The anxiety inherent in self-disclosure, the discomfort engendered by the intimacy and dependency of the therapy situation, and the escalating cost of treatment naturally call for hesitation, and the client's anticipation of relief must be strong to counter these factors.

But will clients return for a second or third appointment after the initial visit? And if they do, will they "go through the motions" of therapy, or will attendance represent a deepening involvement in a therapeutic process? Will participation in psychotherapy eventually result in the beneficial relief of symptoms, or will clients simply be caught in an unproductive relationship, as sometimes evolves between helper and client (Bergin & Lambert, 1978)?

The construct of commitment, drawn from the literature in sociology (Becker, 1960) and social psychology (Festinger, 1957; Gerard, Connolley, & Wilhelmy, 1974; Brickman, Note 1) is eminently suited for considering such questions. Whether we consider the choice of persisting in therapy or

187

dropping out, actively investing oneself in a helping relationship or passively resisting help, we are dealing with the issue of commitment, or the development and maintenance of a consistent line of activity over time.

What do we mean when we say that a client is committed to a helping relationship? Inherent in such a statement is an appreciation for the time-binding capacity of humans—the anticipation of a better future motivating persistence in the current endeavor, in this case, perseverance in therapy according to the model of a particular helper. Commitment sets limits on the situational specifity of behavior (Brickman, Note 1). If not for the time-binding nature of commitment, each visit to the therapist and each inter-change within the session would entail a new decision about whether to return or cooperate in treatment. Commitment also implies the experience of costs as well as rewards, thus distinguishing it from the complacent pursuit of a behavioral course involving no costs. In fact, persistence in therapy would be no issue were the enterprise a purely pleasurable one where symptom relief and personal growth were achieved without effort or anxiety. Commitment thus encompasses the choice and maintenance of a behavioral course about which one is initially ambivalent.

Elements of Commitment

In Brickman's conception (Note 1), commitment entails three elements: (*a*) positive aspects of an individual's experience, (*b*) negative aspects of that experience, and (*c*) a bond between these two that serves to impel the behavioral course. Commitment exists when people make a choice (an act that specifies a positive element) despite costs (a negative element) that they recognize and accept as entailed by that choice (establishing a bond between the positive and the negative elements).

The elements in this definition of commitment are drawn from several traditions. Becker (1960) represents the earliest effort within sociology to define the concept; according to Becker, commitments arise when, by making a "side bet," a person links extraneous interests with a consistent line of activity. With the accumulation of side bets, the consequences of incon-sistency become so expensive that "inconsistency . . . is no longer a feasible alternative [p. 35]." If individuals remain in an aversive situation, despite opportunities to leave, it is because they have implicitly made something they value a good deal (e.g., their self-respect, or career advancement) contingent upon remaining in that situation. Thus, the aspiring analyst who has invested thousands of dollars in a personal analysis, the completion of which has become a condition for entering the fold of the psychoanalytic elite, is likely to be zealously committed to the final unraveling of his Oedipus complex. In this as in all cases, an understanding of this man's commitments entails "an analysis of the system of values or . . . valuables with which bets can be made in the world he [or she] lives in [Becker, 1960, p. 39]." For Becker, side bets and consistent activity are in principle distinguishable, thus avoiding the tautological use of the commitment construct.

The research on dissonance and self-perception calls attention to a complementary process by suggesting that people attach greater value to goals when they see themselves as incurring costs and making sacrifices in their pursuit. From the dissonance theory perspective, consistency between or among cognitions is viewed as pleasurable, whereas inconsistency is seen as dissonant and unpleasant, impelling the person to change cognitions and/or behavior in the direction of greater consonance (Gerard *et al.*, 1974). The man who has voluntarily invested in personal analysis would experience dissonance at the thought of the process being a useless one; dissonance theorists would emphasize the unique constellation of cognitions brought into relationship with each other in the context of the helping situation, and would understand his persistence in terms of dissonance reduction.

In another social-psychological analysis of commitment, Kiesler (1971) suggests that once people take responsibility for having chosen a behavioral course, they feel compelled to explain any change in behavior to others, or at least to themselves. Since people wish to avoid such explanations and the concomitant negative evaluations of self, their behavior becomes more resistant to change.

In this chapter, we apply the construct of commitment to achieve a better understanding of the pursuit of psychotherapy. In the following section, traditional descriptions of stages of psychotherapeutic involvement are presented and reframed as stages of commitment to the helping relationship. Subsequently, research on variables related to dropout from psychotherapy is discussed and related to commitment theory. Then we consider approaches to inducing and maintaining commitment, drawn from the literature in social psychology, and apply these to psychotherapy. Finally, we summarize and discuss briefly the clinical and research implications of a commitment perspective.

Traditional and Alternative Views of Perseverance in Therapy

From the psychoanalytic tradition springs the most detailed account of the course of the therapeutic relationship, unrivaled in regard to either the specification of stages in therapy or the theoretical import with which they are imbued. In their focus on the nature of the client–helper relationship as it changes over time, psychoanalysts have come remarkably close to a commitment analysis of therapy stages. Fine (1973) describes the main stages of psychoanalysis as those of "establishing a relationship, having an analytic honeymoon, experiencing a first treatment crisis, deepening of therapy, working through (usually the longest period) and termination [p. 20]." Similarly, we see commitment to a helping relationship as initially involving strong positive attraction to the therapeutic endeavor, followed by several phases of ambivalence and resolution of the contradictory feelings aroused by the therapy situation. Our discussion will demonstrate the marked similarity between stages in psychoanalysis and stages of commitment to any behavioral course (Brickman, Note 1).

STAGES IN PSYCHOANALYSIS

In his eloquent treatise on modern psychoanalytic technique and practice, Greenson (1967) described characteristic phases of treatment, specifying the role of both helper and client in facilitating or impeding transitions through these phases. Greenson's discussion is replete with references to "polarities," "dialectic" processes, and paradoxical demands for the helper to alternatively foster "two opposing relationships between analyst and patient [p. 379]," one of indulgence and one of frustration, in order "to facilitate the growth of the transference neurosis as well as the working alliance . . . [which are] of equal importance for the development of the optimal analytic situation [p. 396]." Focusing on the client's contribution to the therapeutic dyad, Greenson argues that the client must bring to the helping relationship the experience of pain as well as the anticipation of pleasure. Since negative feelings about analytic treatment are inevitable, neurotic suffering on the part of the client is essential, since "only such a person will be willing *to try* to enter and work in the analytic situation [p. 360]."

The first stage in the analytic relationship involves establishing a working alliance between the patient and analyst that enables them to work purposefully together in the analytic situation (p. 192). The helper's nurturing of this working alliance takes the form of being relatively accessible, warm, and self-disclosing early in treatment and only retreating to a stance of greater distance and deprivation once a sufficient alliance has been formed, a psychoanalytic example of the "low-ball" approach to inducing commitment (Cialdini, Cacioppo, Bassett, & Miller, 1978). With a working alliance established, the patient attends therapy, cooperates in attemping to free associate and confront resistances, and conforms to other expectations of this model. In establishing this alliance the helper both implicitly and explicitly presents a psychoanalytic world view that encompasses both the the client's symptoms and anticipated relief, and the client either tentatively accepts this model or at least willingly suspends judgment.

Ideally, client resistances emerge as a major aspect of the therapeutic relationship only after a working alliance is established. The working alliance provides the helper with necessary leverage to confront the client's resistances, that is, "all the forces within the patient which oppose the procedures and processes of psychoanalytic work [Greenson, 1967, p. 35]," or, in commitment terms, all the negative elements inherent in the therapy experience. The helper interprets the client's hesitation within the psychoanalytic framework as defensively functioning to shield the client from more painful levels of awareness, and carefully balances support and confrontation, lest "the deprivation and frustration of the analytic situation exceed the patient's ability to withstand such stress [p. 377]."

It is through the analysis of resistances that the "transference neurosis" emerges. For the client, a gamut of feelings from attraction to hostility toward the therapist emerge, as positive transference precedes and intermingles with negative transference. The helper interprets all expressions of feeling by the client toward the helper as distortion of reality based on the client's early relationships with parental figures. To the extent that the client accepts such a perspective, commitment to the *real* relationship between client and helper goes unquestioned and perseverance in therapy, to unravel to distortions of transference, is enhanced.

The heart of psychoanalysis is in the "working through" of the transference, a lengthy phase that involves the "repetitive, progressive, and elaborate exploration of the resistances which prevent an insight from leading to change [p. 42]." Continued contemplation of the nature of the psychoanalytic relationship is encouraged, but always as a means of understanding the client's problems. By working through the transference, the client translates insights about past relationships, as experienced in the therapeutic dyad, into new attitudes and behaviors. Within the psychoanalytic framework, as long as the helper is successful in fostering and maintaining the client's psychoanalytic world view, the client can only view leaving therapy before such working through as resistance, and perseverence in treatment becomes the only face-saving course.

Termination is the natural culmination of all of these stages and is considered premature if all stages have not been experienced. The client's desire to terminate, especially early in treatment, would generally be viewed as resistance since "intense and prolonged hateful reactions toward the analyst should emerge and be analyzed before one should think of terminating [p. 235]." Ideally, termination of treatment is contingent upon the helper's judgment that all neurotic material has been worked through, and on the client's total acceptance of the meaning of both positive and negative aspects of the therapy experience in psychoanalytic terms.

BRICKMAN'S STAGES OF COMMITMENT

Brickman (Note 1) proposed that the negative elements important to commitment change over time and that, as a consequence, commitments characteristically pass through several stages. The first stage is an exploring or tentative one that parallels the establishment of a working alliance in Greenson's (1967) discussion of psychoanalysis. In Stage I commitment, no negative aspects of therapy are especially salient and the pain of symptoms and hope for relief are sufficiently intense to impel the client to become involved in a helping relationship. The surge of relief experienced early in treatment as a function of newfound social support enhances the positive aura of this phase.

The second commitment stage follows the initial honeymoon of commitment, as the emotional and financial costs of treatment become more salient with amelioration of the client's acute distress. This period is one of testing or challenging, in which the client faces obstacles to the pursuit of therapy and begins to question the value of further involvement. Whether the difficulties confronted involve financial sacrifices or painful emotions, the ambivalence of this phase can readily be seen as parallel to the experience of resistance in the psychoanalytic framework.

If the client is to persist in therapy beyond the ambivalence of Stage II, the positive rewards from therapy must be perceived as sufficiently large, important, and accessible to warrant the costs entailed in their pursuit. For example, a client may decide that the anxiety aroused by self-disclosing the details of her personal problems is "worth it" as she experiences the nonjudgmental response of the helper and accepts the helper's word that such anxiety is a necessary part of getting better. Thus, a resolution of ambivalence is the essence of Stage III commitment, which tends to be passionate and intense, reminiscent of positive transference in psychoanalysis.

Brickman postulates a subsequent stage, parallel to negative transference in psychoanalysis, in which the client recognizes problems with the enthusiasm of Stage III. Boredom is often characteristic of this phase, and disinterest may be a real threat to persistence. This is followed by a final stage in which a new resolution of the positive and negative elements experienced in the therapy relationship is achieved (Stage V), and a sense of completion and fulfillment predominates. Just as in the psychoanalytic example where positive and negative tranference intermingle and are worked through, here again we have a fluctuation between the recognition of negative and positive elements of the experience and the cognitive reorganization that fosters persistence in the face of ambivalence.

Eidelson's (1980) work on the development of dyadic relationships suggests that the positive and negative elements most critical for understanding the development of client commitment to the helping relationship may be conflicting motivations for affiliation and independence. He sees relationships as developing positively at first with the satisfaction of affiliative needs, followed by a period of decreasing satisfaction as the client experiences restricted independence. A subsequent phase of evaluation and internalization entails the resolution of positive and negative feelings. Within this model, a client's commitment to the therapeutic relationship at a given point in time is seen as the result of the interaction of affiliative rewards and restrictive costs, and the individual client's sensitivities to these outcomes. For commitment to the relationship to continue in the face of the restrictive costs, the client must employ "a new frame of reference ... which includes the particular relationship as a 'given' in the individual's social environment [Eidelson, 1980, p. 461]." One consequence of this new level of commitment is seen as a decrease in tension and ambivalence as the client reduces dissonance by deemphasizing the limitations and restrictions entailed by the relationship.

Eidelson's affiliation–independence model supplements the psychoanalytic example by providing another description of the interplay of positive and negative elements embodied within the commitment framework. Clearly, the phenomena psychoanalysts have described in terms of *working alliance*, *resistance*, *transference*, and *working through* may be acknowledged within the broader commitment context, without being accepted as proof of the validity of the psychoanalytic perspective. The commitment framework emphasizes the processes entailed in persistence in any behavioral course, without restricting the nature of positive and negative elements to those postulated within a particular theoretical domain.

COMMITMENT TO A WORLD VIEW

The role of the helper in fostering client commitment to psychotherapy is crucial. Specifically, to enhance persistence in treatment the helper must offer the client an interpretation of experience (or world view) that conceptually integrates the rewards and costs clients experience and anticipate within the helping relationship, and delineates the essential role of the helper–client dyad in achieving the client's goals. For example, the psychoanalyst may suggest to a client struggling with the tensions of the therapeutic situation that such obvious unresolved ambivalence toward parental figures can only be overcome via continued analysis with an expert who can recognize and interpret resistance. A Rogerian therapist, on the other hand, working within a belief system that emphasizes the role of the helper's unconditional positive regard for the client, may suggest to a client that self-acceptance and symptom relief can only be realized through self-disclosure within the context of a nonjudgmental therapeutic relationship.

We believe that for persistence in treatment the particular content of the world view is incidental, whereas what is critical is that a view is communicated whose content and manner of presentation are maximally acceptable to a particular client. Although a shared world view between helper and client has been emphasized as critical for psychotherapeutic gain (Frank, 1974; Torrey, 1972), here we emphasize its role in fostering perseverance in the therapeutic process.

Dropping Out of Treatment

To demonstrate the utility of our approach, we consider the literature on dropping out of treatment in terms of the commitment model. If Brickman's (Note 1) concept of commitment is fruitful in this regard then it should be possible to translate the variables identified as predictive of dropout into the terms of the model (as is, in fact, the case). The commitment concept provides a framework for integrating intrapsychic, relationship, and environmental factors usually discussed in relative isolation from each other. Furthermore, by encompassing both personal and situational factors, this framework may help therapists to avoid the "fundamental attributional error" (Ross, 1977) of overemphasizing personal factors and "blaming the victim" for an aborted therapy relationship.

Before pursuing the relationship between commitment processes and dropout, a caution is in order. In general, clients are considered dropouts if they fail to continue in therapy as long as the helper or researcher deems satisfactory, whereas from the clients' perspective one or two sessions may suffice. Several researchers have noted marked symptomatic relief in less than five sessions (Rosenthal & Frank, 1958; Uhlenhuth & Duncan, 1968) and even from a single session (Frank, 1963; Smith & Glass, 1977), findings consistent with the experiences of clinicians who treat clients under acute situational stress. Just one or two visits can also have a powerful impact on a client who imbues therapy seeking with special symbolic significance. For example, one of the authors (JPL) had a client suffering from a chronic "workaholic" life-style who attended only four sessions before dropping out. In a serendipitous social encounter several months later, the client reported that therapy had been extremely helpful because in the act of coming she realized that she could take time for herself. Although her helper saw her as a dropout, she was, in fact, a satisfied consumer, off on a European vacation that she thought was facilitated by her brief sojourn in therapy. Research on dropout could have a different flavor entirely were the perspective that of consumers rather than purveyors of therapy. Thus, in considering this literature one should be careful to avoid the assumption that dropout and therapeutic failure are synonymous.

Baekeland and Lundwall (1975) have critically reviewed the research on psychiatric patients dropping out of treatment from a variety of inpatient and outpatient facilities. Implicated in dropout were 15 variables falling into three general categories: (1) *characteristics of clients* (age, sex, socioeconomic status, social isolation, social instability, symptom level, motivation, psychological-mindedness, behavioral and/or perceptual dependence, and specific symptoms such as aggressiveness, sociopathy, and drug dependence), (2) *characteristics of helpers* (therapist attitudes and behaviors and discrepant treatment expectations of helper and client), and (3) *characteristics of the environmental context* of therapy (family pathology, attitudes, and behavior).

Some of the variables related to dropout directly contribute positive and/or negative elements to the therapeutic endeavor. Others contribute to perserverance or dropout by facilitating conceptual bonding of positive and negative elements in the therapy experience. Each of these will be discussed in turn, with references to the literature as reviewed and summarized by Baekeland and Lundwall.

CONTRIBUTION OF POSITIVE AND NEGATIVE ELEMENTS

Variables related to dropout contribute positive and negative elements to the cost–benefit analysis in which every client engages in the pursuit of psychotherapy. For example, some clients may be more sensitive than others to the positive elements of a warm, supportive relationship with a helper. More socially isolated individuals, prone to drop out, have difficulties forming relationships in the first place, they may therefore be either less enticed by the benefits of a therapy relationship or less able to handle a supportive relationships in the first place; they may therefore be either less enticed by the anxiety, who tend to persevere, may represent cases in which the positive benefits of a supportive therapy relationship are especially salient. Finally, aggressive, drug-dependent, and/or sociopathic clients may so disturb their helpers as to inhibit whatever investment of time, energy, and empathetic support they might otherwise provide, an example of how client and helper characteristics may jointly determine the "positives" available to the client from participation in therapy.

Since characteristics of helpers directly affect the quality of care offered to clients, it is hardly surprising that therapist ethnocentrism, boredom, and dislike of clients have been implicated in dropout, or that therapists who give poor instructions, cancel appointments, or do not support judicious use of medicine as an adjunct to therapy fail to hold clients.

The environmental context in which therapy takes place also contributes to clients' decisions about disengaging from therapy. When a person has a strong commitment to a pathological family system, the threat of its disruption or the opposition of important family members impedes compliance with therapeutic instruction (Schultz, 1980) and may actually impel the client out of treatment (Baekeland & Lundwall, 1975). Attesting to the importance of establishing side bets in the family arena is the extensive family systems literature, replete with methods for challenging clients' commitments to pathological family systems.

CONTRIBUTIONS TO BONDING PROCESSES

Many of the variables related to dropout may affect the bonding process in the commitment model: the process by which the positive and negative elements of therapy, experienced or anticipated at any point in time, are conceptually integrated and the role of the helper–client dyad in achieving a better future is defined. Client characteristics may be related to bonding difficulties. For example, sociopaths are notoriously difficult to hold in treatment. Their impulsive terminations may be understood as behavioral manifestations of their difficulties in forming conceptual bonds between the requirements of the current situation (following the rules of treatment) and their long-term goals (keeping out of trouble in the future). In addition, the sociopath lacks the anxiety that would enhance susceptibility to whatever conceptual framework the helper has to offer.

Characteristics of the therapist may either enhance or detract from the client's acceptance of the helper's ideas. The fact that more likable and less aloof therapists hold clients better may reflect the greater credibility of communicators who are perceived as attractive and trustworthy (Zimbardo, Ebbesen, & Maslach, 1977). Clients may well be more receptive to inter- pretations about the inevitable ups and downs of the therapy experience when these are offered by helpers they like and whom they believe to be interested in their care.

The contribution to dropout of discrepant expectations of client and helper may also be understood in terms of bonding processes. For example, clients from lower socioeconomic groups who expect symptom relief and medication have high dropout rates from clinics offering psychoanalytically oriented psychotherapy emphasizing insight and self-exploration of a long-term nature. Unless special attention is given to winning over such clients, it is unlikely that they are going to be convinced that their helpers' perspective is relevant to their concerns in therapy. In a similar vein, the fact that less psychologically minded clients are less likely to persevere in treatment makes sense given the psychological world views promulgated by helpers in the mental health industry.

What constitutes a major concern requiring conceptual bonding for a particular client to persevere in treatment varies from one person to the next. A staunch Protestant who believes that good things come only through suffering and self-denial may have no difficulty with the expense of therapy or an hour's drive to the therapist's office for lengthy insight-oriented therapy. The same individual may bolt if a suggestion is made to bring her family to treatment, since she believes she should not "burden" her husband and children when "the only problem is my nerves." Helper–client matching may forestall dropout by enhancing the likelihood that clients will be offered conceptual frameworks in therapy that they find relevant to their pre- dominant concerns.

Social-Psychological Approaches to Commitment

Having demonstrated the utility of the commitment framework in our consideration of the stages of psychotherapy and the research on psychotherapy dropout, we turn now to the social-psychological literature and review methods for inducing initial commitment and for maintaining commitment to the pursuit of psychotherapy.

INDUCING INITIAL COMMITMENT

All of the methods for inducing commitment that we will discuss aim at eliciting initial behavior on the basis of which subsequent commitment to therapy can be forged. The approaches vary, however, in whether the initial behavior is more or less extreme than the ultimate behaviorial target.[1] We and, in cases where a different behavior is initially sought, in whether this behavior is more or less extreme than the ultimate behavioral target.[1] We believe that the methods we review are especially relevant to the early phases of therapy, when clients first become aware of its emotional and financial costs and the ambivalence of Stage II threatens perseverance in treatment. As our review indicates, the degree to which clients experience an aspect of therapy as positive or negative and the conceptual constellation they use to relate these elements to ongoing behavior are malleable and can readily be influenced by systematic attempts on the part of the therapist.

Focus on the Actual Target Behavior

Festinger's (1957) cognitive dissonance theory formed the basis for much of the early work on inducing commitment. This initial research typically used a "forced compliance" paradigm, first paying subjects varying amounts of money to publicly express an opinion counter to their actual attitudes and then reassessing their attitudes (e.g., Festinger & Carlsmith, 1959; Linder, Cooper, & Jones, 1967). Consistent with dissonance theory predictions, these studies generally found an inverse relationship between the amount of reward and the amount of attitude change in the direction of the publicly expressed opinion: The less money offered, the greater the subsequent attitude change (cf. Gerard *et al.*, 1974). The dissonance explanation rests on the assumption that people experience cognitive dissonance when their behavior is not sufficiently justified (Cohen, 1962; Gerard *et al.*, 1974). If subjects receive $20 for writing counterattitudinal essays, for example, the large extrinsic incentive may provide sufficient justification. If they receive only a few cents for making the same statement, however, the extrinsic incentive is insufficient to justify saying something they do not believe, cognitive dissonance is aroused, and in

---

[1]We exclude from our discussion methods that initially focus on more extreme versions of the target behavor. Research indicates that people who refuse a larger initial request are more likely to agree to a smaller second request than are people not first presented with the large initial request (Cialdini, Vincent, Lewis, Catalan, Wheeler, & Darby, 1975). Such "door-in-the-face" techniques have limited applicability in clinical settings and raise ethical issues beyond the scope of this chapter.

order to reduce this tension subjects justify their behavior by finding another explanation for it (e.g., that they really *do* believe what they just said).[2]

Closely related to the forced compliance studies is research on the relationship between severity of initiation and attraction. This research has demonstrated that the more effort voluntarily expended in pursuing a freely chosen behavioral course, the stronger one's attraction to that course (Aronson, 1961; Aronson & Mills, 1959; Gerard & Mathewson, 1966).

The key to enhancing commitment through insufficient justification lies in the person's perception of a *high degree of choice* in performing the target behavior, with minimal extrinsic justification (Gerard *et al.*, 1974; Wicklund & Brehm, 1976). Whether one takes the dissonance or self-perception perspective, insufficient justification procedures can be viewed as inducing commitment by putting cognitive consistency at stake for the individual, who becomes subsequently committed to a particular course of action through the need to preserve consistency between attitude and behavior. Although the target behavior must have at least a minimal appeal, this paradigm suggests how it may become more attractive as a function of changing costs and rewards incurred in its pursuit. Emphasizing to the client that whether to pursue treatment or not is their free choice, while requiring effort to persist and only the minimal effective external justification for doing so, should increase the client's sense of commitment. And if Kanter (1968) is correct in her contention that sacrifice by the client promotes commitment, then clients' perceptions that they are voluntarily paying a considerable sum of money for therapy should lead them to become more commited to the endeavor.

The low-ball technique (Cialdini *et al.*, 1978) is another mechanism for fostering commitment that focuses on inducing commitment to the target behavior right from the start. This procedure involves first offering sufficient extrinsic incentives to induce an individual to make an active decision regarding a given course of behavior, and then removing the extrinsic incentives. Despite the lower rewards, the person will tend to remain committed to the initial decision and will be more likely to continue the decided-upon behavior without the extrinsic rewards than someone presented with only the more costly request. A parallel body of dissonance research indicates that negative consequences of behavior that people foresee only after commitment to a course of action often lead to enhanced efforts to justify the course of action chosen (Cooper, 1971; Goethals & Cooper, 1975; Goethals, Cooper, & Naficy, 1979).

[2]Bem's (1967) self-perception theory provides an alternative explanation for these findings. According to self-perception theory, in the absense of clear situational influences, people make inferences about their attitudes, beliefs, and motives by observing their own behavior. Thus, perceiving onself as having chosen to write a counterattitudinal essay for only a few cents would lead a person to conclude that he or she must actually believe in the newly expressed opinion. Shifting self-perceptions presumably underlie attitude change. Supporting this interpretation, explicitly labeling donors as charitable produces greater rates of subsequent donation than procedures without explicit labeling (Kraut, 1973).

The low-ball approach is frequently used by modern psychoanalysts. Although clients who begin pursuing psychoanalysis with a warm analyst with whom they talk face-to-face may be surprised when their therapist becomes more "depriving" and requests a shift to the couch, they are nevertheless more likely to persevere than clients plunged directly into the classical psychoanalytic relationship without such preparation.

The explanation first offered for this low-ball effect was that the initial commitment to an uncoerced decision persists over time by creating self-perceptions of favorability toward the decision, which increase willingness to comply with higher costs (Cialdini *et al.*, 1978). However, a more recent series of experiments (Burger & Petty, 1981) suggests that an unfulfilled obligation to to the requester, rather than a commitment to the target behavior, may be responsible for the success of the low-ball technique. Burger and Petty found that the low-ball strategy was effective only when both the first request and the second, more costly request were made by the same person. Furthermore, subjects were more likely to comply with a second, more costly request when it was made by the same person, even if the second request was unrelated to the initial one. This evidence clearly indicates that commitment to the requester, and not to the behavior initially requested, underlies the low-ball phenomenon.

Focus on a Less Extreme Version of Target Behavior

Several other procedures for inducing commitment operate on the principle that people strive to maintain consistency between self-perceptions and behavior. For instance, many studies have found that people are more likely to comply with a large request if they have previously agreed to a smaller initial request (Pliner, Hart, Kohl; & Saari, 1974; Seligman, Bush; & Kirsch, 1976; Snyder & Cunningham, 1975). In a fund drive for the Cancer Society, for example, asking people to comply with the simple initial request to wear a pin publicizing the campaign nearly doubled the rate of subsequent donation (Pliner *et al.*, 1974). One explanation for this "foot-in-the-door" effect is that initial compliance under conditions of low external pressure heightens the self-perception that one is a helpful, compliant person, thus making one more likely to comply with a subsequent larger request (see DeJong, 1979). As with the insufficient justification effect, the amount of external pressure used to induce initial compliance is crucial. If people perceive a sufficient extrinsic justification for having agreed to the initial request, then they will not make self-inferences of compliance and may be less willing to comply with the subsequent request (Zuckerman, Lazzaro, & Waldgeir, 1979).

Many a helper has used the foot-in-the-door approach to induce client commitment without labeling it as such. For example, the first author routinely requests that a client make a decision to come to only three sessions and actually discourages the client from making any longer-term commitment without the experience this trial would provide. This approach has several virtues. The initial small request is easier to comply with than a request to embark on a lengthy course of therapy. Secondly, the subsequent decision to pursue treatment beyond the initial three visits is based more on the clients' perception of their *own* behavior during the initial sessions than on simple adherence to pressure or persuasion by the helper. Finally, once consistency between self-image and behavior is a side bet for an individual, refusal to continue treatment threatens his or her self-image as a "good patient."

The effectiveness of the procedures discussed for inducing commitment—through focusing on the actual target behavior (insufficient justification, lowball) or through focusing on a less extreme version of the target behavior (foot-in-the-door)—all depend on the individual's perception of a high degree of personal choice. Perceptions of choice presumably foster self-attributions of responsibility for behavior (Wicklund & Brehm, 1976). This assumption is consistent with recent attributional formulations (e.g., Mayer, Duval, & Duval, 1980) that stress the importance of perceived personal responsibility as an antecedent of commitment. Feeling that one has personally chosen a behavioral course apparently mediates the effectiveness of commitment-inducing procedures (cf. Kiesler, 1971).

MAINTAINING COMMITMENT

In the previous section we reviewed methods for enhancing the initial commitment among clients facing the ambivalence characteristic of the early phase of treatment. We now focus on the role of attributions and expectancies in enhancing persistence beyond these first confrontations with ambivalence. We believe that the attributions and expectancies that clients bring to therapy, and those shaped by the helper in the early stages of treatment, are especially critical for weathering the inevitable recurrence of peaks and valleys at different points in the therapy experience.

Causal and Moral Attributions

A fundamental premise of attribution theory is that persistence is mediated by the perceived causes of behavioral outcomes. A person who attributes failure in an endeavor to insufficient ability, for example, is likely to give up sooner than one who attributes failure to insufficient effort. Studies of achievement behavior (Rest, Nierenberg, Weiner, & Heckhausen, 1973; Weiner, Heckhausen, Meyer, & Cook 1972) confirm that effort attributions underlie achievement motivation and persistence. Procedures that emphasize insufficient effort as a cause of failure have been found to produce greater persistence in the face of failure than procedures that do not (Dweck, 1975; Dweck & Repucci, 1973), consistent with the notion that self-attributions of responsibility enhance commitment (Kiesler, 1971; Mayer *et al.*, 1980).

Brickman, Rabinowitz, Karuza, Coates, Cohn, and Kidder (1982) have recently modified the traditional perspective on causal attribution by distinguishing between attributions of responsibility for the *problem* and attributions of responsibility for the *solution*. Within this framework, they propose that helping relationships be classified according to those that emphasize personal responsibility for: (*a*) both the problem and the solution (called the "moral model"); (*b*) only the problem, but not the solution (the "enlightenment model"); (*c*) only the solution, but not the problem (the "compensatory model"); and (*d*) neither the problem nor the solution (the "medical model"). (See Chapter 6, by Karuza, Zevon, Rabinowitz, & Brickman in this volume.) Clients and helpers are seen as implicitly holding to one of these four models. To enhance persistence in therapy, the helper would do well to assess the type of model held by the client and to tailor the therapeutic approach accordingly. As Fish (1973) noted, "By allowing the success of therapy to hinge on the weakening or destruction of a patient's cherished beliefs, the therapist has greatly diminished the chances of success [p. 95]."

Certain attributions may nevertheless be more conducive to both persistence and symptom relief than others. For example, teaching clients to attribute improvement to personal effort produces greater benefits (Chambliss & Murray, 1979; Davison & Valins, 1969; Liberman, 1978), whereas stressing external responsibility for improvement yields, at best, only temporary gains (Jeffrey, 1974; Miller, Brickman, & Bolen, 1975; Nentwig, 1978). Positive attributional sets apparently facilitate commitment by providing clients with a useful means of conceptually bonding positive elements (such as the anticipation of relief) with negative elements (such as the experience of pain) so as to provide a rationale for persistent involvement.

Brickman *et al.* (1982) conclude from their review of the literature that attributions of responsibility for *solutions* mediate persistence and improvement, a hypothesis we are currently pursuing in a therapy analogue laboratory study (Bryant, Lemkau, & Brickman, Note 2).

An example from the practice of one of the authors (JPL) illustrates the role of attributions for solutions at a critical point in treatment. An extremely depressed middle-aged man repeatedly and belligerently asked his therapist, "Have you got your magic wand yet?" In response to her consistent refusal (and inability!) to produce a magic solution, the man finally said in exasperation, "I guess you can fall into a ditch but you can't fall out!" From that point on, he energetically pursued his *own* solutions, using the therapist as a consultant to his efforts, only occasionally baiting her with entreaties to "turn the ditch over and let me out!" Such attributional transitions in therapy may be risky times for dropout if the client's expectations of the therapist are dashed before a new type of relationship is perceived as possible and desirable.

One specific method for changing clients' attributional styles so as to facilitate persistence and therapeutic benefit is that of "reattribution training" (Abramson, Seligman, & Teasdale, 1978; Dweck, 1975; Ross, Rodin, &

Zimbardo, 1969; Valins & Nisbett, 1971). This approach involves teaching people to make more adaptive attributions for environmental and behavioral outcomes. For example, training children with learning difficulties to attribute their failures to insufficient effort produced greater subsequent persistence and performance improvement in the face of failure than did only giving them experience with success (Dweck, 1975). Clinicians have reported positive results using similar, cognitive restructuring procedures in the treatment of depression (Beck, 1976, Shaw, 1977), neurosis (Ellis, 1962), and paranoia (Davison, 1966).[3]

Expectations

Another determinant of persistence is the individual's expectation of success. Whereas high expectations of the results of therapy may contribute to the client's return for a second or third visit, positive expectations alone may be insufficient to maintain long-term commitment, and may actually undermine persistence by leaving the client unprepared for the inevitable slumps in the therapeutic course. Positive expectations need to be tempered by realistic anticipation that "one step backward" often comes with the "two steps forward."

Our perspective is consistent with issues raised in the research literature. In general, people with high expectations persist longer and perform better than people with low expectations. People with high expectations of success not only work harder and persist longer, but also do better following failure than people with low expectations of success (Brickman & Hendricks, 1975; Means & Means, 1971; Miller *et al.* 1975; Shrauger & Sorman, 1977). Conversely, people who expect to fail often show performance decrements even before receiving explicit feedback (Hiroto & Seligman, 1975; Roth & Kubal, 1975).

Wortman, and Brehm (1975) contend that persistence in the face of failure is a direct function of expectation of control: The higher the initial expectation, the greater the resultant motivation to persist to exert control. Unrealistically high expectancies, however, when dashed, can lead to dissatisfaction, demoralization, and dropout. As Wortman and Brehm suggest, the magnitude helplessness experienced when quitting in the face of failure is also a direct function of expectation of control: The higher the initial expectation, the greater the subsequent helplessness effects. Paralleling Wortman and Brehm's model, a recent review of research on performance expectations (Linsenmeier &

---

[3]Although attributions that enhance persistence are adaptive in objectively controllable situations where the client's efforts will ultimately be rewarded, they are maladaptive in objectively uncontrollable situations (cf. Janoff-Bulman & Brickman, 1981; Wortman & Brehm, 1975). For example, the woman who accepts her therapist's suggestion that only by choosing to be sexually involved with him will she find solutions to her problems, may persist in therapy and even pay for such "help." Several authors have suggested "immunization training" in which people are taught to differentiate between controllable and uncontrollable outcomes (cf. Janoff-Bulman & Brickman, 1982; Wortman & Brehm, 1975).

Brickman, Note 3) suggests that expectations of success have both positive and negative consequences. Paradoxically, higher expectations produce better performance but also generate lower satisfaction with outcomes; lower expectations produce poorer performance but also generate greater satisfaction with outcomes.

In considering the implications of this literature for the psychotherapeutic dyad, it is critical to distinquish between expectations for achieving the ultimate goals of therapy and expectations for the more immediate course. By raising expectations about ultimate success (e.g., stressing that the client will undoubtedly improve by the end of therapy) while simultaneously reducing expectations about the course of the therapeutic course (e.g., stressing that improvement may very well involve some necessary setbacks), the therapist can capture the benefits of both high and low expectancies as well as counteract their disadvantages. As Fish (1973) writes,

> a therapist can mention that because of the nature of psychological problems, on rare occasions a patient may regress if he has reached a point where such regression enables him to learn to cope with his problems. If the patient gets worse, the therapist can sympathize with him over how painful progress can be, while suggesting that once he has benefited from his therapeutic regression, he will be able to make still greater and less painful strides [p. 37].

We would expect this paradoxical approach to increase commitment to the helping relationship, for when clients hold expectations of both ultimate relief and suffering and setbacks in the process, they have a cognitive map to facilitate the continuous integration of positive and negative elements experienced along the way.

Conclusion

Commitment is at the heart of the psychotherapeutic enterprise. As clients readily attest, therapy is *work*, often involving arduous assignments, painful emotions, and considerable expense. Given the inevitable costs faced by psychotherapy clients, and the fact that helpers rarely choose to treat their clients with only one or two sessions, the development and maintenance of commitment is crucial for helper and client alike.

We began by defining commitment in terms of a person's choice of a behavioral direction and his or her persistence on that course in the face of ambivalence. By reframing psychoanalytic descriptions of stages of therapy, we demonstrated the relevance of commitment processes to the therapeutic dyad, whatever the particular helper's philosophy of treatment. Factors predictive of psychotherapy dropout were also discussed with reference to positive and negative elements in therapy and the integration of these within the commitment framework. We suggested that by attending to commitment processes, helpers enhance the likelihood that their clients will remain in treatment and weather the inevitable fluctuations in the therapeutic course, and we illustrated the applicability of paradigms for inducing and maintaining commitment, drawn from the literature of social psychology applied to the psychotherapy setting. From the literature on causal and moral attributions we were reminded of the importance of fostering clients' beliefs that their own efforts in therapy will result in the personal changes they desire and of attending to the world view of the client in considering any interventions. Finally, the literature on expectations underlined the role of the helper in maintaining high client aspirations for ultimate success while tempering expectations for the more immediate future. We conclude by suggesting that helpers need to design interventions to help clients integrate their stage in therapy with expectations of ultimate benefit.

We think that commitment processes are the very essence of psychotherapy. Although this is a sweeping assertion, we find nothing in the clinical or social-psychological literature that compels us to think otherwise. Moreover, we are confident that even those who believe that fostering client commitment is only a means to hold clients in therapy long enough so that change may be effected through other avenues will agree that commitment processes should be high on our clinical and research agendas.

Reference Notes

1. Brickman, P. *Commitment.* Unpublished manuscript, University of Michigan, 1981.
2. Bryant, F., Lemkau, J. P., & Brickman, P. *Effects of expectancies and causal attributions for problem and solution on persistence at a therapy analogue task.* Work in progress, University of Michigan, 1981.
3. Linsenmeier, J., & Brickman, P. *Expectations, performance and satisfaction.* Unpublished manuscript, University of Michigan, 1981.

References

Abramson, L. Y., Seligman, M. E. P., & Teasdale, J. D. Learned helplessness in humans: Critique and reformulation. *Journal of Abnormal Psychology*, 1978, *87*, 49–74.

Aronson, E. The effect of effort on the attractiveness of rewarded and unrewarded stimuli. *Journal of Applied Social Psychology*, 1961, *63*, 375–380.

Aronson, E., & Mills, J. The effect of severity of initiation on liking for a group. *Journal of Applied Social Psychology*, 1959, *59*, 177–181.

Baekeland, F., & Lundwall, L. Dropping out of treatment: A critical review. *Psychological Bulletin*, 1975, *82*, 738–783.

Beck, A. T. *Cognitive therapy and emotional disorders.* New York: International Universities Press, 1976.

Becker, H. S. Notes on the concept of commitment. *American Journal of Sociology*, 1960, 66, 32–40.

Bem, D. J. Self perception: An alternative interpretation of cognitive dissonance phenomena. *Psychological Review*. 1967, 74, 183–200.

Bergin, A. E., & Lambert, M. J. The evaluation of therapeutic outcomes. In S. L. Garfield & A. E. Bergin (Eds.), *Handbook of psychotherapy and behavior change: An empirical analysis* (2nd ed.). New York: Wiley, 1978.

Brickman, P., & Hendricks, M. Expectancy for gradual or sudden improvement and reaction to success and failure. *Journal of Personality and Social Psychology*, 1975, 32, 893–900.

Brickman, P., Rabinowitz, V. C., Karuza, J., Jr., Coates, D., Cohn, E., & Kidder, L. Models of helping and coping. *American Psychologist*, 1982, 37, 368–384.

Burger, J. M., & Petty, R. E. The low-ball compliance technique: Task or person commitment? *Journal of Personality and Social Psychology*, 1981, 40, 497–499.

Chambliss, C. A., & Murray, E. J. Efficacy attribution, locus of control, and weight loss. *Cognitive Therapy and Research*, 1979, 3, 349–353.

Cialdini, R. B., Cacioppo, J. T., Bassett, R., & Miller, J. A. Low-ball procedure for producing compliance: Commitment then cost. *Journal of Personality and Social Psychology*, 1978, 36, 463–476.

Cialdini, R. B., Vincent, J. E., Lewis, S. K., Catalan, J., Wheeler, D., & Darby, B. L., Reciprocal concessions procedure for inducing compliance: The door-in-the-face technique. *Journal of Personality and Social Psychology*, 1975, 31, 206–215.

Cohen, A. R. An experiment on small rewards for discrepant compliance and attitude change. In J. W. Brehm & A. R. Cohen (Eds.), *Explorations in cognitive dissonance*. New York: Wiley, 1962.

Cooper, J. Personal responsibility and dissonance: The role of foreseen consequences. *Journal of Personality and Social Psychology*, 1971, 18, 354–363.

Davison, G. Differential relaxation and cognitive restructuring in therapy with a "paranoid schizophrenic" or "paranoid state." *Proceedings of the American Psychological Association 74th Annual Convention* 1966, 177–178.

Davison, G. C., & Valins, S. Maintenance of self-attributed and drug-attributed behavior change. *Journal of Personality and Social Psychology*, 1969, 11, 25–33,

DeJong, W. An examination of self-perception mediation of the foot-in-the-door effect. *Journal of Personality and Social Psychology*, 1979, 37, 2221–2239.

Dweck, C. S. The role of expectations and attributions in the alleviation of learned helplessness *Journal of Personality and Social Psychology*, 1975, 31, 674–685.

Dweck, C. S., & Repucci, N. D. Learned helplessness and reinforcement responsibility in children. *Journal of Personality and Social Psychology*, 1973, 25, 109–116.

Eidelson, R. J. Interpersonal satisfaction and level of involvement: A curvilinear relationship. *Journal of Personality and Social Psychology*, 1980, 39, 460–470.

Ellis, A. *Reason and emotion in psychotherapy*. New York: Lyle Stuart, 1962.

Festinger, L. *A theory of cognitive dissonance*. Stanford: Stanford Univ. Press, 1957.

Festinger, L., & Carlsmith, J. M. Cognitive consequences of forced compliance. *Journal of Abnormal and Social Psychology*, 1959, 58, 203–210.

Fine, R. Psychoanalysis. In R. Corsini (Ed.), *Current psychotherapies*. Itasca, Ill.: Peacock, 1973.

Fish, J. M. *Placebo therapy*. San Francisco: Jossey-Bass, 1973.

Frank, J. D. Immediate and long-term symptomatic course of psychiatric outpatients. *American Journal of Psychiatry*, 1963, 120, 429–439.

Frank, J. D. *Persuasion and healing* (Rev. ed.). New York: Schocken, 1974.

Gerard, H. B. Conolley, E. S., & Wilhelmy, R. A. Compliance, justification, and cognitive change. In L. Berkowitz (Ed.), *Advances in experimental social psychology* (Vol. 7). New York: Academic Press, 1974.

Gerard, H. B., & Mathewson, G. D. The effects of severity of initiation on liking for a group: A replication. *Journal of Experimental Social Psychology*, 1966, 2, 278–287.

Goethals, G. R., & Cooper, J. When dissonance is reduced: The timing of self-justificatory attitude change. *Journal of Personality and Social Psychology*, 1975, 32, 361–367.

Goethals, G. R., Cooper, J., & Naficy, A. Role of foreseen, foreseeable, and unforeseeable behavioral consequences in the arousal of cognitive dissonance. *Journal of Personality and Social Psychology*, 1979, *37*, 1179–1185.

Greenson, R. R. *The technique and practice of psychoanalysis* (Vol. 1). New York: International Universities Press, 1967.

Hiroto, D. S., & Seligman, M. E. P. Generality of learned helplessness in man. *Journal of Personality and Social Psychology*, 1975, *31*, 311–327.

Janoff-Bulman, R., & Brickman, P. Expectations and what people learn from failure. In N. T. Feather (Ed.), *Expectations and actions*. Hillsdale, N. J.: Erlbaum, 1982.

Jeffrey, D. B. A comparison of the effects of external control and self-control on the modification and maintenance of weight. *Journal of Abnormal Psychology*, 1974, *83*, 404–410.

Kanter, R. M. Commitment and social organization: A study of commitment mechanisms in Utopian communities. *American Sociological Review*, 1968, *33*, 499–517.

Kiesler, C. A. *The psychology of commitment*. New York: Academic Press, 1971.

Kraut, R. E. Effects of social labeling on giving to charity. *Journal of Experimental Social Psychology*, 1973, *9*, 551–562.

Liberman, B. L. The role of mastery in psychotherapy: Maintenance of improvement and prescriptive change. In J. D. Frank, R. Hoehn-Saric, D. D. Imber, B. L. Liberman, & A. R. Stone, *Effective ingredients of successful psychotherapy*. New York: Brunner/Mazel, 1978.

Linder, D. E., Cooper, J., & Jones, E. E. Decision freedom as a determinant of the role of incentive magnitude in attitude change. *Journal of Personality and Social Psychology*, 1967, *6*, 245–254.

Mayer, F. S. Duval, S., & Duval, V. H. An attributional analysis of commitment. *Journal of Personality and Social Psychology*, 1980, *39*, 1072–1080.

Means, R. S., & Means, G. H. Achievement as a function of the presence of prior information concerning aptitude. *Journal of Educational Psychology*, 1971, *62*, 185–187.

Miller, R. T., Brickman, P., & Bolen, D. Attribution versus persuasion as a means of modifying behavior. *Journal of Personality and Social Psychology*, 1975, *31*, 430–441.

Nentwig, C. G. Attribution of cause and long-term effects of the modification of smoking behavior. *Behavioral Analysis and Modification*, 1978, *2*, 285–295.

Pliner, P., Hart, H., Kohl, J., & Saari, D. Compliance without pressure: Some further data on the foot-in-the-door technique. *Journal of Experimental Social Psychology*, 1974, *10*, 17–22.

Rest, S., Nierenberg, R., Weiner, B., & Heckhausen, H. Further evidence concerning the effects of perceptions of effort and ability on achievement evaluation. *Journal of Personality and Social Psychology*, 1973, *28*, 187–191.

Rosenthal, D., & Frank, J. D. The fate of psychiatric clinic outpatients assigned to psychotherapy. *Journal of Nervous and Mental Disease*, 1958, *127*, 330–343.

Ross, L. The intuitive psychologist and his shortcomings. In L. Berkowitz (Ed.), *Advances in experimental social psychology* (Vol. 10). New York: Academic Press, 1977.

Ross, L. D., Rodin, J., & Zimbardo, P. G. Toward an attribution therapy: The reduction of fear through reduced cognitive–emotional misattribution. *Journal of Personality and Social Psychology*, 1969, *12*, 279–288.

Roth, S., & Kubal, L. The effects of noncontingent reinforcement on tasks of differing importance: Facilitation and learned helplessness. *Journal of Personality and Social Psychology*, 1975, *32*, 680–691.

Schultz, S. K. Compliance with therapeutic regimes in pediatrics. *Social Work in Health Care*, 1980, *5*, 267–278.

Seligman, C., Bush, M., & Kirsch, K. Relationship between compliance in the foot-in-the-door paradigm and size of first request. *Journal of Personality and Social Psychology*, 1976, *33*, 517–520.

Shaw, B. F. Comparison of cognitive therapy and behavior therapy in the treatment of depression. *Journal of Consulting and Clinical Psychology*, 1977, *45*, 543–551.

Shrauger, J. S., & Sorman, P. B. Self-evaluations, initial success and failure, and improvement as determinants of persistence. *Journal of Consulting and Clinical Psychology*, 1977, *45*, 784–795.

Smith, M. L., & G.ass, G. V. Meta-analysis of psychotherapy outcome studies. *American Psychologist*, 1977, *32*, 752–760.

Snyder, M., & Cunningham, M. R. To comply or not to comply: Testing the self-perception explanation of the "foot-in-the-door" technique. *Journal of Personality and Social Psychology*, 1975, *31*, 64–67.

Torrey, E. F. *The mind game: Witch doctors and psychiatrists*. New York: Emerson Hall, 1972.

Uhlenhuth, E. H., & Duncan, D. B. Subjective change with medical student therapists: II. Some determinants of change in psychoneurotic outpatients. *Archives of General Psychiatry*, 1968, *18*, 532–540.

Valins, S., & Nisbett, R. E. *Attribution processes in the development and treatment of emotional disorders*. Morristown, N.J.: General Learning Press, 1971.

Weiner, B., Heckhausen, H., Meyer, M., & Cook, R. E. Causal ascriptions and achievement behavior: Conceptual analysis of effort and reanalysis of locus of control. *Journal of Personality and Social Psychology*, 1972, *21*, 239–248.

Wicklund, R. A., & Brehm, J. W. *Perspectives on cognitive dissonance*. New York: Wiley, 1976.

Wortman, C. B., & Brehm, J. W. Responses to uncontrollable outcomes: An integration of reactance theory and the learned helplessness model. In L. Berkowitz (Ed.), *Advances in experimental social psychology* (Vol. 8). New York: Academic Press, 1975.

Zimbardo, P. G., Ebbesen, E. B., & Maslach, C. *Influencing attitudes and changing behavior* (2nd ed.). Reading, Mass.: Addison-Wesley, 1977.

Zuckerman, M., Lazzaro, M. M., & Waldgeir, D. Undermining effect of the foot-in-the-door technique with extrinsic rewards. *Journal of Applied Social Psychology*, 1979, *9*, 292–296.

PART III

SOCIAL SUPPORT
AND HELP SEEKING

Several sources of evidence have suggested that support from informal social networks is a major factor in people's coping and adaptation. Studies of community samples have shown that persons experiencing psychological distress tend to seek help from friends and family members, and that professional therapists typically are consulted only after other sources of help have been exhausted (see Wills, in press). That informal help may be a significant factor in professional helping relationships is suggested in studies of psychotherapy outcome, which usually show a surprising amount of improvement in the control groups (Luborsky, Singer, & Luborsky, 1975; Strupp & Hadley, 1979), and in studies of "spontaneous remission," which show a notable rate of improvement of psychological distress in untreated samples (Lambert, 1976). The factors involved in the contribution of social support to psychological well-being, however, and the variables that shape people's decisions about help seeking from formal or informal sources, have been investigated only recently. The following chapters provide a comprehensive examination of social support research and its implications for helping relationships.

Chapter 10, by Moos and Mitchell, introduces a conceptual framework for defining and measuring social network resources and shows how social

Basic Processes in Helping Relationships

support provides a source of strength to persons who are coping with stress and difficulty in various areas of life. One of the contributions of this research is to show the substantial level of informal helping resources available in the community. Support is potentially available through a variety of interpersonal relationships—from a husband or wife, friends, family, or work partners—and it is not uncommon for persons in distress to seek and obtain help from ministers, medical practitioners, and other community resources. In addition to providing evidence about the availability of social support, research by Moos and Mitchell and others is beginning to delineate the different functions that are provided by social networks; these include provision of tangible assistance (e.g., money or household services), cognitive guidance, or self-esteem enhancement and emotional support. The function that is most relevant for a particular person appears to depend on the type of problem, with work site support, for example, more important for work-related stress and family support more relevant for interpersonal problems. Chapter 10 shows that social support constructs provide a rich area for interdisciplinary research, for a complete understanding of social networks requires attention to ecological and architectural factors, to personality factors and general coping patterns, to family relationships, to attitudinal orientations toward help seeking, and to general sociodemographic factors. Moos and Mitchell raise some interesting questions about the relative effectiveness of informal support systems and formal helping agencies, and provide a thought-provoking discussion of how professional helpers may work with social networks to enhance the ability of persons to cope with life stresses.

In Chapter 11, Antonucci and Depner provide a detailed presentation of research on the structure and function of social support networks in a variety of populations, including school teachers and elderly persons. Their chapter illustrates the methodological advances in current research, distinguishing properties of social networks such as amount of support, connectedness of networks, stability over time, and symmetry. In several studies, findings on the functions of social support suggest that the most important general function is interpersonal liking and emotional support from others, consistent with the research of Moos and Mitchell (Chapter 10 in this volume) and with evidence from studies of professional helping relationships (see Wills, Chapter 17 in this volume). The research of Antonucci, Depner, and colleagues has also indicated significant individual differences in social support, with women tending to have larger and more diversified networks, and older persons tending to have smaller networks and less reciprocated support. The authors provide a valuable discussion of life-span issues in social support, showing how role relationships and social support needs may change across different stages of the life cycle; this discussion, together with the findings reported on age differences in support, clarifies the particular need of elderly persons for effective social support systems. Antonucci and Depner conclude by discussing conceptual issues important for further research on social support, such as the operative mechanism in the relationship between social support and psychological well-being, and the "buffering hypothesis," which suggests that social support serves a protective function for persons facing a high level of stress (cf. Cohen & McKay, in press). Finally, the authors discuss methodological issues in obtaining valid assessments of social support resources. They make suggestions about obtaining measures of social support as it is perceived by respondents, which requires attention to the exact wording of questions, to the difference between current support interactions and potentially available support, and to the measurement of reciprocity in social support exchanges. These suggestions should be useful for further research on social support in natural settings.

Chapter 12, by DePaulo, reports one of the first experimental research programs on variables involved in the decision to seek help. This research may serve to clarify findings from epidemiological and community studies of help seeking, in which the external validity of the findings is high but the nature of the processes that mediate the observed results is sometimes unclear. DePaulo's chapter presents the approach of experimental social psychology, which institutes rigorous control of particular variables and provides tests of specific theoretical models of factors in help seeking decisions, such as perceived inadequacy, indebtedness, or values concerning self-reliance. It is evident from the work of DePaulo and others (cf. Fisher & Nadler, Chapter 7 in this volume) that help seeking has implications for a person's self-esteem and that self-defensive considerations are an important factor in help-seeking decisions. This aspect of help seeking is moderated, however, by sex differences, with women seeming to respond more to the social and interpersonal aspects of a helping relationship and men having more of a task-oriented approach to helping. In addition, for reasons that are still unclear (see Wills, in press), people evidently prefer to seek help from others they are close to, such as friends and family members, rather than from strangers. Throughout the chapter DePaulo emphasizes that help seeking is not simple; persons weigh carefully the potential costs and benefits of helping before arriving at a decision, which in many cases may be not to seek help, and from the available evidence it is apparent that there are a number of factors that may act to inhibit help seeking. Hypotheses from laboratory research can be examined in further research in clinical and community settings to determine how particular factors apply in the decisions of distressed persons to seek help. Such studies will provide a fuller understanding of the complex pathways through which clients arrive in the offices of professional helpers.

References

Cohen, S., & McKay, G. Social support, stress, and the buffering hypothesis. In A. Baum, J. E. Singer, & S. E. Taylor (Eds.), *Handbook of psychology and health* (Vol. 4). Hillsdale, N. J.: Erlbaum, in press.

Kadushin, C. *Why people go to psychiatrists*. New York: Atherton, 1969.

Lambert, M. J. Spontaneous remission in adult neurotic disorders: A revision and summary. *Psychological Bulletin*, 1976, *83*, 107–119.

Luborsky, L., Singer, B., & Luborsky, L. Comparative studies of psychotherapies. *Archives of General Psychiatry*, 1975, *32*, 995–1008.

Strupp, H. H., & Hadley, S. W. Specific vs. nonspecific factors in psychotherapy: A controlled study of outcome. *Archives of General Psychiatry*, 1979, *36*, 1125–1136.

Wills, T. A. Social comparison in coping and help seeking. In B. M. DePaulo, A. Nadler, & J. D. Fisher (Eds.), *New directions in helping* (Vol. 2): *Help-seeking*. New York: Academic Press, in press.

chapter 10

Social Network Resources and Adaptation: A Conceptual Framework[1]

RUDOLF H. MOOS
ROGER E. MITCHELL

Introduction

The pervasiveness of stressful conditions in modern life prompted Antonovsky's (1979) query: How do any of us manage to stay healthy? How can the majority of people continue to function adequately in the face of omnipresent stressors that are thought to cause or predispose individuals to develop physical and mental illness? These questions led Antonovsky (1979) to propose that health researchers alter their focus from pathogenesis (the development of abnormal functioning or illness) to "salutogenesis" (the maintenance of health). In addressing this issue, theorists have implicated two related sets of resources in the maintenance of adequate functioning as individuals encounter life transitions and crises: coping resources and social network resources. In this chapter we focus on social network resources and on their determinants and effects.[2]

[1]Preparation of this chapter was supported by NIMH Grant MH 28177, NIAAA Grant AA02863, and Veterans Administration Medical Research Funds.

[2]For an overview of recent work on coping resources, see Moos and Billings (in press).

Basic Processes in Helping Relationships

Historical Antecedents of Social Network Concepts

Current conceptions of social networks have emerged from three related areas: sociometric analysis, social network analysis, and crisis theory. The historical roots of these three areas can be traced to the ecological perspective that emerged from psychological field theory over 50 years ago. Sociometric analysis emanated from Moreno's (1934) attempts to describe the "psychological geography" of groups and communities by examining the relationships between individuals. He developed sociometric procedures by which individuals report actual or desired interactions with each other. The resulting data are arranged into a sociogram, that is, a picture in which persons are represented by circles and the interactions among them by lines. The sociogram makes it possible to depict the positions of individuals and their interactions in a pattern of social structure. Moreno's ideas have been used widely to understand the positions of individuals in social settings (for instance, as "stars" or "isolates") and to influence cohesion and productivity in different types of groups and communities (Cartwright & Zander, 1968).

Social network analysis developed from attempts by social anthropologists to understand patterns of interaction that were not based on membership in kinship and institutional groups. For instance, in studying a parish on a Norwegian island, Barnes (1954) mapped out patterns of relationships and introduced the concept of a social network, which is very similar to a sociogram: "The image I have is a set of points, some of which are joined by lines. The points of the image are people, or sometimes groups, and the lines indicate which people interact with each other [p. 43]." These network links were seen as providing access to varied types of information and resources (such as jobs), as well as exerting normative pressure to assume particular values.

These ideas concerning networks were developed further and used to explore a variety of phenomena, such as migration, use of power to resolve work group conflicts, and emergence of support during bereavement (J. Mitchell, 1969). The degree to which marital partners had "close-knit" and overlapping social networks, for example, was found to be related to their conjugal role relationships (Bott, 1971). Following the framework of Lewin's field theory, Bott (1971) conceptualized the social network as "standing between" the overall social environment and family functioning. Most recently, investigators have focused on the influence of social network characteristics upon people's ability to cope with life crises and transitions (Barrera, 1981; Hirsch, 1980; Wilcox, 1981).

These developments have begun to merge with a third strand of more clinically oriented research in the area of crisis theory, which was pioneered by Erich Lindemann (1979). Trained in the tradition of Gestalt psychology,

Lindemann believed that individuals were influenced by a web of social forces. He saw effective utilization of the existing social field as enhancing individual adaptation in crisis situations. A life crisis presents both an opportunity for psychological growth and a danger of psychological deterioration. Since a person is thought to be more susceptible to influence by others during a crisis than during periods of more stable functioning, the outcome of the crisis may depend in part on the support available from significant others in the community. For instance, Lindemann felt that bereaved family members could be helped to cope with the loss of their loved ones through the assistance of community caretakers such as clergy and friends.

Crisis theorists have recognized that the majority of persons who experience psychological problems do not seek out mental health professionals for help. They tend instead to use alternative resources such as family, friends, and employers or community helpers such as clergy, lawyers, teachers, and family practitioners. These findings have led to the suggestion that "spontaneous" remission is due in part to the advice and support people receive from lay helpers and that formal treatment may be needed primarily to compensate for a lack of alternative environmental resources. Furthermore, patients who experience an exacerbation of symptoms after treatment may obtain effective help from their friends and relatives rather than from the use of additional health and welfare services.

Indications of the positive functions of informal social resources have fostered research on their role in the connection between life stressors and adaptation. For instance, Berkman and Syme (1979) found that persons who lacked social and community ties were more than twice as likely to die during a 9-year follow-up period than were those with more extensive social contacts. The authors found a consistent pattern of increased mortality rates associated with each decrease in social "connectedness" and noted that the presence of more intimate ties of marriage and contact with friends and relatives was more strongly related to lower mortality rates than were the ties of church and group membership. Brown and Harris (1978) concluded that the presence of an intimate relationship with a husband or boyfriend afforded "protection" against depression for working-class women who were faced with life stress. Other research has shown that persons who are integrated into the social system are likely to experience a more supportive milieu during life crises, and thus are better able to cope with the impact of stressful events (Myers, Lindenthal, & Pepper, 1975). These studies highlight the role of social network resources in maintaining mental and physical health, and they also raise questions about the dimensions by which such resources should be characterized and the factors involved in understanding their determinants and effects.

The Structure and Functions of Social Networks

In this section we describe some procedures that have been used to assess the structure and functions of social networks. These procedures typically encompass one or more of the following three steps: constructing a list of network members, measuring structural dimensions of the network (such as size) as well as characteristics of specific linkages (such as frequency of contact), and examining the content of the exchanges that occur (such as emotional support).

One strategy for constructing a network list involves asking respondents to name "important" or "significant" individuals with whom they have been in contact recently. Respondents then rate each relationship on dimensions that tap such issues as the frequency of contact with the individual, the strength, valence (positive or negative), and perceived reciprocity of the relationship, and the degree of emotional and tangible support provided by the network member (Pattison, Llamas, & Hurd, 1979). Whereas this approach specifies the social network and then focuses on the type of support and degree of reciprocity of each relationship, an alternative strategy is to define the core social network in terms of individuals with whom the respondent has specific types of exchanges. For instance, the Arizona Social Support Interview Schedule involves asking the respondent to name persons who provided such interpersonal exchanges as discussion of personal feelings, positive feedback, advice and information, and physical assistance during the past month (Barrera, 1981).

STRUCTURAL CHARACTERISTICS OF SOCIAL NETWORKS

The information obtained by these procedures can be summarized along several dimensions. The dimensions of size and density (the extent to which individuals in a network know and contact one another independently of the focal individual) are structural characteristics that describe the entire network, although they can also characterize subsets of it (such as family and nonfamily relationships). A second set of dimensions describe characteristics of specific linkages (relationships) such as (a) multidimensionality (the extent to which a relationship involves more than one type of exchange, such as socializing *and* verbal expression of personal concern), (b) the reciprocity or mutuality in a relationship, and (c) intensity (the strength or commitment of the relationship). These dimensions imply the existence of exchange processes and have been related to adaptation in studies of psychiatric and nonpsychiatric populations (see Hammer, 1981; Mitchell & Trickett, 1980). Other characteristics of linkages that have received less attention include (d) homogeneity (the similarity of social network members on sociodemographic and personal factors), (e) proximity (how close the focal individual lives to the network member), (*f*) duration (the length of time the focal individual has known each network member), and (*g*) frequency of contact. In addition to these characteristics of network ties, researchers have also examined the content of the exchanges that occur within relationships and the functions they serve.

NETWORK FUNCTIONS

In general, initial efforts to measure social connectedness or social support relied upon unidimensional measures. For instance, Gore (1978) constructed a summary index covering an individual's perception of the supportiveness of friends and relatives, the frequency of social activity with these individuals, and the respondent's participation in emotionally satisfying social activities (see also Berkman & Syme, 1979; Lin, Simeone, Ensel, & Kuo, 1979). However, some work has indicated that social networks can serve a number of different functions (Caplan, 1974; Weiss, 1974).

Although various categorizations of social network functions have been suggested (Mitchell & Trickett, 1980), the basic types of interpersonal exchanges that occur among network members can be described in five major categories: (1) *social companionship* (joint participation in recreational and social activities), (2) *emotional support* (the approval and esteem given to or provided by another person and the mutual provision of a "climate of understanding"), (3) *cognitive guidance and advice* (the reciprocal clarification of expectations, access to information and information sharing, and the mutual provision of role models for specific learning activities), (4) *material aid and services* (the provision or acceptance of specific aid such as helping an individual clean house or lending money), and (5) *social regulation* (the expectation of and support for the maintenance of daily routines and interactions and the reaffirmation of an individual's role obligations). While these network functions are generally thought of as interpersonal resources, network members can also exert demands upon individuals which may constrain them from assuming particular roles or accomplishing valued goals.

Some recent work provides empirical support for the notion of distinguishing among such processes. Schaefer, Coyne, and Lazarus (in press) found that emotional and informational support were positively related to each other, but were essentially unrelated to tangible support. Tangible support was found to be related to level of depressive symptoms, whereas the other types of support showed no such relationship. In a related fashion, it may also be important to distinguish among sources of support (such as co-workers, family, and friends).

In this connection, we have constructed a set of Social Climate Scales to evaluate the social environments of such settings as families and work units, classrooms and student living groups, and residential care settings for psychiatric and geriatric patients (Moos, 1974, 1979, 1980). In addition to measuring the overall goals and organization of a setting, these scales assess the perceived quality of interpersonal support provided in the setting. For instance, the Family Relationships Index (FRI) is derived from the Family Environment Scale (FES) and measures how helpful and supportive family members are toward each other and the extent to which they express their feelings openly (Moos & Moos, 1981). An analogous Work Relationships Index (WRI) is derived from the Work Environment Scale (WES) and measures the supportiveness of interpersonal relationships among employees and supervisors (Holahan & Moos, 1981, Moos, 1981). These indices allow researchers to assess the perceived quality of an individual's social relationships in each of several settings.

We have reviewed several ways in which investigators have tried to assess the impact of informal social relationships upon individual adaptation. As described earlier, social network analysis is a technique that has focused on collecting information from individuals about their specific network members. This information is then used to describe structural characteristics of the network (such as density) as well as aspects of the linkages (such as exchange of information and support). The term *social network resources* is used here to refer to indices developed from network analysis techniques, as well as to measures of social connectedness based on such factors as marital status, the quality of contacts with close friends and relatives, and membership in social and community groups (Berkman & Syme, 1979; Holahan & Moos, 1981; Lin, Simeone, Ensel, & Kuo, 1979). This usage is employed as a convenient way of referring to a diverse set of measures that have in common an attempt to assess the characteristics of social relationships.

The foregoing work indicates that developments are being made in defining some aspects of social ties. However, there is less clarity about the processes by which such ties are developed and maintained and about the ways in which they exert their impact. To address these issues, we formulate here a conceptual framework that considers the personal and environmental factors that affect social network resources as well as their influence on adaptation. We then examine some of the determinants of such resources and explore implications for research and practice.

An Integrative Conceptual Framework

The domains of variables needed to conceptualize the determinants and effects of social network resources are integrated in the framework shown in Figure 10.1. Although a considerable body of research has focused on the beneficial effects of social network resources on adaptation (Path E in Figure 10.1), little is known about how the development of these resources can be affected by the preceding sets of personal and environmental factors. With

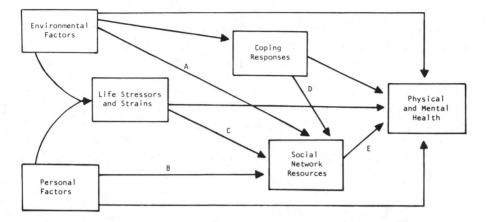

Figure 10.1. A conceptual framework of the determinants and effects of social network resources.

respect to *environmental factors*, for example, geographic proximity between individuals tends to increase the frequency and intensity of their relationship, whereas living in a sociodemographically incongruent neighborhood can inhibit social interaction and the development of friendships (Path A). Such *personal factors* as an extroverted life-style and an orientation toward social affiliation can help an individual create network resources. A tendency toward impulsivity, on the other hand, is related to an increased frequency of major life changes (moving, switching jobs) that can disrupt network ties (Path B).

The *life events domain* is composed of relatively discrete stressors (such as an argument with the boss at work) as well as sequential combinations of such stressors (separation, divorce, child having problems in school) and chronic life strains (being trapped in a monotonous job or a stultifying marriage). The model hypothesizes that both life strains and the coping responses used to handle such strains can affect social network resources (Paths C and D). For instance, stressful events can result in the mobilization and extension of an individual's network and a concomitant increase in social support. Such *coping responses* as seeking information or advice are likely to elicit interpersonal help, whereas attempts to avoid stress or to reduce the tension associated with it by venting one's anger may alienate potentially helpful individuals.

In hypothesizing four sets of determinants of social network resources, the model suggests that part of the relationship between such resources and functioning (Path E) may be due to one or more of these sets of factors. For instance, the protective influence of a cohesive family relationship may be a function of contextual factors (people who experience life events but do not become depressed may live in more culturally congruent neighborhoods), of sociodemographic and personal factors (extroverted individuals may be more adept at mobilizing support), of life stressors (depression-prone individuals are more likely to be experience marital separation and unemployment), and of coping responses (depressed persons may discharge emotion by crying and threatening suicide and thereby alienate supportive confidants).

Many studies have focused on social networks and social support as a given, without attending to the personal and environmental context within which supports are sustained (Mitchell & Trickett, 1980). An examination of such factors may provide clues as to how network ties develop and how they can be enhanced. Following the model shown in Figure 10.1, we discuss the four domains of determinants of social network resources: (1) environmental factors, (2) sociodemographic and personal factors, (3) life stressors and strains, and (4) coping responses.

ENVIRONMENTAL FACTORS

The environmental factors that affect social network resources can be divided into four types: physical and architectural features, organizational factors, suprapersonal characteristics (that is, the average characteristics of the individuals who inhabit a setting), and social–environmental factors (Moos, 1976). We use these four types of factors to describe how neighborhood settings can influence the process and quality of social interaction.

Social scientists have long been interested in how characteristics of communities such as urbanization and residential mobility can influence the quality of life and, in particular, the quality of social ties (Kasarda & Janowitz, 1974; Wellman & Leighton, 1979). There are at least three processes through which specific neighborhood factors can affect the availability and provision of social resources:

1. The physical and organizational features of neighborhoods facilitate and constrain the contexts for meeting and interacting with people.
2. Neighborhood settings define a pool of people (the suprapersonal environment) that is an important source for the recruitment of potential network members.
3. Such settings exert social norms that influence beliefs about the appropriate ways in which support is to be exchanged.

Physical and architectural features have been consistently linked to the development of neighborhood friendship patterns. Studies of student housing complexes have found that next-door neighbors are chosen most often as friends and that friendship choices decline rapidly with increasing distance. Similarly, familiarity among suburban neighbors has been related to the physical closeness and the direct face-to-face orientation of doorways or "fronts" of houses. The more indirect the orientation of two doorways, the less interaction is likely to occur. Life cycle patterns can affect these findings. It is primarily among young married couples with small children that friendships with persons close at hand are likely to be emphasized, in part because young mothers may be more dependent on individuals in the immediate neighborhood for social interaction (Moos, 1976, Chapter 4).

The suprapersonal characteristics of neighborhoods help define the types of available social network resources by influencing the amount of neighborhood social interaction. For example, Bott (1971) has suggested that neighborhoods characterized by high social-status homogeneity and low population turnover are likely to have more close-knit and localized networks. In a recent study, residents in socially homogeneous neighborhoods with low turnover were more likely to be actively involved with each other (Warren, 1978). Other research has shown that access to people of similar ethnicity, life-cycle stage, and religious affiliation may be important in the receipt of certain types of support (Wechsler & Pugh, 1967).

Communities that differ in their internal organization and social environment may also differ in the availability of supportive social ties (Garbarino & Sherman, 1980). Warren (1978) described six neighborhood "types" (integral, parochial, diffuse, stepping stone, transitory, anomic) on the basis of three dimensions: identity (a feeling of belongingness to the neighborhood), interaction (frequency of contact with neighbors), and linkage (association and contacts with individuals and groups outside the local neighborhood). The integral neighborhood is characterized by high identity, high interaction, and high linkage. Mutual neighbor aid is highest in such neighborhoods, probably because people are likely to know one another and persons in need of help are more likely to be visible. Use of formal services is also relatively high, since many residents have contacts with institutions in the larger community. In parochial neighborhoods (high identity, high interaction, low linkage) mutual neighbor aid is high, but use of formal resources is low. The transitory neighborhood (low identity, low interaction, high linkage), with its relatively inactive internal life, shows little mutual assistance among neighbors. Persons entering such neighborhoods are likely to find fewer existing informal networks through which they can develop ties. Although this reflects only one approach, it nonetheless highlights the potential impact of differences in neighborhood organization and climate upon patterns of helping and support.

PERSONAL FACTORS AND SOCIODEMOGRAPHIC CHARACTERISTICS

The relationships between sociodemographic factors and social networks suggest that there are social processes that facilitate and constrain people's ability to maintain access to social support. For instance, social class and life-cycle factors influence the pattern of opportunities for social involvement. As Fischer, Jackson, Stueve, Gerson, Jones and Baldassare (1977) note:

> Being married, and especially having children, influences both people's need for local involvement and their opportunities to achieve such involvement. Children,

for example, connect their parents to the neighborhood in a variety of ways: they demand supervision (which means being with them in the local area), promote informal contact with residents through the children's friends, generate parental interest in the neighborhood and membership in community organizations [p. 147].

In a study of the social networks of over 1000 randomly sampled community residents, Fischer and Phillips (in press) asked participants to name all network members with whom they exchanged instrumental or expressive support. The authors then identified the demographic variables associated with social isolation. The background characteristics of age, social class, and marital status were related to isolation, although the pattern of results varied somewhat as a function of gender and type of isolation (that is, kin or nonkin). In comparison to younger men, older men reported fewer kin and nonkin relationships, but there was no relationship between social isolation and age among women. High income and education were associated with fewer kin relationships, but more nonkin relationships, among both men and women.

Marital status and gender showed complex relationships to isolation. Marital status was related to more kin relationships among men, but not among women. Although married individuals generally had fewer extra-household confidants, married women were more likely than married men to have confidants in addition to their spouse. In a group of community residents aged 50 and over, Depner and Ingersoll (Note 1) also found that women reported more emotionally supportive friends and relatives than did men. In contrast, men relied on exchanges with their spouses for emotional support. Schaefer et al. (in press) examined the level and type of support received in addition to the number of network members who provided support. They found that gender was related to the source rather than the level of emotional support. The spouse provided the most emotional support for men, whereas friends and relatives provided women with as much emotional support as their husbands did. In comparison to nonemployed women, employed women received less emotional support from their husbands, but they tended to obtain emotional support from co-workers and supervisors instead.

The processes that underlie these relationships are still unclear. One possibility is that individuals in particular demographic categories are likely to experience more "network-disruptive" life events. Older men may obtain less support because of the disruptive effects of retirement, physical infirmity, and the death of friends and relatives. Fischer and Phillips (in press) categorize their findings more generally: Such variables as age, income, education, and marital status influence access to and participation in social contexts, thereby structuring opportunities and constraints that shape people's social networks.

Personal Resources and Psychological Functioning

In addition to sociodemographic variables, there are other personal factors that influence the structure and supportiveness of an individual's network.

Individuals may have different levels of personal resources that affect their ability to establish and maintain preferred network structures. They may also have varying network orientations, that is, preferences and beliefs about appropriate ways of developing, maintaining, and utilizing social ties. As Politser (1980) states: "The social network is then not merely an environment that affects a passive individual, but is also a *result* of the individual's interpersonal negotiations in pursuit of his/her goals and well-being [pp. 71–72]."

Such personal resources as self-esteem, sense of self-efficacy, and social competence can influence the development of social network resources. For example, we have shown that self-confidence is positively related to social network resources in family and work settings (Billings & Moos, in press a) and that interpersonal problem-solving skills are positively related to the number of intimates cited by psychiatric clients (Mitchell, in press). In addition, consistent relationships have been found between interpersonal behavior and the cognitive style of field dependence (that is, the degree to which one uses the external field as a referent). Field-dependent persons are more likely than those who are field independent to prefer interpersonal over impersonal situations, to be sensitive to social cues, and to develop supportive relationships (Witkin & Goodenough, 1977).

Beyond the mere absence of skills, maladaptive styles or problems in functioning may decrease support by eliciting negative reactions in network members. In a study of the interpersonal effects of depression, Coyne (1976) arranged for normal individuals to talk to either a depressed or nondepressed patient. Following the conversation, persons who had spoken to depressed patients were themselves significantly more depressed, anxious, and rejecting. The impact of depression on more established interpersonal ties was discussed by Coates and Wortman (1980), who suggested that network members respond with a variety of strategies (such as sympathy, concern, distraction, cheering up) designed to minimize the focal individual's depressive symptoms. When the individual continues to show depressive symptoms, network members may feel frustrated and eventually minimize contact with the depressed person.

Network Orientation

Although clinical literature has noted the influence of individual style upon social relationships, Tolsdorf (1976) was the first to describe different orientations toward the development and utilization of network ties. In comparing the network structures of Veterans Administration medical and psychiatric first admissions, he found the psychiatric patients to have fewer intimate relationships, less reciprocity in relationships, and less ability or willingness to utilize their networks in times of crisis. He described this latter characteristic as a "network orientation," a "set of beliefs, attitudes and expectations concerning the potential usefulness of his network members in helping him cope with a life problem [p. 413]." Whereas medical patients were able to utilize supportive ties and to withdraw selectively from stress-inducing relationships, psychiatric patients showed a pattern of indiscriminate withdrawal in response to interpersonal stress.

A study by Brown (1978) also suggests relationships between negative views concerning help seeking and personal and social resources. Drawing from a longitudinal survey of adults, Brown (1978) focused on differences between persons who sought help from informal or formal support systems in response to troublesome life changes and those who handled problems without seeking assistance. Persons who did not seek help were classified into two groups: the *self-reliant*, who thought they could manage without help, and the *reluctant nonseekers*, who felt that no effective help was available. Reluctant nonseekers reported the lowest self-esteem and least effective coping repertoire. As expected, they also had comparatively unreliable informal networks and strong reservations about discussing their problems with others. The failure of such individuals to maintain network ties probably results in a lack of network support during times of crisis and thus confirms their negative view of help seeking.

An interactional perspective can help to explain the impact of sociodemographic and personal factors upon people's access to social support. These factors may influence opportunities for socialization and the development of interpersonal skills. In addition, they may influence an individual's attractiveness to others, thereby affecting people's willingness to become involved as network members. Thus, persons with few interpersonal skills are less likely to create opportunities for social involvement and less likely to receive a positive response when they do so. A person who develops a negative network orientation is likely to avoid opportunities for enhancing interpersonal skills and resources. Such avoidance serves to accurately reflect as well as to sustain the individual's social world.

LIFE STRESSORS AND STRAINS

Although the literature has emphasized the role of social support in buffering the impact of stressful life events, it is clear that stressors can affect the structure and supportiveness of social networks. Major life events (such as bereavement and geographic relocation) or persistent life strains (such as a spouse's chronic depression) are frequently associated with decreased social support. On the other hand, certain stressors can increase support by prompting the individual's network to mobilize and provide help in response to a discrete life event.

The potential negative effects of major life changes on an individual's social network seem obvious. Job loss, geographic relocation, and other similar events can disrupt established patterns of social ties and limit access to usual sources of support (Schaefer *et al.*, in press). In addition, difficulties in remaining relationships can develop when events (such as job loss) result in negative changes in the individual (for example, depression and loss of self-esteem). Stress can also have an impact through less dramatic but persistent difficulties in important role areas. Financial strain, continuing job dis-satisfaction, and chronic health problems all can serve to decrease one's motivation and ability to maintain network ties, thereby reducing the pool of individuals from whom help can be sought (Pearlin & Lieberman, 1979).

The potential support mobilization role of stressors is suggested by Carveth and Gottlieb (1979), who examined the relationship between stress and social support among mothers shortly after the birth of their first infant. They found moderate positive relationships between stress and social support (that is, rate of contact with friends, amount of problem-centered feedback) and speculated that support had been mobilized but not yet had an impact (see also Barrera, 1981). Supportive behaviors may increase in response to stress either through the initiative of network members or the help-seeking efforts of the focal individual. However, network members may be more willing to provide help in response to normative life changes (such as pregnancy and bereavement) than to nonnormative and less socially accepted events (such as bankruptcy).

COPING RESPONSES

The manner in which stress affects social support is shaped by an individual's coping responses. More adequate coping behavior tends to be associated with greater levels of available support. Billings and Moos (1981) categorized coping responses into three types: active–cognitive (considered several alternatives for handling the problem); active–behavioral (talked with friend about the situation); and avoidance (prepared for the worst, kept my feelings to myself). In groups of alcoholic patients and community residents, individuals who used active coping responses to handle life stressors reported more social network resources, whereas those who used avoidance responses reported fewer resources. Avoidance coping responses are less likely to mobilize support, since they do not permit the individual to acknowledge the need for help.

Individual coping responses vary in the degree to which they encourage the development and utilization of network ties in stressful circumstances, par-ticularly those that involve the loss of support. One series of studies has examined the coping behaviors of wives in response to the job-related absences of their husbands (Boss, McCubbin, & Lester, 1979; McCubbin, 1979) as well as to the general stresses of being married to men in particular professions, such as law enforcement (Maynard, Maynard, McCubbin, & Shao, 1980). Some wives coped by being self-reliant and using their personal resources, or by attempting to build family resources, whereas others tried to develop relationships outside the family by involving themselves in social activities and sharing their personal feelings with others. These varying patterns are likely to influence the structure and quality of a woman's network ties as well as her subsequent adaptation.

We have used a conceptual framework similar to that shown in Figure 10.1 to focus on the determinants of social resources in family settings. Among treated alcoholic patients, for example, we found that the reliance on active problem-solving coping responses, which may promote positive interactions among family members, was associated with perceptions of enhanced family supportiveness. Further analyses showed that families in which the alcoholic member was functioning more poorly, and in which family members experienced more negative life events and higher stress at work, were lower on cohesion and support and showed less agreement about their family environment (Cronkite & Moos, 1980; Moos & Moos, 1981). These results further illustrate the impact of personal functioning, life stressors, and coping responses on family social network resources.

Implications for Research and Practice

In this section we address several themes that emerge from the foregoing material and explore their implications for interventions aimed at enhancing social ties.

THE POTENTIAL UTILITY OF SOCIAL NETWORK ANALYSIS

In the historical overview we noted that three relatively independent strands of research are beginning to merge and to foster more comprehensive approaches to analyzing social support. Such approaches can help to specify what actually transpires within social relationships and to identify the precise exchanges that distinguish supportive from nonsupportive ties. In addition, a focus on social networks enables researchers and clinicians to examine the broader social context within which supportive ties are developed and maintained, as well as to consider the demands and constraints that social relationships exert upon individuals. Social network analysis is an inclusive technique for assessing both the structure of individuals' relationships and the types of exchanges that occur within them (Hammer, 1981; Mitchell & Trickett, 1980).

An analysis of structural dimensions can provide information that is instructive in understanding the dynamics of interpersonal relationships. For example, Wilcox (1981) found that women who were judged to be adjusting less well to divorce had smaller and denser postseparation networks than women judged to be adjusting more positively, even though there were no preseparation differences between the groups on these dimensions. However, the less well adjusted women had shown greater overlap with their spouses' networks prior to separation. Wilcox (1981) suggests that network ties dependent upon the link between the husband and the wife are likely to erode with the strife of marital separation. Similarly, Moos and Fuhr (1982) described a clinical case study in which an adolescent's perception of minimal parental support seemed explainable in terms of her parents' extensive connections to their work. Although still speculative, such network-oriented analyses may provide information on how supportive and nonsupportive ties are developed and maintained.

The specification of network processes goes beyond measures that assess support by identifying variants of help-seeking behavior. What is helpful or supportive may not be explicitly recognized as help by the individual (for example, companionship). In addition, help seeking may reflect a deficiency of network support. In one large-scale community survey, for example, help seeking was found to be a less effective coping technique than self-reliance (Pearlin & Schooler, 1978). The authors suggest that "those who actually get help [are] so thoroughly embedded in a supportive network that they neither have to solicit help in order to receive it nor are necessarily aware of having been a recipient [Pearlin & Schooler, 1979, p. 204]." Social network analysis makes it possible to focus on these kinds of issues and encourages a broader perspective on interpersonal stressors as well as resources.

INTERRELATING NETWORK STRUCTURE AND FUNCTIONS

Although it is assumed that network structure influences network functions, research has yet to clarify the ways in which structural characteristics of networks are related to the provision of support. For instance, only small positive relationships have been reported between network size and perceived support (Barrera, 1981; Schaefer *et al.*, in press). In addition, density seems to be related to perceived support in different ways, depending upon the context. Although network density was associated with more support among students dealing with the stress of exams (Hirsch, 1979), it was related to less emotional support among women undergoing the major life transitions of recent widowhood or midlife resumption of full-time undergraduate studies (Hirsch, 1980). One explanation is that higher-density networks may put more normative pressures on members to maintain existing roles than do less dense networks. In addition, low-density networks can also provide access to a more diverse set of nonfamily roles and activities, some of which may be helpful in establishing alternative social identities. Density may reinforce existing norms and thereby help maintain high or low levels of support, depending upon the nature of these norms.

Similarly, in our studies of representative groups of normal and alcoholic families, we found little relationship between indices of network structure (primarily network size and frequency of contact with friends and relatives) and individuals' perceptions of support in their family and work settings. These findings indicate that structural dimensions cannot be used as indices of the quality of social network resources. However, an analysis of network structure can provide information that is complementary to that obtained from measures of perceived support. A divorcee might report relatively low levels of support, for example, despite having had frequent contact with friends. If most of these individuals were initially members of the spouse's network, their failure to provide support may be due to their continuing ties to the spouse (Wilcox, 1981). An analysis of network structure may help one understand why support is or is not provided.

SPECIFICITY OF RELATIONSHIPS
BETWEEN NETWORK FACTORS AND ADAPTATION

In designing interventions aimed at bolstering interpersonal resources, practitioners need to consider differential effects depending upon the kind of problem and the type and source of support. In his study of women undergoing major life changes, Hirsch (1980) found that adjustment was more strongly related to satisfaction with cognitive guidance than satisfaction with other types of support. The development of coping strategies and plans may be a primary task for women in role transition, so that cognitive guidance is an especially salient form of assistance. Schaefer and her colleagues (in press) showed that tangible assistance was a significant "buffer" against depressive symptoms among community residents, although emotional support was not. Although these findings have yet to be replicated, they suggest that interventions should not focus solely on emotional support.

The relationship between social resources and adaptation may vary as a function of both the source of stress and the source of support (House, 1981). For example, LaRocco, House, and French (1980) found that work-related sources of support were strongly related to reduced levels of job strain, whereas nonwork sources were of equal or greater prominence when general health outcomes were considered. The authors conclude:

> The more specific the type of stress or strain in question, the more likely it is to be affected primarily or only by a limited set of sources of support closely related to the stress or strain in question . . . . We would expect familial stresses and strains to be more affected by sources of support in the family or the network of intimate relatives and friends [p. 214].

The importance of the source of support was also noted by Holahan and Moos (1981), who found that family support was a more effective moderator of the relationship between stress and dysfunction among women, and work support was more important among men. Attending to these issues may enable clinicians to develop more realistic expectations about the impact of particular interventions. Although a support group for new parents may relieve some of the stress associated with parenting, it may not affect more general aspects of family functioning or individual well-being.

In considering these issues, it is important to note that there are a variety of conditions that may affect the relationship between social network factors and adaptation. Network processes may have a general positive effect on functioning whether or not the individual is under stress. The buffering or moderating effect hypothesized by most investigators, however, implies that social resources are most salient under conditions of high stress. Social resources may also affect health by preventing or reducing the occurrence of stressful life events. For example, there is some evidence that people who enjoy high levels of family and work support experience fewer stressful life events (Billings & Moos, in press b).

Although there is conflicting evidence about the conditions under which such effects may occur, a clinician's implicit attitude about how these processes operate can influence program design. Practitioners who believe that increases in network resources will have generally beneficial effects may be more inclined to design broad-based programs. Those who assume that social resources have more impact on persons under stress will probably design intervention efforts targeted toward persons who are experiencing life crises or transitions. A related issue stems from the suggestion that one close relationship is protective and that additional support derived from other sources may not afford much increased benefit. If so, maximally effective interventions should attempt to develop a "safety network" for individuals who have no current source of support.

THE PRACTICAL VALUE OF A CONCEPTUAL FRAMEWORK

The conceptual framework we have presented can help to guide planning for future research and intervention. In addition to enabling a researcher to explore the relative importance of social network resources on adaptation, the framework can help to examine the way in which such resources are linked to and mediate the influences of environmental and personal variables. By identifying a broad set of factors that influence the development and effects of social ties, the model clarifies the fact that the connection between social ties and adaptation may be a function of prior environmental and personal conditions. We have illustrated the utility of this type of model in focusing on the functioning of alcoholic patients (Cronkite & Moos, 1980), as well as in examining adaptation in educational, residential, and community care settings (Moos, 1979, 1980).

Since most of the determinants of social network factors are potentially alterable, the model is rich with implications for intervention at both the environmental and the individual level. At the environmental level, attempts can be made to change work and educational settings to enhance the existing quality of network ties (for example, see Moos, 1979, 1981). At the personal level, programs can be developed to enable people to use their personal resources and coping skills more effectively to sustain supportive social networks. In recognizing that people take an active part in developing and maintaining their social networks, the framework responds to Antonovsky's (1979) call for a focus on salutogenesis and enables researchers and clinicians to explore the factors that maintain health in addition to those that moderate dysfunction.

ACKNOWLEDGMENTS

We wish to thank Andy Billings and Ruth Cronkite for their valuable comments on an earlier draft of the manuscript.

Reference Note

1. Depner, C., & Ingersoll, B. *Social support in the family context.* Paper presented at the thirty-third annual meeting of the Gerontological Society of America, San Diego, Calif., November 1980.

References

Antonovsky, A. *Health, stress, and coping.* San Francisco: Jossey-Bass, 1979.

Barnes, J. A. Class and communities in a Norwegian island parish. *Human Relations*, 1954, 7, 39–58.

Barrera, M. Social support in the adjustment of pregnant adolescents: Assessment issues. In B. H. Gottlieb (Ed.), *Social networks and social support.* Beverly Hills, Calif.: Sage, 1981.

Berkman, L., & Syme, S. Social networks, host resistance and mortality: A nine-year follow-up study of Alameda County residents. *American Journal of Epidemiology*, 1979, 109, 186–204.

Billings, A., & Moos, R. The role of coping responses and social resources in attenuating the stress of life events. *Journal of Behavioral Medicine*, 1981, 4, 139–157.

Billings, A., & Moos, R. Work stress and the stress-buffering roles of work and family resources. *Journal of Occupational Behavior*, in press. (a)

Billings, A., & Moos, R. Social support and functioning among community and clinical groups: A panel model. *Journal of Behavioral Medicine*, in press. (b)

Boss, P., McCubbin, H., & Lester, G. The corporate executive wife's coping patterns in response to routine husband–father absence. *Family Process*, 1979, 18, 79–86.

Bott, E. *Family and social network: Norms and external relationships in ordinary urban families* (Rev. ed.). London: Tavistock, 1971.

Brown, B. Social and psychological correlates of help-seeking behavior among urban adults. *American Journal of Community Psychology*, 1978, 6, 425–439.

Brown, G., & Harris, T. *Social origins of depression: A study of psychiatric disorder in women.* New York: Free Press, 1978.

Caplan, G. *Support systems and community mental health.* New York: Behavioral Publications, 1974.

Cartwright, D., & Zander, A. *Group dynamics: Research and therapy* (3rd ed.). New York: Harper & Row, 1968.

Carveth, W., & Gottlieb, B. The measurement of social support and its relation to stress. *Canadian Journal of Behavioral Science,* 1979, *11*, 179–187.

Coates, D., & Wortman, C. Depression maintenance and interpersonal control. In A. Baum & J. Singer (Eds.), *Advances in environmental psychology* (Vol. 2). Hillsdale, N.J.: Erlbaum, 1980.

Coyne, J. Depression and the response of others. *Journal of Abnormal Psychology,* 1976, *85*, 186–193.

Cronkite, R., & Moos, R. Determinants of the posttreatment functioning of alcoholic patients: A conceptual framework. *Journal of Consulting and Clinical Psychology,* 1980, *48*, 305–316.

Fischer, C., Jackson, R., Stueve, C., Gerson, K., Jones, L., & Baldassare, M. *Networks and places: Social relations in the urban setting.* New York: Free Press, 1977.

Fischer, C., & Phillips, S. Who is alone? Social characteristics of people with small networks. In L. Peplau & D. Perlman (Eds.), *Loneliness: A sourcebook of current theory, research, and therapy.* New York: Wiley, in press.

Garbarino, J., & Sherman, D. High-risk neighborhoods and high-risk families: The human ecology of child maltreatment. *Child Development,* 1980, *51*, 188–198.

Gore, S. The effect of social support in moderating the health consequences of unemployment. *Journal of Health and Social Behavior,* 1978, *19*, 157–165.

Hammer, M. Social supports, social networks, and schizophrenia. *Schizophrenia Bulletin,* 1981, *7*, 45–57.

Hirsch, B. Psychological dimensions of social networks: A multimethod analysis. *American Journal of Community Psychology,* 1979, *7*, 263–277.

Hirsch, B. Natural support systems and coping with major life changes. *American Journal of Community Psychology,* 1980, *8*, 159–172.

Holahan, C., & Moos, R. Social support and psychological distress: A longitudinal analysis. *Journal of Abnormal Psychology,* 1981, *90*, 365–370.

House, J. *Work stress and social support.* Reading, Mass.: Addison-Wesley, 1981.

Kasarda, J., & Janowitz, M. Community attachment in mass society. *American Sociological Review,* 1974, *39*, 328–339.

LaRocco, J., House, J., & French, J. Social support, occupational stress and health. *Journal of Health and Social Behavior,* 1980, *21*, 202–218.

Lin, N., Simeone, R., Ensel, W., & Kuo, W. Social support, stressful life events, and illness: A model and an empirical test. *Journal of Health and Social Behavior,* 1979, *20*, 108–119.

Lindemann, E. *Beyond grief: Studies in crisis intervention.* New York: Jason Aronson, 1979.

Maynard, P., Maynard, W., McCubbin, H., & Shao, D. Family life and the police profession: Coping patterns wives employ in managing job stress and the family environment. *Family Relations,* 1980, *29*, 495–501.

McCubbin, H. Integrating coping behavior in family stress theory. *Journal of Marriage and the Family,* 1979, *41*, 237–244.

Mitchell, J. (Ed.). *Social networks in urban situations.* Manchester, Éng.: Manchester Univ. Press, 1969.

Mitchell, R. Social networks of psychiatric patients: The personal and environmental context. *American Journal of Community Psychology,* in press.

Mitchell, R., & Trickett, E. Social networks as mediators of social support: An analysis of the effects and determinants of social networks. *Community Mental Health Journal,* 1980, *16*, 27–44.

Moos, R. *The social climate scales: An overview.* Palo Alto, Calif.: Consulting Psychologists Press, 1974.

Moos, R. *The human context: Environmental determinants of behavior*. New York: Wiley, 1976.

Moos, R. *Evaluating educational environments: Procedures, methods, findings and policy implications*. San Francisco: Jossey-Bass, 1979.

Moos, R. Specialized living environments for older people: A conceptual framework for evaluation. *Journal of Social Issues*, 1980, *36*, 75–94.

Moos, R. *Work Environment Scale manual*. Palo Alto, Calif.: Consulting Psychologists Press, 1981.

Moos, R., & Billings, A. Conceptualizing and measuring coping resources and processes. In L. Goldberger & S. Breznitz (Eds.), *Handbook of stress: Theoretical and clinical aspects*. New York: MacMillan, in press.

Moos, R., & Fuhr, R. The clinical use of social–ecological concepts: The case of an adolescent girl. *American Journal of Orthopsychiatry*, 1982, *52*, 111–121.

Moos, R., & Moos, B. *Family Environment Scale manual*. Palo Alto, Calif.: Consulting Psychologists Press, 1981.

Moreno, J. *Who shall survive: A new approach to the problem of human interrelations*. Washington, D.C.: Nervous and Mental Disease Publishing, 1934.

Myers, J., Lindenthal, J., & Pepper, M. Life events, social integration and psychiatric symptomatology. *Journal of Health and Social Behavior*, 1975, *16*, 421–427.

Pattison, E., Llamas, R., & Hurd, G. Social network mediation of anxiety. *Psychiatric Annuals*, 1979, *9*, 56–67.

Pearlin, L., & Lieberman, M. Social sources of emotional distress. In R. Simmons (Ed.), *Research in community and mental health* (Vol. 1). Greenwich, Conn.: JAI Press, 1979.

Pearlin, L., & Schooler, C. The structure of coping. *Journal of Health and Social Behavior*, 1978, *19*, 2–21.

Pearlin, L., & Schooler, C. Some extensions of "The structure of coping": A reply to comments by Marshall and Gore. *Journal of Health and Social Behavior*, 1979, *20*, 202–205.

Politser, P. Network analysis and the logic of social support. In R. Price & P. Politser (Eds.), *Evaluation and action in the social environment*. New York: Academic Press, 1980.

Schaefer, C., Coyne, J., & Lazarus, R. Health-related functions of social support. *Journal of Behavioral Medicine*, in press.

Tolsdorf, C. Social networks, support, and coping: An exploratory study. *Family Process*, 1976, *15*, 407–417.

Warren, D. Explorations in neighborhood differentiation. *Sociological Quarterly*, 1978, *19*, 310–331.

Wechsler, H., & Pugh, T. Fit of individual and community characteristics and rates of psychiatric hospitalization. *American Journal of Sociology*, 1967, *73*, 331–338.

Weiss, R. The provisions of social relationships. In Z. Rubin (Ed.), *Doing unto others*. Englewood Cliffs, N.J.: Prentice-Hall, 1974.

Wellman, B., & Leighton, B. Networks, neighborhoods, and communities: Approaches to the study of the community question. *Urban Affairs Quarterly*, 1979, *14*, 363–390.

Wilcox, B. Social support in adjusting to marital disruption: A network analysis. In B. Gottlieb (Ed.), *Social networks and social support*. Beverly Hills, Calif.: Sage, 1981.

Witkin, H., & Goodenough, D. Field dependence and interpersonal behavior. *Psychological Bulletin*, 1977, *84*, 661–689.

chapter 11

Social Support and
Informal Helping Relationships

TONI C. ANTONUCCI
CHARLENE E. DEPNER

Introduction

The potential of the informal social network as a source of helping relationships holds great promise. All problems are not optimally handled through formal services; furthermore, formal services are less likely to be available to a wide range of the population. As we study the importance of informal support relationships, it becomes necessary to understand how they operate, what contributes to a successful network of support relationships, and how one identifies the "successful" as opposed to the "unsuccessful" network. Similarly, if informal support is to be optimally effective for prevention and intervention, it is important to predict the support needs of an individual and understand how support interactions develop into successful relationships over time. This chapter focuses on these issues and provides research evidence pertinent to these points. Our premise is that social support has far-reaching implications for peoples' adaptation to the stresses they experience over the course of life.

Basic Processes in Helping Relationships

Structural, Functional, and Reciprocal
Properties of Social Networks

One of the most basic characteristics of the support network is structure. Structural properties include size, connectedness, symmetry, and stability. It is important to begin with some idea of the structural properties of support networks that might be considered normative, and to that end we shall review some of the findings from our research endeavors, noting the strengths and limitations of the methods used.

In our program at the Institute for Social Research we have been engaged in several studies that focus on social support. Each of these studies utilizes different measurement techniques. The first, "Attachment and the Aging Process: A Lifespan Framework" (Antonucci, Note 1; Antonucci and Beals, Note 2) is a secondary analysis of items from several large datasets that might be regarded as measures of attachment and social support. Thus, within the 2-year duration of that project we have been able to explore the supports perceived by national samples of Americans in 1957, 1971, 1976, and 1978. The samples span a wide spectrum of experiences. However, the approach has several limitations. Each of the investigations used for the secondary analysis was not designed specifically to study social support. In addition, there is considerable variation across studies in the kinds and depth of information obtained. However, the secondary analysis method is useful as an exploratory technique and as a guide for primary data collection on the social support concept.

In our study entitled "Support Networks among New Teachers" (Kahn, Antonucci, & Depner, Note 3) a self-administered questionnaire was developed to measure both the qualitative and quantitative aspects of social support of people trained in secondary education in six major Michigan universities. As shown in Figure 11.1, the information was structured around role relationships. Respondents listed those people important to them in the categories spouse/partner, family/relative, co-workers, and so on. This means of organizing network information is designed by the investigator. It lists "valid" kinds of categories and provides space for a finite number of relationships. We know little about how well this schematic view matches the way the respondent thinks about network structure. Even if the match is a close one, there may be restrictions imposed by the amount of space provided for each kind of relationship. For example, is it reasonable to leave the same number of spaces for family and friends? A further limitation of this method is that it requires a fair level of literacy.

In a third approach used in our study entitled "Supports of the Elderly" (Kahn & Antonucci, Note 4), we developed the instrument pictured in Figure 11.2. This method imposes less restriction on the individual's perception of his or her social network. The diagram, which is designed to be shown to the respondent by the interviewer, has the advantage of offering a visual prompt that hierarchically organizes the network (in this case along the dimensions of closeness and importance). Methodologically, it has the advantage of requiring less in the way of verbal ability, visual acuity, and literacy. Responses may be dictated to an interviewer, with the respondent following along and verifying that answers are recorded correctly.

In "Supports of the Elderly," we examined in detail the support networks of a nationwide sample of people 50 years of age and older. When structural properties of the network were examined (Ingersoll & Depner, Note 5), we found that most respondents had fewer than 10 people in their networks; that network size varied; though not substantially, by age and sex; that most people had relatively well-connected and symmetrical networks; and that there may have been some life cycle differences in late adulthood. These properties are considered in greater detail below.

In listing members of their support network, respondents were asked to include network members at three different levels, represented by three concentric circles. The inner circle represented people to whom they were very close; the middle circle, those to whom they were pretty close; the outer circle, those to whom they were "close—but not quite that close." It is clear that our use of the term *close* connoted family rather than friendship ties to our respondents, since over 80% of the sample nominated a majority of family members in their network.

In this sample there tended to be less than 10 people in the network, with an average of 8.9 (Ingersoll & Depner, Note 5). Men, in general, tended to have fewer network members than women; with one exception, networks tended to be larger in the younger age groups than in the older one (age groups were 50–64, 65–74, and 75+). Since most network members were also family members, it is not surprising that most people reported that their network members knew each other. The measure of symmetry asked who was more likely to initiate contact, the respondent (R) or network members; symmetry was defined as equal initiation from both parties. Most respondents had a fair degree of symmetry in their networks. However, interesting age and sex differences emerged. Women generally reported consistent symmetry across the three age groups. Men, on the other hand, reported the same degree of symmetry as women in the youngest age group (50–64), but the reverse in the next two age groups. In the middle age group (65–74, they reported contacting over half of their network either most or all of the time, rather than half-and-half or less than half. In the oldest age group (75+) over half the men reported contacting either none or few of their network members first. Thus, women showed consistency over these limited sections of the life cycle, but men varied showing symmetry in the younger age group and a lack of symmetry in the two older age groups (for further details see Antonucci, 1981; Depner & Ingersoll, Note 6).

When aggregate data were examined in the study of "Support Networks

SECTION G. PERSONAL NETWORKS

THE NEXT QUESTIONS ARE ABOUT YOUR SITUATION AT THE PRESENT TIME. THEY ARE ABOUT YOUR "PERSONAL NETWORK"

G1. Please list, by first name or initials, the people in each of the categories below who are important to you or to whom you are important. The categories are SPOUSE/PARTNER, FAMILY/RELATIVE, CO-WORKER, SUPERVISOR PROFESSIONAL (E.G., CLERGY, DOCTOR, PSYCHOLOGIST PSYCHIATRIST, SOCIAL WORKER, ETC.) FRIEND. If no people in a category are important to you, leave it blank.

(For each person whose name or initials you list, answer the questions in columns A through E)

	A	B	C			D					E				
	AGE	SEX	WAS THIS PERSON IN YOUR NETWORK LAST YEAR? (check one)			HOW IMPORTANT IS THIS PERSON TO YOU? (check one)					HOW IMPORTANT DO YOU THINK YOU ARE TO THIS PERSON? (check one)				
	in years	M or F	Yes	No	Don't know	Very impor- tant		Important		Not very impor- tant	Very impor- tant		Important		Not very impor- tant
			1	2	3	1	2	3	4	5	1	2	3	4	5
a. SPOUSE/PARTNER															
1.															
b. FAMILY/RELATIVE															
1.															
2.															
3.															
4.															
5.															

c. CO-WORKERS (Include friends who are co-workers here)

1.
2.
3.
4.
5.

d. SUPERVISORS

1.
2.
3.
4.
5.

e. PROFESSIONALS (Instead of name, enter profession of person — e.g., doctor, psychologist, clergy, psychiatrist, social worker, etc.)

1.
2.
3.
4.
5.

f. FRIENDS (not already mentioned)

1.
2.
3.
4.
5.

G2. NOW, PLEASE GO BACK AND CIRCLE THE PERSON IN EACH GROUP WHO IS MOST IMPORTANT TO YOU.

Figure 11.1 Measure of social support used with a college-educated population in a mail-in.

237

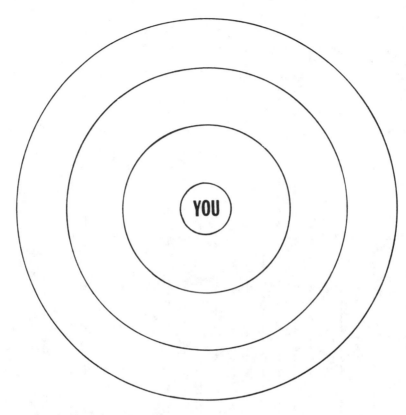

Figure 11.2. Measure of social support used with people 50 years of age or older in face-to-face hour-long interview.

among New Teachers" (Kahn *et al.*, Note 7) the structural network properties remained fairly stable over a 2-year period of major life transition. There were few changes in the number of respondents listing spouses or in the number of family members reported in the network; slightly more co-workers and supervisors were in the network. In this study the effect of the measurement method is again evident, since nonfamily members (i.e., friends, co-workers, and supervisors) appeared in the network listing when we asked about them specifically. Even considering these additions to the network structure, once again the data indicated that networks consist mainly of family who are relatively well connected (know each other) and are stable members of the network structure. Sex differences in this sample have not yet been examined.

The third data source, "Attachment and the Aging Process: A Lifespan Framework" (Antonucci & Beals, Note 2), includes datasets with special and unique characteristics. The three datasets are "Americans View Their Mental Health" (Gurin, Veroff, & Feld, 1960; Veroff, Douvan, & Kulka, 1981). "Quality of American Life" (Campbell, 1981; Campbell, Converse, & Rodgers, 1976), and "Incorporating Time Use Data into Economic and Social Accounts" (Juster & Robinson, Note 8). These studies all used national samples, and the first two included two cohorts, that is, representative samples of the same age groups at different points in time. In these data men tended to report being more satisfied with their marriage and their friendships than women did. Younger people, both men and women, reported being less satisfied with their support than older people. This may have to do with the kinds of supportive functions exchanged within the network. For example, our secondary analysis study identified network satisfaction as a strong predictor of psychological well-being. Increased amounts of social support were associated with higher levels of both life satisfaction and happiness. Although this relationship was true for both men and women, the finding was stronger for women than men, again across all datasets. Finally, although the age pattern is too complex to report here, it is important to mention that the direction of this effect was not linearly related with age. Indeed, considering the family cycle, it seemed that variations in the relationship were particularly connected to family life-cycle events such as marriage, birth of first child, teenage years of children, and adulthood of children (for details, see Tamir & Antonucci, 1981; Antonucci & Beals, Note 2; Beals & Antonucci, Note 9).

As we turn to the functional aspects of support, it is again apparent that different levels of information are available according to the type of questions and methodology employed. In the "Supports of the Elderly" study (Ingersoll & Depner, Note 5), we asked respondents about six specific functions of their network. These concerned people they confided in; people who reassured them; who made them feel respected; who would care for them if they were ill; who would talk with them if they were upset, nervous or depressed; and who would talk with them about their health. We also asked if they provided others with these six specific functions. To study the concept of reciprocity, we identified network members whom the respondent indicated both provided and received each form of support.

The responses indicated several consistent trends. First, women of almost all ages reported that they receive more of each of these functions than men. That is, women were more likely to report that they confide in more people, are reassured by more people, feel respected by more people, feel as though they would be cared for by more people if they were ill, could talk with more people when they were upset, and could talk with more people about their health. Similarly, although the pattern was not as consistent, respondents in this study reported a general decline with age in functions received. Generally, respondents in the oldest age group (75+) reported receiving fewer functions than did respondents in the other two groups (50–64 and 65–74).

One final note on the receipt of functions is pertinent. Summarizing across age and sex, respondents reported, receiving functions in the following rank order (from most to least): respect, care when ill, confiding, reassurance, talk about health, and talk when upset. It is also worth mentioning that our respondents reported that a substantial proportion of the total support functions they receive are provided by members of their social network. With regards to help-seeking behavior, the respondents felt that they are most likely to receive respect but *least* likely to have someone to talk with when they are upset. This has important implications for the role of support networks and areas for possible intervention.

Examining our respondents' reports of the functions they provide to others reveals an interesting and complementary picture. Again, women reported that they provide each of the six functions to more people than men. There was a decline in the number of people our respondents provide support to as they get older. In fact, decline with age in support provided by our respondents was more marked than was the reported decline with age in the functions provided to them by others. The rank ordering of functions given, as reported by our respondents, generally parallels that reported previously. Again, we should note that the forms of support least likely to be provided were basically related to personal concerns.

The "Supports of the Elderly" survey is one of the few studies that actually explored the existence of reciprocal support. The criteria for reciprocity were quite stringent. If Respondent A reported being a confidant of Person #1, and if Person #1 were a person with whom he or she confided, the respondent received a score for reciprocity. The amount of reciprocal support thus calculated was consistently and considerably less than the amount of support our respondents reported they either received or provided. Unanimously, our respondents reported that they provide more supports than they receive across all six functions. Of course, it is impossible to assess whether this impression is corroborated by network members. All the previously established findings remained the same. Women tended to report more reciprocated support than men. Older people reported less reciprocated support than younger people. In addition the rank ordering of reciprocated functions paralleled that reported previously for giving and receiving (see Depner & Ingersoll, Note 6, for more details).

As Kahn and Antonucci (1980) suggested, reciprocity is an important element in the normal functioning of a support network. These findings suggest that the elderly, and perhaps other special groups, are at risk for and may participate in support networks that are unidirectional. This unidirectionality, the receipt rather than the provision of functions, may dramatically affect the operation and effectiveness of the informal support network.

In the study of "Support Networks among New Teachers" (Kahn *et al.*, Note 7), respondents were asked how much others provided them with nine different types of support. These included making you feel loved–liked, approving of the way you do things, giving you advice, making you feel respected, seeing things the way you do, willing to lend you money, showing fondness for you, sizing up people the way you do, and willing to take care of you when ill. Some of these functions, such as respect and care when ill, are identical to those reported in the "Social Networks in Adult Life" study. Interestingly, although the functions measured were not all the same, the rank order reported by respondents in this study is very similar to that of the "Social Networks in Adult Life" study. In short, people reported that others provide what we term *affect* most, *aid* next, and *affirmation* least. Specifically, in hierarchial order, new teachers said that others make them feel liked, show fondness for them, respect them, will lend them money and take care of them when ill, approve of the way they do things and give advice, see things the way they do and size up people the way they do. In the two waves of data 1 year apart, the rank orderings did not change substantially.

Implications for Helping Relationships

The previous sections have described the social support network as a complex system of personal relationships. We have seen that there are numerous possibilities for the structural configuration of the network, and even when networks have similar structural properties, they may vary a great deal in function. In this section, we consider the antecedents and consequences of the structural and functional characteristics of the social support network.

POSITIVE EFFECTS OF SOCIAL SUPPORT NETWORKS

A substantial body of research links the presence of supportive interpersonal relationships with successful resolution of stressful experiences and with overall psychological well-being (for reviews see Cobb, 1976; Heller, 1979; Kahn & Antonucci, 1980; Silver & Wortman, 1980). Although it is generally assumed that social support has beneficial effects, specific mechanisms that account for the relationship between support and well-being have yet to be demonstrated. Specification of such mechanisms is crucial for the development of psychological theory and intervention strategies.

Social support is presumed to work in at least two different ways: (1) *social integration*, effects attributable to the mere existence of a social relationship, and (2) *social interaction*, effects that come about as a result of some exchange within a relationship. Social integration is assumed to promote well-being through its effects on self-definition and continuity of meaning. Inclusion in a social system provides a sense of identity, a "niche," a definition of mutual responsibility. Furthermore, the mere existence of certain relationships, such as marriage and parenthood, provides important rites of passage that define the individual as an appropriately functioning member of society. In addition, one's network of relationships is likely to carry with it certain regularized norms, expectations, and obligations such that the individual develops a rather secure sense of the content and meaning of future interactions. Cobb (1976) identifies one positive effect of support as membership in "a network of mutual obligation." Marris (1975) speaks of the importance of maintaining a network of relationships characterized by predictability and stability. It is such a network that provides continuity of meaning and acts as the framework within which events are interpreted. Such a function is valuable from a psychological standpoint, freeing the individual from continuous negotiation and interpretation of new stimuli. The network's role in interpreting social behavior is also noted by Mitchell (1969). Through these mechanisms and others the simple existence of social bonds is thought to have beneficial effects on well-being. In fact, the absence of social ties has been linked to mortality (Berkman, 1977; Berkman & Syme, 1979; Durkheim, 1957; Lalley, Black, Thornock, & Hawkins, 1979).

Social interaction refers to the specific supportive behaviors that may have positive effects on well-being. Much of the research in this area has not been linked to specific work on social networks. Social psychologists have documented that the presence of others may have beneficial effects through such processes as social comparison, social facilitation, and affiliation. The literature on social support identifies specific forms of support that are considered beneficial. Cobb (1976) identifies emotional support, such as feeling loved and cared for, and esteem support, which contributes to a sense of personal worth. Kahn and Antonucci (1980) classify support as *affect* (similar to Cobb's definition of emotional support), *aid* (which may be advice, information, or direct intervention in problem solving), and *affirmation* (contributing to the individual's sense that he or she is interpreting events correctly). In their review of the forms of support most useful to victims of uncontrollable aversive events, Dunkel-Schetter and Wortman (1981) identify the two more important forms as (1) ventilation, the opportunity to express feelings fully, and (2) validation, similar to Kahn and Antonucci's affirmation. Definitions of social support by Caplan (1974) and Caplan and Killiea (1976) also include validation and feedback, adding need fulfillment and reciprocity. Wellman (1981) notes that the social network provides important links to needed instrumental resources.

NEGATIVE EFFECTS OF SUPPORT NETWORKS

The effects of the social support network may not always be beneficial, however. Any relationship may have both positive and negative features. It has often been noted, for example, that family members are sources of stress as well as support (Croog, 1970). When we view the social support network as a system of mutual obligation, it can be seen that the network not only provides support but demands it as well. This natural giving and receiving of support has been termed a "support bank" (Kahn & Antonucci, Note 10), a resource from which one draws and to which one contributes. For the most part, the net effect of this exchange of support is probably beneficial. However, in some instances, the demands of the network may be excessive and burdensome. In our study of "Supports of the Elderly," people in the youngest age group (50–64) reported that their network was too demanding. However, this tendency decreased with age. A lack of balance between support provided and received is one potentially negative effect of the support network.

Another negative effect of the network is more structural in nature. Although social integration—the formation of social bonds—is generally regarded as beneficial, it has been noted that some bonds have harmful side effects. For example, the isolation and low prestige of the housewife role has been cited by many as the cause of married women's deficit on measures of emotional and physical well-being (Bernard, 1973). In addition, the formation of some bonds—such as marriage—may establish additional bonds that are not voluntarily chosen (e.g., spouse's friends and family) and may be problematic in nature. Furthermore, the network's ability to define meaning may also have negative consequences. An individual may become a scapegoat of the network, or the network may label the individual in some other negative fashion. Similarly, the network's power to assign meaning to events might promote deviant or maladaptive behavior, as in "socialized" juvenile delinquency.

Although members of the support network are valuable resources for personal well-being, there may be concomitant negative consequences of network membership. One must be responsive to the needs of other network members, and such demands may be excessive. Also, supportive benefits are not always evenly distributed within the social network. Certain social bonds are less beneficial to the individual than others. Finally, although there may be concerned and well-meaning people in an individual's support network, their efforts to meet his or her needs for support may not always be successful. In fact, some efforts at support may make the situation worse. Such negative aspects of support also enter into the calculus of the effects of social support.

INDIVIDUAL DIFFERENCES IN THE EFFECT OF SUPPORT

It has been noted that social support seems to "work" more effectively in some circumstances than in others and that we are far from identifying the most effective match of support and situation. In attempting to solve this puzzle, researchers have identified certain sources of variation that affect the way in which support operates. These include individual differences in the need for support, sex differences, and life cycle differences in support networks.

Some data indicate that the quality and quantity of available support vary considerably across individuals. There is also literature that suggests that there is considerable variation in dispositional needs for social support (Antonovsky, 1979; Green, 1975; Hinkle, 1974; Murray, 1938). Further, even if social relationships are a major source of an individual's personal gratification, it does not necessarily follow that such an individual will adopt a coping style that emphasizes reliance on interpersonal resources. Social support may be an integral part of the individual's coping style or it may be completely incompatible with long-term mechanisms of coping and defense, such as denial (Heller, 1979). Finally, circumstances dictate whether social support will be a reasonable or efficient means of addressing certain problems. Dunkel-Schetter and Wortman (1981) observe that some circumstances (e.g., terminal illness) are likely to frighten off potential supporters because they may feel vulnerable to the same fate and/or incapable of solving the problem. There may in fact be distinctions in the usefulness of support for normative versus nonnormative events. Support may be helpful and abundant for anticipated life transitions such as marriage, parenthood, and retirement. However, many networks may be ill equipped to deal with more traumatic or atypical events, such as severe physical impairment and financial crises (Neugarten & Hagestad, 1976). Therefore, the nature of the problem may define the feasibility of human intervention as well as the pool of support available.

SEX DIFFERENCES IN SOCIAL SUPPORT

Much of what has been written about the social relationships of men and women suggests that there will be both qualitative and quantitative sex differences in social support networks. Researchers have noted that whereas men's social networks seem to be large and diffuse, the networks of women are smaller and more intense (Hess, 1979).

Although men tend to have a wider network of casual acquaintances, there is some evidence that their network of close personal relationships is more restricted. Some research has shown that men tend to rely on one key relationship, usually their relationship with their spouse, as the source of confiding and as the nexus of the fuller range of social relationships (Komarovsky, 1974; Lopata, 1975; Lowenthal & Haven, 1968; Lowenthal & Robinson, 1976; Longino & Lipman, 1981).

This research implies that in addition to structural differences the network is likely to function quite differently for men and women, with men relying on a smaller number of relationships for at least some resources.

AGE-RELATED DIFFERENCES IN SOCIAL SUPPORT

Aggregate-level observations of samples spanning a wide age range may obscure support needs and resources that are unique to specific points in the life course. Developmental changes at every level—biological, psychological, and social—have implications for the nature of the support network and the ways in which it is used.

We view the social support network as evolving over time. Many network connections are established and maintained via social roles (e.g., employment, marriage, parenthood, friendship, organizational membership). The early phases of the life course are marked by the acquisition of such roles and the formation and consolidation of key relationships linked to these roles. It is in the later years when marked losses and changes in the network are most likely to take place. Relationships founded in role contexts, such as co-worker relationships, may dissolve or need to be reformulated on a different basis. Mortality of network members is a source of loss and may bring about key changes in other relationships in the network. Widows, for example, suffer not only the loss of the spouse but may also find that they are not included in social circles in which they participated with the spouse.

This line of reasoning suggests that there will be distinct age-related differences in the presence–absence–loss of key social relationships. Furthermore, the duration of existing bonds is likely to vary with the age of the focal individual. This has implications for the functioning of such bonds. For example, long-term relationships are apt to be more comfortable. Interactions are regularized, expectations clear, and there is a mutuality and shared experience that makes negotiation less necessary. Younger individuals are not likely to have many, if any, bonds of this nature, whereas older people may have already suffered the loss of such bonds.

Age-related variations in the need for social support may also be cited. The acquisition of certain roles (e.g., employment, parenthood) involves unique requirements for support. Similarly, the loss of certain roles may prompt the individual to look to the network as an alternate source of certain need gratification. Aging also may bring about changes in health, mobility, financial resources, etc., that will affect what the individual requires from and can provide to the network. In addition to being related to changes in resources needed from the network, age may also change the ability of the network to respond to such needs. In a highly homogenous network, needs of network members may be similar and resources to meet them commensurately scarce. That is, an aging network may find it difficult to meet the needs of the aging individual. Our data indicating that older people tend to provide less support to their network members and receive more support than they provide suggest that a support decrement may occur with age. Finally, Dunkel-

Schetter and Wortman (1981) suggest that the needs of the elderly are precisely of the nature most unreceptive to social support. In their work on victimization, these authors find that people avoid intervention in situations in which they may feel vulnerable to a similar fate and/or helpless in solving the problem. Dunkel-Schetter and Wortman suggest that many of the support needs of the aged have one or both of these characteristics. If they are correct, the support networks of the elderly are not only ravaged by time but also are less motivated and equipped to meet supportive needs.

SOCIAL SUPPORT AND WELL-BEING

In the preceding sections we have reviewed the evidence for the strong effects of social support. Relationships with those close to us have important implications for the way we feel about ourselves and our lives. In this section we will attempt to specify the link between social support and well-being.

Well-being may be defined in many different ways. One obvious distinction is between well-being as measured objectively through indicators quantifiable by an outside party (e.g., income, absence of disease, etc.) and well-being as measured subjectively, that is, the individual's subjective evaluation of experiences (e.g., satisfaction with income or health). Although objective and subjective measures are usually related, they are far from interchangeable. Whether measured objectively or subjectively, well-being may be operationalized as how the individual is doing in any of a number of domains (or using some combination of all domains). Campbell (1981) cites some of the domains that are most closely linked to a generalized, global feeling of life quality: feelings about self, standard of living, family life, marriage, friends, and work. Each of these many definitions is suitable for some purposes. In this chapter, we will use a global definition of well-being that may represent any of the numerous operationalizations.

Some researchers (House, 1981; LaRocco, House, & French, 1980) have begun to specify the various effects of support. Our notion of the relationship between support and well-being is portrayed in Figure 11.3.

A *life event* may be literally any change in the experience of the individual. It may be a traumatic event, such as the loss of a job, or a life transition, such as turning 65, or any other change in the status quo. *Objective stress* is a feature of the event that is quantifiable by an outside party. For example, if an individual loses a job, objective stress might be indicated by loss of income. *Subjective stress* involves the reaction of the focal individual, his or her own assessment that the event is stressful or unpleasant. *Well-being* may be a psychological or physiological indicator (objective or subjective). For example, it may be measured as the individual's self-esteem, the absence of physiological symptoms such as stomach pain or headache, or more global assessments of life quality. According to our model, social support has its own direct effects

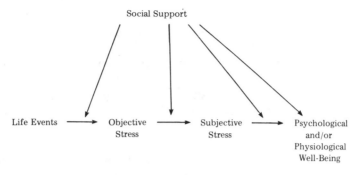

Figure 11.3. The relationship between social support and well-being.

on well-being as well as the potential for intervention at several points in the life-events–well-being sequence.

Direct Effects

As can be seen from our model of the support–well-being relationship, many of the hypothesized effects of support may be categorized in one of two ways: a main effect or a conditioning effect. The main effect describes support as affecting well-being in its own right. For example, Wood and Robertson (1978) found that elderly people with good relationships with family and friends had heightened feelings of life satisfaction. Conversely, the actions of network members may have direct negative effects on well-being. For example, trouble in the marital relationship may diminish well-being. Such direct effects can be assessed quite straightforwardly by determining the relationship between measures of support and measures of well-being.

Conditioning Effects

Other theories of social support may be categorized as conditioning effects. They portray social support as moderating or conditioning the effects of other forces on well-being. For example, Lowenthal and Haven (1968) report that having a confidant facilitates adaptation to such transitions as retirement and widowhood. In the most simple case, the conditioning hypothesis predicts that individuals with good support will not be affected by stress, whereas those with poor support will suffer diminished well-being in the presence of stress. There is not complete consensus in the literature about the point at which support is thought to intervene. We make a distinction between insulating and buffering effects.

An *insulating* hypothesis would hold that support intervenes prior to the subjective perception of stress (Jackson, Note 11). For example, in the case of the person who loses a job, members of the network might have the power to forestall the crisis by preventing the job loss. In the event of job loss, network members might objectively change the situation (e.g., by providing financial aid or lining up a new job) so that the situation does not become an objectively stressful one. On the other hand, the situation might be objectively stressful but the network could act to affect the individual's perception of the situation so that it is not subjectively stressful. Network members might offer encouragement or help the individual to view the job change in its most positive light. Such explanations of the effects of social support portray it as shielding the individual from the experience of subjective stress by modifying the actual or perceived aspects of the situation.

The *buffering* hypothesis regards support as affecting the relationship between subjective stress and well-being. In this case, the stress is both objectively and subjectively experienced, but something about the social support system allows the individual to cope with the stressful situation. To follow the job loss example, the network might offer instrumental aid in job hunting, do things to bolster the individual's self-esteem, or take other action to render the effects of stress less devastating. For both insulating and buffering effects, well-being is a function of the interaction of support and subjective stress.

A saturated model, specifying all possible main and interaction effects (as well as possible control variables) could also be tested. This model would be the specification of the full model depicted in Figure 11.3. Each of these examples portrays the effects of support as beneficial. We need not be limited to this hypothesis. Essentially, however, the format of the test is the same, only the specification of the interaction between support and well-being changes.

Ongoing Issues in the Study of Social Support

Thus far we have considered theoretical models and empirical data without great attention to their limitations. We turn now to a consideration of conceptual and methodological issues that affect both the type of model one adopts and the kind of data one acquires (for an extended discussion of these issues, see Antonucci & Depner, Note 12).

THE DEFINITION OF SUPPORT

Although the terms *social support* and *support networks* have colloquial meaning, there are a variety of ways to define these concepts. Thus, one can measure levels of intimacy, the kinds of support provided, or the kinds of relationships (e.g., family, friends) people have. Each definition leads to a method that introduces some kind of structure and imposes criteria that the respondent will use in formulating replies. The actual words used to ask the questions concerning social support or support networks are significant and may produce very different types of responses.

For example, the researcher might operationalize support as closeness (which may be confused with physical proximity), importance (which may include those with personal control over the respondent's fate), frequency of contact (which may exclude important individuals rarely seen in person), use in problem solving (which may be highly situationally specific), or the provision of certain forms of support (which may combine those who provide support voluntarily with those who do so as part of official role requirements).

These examples illustrate the many ways in which social support might be measured. They all have some validity, perhaps because each taps some aspect of a "supportive" relationship. Investigations that use different operational definitions are measuring subtly different things.

LIMITS IMPOSED BY MEASUREMENT TECHNIQUES

The knowledge gained in research is constrained by the types and form of questions asked. Whole features of a problem may go unexamined simply because no questions are asked about them. Other features may receive excessive attention in a study because they are the subject of probes and special emphasis.

Constraints on the depth of response, such as limiting response options to precoded categories, affect what and how much can be reported. Without such constraints, a person might list an unwieldy number of people as members of his or her network but not have a close relationship with any of them. Conversely, predefined response categories might exclude an important network member who does not readily fit into the classification. Such a problem has developed in studies of friendship networks. Despite a close, intimate relationship with a spouse or other relative, they are not labeled "friend" by the respondents; the framework provided effectively ruled out the very relationships of interest (Candy, Troll, & Levy, 1981).

Clearly, only a compromise can be achieved. The investigator must impose a framework that organizes information and prompts the respondent for important information. However, if questions are constructed with insight and pretested thoroughly they will measure a perspective that is not radically different from that used by most respondents.

ACTUAL VERSUS POTENTIAL AND OBJECTIVE VERSUS SUBJECTIVE SUPPORT

Our respondents want to report not only what they actually do for others but also what they *would* do if asked. Similarly, when reporting what others did for them, our respondents want to report not only what others actually did, but also what they *could* ask others to do. During debriefing they told us they had no difficulty separating the concepts of actual versus potential support, but that the distinction seemed artificial and misleading. For example, respondents were uncomfortable saying that a network member did not listen to their problems when they were reasonably certain the network member would gladly do so if asked.

As we collected information about the functions social networks serve, we also became increasingly sensitive to the differences between objective and subjective levels of support. An individual may value some forms of support more highly than others. Furthermore, the same form of support may be evaluated differently when it comes from different network members. For example, an adult daughter who cooks and cleans for her mother every day may be reported by her mother as not helping much, compared with the distant son who phones weekly and is reported as a great source of support because he gives advice and would help in other ways if he were asked.

RECIPROCITY

Our work has been directed toward the effects of the exchange—giving and receiving—of social support. Colloquial wisdom suggests that a satisfactory relationship involves reciprocity. However, the study of reciprocity is difficult.

One can study the return-in-kind of specific supportive functions or complementary supportive functions. If the questionnaire suggests that support is given but not received, this may be a valid impression or it may simply reflect the omission of the reciprocal function in the instrument. Only a comprehensive list of functions would solve this problem, but the most complete measures are also the most lengthy and tedious. Clearly, every investigation must try to strike a balance between these two concerns.

Earlier, we alluded to difficulties in evaluating objective and subjective support. Feelings of reciprocity are also subject to this problem. What may be viewed as exceedingly inequitable from "objective" indicators may be perceived as satisfactory by the respondent, for reasons not revealed in the measures used.

MEASURING THE EFFECTS OF SUPPORT

Several methodological problems have been encountered by researchers attempting to empirically demonstrate the effects of support. Many problems evolve from the limitations of cross-sectional design. The respondents are asked to report events in the past (subject to recall error) and about the behavior of those close and important to them (subject to social desirability bias) in one data collection. This may or may not encompass a time frame long enough to register long- as well as short-term effects.

Further research must emphasize the testing of specific mechanisms thought to account for support effects. Much of the body of social support research rests on simple correlation evidence of the coexistence of support and well-being. Heller (1979) points out that this is not evidence of the impact of support. The relationship may be the result of both support and well-being being related to another exogenous variable, such as social competence. For example, those who have a satisfying life and cope well with difficulties may also be adept at forming satisfying relationships, but social support might not be the reason for enhanced well-being. Recent research strengthens the case that the relationship between support and well-being is not spurious. Holahan and Moos (1981) report a relationship between changes in support and changes in psychological adjustment, after appropriate statistical controls have been implemented. Still, the reasons for the relationship need to be empirically demonstrated. The testing of specific mechanisms, however, will be a demanding process. Self-report measures of components of our model, such as support, well-being, and so on may be so similar operationally that it is doubtful that independent constructs are being assessed. The respondent may view them as fundamentally the same question. The possibility of such artifacts calls for research designs that include multiple measures of key constructs from independent sources, measures that would optimally be prospective rather than retrospective in nature. Even though correlations between measures of the constructs in the model may be artificially inflated because of the shared-methods error, the components of the model do not account for all the variance on the dependent measure. We know that well-being is a multiply determined phenomenon (Andrews & Withey, 1976; Campbell, 1981). This makes sense conceptually, but methodologically it makes effects difficult to establish.

These are but a few of the methodological issues that affect research on social support. Investigators should be cognizant of these issues when designing research and drawing inferences from data.

Conclusion

In the preceding pages we have attempted to underscore the importance and utility of the social support concept. Although the effects of support make sense inherently, we have noted the difficulties of rigorously documenting social support processes. We have made several suggestions for improving research in this area, but certain difficult problems remain to be solved. Their resolution and continued research, however, will be a tremendous contribution to a field with much promise both for theory and practice.

Reference Notes

1. Antonucci, T. *Attachment in the aging process: A lifespan framework.* Final Report to the National Institute on Aging, 1981.
2. Antonucci, T., & Beals, J. *Attachment in the aging process: A lifespan framework.* Paper presented at the meeting of the Gerontological Society of America, San Diego, November 1980.
3. Kahn, R. L., Antonucci, T., & Depner, C. *Support networks among new teachers.* Current study at the Survey Research Center, University of Michigan, Ann Arbor, 1979.
4. Kahn, R. L., & Antonucci, T. *Supports of the elderly.* Current study at the Survey Research Center, University of Michigan, Ann Arbor, 1979.
5. Ingersoll, B., & Depner, C. *Support networks of middle-aged and older adults.* Paper presented at the meeting of the American Psychological Association, Montreal, September, 1980.
6. Depner, C., & Ingersoll, B. *Social support in the family context.* Paper presented at the meeting of the Gerontological Society of America, San Diego, November 1980.
7. Kahn, R. L., Antonucci, T. C., & Depner, C. *Interim report: Social support networks among new teachers.* Ann Arbor: Institute for Social Research, University of Michigan, 1981.
8. Juster, F. T., & Robinson, J. P. *Incorporating time use data into economic and social accounts.* Proposal submitted to National Science Foundation, 1974.
9. Beals, J., & Antonucci, T. *Age and family life cycle issues.* Paper presented at the meeting of the American Psychological Association, Montreal, September 1980.
10. Kahn, R. L., & Antonucci, T. C. *Applying social psychology to the aging process: Four examples.* Paper presented at the Conference on Training Psychologists for Work in Aging, Boulder, Colorado, June 1981.
11. Jackson, J. S. *Three generation life-cycle analysis of black aging* (Addendum to grant application). Ann Arbor: Institute for Social Research, University of Michigan, 1980.
12. Antonucci, T., & Depner, C. *Social support through the life course: Conceptual and methodological issues.* Paper presented at the meeting of the American Psychological Association, Montreal, September 1980.

References

Andrews, F. M., & Withey, S. B. *Social indicators of well-being: Americans' perceptions of life quality.* New York: Plenum, 1976.

Antonovsky, A. *Health, stress, and coping.* San Francisco: Jossey-Bass, 1979.

Antonucci, T. C. Frontiers in aging: Attachment and social support across the life span. *Frontiers in Aging Symposium Proceedings,* 1981.

Berkman, L. F. *Social networks, host resistance and mortality: A follow-up study of Alameda County residents.* Unpublished doctoral dissertation, University of California, Berkeley, 1977.

Berkman, L. F., & Syme, S. L. Social networks, host resistance and mortality: A nine-year follow-up study of Alameda County residents. *American Journal of Epidemiology,* 1979, *109*, 186–204.

Bernard, J. *The future of marriage.* New York: Bantam Books, 1973.

Campbell, A. *The sense of well-being in America: Recent patterns and trends.* New York: McGraw-Hill, 1981.

Campbell, A., Converse, P. E., & Rodgers, W. L. *The quality of American life*. New York: Russell Sage Foundation, 1976.

Candy, S. G., Troll, L. E., & Levy, S. G. A developmental exploration of friendship functions in women. *Psychology of Women Quarterly*, 1981, *5*, 456–473.

Caplan, G. *Support systems and community mental health*. New York: Behavioral Publications, 1974.

Caplan, G., & Killilea, M. (Eds.). *Support systems and mutual help*. New York: Grune & Stratton, 1976.

Cobb, S. Social support as a moderator of life stress. *Psychosomatic Medicine*, 1976, *38*, 300–314.

Croog, S. H. The family as a source of stress. In S. Levine & N. A. Scotch (Eds.), *Social stress*. Chicago: Aldine, 1970.

Dunkel-Schetter, C., & Wortman, C. Dilemmas of social support: Parallels between victimization and aging. In S. B. Kiesler, J. N. Morgan, & V. K. Oppenheimer (Eds.), *Aging: Social change*. New York: Academic Press, 1981.

Durkheim, E. *Suicide*. Glencoe, Ill.: Free Press, 1957.

Green, W. Effects of brief psychotherapy during the hospitalization period on the recovery process in heart attacks. *Journal of Consulting and Clinical Psychology*, 1975, *43*, 223–232.

Gurin, G., Veroff, J., & Feld, S. *Americans view their mental health*. New York: Basic Books, 1960.

Heller, K. The effects of social support: Prevention and treatment implications. In A. P. Goldstein & F. H. Kanfer (Eds.), *Maximizing treatment gains: Transfer enhancement in psychotherapy*. New York: Academic Press, 1979. Pp. 353–382.

Hess, B. B. Sex roles, friendship and the life course. *Research on Aging*, 1979, *1*, 494–515.

Hinkle, L. E., Jr. The effects of exposure to cultural change, social change and changes in interpersonal relationships on health. In B. Dohrenwend & B. Dohrenwend (Eds.), *Stressful life events: Their nature and effects*. New York: Wiley, 1974.

Holahan, C. L., & Moos, R. H. Social support and psychological distress: A longitudinal analysis. *Journal of Abnormal Psychology*, 1981, *90*, 365–370.

House, J. *Work stress and social support*. Reading, Mass: Addison-Wesley, 1981.

Kahn, R. L., & Antonucci, T. C. Convoys of social support: A life-course approach. In P. B. Baltes & O. G. Brim (Eds.), *Life-span development and behavior* (Vol. 3). New York: Academic Press, 1980.

Komarovsky, M. Patterns of self-disclosure of male undergraduates. *Journal of Marriage and the Family*, 1974, *36*, 677–686.

Lalley, M., Black, E., Thornock, M., & Hawkins, J. D. Older women in single room occupant (SRO) hotels: A Seattle profile. *The Gerontologist*, 1979, *19*, 67–74.

LaRocco, J. M., House, J. S., & French, J. R. P., Jr. Social support, occupational stress, and health. *Journal of Health and Social Behavior*, 1980, *21*, 202–218.

Longino, C. F., Jr., & Lipman, A. Married and spouseless men and women in planned retirement communities: Support network differentials. *Journal of Marriage and the Family*, 1981, *43*, 169–177.

Lopata, H. Z. Support systems of elderly urbanites: Chicago of the 1970s. *The Gerontologist*, 1975, *15*, 35–41.

Lowenthal, M. F., & Haven, C. Interaction and adaptation: Intimacy as a critical variable. *American Sociological Review*, 1968, *33*, 20–30.

Lowenthal, M. F., & Robinson, B. Social networks and isolation. In R. H. Binstock & E. Shanas (Eds.), *Handbook of aging and the social sciences*. New York: Van Nostrand-Reinhold, 1976. Pp. 432–456.

Marris, P. *Loss and change*. Garden City, N.Y.: Anchor Books, 1975.

Mitchell, J. C. (Ed.). *Social networks and urban situations*. Manchester, Eng.: Manchester Univ. Press, 1969.

Murray, H. *Explorations in personality*. New York: Oxford Univ. Press, 1938.

Neugarten, B. L., & Hagestad, G. O. Age and life course. In B. H. Binstock & E. Shanas (Eds.), *Handbook of aging and the social sciences*. New York: Van Nostrand-Reinhold, 1976.

Silver, R. L., & Wortman, C. B. Coping with undesirable life events. In J. Garber & M.E.P. Seligman (Eds.), *Human helplessness*. New York: Academic Press, 1980.

Tamir, L. M., & Antonucci, T. C. Self-perception, motivation, and social support through the family life course. *Journal of Marriage and the Family*, 1981, *43*, 151–160.

Veroff, J., Douvan, E., & Kulka, R. *The inner American*. New York: Basic Books, 1981.

Wellman, B. Do networks support? A structural perspective. In B. Gottlieb (Ed.), *Social networks and social support in community mental health*. Beverly Hills, Calif.: Russell Sage Foundation, 1981.

Wood, V., & Robertson, J. Friendship and kinship interaction: Differential effects on the morale of the elderly. *Journal of Marriage and the Family*, 1978, *40*, 367–375.

chapter 12

Social-Psychological Processes
in Informal Help Seeking[1]

BELLA M. DePAULO

Introduction

A basic fact about helping is that people with problems—even potentially debilitating problems—often do not seek the help that they need (e.g., Bergin, 1971; Dohrenwend, Dohrenwend, Gould, Link, Neugebauer, & Wunsch-Hitzig, 1980). These problems might include medical conditions that are continually worsening, severe financial difficulties, or a variety of personal coping problems, often precipitated by stressful life events. Although the seriousness of these problems might be expected to act as a facilitator of help seeking, it is also clear that there are costs associated with seeking help that act as deterrents. People in need of medical or psychiatric care, for example, may fear what they might find out about themselves, about their condition, and about what steps they should take in order to deal effectively with their problems. Furthermore, the financial costs of professional assistance may be substantial, and matters of inconvenience can further inhibit tendencies to seek help. Social and cultural stereotypes can also deter the potential help

[1]Preparation of this chapter was supported by grants from the National Institute of Mental Health and the University of Virginia Research Council.

Basic Processes in Helping Relationships

seeker, particularly if these stereotypes are part of the normative structure of the individual's reference group. Thus, for example, "diseased" people are sometimes believed to be dirty or weak; people who seek psychological assistance risk being labeled as crazy, unpredictable, and untrustworthy; and recipients of material assistance (e.g., welfare recipients) are often perceived as lazy, inept, or morally inferior. In a sense, then, it is understandable that people with problems of great personal consequence sometimes hesitate to seek help.

Having considered some of the more serious types of needs, I will turn to more mundane instances. Consider the following casual observations of some of my friends and pilot study subjects:

1. John Doe and Mary Smith go on occasional excursions to far-away skiing slopes that they have never been to before. Not infrequently, they get lost. An argument then ensues over which of them will ask for help. Often they drive around aimlessly, as neither will consent to ask a stranger for directions.

2. Upon entering a new supermarket, Susie Cue searches every aisle rather than asking a clerk for assistance in locating the one desired item.

3. In a pilot study with undergraduate women, subjects were recruited to participate in what was described as a visual perception experiment. Subjects, tested individually, were given five wooden sticks of varying sizes. They were to take each stick in turn, stand it up at one end of a table, and then walk to the other end of the table to draw their estimate of the size of the stick on a piece of paper. Meanwhile, another subject (actually a confederate), who had presumably just completed the task with the sticks, sat quietly nearby completing a questionnaire. Subjects proceeded smoothly in their drawing of the first two sticks. The problem arose with the third stick, which had been slightly rounded at the bottom so that it would not stand up. As in a previous study (Stokes & Brickman, 1974), approximately half the women asked the confederate for help in standing up the stick. However, our study included males, who devised a remarkable number of ingenious and illicit ways to get the stick to stand (e.g., searching the experimental room for scraps of paper to prop under the stick and drawing the stick lying down, thereby defying very explicit experimental instructions); but 11 of the 12 never asked the confederate for help.

These are indeed mundane instances. The individuals in all three examples can, and do, get along quite well without help. Their "needs" do not become that much more pressing when they put off asking for help. In short, the facilitators of help seeking in these instances are not very powerful. These people do, though, suffer certain inconveniences: They take needless, time-consuming detours, meanwhile putting off highly pleasurable activities; they engage in frustrating and time-consuming supermarket searches; and they spend more time in their psychology experiments than they have to. Why do they tolerate these inconveniences, minor though they may be? Why *not* ask for help? Perhaps the costs of asking for help in these instances, in which help is merely convenient rather than necessary, are much more subtle than in situations in which the needs of the help seekers are greater (cf. Gross & McMullen, 1981). These situations seem to be telling us something important about the process of help seeking. They provide a point of departure for learning more about why people do or do not seek help.

People's unwillingness to ask for help—whether with major problems or minor ones—is of interest theoretically because by refusing to obtain useful resources, people are in a sense working against their own self-interest (Gross & McMullen, 1981). This phenomenon is all the more intriguing with respect to everyday help seeking, in which the costs of asking for help are fewer or more subtle.

APPROACHES TO STUDYING HELP SEEKING

Until recently, research on help seeking has focused on medical help seeking, psychiatric help seeking, and help seeking as a response to stressful life events. Research on help seeking from professional helpers or from formal helping institutions has been primarily an investigation of demographic and attitudinal correlates of help seeking or help utilization. Thus, for example, it has been shown consistently that people who seek medical care, dental care, and psychological assistance, who utilize social services facilities and legal facilities, or who join self-help groups tend to be well-educated, white, middle-class, and female (for reviews, see Gottlieb, 1976; Gourash, 1978; Greenley & Mechanic, 1976; Kadushin, 1969; McKinlay, 1972). Attitudinal correlates of psychiatric help seeking include readiness to acknowledge one's need for help, interpersonal openness, desire for feedback about oneself, and confidence in mental health professionals (e.g., Fischer & Turner, 1970; Snyder, Ingram, & Newburg, Chapter 13 in this volume). Internal locus of control is one attitudinal predictor of medical help seeking (e.g., Wallston, Maides, & Wallston, 1976). Although medical and psychiatric help seeking are often studied independently, it is clear that people who seek help often present a mixture of physical complaints and psychological problems (Pennebaker & Skelton, 1978; Tessler & Mechanic, 1978).

Recently, researchers have shown increasing interest in help seeking from nonprofessional sources (see Moos & Mitchell, and Antonucci & Depner Chapters 10 and 11, respectively, in this volume). In the social support research domain, however, the focus is on life events that are more stressful and serious than the ones discussed here. The same kinds of questions that are central to the study of serious life events also need to be addressed in the study of help seeking in everyday life situations. These questions include: Who asks for help? What kinds of helping situations are psychologically similar from the point of view of the help seeker? What kinds of people are asked for help?

And, in their views of the helping process, how similar are the perspectives of the helper and the help seeker? These are some of the questions I have addressed in my research program. In the next sections, I report findings from several of the initial studies in this program. At this early phase, a questionnaire approach seemed appropriate for developing a broad overview of everyday helping interaction. These self-report studies were then used as a strong, data-based foundation to guide future behaviorial investigations of specific psychological mechanisms.

Help Seeking in Everyday Life Situations

Since research on help seeking for noncrisis needs had been so meager prior to this investigation, I wanted to sample a wide variety of helping situations and a fairly large number of respondents of both sexes and from several different age levels. For each of the situations, I wanted the respondents to give some indication of the kind of person from whom they would be most likely to seek help. Furthermore, I wanted to begin to investigate some hypotheses about the kinds of processes that might be operating in help-seeking interactions. One assumption I made was that people's willingness to ask for help might be related not only to their own feelings about help seeking, but also to their perceptions of how their helper might feel about giving them help. Also, an extensive body of research and writings from psychology, anthropology, and sociology led me to believe that reciprocity considerations might be influential in the help-seeking process (for a review, see Greenberg, 1980). Finally, I also looked at the relationship between the help giver's and the help seeker's perspectives.

Respondents who provided the recipient's perspective were 303 males and females from four different age levels. All four samples were predominantly middle-class. The youngest group (mean age = 12.9 years) was 96 junior high school students, and the next youngest group was 98 high school students (mean age = 15.6). The two older samples included 51 college students (mean age = 19.8) and 58 adults (mean age = 41.6). Most of the adults were teachers, clerical workers, or salespersons.

The assessment tool was an inventory of 48 items describing specific situations in which a person might decide to ask for help (DePaulo, 1978c). Although the inventory included a number of rather serious situations, such as medical or psychological crises, most of the items described more mundane instances, such as requests for directions, for advice, for a ride, for small or large amounts of money, or for help in moving a bookcase.

The 48 items were selected from a pool of 63 by four judges. The judges were instructed to maximize the diversity of the items by choosing situations that varied widely along such dimensions as the urgency of the need, the degree to which help seeking would be burdensome to the help giver, and the degree to which help seeking would be demeaning to the help seeker.

Thirteen items were designed to be particularly appropriate to high school and college students (e.g., requests for academic advice); 13 others were designed to be particularly appropriate for adults (e.g., seeking advice on buying a car). These items were not included on the junior high school questionnaire. In this chapter, I focus primarily on the data from the 22 items that were answered by respondents at all four age levels. The patterns of results based on the remaining items were very similar to those reported here.

For each of the 22 situations, respondents were asked to indicate the type of person from whom they, personally, would ask for help. They were to select one alternative from each of the following sets: (*a*) someone you like, someone you dislike, someone you are neutral towards; (*b*) someone who likes you, someone who dislikes you, someone who is neutral about you; (*c*) male, female; (*d*) child, teenager, adult, elderly person; and (*e*) stranger, acquaintance, friend, or family member.

Subjects also answered five other questions about each situation. The questions were:

1. How important is it for you to get help in this situation? (Response alternatives ranged from "not at all important" to "extremely important.")
2. How do you feel about asking for help in this situation? (I enjoy it, I don't mind, I don't like it.)
3. How will the person you ask feel about helping you in this situation? (S/he will enjoy it, s/he won't mind, s/he won't like it.)
4. If you ask this person for help, do you think s/he will then be likely to ask you for help if s/he gets into a similar situation in the future? (yes, no)
5. Actually, I probably would not ask for help in this situation. (true, false)

In sum, respondents answered 10 questions about each of 22 different situations. All inventories were completed anonymously.

DO HELP SEEKERS CONSIDER THE HELPER'S FEELINGS?

The data clearly supported the prediction that help seekers' reactions would be related to their perceptions of their helpers' probable reactions. One of the strongest relationships in all of the data was between the help seekers' reported feelings about asking for help and their expectations about their helpers' feelings about giving help: Respondents reported feeling better about asking for help when they believed that their helpers would not mind giving help. Furthermore, when respondents believed that their helpers would mind helping, they were more likely to not ask for help at all.

Subjects believed that their helpers would feel better about helping in those situations in which it was especially important to obtain help. That is, if the help seekers themselves thought that it was not very important to get help, they predicted that their helpers would not feel very positive about giving them help. And in keeping with the assumption that helpers' feelings importantly affect people's help-seeking decisions, respondents indicated that in those situations in which it was not important for them to obtain help, they would not be likely to seek help.

One other set of findings relevant to the helper's behavior emerged strongly from our data. Respondents indicated that they would be more willing to ask for help, and would feel more comfortable about asking, when they believed that the helper would not hesitate to ask them for help in return.

The obtained results pertaining to the helper's reactions fit closely with an indebtedness formulation (Greenberg, 1980), which suggests that feelings of obligation figure prominently in helping interactions. Indebtedness is a state that individuals usually try to avoid. When helpers are perceived as enjoying the helping relationship, and as willing to obligate themselves to the help seeker in the future, help seekers' anticipation of their indebtedness is probably reduced. This reduction in anticipated indebtedness may then serve as an important facilitator of help seeking.

WHAT ARE THE DIMENSIONS OF HELP-SEEKING SITUATIONS?

It seemed possible that subjects' perceptions of the different situations would differ with different aspects of the help-seeking process; when answering one kind of question about help seeking, respondents might categorize the situations differently than when considering a very different kind of question. Thus, a separate factor analysis of the 22 situations was computed for the responses to each of the 10 questions. Results indicated that the *seriousness* or *importance* of the situation was an important dimension to respondents when they indicated their own feelings about asking for help or their willingness to ask for help. In considering other aspects of the helping process, however, respondents seemed to view the situations differently. For example, in answering the reciprocity-oriented question ("Would the helper ask you for help in the future?"), the most important aspect of the situations was not their seriousness, but whether or not they involved some special helping skill. Another example is the question concerning the choice of a male or female helper; in answering this question, respondents categorized the situations according to whether they seemed to involve some stereotypic sex-typed activity.

In summary, although certain sets of situations were viewed in similar terms (e.g., seriousness, whether a special skill was involved), the overriding generalization seems to be that the dimensionality of help seeking varies with the aspect of helping in question. Perhaps, then, no single typology of help-seeking situations will be attainable.

WHO ASKS FOR HELP?

Consistent with the literature on help seeking from professional helpers (e.g., Gourash, 1978), males (compared to females) more often indicated that they would not ask for help at all in these situations. This was particularly true when the situations were unimportant ones; males felt somewhat better about asking for help in serious situations. Though females overall found it more important to get help, males attached relatively greater importance to obtaining help in the situations that were task-oriented (e.g., situations in which help would be instrumental to achieving a specific goal). Males, then, are more reluctant to seek help than are females, but will do so a bit more willingly if the situation is important or task-oriented.

Since women seek help more than men and find it more important to get help, it might be hypothesized that for women the state of obligation is sometimes actively sought out. Obligation involves not only a tension motivating one to reciprocate; it also implies the maintenance of a social bond until that reciprocation has occurred (cf. Clark & Mills, 1979). The females in this study were also more likely than the males to expect their helpers to ask them for help in return. Perhaps, then, females are less averse to indebtedness because they expect it to be short-lived. Perhaps men regard help-seeking as a threat to their competence or independence; women, in contrast, may see it as a means of sustaining interpersonal relationships. Consistent with this orientation toward seeking help, females in this study perceived their helpers as more positively disposed toward giving them help.

There were no overall age differences in willingness to seek help, in the perceived importance of obtaining help, in reported feelings about asking for help, or in the perceptions of the helpers' feelings about giving help. However, there were important age effects in the choice of helpers. We turn next to these data.

WHAT KINDS OF PEOPLE ARE ASKED FOR HELP?

In indicating their preferred helpers, respondents reported a strong preference for seeking help from people who were the same age and same sex as themselves and with whom they enjoyed mutual attraction. That is, people chose to seek help from others whom they like and who like them. Usually, these helpers were described as friends rather than strangers or acquaintances. Although this evidence is intuitively compelling and also consistent with social support research, it deserves special note as a point of contrast with certain findings that have been reported consistently in the literature on reactions to aid (see, for example, Fisher & Nadler, Chapter 7 in this volume).

It has been noted there that unsolicited help offered by an attitudinally similar other (e.g., Fisher & Nadler, 1974) or by a person with a similar (versus greater) degree of task-relevant experience (e.g., Fisher, Harrison, & Nadler, 1978) can have esteem-threatening implications and lead to negative recipient responses, such as a decrement in self-esteem and derogation of the helper or the help.

The situations modeled in the Fisher and Nadler studies differ from many of the ones described in the help inventory used in this study in that they were all very competence-relevant; that is, the tasks were often described as relevant to intelligence or professional success. Thus, an offer of help from a similar other may have underlined the recipient's relative inadequacy and inferiority. It should also be noted that these were studies in which help was offered, rather than solicited, and that all of the helpers—even the "similar" ones— were strangers rather than friends. Perhaps when choosing a helper with a task that has implications for important aspects of the self, people will choose someone with more (rather than similar) task-relevant experience when choosing among strangers or acquaintances, but whenever possible will approach a friend instead. It is clear from the social support literature that people dealing with stressful life events tend to seek help first from their network of family and friends; however, once they have decided to seek help from strangers (i.e., professional helpers), presumably they search for the person most competent to deal with their particular problem (i.e., helpers with an impressive amount of task-relevant experience). Fisher and Nadler's findings may be more relevant to professional helping relationships, whereas the present findings seem applicable to informal helping situations.

Blau's (1955) observations of patterns of consultation in a government agency are also relevant here. Workers performed complex tasks that involved a great deal of subjective judgment. Help seeking and help giving were quite frequent. Blau found that on a day-to-day basis, workers engaged in reciprocal consultations with fellow workers who were very similar to themselves in expertise, even though workers with much greater expertise were available. However, for help with extremely difficult and intricate problems, workers would approach the "expert helpers," rather than their everyday partners.

In the situations described in the help inventory, respondents indicated that they would more frequently ask females for help than males. This was especially true when the situations involved a feminine sex-typed task and when it was particularly important to the help seekers to succeed in obtaining help. In situations in which help was more commonly sought from males than from females, respondents often indicated that they probably would not ask for help at all.[2]

---

[2]A similar positivity effect in the perception of female helpers has also been reported in a help-seeking study involving a very different paradigm (DePaulo & Dull, Note 5). In that study, male and female participants were to call males and females whose names had been selected at random from a telephone directory and ask them to fill out and return a questionnaire. Before placing

Preferences for seeking help from family, as compared to friends, differed considerably with age. The youngest (junior high school) and oldest (adult) samples indicated a relatively greater preference for seeking help from family, whereas the two middle groups (the high school and college students) were more likely to seek help from friends. During the high school and college years, the reluctance to seek help from family members was especially characteristic of the males. The teens may be particularly important years for affirming masculine independence; probably few acts are as inconsistent with that goal as asking "mommy" or "daddy" for help.

Although respondents preferred overall to seek help from same-sex helpers, help seekers in the adult samples were relatively more likely to seek help from the opposite sex. This finding, combined with the consistent finding of preferences for same-age helpers, suggests that adults seek help frequently from their spouses or spouse equivalents. However, we did not ask that directly in this study.

WHY DO PEOPLE NOT ASK FOR HELP
MORE OFTEN IN EVERYDAY LIFE SITUATIONS?

Looking back at the examples of people who were reluctant to make requests for small favors, what can the data suggest about the reasons for this reluctance? One possibility is that people were hesitant to seek help with these small matters in part because they were so small. Respondents who completed the help-seeking inventory indicated that they would prefer not to seek help at all if it was not very important for them to get help. They also believed that their helpers would be less positively disposed toward helping if the requests were not very important ones. This is especially noteworthy in view of the finding that help seekers' own feelings about asking for help were best predicted by their perceptions of the helpers' feelings about giving them help.

The finding that people feel especially reluctant to ask for small favors is in some ways counterintuitive. Certainly, larger requests would be a greater imposition on the helper and would produce greater indebtedness in the recipient, and both imposition and indebtedness are factors that should *inhibit* help seeking. Perhaps the true relationship is actually curvilinear; that is, help seekers are most reluctant to seek help if the request is especially large or especially small. Some suggestive evidence has been found that is consistent with this hypothesis. In a study by DePaulo and Fisher (1980), participants

---

their calls, participants predicted the reactions (to the help requests) of the people they called. Participants of both sexes anticipated more positive responses from women than from men. Actually speaking to a person did not alter help seekers' perceptions; although all callers indicated that that they would return the questionnaire, help seekers still expected more women than men to actually do so. (In fact, the return rates were not significantly different for women than for men.)

were given an opportunity to seek help with the task of identifying emotions depicted in photographs of facial expressions and body postures. This judgmental task varied in difficulty in two ways: The content of the photographs was either particularly easy or particularly difficult to decode, and the structure of the response alternatives rendered the task either particularly easy (i.e., the correct alternative stood out from the rest) or particularly difficult (i.e., the response alternatives were all very similar). Participants were especially reluctant to disturb a preoccupied helper when their task was either easy in both ways or difficult in both ways. The authors suggested that when the problems were doubly easy, participants may have felt that they were simply too easy to warrant bothering a busy helper; when they were doubly difficult, they might demand too much of the helper's time.

The curvilinearity hypothesis may be an accurate description of help seeking from *non*professionals. When people face extremely difficult, time-consuming, and important life problems, they may in fact hesitate to burden someone who is not otherwise compensated for their helping efforts. In these situations, people may do without help or they may bring their problems to paid professionals.

The subjects in the pilot study (who were reluctant to ask for directions or for help in standing up a stick) might have been hesitant for still another reason—because the people from whom help was to be sought were strangers to them, people whom they would probably never see again and with whom they shared no affective ties. As noted previously, people seem to prefer to seek help from people whom they like and who like them; for example, good friends. It was also suggested that women especially might like to participate in helping relationships as a way of developing and maintaining social bonds. This particular function of help seeking is precluded by transactions in which the helper will never again be seen. This suggests another reason why the stranger status of the helpers in our examples may have inhibited help seeking: Since ordinarily we do not arrange to repay strangers for very small favors, there is no opportunity to reduce indebtedness by direct behavioral reciprocity.

Finally, our data suggest a few additional reasons why the males in the "visual perception" experiment may have been reluctant to ask for help. For reasons that are not yet clear, males in general seem to be unwilling help seekers. Our data suggest that this might be particularly true when the problem for which help might be sought is not very important and does not contain instrumental cues. In the visual perception study, there were no special rewards offered for successful task performance, nor were any special costs attached to success achieved by illegal means. Help seeking, then, was not instrumental to the attainment of any important goal. Instead of asking for help, the males fumbled on their own or designed devious ways to circumvent the rules of the task.

THE HELPER'S PERSPECTIVE

To begin to examine the helper's perspective on everyday helping inter-actions, the same inventory of 22 situations was administered to respondents at the same four age levels. (Respondents were randomly assigned to take the role of the helper or the help seeker.) Helper respondents were 113 junior high school students, 111 high school students, 44 college students, and 51 adults. The "helpers" were asked to answer the following eight questions about each situation, on rating scales comparable to those used by the help seekers.

1–2. How important would a girl/woman (boy/man) your age think it was to get help in this situation?

3–4. How would you feel about helping a girl/woman (boy/man) your age in this situation?

5–6. If a girl/woman (boy/man) your age asked you for help in this situation, would you be likely to ask him/her for help if you found yourself in a similar situation in the future?

7–8. How do you think a girl/woman (boy/man) your age would feel about asking for help in this situation?

The data generated by the helper respondents complemented those generated by the help seekers. First, just as the help seekers said that they would feel better about asking for help in those situations in which they believed that their helpers would feel better about giving help, the helper respondents, in an analogous way, indicated that they would feel better about giving help in those situations in which they believed that the help seekers would feel better about seeking help. Second, helpers indicated that they would be more likely to ask for help themselves in those situations in which they felt particularly good about giving help to others.

Another strong finding from the help-seeking data was that helpers were perceived as feeling more positive about helping in those situations in which help seekers found it particularly important to obtain help. Paralleling this result, respondents considering the situations from the perspective of the helper reported that they would feel better about giving help in those situations in which they believed that it would be particularly important for the help seeker to obtain help.

It appears from these results that people feel especially good about giving when what they have to offer is considered important by the recipient. At the same time, they do not like the recipient to feel uncomfortable about asking for help. Help seekers, for their part, feel particularly comfortable about seeking help when it is important to them to obtain the desired aid; they are less comfortable in helping interactions when they perceive their helpers as ill at ease about giving.

Although these analyses suggest in a general way that help seekers and helpers bring certain similar perspectives to helping interactions, it is possible to assess the correspondence between the helpers' perceptions of the help seekers, and the help seekers' reports of their own feelings, in a more specific way. I turn to these data next.

HELPERS' PERCEPTIONS OF HELP SEEKERS: HOW ACCURATE ARE THEY?

Since a substantial number of respondents indicated their feelings about asking for help and the importance to them of obtaining help across a variety of situations, this data base can be used as a normative criterion with which to assess the accuracy of the helper respondents in predicting the responses of the help seekers (DePaulo, 1978b). The question is: How accurate were the helpers in perceiving the variations in help seekers' feelings across the different kinds of situations? We assume that this kind of skill could be quite important in helping relationships, in that helpers who can accurately perceive variations in help seekers' feelings and needs from situation to situation may be better able to render assistance effectively. Furthermore, when the helpers understand help seekers in this way, both parties may be more comfortable in the interaction and may experience more successful outcomes.

All accuracy scores were correlation coefficients (Cronbach, 1955) assessing the relationship between help givers' predictions for the 22 situations and the actual mean responses of male and female help seekers in the same age bracket as the help giver. For example, a college female would predict, for each of the 22 situations, how important a man her age and a woman her age would think it was to get help. She would also predict how a man and a woman her age would feel about asking for help in each of the 22 situations. These four sets of predictions would be correlated with the corresponding means of the actual responses of male and female help seekers her age.

Overall, helpers showed substantial accuracy at every type of prediction that they made. Helpers were more accurate at predicting the responses of females than they were at predicting responses of males, and female helpers were more accurate predictors than were male helpers.

We noted earlier that (*a*) female respondents said that they would ask for help in these situations significantly more often than male respondents, and (*b*) help seekers of both sexes reported a much greater willingness to seek help from females than from males. Perhaps, then, more experience in helping interactions leads to more accurate judgments of the affective responses of help seekers. Women, for example, ask for help more often than men and are asked to help more than men in these situations. Perhaps this apparently greater openness about their needs, and greater involvement in the helper role, enables women both to judge more accurately and to be judged more accurately. If women are more skillful because they have more experience in helping situations, then perhaps those men who have a great deal of experience in helping are good judges, too. Studies of counselors, psychiatrists, medical practitioners, and other workers in the helping professions may prove instructive in this regard.[3]

A second study, involving 39 college students who predicted help seekers' responses, adds to the picture of the accurate judge. In addition to predicting help seekers' responses to the 22 situations, these students completed a number of personality scales, and their nonverbal decoding skills were assessed by several standardized instruments. Students who were especially accurate at predicting situational variations in help seekers' responses were more tolerant of diverse points of view (Jackson, 1971), more likely to perceive human nature as complex rather than simple (Wrightsman, 1964), and less Machiavellian (Christie & Geis, 1970). They did not differ from less accurate judges in self-esteem or in social participation, that is, in their tendency to be outgoing and gregarious and to join a variety of social groups (Jackson, 1971). Accurate judges also were not notably skilled at judging nonverbal cues communicated by face, body, or tone of voice; however, they were particularly adept at discerning *discrepancies* between tone of voice cues and visual cues (DePaulo, Rosenthal, Eisenstat, Rogers, & Finkelstein, 1978). It appears, then, that people who understand the ways in which help seekers' feelings vary from situation to situation are generally well-attuned to the intricacies of social life. They perceive people as complex rather than simple, they are open to many different points of view, and they can discern subtle inconsistencies in other people's communications.

The Process of Asking for Help

Various models of the help-seeking process have been proposed, including models of medical help seeking (e.g., Rosenstock, 1974), psychiatric help seeking (e.g., Albers & Scrivner, 1977; Kadushin, 1958), and several models less specifically tied to a particular help-seeking domain (e.g., Brickman, Rabinowitz, Karuza, Coates, Cohn, & Kidder, 1982; Gross, Fisher, Nadler, Stiglitz, & Craig, 1979; Gross & McMullen, 1981). Although these models differ somewhat in their details, a small number of steps in the help-seeking process described by most of these models can readily be identified.

The help-seeking process is triggered by the help seeker's recognition of his or her need for help. In the case of necessary help, this might include an

---

[3]Alternatively, perhaps greater skill at judging leads to greater involvement in helping interactions, rather than the reverse. More accurate judges may volunteer to help more often, they may be approached for help more frequently, and they may be more likely to ask for help themselves. Probably the causality is bidirectional: More experience leads to greater skill *and* greater skill leads to more frequent helping experiences.

acknowledgment of the severity of one's problem and an admission of one's own inability to cope (cf. Snyder, Ingram,& Newburg, Chapter 13 in this volume). In the case of convenient help, this step might involve the recognition that help would be useful in some way, although not absolutely necessary. The same "objective" need might be interpreted quite differently (cf. Gross & McMullen, 1981): There are important individual differences in perceptions of internal states (e.g., Pennebaker & Skelton, 1978) and in the labeling of internal states and of personal situations as conditions for which help might be appropriate.

Once the possibility of help seeking is allowed (step 1), the help seeker must then (2) decide whether or not to actually seek help, (3) select an appropriate source of help, (4) initiate and execute the help request, and (5) react in some way to the helper's response (e.g., comply with the help if help is offered, seek a different helper if help is refused, etc.). These are not necessarily linear sequential steps. For example, the decision to seek help might be influenced by the availability of an acceptable source of help and by previous helpers' reactions to help requests (cf. Gross & McMullen, 1981).

Virtually all of the research on help seeking from experimental social psychology has focused on the second step, that is, deciding whether or not to ask for help. In the following sections, I will describe what I believe to be some of the major psychological[4] inhibitors and facilitators of help seeking, summarizing the relevant experimental findings when such findings exist.

ACHIEVEMENT MOTIVATION

The motivation to achieve goals independently is part of the tradition of rugged individualism that characterizes most Western cultures. One by-product of this motivation for independent accomplishments might be a reluctance to ask for help. In a study by Tessler and Schwartz (1972), in which subjects received failure feedback as they attempted to rate ambiguous dialogues, achievement motivation was a strong negative predictor of help seeking: Subjects high in achievement motivation were very unlikely to consult a set of guidelines designed specially to facilitate performance at this task. Thus, this study provides some support for the postulation of achievement motivation as an inhibitory factor in the help-seeking process.

However, it might also be hypothesized that high-need-for-achievement people will persist in their attempts to remain self-reliant only when there is a reasonable possibility that they *can* succeed on their own. People high in need for achievement characteristically choose moderate challenges and risks,

---

[4]Some of the important factors that can facilitate or inhibit a help request are not very psychological in nature. For example, people may refrain from seeking help because appropriate aid is (or is believed to be) unavailable or unaffordable, or because the problem in question is not one that can be alleviated.

rather than tasks that are either extremely easy or virtually impossible. Thus, when independent success is very unlikely, achievement motivation may be directly, rather than inversely, related to help seeking.

PERCEIVED INADEQUACY

Sociologists such as Blau (1955) and Homans (1961) have suggested that help seeking is avoided in part because the act of requesting help is often regarded as an open admission of personal inadequacy. Apparently the inadequacy that is exposed by the need for help is even more salient and embarrassing when help is actively requested than when an offer of help is accepted. This notion is supported both by a laboratory study (Broll, Gross, & Piliavin, 1974) and by a field experiment involving welfare recipients (Piliavin & Gross, 1977); in both studies, people who had to initiate the helping interaction by requesting help obtained less aid than people who were offered help by others.

Many experimental investigators of the relationship between perceptions of inadequacy and willingness to ask for help have manipulated the degree to which the act of asking for help might be perceived as an admission of incompetence. For example, participants might be told that either a very large or very small percentage of previous subjects needed help with the task (Broll *et al.*, 1974; Nadler & Porat, 1978; Shapiro, 1980), or they might be told that their particular problem is either very common or very uncommon (Snyder & Ingram, Note 1). Or the manipulation might be even more subtle; for example, in the study by Gross *et al.* (1979), women were informed of the availability of a women's counseling service by letters that implied that their problems were normative ("many of us women") or nonnormative ("you are probably . . ."), their fault ("your situation") or society's fault ("the situation society has created"). These kinds of manipulations either suggest to people that they should be able to get along adequately without help (since almost everyone else can) or provide an excuse for needing help (e.g., almost no one can deal with this problem alone; the problem was imposed by society and was not their doing).

People might refuse to ask for help so as to avoid admitting incompetence to themselves, or to avoid *appearing* incompetent to others. Studies that manipulated the normativeness of the need for help (Broll *et al.*, 1974; Gross *et al.*, 1979; Nadler & Porat, 1978; Shapiro, 1980; Tessler & Schwartz, 1972) suggest that a normativeness manipulation will be effective only if the help seeker can remain anonymous. It appears than when people deciding whether to seek help know that they will be identifiable or observed, they are reluctant to seek any help at all, and find normative information of little consolation. However, when their help requests are anonymous and they therefore have only their own feelings of inadequacy to worry about, they can be persuaded to seek help by the knowledge that the need for help is not unusual.

Other kinds of information can also be used to suggest to potential help seekers that they *should* be able to solve their problem without help. For example, Tessler and Schwartz (1972) told subjects that success at the experimental task was or was not related to intelligence and mental health; high-self-esteem subjects asked for less help when the task was described as related to these "central" attributes. (Low-self-esteem subjects asked for help equally in both conditions.) Morris and Rosen (1973) told participants directly that they should have done better at the task, or that they had performed well. The former participants, who were made to feel inadequate, were less willing to seek further help at the task. In two studies, adults (who seem to believe that they should be able to perform virtually any task more successfully than a child) were more reluctant to seek aid from a child helper than from an adult helper, even though the child showed evidence of being as competent as the adult helper and more competent than the subjects themselves (DePaulo, 1978a; Druian & DePaulo, 1977). Finally, aspects of the task itself could serve as clues to subjects as to whether or not help might appropriately be sought; presumably, subjects generally will find it more appropriate to seek help with problems that are difficult than with problems that are easy. In a study in which subjects worked on numerous problems varying in difficulty, more help was sought on the more difficult problems (DePaulo & Fisher, 1980).

In summary, we are suggesting that certain aspects of one's identity, or of one's current situation, demand independent and successful task performance. Asking for help in any of these situations can constitute an overt admission of the possibility that one is not as competent as one has in some sense claimed to be; this can be a threat to one's own self-concept and an embarrassment to one's public identity.

Thus, the traditional practice of helping agencies of keeping the helping process confidential seems to be well-advised. But after people have asked for help, they may still have anxieties about whether the helper will come to see them as incompetent (DePaulo & Fisher, 1980). There is indeed evidence that these fears are not unfounded: helpers sometimes do develop unflattering views of the people they have assisted (Wills, 1978, Note 2).

INDEBTEDNESS

The need to seek help not only can make people feel inadequate, it can also cast them into a state of indebtedness (Greenberg, 1980). Relevant empirical work is generally supportive of the hypothesized role of indebtedness in inhibiting help requests. Greenberg and Shapiro (1971) and Morris and Rosen (1973) have shown that people are more likely to put off asking for help, and are less likely to ask for help at all, when they anticipate no opportunity to repay than when reciprocity will clearly be possible. Castro (1974) qualified this finding by showing that reciprocity considerations are important primarily when the cost to the helper of giving aid is high. She also showed that the opportunity to reciprocate facilitates help seeking even when reciprocity can only be made to a third party, and not to the actual helper.

The closeness of the ties between helper and help seeker also importantly moderate the indebtedness process. People perceive relatives and friends (as opposed to strangers and acquaintances) as more obligated to provide needed help, and they report feeling less gratitude for the help that is received (Bar-Tal, Bar-Zohar, Greenberg, & Hermon, 1977). Consistent with this finding, it has also been demonstrated that help seeking from friends is not sensitive to the costs to the helper of providing help (Shapiro, 1980), as it is when the helper is a stranger (Castro, 1974; DePaulo & Fisher, 1980).

In summary, a state of indebtedness from which no immediate escape is forseen inhibits help seeking. Also in line with indebtedness notions, people are reluctant to seek help when the provision of aid will be costly to the helper. However, considerations of costs and of immediate opportunities for repayment seem to be less important in close relationships (cf. Clark & Mills, 1979). Perhaps this is because participants in such relationships believe in a higher-order reciprocity (i.e., inequities occur constantly, but they are continually shifting in direction, and in the long run they "even out").

OTHER SELF-PRESENTATIONAL CONCERNS

In addition to their concerns about projecting and protecting an image of status and competence, help seekers might also worry about their likability. That is, they might hesitate to ask for help because of a concern that the helper or other onlookers will come to view them as a pest, or an annoyance, or a burden (cf. Kalish, 1967). Fear of refusal may also be a major inhibitor of help seeking. Refusal might imply that the helper perceived the help seeker's request as illegitimate or ill timed, that the helper dislikes the help seeker and is avoiding personal contact, or any of a number of other unpalatable possibilities.

Whereas an achievement or inadequacy formulation of help-seeking inhibitions might predict that individuals will avoid seeking help in order to appear more autonomous and competent, an impression management perspective would suggest that people will try to present themselves in the ways that are most valued and most rewarded by others (cf Jellison & Gentry, 1978). This could imply, in some instances, that people will *want* to create an image of inferiority and dependency with respect to the helper (cf. Jones & Pittman, in press). For example, traditional sex-role stereotypes suggest that females should be relatively more dependent, particularly vis-à-vis males. Thus in opposite-sex interactions— particularly with attractive others, whose attractiveness may intensify self-presentational concerns—males may garner the most favorable image by refusing to ask for help and females may fare far better in the eyes of others by willingly seeking help. Research supports this formulation. Whereas both males and females ask for less help from attractive same-sex helpers than from unattractive same-sex helpers (Nadler, 1980; Nadler, Shapira, & Ben-Itzhak, 1982; Stokes & Brickman, 1974)[5] the sexes diverge in opposite-sex interactions. Males ask for less help from attractive than from unattractive females, but females seek more help from attractive than from unattractive males (Nadler *et al.*, 1982).

In seeking help, people often must divulge information about themselves. This necessity can function as one of the costs of asking for help. People may be especially reluctant to divulge negative information, but people who prefer privacy may be reluctant to share even positive or neutral facts about themselves. This may be particularly important for persons who are shy (cf. Leary & Schlenker, 1981). People might also hesitate to ask for help out of a fear of what they might find out themselves (cf. Snyder, Ingram, & Newburg, Chapter 13 in this volume). These kinds of concerns may seem most relevant to help seeking in medical or psychiatric settings, but actually they might be much more pervasive. For example, students seeking academic assistance may find that they know even less about the subject matter than they thought; or, even worse, they may find out that even with help they still are not competent enough to learn the relevant skills, or perhaps not even competent enough to understand the helper's explanations of the material.

HELPER-ORIENTED CONCERNS

Potential help seekers may be inhibited not only by the costs that they themselves might incur in the help-seeking process, but also by the costs that their helper might incur. Most notably, help seekers might worry that their help request might be an *imposition*. Accordingly, it has been shown that people sometimes seek less help when helping entails more work or a greater sacrifice (Castro, 1974; Shapiro, Note 3) on the part of the helper, or when the helper is already preoccupied (DePaulo & Fisher, 1980). Although this evidence (that people are reluctant to seek help that would be costly for the helper to give) was presented earlier as supportive of indebtedness dynamics, it is also consistent with an imposition formulation.

Imposition can be characterized as a selfless concern about the helper's outcomes, but it is probably also strongly infused with apprehensiveness about the threat of being negatively evaluated by the helper (i.e., the helper might perceive the help seeker as a bothersome person to be avoided in the future). Indirect support for this notion comes from studies of the role of

---

[5] Consistent with the notion that the effects of attractiveness are mediated by self-presentational concerns, the helper's attractiveness has no impact on help seeking when the help seeker will never meet the helper (Nadler, 1980) or when the helper is simply carrying out the duties of an assigned helper role (Stokes & Bickman, 1974).

nonverbal sensitivity in help seeking. People who are willing to ask for help (compared to those who are reluctant to do so) are more sensitive to polite, controlled, overt nonverbal cues (such as those that might be given off by a helper who feels imposed upon, but is trying to mask that fact) and relatively insensitive to the more covert and unintended cues that might reveal the helper's true displeasure (DePaulo & Fisher, 1981; Depaulo, Leiphart, & Dull, in press; DePaulo & Rosenthal, 1979).

Helper-oriented concerns that can inhibit help seeking also include less charitable considerations than the ones described thus far. For example, help seekers may realize that a request for help might validate a helper's claim to superior status, power, or expertise, and may be reluctant to provide such validation. Conversely, this validational function can serve as a facilitator of help seeking, as when people use help seeking as a tactic of ingratiation (cf. Jones, 1964).

INSTRUMENTAL FACTORS

Perhaps the major *facilitator* of help seeking is an instrumental factor: People who ask for help enjoy a greatly improved chance of obtaining what they want or need, compared to people who do not seek help. In addition to this primary motivator of help seeking, many of the motivations that were described earlier as inhibitors of help seeking can be reconceptualized as facilitators. For example, help seeking can be suitable grist for the mill of *achievement motivation*, if obtaining a goal is seen as a challenge and help seeking is viewed as a clever and resourceful means of meeting that challenge.

Indebtedness is another factor that can function to inhibit or to facilitate help seeking. People who are indebted often maintain a relationship with the helper until the debt is repaid. In this way, help seeking can serve as a "starting mechanism" for *establishing an interpersonal relationship*, or it can be used as a way of maintaining or strengthening an already existing relationship (cf. Clark & Mills, 1979; Gouldner, 1960).

Help seeking can also serve *informative* and *image-enhancing* functions. It is informative when it is used as a means of finding out more about oneself, and it can be image-enhancing when it is used as a means of establishing an association with a more knowledgeable or attractive person.

Extensions and Implications

The evidence reviewed suggests that in a wide variety of informal situations people are reluctant to ask for help. Several important psychological factors contribute to this reluctance. When the task in question involves a skill, help-seeking inhibitions sometimes stem from a desire to achieve success completely independently. Aspects of individuals' identities can lead them to feel that they *should* be competent at certain kinds of tasks or that they should be more competent than certain other classes of people; these kinds of feelings can also inhibit help seeking. For example, it has been shown that people with high self-esteem do not like to admit that they need help with tasks that measure intelligence or adjustment. In part because help seeking sometimes reflects unfavorably on the help seeker's competence, people are especially reluctant to ask for help when they are observed. When help seeking is private, people seek help a little more readily when they know that many other people in their situation have needed help, too.

Even when a help request would not be particularly threatening to the help seekers' feelings of competence, or to their status vis-à-vis the helper, there are still other factors that operate to inhibit help seeking. For example, in addition to any gratitude they might feel for any help received, help seekers often feel indebted to their helpers in a less positive way; that is, they may experience an aversive sense of obligation to repay. Accordingly, it has been shown that people are unwilling to ask for help when they believe that their benefactor either will not need their help in the future or would not be willing to ask for it. Finally, help seekers seem to worry about imposing upon their helpers, in that they are especially unlikely to ask for help when their requests would be particularly time-consuming, bothersome, or costly to their helpers. Furthermore, people obtain more needed help when the helper offers them help than when they themselves have to initiate the request.

The findings discussed in this chapter describe the dynamics of help seeking from nonprofessional helpers in informal situations. I can only speculate on the extent to which these findings may or may not generalize to professional helping relationships. Of course, formal and informal relationships differ in many ways. To cite just a few differences, formal helping relationships tend to involve more serious problems, they are more often conducted in private, and they tend to be governed by norms of confidentiality and continuity (i.e., the help seeker is expected not to "shop around" for another helper once the helping process is formally initiated; cf. Merton, 1976). Informal helping, on the other hand, tends to involve a greater diversity of helpers in a wider range of settings. Also, many of the requests made in informal relationships are for help that can be rendered readily and effectively; thus, there is often less ambiguity about the eventual usefulness of the assistance.

In extending the findings on informal help seeking to professional helping relationships, the dynamics of perceived inadequacy may be most in need of qualification. In informal situations, as noted earlier, individuals hesitate to seek help when they feel that they should be able to succeed on their own. However, when they become extremely inadequate at handling a problem that is very important to them, they may be especially primed to seek help from a professional. In instances of extreme inability to cope, the bases for evaluating the needy individual's actions may also change. When the problem is manageable, the response most respected by others might be to deal with the problem independently; however, as attempted coping strategies fail and the problem worsens, the needy individual might lose respect by *not* seeking outside help.

The initial step of seeking professional help may be much more difficult than the initial step of seeking informal assistance, in part because the inadequacy that one is admitting is usually much greater; however, once a professional relationship is initiated, the help seeker may find that some of the costs of aid in informal settings are less relevant in professional settings. For example, concerns about imposition are probably greatly diminished in professional settings. Helping sessions are usually scheduled at the helper's (and help seeker's) convenience; and since it is the helper's role to help, help seekers need not worry about the appropriateness of approaching this particular person for assistance. Furthermore, feelings of indebtedness are probably diminished, too, since professional helpers receive tangible compensation for their efforts. The implication of this is that help seeking in many everyday life situations might be facilitated by the availability of persons or agencies whose role it is to give help for these kinds of needs. Some of these types of helpers and services already do exist. For example, in certain regions, people can "Dial-A-Ride" when they need one, and the elderly can avail themselves of helpers to do household chores and other errands. Some of these services also function—perhaps coincidentally—to help their clients establish and maintain interpersonal contacts.[6]

Clearly, however, it would be impractical, if not impossible, to recruit helpers to be available to deal with every possible need. How, then, might people function more effectively as helpers and help seekers across the wide variety of helping situations that arise in their everyday lives? Only a few suggestions will be forwarded here; there are many possibilities, but few have been systematically researched. Helpers, for their part, might attempt to offer help when individuals clearly seem to need it, so as to relieve them of the psychological burden of initiating the request themselves. Even this seemingly kindly course of action would need to be implemented with a great deal of interpersonal sensitivity. A well-intentioned offer of assistance with a skilled

---

[6]Falling between the informal helping relationships described in this chapter and the traditional one-on-one professional relationships are other kinds of semiformal helping arrangements. One particularly interesting variety is the groups of people (e.g., abused wives, parents of "problem" adolescents, "Straight Partners") who join together to deal with a common problem. In these groups, the aversiveness of help seeking is reduced in a number of ways. For example, each person is giving help as well as receiving help (thus reducing feelings of inferiority and indebtedness); normativeness information (i.e., information that other people have this problem too) is available and salient; and the probability of being refused is minimal. Furthermore, participants may derive a sense of achievement from their active attempts to cope with their situation, and they may also establish important interpersonal bonds.

task can be interpreted by recipients as an insult to their competence (cf. DePaulo, Brown, Ishii, & Fisher, 1981; Fisher, DePaulo, & Nadler, 1981; Nadler, Sheinberg, & Jaffe, 1981); and even with unskilled tasks, people who offer to help *too* frequently can quickly become burdensome and annoying (cf. DePaulo, Brittingham, & Kaiser, Note 4). Also, people who are likely to be asked for help (a category that excludes very few) might make it easier for others to approach them by indicating, in their day-to-day activities, that they, too, are willing to seek help from others.

Help seekers can also find ways to make help seeking easier for themselves. Since the reaction of the helper is often very important to help seekers, they can make special efforts to approach the helper at a time that is likely to be convenient to the helper, and in a way that is likely to be accommodating. In many instances, help seekers may be able to obtain useful aid while enhancing the self-esteem of the person they approach for help. For example, adults might ask their children or elderly parents for help with gardening. The children might be eager to participate in this "grown-up" activity, and the elderly might be happy to have this increasingly rare opportunity to be a helper rather than a recipient. In our eagerness to find ways to help needy populations (such as the elderly and the handicapped), perhaps we have too often overlooked one of the most genuinely rewarding and mutually satisfying arrangements—encouraging the "needy" to give useful help as well as to receive it.

Reference Notes

1. Snyder, C. R., & Ingram, R. E. *The impact of consensus information upon help-seeking behavior.* Unpublished manuscript, University of Kansas, 1981.
2. Wills, T. A. *Perceptual consequences of helping another person.* Paper presented at the meeting of the American Psychological Association, Washington, D.C., September 1976.
3. Shapiro, E. G. *Willingness to request help from others: Effects of mode of interaction and size of request.* Paper presented at the meeting of the American Sociological Association, New York, August 1980.
4. DePaulo, B. M., Brittingham, G. L., & Kaiser, M. K. *When too good is not good.* Manuscript in preparation, University of Virginia, 1982.
5. DePaulo, B. M., & Dull, W. R. *Shyness and help-seeking.* Manuscript in preparation, University of Virginia, 1982.

References

Albers, R. J., & Scrivner, L. L. The structure of attrition during appraisal. *Community Mental Health Journal*, 1977, *13*, 325–332.
Bar-Tal, D., Bar-Zohar, Y., Greenberg, M. S., & Hermon, M. Reciprocity in the relationship between donor and recipient and between harm-doer and victim. *Sociometry*, 1977, *40*, 293–298.

Bergin, A. E. The evaluation of therapeutic outcomes. In A. E. Bergin & S. L. Garfield (Eds.), *Handbook of psychotherapy and behavior change: An empirical analysis*. New York: Wiley, 1971.

Blau, P. M. *The dynamics of bureaucracy*. Chicago: Univ. of Chicago Press, 1955.

Brickman, P., Rabinowitz, V. C., Karuza, J., Jr., Coates, D., Cohn, E., & Kidder, L. Models helping and coping. *American Psychologist*, 1982, *37*, 368–384.

Broll, L., Gross, A. E., & Piliavin, I. Effects of offered and requested help on help-seeking and reactions to being helped. *Journal of Applied Social Psychology*, 1974, *4*, 244–258.

Castro, M. A. Reactions to receiving aid as a function of cost to the donor and opportunity to aid. *Journal of Applied Social Psychology*, 1974, *4*, 194–209.

Christie, R., & Geis, F. L. (Eds.), *Studies in Machiavellianism*. New York: Academic Press, 1970.

Clark, M. S., & Mills, J. Interpersonal attraction in exchange and communal relationships. *Journal of Personality and Social Psychology*, 1979, *37*, 12–24.

Cronbach, L. J. Processes affecting scores on "understanding of others" and "assumed similarity." *Psychological Bulletin*,, 1955, *52*, 177–193.

DePaulo, B. M. Accepting help from teachers—when the teachers are children. *Human Relations*, 1978, *31*, 459–474. (a)

DePaulo, B. M. Accuracy in predicting situational variations in help-seekers' responses. *Personality and Social Psychology Bulletin*, 1978, *4*, 330–333. (b)

DePaulo, B. M. Help-seeking from the recipient's point of view. JSAS *Catalog of Selected Documents in Psychology*, 1978, *8*, 62. (Ms. No. 1721) (c)

DePaulo, B. M., Brown, P. L., Ishii, S., & Fisher, J. D. Help that works: The effects of aid on subsequent task performance. *Journal of Personality and Social Psychology*, 1981, *41*, 478–487.

DePaulo, B. M., & Fisher, J. D. The costs of asking for help. *Basic and Applied Social Psychology*, 1980, *1*, 23–35.

DePaulo, B. M., & Fisher, J. D. Too tuned-out to take: The role of nonverbal sensitivity in help-seeking. *Personality and Social Psychology Bulletin*, 1981, *7*, 201–205.

DePaulo, B. M., Leiphart, V. M., & Dull, W. R. Help-seeking and social interaction: Person, situation, and process considerations. In D. Bar-Tal, J. Karylowski, J. Reykowski, & E. Staub (Eds.), *The development and maintenance of prosocial behavior*. New York: Plenum, in press.

DePaulo, B. M., & Rosenthal, R. Ambivalence, discrepancy, and deception in nonverbal communication. In R. Rosenthal (Ed.), *Skill in nonverbal communication*. Cambridge, Mass.: Oelgeschlager, Gunn & Hain, 1979.

DePaulo, B. M., Rosenthal, R., Eisenstat, R. A., Rogers, P. L., & Finkelstein, S. Decoding discrepant nonverbal cues. *Journal of Personality and Social Psychology*, 1978, *26*, 313–323.

Dohrenwend, B. P., Dohrenwend, B. S., Gould, M. S., Link, B., Neugebauer, R., & Wunsch-Hitzig, R. *Mental illness in the United States: Epidemiological estimates*. New York: Praeger, 1980.

Druian, P. R., & DePaulo, B. M. Asking a child for help. *Social Behavior and Personality*, 1977, *5*, 33–39.

Fischer, E. H., & Turner, T. L. Orientations to seeking professional help: Development and research utility of an attitude scale. *Journal of Consulting and Clinical Psychology*, 1970, *35*, 79–90.

Fisher, J. D., DePaulo, B. M., & Nadler, A. Extending altruism beyond the altruistic act: The mixed effects of aid on the help recipient. In J. P. Rushton & R. M. Sorrentino (Eds.), *Altruism and helping behavior*. Hillsdale, N.J.: Erlbaum, 1981.

Fisher, J. D., Harrison, C., & Nadler, A. Exploring the generalizability of donor–recipient similarity effects. *Personality and Social Psychology Bulletin*, 1978, *4*, 627–630.

Fisher, J. D., & Nadler, A. The effect of similarity between donor and recipient on reactions to aid. *Journal of Applied Social Psychology*, 1974, *4*, 230–243.

Gottlieb, B. H. Lay influences on the utilization and provision of health services: A review. *Canadian Psychological Review*, 1976, *17*, 126–136.

Gouldner, A. W. The norm of reciprocity: A preliminary statement. *American Sociological Review*, 1960, *25*, 161–178.

Gourash, N. Help-seeking: A review of the literature. *American Journal of Community Psychology*, 1978, *6*, 413–424.

Greenberg, M. S. A theory of indebtedness. In K. J. Gergen, M. S. Greenberg, & R. H. Willis (Eds.), *Social exchange: Advances in theory and reserch*. New York: Wiley, 1980.

Greenberg, M. S., & Shapiro, S. Indebtedness: An adverse aspect of asking for and receiving help. *Sociometry*, 1971, *34*, 290–301.

Greenley, J. R., & Mechanic, D. Social selection in seeking help for psychological problems. *Journal of Health and Social Behavior*, 1976, *17*, 249–262.

Gross, A. E. Fisher, J. D., Nadler, A., Stiglitz, E., & Craig, C. Initiating contact with a women's counseling service: Some correlates of help utilization. *Journal of Community Psychology*, 1979, *7*, 42–49.

Gross, A. E., & McMullen, P. A. The help-seeking process. In V. Derlega & J. Grzelak (Eds.), *Living with others*. New York: Academic Press, 1981.

Homans, G. C. *Social behavior: Its elementary forms*. New York: Harcourt, 1961.

Jackson, D. N. *Jackson Personality Inventory*. New York: Research Psychologists Press, 1971.

Jellison, J. M., & Gentry, K. W. A self-presentation interpretation of the seeking of social approval. *Personality and Social Psychology Bulletin*, 1978, *4*, 227–230.

Jones, E. E. *Ingratiation*. New York: Irvington, 1964.

Jones, E. E., & Pittman, T. S. Toward a general theory of strategic self-presentation. In J. Suls (Ed.), *Psychological perspectives on the self*. Hillsdale, N.J.: Erlbaum, in press.

Kadushin, C. Individual decisions to undertake psychotherapy. *Administrative Science Quarterly*, 1958, *3*, 329–411.

Kadushin, C. *Why people go to psychiatrists*. New York: Atherton, 1969.

Kalish, R. A. Of children and grandfathers: A speculative essay on dependency. *Gerontologist*, 1967, *7*, 65–70.

Leary, M. R., & Schlenker, B. The social psychology of shyness: A self-presentation model. In J. T. Tedeschi (Ed.), *Impression management theory and social psychological research*. New York: Academic Press, 1981.

McKinlay, J. B. Some approaches and problems in the study of the use of services: An overview. *Journal of Health and Social Behavior*, 1972, *13*, 115–152.

Merton, R. K. *Sociological ambivalence*, New York: Free Press, 1976.

Morris, S. C., III, & Rosen, S. Effects of felt adequacy and opportunity to reciprocate on help-seeking. *Journal of Exeperimental Social Psychology*, 1973, *9*, 265–276.

Nadler, A. "Good looks do not help": Effects of helper's physical attractiveness and expectations for future interaction on help-seeking behavior. *Personality and Social Psychology Bulletin*, 1980, *6*, 378–383.

Nadler, A., & Porat, I. Names do not help: Effects of anonymity and locus of need attribution on help-seeking behavior. *Personality and Social Psychology Bulletin*, 1978, *4*, 624–626.

Nadler, A., Shapira, R., & Ben-Itzhak, S. Good looks may help: Effects of helper's physical attractiveness and sex of helper on males' and females' help-seeking behavior. *Journal of Personality and Social Psychology*, 1982, *42*, 90–99.

Nadler, A., Sheinberg, O., & Jaffe, Y. Seeking help from the wheelchair. In C. Spielberger & I. Sarason (Eds.), N. Milgram (Guest Ed.), *Stress and anxiety* (Vol. 8). Washington, D.C.: Hemisphere, 1981.

Pennebaker, J. W., & Skelton, J. A. Psychological parameters of physical symptoms. *Personality and Social Psychology Bulletin*, 1978, *4*, 524–530.

Piliavin, I. M., & Gross, A. E. The effects of separation of services and income maintenance on AFDC recipients' perceptions and use of social services: Results of a field experiment. *Social Service Review*, 1977, *9*, 389–406.

Rosenstock, I. M. The health belief model and preventive health behavior. *Health Education Monographs*, 1974, *2*, 354–386.

Shapiro, E. G. Is seeking help from a friend like seeking help from a stranger? *Social Psychology Quarterly*, 1980, *43*, 259–263.

Stokes, S., & Bickman, L. The effect of the physical attractiveness and role of the helper on help-seeking. *Journal of Applied Social Psychology*, 1974, *4*, 286–293.

Tessler, R., & Mechanic, D. Psychological distress and perceived health status. *Journal of Health and Social Behavior*, 1978, *19*, 254–262.

Tessler, R. C., & Schwartz, S. H. Help-seeking, self-esteem, and achievement motivation: An attribution analysis. *Journal of Personality and Social Psychology*, 1972, *21*, 318–326.

Wallston, K. A., Maides, S., & Wallston, B. S. Health-related information seeking as a function of health-related locus of control and health value. *Journal of Research in Personality*, 1976, *10*, 215–222.

Wills, T. A. Perceptions of clients by professional helpers. *Psychological Bulletin*, 1978, *85*, 968–1000.

Wrightsman, L. Measurement of philosophies of human nature. *Psychological Reports*, 1964, *14*, 743–751.

PART IV

PROCESSES IN
THERAPEUTIC RELATIONSHIPS

How do clients benefit from receiving help? What processes are responsible for improvement in psychotherapy? The following section reports recent research addressed to these questions. It is clear that persons do benefit in various ways from receiving help; the issue is exactly what processes are responsible for therapeutic gain and how these processes operate in the context of the interpersonal relationship between helper and client. The chapters in this section consider several basic issues in how clients respond to or react against help, how a helping relationship develops, and how the helper–client interaction is related to therapy outcome. A general finding in this work, as in the previous sections on help seeking and reactions to help, is that a helping relationship is not a one-sided transaction but rather is a complex relationship, involving helper and client processes that may either facilitate or inhibit therapeutic gain. The ultimate outcome of helping probably is based on a combination of facilitating and inhibiting processes.

In Chapter 13, Snyder, Ingram, and Newburg integrate their research on how people respond to personality feedback. This work represents a bridge between help seeking and involvement in therapy, because there are large individual differences in desire for feedback about the self, and persons with a low desire for feedback are unlikely to seek professional help at all.

Basic Processes in Helping Relationships

Copyright © 1982 by Academic Press, Inc.
All rights of reproduction in any form reserved
ISBN 0-12-757680-0

Personality variables such as locus of control and beliefs about the nature of one's problem seem to be important in regard to help seeking. Once a client has entered therapy, feedback from the therapist about personality attributes or therapeutic progress may serve to enhance the effect of treatment, probably by increasing clients' expectations about their ability to change; the authors make several valuable suggestions about how feedback may be communicated with consideration for clients' characteristic defense mechanisms. This process is not an unmixed blessing, however, for studies by Snyder and others have shown that people have a strong tendency to accept as uniquely true for themselves "Barnum statements," personality descriptions worded so generally that they are true of virtually everyone. Surprisingly, people show comparable acceptance of positive or negative personality descriptions, and this tendency is most pronounced for persons who have a high level of insecurity and when the feedback is delivered by a prestigious, authoritative source—conditions that probably obtain for the majority of psychotherapy clients.

Once clients have entered a formal helping relationship, their participation and adherence to the recommendations of the therapist are not always wholehearted or consistent. In Chapter 14, DiNicola and DiMatteo consider the processes that produce resistance to treatment by clients. This phenomenon has been studied most extensively in medical settings, where objective studies have shown a surprisingly high level of noncompliance with treatment regimens. The determinants of client resistance appear to be multidimensional, involving beliefs about treatment and treatment alternatives, psychological processes such as reactance against influence, situational factors, and the attitudes and behavior of the therapist. The authors note the importance of factors in the interpersonal relationship between therapist and patient, such as therapist–patient communication processes, for increasing adherence to treatment, and make a number of specific suggestions about social influence and cognitive–behavioral procedures that can be applied to reduce clients' resistance. Although the bulk of the evidence considered by DiNicola and DiMatteo is drawn from primary medical care settings, the findings are generally comparable to what is known from studies of psychotherapy, and there is reason to expect that many of their conclusions have wide generality.

To understand how a helping relationship makes an impact on clients, it is necessary to know how helpfulness is communicated. This issue is addressed in a recent research program by Elliott and colleagues, based on analysis of the verbal interaction between therapists and clients. Their findings are discussed in Chapter 15. Using a response mode analysis of helper–client communications, these investigators have examined helping communications from several different perspectives. Stiles has employed response mode analysis to examine the correlates of client satisfaction in a wide variety of helping relationships, including counseling and psychotherapy sessions, conversations between physicians and patients, and parent–child interactions. This research has found that the greatest consistency across settings is in *clients'* response mode usage, suggesting that client factors may be an important commonality in helping relationships. Stiles has also found that helping relationships go through definite stages, with systematic changes in helping behavior. Elliott has studied how clients perceive helpfulness and has identified empirical clusters that represent different types of helping behaviors; these include cognitively oriented communications (e.g., problem solving) in addition to the empathy and emotional support dimensions that have been the focus of previous research, as well as several types of behavior that are perceived as decidedly nonhelpful by clients. Work by Shiffman has investigated whether therapists' communication styles change as a result of clinical training; his results are provocative, for they show no major changes in clinical trainees' behavior, although the clinicians do differ significantly from nonclinical students, which suggests a self-selection process. Barker has pursued an interesting extension of this work by investigating helping communications among laypersons. A study of helping responses of married couples indicates that variables found to be important in clinical settings are also correlated with relationship satisfaction in informal helping relationships. The contributions of the various authors provide a number of stimulating ideas for further research on helping communications by professional helpers and in everyday helping situations.

Because of the central role of the helper–client relationship in therapeutic endeavors, the similarity between helper and client assumes a particular importance. Laboratory research has consistently indicated a correlation between attitude similarity and interpersonal attraction, suggesting that a comparable process might occur in professional helping relationships. Chapter 16, by Abramowitz and colleagues, provides a systematic examination of evidence on similarity effects in clinical settings. There are some instances in which complementarity between helper and client seems preferable (particularly with regard to interaction style), but similarity of attitudes and values seems more generally relevant for effective helper–client relationships. The authors suggest an interesting conclusion, for they note that the *initial* similarity of helper and client is not necessarily a major factor in professional helping relationships; trained clinicians show an ability to work effectively with clients who differ in race, sex, and perhaps in social background. More important than initial similarity, however, is a body of evidence showing a marked tendency for clients to become more similar to the therapist's beliefs and values over the course of therapy. This *convergence* process has been observed consistently both for general attitudes and values (see Beutler, 1981) and for expectations about treatment (see Duckro, Beal, & George, 1979). Moreover, the amount of therapist–client convergence is related to therapy outcome. This convergence phenomenon may be derivable from theoretical formulations of helper's and client's attributions (see Part II of this volume, "Social-Psychological Processes"), and the current evidence suggests that this is an important process in many types of treatment. Abramowitz *et al.*

summarize the domains of personality and interpersonal behavior in which complementarity or similarity effects seem to be relatively more important, and conclude by suggesting several research approaches that will increase our understanding of the role of similarity in helping relationships.

In Chapter 17 I consider the issue of nonspecific factors in helping relationships. One of the most striking findings about psychotherapy has been the comparable effectiveness of many different therapies, each with a completely different theoretical rationale, method of treatment, and (until now) band of adherents who believed that it was the only way to really benefit clients. Why such different therapies are all effective and what processes are actually responsible for therapeutic gain are discussed in detail in the chapter. I consider the mechanisms through which the therapeutic relationship increases clients' self-esteem and provides an arena in which a client can model the interpersonal behaviors of a reasonably adjusted person and can receive reasonably objective feedback about his or her own behavior. I discuss evidence showing the importance of clients' expectations, attributions, and belief systems for therapy and suggest how these variables are modified in the context of an interpersonal relationship. Finally, I propose an (admittedly crude) explanation for evidence on the comparable effectiveness of professional and nonprofessional helpers and suggest further research that will delineate the unique advantages of each type of helper. As a theme in the chapter, I note that the processes considered seem to be just as important for behavior therapy as for traditional psychotherapy; thus, the evidence on nonspecific factors is no less relevant now than it was in former years.

A complete understanding of helping relationships must consider the environmental context in which helping occurs, and for inpatient settings in particular, the specific nature of the social interaction between helpers and clients. In Chapter 18 Baltes reports results from investigations of staff–client interaction in nursing homes, using observational as well as experimental methodology. The power of direct observation methods is well demonstrated in this research program, for this work has provided not only precise data on the absolute frequency of various interactional behaviors, but also an analysis of sequential aspects of the interaction. The research by Baltes and colleagues bears on the issue of how helpers support independence versus dependence by clients; the results are informative, for they indicate a tendency by nursing home staff to reinforce dependent behavior by residents. It is noteworthy that this is not an isolated finding, but one that has been replicated across several different studies. In addition, data on the absolute frequency of social interaction indicate that the majority of staff members' social interaction was with other staff, rather than with residents. The implications of this methodological approach, and of the substantive findings, seem particularly important for the study of helping relationships, for it is the actual helper–client interaction (rather than more remote variables such as the helper's theoretical orientation) that determines the impact of helping on the recipient.

References

Beutler, L. E. Convergence in counseling and psychotherapy: A current look. *Clinical Psychology Review*, 1981, *1*, 79–102.

Duckro, P., Beal, D., & George, C. Research on the effects of disconfirmed client role expectations in psychotherapy: A critical review. *Psychological Bulletin*, 1979, *86*, 260–275.

chapter 13

The Role of Feedback in Help Seeking and the Therapeutic Relationship

C. R. SNYDER
RICK E. INGRAM
CHERYL L. NEWBURG

> A good listener is not only popular everywhere, but after a while he gets to know something.
>
> —Wilson Mizner (1942)

Introduction

Learning about oneself through *listening* to others—whether a trained therapist or an understanding friend—is an important process. If self-relevant information can be heard and meaningfully understood, the listener may adjust his or her actions so as to achieve more benefit and satisfaction from life. The effective use of self-relevant information, or feedback, becomes especially relevant in helping relationships, in which the individual makes some effort to improve his or her life situation.

In the past, several authors have advocated the importance of the feedback process to human functioning. According to Bernard (1974), for example, "Feedback is . . . needed not only in individual growth but in families, communities, and government. Feedback may be negative, positive or equivocal, but it is essential to normal functioning [p. 289]." In the area of social

287

comparison theory, other writers have proposed that people are highly motivated to acquire feedback about themselves (e.g., Festinger, 1954; Homans, 1961; Rotter, 1954; Suls & Miller, 1977; Thibaut & Kelley, 1959). Through discussion of these theories, the authors describe feedback as any information concerning a person's attitudes, behaviors, beliefs, physical attributes, or psychological characteristics relative to other people. The general assumption behind such theories is that people desire to obtain feedback because of the essential information it can provide in learning about acceptable and unacceptable behavior.

From a more applied perspective, the importance of the feedback process seems to be a basic assumption within the helping professions. Although theoretical orientations and approaches to therapy differ markedly among therapists of different disciplines, there is a common thread: *All therapists provide feedback* to the individual who is experiencing problems. The helping relationship can, indeed, be defined as a feedback process (see Ingram, McNeill, & Saccuzzo, 1979). There is a recipient, the client, who seeks to obtain feedback from a sender, the therapist, which will help him or her to overcome some difficulties. (Such a desire is often reflected in the presenting problems and subsequent verbal statements of clients, for example, "Tell me what I'm doing wrong." "Am I crazy?" "How can I make things better?") And there is a sender, the therapist, who provides feedback designed to meet the recipient's needs. Although the form of the feedback may differ across therapeutic approaches and individual psychotherapists, its overall goal is the same: to help the client learn about, and adaptively modify, his or her behavior, thoughts, and feelings. Thus, in theory and clinical application, feedback has been recognized as having important implications for helping relationships (see Goldfried, 1980).

This chapter explores the role of feedback within the helping relationship from both an empirical and a conceptual standpoint. For purposes of exposition, the helping process will be described in terms of three chronological phases: seeking of psychological help, assessment at the beginning of therapy, and therapeutic intervention. The role and importance of feedback within each of these phases will be examined.

Feedback and Psychological Help Seeking

Empirical evidence has shown that helping relationships are effective for reducing or eliminating an individual's psychological difficulties (see Bergin & Lambert, 1978; Smith & Glass, 1977). Before such a relationship can proceed, however, it must be initiated. Hypothetically, the initiation of help seeking should be quite straightforward: If an individual is experiencing problems, he or she should take the steps needed to alleviate those problems, including, if necessary, the seeking of psychological help.[1] Empirical studies indicate, however, that the process is rarely so simple. Many individuals do not seek the psychological help when they need it (Bergin & Lambert, 1978; Dohrenwend, Dohrenwend, Gould, Link, Neugebauer, & Wunsch-Hitzig, 1980), but choose to suffer in solitude or attempt to deal with their problems in other ways.

Research in this area suggests that several factors associated with feedback may be quite important to a person's decision to seek psychological help. In the following section, we will examine personality and situational feedback-related factors that are relevant to the help-seeking phenomenon.[2]

AN EXAMPLE OF PERSONALITY FACTORS: INDIVIDUAL DIFFERENCES IN DESIRE FOR FEEDBACK

Since therapy is recognized as a feedback-oriented process by potential clients (see Ingram *et al.*, 1979), one personality factor that may influence help seeking is the individual's desire for feedback. It seems reasonable to hypothesize that people with a high desire for feedback about themselves will be particularly likely to seek professional help when psychological difficulties arise; conversely, individuals with a low desire for feedback should tend to avoid seeking help and the feedback it entails. Available data in this area support this hypothesis. In a study exploring the motivational properties of individual differences in desire for feedback, our research group (Snyder, Ingram, Handelsman, Wells, & Huwieler, Note 1) found that college students who had self-reported a low (compared to high) desire for feedback about themselves[3] also reported significantly less psychological help-seeking behavior in the past and a significantly lower likelihood of seeking psychological help in the future. We also found, among Veterans Administration (VA) inpatients with a diagnosis of alcoholism, that those who had not volunteered for an inhouse treatment program reported a significantly lower desire for feedback, compared with those who had volunteered for the same program.

Given these findings, it is interesting to consider why some individuals have a low desire for feedback. For reasons outlined in the beginning of this

---

[1]Some "helping" relationships are not initiated by the individual in question, however. An institution, such as the court system, may take the initiator's role.

[2]Although personality and situational factors will be discussed separately at several junctures in this chapter, it should be noted that these factors often *interact* to influence the various phases of the helping process. Unfortunately, little research has been devoted to investigating such interaction, and thus, any discussion of that interaction will be limited.

[3]Desire for feedback was measured by giving 1000 undergraduate students a single 9-point Likert item on which they rated their desire for feedback about themselves across a variety of situations (1 = not at all interested in feedback, 9 = extremely interested in feedback). The low-desire-for-feedback people had an average of 2 on this item and the high-desire-for-feedback people had an average of 9.

chapter, we believe that a low desire for feedback may hinder a person from functioning at an optimal level, especially if he or she is in need of psychological help and chooses not to seek it. Why then do some people prefer not to seek feedback that may be beneficial to them? One possibility is that negative past experiences with feedback lead to a generally lowered desire for it. It may be that individuals who have had such experiences come to perceive the feedback process itself negatively, and thus avoid future feedback-related situations. This possibility is supported by the finding that VA inpatients who did not volunteer for treatment services (and who had a significantly lower desire for feedback than volunteer inpatients) also reported receiving more negative and less relevant past feedback than did those in the volunteer group (Snyder et al., Note 1). Another possible reason why many people do not seek potentially useful feedback is that they feel unable to act effectively upon the feedback they receive. That is, a low desire for feedback may be caused by the belief that one cannot help oneself. If an individual believes that he or she lacks the capabilities to change, a reduced motivation to seek feedback may naturally follow. It is also possible that feelings of helplessness affect help seeking irrespective of desire for feedback. If individuals truly believe that they are helpless, help seeking may be perceived as a waste of time, and desire for feedback may be lowered as a corollary. Such a relationship, however, has yet to be empirically explored (for a review of learned helplessness, see Garber & Seligman, 1980).

In all likelihood, there are a variety of other feedback-related personal variables that influence psychological help seeking. Locus of control, previous dealings with psychological difficulties, past experience with psychological help seeking, and the perceptions of the nature of the problem are all examples of potentially influential variables. In fact, any personality or individual difference dimension that affects the perception of the role of feedback in therapy, or in one's life in general, may have an impact on psychological help seeking. Further research is needed to elucidate how personality variables influence the seeking of psychological help.

AN EXAMPLE OF SITUATIONAL FACTORS:
CONSENSUS INFORMATION ABOUT ONE'S PROBLEM

As an example of a situational-feedback-related factor that may have an impact upon help-seeking behavior, consider the role of consensus feedback. By definition, consensus (or actuarial) feedback is information about the base-rate prevalence of a problem within the population (see Kelley, 1971, 1973). High-consensus feedback indicates that an individual's problem is widely experienced in the population, whereas low-consensus feedback indicates that an individual's difficulties are rarely experienced by others.

In a study of the effect of consensus information on psychological help-seeking behavior, we hypothesized that high-consensus feedback facilitates help seeking (Snyder & Ingram, Note 2). In this study, it was predicted that high-consensus feedback would have a reassuring effect, allowing people to acknowledge the seriousness of their problems along with the inadequacy of their coping response. Conversely, we predicted that low-consensus feedback would *not* have a reassuring effect because it would arouse defensiveness, inhibiting acknowledgment of the seriousness of difficulties and the inadequacy of coping responses. These predictions were explored with a group of highly test-anxious college students as follows. Participants were given feedback by an experimenter that they had test anxiety, along with either high- or low-consensus information regarding the prevalence of test anxiety within the college population. They were then asked to indicate their willingness to seek psychological help for their test anxiety. Consistent with predictions, the individuals who received feedback that their problem was common (high consensus), as compared to uncommon (low consensus), expressed more interest in psychological help. Furthermore, these effects appeared to be mediated by perceptions of problem seriousness and personal coping such that the high-consensus-feedback individuals also reported more problem seriousness and less coping. Thus, consensus feedback, perhaps through mediating perceptions of seriousness and coping, appears to have an effect on help seeking.

Many other types of situational factors may also have an impact on psychological help-seeking behavior. For example, local mental health resources, friends' reactions, and current living conditions may be influential. In fact, any situational dimension that fosters ideas about psychological problems or the value of help seeking may influence an individual's motivation to seek out a helping relationship. Future research efforts are warranted in order to determine how various situational factors affect psychological help seeking.

Feedback and Assessment

Psychological assessment is often an integral part of the process of psychotherapy. Such assessment may involve any combination of projective tests, personality inventories, behavioral observations, and client self-reports. Once completed, assessment results typically become the basis for subsequent feedback to the client during therapy. Sometimes the therapist may plan a session specifically designed to give the client assessment-derived feedback.[4]

[4] In actual clinical practice, the feedback session approach is not often utilized. Some writers, however, have argued that it is the most ethical and therapeutically useful way to give personality feedback to clients (Craddick, 1972; Fischer, 1970, 1978). This feedback process is more typically employed when assessment is undertaken just for the sake of assessment rather than as the beginning of therapy. This occurs most often when the clinician has received an evaluation referral from another professional, in guidance–counseling settings, and in the case of employee appraisals. In these latter instances the assessment results are frequently interpreted directly to the assessee.

More commonly, the therapist gradually incorporates assessment-derived feedback into the overall treatment plan. In any case, clinicians are likely to give personality feedback to their clients based on initial and ongoing assessments. This section will describe some of the personality and situational factors that may be important for clients' utilization of feedback derived from psychological assessment.

PERSONALITY FACTORS

Information about personality factors that may influence reactions to assessment-derived feedback comes primarily from studies of the "Barnum effect." Paul Meehl coined the term *Barnum effect* in 1956 to describe the tendency of most people to accept personality feedback composed of vague statements that are true of virtually everyone in the general population (e.g., "You have a tendency to be critical of yourself," or "Security is one of your major goals in life"). In the typical Barnum effect research paradigm, participants (*a*) complete a personality test, (*b*) wait for the test to be scored, (*c*) receive feedback purportedly derived from the test but actually composed of "Barnum" (vague, high base-rate) statements, and (*d*) rate the accuracy of the feedback and their acceptance of it. Empirical research using this paradigm burgeoned in the 1970s, when over 40 papers on the topic appeared in the psychological literature (for a review see Snyder, Shenkel, & Lowery, 1977), and many of these studies addressed the issue of personality factors related to feedback acceptance.

Through the use of this paradigm, several studies have found that traditional individual difference measures, such as sex, age, and occupational background, do not influence acceptance of feedback (see Snyder *et al.*, 1977). Certain personality dimensions, on the other hand, do appear to be related to acceptance. First, individuals with an external as compared to internal locus of control are more prone to accept feedback (Snyder & Larson, 1972; Snyder & Shenkel, 1976). Second, people who report a high level of insecurity in their lives are more accepting of feedback (Snyder & Clair, 1977). Third, a person's desire for feedback interacts with the favorability of the feedback to influence his or her acceptance. With regard to this third dimension, we have found that both positive and negative feedback were less accepted by low- as compared to high-desire-for-feedback research participants (Snyder *et al.*, Note 1). In addition, high-desire-for-feedback individuals accepted positive feedback more than negative feedback, and low-desire-for-feedback individuals showed *no difference* in their acceptance of positive and negative feedback. These latter results suggest that people with a high desire for feedback may be especially sensitive to personally relevant feedback, whereas people with a low desire for feedback may be cognitively "turned off" to the assessment feedback process.

Taken together, the results of this research suggest that people may be quite accepting of, and sensitive to, the assessment-derived feedback they receive. Since psychological help seekers may be likely to possess the personality factors of an external locus of control, heightened insecurity, and a heightened desire for feedback, they should be particularly accepting of the personality feedback their therapists may offer.

SITUATIONAL FACTORS

Additional related research has been conducted under the label of the acceptance phenomenon. Unlike the Barnum effect, which only considers the acceptance of feedback that has a high base-rate accuracy, the acceptance phenomenon considers the acceptance of feedback that does and does *not* have a high base-rate accuracy. In the research on the acceptance phenomenon, the situations under which feedback is most readily accepted have been specifically examined. To date, several important situational factors have been empirically identified. First, the perceived situational relevance of feedback has been found to influence acceptance. In a study by Snyder and Larson (1972), for example, research participants were given bogus personality feedback and told either that the feedback was derived specifically for them (the high-personal-relevance condition) or that it was generally true of all people (low personal relevance). Results demonstrated that people who received the high-relevance feedback rated it as being a more accurate characterization of their own personalities than people who received the low-relevance feedback. Similar results have been found in several other investigations (e.g., Collins, Dmitruk, & Ranney, 1977; Layne, 1978; Snyder, 1974; Snyder, Larsen, & Bloom, 1976).

An additional situational variable that can affect feedback acceptance is the sense of self-disclosure individuals experience in diagnostic situations. In a study by Handelsman and Snyder (in press), half of the research participants were informed, after the completion of a psychological test, that they had been very self-disclosing. The remaining participants were given no self-disclosure information. Results showed that people in the self-disclosure condition accepted feedback supposedly derived from the psychological test at a significantly higher rate than those in the no-self-disclosure-information condition.

Another situational factor that has been found to affect acceptance of personality feedback is the sense of security promoted by the feedback situation. In a study examining this variable, Snyder and Clair (1977) manipulated research participants' sense of security by altering the experimental setting. In a high-insecurity setting, people were administered a psychological test in a brightly lit room equipped with cameras, a microphone, and a two-way mirror through which they were supposedly being observed. In the low-insecurity setting, people completed the same test in a plain room without the anxiety-inducing objects. Results showed that people in the high-insecurity setting were more acceptant of subsequent personality feedback than were people in the low-insecurity setting.

The status of the person giving feedback has also been identified as an important situational variable. Halperin, Snyder, Shenkel, and Houston (1976) found that the status of the diagnostician interacted with the favorability of feedback to influence acceptance ratings. Research participants in this study were given either positive or negative feedback by either a high-status or low-status diagnostician. In the positive-feedback condition, the feedback was highly accepted regardless of the diagnostician's status. In the negative-feedback condition, however, the high- as compared to low-status diagnostician elicited significantly higher levels of acceptance. These findings have been replicated with individuals participating in groups (Snyder & Newburg, 1981).

Taken together, the above findings suggest that the nature of the helping relationship may make acceptance of assessment-derived feedback particularly likely.[5] Overall, such assessment feedback is typically described as personally relevant; clients are likely to view themselves as, and perhaps strive to be, self-disclosing during the assessment process; actual clinical–diagnostic settings can easily engender a high level of insecurity in clients; and mental health diagnosticians are likely to be perceived as having high status. (The status of the diagnostician may be especially important when the feedback is negative, which is often true of clinical feedback.) With all of these situational factors having the potential to enhance feedback acceptance in the helping relationship, Snyder and Newburg (1981) warn mental health professionals to "speak softly because [you] carry a big stick [p. 628]."

In order to explain the fact that people tend to accept Barnum personality

---

[5]At this point, it may be important to note that Layne (1979) has argued that the findings in the acceptance literature are not powerful enough to warrant concern in actual clinical settings. He states, for example, that "Relevance typically raises acceptance from a rating of around 'good/average' or 'neutral/accurate' to a rating of slightly better than 'good' or 'accurate/neutral,' respectively [p. 220]." He then infers that actual clients would similarly only slightly adjust their acceptance of feedback in response to situational variables. This inference is questionable, however, on empirical, methodological, and theoretical grounds. Empirically, Layne's inference was based upon only a relevance manipulation and yet was used to draw conclusions about the entire set of situational factors that influence the acceptance phenomenon. Methodologically, such a conclusion is inappropriate since the observed "slight" adjustment of acceptance ratings may be a function of weak or insensitive dependent measures. On the theoretical level, it can be argued that the findings of analogue studies are likely to be magnified in actual clinical settings. As compared to college students who serve as research participants in required experiments, actual clients may be more insecure, more self-disclosing and more highly impressed with the status and abilities of the diagnostician–feedback-provider. All of these situational factors seem to promote heightened feedback acceptance.

descriptions that are not based upon actual assessment-derived information, several researchers have invoked the notion of gullibility (e.g., Forer, 1949; Lattal & Lattal, 1967; Stagner, 1958), positing that research participants accept Barnum feedback because they are gullible and nondiscriminating. Recent research and theory, however, have moved away from this notion. Instead, present theory argues that individuals are behaving *rationally* if they accept Barnum personality descriptions (Layne, 1979; Snyder, Newburg, Ingram, Handelsman, & Mangione, Note 3). Indeed, by definition, Barnum feedback consists of statements that have a high base-rate of accuracy in the general population. Therefore, Barnum feedback, like P.T. Barnum circuses, is bound to have "a little something for everybody," and thus be reasonably descriptive of almost anyone. The empirical work of Snyder and Shenkel (1976) certainly supports the idea that it is rationally perceived, high-base-rate accuracy that accounts for the acceptance of Barnum feedback rather than participant gullibility. In their study of feedback acceptance, Snyder and Shenkel found that statistical control of the base-rate accuracy of feedback statements significantly attenuated the degree to which such statements were accepted. In other words, the base-rate accuracy of such statements for people in general largely determined how accurate these statements were viewed by a given individual.

The rationality explanation for feedback acceptance has also been applied to the acceptance phenomenon as a whole (e.g., Layne, 1979), wherein feedback does not necessarily have a high base-rate accuracy, and situational variables seem capable of enhancing or reducing feedback acceptance. We do not find the rationality explanation as compelling, however, when considered in terms of the entire acceptance phenomenon (see Snyder *et al.*, Note 3). Presumably, if people are capable of "rationally" assessing the accuracy of feedback about their own personalities and characteristics, then the situation in which the feedback is provided should be irrelevant. As previously reviewed, this is not always the case. Thus, we would invoke the concept of *situational persuasibility* to explain current research findings on the acceptance phenomenon. According to a situational persuasibility explanation, although individuals may be quite discerning of feedback under a variety of circumstances, certain situations have the capacity to promote an elevated level of feedback acceptance. As described earlier, many of these situations are closely linked to helping relationships. Because of the situational factors that produce a high level of client acceptance of assessment-derived feedback, mental health professionals should be careful not to construe this acceptance as reflecting validation of either the assessment procedures or the assessor (Snyder *et al.*, 1977). It should also be noted, however, that client persuasibility may increase the probability that the diagnostic input will be incorporated. This latter step is an important one that may facilitate subsequent therapeutic interventions.

Feedback and the Therapeutic Intervention Process

At no time may the role of feedback be more important than during actual therapeutic intervention (Goldfried, 1980; Korchin, 1976; Sundberg, 1977). Once a helping relationship has been initiated and assessment completed, the intervention process typically involves giving substantial feedback to the client, and, ideally, the effective use of that feedback by the client. It becomes apparent, then, that the client's assimilation and utilization of feedback obtained from therapy must play a major role in determining the efficacy of therapeutic intervention. A client who is receptive to feedback, for instance, is far more likely to profit from the helping relationship than the client who is not. Accordingly, we now turn to an examination of two related areas of theory and research regarding the impact of feedback in the therapeutic intervention process. The first area addresses personality variables that may mediate the effect of feedback within the helping relationship; the second area considers the relationship between situational feedback and therapeutic outcome.

PERSONALITY FACTORS

Clearly, all individuals do not process and react to feedback in the same manner. Although the personality factors described in this section certainly do not exhaust the list of all possible factors, they should illustrate the impact that individual differences can have on response to feedback obtained through the therapy process.

Desire for Feedback and Client Expectancies

One well-established influence upon therapeutic outcome is the set of expectations the client brings to therapy (Shapiro & Morris, 1978). More specifically, high as opposed to low expectations regarding one's ability to change have been found to foster positive therapeutic outcomes (Frank, Hoehn-Saric, Imber, Liberman, & Stone, 1978). According to our recent work (Snyder et al., Note 1), an individual's desire for feedback may be similarly related to therapeutic change. As part of a large intake questionnaire, incoming clients to a major university psychological clinic were asked to rate their desire for feedback, their motivation for therapy, and their expectation that their therapist would be helpful. Both the motivation and expectancy measures were found to correlate positively with clients' desire for feedback. Thus, it appears that the individual who possesses a high desire for feedback is also more likely to be motivated for therapy and to have positive expecta-tions.[6] When the evidence concerning the impact of expectation sets upon

---

[6]This is not to say that a high desire for feedback *causes* these other variables to increase. It may simply be part of a constellation of factors (i.e., high desire for feedback, high motivation, positive expectancies) that are interrelated and perhaps influenced by other currently unknown variables.

therapy outcome is considered, these findings suggest that the individual with a high desire for feedback may be especially primed for a successful therapy experience.

Client Problems

There are many different types of problems that bring people into therapy. The nature of these problems may exert some systematic influence upon how feedback is processed and evaluated during therapeutic intervention. Perhaps the foremost example of a problem that might lead to systematic feedback distortion is depression. On a conceptual level, several writers have argued that depressed individuals have a proclivity for distorting information in a negative manner (Beck, 1976; Beck, Rush, Shaw, & Emery, 1979; Mendels, 1970). According to Beck, for example, depressed individuals are inclined to distort environmental information so that they view themselves, their life situations, and their futures in a more negative fashion than is veridical. Thus, feedback given to the depressed client during therapy may be negatively distorted. This proposition has been supported empirically in a study by Nelson and Craighead (1977). These researchers found that individuals who had previously self-reported high levels of depression were, relative to nondepressed individuals, more likely to recall feedback that reflected negatively upon them. Analogous results have also been found in more recent research by Ingram, Smith, Brehm, and Stucky (Note 4).

Although depression is the most common example of a problem that might influence feedback processing, other client problems may also exert characteristic influences. Individuals with a high level of anxiety, for example, may be cognitively receptive to certain kinds of feedback (Smith, Ingram, & Brehm, Note 5). Unfortunately, research attention has yet to be turned to the feedback evaluation process associated with many problems other than depression. Further research is needed to determine how people with different problems typically process feedback and what types of feedback are most therapeutically effective with different problem constellations.

Characteristic Defense Mechanisms

As the term is commonly used today, *defense mechanisms* are regarded as strategies that are designed to reduce anxiety promoted by external situations.[7] One external situation that may be very anxiety-provoking is the psychological helping relationship. Although the therapy goal may be to reduce anxiety, the helping situation may engender a good deal of anxiety itself due to the self-exploration and self-confrontation involved, the push to carry out these processes in the presence of a high-status yet ambiguous authority figure (i.e.,

---

[7]As they were initially conceived, defense mechanisms were thought to help ward off internally generated sources of anxiety. Alfred Adler, however, popularized the notion that defense mechanisms are devices that serve to attenuate externally provoked anxiety (see Ansbacher & Ansbacher, 1967).

the therapist), and the prospect of receiving feedback about personal in-adequacies and deficiencies. Thus, to the extent that the helping relationship in general and feedback in particular promote anxiety, several writers have suggested that characteristic defense mechanisms will affect the way in-dividuals process feedback within therapy (e.g., Berger, 1970; Yenawine & Arbuckle, 1971).

Kipper and Ginot (1979) have elaborated on the these concepts and proposed that defenses distort feedback in a systematic fashion. To test this possibility, they identified people who characteristically used one of five defense clusters: projection, reversal (including denial, reaction formation, and repression), turning against self, principalization (including intellectual-ization, isolation, and rationalization), and turning against object (displace-ment). Once identified according to their characteristic defense, people were videotaped in two role-playing sessions and later asked to observe themselves on tape and rate their performances along a number of dimensions. Research participants' ratings were then compared to the ratings of three independent observers, and discrepancies were analyzed. Consistent with predictions, several of the defense groups were found to distort ratings of the videotape feedback in ways that were consistent with their defense mechanisms. The projection group, for instance, was found to produce the most extreme overall distortions, whereas members of the turning-against-self group were par-ticularly likely to underestimate their own performances. Although the reversal and turning-against-object groups did not distort the feedback in a systematic manner, Kipper and Ginot's results do suggest that an individual's predilection for a particular defense may have an impact on the processing and evaluation of feedback within therapy.

SITUATIONAL FACTORS

There are probably many situational factors that are related to feedback during therapeutic intervention. Two of these factors have been selected to illustrate the impact of feedback during therapy.

Monitoring Behavior

One of the basic tenets of behavioral psychotherapy approaches is that observable indices of psychological problems can and should be monitored and recorded (e.g., Goldfried & Sprafkin, 1974; Thoresen & Mahoney, 1974). In fact, one of the first goals in behavior therapy is to define the problem in measurable terms so that the client can then be taught to make observational records or behavioral counts of the problem (Wolpe & Lazarus, 1966). From our point of view, this recording and counting process is simply a systematized feedback procedure.

Although initial behavioral monitoring is typically described as a baseline period from which to judge the efficacy of subsequent therapeutic interventions, it has been observed that merely monitoring one's problem can serve to lessen it (Kazdin, 1974; Mahoney, Moore, Wade, & Moura, 1973; McFall, 1970; Sundberg, 1977). One possible reason for this phenomenon is that behavioral monitoring serves as a vivid feedback procedure that encourages the client to mobilize his or her adaptive coping skills (see Kanfer, 1980). In this sense, the assessment-like feedback process may actually generate self-stimulated therapeutic improvement.

Behaviorally oriented therapists, and those of other theoretical orientations as well, typically continue to monitor the client's problem throughout therapy. This is done in order to give clients feedback about their progress and to estimate the usefulness of a particular therapeutic intervention. The continual exchange of feedback information is the vehicle by which client and therapist keep informed as to the success of the helping relationship.

Enhancing Expectations

One of the emerging viewpoints in the therapeutic intervention literature is that the client's expectations for success should be elevated during the helping process in order to maximize the potential for change (Frank et al., 1978). According to this viewpoint, by imparting feedback to the client that he or she can improve, motivation will increase, and the client becomes more likely to change. The empirical work of Halperin and Snyder (1979) has provided some support for this contention. In their study of a snake-phobic population, one group of individuals was provided with a desensitization treatment along with diagnostic personality feedback (purportedly derived from a personality test) indicating that they had a strong capacity for change and could benefit from treatment. A second group received the desensitization treatment only; a third group served as a waiting list control. On a subsequent behavioral avoidance test, when all participants were asked to approach a live snake, those in the desensitization-plus-feedback group were found to approach the snake significantly more closely than were individuals in either of the other groups. These results suggest that it may be possible to enhance an individual's expectations and subsequent treatment outcome through the provision of certain kinds of diagnostic feedback. Such feedback may help to convince the client that he or she is a responsible person capable of changing.

Future Conceptual and Research Issues

The foregoing discussion has outlined many areas of research and conceptualization that describe feedback in the helping process. Although advances in these areas have helped to identify several important variables pertaining to the relationship between feedback and the various components of the helping process, many significant issues have yet to be adequately explored. In this section, we will suggest some promising and needed areas of investigation. Since, as should be clear from previous sections, feedback and the helping relationship are related in numerous ways, the suggestions are not meant to be exhaustive. Instead, they are intended to provide a starting point for establishing a better understanding of the role of feedback in the helping relationship.

PERSONALITY ISSUES

A fundamental, but insufficiently explored, personality issue concerns the desire for feedback. We have assumed that it is adaptive for people to be desirous of feedback because feedback generates the very information by which we learn about our world and ourselves. Empirically, however, there is very little information on the "average" desire for feedback, and much less on individual differences in this variable. This paucity of information is remarkable when one considers the potential impact that individual differences in desire for feedback may have on psychological helping relationships as well as on the broader spectrum of learning environments.

At present, therefore, there is a great need for the development of a scale to tap individual differences in the desire for feedback. In the past, researchers have used a simple one-item Likert question in order to measure individual differences on the variable (see Snyder *et al.*, Note 1). Although there is some empirical evidence attesting to the ability of this item to measure desire for feedback, a psychometrically validated scale is more desirable for future research.

Once a suitable desire-for-feedback scale is available, research can proceed to investigate the developmental and psychological underpinnings of desire for feedback. Previous research suggesting that an elevated desire for feedback may facilitate the entire helping process (from seeking help to undergoing therapy) needs to be replicated. If such research reveals that a low-desire-for-feedback person does not seek help or does not profit from the helping process, it will become particularly important to investigate the differences between high- and low-desire-for-feedback individuals. Although it has been suggested that a sense of helplessness may accompany a low desire for feedback and underlie some of the behaviors associated with it (e.g., low help seeking, low therapy motivation), this suggestion should be empirically investigated.

Also with regard to the desire for feedback, it seems worthwhile to explore the behavioral and cognitive correlates of high versus low desire orientations. For example, we might ask about the arenas in which the behavior of low-desire-for-feedback persons differs markedly from their high-desire-for-feedback counterparts. Does the low-desire-for-feedback individual behaviorally avoid potential feedback situations? From a cognitive standpoint, we might ask about how low-desire-for-feedback individuals process feedback in light of their tendency to be less accepting of personality feedback. Does feedback, for example, have an impact on such people even though it is verbally dismissed? What other cognitive characteristics might be correlated with desire for feedback? These questions represent prime targets for future research on the desire for feedback.

SITUATIONAL ISSUES

Psychological Help Seeking

A helping relationship is usually established by people who are willing to seek professional assistance. Earlier, we discussed how the individual differences variable of desire for feedback and the situational variable of consensus information relate to psychological help seeking. One goal of future research would be to delineate other individual difference and situational variables that may influence psychological help seeking. Research should not only seek to identify additional factors, however, but also attempt to specify how those factors interact to either facilitate or inhibit help seeking. Additionally, since help may not be initiated until the potential client can admit the severity of the problem and his or her inability to cope, future research should consider the situational factors that might lead to such a cognitive emotional appraisal. And finally, investigators would be well advised to develop testable theoretical frameworks to explain the role of feedback in the help-seeking process. Psychological help seeking is certainly a vital research area since there are undoubtedly a large number of people who need help and could seek it, but choose not to do so.

Assessment

In the area of assessment, recent research has focused on situations that influence peoples' receptivity to diagnostic feedback. In so far as these research efforts have been productive, future research should be directed toward discovering other situational influences. Research that addresses the generality of the acceptance phenomenon to actual clinical settings is also important. As noted earlier, previous research has been criticized on the grounds that its generality to applied settings is limited (Layne, 1979), but this claim needs to be empirically tested. We propose that the bulk of the findings reviewed in this chapter will be found to obtain in clinical settings. However, it is true that in these settings feedback occurs in a discussion format, for the most part, as compared to the unilateral model of feedback that current research has followed. One way to address this issue would be to study feedback that is initiated by the assessor, but is then collaboratively discussed until both parties understand how the findings are true of a particular person (Fischer, 1981).

Theoretical formulations are also needed to explain how and why certain situations lead to increased acceptance of feedback. Although the notion of "situational persuasion" is appealing as a descriptive label for these findings, its power as an explanatory mechanism is limited. An adequate theoretical explanation must not only specify the critical individual difference variables in the acceptance phenomenon, but also predict those situations in which the acceptance of feedback will be enhanced. Perhaps a fruitful approach to promote better understanding of the acceptance phenomenon would be to ascertain the cognitive–emotional state that allows a person to accept feedback. With recent advances in the information–processing techniques of cognitive psychology, researchers may now have more satisfactory means of investigating hypothesized cognitive–emotional factors. Once these are better understood, investigators could turn to the individual differences and situational variables that contribute to their presence and attendant mediational properties.

Therapeutic Interventions

Feedback is also at the core of the actual therapeutic intervention process. Therapists typically determine some criterion of change, whether explicitly or implicitly, and use it to evaluate therapeutic progress. If the client and therapist can not share a feedback monitoring process, however, successful intervention becomes less likely. Sometimes this is the case because the client or therapist cannot accurately give feedback; sometimes this is the case because the client and therapist cannot develop or agree upon a feedback process. Empirical investigation of ways to optimally achieve a shared feedback-monitoring system between therapist and client would certainly be a worthwhile research direction.

Beyond the use of feedback in the aforementioned monitoring process, feedback is used as an actual intervention strategy to induce client change. There is obviously a great deal of extant research on intervention strategies, and much more will be completed in the future. In this vein, it may be appropriate to ask future researchers to explore the possibility that a *common* cognitive–emotional reaction to various feedback interventions may result in an adaptive response to feedback. It may be that, although specific intervention feedback strategies vary, effective client response is preceded by a typical cognitive–emotional mediational set. To the extent that such a mediational set is understood, we should be better able to refine the effective components of feedback interventions.

Concluding Statement

Throughout this chapter it has been suggested that a common cognitive–emotional set may facilitate psychological help seeking, acceptance of assessment-derived feedback, and therapeutic change. Perhaps this cognitive–emotional set is similar to the attentional state of *listening*. To paraphrase Mizner (1942), a person who listens to feedback is primed to learn about himself or herself. Indeed, helping relationships may be built on this premise.

ACKNOWLEDGMENTS

The authors gratefully acknowledge the input of Constance T. Fischer, Christopher Layne, Timothy W. Smith, and Thomas Ashby Wills on this chapter. Listening to the feedback of these reviewers resulted in an improved chapter.

Reference Notes

1. Snyder, C. R., Ingram, R. E., Handelsman, M. M., Wells, D. S., & Huwieler, R. *Desire for personal feedback: Who wants it and what does it mean for therapy?* Unpublished manuscript, University of Kansas, 1981.
2. Snyder, C. R., & Ingram, R. E. *The impact of consensus information upon help-seeking behavior.* Unpublished manuscript, University of Kansas, 1981.
3. Snyder, C. R., Newburg, C. L., Ingram, R. E., Handelsman, M. M., & Mangione, L. *The Barnum effect and rationality versus the acceptance phenomenon and situational gullibility.* Unpublished manuscript, University of Kansas, 1981.
4. Ingram, R. E., Smith, T. W., Brehm, S. S., & Stucky, R. J. *Depression and self-referent information encoding.* Paper presented at the meeting of the Rocky Mountain Psychological Association, Denver, Colorado, April 1981.
5. Smith, T. W., Ingram, R. E., & Brehm, S. S. *Social anxiety, anxious self-preoccupation and recall of self-relevant information.* Unpublished manuscript, University of Kansas, 1981.

References

Ansbacher, H. L., & Ansbacher, R. R. *The individual psychology of Alfred Adler.* New York: Harper & Row, 1967.
Beck, A. T. *Cognitive therapy and the emotional disorders.* New York. International Universities Press, 1976.
Beck, A. T., Rush, A. J., Shaw, B. F., & Emery, G. *Cognitive therapy of depression.* New York: Guilford Press, 1979.
Berger, M. M. Confrontation through videotape. In M. M. Berger (Ed.), *Videotape techniques in psychiatric training and treatment.* New York: Brunner/Mazel, 1970.
Bergin, A. R., & Lambert, M. J. The evaluation of therapeutic outcomes. In S. L. Garfield & A. E.

Bergin (Eds.), *Handbook of psychotherapy and behavior change: An empirical analysis* (2nd ed.). New York: Wiley, 1978.

Bernard, H. W. *Personality: Applying theory*. Boston: Holbrook, 1974.

Collins, R. W., Dmitruk, V. M., & Ranney, J. T. Personal validation: Some empirical and ethical considerations. *Journal of Consulting and Clinical Psychology*, 1977, *45*, 70–77.

Craddick, R. A. Humanistic assessment: A reply to Brown. *Psychotherapy: Theory, Research and Practice*, 1972, *9*, 107–110.

Dohrenwend, B. P., Dohrenwend, B. S., Gould, M. S., Link, B., Neugebauer, R., & Wunsch-Hitzig, R. *Mental illness in the United States: Epidemiologic estimates*. New York: Praeger, 1980.

Festinger, L. A theory of social comparison processes. *Human Relations*, 1954, *7*, 117–140.

Fischer, C. T. The testee as co-evaluator. *Journal of Counseling Psychology*, 1970, *17*, 70–76.

Fischer, C. T. Personality and assessment. In R. S. Valle & M. King (Eds.), *Existential–phenomenological alternatives for psychology*. New York: Oxford Univ. Press, 1978.

Fischer, C. T. *Individualized assessment: An introduction*. Monterey, Calif.: Brooks/Cole, 1981.

Forer, B. R. The fallacy of personal validation: A classroom demonstration of gullibility. *Journal of Abnormal and Social Psychology*, 1949, *44*, 118–123.

Frank, J. D., Hoehn-Saric, R., Imber, S. D., Liberman, B. L., & Stone, A. R. *Effective ingredients of successful psychotherapy*. New York: Brunner/Mazel, 1978.

Garber, J., & Seligman, M. E. P. (Eds.). *Human helplessness: Theory and applications*. New York: Academic Press, 1980.

Goldfried, M. R. Psychotherapy process: Some views on effective principles of psychotherapy. *Cognitive Therapy and Research*, 1980, *4*, 280–285.

Goldfried, M. R., & Sprafkin, J. N. *Behavioral personality assessment*. Morristown, N.J.: General Learning Press, 1974.

Halperin, K. M., & Snyder, C. R. Effects of enhanced psychological test feedback on treatment outcome: Therapeutic implications of the Barnum effect. *Journal of Consulting and Clinical Psychology*, 1979, *47*, 140–146.

Halperin, K. M., Snyder, C. R., Shenkel, R. J., & Houston, B. K. Effects of source status and message favorability on acceptance of personality feedback. *Journal of Applied Psychology*, 1976, *61*, 85–88.

Handelsman, M. M., & Snyder, C. R. Is "rejected" feedback really rejected?: Effects of informativeness on reactions to positive and negative personality feedback. *Journal of Personality*, in press.

Homans, G. C. *Social behavior: Its elementary forms*. New York: Harcourt, 1961.

Ingram, R. E., McNeill, B. W., Saccuzzo, D. P. Perceptions of the process of psychotherapy by non-mental health professionals. In L. E. Nelson & E. D. Anderson (Eds.), *Helping people: Selected readings about casework, counseling, and psychotherapy*. Johnson City, Tenn.: University Press, 1979.

Kanfer, F. H. Self-management methods. In F. H. Kanfer & A. P. Goldstein (Eds.), *Helping people change* (2nd ed.). New York: Pergamon, 1980.

Kazdin, A. E. Self-monitoring and behavior change. In M. J. Mahoney & C. E. Thoresen (Eds.), *Self-control: Power to the person*. Monterey, Calif.: Brooks/Cole, 1974.

Kelley, H. H. *Attribution in social interaction*. Morristown, N.J.: General Learning Press, 1971.

Kelley, H. H. The process of causal attribution. *American Psychologist*, 1973, *28*, 107–128.

Kipper, D. A., & Ginot, E. Accuracy of evaluating videotape feedback and defense mechanisms. *Journal of Consulting and Clinical Psychology*, 1979, *47*, 493–499.

Korchin, S. J. *Modern clinical psychology*. New York. Basic Books, 1976.

Lattal, K. A., & Lattal, A. D. Student "gullibility": A systematic replication. *Journal of Psychology*, 1967, *67*, 319–322.

Layne, C. Relationship between the "Barnum effect" and personality inventory responses. *Journal of Clinical Psychology*, 1978, *34*, 94–97.

Layne, C. The Barnum effect: Rationality versus gullibility? *Journal of Consulting and Clinical Psychology*, 1979, *47*, 219–221.

Mahoney, M. J., Moore, B. S., Wade, T. C., & Moura, N. G. M. Effects of continuous and intermittent self-monitoring on academic behavior. *Journal of Consulting and Clinical Psychology*, 1973, *41*, 65–69.

McFall, R. M. Effects of self-monitoring on normal smoking behavior. *Journal of Consulting and Clinical Psychology*, 1970, *35*, 135–142.

Meehl, P. E. Wanted—A good cookbook. *American Psychologist*, 1956, *11*, 263–272.

Mendels, J. *Concepts of depression*. New York: Wiley, 1970.

Nelson, R. E., & Craighead, W. E. Selective recall of positive and negative feedback, self-control behaviors, and depression. *Journal of Abnormal Psychology*, 1977, *86*, 379–388.

Rotter, J. B. *Social learning and clinical psychology*. Englewood Cliffs, N.J.: Prentice-Hall, 1954.

Shapiro, A. K., & Morris, A. The placebo effect in medical and psychological therapies. In S. L. Garfield & P. E. Bergin (Eds.), *Handbook of psychotherapy and behavior change: An empirical analysis* (2nd ed.). New York: Wiley, 1978.

Smith, M. L., & Glass, G. V. Meta-analysis of psychotherapy outcome studies. *American Psychologist*, 1977, *32*, 752–760.

Snyder, C. R. Acceptance of personality interpretations as a function of assessment procedures. *Journal of Consulting and Clinical Psychology*, 1974, *42*, 150.

Snyder, C. R., & Clair, M. Does insecurity breed acceptance?: Effects of trait and situational insecurity on acceptance of positive and negative diagnostic feedback. *Journal of Consulting and Clinical Psychology*, 1977, *45*, 843–850.

Snyder, C. R., Larsen, D., & Bloom, L. J. Acceptance of personality interpretations prior to and after receiving diagnostic feedback supposedly based on psychological, graphological, and astrological assessment procedures. *Journal of Clinical Psychology*, 1976, *32*, 258–265.

Snyder, C. R., & Larson, G. R. A further look at student acceptance of general personality interpretations. *Journal of Consulting and Clinical Psychology*, 1972, *38*, 384–388.

Snyder, C. R., & Newburg, C. The Barnum effect in a group setting. *Journal of Personality Assessment*, 1981, *45*, 622–629.

Snyder, C. R., & Shenkel, R. J. Effects of "favorability," modality, and relevance upon acceptance of general personality interpretations prior to and after receiving diagnostic feedback. *Journal of Consulting and Clinical Psychology*, 1976, *44*, 34–41.

Snyder, C. R., Shenkel, R. J., & Lowery, C. R. Acceptance of personality interpretations: The "Barnum effect" and beyond. *Journal of Consulting and Clinical Psychology*, 1977, *45*, 104–114.

Stagner, R. The gullibility of personnel managers. *Personnel Psychology*, 1958, *11*, 347–352.

Suls, J. M., & Miller, R. L. (Eds). *Social comparison processes: Theoretical and empirical perspectives*. Washington, D. C.: Hemisphere, 1977.

Sundberg, N. D. *Assessment of persons*. Englewood Cliffs, N.J.: Prentice-Hall, 1977.

Thibaut, J. W., & Kelley, H. H. *The social psychology of groups*. New York: Wiley, 1959.

Thoresen, C. E., & Mahoney, M. J. *Behavioral self-control*. New York: Holt, 1974.

Wilson, M. In H. L. Mencken (Ed.), *A dictionary of quotations on historical principles from ancient and modern sources*. New York: Knopf, 1942.

Wolpe, J., & Lazarus, A. A. *Behavior therapy techniques: A guide to the treatment of neuroses*. New York: Pergamon, 1966.

Yenawine, G., & Arbuckle, D. S. Study of the use of videotape and audiotape as techniques in counselor education. *Journal of Counseling Psychology*, 1971, *18*, 1–6.

chapter 14

Communication, Interpersonal Influence, and Resistance to Medical Treatment[1]

D. DANTE DiNICOLA
M. ROBIN DiMATTEO

Introduction

In their role as healers, physicians often recommend complex treatment regimens to their patients, calling into play many of the advances that have brought medicine to the scientific forefront during the past 40 years. Patients with heart disease, once likely to die prematurely, are now offered treatments that can prolong their lives and even restore their health and vigor. Persons with high blood pressure, once at the mercy of impending stroke and heart attack, can now through treatment avoid disability. Diabetics can live essentially normal and productive lives with new forms of medical care. Typically, patients are concerned enough about their well-being to seek medical help. However, after their physicians have puzzled through elaborate diagnoses and have offered treatment recommendations, many patients ignore the advice they have been given. Indeed, recent research indicates that few physicians who merely give advice are able to effect healing.

[1]Preparation of this chapter was supported in part by Intramural Research Funds and Intercampus Opportunity Funds from the University of California, Riverside.

Basic Processes in Helping Relationships

PREVALENCE OF NONCOMPLIANCE

Noncompliance with medical care involves a wide range of behaviors. Individual patients may (purposely or not) ignore, forget, or misunderstand a medical recommendation, such as to take medication, follow a restrictive diet, engage in an exercise program, or continue to show up for clinic appointments. Empirical studies have shown that noncompliance by patients is found with substantial frequency in private medical practice as well as in public clinics, among those who are advantaged as well as disadvantaged socioeconomically, and among those who are acutely ill as well as among the chronically afflicted (Haynes, 1979; Sackett & Snow, 1979). Studies have also shown that compliance is related to the complexity of the treatment regimen. Complex recommendations (such as changes in life-style) are less frequently followed than simple assignments such as taking medication. Short-term regimens, such as a 10-day treatment course of an antibiotic, are more likely to be followed than long-term regimens such as medication for hypertension. The latter treatment may last the entire lifetime of the patient (Haynes, 1979). Patients adhere to short-term medication regimens at average rates of 70% to 80% when the regimen is curative (e.g., for a throat or urinary tract infection), and 60% to 70% when the regimen is preventive (Sackett & Snow, 1979). With lifetime medication regimens and with long-term behavioral scheduling (such as eating a restricted diet to prevent or control symptoms in diabetes or hypertension), compliance is initially low (about 50%) and diminishes as the therapy continues (Sackett & Snow, 1979; Haynes, 1979).

Another area in which compliance is important involves preventive health measures. Despite knowledge of health risks, and despite medical advice, people continue to smoke, overeat, drink too much, avoid exercise, and avoid wearing safety belts in their automobiles (see, e.g., Farquhar, 1978; Henderson, Hall, & Lipton, 1979). Moreover, people typically engage in combinations of these unhealthy behaviors (Langlie, 1977). This "preventive" category of noncompliance is the most problematic because the required regimens extend into every aspect of the patient's life and the threat of disease is far removed from the present time (Surgeon General, 1979).

Noncompliance is increasingly regarded as an important issue, not only because it may be dangerous for the patient but also because it is costly to the health care system. The failure of patients to keep their appointments is expensive because clinicians' time is wasted. When patients drop out of treatment, histories, physical exams, and tests must be repeated when they seek other physicians or other health care settings (DiMatteo, Prince, & Taranta, 1979; Kasteler, Kane, Olsen, & Thetford, 1976). Research on appointment keeping in medical settings (reviewed by Sackett & Snow, 1979) has shown that only 40% to 50% of patients comply with appointments for preventive regimens while 60% to 70% comply with appointments for curative regimens. These rates are comparable to dropout rates in general psychiatry clinics, where 20% to 57% of patients fail to return after the first visit and 31% to 56% attend no more than four times (Baekeland & Lundwall, 1975).

AN ANALYSIS OF RESISTANCE

If medical care involved merely arriving at decisions and giving advice, medicine would be a purely technical enterprise. Diagnoses would be made by weighing the appropriate evidence, and treatment regimens would be planned with optimal biomedical considerations. Ideally, the advice would be taken by the patient and put into practice so that the illness would be cured or the preventive regimen engaged. This ideal state rarely exists, however. A purely technical approach to patient care ignores the fact that patients are human beings who, for many and varied reasons, may resist efforts to care for them (DiMatteo & Friedman, 1982; Friedman & DiMatteo, 1979).

A major problem in medicine, as in all forms of therapy (Meichenbaum, 1977), is the problem of resistance. In medicine or in psychotherapy, this resistance can take one of two major forms. In the first form, the patient might *resist the influence of the provider* of care because of the provider's characteristics as a person, because of the quality of the therapeutic relationship, or because of the patient's rejection of the provider's position of authority. Such resistance is likely to be manifested in patients' rejection of treatment. They may fail to show up for appointments or may drop out of treatment and seek another therapist, health professional, or alternative healer (Baekeland & Lundwall, 1975; Hayes-Bautista, 1976). The second type of resistance involves acceptance of the provider of treatment but *rejection of the specific advice*. It is often manifested in patients' continued return for treatment after having failed to follow the prescribed regimen or to stop an unhealthy practice proscribed by the medical practitioner. In the second case, patients are assumed to be motivated to change, but are seemingly unable to control their behavior. Thus, in the first case the patient's commitment to treatment is in doubt; in the second case this is not so. In this chapter, we examine the factors that contribute to both forms of patient resistance to therapists' recommendations. In addition, because there are essential similarities in resistance to medical treatment and to psychotherapy, we shall draw on evidence from both settings.

CAUSES OF NONCOMPLIANCE

Researchers and practitioners who have examined noncompliance have hypothesized a plethora of competing theories to explain the phenomenon of patient resistance to therapeutic advice. These explanations tend to fall into three broad categories.

Intrapsychic Factors

Many theories of compliance propose that thoughts, feelings, and/or attitudes dispose patients favorably or unfavorably toward specific treatments or therapists. Motivational theories lean heavily on psychodynamic explanations and suggest that patient resistance can be understood in terms of rejection of authority, disease denial, or rationalization of unhealthy behavior (Appelbaum, 1977; Stimson, 1974). Beliefs and attitudes regarding both one's susceptibility to disease and the severity of disease influence compliance. So too do patients' beliefs about the costs versus the benefits of treatment (Becker, 1974). Misinformation and inaccurate beliefs (such as from culturally accepted, nonmedical sources) are also implicated in the search for causes of noncompliance (Stone, 1979). It has also been hypothesized that patients resist medical advice in order to achieve control in a situation in which they have lost control. They may engage in an active search to restore their lost freedom (called psychological reactance; Brehm, 1966) or try to avoid developing a dependency to which they know from past experience they are prone (Blane, 1968). From a cognitive dissonance perspective (Festinger, 1957), it has been suggested that patients seek to maintain their commitment to a bad decision (e.g., a course of behavior such as smoking) by resisting persuasion to change it. By resisting therapeutic recommendations, patients attempt to balance the power and control in the therapist–client (or physician–patient) relationship. In this view, resistance is seen as part of the therapist–patient power struggle that is inevitable in therapy. As Haley (1963) noted, "The interchange between therapist and patient will inevitably center upon who is to set [the] rules. . . . It is of crucial importance that the therapist deal successfully with the question whether he or the patient is to control what kind of relationship they will have. No form of therapy can avoid this problem, it is central, and in its resolution is the source of therapeutic change [p. 19]."

Environmental Factors

A second category of explanations for resistance involves the patient's environment and its effects on his or her behaviors and habits. Research evidence suggests that barriers to compliance include demands (of time, money, interest, and attention) made on the patient's resources. Related to this are sociocultural models of patient compliance that point to cultural and social supports as necessary to the enhancement of compliance (Stone, 1979). Finally, behavioral approaches stress environmental supports and reinforcements as necessary for continued healthy behavior.

Physician–Patient Relationship

A third type of theory emphasizes therapist (or physician) behavior as a determinant of resistance. Waitzkin and Stoeckle (1972) explain patient resistance in terms of reciprocation. If the physician controls information and refuses to share it with the patient, the patient responds with resistance. Other approaches also focus on faulty communication between physician and patient, but deemphasize the intentionality of the physician's witholding of information (Svarstad, 1976). Further, lack of participation by patients in decisions made about their own course of treatment has been suggested as a cause of resistance (Stone, 1979). Finally, the absense of caring, warmth, and understanding on the part of the therapist has been implicated as a cause of patient resistance to therapy (e.g., Frank, 1961). In a similar vein, the technique-centered character of today's medical care (in contrast to earlier years) has been blamed for resistance because of the alienation now experienced by patients when they receive medical care (Rodin & Janis, 1979).

These three categories are similar to the three "vectors" conceptualized by Baekeland and Lundwall (1975) to explain patient dropout from psychiatric treatment and from rehabilitation for drug and alcohol abuse. These vectors illustrate the diversity of theories that attempt to explain patient resistance to fulfilling prescribed treatments. This diversity in the available explanations for resistance may seem confusing at first. We believe, however, that the preponderance of explanations tends to balance off a tendency of medical professionals to conceptualize noncompliance as a unitary phenomenon, having a specific cause, diagnosis, and treatment (Gillum & Barsky, 1974). As we demonstrate in this chapter, patient resistance to medical regimens does not lend itself to solution by a single technique (for example, simply improving the communication of information or the delivery of social support). Although noncompliance can be understood in terms of a limited number of dimensions (approximately six; Cummings, Becker, & Maile, 1980), the development and maintenance of behavior change is nevertheless complex. Patient compliance is embedded in a web of social and psychological factors.

Understanding compliance behavior in a social-psychological framework reminds us, of course, that a patient's less than wholehearted acceptance of medical advice is not all all surprising. This is because the giving of medical advice and the prescription of a medical regimen involve an influence attempt which is not certain to work.[2] It is possible, however, to delineate the conditions under which the suggestions of one person will be manifested as behavioral change by another person. This is our goal in this chapter.

UNDERSTANDING PATIENT RESISTANCE—A COMPREHENSIVE MODEL

In this chapter, we are concerned with adherence to medical recommendations made in face-to-face interactions between health professionals

---

[2] Although the giving of medical advice may not be viewed by the therapist as an explicit attempt to influence, it may well be so viewed by the patient.

(physicians, nurses, nurse practitioners) and their patients.[3] Our conceptual approach to compliance with medical regimens reflects our attempt to represent accurately the empirical findings of the research on patient compliance. We describe various factors to which physicians and other health professionals must attend in their care of patients. The concepts are examined in a manner that may help to guide clinicians' assessments of patient resistance and to suggest interventions to improve cooperation.

In the following pages, a summary of research on patient resistance to medical regimens is presented. Our implicit focus is on a social-psychological approach to compliance behavior, in which the patient's beliefs and attitudes are understood within the context of the social and physical environment and the interpersonal relationship with the health professional.

Variables in Resistance to Medical Regimens

THE THERAPEUTIC RELATIONSHIP: COMMUNICATION

It may seem trite to point out that patients will have difficulty complying with medical regimens they do not understand. Life-style alterations and habit changes can take place only if the patients have a precise understanding of the new behaviors they are required to enact. Without this understanding, they are likely to become frustrated and lose their motivation to comply. This issue is not trivial. Poor communication was cited by Baekeland and Lundwall (1975) as a major cause of patients' dropping out of psychiatric treatment. Correspondingly, studies of medical patients have shown that as many as 60% of patients interviewed immediately after their visit with the doctor had misunderstood the therapeutic regimen that had just been explained to them (Boyd, Covington, Stanaszek, & Coussons, 1974; Svarstad, 1976). This misunderstanding stems partly from the limited conceptual explanations that most physicians give their patients (Ley & Spelman, 1967). These limited explanations arise from physicians' beliefs that their patients have little medical knowledge and understanding. Studies of physician–patient com-

---

[3] In such a situation, interpersonal influence and issues of communication exchange are most relevant. We recognize, of course, that people may receive many health recommendations from written materials, broadcasts, and various community health education programs. Such messages are oftentimes very successful (see Kelley, 1979, for an overview), for they provide individuals with cues to action and a social norm to which they can compare themselves and aspire. This may not be enough, however, for each individual patient's intrapsychic life (beliefs, defenses) and environmental constraints (the social and physical environment) must also be considered. Careful monitoring of the individual health-professional–patient relationship is needed. These factors are all relevant in understanding and overcoming patient resistance; thus, an individualized approach is needed.

munication have shown that whereas patients' medical knowledge and ability to understand conceptual explanations is higher than their physicians believe to be the case, patients' knowledge of medical *jargon* and medical terms is rather limited (Samora, Saunders, & Larson, 1961). Patients often confuse medical terminology or have no idea what it means. It is in this very terminology, however, that medical recommendations are typically explained to them (Barnlund, 1976; Korsch, Gozzi, & Francis, 1968). Of course, it has been suggested (Stone, 1979; Waitzkin & Stoeckle, 1972) that there are disadvantages to providing patients with too much information about their medical care. Patients might misunderstand or become confused and fearful, and medical professionals may feel that they need to maintain a position of power and superiority by maintaining control of medical information.

Difficulties and limitations in physician–patient communication do not involve only the use of jargon. A major problem in medical care is the commonly voiced complaint by patients that their physicians do not listen to them (Eisenberg, 1977), an assertion that has some empirical support (Davis, 1971; Freeman, Negrete, Davis, & Korsch, 1971; Stiles, Putnam, Wolf, & James, 1979). Asking a patient closed-ended, specific questions, awaiting an exact response, and discouraging elaboration tends to be unsatisfactory from the point of view of the patient. Instead, patient satisfaction results when physicians listen to their patients, allowing them to tell their story in their own words (at least in the initial phases of the visit) (Stiles *et al.*, 1979). In addition to promoting patient satisfaction (which in itself is likely to enhance patient cooperation—Korsch *et al.*, 1968), listening to the patient is likely to contribute to an accurate diagnosis and treatment (Osler, 1899). In many cases, an accurate medical history may be the best predictor of the patient's present medical problem. Furthermore, by listening fully to what the patient has to say, and only then consolidating the information into a diagnosis, the physician can help to prevent the common problem of formulating a theory about the patient's problem too quickly and then fitting all of the subsequently collected data into that theory (Elstein, 1976). Formulating a theory only after collecting all the empirical evidence could help to prevent a premature diagnosis. Of course, listening to the patient's story, told in his or her own words, also shows that the physician respects the patient as a person and is willing to share control of the interview, a factor that in itself is likely to promote continued compliance (Stone, 1979).

Research evidence suggests that in short-term medication regimens such as taking an antibiotic for 10 days, the communication of information (i.e., that the regimen must be carried out for the entire prescribed time, even after the symptoms have disappeared), combined with obtaining feedback about what the patient understands, is the most important factor in bringing about patient cooperation (Haynes, 1980). If the regimen involves simply remembering to take about 40 pills and does not require difficult life-style changes, few of the other factors examined in this chapter (environmental, social, attitudinal, etc.)

need even be considered. Of course, as we have seen in this section, even the simplest communications between doctors and patients are plagued with problems.

THE THERAPEUTIC RELATIONSHIP: INTERPERSONAL RAPPORT

Psychiatrist Jerome Frank (1961) has suggested that the interpersonal relationship between helper and client is the primary ingredient of therapeutic change, regardless of the type of therapy employed. The literature examining patient compliance in the light of the therapeutic relationship supports Frank's assertion. Numerous studies have shown that the quality of the health-professional–patient relationship is a key factor in patient compliance (Aday & Andersen, 1974; Davis, 1968; Engel, 1977; Hulka, 1979; Vuori, Aaku, Aine, Erkko, & Johansson, 1972).

Rapport between patient and therapist tends, not surprisingly, to influence the patient's commitment to the therapeutic relationship. DiMatteo *et al.* (1979) found that the feelings among patients that their physicians cared about them influenced their intent to return for treatment. Alpert (1964) similarly found that appointment keeping in a pediatric clinic was influenced by the mother's feelings that there was a doctor at the clinic with whom she could talk and who cared about the welfare of her and her child. Baekeland and Lundwall (1975) found that patients were less likely to return to psychotherapy if they and their therapists held different expectations about treatment, and if their therapists were detached, relatively inactive, and impersonal. The therapist or physician who avoids the development and maintenance of rapport with patients and who communicates boredom or disinterest toward patients is likely to experience a high level of patient dropout.

The connection between physician–patient rapport and patients' compliance with specific behavioral recommendations may be less obvious than the connections between rapport and staying in treatment, but it can certainly be explained. Some studies have found patients' compliance to be partly a function of their belief in the therapist's ability (Becker, Drachman, & Kirscht, 1972), as well as of their perceptions of the therapist's friendliness (Francis, Korsch, & Morris, 1969; Korsch & Negrete, 1972). Patients' perceptions of the therapist's interest in them also affect compliance positively (Becker *et al.*, 1972; Kincey, Bradshaw, & Ley, 1975). Noncompliance tends to be promoted when continued tension is built up and not released during the medical visit (Davis, 1971). Rapport may be a critical factor in patient compliance because of the tendency for positive interpersonal factors in the health-professional–patient relationship to minimize the need for patients to balance off an unpleasant power differential with the physician or therapist. If the therapist is trusted, the reactance that patients might normally feel in response to a restriction of their freedom is minimized (cf. Ben-Sira, 1980).

Research on physician-patient rapport suggests that the communication of warmth and caring to patients can be enhanced by the physician's recognition and control of nonverbal expressions (Friedman, 1979). This nonverbal control can strongly affect patients' satisfaction with medical care (DiMatteo, 1979a, 1979b; DiMatteo, Taranta, Friedman, & Prince, 1980), and their return to the clinic for their appointments (DiMatteo & Prince, Note 1). Research in counseling has been able to identify important therapist behaviors such as eye contact, open-arm position, smiling, forward lean, and head nodding (LaCrosse, 1975; Tepper & Haase, 1978; Seay & Altekruse, 1979). Physician sensitivity to nonverbal communication by others (implying empathy or an ability to understand emotional communications from patients) may be critically important to compliance as well. Sensitivity is required in order to recognize patients' emotional distress and discomfort when the treatment regimen is first prescribed or discussed. It helps the physician to recognize issues which concern the patient and to modify the treatment if necessary to accommodate the patient's capabilities. Later in the course of therapy, this sensitivity may help to uncover patients' difficulties in compliance expressed in cues of discomfort or confusion. Research by DiMatteo *et al.* (1980) has demonstrated that physician sensitivity to nonverbal communication is extremely important in bringing about patient satisfaction with the affective components of medical care.

PATIENTS' BELIEFS AND ATTITUDES

Many physicians are convinced that there exists a "resistant" or "non-compliant" personality among patients. In clinical practice, a certain type of patient—characterized by belligerence and/or passive–aggressive maneuvering—is typically perceived as a noncomplier. In fact, the majority of physicians surveyed by Davis (1966) pointed to the patient's personality as the major cause of patient noncompliance. Research evidence suggests that these assessments are incorrect, however. No personality variables have emerged as consistent predictors of patient noncompliance. Yet, it is easy to see how health care professionals may draw such inferences, since consistencies and behavioral patterns tend to emerge frequently among patients. Patients who have trouble controlling their weight may also be negligent in taking hypertensive medication or in following a low-salt diet. This consistency may stem not from personality, but from relatively stable (although certainly changeable) cognitive factors of attitudes and beliefs. The operation of such stable cognitive factors has been formalized in the Health Belief Model (Becker, 1974; Rosenstock, 1975).

The Health Belief Model has contributed much to our understanding of the role of cognitive factors in patient compliance with preventive and re-habilitative measures. The model identifies at least four factors that are posited to be central to health behavior. These are the person's belief in his or her own *susceptibility* to negative health consequences as a result of not cooperating with treatment, the person's belief in the *severity* of the health problems to result, the person's belief in the *cost* of the following the treatment regimen (in terms of time and effort as well as money), and the person's belief in the *efficacy* of the treatment. The Health Belief Model explains the contributions to compliance of factors that look deceptively like personality. This model helps to focus attention on individual cognitive factors that are amenable to change.

Health beliefs are subject to influence through effective persuasion. Fear arousal, one method that physicians use (sometimes indiscriminately) to persuade, requires a very specific set of conditions in order to be effective. Well-defined recommendations must be given, and the person must have a sense of self-efficacy. Persuasion and attitude change require that the persuader possess certain characteristics such as likability and trustworthiness. A positive therapeutic relationship is essential, and only with it can the health professional function as a social normative force in the patient's life. These factors are all necessary to change patients' attitudes and beliefs—factors which have been demonstrated time and again (in the research on the Health Belief Model as well as in research on other models; see Ajzen & Fishbein, 1980; Triandis, 1977; and Wallston & Wallston, 1981) to be applicable to patient compliance.

SOCIAL NORMS AND RESISTANCE

Beliefs appear to be important factors in compliance, but they do not operate alone. Social normative factors also help to overcome resistance. They may serve to encourage patients in their intentions to carry out therapeutic recommendations.

Social and cultural factors in the patient's background appear to be important in understanding compliance. Behavior change is likely to take place only within the social, cultural, and environmental context of the patient's life because this context controls the character of health-related information that the patient receives and is willing to accept. Interestingly, patient resistance to medical advice does not typically reflect a general lack of concern among people about health matters. Rather, it often reflects an anxiety about health. This anxiety leads individuals to seek advice from many varied sources in their environment. These sources may include (*a*) mass media (e.g., advertisements on radio and television promising instant cures for all kinds of ills); (*b*) the lay referral network, which includes individuals in the family or community who help the patient to decide whether to seek medical care at all and what aspects of medical advice to accept and follow (Zola, 1973); (c) the family, which more than any other institution influences the individual's health beliefs, values, and habits (Pratt, 1976); and (d) cultural norms for behavior, such as dietary habits, which affect the acceptability of the prescribed treatment (Nall & Speilberg, 1967; Snow, 1974). Resistance is likely to result when input to the patient from trusted, familiar sources (such as family and culture) conflicts with medical recommendations. The patient is likely to follow advice from the former source. When medical treatment is designed to fit the cultural and social norms of the patient and to call into play the support of the family and cultural group, resistance is minimized (McKinlay, 1973). The sheer strength of social and cultural influence suggests that health professionals should strive to remain acutely aware of patients' norms for behavior and should design therapeutic regimens consistent with these factors (see Quesada, 1976; Twaddle, 1969).

THE HEALTH PROFESSIONAL: ATTITUDES AND RESISTANCE

Health professionals' reactions (on cognitive, affective, and behavioral dimensions) are also likely to figure significantly in patients' responses to the demands of health care. The process of caring for highly distressed patients in a medical setting demands the careful management of emotions by the professional (Goffman, 1959). The physician must exert control in order to suppress his or her expressions of embarrassment (Emerson, 1970) and of sympathy and distress (Glaser & Strauss, 1965). Physicians are typically trained to repress or resist their feelings toward patients in the name of efficiency (Daniels, 1960; Lief & Fox, 1963). In fact, Cartwright (1979) and Rosenberg (1971) have noted that medical training demands compulsivity, intellectualization, and denial of emotions. Short-term coping is based on the denial of emotional responses. The literature on burnout (see Chapter 20, by Pines, in this volume) has noted that denial does not work as a long-term solution, however. At the very least, when physicians attempt to preserve their own psychological equilibrium they become highly resistant to their patients' psychological needs and concerns. As we have seen, however, consideration of issues along those psychosocial dimensions is critically important, since both the expression of concern and the affective component of patient care may strongly affect compliance.

Particularly when the benefit from engaging in certain health behaviors is in question (e.g., the benefits of exercise or weight control) health care professionals' beliefs may be highly relevant. These beliefs are likely to influence the specific recommendations that are given to patients (Cockerham, Creditor, & Creditor, 1980; Shangold, 1979). Health professionals' own success at self-control will likely influence the enthusiasm with which they make behavioral recommendations to their patients. This enthusiasm may manifest itself behaviorally in the consistency with which health professionals apply reinforcement and attend to the components of the operant process with their patients. Indeed, this consistency is one of the most important factors in the success of any behavioral program (Mahoney & Thoreson, 1974). Finally, the health professional's own behavior is likely to be particularly important in serving as a model of self-control to patients and is likely to be emulated by them.

The health professional's success in influencing patients' behavior demands a belief in the inherent changeability of people, regardless of their demographic characteristics. Unfortunately, as Pratt (1970) has found, physicians often respond negatively to patients of low social class. Roth (1972) also observed that medical emergency room staff members felt that the bulk of their lower-class patients were undeserving of care. Wills (1978) noted that professional helpers generally perceive clients less favorably than they perceive themselves, and regard clients less favorably than do lay persons. In addition, how the patient reacts in relation to the health professional is critically important. Health professionals in general tend to express dislike for patients who are assertive and dominant ("bad patients"), and for those who present any resistance to their efforts, however minimal. Persons regarded as "good patients," on the other hand, are those who appear submissive and unassuming and never ask questions or exhibit resistance. These labels are significant for they influence the treatment of the patient by the health professional (Lorber, 1975; Taylor, 1979). These attitudes and behaviors also have a significant effect on patients' tendencies to drop out from treatment.

Wills (1978) has noted a personalistic tendency on the part of helpers to attribute the behavior of clients to their personality characteristics and to minimize the contribution of the situation or environment. The actor–observer effect (Jones & Nisbett, 1971) suggests that this phenomenon is not unique to health professionals. Misunderstandings can easily occur when patients attribute their behavior (e.g., difficulties in following a treatment regimen) to environmental problems and situational factors at the same time that their health professionals see patients' personalities as responsible for their noncompliance (Davis, 1966). An approach to compliance such as that presented in this chapter seeks to focus attention on the situational factors that affect patient compliance, and thus helps to avoid blaming patients for their difficulties in following the treatment regimen.

A final aspect of the health professional's attitudes that influences patient compliance involves the need of the health professional for control in the relationship. Stone (1979) has posited the importance of shared control in the health transactions model, but according to Waitzkin and Stoeckle (1972), shared power is normally unacceptable to health professionals, who prefer to remain in complete control over their patients. As we noted earlier, Haley (1963) warned against such an orientation by arguing that insistence upon a superior position vis-à-vis a patient is likely to provoke a sense of contest and to place the therapist at a disadvantage.

The Assessment of Resistance

Theoretical and empirical literature suggests almost unequivocally that patient resistance is difficult to overcome. The bulk of evidence supports the multidimensonality of the resistance problem and suggests that solutions must take into consideration many facets of the patient's life—beliefs, attitudes, social roles and norms, and, as we will consider below, behavioral supports, skills, and cognitive control. Physicians' awareness of many aspects of the problem of noncompliance is typically quite deficient, however. Although they report that their greatest dissatisfaction in practice comes from being unable to exert control over their patients (Ford, Liske, Ort, & Denton, 1967), physicians' assessments of the extent of the problem of noncompliance, as well as its cause, are usually inaccurate. Physicians overestimate the degree to which their patients adhere to recommendations (Charney, 1972) and are unable, for the most part, to judge which of their patients are not adhering to their therapeutic regimens (Kasl, 1975). Empirical evidence points, however, to the importance of physicians' awareness of noncompliance. Inui, Yourtee, and Williamson (1976) found that a tutorial session informing physicians of the problem of noncompliance among hypertensives and of strategies for dealing with it helped significantly to improve the compliance behavior of their patients. Svarstad (1974) found too that physicians' careful monitoring of patient compliance was very effective in improving it. Thus, the accurate assessment of patient compliance is a critical first step to its improvement.

The precise level of a patient's cooperation with a treatment regimen is sometimes difficult to measure. Subjective estimates such as judgments by the health professional and self-reports of the patient tend to indicate higher levels of compliance than do objective measures such as pill counts and direct (urine or blood) assay of the medication in the patient's body. The assessment of compliance where other sorts of regimens are concerned (e.g., diet and exercise) is more problematic, for it requires subjective reports of complex behaviors. Most researchers and clinicians who are aware of the assessment problem shun self-reports from their patients as misleading, and assume that patients cannot be trusted to tell them the truth. Gordis, Markowitz, and Lilienfeld (1969) have pointed to the need for indirect measures by demonstrating the preponderance of inaccurate answers obtained when patients are asked about their compliance. Sackett (Note 2) has argued, however, that efforts to devise indirect measures of compliance are a waste of time and resources because the problem of assessment lies not in the measures themselves but in the philosophy behind them. Sackett argues that asking the patient can be the most accurate as well as the most economical method for determining compliance, and it will yield accurate results if health-professional–patient rapport exists. Interview measures of compliance can be quite accurate if patients feel that it is acceptable for them to admit compliance difficulties. Any therapeutic relationship in which the patient is cast in the role of the naughty child and the health professional in the role of the parent is likely to enhance patients' resistance to telling the truth and admitting difficulties. On the other hand, an open, honest partnership between physician and patient (e.g., the health transactions model of Stone, 1979) is likely to eliminate the punitiveness associated with noncompliance and help both patient and health professional deal with the difficulties involved in attempting any life-style change.

Reducing Resistance and Achieving Behavior Change

PERSUASION

Persuasion toward the goal of behavior change involves a number of steps. Haley (1963) defined three. First, the therapist or health professional must persuade the patient that a positive change might occur, that is, that it is indeed possible for the person to change. Second, the therapist must persuade the patient to let him or her exert influence or help to bring about the change. Third, the therapist must persuade the patient to carry out the steps necessary to make the change. Resistance to persuasion is likely to occur at any step, of course (Haley, 1963). Social-psychological research on attitude change and persuasion has identified factors that figure prominently in efforts to forestall or overcome resistance. These involve establishment of an interpersonal relationship, as well as the delivery of appropriate arguments that present both sides of the issue instead of only one (Zimbardo, Ebbesen, & Maslach, 1977). In psychotherapy, Haley (1963) has focused on the problem of resistance, suggesting that a major key to overcoming it involves placing the responsibility for change back into the hands of the patient. For example, one approach involves asking patients *when* they want to change. In addition, resistance can be overcome by accepting it and even encouraging it. This may involve telling patients that they are unlikely to be able to follow the full treatment regimen right away, deeming any deviations from it acceptable. Thus, the therapist gains control of the resistance by participating in it.

Resistance will almost surely occur if the patient or client feels coerced. According to Haley (1963), therapists who "make an issue" of being in a superior position by insisting that the patient accept their superiority are going to be at a disadvantage in the relationship. If the patient has a need to take control in the interaction and to occupy the superior position, the therapist should allow this to happen. Therapists should refuse to let the patient's resistance provoke them, and should not allow resistance to be the method by which the patient gains control in the relationship. Thus, a central question in the problem of resistance (and indeed in understanding human behavior in general) involves how much influence a person will permit another to have over him or her. Once that issue is determined, therapeutic change can be achieved within the limits of that permitted influence.

THE COMMITMENT TO COOPERATE

Many current theories propose that an essential component of behavior change is the statement of an *intention*. Commitment represents the point at which the concepts of resistance and noncompliance diverge in meaning, for with the statement of an intention, conscious resistance has been overcome. Ajzen and Fishbein (1980) explain in their "theory of reasoned action" that the statement of an intention is a natural outgrowth of social normative pressures and positive beliefs regarding the intended behavior. The behavioral intention provides the key link between cognitive and social factors, on the one hand, and actual behavior change on the other. Indeed, studies of overt commitment have typically demonstrated the importance of intentions in achieving patient compliance (Bandura, 1969; Farquhar, 1978).

Commitment typically involves one of the three forms: a verbal promise to the health professional (Levy, Yamashita, & Pow, 1979), a written promise (Levy, 1977; Wurtele, Galanos, & Roberts, 1980), or a contingency contract in which the health professional agrees to deliver some reinforcement (e.g., attention, time, money) in return for patient compliance within some mutually agreed upon time frame (see Becker & Maiman, 1980, for a review). The research shows that contingency contracts are particularly successful even with relatively complex, long-term compliance conditions. One problem associated with these contracts, however, is the extinction of compliance behavior once the contingent reinforcements are removed. (For a detailed discussion of other approaches to building commitment in therapeutic relationships see Lemkau, Bryant, & Brickman, Chapter 9 in this volume.)

MAINTENANCE OF BEHAVIOR CHANGE

The acquisition and self-maintenance of long-term health behaviors in the absence of contingent reinforcement from the environment remains difficult for many people (Becker & Maiman, 1980). Commitment to behavior change represents the overcoming of resistance as the patient states a determination to carry out the behavior prescribed. Yet, the patient's behavior may fall short of that which is expected and desired by the clinician. It is often very difficult to translate intentions into behavior. Rosenstock and Kirscht (1979) have noted that compliance with therapeutic regimens or with prescriptions for healthy living requires much more than commitment, because most health behaviors result from habit. Fulfillment and maintenance of treatment recommendations demand the skill of operant conditioning and self-regulation. Too often, theoretical and clinical approaches overlook this important issue. Thus, in many ways compliance is a behavior problem (Kasl, 1975; Zifferblatt, 1975). Behavioral change requires multifaceted treatment programs and self-regulation by the patient (Dunbar, Marshall, & Hovell, 1979; Karoly, 1975; Mahoney, 1974).

One major obstacle to achieving behavior change is the patient's fear of the unknown. For a patient who has never engaged in any physical exercise, the recommendation to "start taking walks every day" may be met with polite but noncommittal agreement. When the patient returns home, the lack of knowledge regarding when to walk, how fast to walk, how far, etc., may be so problematic that the patient is dissuaded from doing anything. In addition, the patient may feel embarrassed about the behavior (e.g., uncomfortable or distressed at letting other people see him or her walking, moving about, exercising). The difficulties might be compounded further if the patient experiences discomfort while enacting the behavior (such as shortness of breath when walking). As a result the patient may feel that compliance is simply not worth the trouble.

Closer coordination between health professionals' recommendations and their patients' attempts to engage in prescribed behavior is necessary if noncompliance is to be overcome. What does this closer coordination involve? Surely, clear explanations of the intended behaviors are necessary if patients are to know what they must do. It may also be necessary to show patients directly what to do, and to consider all the possible avenues for avoidance of the behavior. Potential barriers to compliance must be considered. In a study by Atkins (Note 3), for example, a health counselor worked individually with COPD patients (chronic obstructive pulmonary disease includes asthma, chronic bronchitis, and emphysema) in an effort to increase their compliance with an exercise prescription designed to improve their lung capacity. During a home visit, the health counselor reviewed a typical daily schedule with the patient in order to identify the most appropriate times during which to walk. The counselor also uncovered other potential barriers to compliance, such as not having a safe place to walk and not having appropriate shoes to wear. Patients received instruction in behavioral self-monitoring, evaluation, and reinforcement (considered in more detail below). No coercion was involved because patients had already stated their commitment to the exercise routine. Patients were taught basic self-regulatory skills, and their relationship with the health professional maintained their dignity in a process of mutual cooperation.

Self-regulatory factors are critically important to compliance with behavior change regimens (Kanfer, 1975). There are three stages in the process of self-regulation, and compliance as a "behavioral skill" demands the development of these three components. The first, *self-monitoring* or self-observation, involves deliberate and careful attention to one's own behavior. Patients might be encouraged to become aware of precisely how much they eat, when they smoke, as well as the antecedent and consequent events. The analysis of behavior patterns is the first critical step to behavior change. The second stage involves *self-evaluation*, the comparison of one's behavior with a criterion or ideal. Self-evaluation can result in the correction of the target behavior if *self-reinforcement* is administered. Thus, behavior change requires very specific assessments of behavior as well as clear performance criteria (e.g., how many calories a day to consume, how many miles a day to walk). In addition, specific information about reinforcement is required (e.g., that reinforcement should be delivered after, not before, the required behavior is done). Patient education regarding all aspects of self-regulation can thus be extremely important.

COGNITIVE FACTORS AND BEHAVIOR CHANGE

Behavioral intervention alone is not sufficiently effective in maintaining long-term behavior change. Cognitive factors influence the achievement and continuation of health behaviors in a number of ways. For example, the degree to which patients or clients attribute their therapeutic change to themselves versus an external agent, such as the health professional, influences the likelihood that the behavior will be maintained over a long period of time (see Wilson, 1980). Feelings of self-efficacy play an important role in health behavior: What patients say to themselves may be a significant determinant of their ability to change their behavior. Negative self-statements, for example, can easily ruin an excellent program of behavioral self-regulation. Patients need help and encouragement to become aware of their own thoughts and self-statements. They need to learn how to collect data to refute their negative self-statements and to produce self-instructions compatible with success instead of failure. Although operant methods and behavior shaping have been used successfully in bringing about compliance with medical regimens (Zifferblatt, 1975), cognitive components may be particularly important when the frequency of contact between health professional and patient cannot be high.

SOCIAL SUPPORT AND THE FAMILY

"The patient's family still remains a largely unexploited means for reminding, assisting, encouraging, and reinforcing the patient with respect to following medical advice [Becker & Maiman, 1980, p. 129]." Theory and research on the role of family support in health and illness behavior suggest that the family may be very important in influencing both behavioral and cognitive factors in compliance. For example, studies of compliance have found that individuals with unstable family situations, and those who live alone or are socially isolated, have considerably more trouble complying with their prescribed medical regimens than do those who live with supportive, stable families (Baekeland & Lundwall, 1975; Haynes, Taylor & Sackett, 1979). Even in serious illness, family support may help the patient manage the condition, although in serious illness as in the maintenance of health behavior, it is not yet clear precisely how social support operates or under what conditions family involvement might even be detrimental to the patient. Family members may be very helpful in reducing patient anxiety (Kosa & Robertson, 1975) and may provide both psychological and physical support (Caplan, 1979). Of course, close individuals may also interfere with the behavior change regimen either by providing psychological barriers (e.g., disparagements) or physical barriers (using resources needed to bring about or maintain the behavior change).

BEHAVIOR AND ATTITUDE CHANGE: A FEEDBACK LOOP

The influence of behavior change on attitude change is the final component in the process of achieving patient compliance. Self-perception theory (Bem, 1967) and the theory of cognitive dissonance (Festinger, 1957) both predict that once engaged in the new healthy behavior, a patient is likely to come to value it more than ever before, and as a result continue to engage in it. Healthy beliefs develop from healthy behavior.

The relationship between behavior change and subsequent attitude change suggests that the overcoming of resistance involves an iterative process in which a change in behavior is made and then attitudes and beliefs are realigned. As a result of these attitude shifts, further behavioral changes are facilitated. In a similar vein, the health professional's approach may involve a "foot-in-the-door" technique (Freedman & Fraser, 1966) in which certain simple behavior changes are encouraged. These changes set the pattern for cooperation with the health professional (and perhaps a positive feeling toward him or her, brought about partly in response to the act of cooperating). The patient also recognizes that it is indeed possible for him or her to make behavioral changes. This principle is the basis for the therapeutic technique for overcoming resistance that involves bringing about some (perhaps minor) behavioral change within the therapy session (Haley, 1973). Such a change helps to establish both the power of the therapist and patients' control over their own behavior.

CONCLUSIONS

Patient compliance with prescribed regimens is a complex process that is influenced by many things, including intrapsychic, behavioral, environmental, and social factors in patients' lives. Compliance is also strongly affected by the character of the health-professional–patient relationship. Consideration of these factors is essential if health professionals are to avoid attributing patients' difficulties in following treatment regimens to patients' personality deficiencies. Instead, an emphasis on the complete range of factors involved in bringing about patient cooperation is likely to help focus attention on important situational and environmental factors in patients' lives.

An emphasis on psychosocial factors and behavioral skills is needed in the quest for patient compliance. This emphasis expands the realm of expertise demanded of health professionals, of course, and points to many deficiencies in traditional medical training and practice. In the midst of highly dramatic activities of medical care, health professionals often lose sight of the most basic principle of patient care—that the whole patient must be treated. Any worthwhile approach to patient care must emphasize the interaction of the mind and the body.

Much is still missing from our understanding of resistance to medical advice. Although many factors related to patient compliance or noncompliance have been identified, more knowledge about the process of building cooperation and preventing resistance is needed. In this chapter we have suggested some ways in which social-psychological knowledge might be applied to minimize resistance to medical treatment.

The problem of resistance is manifested in medicine as well as in psychotherapy with definable similarities in the two settings. Although the substantive issues in these two patient care fields may be somewhat different, the basic processes are similar in many ways. In both medicine and psychotherapy, successful treatment requires the commitment of the patient to the therapeutic relationship and acceptance of the therapist's influence. It is only after this initial commitment is made that specific behavioral goals can be defined and achieved. Of course, compliance in psychotherapy and compliance in medicine do differ in some important ways. In psychotherapy, problems are typically presented as psychosocial in character. In medicine, on the other hand, psychosocial issues often exist but are either secondary to the presenting medical problem or else are obscured by it. Medical patients, unlike psychotherapy patients, might be experiencing physical pain. Psychotherapy patients, on the other hand, are likely to expect to disclose psychosocial information while medical patients are not. Psychotherapy patients may thus be more comfortable with a therapeutic focus on their behavior. It should be noted, of course, that the physicians themselves, not their patients, may be the ones who resist a psychosocial emphasis in medicine. All in all, a more precise understanding of the differences and similarities between medical care and psychotherapy is necessary for a complete analysis of resistance. This endeavor represents a promising area for further research.

The empirical literature on patient resistance to medical influence and behavior change has identified various factors that "postdict" compliance. Differences have been found between individuals who follow medical advice and those who do not. These differences usually involve their attitudes toward various aspects of health care, their social norms and roles, and their intentions. Such factors are not established as predictors or "causes" of noncompliance because their direct link to the behavior in question has never been established experimentally. Therefore, intervention studies are needed (Becker, Note 4) if recommendations are to find appropriate clinical application. Partly because of their training and partly because of the nature of patient care, physicians and health professionals are likely to accept and initiate only interventions which have been documented to be effective in randomized clinical trials. Sackett (Note 2) has even suggested that because of their expense and trouble, programs to increase patient cooperation should not be instituted unless their efficacy has been clearly demonstrated in experimental research.

It is easy to understand the reluctance with which psychologists and other researchers approach experimentation on a topic as complex as patient resistance to medical regimens. Researchers have tended to measure as many factors as possible, hoping that some of them will be significantly correlated with compliance; experimental studies are done rarely. (A good example of a worthwhile study of this nature is that by Atkins, Note 3.)

Of course, a middle ground exists on which researchers and clinicians might meet. It is the approach emphasizing "reforms as experiments" (Campbell, 1969). Promising interventions established from theory and correlational research can be instituted as reforms but at the same time can be evaluated (for example, in an experimental group that receives the treatment intervention while the rest of the population acts as a control). If it is efficacious, some proportion of the clientele will have already received the treatment and benefited from it. If it is not, it is better to know this before instituting the change as a policy for the entire population. Of course, field experiments in any area of study require a great deal of effort. Developing and administering treatments while controlling extraneous variables in the clinic or hospital or in the patients' natural environment is a challenge to the researcher's skill. Just as in counseling and psychotherapy, research on interpersonal influence in the medical setting requires direct involvement in and careful examination of the therapeutic process.

Although there is much yet to learn about patient compliance, much is presently known. A number of our assertions are, however, based on weaker than ideal methodologies. As Rosenstock (1975) has concluded, although we cannot yet derive a single universal strategy for improving patient compliance from the research, the knowledge gained to date may help a clinician to develop a strategy that will be better than one selected at random. It is very important for a clinician to know, for example, that in order for patients to comply, they must be interested in their health, believe and understand the diagnosis, assess correctly its potential impact, and believe in the efficacy of the treatment. Patients must also find ways of using their prescribed medication that are not more trouble than the illness itself, and must know precisely how and how long to take the medication. Patients respond to prescribed treatment within their own life framework. Therefore, it is within that life framework that clinicians must be involved.

ACKNOWLEDGMENTS

The authors wish to thank Thomas Ashby Wills for his very helpful comments on an earlier draft of this chapter, and Deanna DiNicola for her assistance in reviewing the literature.

Reference Notes

1. DiMatteo, M. R., & Prince, L. M. Physician expressiveness and patient behavior. Manuscript in preparation, University of California, Riverside, 1982.
2. Sackett, D. L. Future applications and hypotheses from old research. Paper delivered at the conference on New Directions in Patient Compliance, French Lick, Indiana, August 8–10, 1978.
3. Atkins, C. J. *Improving exercise compliance among chronic lung patients: A comparison of cognitive and behavioral approaches.* Paper presented at the meeting of the Western Psychological Association, Los Angeles, April 1981.
4. Becker, M. H. Lecture to medical students, University of California, Los Angeles, School of Medicine, February 23, 1981.

References

Aday, L. A., & Andersen, R. A framework for the study of access to medical care. *Health Services Research*, 1974, *9*, 208–220.

Ajzen, I., & Fishbein, M. *Understanding attitudes and predicting social behavior.* Englewood Cliffs, N.J.: Prentice-Hall, 1980.

Appelbaum, S. A. The refusal to take one's medicine. *Bulletin of the Menninger Clinic*, 1977, *41*, 511–521.

Alpert, J. J. Broken appointments. *Pediatrics*, 1964, *34*, 127–132.

Baekeland, F., & Lundwall, L. Dropping out of treatment: A critical review. *Psychological Bulletin*, 1975, *82*, 738–783.

Bandura, A. *Principles of behavior modification.* New York: Holt, 1969.

Barnlund, D. C. The mystification of meaning: Doctor–patient encounters. *Journal of Medical Education*, 1976, *51*, 716–725.

Becker, M. H. (Ed.).*The health belief model and personal health behavior.* Thorofare, N.J.: Slack, 1974.

Becker, M. H., Drachman, R. H., & Kirscht, J. P. Predicting mothers' compliance with pediatric medical regimens. *Journal of Pediatrics,* 1972, *81,* 843–854.

Becker, M. H., & Maiman, L. A. Strategies for enhancing patient compliance. *Journal of Community Health,* 1980, *6,* 113–135.

Bem, D. J. Self-perception: An alternative interpretation of cognitive dissonance phenomena. *Psychological Review,* 1967, *74,* 183–200.

Ben-Sira, A. Z. Affective and instrumental components in the physician–patient relationship: An additional dimension of interaction theory. *Journal of Health and Social Behavior,* 1980, *21,* 170–180.

Blane, H. T. *The personality of the alcoholic: Guises of dependency.* New York: Harper & Row, 1968.

Boyd, J. R., Covington, T. R., Stanaszek, W. F., & Coussons, R. T. Drug-defaulting. II. Analysis of noncompliance patterns. *American Journal of Hospital Pharmacy,* 1974, *31,* 485–491.

Brehm, J. W. *A theory of psychological reactance.* New York: Academic Press, 1966.

Campbell, D. T. Reforms as experiments. *American Psychologist,* 1969, *24,* 409–429.

Caplan, R. D. Patient, provider, and organization: Hypothesized determinants of adherence. In S. J. Cohen (Ed.), *New directions in patient compliance.* Lexington, Mass.: Heath, 1979. Pp. 75–100.

Cartwright, L. Sources and effects of stress in health careers. In G. C. Stone, F. Cohen, & N. E. Adler (Eds.), *Health psychology.* San Francisco: Jossey Bass, 1979.

Charney, E. Patient-doctor communication: Implications for the clinican. *Pediatric Clinics of North America,* 1972, *19,* 263–279.

Cockerham, W. C., Creditor, M. C., Creditor, U. K., & Imrey, P. B. Minor ailments and illness behavior among physicians. *Medical Care,* 1980, *18,* 164–173.

Cummings, K. M., Becker, M. H., & Maile, M. C. Bringing the models together: An empirical approach to combining variables used to explain health actions. *Journal of Behavioral Medicine,* 1980, *3,* 123–145.

Daniels, M. J. Affect and its control in the medical intern. *American Journal of Sociology,* 1960, *66,* 259–267.

Davis, M. S. Variations in patients' compliance with doctors' orders: Analysis of congruence between survey responses and results of empirical investigations. *Journal of Medical Education,* 1966, *41,* 1037–1048.

Davis, M. S. Physiologic, psychological and demographic factors in patient compliance with doctors' orders. *Medical Care,* 1968, *6,* 115–122.

Davis, M. S. Variations in patients' compliance with doctors' orders: Medical practice and doctor–patient interaction. *Psychiatry in Medicine,* 1971, *2,* 31–54.

DiMatteo, M. R. A social-psychological analysis of physician–patient rapport: Toward a science of the art of medicine. *Journal of Social Issues,* 1979, *35*(1), 12–33. (a)

DiMatteo, M. R. Nonverbal skill and the physician–patient relationship. In R. Rosenthal (Ed.), *Skill in nonverbal communication.* Cambridge, Mass.: Oelgeschlager, Gunn & Hain, 1979. (b)

DiMatteo, M. R., & Friedman, H. S. *Social psychology and medicine.* Cambridge, Mass.: Oelgeschlager, Gunn, and Hain, 1982.

DiMatteo, M. R., Prince, L. M., & Taranta, A. Patients' perceptions of physicians' behavior: Determinants of patient commitment to the therapeutic relationship. *Journal of Community Health,* 1979, *4,* 280–290.

DiMatteo, M. R., Taranta, A., Friedman, H. S., & Prince, L. M. Predicting patient satisfaction from physicians' nonverbal communication skills. *Medical Care,* 1980, *18,* 376–387.

Dunbar, J. M., Marshall, G. D., & Hovell, M. F. Behavioral strategies for improving compliance. In R. B. Haynes, D. W. Taylor, & D. L. Sackett (Eds.), *Compliance in health care.* Baltimore: Johns Hopkins Univ. Press, 1979. Pp. 174–190.

Eisenberg, L. The search for care. *Daedalus,* 1977, *106,* 235–246.

Elstein, A. S. Clinical judgment: Psychological research and medical practice. *Science,* 1976, *194,* 696–700.

Emerson, J. Behavior in private places: Sustaining definitions of reality in gynecological examinations. In H. P. Dreitzel (Ed.), *Recent sociology* (Vol. 2). New York: Macmillan, 1970. Pp. 74–97.

Engel, G. L. The need for a new medical model: A challenge for biomedicine. *Science*, 1977, *196*, 129–136.

Farquhar, J. W. *The American way of life need not be hazardous to your health.* New York: Norton, 1978.

Festinger, L. *A theory of cognitive dissonance.* New York: Harper, 1957.

Ford, A. B., Liske, R. E., Ort, R. S., & Denton, J. C. *The doctor's perspective: Physicians view their patients and practice.* Cleveland: Case Western Reserve Univ. Press, 1967.

Francis, V., Korsch, B., & Morris, M. Gaps in doctor–patient communication: Patients' response to medical advice. *New England Journal of Medicine*, 1969, *280*, 535–540.

Frank, J. D. *Persuasion and healing.* Baltimore: Johns Hopkins Univ. Press, 1961.

Freedman, J. L., & Fraser, S. C. Compliance without pressure: The foot-in-the-door technique. *Journal of Personality and Social Psychology*, 1966, *4*, 195–202.

Freemon, B., Negrete, V., Davis, M., & Korsch, B. Gaps in doctor–patient communication: Doctor–patient interaction analysis. *Pediatric Research*, 1971, *5*, 298–311.

Friedman, H. S. Nonverbal communication between patients and medical practitioners. *Journal of Social Issues*, 1979, *35*(1), 82–99.

Friedman, H. S. & DiMatteo, M. R. Health care as an interpersonal process. *Journal of Social Issues*, 1979, *35*(1), 1–11.

Gillum, R. F., & Barsky, A. J. Diagnosis and management of patient noncompliance. *Journal of the American Medical Association*, 1974, *228*, 1563–1567.

Glaser, B., & Strauss, A. *Awareness of dying.* Chicago, Ill: Aldine, 1965.

Goffman, E. *The presentation of self in everyday life.* Garden City, N.Y.: Doubleday, 1959.

Gordis, L., Markowitz, M., & Lilienfeld, A. M. Studies in the epidemiology and preventability of rheumatic fever: IV. A quantitative determination of compliance in children on oral penicillin prophylaxis. *Pediatrics*, 1969, *43*, 173–182.

Haley, J. *Strategies of psychotherapy.* New York: Grune & Stratton, 1963.

Haley, J. *Uncommon therapy: The psychiatric techniques of Milton H. Erickson, M. D.* New York: Norton, 1973.

Hayes-Bautista, D. E. Termination of the patient–practitioner relationship: Divorce, patient style. *Journal of Health and Social Behavior*, 1976, *17*, 12–21.

Haynes, R. B. Introduction In R. B. Haynes, D. W. Taylor, & D. L. Sackett (Eds.), *Compliance in health care.* Baltimore: Johns Hopkins Univ. Press, 1979. Pp. 1–7.

Haynes, R. B. Taking medication: Short and long-term strategies. In W. S. Agras (Ed.), *Promoting long term health behaviors.* New York: Guilford Publications, 1980 (audiotape).

Haynes, R. B., Taylor, D. W., & Sackett, D. L. (Eds.). *Compliance in health care.* Baltimore: Johns Hopkins Univ. Press, 1979.

Henderson, J. B., Hall, S. M., & Lipton, H. L. Changing self-destructive behaviors. In G. C. Stone, F. Cohen, & N. E. Adler (Eds.), *Health psychology.* San Francisco: Jossey-Bass, 1979. Pp. 141–160.

Hulka, B. S. Patient–clinician interactions and compliance. In R. B. Haynes, D. W. Taylor, & D. L. Sackett (Eds.), *Compliance in health care.* Baltimore: Johns Hopkins Univ. Press, 1979. Pp. 63–77.

Inui, J. F., Yourtee, E. L., & Williamson, J. W. Improved outcomes in hypertension after physician tutorials. *Annals of Internal Medicine*, 1976, *84*, 646–651.

Jones, E. E., & Nisbett, R. E. *The actor and the observer: Divergent perceptions of the causes of behavior.* New York: General Learning Press, 1971.

Kanfer, F. H. Self-management methods. In F. H. Kanfer & A. P. Goldstein (Eds.), *Helping people change.* New York: Pergamon, 1975. Pp. 309–355.

Karoly, P. Operant methods. In F. H. Kanfer & A. P. Goldstein (Eds.), *Helping people change.* New York: Pergamon, 1975. Pp. 195–228.

Kasl, S. V. Issues in patient adherence to health care regimens. *Journal of Human Stress*, 1975, *1*, 5–17.

Kasteler, J., Kane, R. L., Olsen, D. M., & Thetford, C. Issues underlying prevalence of "doctor-shopping" behavior. *Journal of Health and Social Behavior*, 1976, *17*, 328–339.

Kelley, A. B. A media role for public health compliance? In R. B. Haynes, D. W. Taylor, & D. L. Sackett (Eds.), *Compliance in health care*. Baltimore: Johns Hopkins Univ. Press, 1979. Pp. 193–201.

Kincey, J., Bradshaw, P., & Ley, P. Patients' satisfaction and reported acceptance of advice in general practice. *Journal of the Royal College of General Practice*, 1975, *25*, 558–566.

Korsch, B. M., Gozzi, E. K., & Francis, V. Gaps in doctor–patient communication: I. Doctor–patient interaction and patient satisfaction. *Pediatrics*, 1968, *42*, 855–871.

Korsch, B. M., & Negrete, V. F. Doctor–patient communication. *Scientific American*, 1972, *227*, 66–74.

Kosa, J., & Robertson, L. The social aspects of health and illness. In J. Kosa & I. Zola (Eds.), *Poverty and health: A sociological analysis* (rev. ed.). Cambridge, Mass.: Harvard Univ. Press, 1975.

LaCrosse, M. B. Nonverbal behavior and perceived counselor attractiveness and persuasiveness. *Journal of Counseling Psychology*, 1975, *22*, 563–566.

Langlie, J. K. Social networks, health beliefs, and preventive health behavior. *Journal of Health and Social Behavior*, 1977, *18*, 244–260.

Levy, R. L. Relationship of an overt commitment to task compliance in behavior therapy. *Journal of Behavioral Therapy and Experimental Psychiatry*, 1977, *8*, 25–29.

Levy, R. L., Yamashita, D., & Pow, G. The relationship of an overt commitment to the frequency and speed of compliance with symptom reporting. *Medical Care*, 1979, *17*, 281–284.

Ley, P., & Spelman, M. S. *Communicating with the patient*. London: Staples Press, 1967.

Lief, H., & Fox, R. C. Training for detached concern in medical students. In H. Lief (Ed.), *The psychological basis for medical practice*. New York: Harper & Row, 1963.

Lorber, J. Good patients and problem patients: Conformity and deviance in a general hospital. *Journal of Health and Social Behavior*, 1975, *16*, 213–225.

Mahoney, M. J. *Cognition and behavior modification*. Cambridge, Mass.: Ballinger, 1974.

Mahoney, M. J., & Thoreson, C. E. (Eds.). *Self-control: Power to the person*. Monterey, Calif.: Brooks/Cole, 1974.

McKinlay, J. Social networks, lay consultation, and help-seeking behavior. *Social Forces*, 1973, *51*, 275–292.

Meichenbaum, D. H. *Cognitive behavior modification*. Morristown, N.J.: General Learning Press, 1977.

Nall, F., & Speilberg, J. Social and cultural factors in responses of Mexican Americans to medical treatment. *Journal of Health and Social Behavior*, 1967, *8*, 299–308.

Osler, W. Lecture to medical students. *Albany Medical Annals*, 1899, *20*, 307.

Pratt, L. Optimism–pessimism about helping the poor with health problems. *Social Work*, 1970, *15*(2), 29–33.

Pratt, L. V. *Family structure and effective health behavior: The energized family*. Boston: Houghton, 1976.

Quesada, G. M. Language and communication barriers for healthy delivery to a minority group. *Social Science and Medicine*, 1976, *10*, 323–327.

Rodin, J., & Janis, I. L. The social power of health care practitioners as agents of change. *Journal of Social Issues*, 1979, *35*(1), 60–81.

Rosenberg, P. P. Students' perceptions and concerns during their first year in medical school. *Journal of Medical Education*, 1971, *46*, 211–218.

Rosenstock, I. M. Patients' compliance with health regimens. *Journal of the American Medical Association*, 1975, *234*, 402–403.

Rosenstock, I. M., & Kirscht, J. P. Why people seek health care. In G. C. Stone, F. Cohen, & N. E. Adler (Eds.), *Health psychology*. San Francisco: Jossey-Bass, 1979. Pp. 161–189.

Roth, J. A. Some contingencies of the moral evaluation and control of clientele: The case of the hospital emergency service. *American Journal of Sociology*, 1972, *77*, 839–856.

Sackett, D. L. & Snow, J. C. The magnitude of compliance and noncompliance. In R. B. Haynes,

D. W. Taylor, & D. L. Sackett (Eds.), *Compliance in health care*. Baltimore: Johns Hopkins Univ. Press, 1979. Pp. 11–22.

Samora, J., Saunders, L., & Larson, R. F. Medical vocabulary knowledge among hospital patients. *Journal of Health and Human Behavior*, 1961, *2*, 83–89.

Seay, T. A., & Altekruse M. K. Verbal and nonverbal behavior in judgments of facilitative conditions. *Journal of Counseling Psychology*, 1979, *26*, 108–119.

Shangold, M. M. The health care of physicians: "Do as I say and not as I do." *Journal of Medical Education*, 1979, *54*, 668.

Snow, L. Folk-medical beliefs and their implications for care of patients. *Annals of Internal Medicine*, 1974, *81*, 82–96.

Stiles, W. B., Putnam, S. M., Wolf, M. H., & James, S. A. Interaction exchange structure and patient satisfaction with medical interviews. *Medical Care*, 1979, *17*, 667–679.

Stimson, G. V. Obeying doctors' orders: A view from the other side. *Social Science and Medicine*, 1974, *8*, 97–104.

Stone, G. C. Patient compliance and the role of the expert. *Journal of Social Issues*, 1979, *35*(1), 34–59.

Surgeon General. *Healthy people: The Surgeon General's report on health promotion and disease prevention, 1979*. USDHEW Public Health Service, Office of the Assistant Secretary of Health and the Surgeon General.

Svarstad, B. *The doctor–patient encounter: An observational study of communication and outcome*. Unpublished doctoral dissertation, Department of Sociology, University of Wisconsin, 1974.

Svarstad, B. Physician–patient communication and patient conformity with medical advice. In D. Mechanic (Ed.), *The growth of bureaucratic medicine*. New York: Wiley, 1976.

Taylor, S. E. Hospital patient behavior: Reactance, helplessness, or control? *Journal of Social Issues*, 1979, *35*(1), 156–184.

Tepper, D. T., Jr., & Haase, R. F. Verbal and nonverbal communication of facilitative conditions. *Journal of Counseling Psychology*, 1978, *25*, 35–44.

Triandis, H. C. *Interpersonal behavior*. Monterey, Calif.: Brooks/Cole, 1977.

Twaddle, A. C. Health decisions and sick role variations: An exploration. *Journal of Health and Social Behavior*, 1969, *10*, 105–114.

Vuori, H., Aaku, T., Aine, E., Erkko, R., & Johansson, R. Doctor–patient relationship in the light of patients' experiences. *Social Science and Medicine*, 1972, *6*, 723–730.

Waitzkin, H., & Stoeckle, J. D. The communication of information about illness: Clinical, sociological, and methodological considerations. *Advances in Psychosomatic Medicine*, 1972, *8*, 180–215.

Wallston, B. S., & Wallston, K. A. Toward a unified social psychological model of health behavior. In G. Sanders & J. Suls (Eds.), *Social psychology of health and illness*. Hillsdale, N.J.: Erlbaum, 1981.

Wills, T. A. Perceptions of clients by professional helpers. *Psychological Bulletin*, 1978, *85*, 968–1000.

Wilson, G. T. Cognitive factors in lifestyle changes: A social learning perspective. In P. O. Davidson & S. M. Davidson (Eds.), *Behavioral medicine: Changing health lifestyles*. New York: Brunner/Mazel, 1980.

Wurtele, S. K., Galanos, A. N., & Roberts, M. C. Increasing return compliance in a tuberculosis detection drive. *Journal of Behavioral Medicine*, 1980, *3*, 311–318.

Zifferblatt, S. M. Increasing patient compliance through the applied analysis of behavior. *Preventive Medicine*, 1975, *4*, 173–182.

Zimbardo, P. G., Ebbesen, E. B., & Maslach, C. *Influencing attitudes and changing behavior* (2nd ed.). Reading, Mass.: Addison-Wesley, 1977.

Zola, I. K. Pathways to the doctor—From person to patient. *Social Science and Medicine*, 1973, *7*, 677–689.

chapter 15

The Empirical Analysis of Help-Intended Communications: Conceptual Framework and Recent Research[1]

ROBERT ELLIOTT
WILLIAM B. STILES
SAUL SHIFFMAN
CHRISTOPHER B. BARKER
BONNIE BURSTEIN
GERALD GOODMAN

Introduction

This chapter is about the intervention choices that confront helpers during moments in helping situations. A clinical example illustrates the nature of these choices: A young female Asian college student wrote on her intake form that she was feeling depressed, was withdrawing from people, and was having trouble concentrating on her schoolwork. The helper chose to begin by reflecting what the client had written on the intake form ("I understand you're feeling depressed"); she then followed up the client's initial disclosures with a reflection ("You mean you can't find specific things that make you depressed, but yet you aren't feeling good").

The helper had a variety of response options open to her, and may have wondered which strategy was best in the situation. In this case, the client later listened to a tape of the session and identified the interventions that had helped or hindered her. She reported these reflections as two of the most significant helper responses in the session, describing them as supportive and

[1]The material in this chapter is based on a symposium presented at the American Psychological Association Convention, Los Angeles, August 1981.

Basic Processes in Helping Relationships

understanding. From what the client told us about later responses in the session, it was clear that a number of other response options would not have been as useful to her and might even have been seen as hindering: Questions about her situation (e.g., relations with males), interpretations of possible causal factors (e.g., recent arrival in this country), and giving advice (e.g., to keep herself busy) were all perceived by her as "irrelevant," perhaps because she had already heard them too often from friends and relatives.

This chapter describes recent research on the major response options available to helpers in help-intended communication situations. *Help-intended communication situations* refer to a broad class of situations in which one person (helper, counselor, therapist, fellow support group member, friend) interacts with a second person (help seeker, client, patient) with the intention of providing the latter with some form of psychological help. Help-intended communication situations include both professional and nonprofessional helping, as well as certain communications by nonpsychological professionals (e.g., physicians, lawyers) and by intimate friends or family members.

Help-intended communication has three basic aspects: *content, action,* and *style* (Russell & Stiles, 1979); that is, helpers make choices about what to talk *about* (content), what they intend to *do* by what they say (action), and *how* they will say what they have to say (style). Choices of mode of action are referred to by linguists and philosophers as *speech acts* (Searle, 1969) and by us as *response modes*. Of the three aspects of the helping process, it is choice of response mode or action that is probably most salient for helpers (content is usually presented by the client; style is often not attended to).

Research on helper response modes goes back to the first generation of process researchers: Snyder (1945), Bales (1950), and Strupp (1955). These researchers all examined types of verbal action in dyadic or small group situations by dividing communication into small units, generally on the order of the sentence. Much of this early work addressed questions of differences between response mode use patterns displayed by therapists of different therapeutic "schools" or with varying levels of professional experience.

In the 1960s, therapy process researchers turned away from response modes toward more stylistic variables, particularly the facilitative conditions of the client-centered model of therapy (Rogers, Gendlin, Kiesler, & Truax, 1967; Truax & Mitchell, 1971) and client stylistic variables such as Experiencing (Klein, Mathieu, Gendlin, & Kiesler, 1969) and Vocal Quality (Rice & Wagstaff, 1967). Finally, in the early 1970s the pendulum swung back, as systematic packages for training professional and nonprofessional helpers began to appear (e.g., Danish & Hauer, 1973; Ivey & Gluckstern, 1976; Kagan, Note 1). In these packages, attempts were made to break helping behavior into specific defined component skills, such as response modes. Each training package was made up of a different framework of responses; however, research efforts were directed toward validating training packages rather than toward understanding and measuring response modes.

Goodman and Dooley's (1976) paper, "A Framework for Help-Intended Communication," was an attempt to integrate the older process research tradition with the more recent training literature by providing a single comprehensive set of six response modes: question ("How do you feel about that?"), advisement ("It might be useful to tell him how you feel"), reflection ("So what you're saying is that you're angry as well as sad "), interpretation ("I think you're depressed because you can't accept your anger"), self-disclosure ("When you say that, I feel near tears, too"), and silence (5+ sec pause). This framework has now been adapted and used by trainers and researchers. It is simple, which makes it relatively easy to teach to both neophyte helpers and research raters. It is pantheoretical; that is, it can be readily applied to a variety of helping schools and situations. Furthermore, a training package based on the framework is available and widely used (Goodman, 1979).

This framework has provided the major impetus for an approach to studying help-intended communication that is distinguished by careful description of actual helping interactions, by development of psychometrically sound measuring instruments, and by an interest in testing assumptions about the nature of help-intended communication. This chapter summarizes recent research on the response modes, centered around usage patterns, impact on clients, and training effects, as well as study of the framework itself, its categories, and their measurement.

The Response Mode Framework

The close analysis of help-intended communication has led to the development of a whole "family" of closely related methods for measuring response modes, including the addition of modes not in the original Goodman and Dooley framework. Table 15.1 contains a summary of nine modes commonly distinguished by response mode researchers. The table contains the forms typically used, the underlying helping intention, and some of the alternative names and subcategories within each response mode. New additions to the framework include reassurance ("Yes, I think you can do it"), disagreement ("I don't think that's a good idea"), and information ("For many people, a vacation from therapy can be useful"). Researchers studying the response modes typically work with tapes, and/or carefully done transcripts of actual helping interactions.

The unit of analysis commonly used is the verbal sentence or clause. Response mode raters have usually been advanced undergraduate or graduate students, trained 20–50 hours. Reliabilities are generally in the .80s. Major response mode rating systems include (*a*) Stiles' *Verbal Response Mode* (VRM) *System* (1978, 1979), (*b*) Hill's *Counselor Verbal Response Category System* (1978; Hill, Greenwald, Reed, Charles, O'Farrell, & Carter, 1981), (*c*) Elliott's *Helper*

Table 15.1
Summary of Helper Response Modes

Category	Other names/subtypes	Typical forms	Helping intention
Question[a-i]	Open–closed,[c,d,f,g,b] information gathering[g]	Interrogative	Gathering information
Advisement[a-i]	Process,[d,f] general,[d] direct guidance,[c] cognitive–behavioral,[c] command,[c] suggestion[f]	Command, request, suggestion	Transferring guiding information
Reflection[a-i]	Restatement,[c] nonverbal referent,[c] exploration[g]	Repetition, paraphrase, summary	Communicating understanding of message
Interpretation[a-i]	Person–general,[f,c] exploration[g]	Contains new information about help seeker, describes causal links or patterns	Explaining help seeker to self
Self-disclosure[a-i]	Me-too,[e,f] process[d,f]	Refers to helper's experiences or characteristics	Deliberate sharing of self
Information[b-d,g-i]	Edification,[b] explanation,[b] general interpretation[c,f,i]	Refers to third parties	Explaining nonpresent people or giving general information

336

Reassurance[b-i]	Acknowledgment[a,c,e,f,i] confirmation[b]	Agreement, "uh-huh", positive aspects of help seeker	Supporting help seeker, responding positively
Disagreement[c-e,g,i]	Confrontation,[c] criticism,[e] confirmation[b]	Negation, reference to negative states or outcomes	Challenging, disagreeing
Silence[a,c,e,f,i] versus interruption[a,f]		Measurable latency (3–5 sec) versus overtalk, or no interresponse latency	Verbal allowing versus crowding

[a]Original version, Goodman & Dooley, 1976.
[b]Stiles, 1978, 1979.
[c]Hill, 1978; Hill, Greenwald, Reed, Charles, O'Farrell & Carter, 1981.
[d]Elliott, 1979, Note 2; Elliott & Feinstein, Note 7.
[e]Barker & Lemle, Note 3; Barker, 1981.
[f]Burstein, in press.
[g]Shapiro, Barkham, & Irving, Note 9.
[h]Shiffman, 1981.
[i]Whalen & Flowers, 1977.

Behavior Rating System (1979, Note 2), (*d*) Barker & Lemle's (Note 3; Barker, 1981), and (*e*) Burstein's (in press) response mode systems. Methodological details are covered in these sources and those cited in Table 15.1.

Different investigators have focused on different sorts of helping interactions: Professional therapy and counseling sessions (both initial sessions and throughout treatment) have been studied, as have several types of helping "analogue" interviews (e.g., 20-min one-shot helping sessions, and group exercises in which participants took turns as "helper" and "discloser"). In addition, different kinds of helpers have been observed: professionals, paraprofessionals and informal helpers (e.g., couples). In addition, several investigators (Hill, Greenwald, Reed, Charles, O'Farrell, & Carter, 1981; Stiles & Sultan, 1979) have also studied client response mode use. Finally, several researchers have identified higher-order dimensions or factors that organize the response modes: Stiles (1979) describes three conceptual dimensions (see the following section), whereas Shiffman (1981) found two empirical factors, asking and telling, both negatively loading on reflection (see the section entitled "Response Mode Use and Training Effects among Clinical Psychology Graduate Students").

Response Mode Use and Impact
in Psychotherapy and Medical Interviews

The Stiles VRM system is based on a conceptual framework in which three binary dimensions (source of experience, frame of reference, and focus) are used to organize eight response modes as a 2 × 2 × 2 cube (Stiles, 1978, 1979). This version of the response mode framework has been applied to two types of formal helping interactions, psychotherapy (McDaniel, Stiles, & McGaughey, 1981; Stiles, 1979; Stiles, McDaniel, & McGaughey, 1979; Stiles & Sultan, 1979; Stiles, Note 4) and medical interviews (Stiles, Putnam, Wolf, & James, 1979a, 1979b). Unlike the other systems reviewed in this chapter, it has been applied to client behavior, as well as to non-help-intended conversations involving professors and students (Cansler & Stiles, 1981), parents and children (Stiles & White, 1981), married couples (Premo & Stiles, Note 5), and presidential primary campaign speeches (Stiles, Au, Martello, & Perlmutter, Note 6).

PSYCHOTHERAPY

Technical differences among different schools of psychotherapy can be seen in terms of the three binary dimensions. Client-centered therapy (Rogers, 1951) explicitly prescribes staying in the client's internal frame of reference.

This implies that the therapist should use only reflection, acknowledgment (mild reassurances), confirmation (reassurance–disagreement), and edification (information), and avoid advisement, interpretation, question, and disclosure. Gestalt therapy (Perls, 1969) prescribes just the reverse, suggesting that the therapist should always stay in his or her own existential frame of reference. Psychoanalysis (Freud, 1912/1958) represents still a different pattern, pre-scribing modes that concern the patient's experience (question, acknow-ledgment, reflection, and interpretation) and proscribing modes that concern the analyst's own experience (disclosure, edification, confirmation, advisement). In verbatim transcriptions of psychotherapy sessions by prominent practitioners of each of these schools, the therapists conformed to these prescriptions and proscriptions of their own school in 80% to 90% of their utterances (Stiles, 1979).

Despite systematic therapist differences and different topics of conver-sation, psychotherapy clients' mode profiles are remarkably consistent. Most client utterances are disclosure (D) or edification (E) in grammatical form and communicative intent (Stiles & Sultan, 1979). That is, clients use first-person (disclosure form) or third-person (edification or information form) declarative sentences to talk about their own private experience (disclosure intent) and about objective matters (edification or information intent). To illustrate:

> I'm angry at her. D(D)
> She made me angry. E(D)
> She hit me. E(E)
> I hit her back. D(E)

(Note: The form abbreviation is written first, the intent abbreviation is written in parentheses.) In contrast to their therapists, clients very rarely use ques-tions, reflections, advisements, or interpretations.

The systematic differences in mode use found among therapists of different schools (Stiles, 1979) converge with similar findings by other investigators using other response mode systems (Brunink & Schroeder, 1979; Hill, Thames, & Rardin, 1979; Snyder, 1945; Strupp, 1955). The consistency of these results suggests that if there is a common core to psychotherapeutic process, it is unlikely to be found in the therapists' verbal techniques. However, the similarity of client profiles across schools suggests that there might be a common "active ingredient" in the client's verbal behavior.

The most obvious candidate is the client disclosure form with disclosure intent, termed D(D). In using D(D), a client explores his or her own internal frame of reference using the first person ("I") to take personal responsibility for subjective experiences (i.e., to "own" or "accept" them). In a first test of this hypothesis, client percentage D(D) in segments sampled from a wide range of therapy and informational interviews was correlated .58 ($p < .001$) with more global "good process" ratings of the segments on the Experiencing (EXP) scale (Klein *et al.*, 1969), a fully anchored 7-point Likert-type rating scale developed to measure the primary client process variable in the client-centered theory of personality change (Stiles, McDaniel, & McGaughey, 1979). Similarly, clients' percentage of D(D) in a series of sessions was correlated .66 ($p < .001$) with ratings of *client exploration* and .65 ($p < .001$) with ratings of *therapist exploration* based on samples of the same series of sessions (McDaniel *et al.*, 1981).

If D(D) is a major active ingredient in psychotherapy, then clients' use of D(D) in psychotherapy should be positively correlated with therapeutic benefit. However, in a first test of this hypothesis (McDaniel *et al.*, 1981) based on data from the Vanderbilt Psychotherapy Project (Strupp & Hadley, 1979), client D(D) showed no clear or consistent relationship with measures of improvement. However, clients who were more severely disturbed or distressed (e.g., higher MMPI Depression scale scores and higher therapist ratings of overall severity of disturbance and psychic distress) tended to use a higher percentage of D(D).

In another study (Stiles, Note 4), clients' percentage of D(D) in a general sample of outpatient therapy sessions was uncorrelated with Session Evaluation Questionnaire (Stiles, 1980) ratings of the depth and value of sessions, suggesting that there is a discrepancy between external raters' judgments of a session's depth (i.e., of EXP and of "exploration") and the session's impact on participants. Nevertheless, sessions that were high in client D(D) *relative to each client's usual level* were rated on the Semantic Differential scales as relatively "rough," "difficult," and "dangerous" by both clients and therapists.

MEDICAL INTERVIEWS

The VRM profiles of physicians and patients in initial medical interviews changed greatly across three interview segments (Stiles, Putnam, Wolf, & James, 1979b). In the *medical history*, most physician utterances were questions or acknowledgments. Patient uttterances were almost all edification or disclosure in intent (i.e., giving objective or subjective information). However, a substantial minority were acknowledgment (K) in form: K(E) and K(D)— "yes" or "no" answers that communicate objective or subjective information, respectively.

> (Did you have a rash?)   Yes.   K(E)
> (Did it itch?)   Yes.   K(D)

In the *physical examination*, physicians used more advisements ("Open your mouth") and disclosures ("I'm going to check your throat") to direct patients through examination procedures. Patients continued to give information, but with relatively more K(E) and K(D) (i.e., more "yes" and "no") answers.

In the *conclusion*, physicians continued to gather information from patients, shown by physician questions and acknowledgments and patient edifications and disclosures, but there was also a substantial flow of information from physicians to patients, including explanations of illness and treatment, shown by physician edifications and disclosures and patient acknowledgments and questions.

Factor analyses of mode frequencies (Stiles, Putnam, Wolf, & James, 1979a) showed that each interview segment had a clear and simple structure, consisting of two or three distinct "verbal exchange" factors, each of which had an identifiable medical function. For example, the medical history consisted primarily of two types of verbal exchange. In the *exposition exchanges*, with high loadings for patient E(E), D(E), E(D), and D(D), and for physician acknowledgments, patients told their story in their own words (edification and disclosure forms) while physicians facilitated with "mm-hms." In the *closed question exchanges*, with high loadings for physician questions and reflections and for patient K(E) and K(D), physicians asked questions and reflected the sense of answers, while patients answered yes or no. Out of seven verbal exchange factors (two from the history, two from the physical examination, and three from the conclusion, two were significantly correlated with patient satisfaction, measured by subscales of the Medical Interview Satisfaction Scale, which consists of 26 Likert scales (Wolf, Putnam, James, & Stiles, 1978). Exposition exchanges in the history segment were associated with affective satisfaction (feelings of warmth and acceptance; trust in the doctor). Feedback exchanges in the conclusion segment, which consisted mainly of physician edification (information) and patient acknowledgments and questions, were associated with cognitive satisfaction (understanding of illness and treatment).

The Impact of Response Modes on Client-Perceived Helpfulness

Elliott and associates (Elliott, Barker, Caskey, & Pistrang, in press; Elliott & Feinstein, Note 8) have conducted a series of studies aimed at comparing the helpfulness of different helper response modes. The purpose of this research has been to examine the presuppositions of helping skills training programs (Carkhuff, 1969; Danish & Hauer, 1973; Goodman, 1979; Ivey & Gluckstern, 1976), which commonly teach helpers to reduce advisement, question, and interruption and to increase reflection, silence, and self-disclosure.

These studies used an adaptation of Kagan's (Note 1) Interpersonal Process Recall (IPR) technique, in which a recording of a just-completed helping session is played back for the client, enabling the client to remember and describe the momentary experiences that accompanied particular helper responses. As the tape was played back, the client rated each helper response on the Helpfulness Rating Scale (Elliott, in press) and described the helper's response modes (Elliott & Feinstein, Note 7). Finally, trained raters rated response modes using the Elliott version of the response modes (Elliott, 1979, Note 2). Two of the studies involved brief, one-shot helping interviews with undergraduate students; a third study used therapy interviews sampled throughout treatment in a variety of community settings.

The results of three studies applying these methods (Elliott *et al.*, in press; Elliott & Feinstein, Note 8) can be summarized as follows: From the client's point of view, interpretations were generally the most helpful response mode: Significant correlations with helpfulness for client-perceived interpretation obtained in all three studies and for rater-perceived interpretation in two of the three studies.[2] However, the response modes accounted for very little of the variance in client helpfulness ratings. The effects are certainly not large enough to provide a reliable guide for the practice of psychological helping. This negative finding casts doubt on the content of helping skill training packages that attempt to make helpers more helpful by teaching them to switch response modes.

The lack of clear helpfulness differences among modes suggests that other qualitative data are needed to understand the relationship between response modes and client-perceived helpfulness. Thus, the research has moved in two separate directions: cluster analyses of significant events and qualitative analysis of helpful and hindering response modes.

CLUSTER ANALYSES OF SIGNIFICANT EVENTS

The first direction involves using cluster analyses of clients' descriptions to identify types of significant change events, which can then be described in terms of response modes. Elliott & Feinstein (Note 8) obtained clients' descriptions of significantly helpful and nonhelpful helper responses in brief one-shot helping sessions. These descriptions were sorted by students, colleagues, and lay people into categories, which provided the basis for cluster analyses (maximum linkage method, Dixon & Brown, 1979). (See Table 15.2.)

The analyses yielded seven discrete clusters of helpful events termed *new perspective, understanding, problem solution, clarification of problem, reassurance, personal contact,* and *client involvement*. Three of the clusters were found to possess significant patterns of response modes: New perspective events, the most common type, typically contained process advisements and interpretations. Understanding events were characterized by interpretation or reflection. Finally, personal contact events were rated as self-disclosure or information.

The cluster analysis of nonhelpful events yielded five clusters and suggests a

---

[2]Therapists rated helpfulness in the study that involved actual outpatient psychotherapy; although client and therapist helpfulness ratings were not significantly correlated in this study, interpretations also predicted therapist perceived helpfulness.

taxonomy of negative events in help-intended communication: *misperception*, *misdirection*, *negative counselor reaction*, *unhelpful confrontation*, and *disappointment*. Only misperception events were found to have a characteristic response mode pattern: These typically involved question or reflection.

QUALITATIVE ANALYSIS OF HELPFUL AND HINDERING RESPONSE MODES

The second direction of research involves selecting client-perceived helpful and nonhelpful instances of each response mode and studying them qualitatively to discover what distinguishes them. For example, qualitative analyses suggest that helpful questions in formal helping situations are typically open-ended and aimed at helping a cooperative help seeker to explore feelings or personal meanings (e.g., "I wonder, as we're talking now, how you do feel?"). In contrast, low-rated questions typically involve (*a*) sidetracks (e.g., help seeker mentions anthropology in a long list of subjects she does not want to major in, to which helper responds, "How did anthropology get in there?"), (*b*) probes into uncomfortable topics (e.g., female help seeker begins session by very nervously disclosing having just been kissed by a boy for the first time; the male helper's very first response is: "How did that feel, when he kissed you?"), or (*c*) confrontational questions (e.g., helper repeatedly uses exploratory feeling questions to get a frightened help seeker to examine her feelings; the help seeker experiences the helper as unsympathetically trying to pin her down).

Response Mode Use and Training Effects among Clinical Psychology Graduate Students

A surprising recent finding is that graduate training in clinical psychology does not affect trainees' response mode use, except when trainees have had specific training in the response modes. Shiffman (1981) compared the response mode use of clinical trainees and graduate students in nonclinical areas of psychology with a 5-min behavior sampling procedure called the Group Assessment of Interpersonal Traits (GAIT; cf. Goodman, 1972). In the GAIT, three to eight participants take turns acting as helper and help seeker for each other. In a cross-sectional design, trainees spanning 3 years of graduate study were evaluated. The design was replicated 1 year later.

In order to summarize the response mode data, ratings made from tapes of 200 GAIT dyads were factor analyzed. Two stable factors emerged, which accounted for two-thirds of the response mode variance. One factor, labeled *Asking*, was defined by high positive loading for question (open and closed

Table 15.2
Clusters of Significant Events[a]

A. *Helpful Event Clusters*

Cluster 1: New Perspective (N = 28). Client describes seeing something new about self, or becoming more aware.

—What H (helper) said about my concern made a lot of sense; it gave me something to think about. It was a new outlook.

—It made me realize something that I hadn't thought about. It made me open my eyes about myself.

Cluster 2: Understanding (N = 18). Client describes feeling understood by helper:

—It felt good to know that H didn't think that I was crazy. It was nice to have someone understand me.

—H made me think. H hit the nail on the head. That's the way I really am and it made me feel like I was getting across to H what I was talking about.

Cluster 3: Problem Solution (N = 15). Client receives helpful suggestions regarding presenting problems:

—H was giving me an alternative to see if it helps. I was looking for an answer and H threw out a possibility.

—H brought out an option that I had never thought about. It made me think about what actually would happen if I did that, and I realized it wouldn't be as bad as I had thought it would be. Not after, but when H was saying it, it was like a light bulb went on.

Cluster 4: Clarification of Problem (N = 7). Client describes coming to a clearer definition of what client is working toward:

—It started relating my ideas together, started my mind thinking in the direction of a possible solution.

—It made me feel like it was one of the major problems facing me, and as a whole it made my mind clearer.

Cluster 5: Reassurance (N = 7). Client experiences emotional support coming from helper:

—It was kind of a pat on the back. I was recovering from these caustic things and was really feeling hostile, and H picked that up.

—It backed me up. H felt like what I said was a positive thing. It's nice to have positive input. H told me what I wanted to hear.

Cluster 6: Personal Contact (N = 7). Client describes coming to a greater sense of helper as a person:

—H was familiar with it. I felt as though I wasn't the only one.

—H related to it; we both joked about it; it was the first time we weren't serious. What H said struck me differently from all the others (I've talked with). We were having a good time.

Cluster 7: Client Involvement (N = 5). Client is stimulated to become more engaged in the helping process:

—H was asking my opinion on it, and made me want to respond.

—It got the ball rolling. It just kept me going, at the same time putting into perspective what I was going to say.

B. *Nonhelpful Event Clusters*

Cluster 1: Misperception (N = 19). Client describes feeling misunderstood by helper; feels helper has an inaccurate picture of the client's problem or experience:

—It was a source of confusion. I felt that maybe H wasn't understanding me. I didn't know how far back, but I felt that H was confused at what I was saying.

—It was a misinterpretation. It wasn't the way I was thinking.

(continued)

Table 15.2 (*continued*)

Cluster 2: Misdirection (N = 14). Client experiences helper as interrupting or interfering with client's disclosure and exploration:
  —It was an interruption to what I was saying and thinking about. I didn't want to break the flow.
  —I thought that was already taken care of; we had already gotten out of that and it was sort of irrelevant to go back to it.

Cluster 3: Negative Helper Reactions (N = 14). Client describes helper as responding negatively to client, by being either uninvolved or critical:
  —H made a joke of it. H was uninvolved. I was so excited. I wanted H to talk to me but H just kept on saying, "You'll really have to decide for yourself." Then H started giggling. That *really* turned me off.
  —H seemed to be attacking me. H made it seem like I was looking at my problem from a narrow, one-sided point of view.

Cluster 4: Unhelpful Confrontation (N = 14). Client experiences unhelpful discomfort as result of helper putting pressure on client to do or think about someting:
  —It was bothersome again. H was asking me what I was going to do. I had to think about it again. It made me want to not think about it at all, the whole situation.
  —I was waiting for a response that didn't come. It was an uncomfortable feeling—you know you're supposed to be talking. I wanted H to say something, let me know what to do next.

Cluster 5: Disappointment (N = 9). Client's expectations for help are not met due to inadequate or nonproductive responses:
  —I was looking for a word to describe how I was feeling. I felt if H knew what I was saying, H would help me. I wanted some verbal guidance
  —It didn't seem to lead me anywhere. It just reemphasized my problem without doing anything about it.

---

[a]From "Cluster analysis of significantly helpful and nonhelpful response modes" by R. Elliott and L. Feinstein. In R. Elliott (Chair), *Recent research on helping communications.* Symposium presented at the American Psychological Association Convention, Los Angeles, August 1981. Copyright © Robert Elliott, 1981. Reprinted by permission.

types) and high negative loading for reflection. The second factor, *Telling*, again had a high *negative* loading for reflection and high positive loading for advisement, explanation (information), and disclosure. This implies that reflection is an alternative to *both* Asking and Telling: One either reflects or asks and tells in various proportions.

The results showed that clinical trainees' performance did not change as they proceeded through training. The clinical trainees' style was consistently and strikingly different from the nonclinical trainees' (Figure 15.1). Nonclinical trainees engaged in a great deal of telling. They told the client about themselves (disclosure), about others (information), and what to do (advisement). Their use of these telling modes was 2½ times that of the clinical trainees, who replaced these telling modes with reflections, which made up nearly half of their responses. Although clinical trainees did about as much asking as their nonclinical peers, they seemed to shift their interrogation toward *open* questions, which allow the client greater freedom in responding.

The nonclinical trainees' response mode use pattern was consistent with that found among lay helpers (e.g., Barker, 1981; Burstein, in press; Dooley, 1974; Reisman & Yamokoski, 1974; Whalen & Flowers, 1977), for whom the most commonly used modes are question, advisement, interpretation, and reassurance. These studies suggest that untrained helpers rarely use reflection, information, self-disclosure, disagreement, and silence. The clinical trainees' response mode profile is consistent with a review of the effects of clinical training and experience (Shiffman, 1981); trained and experienced helpers seem to use fewer questions and advisements and more reflections and silences. However, in contrast to a recent study by Hill, Charles, and Reed (1981), the effects found in the present study appeared to be the result of selection, distinguishing clinical and nonclinical graduate students from the beginning. (The discrepancy between this study and others in the literature probably reflects differences in sample, design, and measurement methods.)

Thus, these data suggest the pessimistic conclusion that advanced training may be unnecessary or that "therapists are born and not made." However, the distinctive performance of seven trainees who had participated in a 10-week workshop on the response modes suggests that response modes *are* trainable beyond this baseline level. As Figure 15.1 shows, workshop graduates were markedly different from other clinical trainees. Especially notable is their diminished use of questions, balanced by their increased use of reflection. Advice giving and information (explanation) have also nearly disappeared. Workshop trainees differ from other clinical trainees in much the same way clinical trainees differ from nonclinical trainees; in effect, they are "more clinical" than other trainees.

The apparent impact of the workshop experience on mode use contrasts with the limited effect of the general graduate training in clinical psychology. Perhaps the response mode system gives trainees a framework for monitoring, evaluating, and changing their clinical style. Without such a concrete language, trainees and their supervisors may communicate unproductively in vague global terms. The instruction to "give the client more room" is not easily carried out; the instruction to ask fewer questions and give less advice is more easily understood and adopted. The specificity of training may be critical to its efficacy.

Effects of Live versus Automated Training on Response Mode Use by Community Adults

The large number of potential nonprofessional counselors often exceeds the capacity of labor-intensive, traditionally administered methods for training psychological helpers. One relatively economical alternative is the use of leaderless, automated communication training packages, in which an audio-

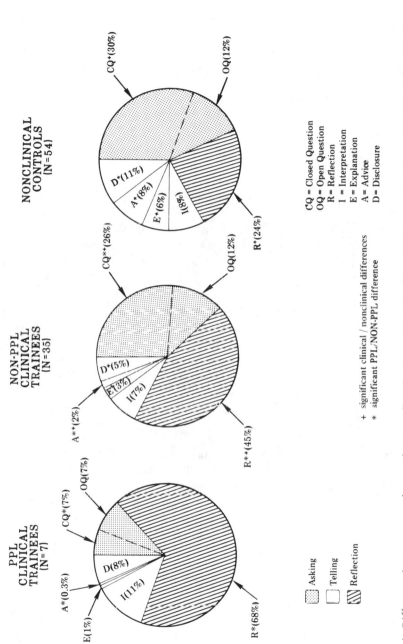

Figure 15.1. Differences in response mode usage between clinical trainees with and without PPL (response modes workshop) and nonclinical controls. (From *The effects of graduate training in clinical psychology on performance in a psychotherapy analogue* [Doctoral dissertation, University of California, Los Angeles, 1981. Copyright © Saul M. Shiffman, 1981. Reprinted by permission.)

tape provides lectures and programs experiential learning exercises for use in small-group situations.

Previous studies of the impact of such automated packages for training helpers have found that they can change attitudes (Lieberman, Yalom, & Miles, 1973), and can teach a single new behavior (Witlin, 1974) or a set of behaviors (Dooley, 1974; Taylor, 1976). These studies encouraged the development of leaderless training packages, culminating in Goodman's (1979) Self-led Automated Series on Helping Alternatives (SASHAtapes). This automated training format has a number of goals, most important of which are (a) to entice helpers into using a broader range of response modes (in particular, reflection and silence), (b) to reduce overused modes (especially question and advisement), and (c) to facilitate the more effective use of each response mode.

In a study designed to evaluate this format, Burstein (in press) addressed two questions: First, can SASHAtapes produce the desired changes in response mode use? Second, how do changes produced by such automated training compare to those resulting from more conventional leader-led training? A heterogeneous group of 160 community adults who volunteered for a free course in help-intended communication were randomly assigned in groups of 5 to 10 to three conditions: automated training groups (SASHAtapes), leader-led training groups (with identical content), and a delayed-training control condition. Participants in the automated and leader-led groups participated in six 2-hr training sessions, each focusing on a different response mode. After training (or an equivalent period of time for the control group), all participants took part in the Group Assessment of Interpersonal Traits (GAIT; Goodman, 1972; cf. Shiffman, 1981). In general, the training had the desired effect of reducing the use of questions and interruptions and increasing the use of reflection, self-disclosure, and silence. With one exception (reflection), these training effects were stronger in the tape-led group than in the leader-led group.

Perhaps the automated training promoted generally stronger gains than live leaders because in the automated training groups, the group becomes its own teacher (e.g., group members take turns as "facilitators"). Participants reported feeling proud of mastering the material together. Groups struggled with the concepts presented, teaching each other rather than passively absorbing material, as they might from a live expert.

Response Mode Use by Intimate Couples

Helping is not confined to the formal efforts of professional or para-professional helpers. A variety of programs exist for enhancing couples' interpersonal communication skills (e.g., Guerney, 1977; Miller, Nunnally, &

Wackman, 1976); overall, such programs appear to have a positive impact on marital satisfaction and communication skills (see Joanning, Brock, Avery, & Coufal, 1980). Many programs focus on skills analogous to informal helping. However, some have argued that not enough is known about informal helping to justify the interventions (e.g., Gottlieb, 1976). Barker (1981; Barker & Lemle, Note 3; Lemle, 1980) studied this process of informal helping, with particular focus on (*a*) the response modes used by couples in trying to give psychological help to each other, (*b*) the helpfulness of these response modes, and (*c*) the effects of a brief training program in helping communication.

Fifty-three nondisturbed, volunteer couples took part in a brief training program adapted from the SASHAtapes for use with couples. The methods used were similar to those in Burstein's study (in press; reviewed above) of the effects of SASHAtape training. Automated and delayed training conditions were used, with random assignment to conditions. An adaptation of the GAIT for couples, the Couples' Helping Exercise, was used to obtain a behavior sample of helping communication before and after either training or a waiting period. In this procedure, each member of the couple takes a turn as helper and help seeker in a 5-min interaction. In addition, couples rated helpfulness and response mode use for these 5-min dyads. Finally, couples' response modes were rated by third-party coders, using Barker & Lemle's (Note 3) adaptation of the response mode framework for informal helping.

Question, interpretation, and advisement were the most frequently used helper response modes. Training was not particularly successful: The only response mode that was affected by it was silence, which increased. The most interesting results involved relations between response modes and ratings of the helpfulness of the 5-min dyads made by the member of the couple who was in the role of help seeker at the time. (See Table 15.3.) Response modes were much poorer predictors of perceived helpfulness than more complex evaluative variables (principally an empathy versus criticalness dimension). Interactions rated by participants as more helpful were rated higher on empathy and lower on criticism (disagreement) by coders. With minor exceptions, helper response mode usage did not predict perceived helpfulness, a finding parallel to that of Elliott *et al.* (in press; reviewed earlier).

Other findings suggest that, among intimate couples, criticism (disagreement) is frequently carried by interpretation (probably in the form of "mindreading" or statements like "You always get upset by little things like that") and by self-disclosures (probably of the confrontational sort, e.g., "I'm uncomfortable with what you've just said"). Training of couples in informal helping needs to be directed toward communicating understanding and avoiding subtle or not-so-subtle cues of disagreement. These findings do not justify programs that teach particular response modes to the exclusion of others.

Table 15.3
Correlations of Process Variables with Ratings by Male and Female Help Seekers[a,b]

Process variable	Helpfulness rating		Relationship satisfaction	
	Male	Female	Male	Female
Empathy versus criticism	.25*	.46***	.05	.33**
Supportive	.26*	.14	.08	.34**
Problem solving	.01	.00	−.06	−.16

[a]From *The helping process in couples: Communication instruction and patterns of informal help* (Doctoral dissertation, University of California, Los Angeles, 1980) by C.B. Barker. *Dissertation Abstracts International*, 1981, *41*, 3365B. Copyright © Christopher B. Barker, 1980. Reprinted by permission.

[b]One-tailed significance tests were performed by correlations with Empathy and Supportive; two-tailed tests were performed for correlations with Problem Solving. Relationship satisfaction was measured using the Locke–Wallace Scale (Locke & Wallace, 1959).

$*p < .05.$
$**p < .01.$
$***p < .001.$

Discussion and Implications

Research on the response modes addresses a diverse set of problems and populations: from theoretical concerns about the measurement of interpersonal events to practical issues of training the next generation of professional and lay helpers; from graduate students talking about personal concerns in a 5-min behavioral sampling task to the behavior of patients in medical examinations. This wide range of application provides evidence that the response modes are a powerful tool for describing help-intended communication. The research described in this chapter addressed three areas: use patterns, impact on clients, and the effects of training.

PATTERNS OF RESPONSE MODE USE

In professional psychological helping relationships (psychotherapy and counseling), the behaviors of therapists vary widely depending on the therapists' school or approach, but the behavior of clients is remarkably consistent, being mostly made up of self-disclosure and information giving. The study of client response modes (e.g., Hill, Greenwald, Reed, Charles, O'Farrell, & Carter, 1981; Stiles & Sultan, 1979) is a promising break with the tradition of seeing the client as the passive object of the therapist.

Among lay and informal helpers, question, advisement, interpretation and reassurance are the most common response modes. This pattern contrasts most strikingly with mode use by client-centered therapists and students influenced by the client-centered tradition. Finally, in medical interviews, the pattern of mode use depends on the phase of the interview and the task being performed (e.g., history taking, physical examination).

IMPACT OF RESPONSE MODES ON HELP SEEKERS

The impact of helper responses on help seekers has critical implications for whether they continue helping interactions and benefit from them in the future. In formal therapy and brief counseling interviews, helper interpretation was a weak but significant predictor of helpfulness ratings. This effect is not powerful enough to be particularly useful for clinical practice. It seems that more focused research questions are needed, particularly those emphasizing the role of response modes in helping contexts, defined perhaps by factors such as the helping task (Rice & Greenberg, in press).

It also appears that in informal helping among couples, criticism (disagreement) has a negative impact on the help seeker, while empathy (accurate reflection) is perceived as helpful. These results have implications for marital therapy and relationship enhancement interventions.

The role of the helping context in determining the impact of response modes is underlined by research on medical interviews in which different sorts of patient satisfaction depended on the use of different response modes in different phases of the interview. More research of this sort is needed to overcome assumptions about the uniformity of the helping process (cf. Kiesler, 1966).

EFFECTS OF TRAINING ON RESPONSE MODE USE

Traditional clinical training such as is meted out to clinical psychology graduate students may not be an effective way of influencing their response mode use; instead, differences in mode seem to reflect (a) selection and self-definition and (b) focused training in the response modes.

The usefulness of focused training in the response modes is further demonstrated by the success of the automated SASHAtape package in teaching adults to broaden their communication styles. However, when a similar package was used with intimate couples, it was not effective, perhaps because the intervention was not strong enough to influence couples' deeply engrained communication habits.

IMPLICATIONS FOR CLINICAL PRACTICE

Systematic research on the response modes is in its infancy; at the same time, clinical practice is highly complex. Thus, it should not be surprising that the major conclusion that can be safely drawn from response mode research is mostly negative: *No helper (or client) response mode is clearly more helpful than any other mode.* Qualitative analyses of types of significant response modes are consistent with what most clinicians already know: The critical thing is not the type of intervention, but rather when it is uttered (context), and how well it is performed (quality). For example, qualitative analyses suggest that effective advisements are long, complex responses, bolstered by interpretations and disagreements with the client's current way of doing things and tempered by reassurance and self-disclosure; furthermore, they are embedded in complex intervention sequences in which they may have been foreshadowed by earlier, simpler advisements. Theoretical statements and training packages that state or imply that some response modes are per se superior to others overstate the facts. Timing and quality of performance are surely more important than mode.

This conclusion has a number of implications for clinical practice and training.

First, helpers should not be discouraged from using certain kinds of response modes. Research on response mode use patterns suggests that both professional and nonprofessional helpers respond in typical, perhaps stereotypical, ways. If that is the case, then it is possible that both kinds of helpers may be missing opportunities for enhancing significant change events using atypical forms of responding. Perhaps efforts should be made to help both professional and nonprofessional helpers break down narrow, stereotyped response patterns (cf. Goodman, 1979).

Second, helpers should be given instruction in or teach themselves how to determine what mode is most likely to be worthwhile in a given context. Helpers should evaluate the context in which they are about to respond, including the nature of the helping task (Rice & Greenberg, in press), the type of significant change event that is desired (e.g., Elliott & Feinstein, Note 8), the quality of the helping alliance (Luborsky, 1976), how the client has reponded to the mode in the past, and what the client is doing at the moment (Hill, Greenwald, Reed, Charles, O'Farrell, & Carter, 1981; Stiles & Sultan, 1979).

Third, helpers should attend to the skillful performance of each response mode. In the absence of an adequate knowledge base defining skillfulness (cf. Liston, Yager, & Strauss, 1981), this means that the helper will have to study the impact of specific interventions on the client, perhaps asking for direct feedback.

IMPLICATIONS FOR RESEARCH ON THE RESPONSE MODES

Despite the somewhat negative conclusions drawn above, it is our position that the response modes are an essential piece of the help-intended communication puzzle. A description of the helping process which omits them is either incomplete or has smuggled them in secretly (e.g., as behavioral descriptors of levels of empathy). Our point is that *the response modes form a necessary but not a sufficient condition for understanding the helping process.* As such, they provide a useful starting place for both training and research on help-intended communication. We recommend/predict that over the next 10 years researchers will build on the response modes to help them address vital questions about psychological helping. One such vital question concerns the characteristics of helpful and nonhelpful response modes (e.g., questions). Another vital question is the nature of the helper's contribution to significant change events in helping relationships. In this way, the response modes will play an important supportive role in the elucidation and refinement of basic change mechanisms in therapeutic approaches of proven effectiveness (e.g., cognitive therapy of depression).

ACKNOWLEDGMENTS

The authors thank Russell Lemle, Larry Feinstein, Clara Hill, and Debbie Borys for their assistance.

Reference Notes

1. Kagan, N, *Interpersonal process recall: A method of influencing human interaction.* Unpublished manuscript, 1975. (Available from author, 434 Erickson Hall, College of Education, Michigan State University, East Lansing, Michigan 48824.)
2. Elliott, R. *Helper Behavior Rating System* (1979 version). Unpublished rating manual, University of Toledo, Department of Psychology, 1979.
3. Barker, C. B., & Lemle, R. Help-intended responses used by intimate couples. In R. Elliott (Chair), *Recent research on helping communications.* Symposium presented at the meeting of the American Psychological Association, Los Angeles, August 1981.
4. Stiles, W. B. Verbal response mode correlates of session impact. In R. Elliott (Chair), *Recent research on helping communications.* Symposium presented at the meeting of the American Psychological Association, Los Angeles, August, 1981.
5. Premo, B. E., & Stiles, W. B. *Familiarity in verbal interactions of married couples and stranger dyads.* Paper presented at the meeting of the Midwestern Psychological Association, St. Louis, Mo., May 1980.
6. Stiles, W. B., Au, M. L., Martello, M. A., & Perlmutter, J. A. *Analysis of campaign oratory: Verbal response mode use in 1980 presidential primary speeches.* Paper presented at the meeting of the Midwestern Psychological Association, Detroit, May 1981.
7. Elliott, R., & Feinstein, L. *Helping intention rating procedure.* Unpublished manuscript, Department of Psychology, University of Toledo, 1978.
8. Elliott, R., & Feinstein, L. Cluster analysis of significantly helpful and nonhelpful response modes. In R. Elliott (Chair), *Recent research on helping communications.* Symposium presented at the meeting of the American Psychological Association, Los Angeles, August 1981.
9. Shapiro, D., Barkham, M., & Irving, L. *Helper behaviour rating manual.* Unpublished manuscript, University of Sheffield, England, MRC Social and Applied Psychology Unit, 1980.

References

Bales, R. F. *Interaction process analysis: A method for the study of small groups.* Reading, Mass.: Addison-Wesley, 1950.
Barker, C. B. The helping process in couples: Communication instruction and patterns of

informal help (Doctoral dissertation, University of California, Los Angeles, 1980). *Dissertation Abstracts International*, 1981, *41*, 3565B. (University Microfilms No. 81-2805)

Brunink, S. A., & Schroeder, H. E. Verbal therapeutic behavior of expert psychoanalytically oriented, gestalt, and behavior therapists. *Journal of Consulting and Clinical Psychology*, 1979, *47*, 567–574.

Burstein, B. The structure of helping language as an outcome of two communication skills training programs: Live vs. automated (Doctoral dissertation, University of California, Los Angeles, 1982). *Dissertation Abstracts International*, in press.

Cansler, D. C., & Stiles, W. B. Relative status and interpersonal presumptuousness. *Journal of Experimental Social Psychology*, 1981, *17*, 459–471.

Carkhuff, R. R. *Helping and human relations*. New York: Holt, 1969.

Danish, S. J., & Hauer, A. L. *Helping skills: A basic training program*. New York: Behavioral Publications, 1973.

Dixon, W. J., & Brown, M. D. (Eds.). *BMDP-79: Biomedical computer programs, P-series*. Berkeley: Univ. of California Press, 1979.

Dooley, D. Effects of response interaction training on the Group Assessment of Interpersonal Traits (Doctoral dissertation, University of California, Los Angeles, 1973). *Dissertation Abstracts International*, 1974, *34*, 3492B–3493B. (University Microfilms, No. 73-32058)

Elliott, R. How clients perceive helper behaviors. *Journal of Counseling Psychology*, 1979, *26*, 285–294.

Elliott, R. Interpersonal Process Recall (IPR) as a process research method. In L. Greenberg & W. Pinsoff (Eds.), *The psychotherapeutic process*. New York: Guilford Press, in press.

Elliott, R., Barker, C. B., Caskey, N., & Pistrang, N. Differential helpfulness of counselor verbal response modes. *Journal of Counseling Psychology*, in press.

Freud, S. [Recommendations to physicians practicing psycho-analysis.] In J. Strachey (Ed. and trans.), *The standard edition of the complete psychological works of Sigmund Freud* (Vol. 12). London: Hogarth Press, 1958. (Originally published, 1912.)

Goodman, G. *Companionship therapy: Studies in structured intimacy*. San Francisco: Jossey-Bass, 1972.

Goodman, G. *SASHAtapes: Self-led automated series on help-intended alternatives*. Los Angeles: UCLA Extension, Department of Human Development, 1979.

Goodman, G., & Dooley, D. A framework for help-intended communication. *Psychotherapy: Theory, Research and Practice*, 1976, *13*, 106–117.

Gottlieb, B. H. Lay influences on the utilization and provision of health services: A review. *Canadian Psychological Review*, 1976, *17*, 126–136.

Guerney, B. G., Jr. *Relationship enhancement: Skill-training programs for therapy, problem prevention, and enrichment*. San Francisco: Jossey-Bass, 1977.

Hill, C. E. Development of a counselor verbal response category system. *Journal of Counseling Psychology*, 1978, *25*, 461–468.

Hill, C. E., Charles, D., & Reed, K. G. A longitudinal analysis of changes in counseling skills during doctoral training in counseling psychology. *Journal of Counseling Psychology*, 1981, *28*, 428–436.

Hill, C. E., Greenwald, C. Reed, K. G., Charles, D., O'Farrell, M. K. & Carter, J. A. *Manual for counselor and client verbal response category systems*. Columbus, Ohio: Marathon Press, 1981.

Hill, C. E., Thames, T. B., & Rardin, D. K. Comparison of Rogers, Perls, and Ellis on the Hill Counselor Verbal Response Category System. *Journal of Counseling Psychology*, 1979, *26*, 198–203.

Ivey, A. E., & Gluckstern, N. B. *Basic influencing skills: Participant manual*. North Amherst, Mass.: Microtraining Associates, 1976.

Joanning, H., Brock, G. W., Avery, A. W., & Coufal, J. D. The educational approach to social skills training in marriage and family intervention. In W. T. Singleton, P. Spurgeon, & R. B. Stammers (Eds.), *The analysis of social skill*. New York: Plenum, 1980.

Kiesler, D. J. Some myths of psychotherapy research and the search for a paradigm. *Psychological Bulletin*, 1966, *65*, 110–136.

Klein, M. H., Mathieu, P. L., Gendlin, E. T., & Kiesler, D. J. *The experiencing scale: A research and training manual* (Vol. 1). Madison,Wis.: Wisconsin Psychiatric Institute, 1969.

Lemle, R. Sex role patterns of informal helping in intimate couples (Doctoral dissertation, State University of New York at Buffalo, 1980). *Dissertation Abstracts International*, 1980, *41*, 355B. (University Microfilms No. 80-16210)

Lieberman, M. A., Yalom, I. D., & Miles, M. D. *Encounter groups: First facts*. New York: Basic Books, 1973.

Liston, E. H., Yager, J., & Strauss, G. D. Assessment of psychotherapy skills: The problem of interrater agreement. *American Journal of Psychiatry*, 1981, *138*, 1069–1074.

Locke, H. J., & Wallace, K. M. Short marital–adjustment and prediction tests: Their reliability and validity. *Marriage and Family Living*, 1959, *21*, 251–255.

Luborsky, L. Helping alliances in psychotherapy. In J. L. Claghorn (Ed.), *Successful psychotherapy*. New York: Brunner/Mazel, 1976.

McDaniel, S. H., Stiles, W. B., & McGaughey, K. J. Correlations of male college students' verbal response mode use in psychotherapy with measures of psychological disturbance and psychotherapy outcome. *Journal of Consulting and Clinical Psychology*, 1981, *49*, 571–582.

Miller, S., Nunnally, E. W., & Wackman, D. B. Minnesota Couples Communication Program (MCCP): Premarital and marital groups. In D. H. L. Olson (Ed.), *Treating relationships*. Lake Mills, Iowa: Graphic, 1976.

Perls, F. S. *Gestalt therapy verbatim*. Lafayette, Calif.: Real People Press, 1969.

Reisman, J. M., & Yamokoski, T. Psychotherapy and friendship: An analysis of the communication of friends. *Journal of Counseling Psychology*, 1974, *21*, 269–273.

Rice, L. N., & Greenberg, L. (Eds.). *Change episodes*. New York: Guilford Press, in press.

Rice, L. N., & Wagstaff, A. K. Client voice quality and expressive style as indexes of productive psychotherapy. *Journal of Consulting Psychology*, 1967, *31*, 557–563.

Rogers, C. R. *Client-centered therapy*. Boston: Houghton, 1951.

Rogers, C. R., Gendlin, E. T., Kiesler, D. J., & Truax, C. B. (Eds.). *The therapeutic relationship and its impact*. Madison: Univ. of Wisconsin Press, 1967.

Russell, R. L., & Stiles, W. B. Categories for classifying language in psychotherapy. *Psychological Bulletin*, 1979, *86*, 404–419.

Searle, J. R. *Speech acts: An essay in the philosophy of language*. Cambridge: Cambridge Univ. Press, 1969.

Shiffman, S. M. The effects of graduate training in clinical psychology on performance in a psychotherapy analog (Doctoral dissertation, University of California, Los Angeles, 1981). *Dissertation Abstracts International*, 1981, *42*, 2084B–2085B. (University Microfilms No. 81-22837)

Snyder, W. U. An investigation of the nature of nondirective psychotherapy. *Journal of General Psychology*, 1945, *33*, 193–223.

Stiles, W. B. *Manual for a taxonomy of verbal response modes*. Chapel Hill: Institute for Research in Social Science, University of North Carolina at Chapel Hill, 1978.

Stiles, W. B. Verbal response modes and psychotherapeutic technique. *Psychiatry*, 1979, *42*, 49–62.

Stiles, W. B. Measurement of the impact of psychotherapy sessions. *Journal of Consulting and Clinical Psychology*, 1980, *48*, 176–185.

Stiles, W. B., McDaniel, S. H., & McGaughey, K. Verbal response mode correlates of experiencing. *Journal of Consulting and Clinical Psychology*, 1979, *47*, 795–797.

Stiles, W. B., Putnam, S. M., Wolf, M. H., & James, S. A. Interaction exchange structure and patient satisfaction with medical interview. *Medical Care*, 1979, *17*, 667–681. (a)

Stiles, W. B., Putnam, S. M., Wolf, M. H., & James, S. A. Verbal response mode profiles of patients and physicians in medical screening interviews. *Journal of Medical Education*, 1979, *54*, 81–89. (b)

Stiles, W. B., & Sultan, F. E. Verbal response mode use by clients in psychotherapy. *Journal of Consulting and Clinical Psychology*, 1979, *47*, 611–613.

Stiles, W. B., & White, M. L. Parent–child interaction in the laboratory: Effects of role, task, and child behavior pathology on verbal response mode use. *Journal of Abnormal Child Psychology*, 1981, *9*, 229–241.

Strupp, H. H. An objective comparison of Rogerian and psychoanalytic techniques. *Journal of Consulting Psychology*, 1955, *19*, 1–7.

Strupp, H. H., & Hadley, S. W. Specific versus nonspecific factors in psychotherapy: A controlled study of outcome. *Archives of General Psychiatry*, 1979, *36*, 1125–1136.

Taylor, R. H. A comparison of conceptual and behavioral formats for interpersonal training (Doctoral dissertation, University of California, Los Angeles, 1976). *Dissertation Abstracts International*, 1976, *36*, 5288B. (University Microfilms No. 76-9019)

Truax, C. B., & Mitchell, K. M. Research on certain therapist interpersonal skills in relation to process and outcome. In A. E. Bergin & S. L. Garfield (Eds.), *Handbook of psychotherapy and behavior change* (1st ed.). New York: Wiley, 1971.

Whalen, C. K., & Flowers, J. V. Effects of role and gender mix on verbal communication modes. *Journal of Counseling Psychology*, 1977, *24*, 281–287.

Witlin, B. A. A comparison of conceptual and experimental input patterns on the effects of interpersonal skills training (Doctoral dissertation, University of California, Los Angeles, 1974). *Dissertation Abstracts International*, 1974, *35*, 1931B. (University Microfilms No. 74-21,122)

Wolf, M. H., Putnam, S. M, James, S. A., & Stiles, W. B. Medical Interview Satisfaction Scale: Development of a scale to measure patient perceptions of physician behavior. *Journal of Behavioral Medicine*, 1978, *1*, 391–401.

chapter 16

Similarity between Clinician and Client: Its Influence on the Helping Relationship

STEPHEN I. ABRAMOWITZ
ALLEN BERGER
GIFFORD WEARY

Introduction

Increasing awareness that social processes are critical to the treatment of psychopathology has ushered in an era of social-psychological applications to psychotherapy. Conceptualizations having the widest range of explanatory convenience, such as the social behavior theories, have deservedly had far-ranging impact on clinical practice (O'Leary & Wilson, 1975). However, despite several noteworthy contributions (Brehm, 1976; Goldstein, 1971; Harvey & Weary, 1981; Johnson & Matross, 1977; Strong, 1978; Weary & Mirels, in press; Wills, 1978), the relevance of more specific social-psychological theories has generally been less well recognized. The aim of this chapter is to consider the question of therapist–patient similarity in relation to therapeutic process and outcome. We discuss various issues raised by attempting to match patients with their therapists on some relevant dimension, review social-psychological processes relevant to similarity effects, and consider pertinent findings from clinical research. In a final section, we discuss implications for theory, research, and practice.

Matching Paradigms for Psychotherapy

The various matching paradigms have always held a certain fascination for students of psychotherapy. If treatment success is indeed a function of therapist, technique, and patient variables (C. V. Abramowitz, S. I. Abramowitz, H. B. Roback, & C. Jackson, 1974), then the clinician theoretically could improve therapeutic outcome by optimizing the fit among the primary factors in the psychotherapeutic equation. In the prototypic matching design, certain patients are paired with certain therapists (across treatment approaches) or with certain treatment approaches (across therapists) to create one "favorably combined" and one "unfavorably combined" group (Berzins, 1977). Although matching has been attempted on a diverse assortment of demographic characteristics, values, personality styles, and cognitive variables, the underlying dimensions of similarity–dissimilarity and complementarity–noncomplementarity offer a heuristic schema for organizing this sprawling literature (Parloff, Waskow, & Wolfe, 1978).

SIMILARITY VERSUS COMPLEMENTARITY

Various self-psychological models of interpersonal attraction and influence suggest that therapist–patient similarity should facilitate positive treatment results (Johnson & Matross, 1977). As we shall explore later, similarity between therapist and patient is thought to enhance interpersonal attraction and thereby foster rapport, treatment persistence, and outcome. Enhancement of behavior change effects associated with similarity is typically expected when the focal variable reflects content on the relatively superficial level of personality, such as personal values or demographic variables that are correlated with those values. Matching to promote similarity usually occurs when the variable in question is symmetrical, in the sense that it has a meaningful conterpart in both dyadic participants (Berzins, 1977). Thus, religious or social values provide a basis for fostering similarity, but the therapist's professional background does not, since no substantive dimension exists for the patient.

In contrast, matching on stylistic variables, which we think reflect a deeper level of personality, rests on the assumption that complementarity (rather than similarity) will have therapeutically facilitative effects. Presumably, complementarity of underlying needs of therapist and patient produces rewards deriving from mutual gratifications, whereas noncomplementarity produces competition for satisfaction of the same needs. Matching to foster complementarity can logically proceed along dimensions that possess asymmetrical as well as symmetrical properties. One such continuum is internal versus external control of reinforcement. Lefcourt (1976) has observed that externally oriented beliefs often serve defensive functions, such as rationalization for failure and for dependent behavior. If endorsement of externality is associated with dependency needs, then these are likely to be better met in early sessions by a therapist who is relatively structured and thus offers complementarity. C. V. Abramowitz *et al.* (1974) indeed found that the success of directive versus nondirective forms of group therapy depended on clients' orientation toward internal or external control. Internally oriented persons improved more in the less directive therapy condition, whereas externally oriented persons derived greater benefit from the relatively directive approach to treatment.

VARIABLES AND MEASURES

Much of the groundbreaking work on the influence of values on psychotherapy must be credited to Goldstein (1960), who studied the fit between the therapist's and the patient's expectations about treatment. More recently, investigators have examined similarity phenomena in relation to values tapped by the Strong Vocational Interest Blank, Ways to Live Scale, Allport-Vernon Study of Values, and Optimal Personality Integration Scale (Pettit, Pettit, & Welkowitz, 1974). The intuitive appeal of pairing on primary demographic indicators of values such as social class (Lorion, 1974), race (Sattler, 1977), and sex (Davidson & Abramowitz, 1980) has been a noteworthy aspect of this literature. Researchers have looked at the impact of clinician–client racial similarity on the process and outcome of insight psychotherapy (Jones, 1978), the effect of congruence between therapist and patient social class on selection for treatment (Kandel, 1966), and same- versus opposite-sex pairing on judgment of diagnostic severity (S. I. Abramowitz & H. R. Herrera, 1981). By contrast, the variables of age and religion have received less attention (Bergin, 1980; Wadsworth & Checketts, 1980).

When the matching is to achieve complementarity on deeper, underlying dimensions, two classes of variables have typically been studied: personality and cognitive styles. Among the instruments that have frequently been used to assess therapist or patient personality are the Myers-Briggs Indicator of Jungian Types (extroversion–introversion, sensing–intuitive, thinking–feeling, and judgmental–perceiving), Fundamental Interpersonal Relations Orientation Scale (expressed–wanted inclusion, control, and affection), and various derivatives of the MMPI.[1, 2] There has also been interest in matching

---

[1] As Parloff *et al.* (1978) have noted, researchers have often been unclear about whether their assessment devices tap cognitive process, content, or structure. Moreover, virtually identical names have been given to seemingly different cognitive variables measured by different operations.

[2] No review of the personality matching literature would be complete without mention of the two-decade saga of the therapist A and B type variable. In 1960, Whitehorn and Betz observed that

on personal contructs as measured by Kelly's Role Construct Repertory Test (Landfield, 1971) and cognitive congruence as determined by scales adapted from the evaluative dimensions of the semantic differential (B. C. Edwards & J. W. Edgerly, 1970).

Similarity–Attraction Processes

Similarity effects and the processes that underlie them have received considerable attention from social psychologists working in both the laboratory and the field. In this section, we introduce some demonstrations of similarity phenomena and point out their relevance for clinical interactions. Psychological processes that have been advanced to explain those phenomena are then presented.

EMPIRICAL DEMONSTRATIONS

There is considerable evidence to support the notion that similarity enhances attraction, including correlational studies, controlled field studies, and experimental laboratory investigations (Byrne, 1971; Griffitt, 1974; Newcomb, 1956). As expressed by the Byrne-Nelson formula, the basic similarity–attraction principle is that liking for a stranger is a function of the proportion of similar attitudes held by that stranger. This formulation was subsequently refined to include the impact of evaluative feedback on attraction (Byrne & Rhamey, 1965).

A recent phenomenon derived from similarity–attraction principles and demonstrated in the laboratory is the assumed similarity or *false consensus* effect. This refers to a general tendency to view others' judgments and behavioral choices that are similar to one's own as relatively common and therefore appropriate (Ross, Greene, & House, 1977). A corresponding process, which has been observed among clinicians (Meehl, 1973), is to view alternative responses as uncommon and therefore deviant. As a consequence of the false consensus phenomenon, responses seen as different from those of the subject are, due to their presumed counternormativeness, viewed as more

---

therapists who tended to be successful with schizophrenic patients differed on a 23-item scale derived from the Strong Vocational Interest Blank from those who tended to be unsuccessful with them. The upshot was an interactional hypothesis that, based on an assumption of complementarity, predicted that schizophrenics improve more with A-therapists and neurotics improve more with B-therapists. Unfortunately, the extensive line of research stimulated by this promising beginning has yielded data that have been characterized as disappointing by a succession of reviewers (Parloff *et al.*, 1978).

revealing of underlying personality dispositions (Ross *et al.*, 1977). Such processes would appear to be consistent with Szasz's (1970) penetrating analysis of the mental health establishment as a norm-regulating institution. In a related vein, Goffman (1961) and Roth (1972) have brought into focus how the "good versus bad" implications of staff and mental patient roles accelerate the process of moral devaluation by reinforcing impressions of dissimilarity.

EXPLANATORY PSYCHOLOGICAL PROCESSES

We now turn to the basic psychological processes that have been advanced to explain the foregoing demonstrations of similarity and attraction phenomena. Although the brief comparative format in which the conceptual frameworks are presented tends to highlight points of departure rather than common ground, Byrne (1971) himself has observed that the different formulations are not necessarily mutually exclusive.

Reinforcement–Affect Approach

Newcomb (1956) proposed that interpersonal attraction is a function of the degree to which reciprocal rewards are present in the interaction. Dislike in this model derives from reciprocal punishments. This formulation was refined by Byrne, who suggested that attraction results from a process similar to classical conditioning; the occurrence of an interpersonal reward engenders positive affect that is directed toward the rewarding person, whereas punishment in an interpersonal circumstance elicits negative social affect (Byrne, 1971).

Cognitive Models

Cognitive models are based on the premise that people tend to prefer consistency over inconsistency (Festinger, 1957). The two major models with relevance for the similarity–interpersonal-attraction relationship are cognitive dissonance and balance theories. The former formulation, for example, suggests that when one individual confronts another with a dissimilar attitude, a state of cognitive dissonance is activated. Because cognitive consistency is the preferred psychological state, the individual will strive to maintain it by evaluating the dissimilar person as unattractive. Balance theory, originally discussed by Heider (1958) and elaborated by Newcomb (1968), makes several predictions for what happens in a dyad when attitudes or opinions about an issue are similar or agreed upon and when there is disagreement or dissimilarity. When two people like each other and they agree on an issue or when they dislike each other and they disagree on an issue, they are in what is referred to as a balanced state. By contrast, when dyadic participants like one another and they disagree about an issue or when they dislike each other but hold a similar opinion about an issue, they are said to be in an imbalanced state. Imbalanced configurations tend to shift toward balanced ones, in that unstable dyadic relationships exert a continuing pressure toward change until they become balanced (Newcomb, 1968; Sussman & Davis, 1975).

Personal Construct Theory

Kelly (1955) viewed all people as behaving analogously to a scientist, who understands the world by generating predictive hypotheses and testing them out. Central to his theory is the personal construct, the way in which a person understands two things as being alike and different from a third. Personal constructs are organized into a personal construct system that has a particular structure and content. As Landfield (1971) noted, knowledge of the structure, or the ways in which construct dimensions are related within the individual, enhances our appreciation for the meaning of the individual dimensions, their relative importance within the system, and the implications the use of one dimension may have for that or another dimension. Landfield (1971) proposed that some degree of commonality, or content overlap, in the construct systems of the therapist and client is crucial in the initial, rapport-building phase of the treatment. However, it is possible that some degree of structural dissimilarity is desirable to expose the patient to the alternative role perspectives offered by the therapist.

Interpersonal Theories

According to Sullivan's (1965) theorem of reciprocal emotions, the needs of the therapist and patient are gratified or frustrated to the degree that they are conjunctive (complementary) or disjunctive. Dyadic communication in psychotherapy thus becomes a function of the interactional situation as integrated by the prepotent needs of both participants. Leary (1957) and Carson (1969) attempted to systematize Sullivan's formulation by classifying predominating personal behaviors along two orthogonal bipolar factors: dominance–submission and love–hate. Dyadic interaction is presumed to be facilitated when one individual reciprocates another's affective orientation and complements the other with respect to dominance–submission. Schutz (1958) introduced the notion of interpersonal compatibility, which is a function of an individual's needs to express or receive inclusion, control, and affection. Three types of compatibility result from this schema. Reciprocal compatibility occurs when each individual's level of expressed behavior matches the other's level of wanted behavior across the three need areas. Originator compatibility refers to complementarity of who wants to originate (express) and who wants to receive. And finally, interchange compatibility depends on the degree of agreement in the perceived importance of a particular need. To illustrate, reciprocal compatibility would prevail when the amount of inclusion, control, and affection expressed by the therapist matched the amount desired by the patient, and vice versa.

Psychoanalytic Concepts

According to psychoanalytic principles of psychotherapeutic process, the patient and the therapist are inclined to see in each other the image of significant figures from their past (Greenson, 1967). Patients tend to view the therapist's attitudes and behaviors as reminiscent of those of their parents and other important authority figures, and react to those impressions with defensive maneuvers that reduced anxiety in the past. Furthermore, therapists tend to respond to the patient's help-seeking requests in ways similar to those in which they themselves were nurtured by their own parents, and deal ineffectively with material that activates their own unresolved conflicts. The patient's perceptual and response distortions of the therapist are referred to as transferences and said to be positive when they facilitate rapport and working through, and negative when they promote resistance. Correspondingly, the therapist's distortions of the patient are referred to as countertransferences, which can be roughly classified as chronic or acute (Reich, 1951). Chronic countertransference represents a habitual need that reflects the therapist's character structure and is therefore manifested with many patients. Acute countertransference is specific to certain material that is anxiety arousing for a particular therapist and varies in intensity depending on the extent to which the therapist identifies with the patient. One kind of acute countertransference reaction is the *negative fit* (Luborsky & Singer, Note 1), which occurs when the therapist actually responds in ways that fit the patient's negative preconceptions about important interpersonal relationships. Another variant is the *therapeutic misalliance* (Langs, 1975), which occurs when the therapist colludes with the patient not to explore a certain conflictual issue because the topic evokes the therapist's anxiety. Since transference and countertransference processes are believed to be affected by the degree to which each participant in the therapeutic interaction does or does not identify with the other, the potential for positive similarity effects is considerable. Counterexamples can be noted, however. A therapist with a working-class background might be expected to be especially tolerant of the reputed help-seeking preferences of lower-class patients for advice giving, medication, and direct problem resolution (Goldstein, 1960). Paradoxically, our clinical experience suggests that it is often therapists of working-class parents who, uncomfortable with the recollections of their disadvantaged background that a lower-class patient conjures up, insist that patients on public assistance are "poor candidates" for psychotherapy.

Similarity and Complementarity Effects in the Clinic

CLINICAL RESEARCH STRATEGIES

Within the context provided by the foregoing conceptual orientations, we now turn to the findings of studies that have attempted to demonstrate similarity phenomena in the clinic. The impetus for the study of similarity effects in clinical settings was Byrne's (1971) attraction paradigm, which is grounded in the methodological traditions of experimental social psychology. In fact, aspects of Byrne's procedures can be traced to Asch's (1946) impression-formation paradigm, in which observers render evaluations of observeds described identically except for the manipulated attribution (e.g., warm-cold). In the popular clinical judgment analogue, the observed's personality description and attribution are replaced with the patient's case materials and class, race or sex. For example, S. I. Abramowitz, C. V. Abramowitz, C. Jackson, and B. Gomes (1973) had counselors and clinicians evaluate the case report of a student seeking psychological assistance and identified as either male or female and either politically left or right. The rater's judgments were expected to reflect their perception of the differential sex-role appropriateness of males and females who engage in left or right political activity.

Byrne's (1971) similarity and attraction model goes a step further by assessing similarity directly rather than merely assuming that observers identify more with persons who appear to share their own values. Thus, Goldstein (1971) randomly assigned prison inmates to four conditions varying in both alcoholism relevance and apparent therapist–subject agreement, or to a control group. Subjects then viewed a 15-min videotape of a psychotherapy session and rated its attractiveness. The combination of random assignment to conditions and experimenter control over the attributional manipulation gives the clinical analogue ample assurance of internal validity.

The remoteness of the typical analogue situation from the real-life arena has spurred the development of the clinical field experiment, in which the similarity manipulation occurs in a modified but genuine clinical context. Thus, Goldstein (1971) randomly assigned clients at a university counseling center to one of three conditions varying in the patients' perceived similarity to their therapist-to-be. Clients in the three groups were informed that they agreed with their prospective therapist on different proportions of the items on a student opinion scale (actually the MMPI F Scale) they had just completed—88% in the high-similarity condition, 50% in the moderate-similarity condition and 12% in the low-similarity condition. Each subject then participated in an initial counseling interview and completed evaluation measures.

It soon became apparent that experimenter-induced similarity effects obtained in interview analogues often were not demonstrable within the natural setting. In coming to grips with his own failures to replicate, Goldstein (1971) conjectured that any enhancement derived from contrived matching on a narrow and not necessarily salient attitudinal dimension might well be offset by the new interpersonal information exchanged in the first few therapy sessions. In a study in which patient–therapist similarity was determined by naturally occurring clinic assignment procedures, D. W. Edwards, L. R. Greene, S. I. Abramowitz, and C. V. Davidson (1979) examined whether patients' social class interacted with therapists' status-relevant characteristics in determining the effectiveness of outpatient treatment offered within the context of an urban community mental health center. Unfortunately, the strength of designs adapted from the experiment is the weakness of the naturalistic motif—the uncertainty that the results obtained can, in the absence of random assignment, be attributed to the similarity inferred from the focal therapist and patient characteristics.

The archival search, a popular variant of the naturalistic approach, deserves special mention. In this clinical derivative of the unobtrusive model (Webb, Campbell, Schwartz, & Sechrest, 1966), the researcher retrieves the data, usually in the form of demographic and treatment-relevant information, from actual institutional archives. This strategy enjoys the twin advantage of maximizing ecological validity while neatly circumventing the problem of social desirability responding by professionals, who could not have known that their clinical notes would become the subject of study. Archival data are nonetheless vulnerable to the notorious unreliability of institutional records, in addition to the aforementioned constraints on internal validity common to all naturalistic methods. However, by using patients' self-reports of their own symptomatology at intake as a statistical control, investigators have been able to rule out such potential threats to the internal validity of their field studies of similarity effects (S. I. Abramowitz & H. R. Herrera, 1981).

THERAPIST–PATIENT EXPECTATIONS

Clinical wisdom teaches that congruence in the therapist's and the patient's expectations about treatment should promote rapport, patient persistence, and outcome itself (Goldstein, 1960). And indeed, similarity of clinician–client expectations has consistently been shown to be related to a lower dropout rate. According to Parloff *et al.* (1978), however, clinician–client congruence in expectations early in therapy has not been a reliable antecedent of ultimate outcome. A similar conclusion was reached by Duckro, Beal, and George (1979), who nonetheless reviewed several findings suggesting that increasing similarity in therapist–patient expectations over the course of treatment facilitates therapeutic progress. The emergence of gradual convergence between clinician and client as a more stable correlate of favorable outcome than initial similarity is a phenomenon to which we will have numerous occasions to return in this section.

The promising results yielded by studies of patients who have been explicitly prepared for psychotherapy nonetheless suggest that outcome may well be enhanced by systematic efforts to bring prospective patients' initial conception of their role in line with their respective treatment roles. The study by Jacobs, Charles, Jacobs, Weinstein, and Mann (1972) is illustrative. Subjects included lower-income patients and psychiatric residents, who underwent a role induction orientation or an orientation from the chief resident that focused on the difficulties some people experience in exploring their feelings, accepting psychological explanations of their problems, and tolerating delays in symptom relief. The results were impressive. The success level attained by the fully prepared dyads was substantially higher than that attained by the dyads in which only one participant had been exposed to the preparation regimen and almost twice as high as that attained by the dyads in which neither participant had been prepared.

As a group, the preparation studies suggest that the creation of expectational congruence between therapist and client appears not only to deter premature termination, but also to facilitate improvement (Parloff *et al.*, 1978). Socialization into psychotherapy has been demonstrated to be especially helpful for the less psychologically sophisticated patient, who is usually of lower social class. Such evidence indicates the presence of an interaction whereby the degree of impact of therapist–patient congruence in expectations depends on the patient's social status (Heitler, 1976; Lorion, 1974). Efforts aimed at bringing the expectations and techniques of the middle-class therapist in line with the preferences of the lower-class patient are as yet rare (Goldstein, 1973), but they would appear to hold promise for further enhancement of the working alliance.

DEMOGRAPHIC CHARACTERISTICS

As social markers providing indirect cues to the patient's and the therapist's values, demographic characteristics have occupied the attention of a large number of researchers committed to priming similarity via matching. This literature was given impetus by the influential work of Hollingshead and Redlich (1958) on the unequal distribution of mental illness across the social classes and by the burgeoning community mental health movement. Thus, investigative energy was initially focused on the effectiveness with lower-class patients of a treatment whose origins were distinctly Victorian and whose practitioners were overwhelmingly middle-class. As the civil rights movement gathered momentum and investigators became sensitized to the inevitable confound of social position with race, concern shifted to cross-racial assess-ment and treatment dyads. The feminist movement subsequently provided critiques and reformulations that became more grist for the empirical politics of psychotherapy.

Social Class

The results of both analogue and field studies have consistently indicated that lower-class patients are less likely to be accepted for treatment, less likely to be given intensive psychotherapy, and more likely to terminate therapy prematurely (Lorion, 1974; Parloff *et al.*, 1978). Thus, Rosenthal and Frank (1958) found through a search of outpatient records that clinicians were more likely to refer to therapy persons most similar to themselves, such as middle-income rather than lower-income patients. Kandel (1966) conducted a related study in which the clinician's socioeconomic background was assessed directly. Kandel found that psychiatric residents of lower-class origin elected to see roughly equal proportions of their middle-class and lower-class patients in therapy, whereas therapists with middle-class family backgrounds under-took treatment with a greater proportion of their middle-class than their lower-class patients.

Naturalistic studies have consistently confirmed the earlier finding of an overrepresentation of lower-class individuals among those diagnosed as mentally ill. Moreover, clinical analogues have typically shown that stimulus patients receive a more severe psychiatric evaluation when they are believed to be lower-class rather than middle-class (C. V. Abramowitz & P. R. Dokecki, 1977). Such data are consistent with field evidence of a correlation between lower socioeconomic status and clinical judgments of severity of disturbance as well as with the interpretation that some portion of the overrepresentation of lower-class individuals among those diagnosed as mentally ill results from labeling bias. However, as has been pointed out elsewhere (C. V. Abramowitz & P. R. Dokecki, 1977), it can be argued that the devaluation of stimulus persons designated as lower-class reflects effective cue utilization rather than bias per se. For example, clinicians who factor into their prognostic equation the likelihood that the lower-class patient will have to contend with poorer nutrition and a less enriching psychosocial environment might well be regarded as astute rather than prejudiced. To reduce the credibility of this alternative explanation, investigators have been counseled to block therapists on a values-related characteristic unlikely to be associated with expertise, such as authoritarianism. They can then demonstrate that the labeling effect is not equivalent in magnitude across the therapist groups (C. V. Abramowitz & P. R. Dokecki, 1977).

Race

The notion that black patients are inevitably shortchanged in therapy with whites is a "heartpothesis" rooted in 200 years of cross-generational wisdom (S.

I. Abramowitz, 1978). Unfortunately, the research literature does not render a simple verdict. The conclusions reached by reviewers have run the gamut from those that implicate white practitioners to those that in effect exonerate them. Perhaps not surprisingly, the direction of the verdict delivered has seemed to vary with the race of the reviewer (S. I. Abramowitz & J. Murray, in press). Thus, Siegel (1974), C. V. Abramowitz and P. R. Dokecki (1977) and Sattler (1977), all white, inferred that the overall evidence does not offer convincing support for the hypothesis of cross-racial bias. However, the most influential black reviewers have interpreted essentially the same data as confirmatory (Griffith, 1977; Griffith & Jones, 1979).

Dividing the findings according to method, we find that archival and other naturalistic designs have in the main suggested that black patients are more likely to drop out of treatment, less likely to be referred for individual psychotherapy, more likely to receive a shorter psychiatric hospitalization, and more reluctant to self-disclose in early sessions with a white therapist (S. I. Abramowitz & J. Murray, in press; Griffith & Jones, 1979; Parloff et al., 1978). In a well-executed field study, Jones (1978) examined the treatment records of matched black and white neurotic females seen by a black or a white therapist. The rates of success achieved with the insight-oriented individual therapy were equivalent regardless of racial match, but noteworthy differences among the dyads emerged along several dimensions of therapeutic process, such as the client's erotic feelings.

By contrast, clinical analogues have turned up relatively meager evidence of cross-racial effects (C. V. Abramowitz & P. R. Dokecki, 1977; Parloff et al., 1978; Sattler, 1977) and even a smattering of seemingly "problack" effects (S. I. Abramowitz & J. Murray, 1981). In the event of such a discrepancy across methods, the internal validity of the experimentally based analogue is traditionally accorded priority over the more externally valid but correlational and confounded field investigation. A persuasive case can be made, however, that professional sensitization to the racial bias analogue and other corrosive factors compromised the integrity of the analogue and tilted the odds against confirmation of cross-racial bias formulations (S. I. Abramowitz & J. Murray, 1981).

Sex

In reviewing the results of studies matching therapists and patients on the basis of sex, it is useful to consider the heated debate over sex bias in clinical judgment separately from the broader issues of process and outcome. Data relevant to the sex bias question have been conspicuously contradictory, inviting gerrymandered interpretations from both political directions. For example, a report prepared by the American Psychological Association Task Force on Sex Bias and Sex-Role Stereotyping in Psychotherapeutic Practice (1975) not only highlighted dramatic but probably unrepresentative anecdotal accounts, but also managed to omit a disproportionate number of the findings inconsistent with sex bias formulations. Stricker (1977) astutely pointed out these limitations of the report but then apparently succumbed to his own proestablishment allegiances by neglecting to mention several worthy studies that yielded results supportive of feminist exhortations to match on sex.

More recently, reviewers have attempted to resolve this dispute by examining the evidence according to method. Some consensus has been reached that the data returned by clinical analogues have been largely disconfirmatory (Davidson & Abramowitz, 1980; Smith, 1980). However, a significant number of the relatively uncontrolled but ecologically valid field studies have generated findings compatible with the position that female patients are dealt with differently by male and female therapists (Davidson & Abramowitz, 1980). In deciding whether the evidence does or does not support the contention of sex-biased clinical inference, observers must therefore weigh the relative merits of the analogue's internal validity, however compromised, against the external validity of the naturalistic study, however confounded.

In an investigation alluded to earlier, S. I. Abramowitz and H. R. Herrera (1981) attempted to determine whether sex effects on clinical judgment obtained in the field could survive a control for the potential confound represented by sex-differential levels of maladjustment at intake. Ratings of patients by medical students undergoing their psychiatric rotation made using the Hopkins Psychiatric Rating Scale were employed as the judgment criteria and the self-reports of patients on the parallel Hopkins Symptom Checklist were employed as the post hoc statistical control. An absence of interactions between therapist and patient sex disconfirmed the notion that female patients are judged especially harshly by (inexperienced) male practitioners. However, several main effects of both therapist and patient sex survived the partialling out of "true" sex differences in presenting symptom complaints. This would appear to suggest that some portion of the sex differences in judgmental severity turned up in previous field studies should not be dismissed as an artifact of biased subsample recruitment.

With respect to the more far-ranging questions of process and outcome, the results suggest that the sex of the therapist and the sex of the patient are both salient parameters but often not in ways consistent with similarity notions. Cartwright and Lerner (1963) reported that the effects of matching on the basis of sex depended on the therapist's experience. Same-sex pairs were associated with greater improvement when the therapist was relatively experienced, whereas opposite-sex pairs were associated with greater improvement when the therapist was inexperienced. Orlinsky and Howard (1976) found that female outpatients of female therapists felt more satisfied with therapy and had had more "helpful experiences" than female outpatients of male therapists. However, they also determined that the facilitative effects of the female–female pairing were for the most part limited to younger, single, and depressed patients. Finally, Kirshner, Genack, and Hauser (1978) found that

97 female patients at a university health service were more responsive to treatment than their 92 male counterparts regardless of the therapist's sex and that female therapists had more satisfied patients than their male colleagues regardless of the patient's sex. However, evidence also showed that female patients paired with a senior female therapist expressed greater satisfaction and manifested greater improvement than did either female patients paired with a senior male therapist or male patients paired with a senior therapist irrespective of sex.

VALUES

Although the number of studies directed at the therapist's and the patient's values has not been large in relation to the significance of the question, the results from matching studies have been straightforward. Patients appear to adopt their therapist's values and, the more they do, the more they improve (Beutler, 1981). Moreover, although neither similarity nor dissimilarity has been clearly predictive of outcome, the bulk of the evidence suggests that initial dissimilarity rather than similarity is related to convergence. To the extent that this evidence is valid, it would appear to necessitate a reformulation of the way in which similarity is thought to influence psychotherapeutic processes. Thus, although the data thus far fail to establish initial similarity in values as a determinant of either treatment process or outcome, they suggest that the social learning mechanisms that presumably foster similarity over the course of treatment (i.e., therapist–patient convergence) play an important role in mediating outcome (Beutler, 1981). This reconceptualization of similarity as a mediator rather than as an independent variable in the psychotherapeutic equation would appear to highlight therapists' own coping resources and their ability to impart adaptive strategies to others as primary curative factors.

The often-cited findings of Pettit *et al.* (1974) would appear to have especially unfavorable treatment implications for the notion of initial similarity as a critical treatment parameter. Lower-income patients who were more submissive to authority were determined to be less likely to drop out of treatment when matched with therapists high in independence, that is, when matched in terms of complementarity rather than similarity of values. Such data would seem to underscore the difficulties encountered in classifying a particular characteristic as a "surface" belief or a "deeper" need and thus in determining whether similarity or complementarity should be the basis for the match.

The weight of the evidence reviewed by Beutler (1981) also raises serious questions about the wisdom of generalizing from findings originally based on laboratory-induced perceptions of similarity to their naturally occurring counterparts in the clinic. Perceptions of attitudinal similarity that are created by experimental manipulation cannot, by definition, be correlated with underlying needs, whereas such naturally occurring perceptions may reflect a host of needs, processes, and defenses. We can only echo Beutler (1981) in encouraging research that looks at the convergence–improvement relationship as a function of initial similarity–dissimilarity and in considering that the widely held assumption of initial similarity as necessarily more facilitative than dissimilarity may have been oversimplified. Moreover, it has become apparent that it is necessary to distinguish between those dimensions that promote identification and are candidates for similarity matching and those that provide a contrast schema against which to reassess conflicts and hence are candidates for dissimilarity matching.

To the extent that we can relinquish our insistence that beliefs are necessarily superficial in favor of the notion that they often provide clues to deeper personality processes, we can close on a more positive note. Considerable evidence has accumulated that externally oriented and internally oriented patients appear to prefer and to benefit more from directive and nondirective forms of group therapy, respectively. These findings with locus of control beliefs recall the negative findings of Pettit *et al.* (1974) regarding similarity and foreshadow the sweeping conclusion drawn from the Indiana Personality Matching Project (Berzins, 1977). Persons who approach treatment passively appear to fare better with a dominant–controlling therapist than with a more passive–following therapist.

PERSONALITY STYLES

Empirical efforts to match patients and therapists on the basis of personality characteristics fall into four general categories: the early studies of matching with standardized, omnibus measures of personality; later, more complex attempts to match on multiple personality attributes; the data on therapist–patient personality convergence; and the extensive program of research undertaken to determine if A-Type and B-Type therapists are differentially effective with schizophrenic and neurotic patients.

As Berzins (1977) and Parloff *et al.* (1978) point out, much of the initial matching research carried out with the MMPI, the Myers-Briggs Type Indicator, and the Fundamental Interpersonal Relations Orientation Scale (FIRO-B) has not been replicated. Although the FIRO-B has generated fewer matching studies than either of the foregoing instruments, it has yielded somewhat more consistent results. Sapolsky (1965) reported an association between supervisors' ratings of improvement and overall dyadic compatibility of psychiatric residents with their female patients. Mendelsohn and Rankin (1969) were unable to replicate this finding in general, but they did observe that, for the dyads involving female clients, 5 of the 10 compatibility scores were related to outcome.

The greater sophistication of matching efforts predicated on an array of personality predictors generated by multiple assessment devices deserves special mention. Dougherty (1976) paired patients with therapists on 11 variables obtained from five psychometric indices including the MMPI and FIRO-B. After cross-validating several predictive equations, he experimentally tested their clinical utility on (a) therapist–patient dyads expected to manifest either optimal or minimal gain, and (b) appropriate control dyads. The results indicated that the regression equations were moderately successful in predicting therapeutic responsiveness. Berzins' (1977) Indiana Matching Project represents the most comprehensive effort at systematic personality matching to date. Patient criteria included four interpersonal roles (avoidance of others, turning against self, dependency, and turning toward others and self), and clinician criteria included factor–analyzed responses to the Personality Research Form. Several hundred college clinic patients were randomly assigned to the 10 project therapists. Overall, better outcome was observed for pairs that maximized therapist–patient need complementarity. Dominant–directive therapists were particularly successful with passive–submissive patients.

Returning to Beutler's (1981) analysis of convergence research, the somewhat thinner evidential base with respect to personality matching nonetheless prompts the same inferences suggested by the values-matching studies. Personality convergence during treatment has tended to correlate with improvement and initial dissimilarity has tended to correlate with convergence. Again, no consistent relationship emerged between initial similarity–dissimilarity and outcome.

COGNITIVE VARIABLES

In examining some representative studies in which an effort was made to match therapists and patients along a cognitive dimension, we find ourselves confronted with many of the conceptual issues that emerged from the reviews of the evidence relating to values and personality. Two investigations indeed support the notion that initial cognitive similarity is associated with therapeutic gain. Carr (1970) reported that compatibility between patients and their therapist in terms of level of conceptual differentiation predicted positive treatment results. Using a different cognitive measure, McLachlan (1972) likewise demonstrated that patients who were initially more congruent with their therapist in regard to conceptual level reported greater improvement than patients in the incongruent dyads.

An impressive study by Landfield (1971) yielded counterintuitive results, however. As the reader may recall from our earlier discussion of personal construct theory, the commonality corollary predicts that initial similarity in the content of the two therapy participants' personal constructs is conducive to the flow of communication and presumably to the building of rapport. The results nonetheless indicated that treatment was more beneficial when the content of the patient's and the therapist's constructs was dissimilar and when the constructs tended to converge over the course of therapy. In addition, improvement was greater when patients shifted their self-conceptions toward the therapist's ideal self, yet another illustration of the convergence phenomenon. Paradoxically, initial content similarity was associated with negative therapist evaluations of the patient.

Parloff *et al.* (1978) attempt to reconcile these seemingly disparate findings by drawing a distinction between the different cognitive variables studied. For example, Carr's (1970) differentiation and McLachlan's (1972) conceptual level can be viewed as criteria of cognitive complexity, whereas Landfield's (1971) construct content is clearly a content index. Consistent with Parloff *et al.* (1978), it may be that similarity in the complexity of cognitive structure facilitates communication and that dissimilarity in cognitive content creates a pressure for therapeutic change.

Conclusions and Recommendations for Research and Practice

The reader is now familiar with the rationale for the matching paradigm in psychotherapy, the seminal laboratory evidence for similarity and attraction effects, the psychological processes believed to be associated with them, and the degree to which they have been demonstrated within the clinical setting. In this closing section, we draw some tentative conclusions and make some initial recommendations concerning conceptual issues, research, and practice.

THEORETICAL CONSIDERATIONS

This chapter underscores the complexity of the issues raised by the matching paradigm in psychotherapy and the need for conceptual refinements to accommodate the empirical returns to date. It seems clear that a model whose base is the "proportion of similar attitudes" alone is insufficient. As Goldstein (1971) conceded, it may be unrealistic to expect similarity effects to generalize to the more complex natural setting without taking into account the location and function of the focal dimension within the observer's (i.e., patient's) personality system. How salient, for example, is the focal dimension to the patient? What is the dimension's "breadth" and how will the perception of similarity in relation to it reverberate to other realms of the personality? Considerable conceptual and interpretive clarity appears to be gained by shifting from the notion of initial similarity as proposed by Byrne (1971) to one of developing similarity, or convergence, as restated by Beutler (1981). The cumulative findings in the realms of expectations, values, personality, and cognition appear to suggest that, regardless of initial similarity, successful patients are more likely to have adopted their therapist's personal qualities. To the extent that this reformulation of similarity as a mediating rather than initial source of outcome variance is borne out by further research, it would seem to underscore the curative role of learning mechanisms and therapists' ability to impart their own coping skills to their patients.

An especially difficult hurdle for observers to overcome remains that of dimensional "depth." Some workers prefer to conceive of beliefs (such as those involving external control) as attributes in and of themselves that exist independently of any underlying personality processes. Others, however, view such beliefs as mere manifestations of underlying needs (e.g., dependency), which are gratified through interactions with persons having complementary rather than similar needs (e.g., dominance). To the extent that the latter is the case (and the clinical research described in this chapter suggests that it well may be), a serious question is raised about the justifiability of generalizing to clinical interactions from laboratory inductions of perceived similarity, which are likely to be independent of the more enduring facets of the subject's personality. In genuine interpersonal encounters, of course, beliefs and values develop over extended periods of time and are organized within an elaborate network of attributions. Laboratory inductions of similarity are thus unlikely to have the same repercussions throughout the personality system.

The assumption of the unidimensionality of impressions of similarity or complementarity can likewise be challenged. As patients become better acquainted with their therapist over the course of treatment, they are likely to become better able to differentiate those attributes that are similar to their own from those that appear to be dissimilar. Psychotherapy researchers, however, still seem reluctant to abandon the intuitive comfort of the original similarity and attraction model. Until we move toward more differential conceptions, we are likely to remain unable to predict when and which kinds of similarities foster identification and enhancement, which and what kinds of dissimilarities serve as blueprints for change, and when convergence phenomena will occur.

RESEARCH

Methodological prescriptions follow largely from the foregoing conceptual considerations. First and foremost, operationalization of similarity should reflect the shift toward greater specification and differentiation at the conceptual level, with measures chosen to lend credibility to claims for breadth and depth. Whenever feasible, efforts should be made to assess the salience to the client of the focal dimension, and its location within the personality system. Manipulation checks (clinical analogue) or process assessments (prospective field study) are desirable to ascertain that, whether by induction or natural occurrence, subjects in the "matched" condition perceive more similarity (or complementary need gratification) than their counterparts in the "unmatched" condition. Such procedures will loom particularly important in those more sophisticated studies in which similarity is intended in some spheres and dissimilarity is intended in others.

More generally, researchers who choose the analogue approach need to concern themselves with the credibility of the stimulus manipulation, as increasing numbers of professionals and trainees become sensitized to the investigative interest in the role of values in psychotherapy. Within the limitations of the modality, such workers would do well to maximize external validity by recruiting experienced clinicians and genuine help seekers, creating a number of representative clinical vignettes, and using rating scales with which clinicians are well acquainted (S. I. Abramowitz & J. Murray, in press; C. V. Davidson & S. I. Abramowitz, 1980). As noted previously, devotees of field research must confront the array of potential confounds introduced by nonrandom assignment of patients to conditions. Proper precautions must be taken to reduce the likelihood that any differences obtained can be explained away as an artifact of selection bias rather than attributed to similarity effects. Given the frequent inability to replicate promising early findings in this area, the call by Parloff *et al.* (1978) for more prospective naturalistic studies in which the attitudinally similar and dissimilar dyads are created before treatment actually begins, rather than recreated on a post hoc basis, seems especially well taken.

We have three specific recommendations for research directions. We second Beutler's (in press) suggestion regarding the need for interactional investigations that examine convergence–improvement effects as a direct function of similarity–dissimilarity. Parallel investigations in which therapeutic orientation is looked at as a moderator of convergence also seem worthwhile. Since treatment approaches tend to vary along a continuum of directiveness, and convergence implies the patient's adoption of the therapist's values, it would be important to know whether more directive modalities (or therapists) promote convergence. And last, we would encourage colleagues to transcend the sensitive issues surrounding therapist–patient matching based on age and religion and fill the empirical gaps in those areas (Bergin, 1980).

PRACTICE

Although recent years have witnessed an overdue sensitivity on the part of practitioners to the salience of race and sex in the face-to-face encounter, the data serve as a reminder that lower-class individuals often seem not to receive a fair shake in the mental health system. In particular, the cumulative evidence suggests the desirability of more than the usual vigilance and restraint in psychiatric labeling and of introducing lower-class patients to the middle-class etiquette of psychotherapy by means of a brief preparation program.

The results of several independent studies, carried out by different investigators using different concepts and measures, converge to suggest that passive–dependent patients do especially well with dominant–controlling therapists. Although one might argue from a clinical standpoint that such need complementarity would not seem to allow for the eventual "weaning" of the patient from the therapist, this concern has not been borne out by the data. In fact, it is noteworthy that, bearing in mind the research limitations and inconsistencies noted above, the evidence thus far suggests that initial complementarity is more facilitative then initial similarity. The preponderance of the evidence further suggests that, regardless of initial similarity, convergence with respect to increasing attitudinal similarity between therapist and patient over the course of treatment is associated with greater improvement. Taken together, such findings compel clinicians to abstain from the temptation to match on the intuitively appealing basis of initial similarity and to focus instead on their ability to foster the patient's acquisition of the adaptive coping strategies represented within their own cognitive and behavioral repertoires. Although the loss of the intuitively comfortable notion of initial similarity and therapeutic attraction will no doubt prove difficult to grieve, many will appreciate their liberation from the dictum that to accept dissimilar patients is necessarily to shortchange them.

Reference Note

1. Luborsky, L. B., & Singer, B. *The fit of therapists' behavior into patients' negative expectations: A study of transference–countertransference contagion.* Unpublished manuscript, University of Pennsylvania School of Medicine, 1974.

References

Abramowitz, C. V., Abramowitz, S. I., Roback, H. B., & Jackson, C. Differential effectiveness of directive versus nondirective group therapy as a function of client interal–external control. *Journal of Consulting and Clinical Psychology*, 1974, *42*, 849–853.

Abramowitz, C. V., & Dokecki, P. R. The politics of clinical judgment: Early empirical returns. *Psychological Bulletin*, 1977, *84*, 460–476.

Abramowitz, S. I. Splitting data from theory on the black patient–white therapist relationship. *American Psychologist*, 1978, *33*, 957–958.

Abramowitz, S. I., Abramowitz, C. V., Jackson, C., & Gomes, B. The politics of clinical judgment: What nonliberal examiners infer about women who don't stifle themselves. *Journal of Consulting and Clinical Psychology*, 1973, *41*, 385–391.

Abramowitz, S. I., & Herrera, H. R. On controlling for patient psychopathology in naturalistic studies of sex bias: A methodological demonstration. *Journal of Consulting and Clinical Psychology*, 1981, *49*, 597–603.

Abramowitz, S. I., & Murray, J. Race effects in psychotherapy. In J. Murray & P. R. Abramson (Eds.), *Bias in psychotherapy*. Berkeley: Univ. of California Press, in press.

American Psychological Association. Task Force on Sex Bias and Sex-Role Stereotyping in Psychotherapeutic Practice. Report of the task force on sex bias and sex-role stereotyping in psychotherapeutic practice. *American Psychologist*, 1975, *4*, 1169–1175.

Asch, S. E. Forming impressions of personality. *Journal of Abnormal and Social Psychology*, 1946, *41*, 258–290.

Baker, E. K. The relationship between locus of control and psychotherapy: A review of the literature. *Psychotherapy: Theory, Research and Practice*, 1979, *16*, 351–362.

Bergin, A. E. Psychotherapy and religious values. *Journal of Consulting and Clinical Psychology*, 1980, *48*, 95–105.

Berzins, J. I. Therapist–patient matching. In A. S. Gurman & A. M. Razin (Eds.), *Effective psychotherapy: A handbook of research*. New York: Pergamon, 1977.

Beutler, L. E. Convergence in counseling and psychotherapy: A new look. *Clinical Psychology Review*, 1981, *1*, 79–101.

Brehm, S. S. *The application of social psychology to clinical practice*. New York: Wiley, 1976.

Byrne, D. *The attraction paradigm*. New York: Academic Press, 1971.

Byrne, D., & Rhamey, R. Magnitude of positive and negative reinforcements as a determinant of attraction. *Journal of Personality and Social Psychology*, 1965, *2*, 884–889.

Carr, J. E. Differentiation similarity of patient and therapist and the outcome of psychotherapy. *Journal of Abnormal Psychology*, 1970, *76*, 361–369.

Carson, R. C. *Interaction concepts of personality*. Chicago: Aldine, 1969.

Cartwright, R. D., & Lerner, B. Empathy, need to change, and improvement in psychotherapy. *Journal of Consulting Psychology*, 1963, *27*, 138–144.

Davidson, C. V., & Abramowitz, S. I. Sex bias in clinical judgment: Later empirical returns. *Psychology of Women Quarterly*, 1980, *4*, 377–395.

Dougherty, F. E. Patient–therapist matching for prediction of optimal and minimal therapeutic outcome. *Journal of Consulting and Clinical Psychology*, 1976, *44*, 889–897.

Duckro, P., Beal, D., & George, C. Research on the effects of disconfirmed client role expectations in psychotherapy. *Psychological Bulletin*, 1979, *86*, 260–275.

Edwards, B. C., & Edgerly, J. W. Effects of counselor–client congruence on counseling outcome in brief counseling. *Journal of Counseling Psychology*, 1970, *17*, 313–318.

Edwards, D. W., Greene, L. R., Abramowitz, S. I., & Davidson, C. V. National health insurance, psychotherapy and the poor. *American Psychologist*, 1979, *34*, 411–419.

Festinger, L. *A theory of cognitive dissonance*. Stanford, Calif.: Stanford Univ. Press, 1957.

Goffman, E. *Asylums*. Garden City, N.Y.: Anchor Books, 1961.

Goldstein, A. P. Therapist and client expectation of personality change in psychotherapy. *Journal of Counseling Psychology*, 1960, *7*, 180–184.

Goldstein, A. P. *Psychotherapeutic attraction*. New York: Pergamon, 1971.

Goldstein, A. P. *Structured learning theory*. New York: Pergamon, 1973.

Greenson, R. R. *The technique and practice of psychoanalysis* (Vol. 1). New York: International Universities Press, 1967.

Griffith, M. S. The influence of race on the psychotherapeutic relationship. *Psychiatry*, 1977, *40*, 27–40.

Griffith, M. S., & Jones, E. E. Race and psychotherapy: Changing perspectives. In J. E. Masserman (Ed.), *Current psychiatric therapies* (Vol. 8). New York: Grune & Stratton, 1979.

Griffitt, W. Attitude similarity and attraction. In T. L. Huston (Ed.), *Foundations of interpersonal attraction*. New York: Academic Press, 1974.

Harvey, J. H., & Weary, G. *Perspectives on attributional processes*. Dubuque, Iowa: Brown, 1981.

Heider, F. *The psychology of interpersonal relations*. New York: Wiley, 1958.

Heitler, J. B. Preparatory techniques in initiating expressive psychotherapy with lower-class, unsophisticated patients. *Psychological Bulletin*, 1976, *83*, 339–352.

Hollingshead, A. B., & Redlich, F. C. *Social class and mental illness*. New York: Wiley, 1958.

Jacobs, D., Charles, E., Jacobs, T., Weinstein, H., & Mann, D. Preparation for treatment of the disadvantaged patient: Effects on disposition and outcome. *American Journal of Orthopsychiatry*, 1972, *42*, 666–674.

Johnson, D. W., & Matross, R. P. Interpersonal influence in psychotherapy: A social psychological view. In A. S. Gurman & A. M. Razin (Eds.), *Effective psychotherapy: A handbook of research*. New York: Pergamon, 1977.

Jones, E. E. Effects of race on psychotherapy process and outcome: An exploratory investigation. *Psychotherapy: Theory, Research and Practice*, 1978, *15*, 226–236.

Kandel, D. B. Status homophily, social context, and participation in psychotherapy. *American Journal of Sociology*, 1966, *71*, 640–650.

Kelly, G. A. *The psychology of personal constructs* (Vol. 2). New York: Norton, 1955.

Kirshner, L. A., Genack, A., & Hauser, S. Effects of gender on short-term psychotherapy. *Psychotherapy: Theory, Research and Practice*, 1978, *15*, 158–167.

Landfield, A. W. *Personal construct systems in psychotherapy*. Chicago: Rand McNally, 1971.

Langs, R. J. Therapeutic misalliances. *International Journal of Psychoanalytic Psychotherapy*, 1975, *4*, 77–105.

Leary, T. *Interpersonal diagnosis of personality*. New York: Ronald Press, 1957.

Lefcourt, H. L. *Locus of control: Current trends in theory and research*. Hillsdale, N.J.: Erlbaum, 1976.

Lorion, R. P. Patient and therapist variables in the treatment of low-income patients. *Psychological Bulletin*, 1974, *81*, 344–354.

McLachlan, J. C. Benefit from group therapy as a function of patient–therapist match on conceptual level. *Psychotherapy: Theory, Research and Practice*, 1972, *9*, 317–323.

Meehl, P. E. Why I do not attend case conferences. In P. E. Meehl (Ed.), *Psychodiagnosis: Selected papers*. Minneapolis: Univ. of Minnesota Press, 1973.

Mendelsohn, G. A., & Rankin, N. O. Client–counselor compatibility and the outcome of counseling. *Journal of Abnormal Psychology*, 1969, *74*, 157–163.

Newcomb, T. M. The prediction of interpersonal attraction. *American Psychologist*, 1956, *11*, 575–586.

Newcomb, T. M. Interpersonal balance. In R. P. Abelson, E. Aronson, W. J. McGuire, T. M. Newcomb, M. J. Rosenberg & P. H. Tannenbaum (Eds.), *Theories of cognitive consistency: A sourcebook*. Chicago: Rand McNally, 1968.

O'Leary, K. D., & Wilson, G. T. *Behavior therapy: Application and outcome*. Englewood Cliffs, N.J.: Prentice-Hall, 1975.

Orlinsky, D. E., & Howard, K. I. The effects of sex of therapist on the therapeutic experiences of women. *Psychotherapy: Theory, Research and Practice*, 1976, *13*, 82–88.

Parloff, M. B., Waskow, I. E., & Wolf, B. E. Research on therapist variables in relation to process and outcome. In S. L. Garfield & A. E. Bergin (Eds.), *Handbook of psychotherapy and behavior change: An empirical analysis* (2nd ed.). New York: Wiley, 1978.

Pettit, I. B., Pettit, T. F., & Welkowitz, J. Relationship between values, social class, and duration of psychotherapy. *Journal of Consulting and Clinical Psychology*, 1974, *42*, 482–490.

Reich, A. On countertransference. *International Journal of Psychoanalysis*, 1951, *32*, 25–31.

Rosenthal, D., & Frank, J. D. The fate of psychiatric clinic outpatients assigned to psychotherapy. *Journal of Nervous and Mental Disease*, 1958, *127*, 330–343.

Ross, L., Greene, D., & House, P. The "false consensus effect": An egocentric bias in social perception and attribution processes. *Journal of Experimental Social Psychology*, 1977, *13*, 279–301.

Roth, J. A. Some contingencies of the moral evaluation and control of clientele: The case of the hospital emergency service. *American Journal of Sociology*, 1972, *77*, 839–856.

Sapolsky, A. Relationship between patient–doctor compatibility, mutual perception, and outcome of treatment. *Journal of Abnormal Psychology*, 1965, *70*, 70–76.

Sattler, J. M. The effects of therapist–client racial similarity. In A. S. Gurman & A. M. Razin (Eds.), *Effective psychotherapy: A handbook of research.* New York: Pergamon, 1977.

Schutz, W. C. *FIRO: A three-dimensional theory of interpersonal behavior.* New York: Holt, 1958.

Siegel, J. M. A brief review of the effects of race in clinical service interactions. *American Journal of Orthopsychiatry,* 1974, *44,* 555–562.

Smith, M. L. Sex bias in counseling and psychotherapy. *Psychological Bulletin,* 1980, *87,* 392–407.

Stricker, G. Implications of research for psychotherapeutic treatment of women. *American Psychologist,* 1977, *32,* 14–22.

Strong, S. R. Social psychological approach to psychotherapy research. In S. L. Garfield & A. E. Bergin (Eds.), *Handbook of psychotherapy and behavior change: An empirical analysis* (2nd ed.). New York: Wiley, 1978.

Sullivan, H. S. *Collected works.* New York: Basic Books, 1965.

Sussman, M., & Davis, J. Balance theory and the negative interpersonal relationship: Attraction and agreement in dyads and triads. *Journal of Personality,* 1975, *43,* 560–581.

Szasz, T. S. *The manufacture of madness: A comparative study of the Inquisition and the mental health movement.* New York: Harper, 1970.

Wadsworth, R. D., & Checketts, K. T. Influence of religious values on psychodiagnosis. *Journal of Consulting and Clinical Psychology,* 1980, *48,* 234–240.

Weary, G., & Mirels, H. (Eds.). *Integrations of clinical and social psychology.* New York: Oxford Univ. Press, in press.

Webb, E. J., Campbell, D. T., Schwartz, R. D., & Sechrest, L. *Unobtrusive measures: Nonreactive research in the social sciences.* Chicago: Rand McNally, 1966.

Whitehorn, J. C., & Betz, B. J. Further studies of the doctor as a crucial variable in the outcome of treatment with schizophrenic patients. *American Journal of Psychiatry,* 1960, *117,* 215–223.

Wills, T. A. Perceptions of clients by professional helpers. *Psychological Bulletin,* 1978, *85,* 968–1000.

chapter 17

Nonspecific Factors in Helping Relationships

THOMAS ASHBY WILLS

Introduction

The varieties of helping relationships are many. Persons who seek counseling, encouragement, or advice may go to highly trained psychotherapists or to paraprofessional helpers. In some cases they may instead consult a family physician or minister or may seek help from informal social networks. At first glance it would appear that the helping processes involved in these various help-giving resources would be dramatically different and would produce widely differing types and kinds of psychological outcomes. Yet this apparently is not the case. Recent research has suggested that the commonality among various approaches to helping is more important than the apparent differences. It now seems evident that formal or informal treatment approaches differing widely in general philosophy, professional training, and specific treatment methods must have basic common elements and that these elements, usually termed *nonspecific factors*, have an important role in producing the beneficial effects of psychotherapy. The purpose of this chapter is to describe and discuss the basic processes in helping relationships that contribute to therapeutic change.

Basic Processes in Helping Relationships

EVIDENCE FOR NONSPECIFIC FACTORS

Evidence for the existence of nonspecific factors in helping relationships is inferential, because the existing research has focused on global comparisons of one treatment method with another, yet it is compelling. One type of evidence is provided by systematic analyses comparing the effectiveness of different types of psychotherapies. Such analyses show that although the various treatment approaches all have significant effectiveness for improving the psychological well-being of clients, no major difference *between* therapies has been found. All the types of therapy that have been studied show essentially comparable effectiveness, implying that whatever is responsible for this effectiveness is not limited to a particular theoretical system or school of psychotherapy. For example, Smith, Glass, and Miller (1980) performed a statistical analysis of the 1766 outcome effect measures reported in 475 controlled studies of psychotherapy. Although analogue studies were included in the analysis, the representativeness of the pool of studies examined was adequate; the average client received 16 hr of therapy from a therapist with 3¼ years of professional experience. Results at the most general level of analysis showed psychotherapy (broadly construed) to be effective, the average client in the treated group being better off than 80% of the untreated control persons. Subsequent analysis at a more specific level, however, showed that although there were some differences between therapies with similar theoretical background (e.g., implosion therapy is inferior to desensitization), there was no major difference between classes of therapy with widely differing theoretical backgrounds. Comparison of behavioral therapies with the broad class of psychodynamic and ego therapies (including psychoanalytic, rational–emotive, and Rogerian therapy) showed no difference between the two classes in overall effectiveness. Also, comparison of estimated effect sizes for typical phobic and neurotic clients showed comparable effectiveness of behavioral and nonbehavioral therapies.[1] These conclusions, which are identical to those of substantive literature reviews (e.g., Luborsky, Singer, & Luborsky, 1975), clearly imply that professional psychotherapists, whatever their training and theoretical orientation, are doing—or accomplishing—essentially similar things when they actually interact with clients.

Additional evidence comes from studies comparing the effectiveness of highly trained, professional therapists with that of paraprofessionals or lay helpers. It was generally assumed that because of the complexity of establishing and maintaining a therapeutic relationship, professional training and experience were required to master the therapeutic skills that are necessary for effective helping. Yet, again, recent research has suggested a different conclusion. A review by Durlak (1979) examined 42 studies comparing the effectiveness of professional therapists (psychologists,

---

[1]There was some superiority for therapies classified as behavior modification, compared with desensitization or psychodynamic therapies.

psychiatrists, or clinical social workers) with that of paraprofessionals (psychiatric aides, medical personnel, untrained college students, or lay adults). Overall, there was no difference in observed effectiveness between professionals and paraprofessionals. If anything, the evidence favored the paraprofessionals and suggested that they were particularly effective with clients who were younger and of lower socioeconomic status—characteristics similar to those of the paraprofessionals. Attempts to fault Durlak's conclusions on methodological grounds have not been compelling, and in fact the most recent studies have continued to show no difference in general outcome between professional and paraprofessional helpers (see Nietzel & Fisher, 1981, and reply by Durlak, 1981). These surprising findings imply that whatever the therapeutic skills possessed by highly trained helpers, these skills are possessed (or rapidly learned by) persons without professional training.

WHAT ARE THE NONSPECIFIC FACTORS?

The evidence just considered shows that whatever processes are important for therapeutic benefit, these factors are present in formal psychotherapies with radically different assumptions about human nature and methods of treatment. Moreover, effective helping interaction can be established by nonprofessional helpers as well as by professionals, so we must infer that helping skills are more widely distributed than had been thought. In the following sections, basic processes are discussed that probably represent the nonspecific factors in many types of helping relationships. The proposals are largely inferential, because studies designed to determine the specific role of particular factors have generally not been conducted, but evidence is available to support the posited role of each process. My approach is inclusive rather than restrictive because it seems important to describe most of the processes that are involved in helping interactions by both professional and nonprofessional helpers. I suggest, in conclusion, that some processes may be more characteristic of professional therapists, whereas others are more operative in helping by lay persons. I argue that these two domains of processes combine in such a way as to produce the observed equivalent effectiveness of professional and lay helpers.

Another issue in this chapter is the importance of nonspecific factors in behavior therapy. Although the behavioral therapies were originally construed as eliminating the role of nonspecific factors (through the application of techniques derived from social learning theory), the recent evidence shows that relationship factors are important for therapies as diverse as systematic desensitization (Kazdin & Wilcoxon, 1976), general behavior therapy (DeVoge & Beck, 1978), behavioral marriage and family therapy (Alexander, Barton, Schiavo, & Parsons, 1976; Jacobson & Margolin, 1979), and smoking cessation (Harris & Lichtenstein, Note 1). Thus, the present chapter emphasizes the extent to which nonspecific factors are involved in behavior therapy as well as in other types of psychotherapy. As Wilson and Evans (1977) have cogently observed, the fact that a process is "nonspecific" does not mean that it is nonexistent, but simply that it has not been described correctly.

Relationship Factors: Self-Esteem Enhancement

One basic premise of this chapter is that therapeutic gain derives from a significant interpersonal relationship with the helper. The question is what dimensions of clients' well-being are affected by the interpersonal relationship and how this occurs. A dimension that is clearly important for helping relationships is the client's self-esteem. Recent research in social psychology has shifted from a concern with cognitive processes to a realization of the general importance of self-enhancing processes in social interaction (e.g., Baumeister, 1982; Greenwald, 1980; Wegner & Vallacher, 1980; Wills, 1981). There is every reason to expect that self-esteem maintenance is equally important in clinical relationships and in general social interaction.

A common feature of many persons seeking help is that they face various types of threats to their self-esteem. They may have a long history of regarding themselves as unworthy or unlikable persons, or may face current situations such as divorce or job problems in which they experience conflict with or rejection by others, presenting them with severe blows to their sense of personal worth and competence (for a discussion of the role of ego-threat in life stress, see Wills & Langner, 1980). Accordingly, a fundamental aspect of a helping relationship is restoration of the client's sense of his or her own worth as a person.

Several sources of evidence suggest that self-esteem enhancement is a major factor in helping relationships. The Smith *et al.* (1980) analysis showed that one of the strongest effects of psychotherapy was on clients' self-esteem. Also, studies of clients' perceptions of therapy (e.g., Strupp, Fox, & Lessler, 1969) have shown that the most salient aspect of therapy from the clients' stand-point is the perception that they are liked or respected by the therapist. Whether this quality is termed *warmth, respect, positive regard, interest,* or *rapport,* it appears consistently across different studies and is empirically correlated with therapy outcome.[2] This is just as true in behavior therapy as in

---

[2]Two methodological points should be noted. First, measures of therapist interpersonal skills (warmth, empathy, and "genuineness") as rated by independent judges typically show no relationship to therapy outcome (see Mitchell, Bozarth, & Krauft, 1977), but when client perceptions of therapy are obtained, therapist variables show consistent relationships with outcome as assessed both by clients and by other sources (Gurman, 1977; Lambert *et al.*, 1978). Second, although these different variables have been conceived as separate dimensions, as perceived by clients they are usually merged in one overall "good therapist" dimension.

other forms of psychotherapy. Ryan and Gizynski (1971) and Sloane, Staples, Cristol, Yorkston, and Whipple (1975) in retrospective studies found that clients of behavioral therapists attached great importance to the therapist's and client's liking for each other; this liking dimension (as rated by clients, therapists, and independent judges) was related to therapy outcome, whereas the therapist's use of specific behavioral techniques showed no such relationship. In a prospective study, Ford (1978) found not only that client ratings of therapist warmth were related to the outcome of time-limited behavior therapy, but also that the same therapist could establish rapport with clients just as effectively whether applying a systematic cognitive–behavioral intervention or focusing exclusively on providing nondirective emotional support. Another replicated finding in these studies (cf. Howard, Orlinsky, & Perilstein, 1976) is that there are consistent differences across therapists in the ability to establish a positive relationship with clients.

A corollary of this formulation is that therapeutic success will depend to a large extent on whether the therapist likes the client, or to frame the question in reciprocal terms, whether the therapist and client like each other. A number of studies have indeed suggested that the therapist's personal liking or positive feelings toward a client are related to assessment of suitability for therapy (e.g., Elstein & Van Pelt, 1968; Fehrenbach & O'Leary, Chapter 2 in this volume; Garfield & Affleck, 1961; Parsons & Parker, 1968; Wallach & Strupp, 1960). Conversely, clients' perceptions that they are not liked, respected, or treated seriously by therapists are strongly related to dropout from therapy (Baekeland & Lundwall, 1975; Rosenzweig & Folman, 1974; J. G. Shapiro, 1974) or unsuccessful therapy outcome (Ford, 1978; A. K. Shapiro, Struening, E. Shapiro, & Barten, 1976; Strupp & Hadley 1979). It also follows that just as therapists' perceptions of clients crystallize rapidly, so also the basic liking versus disliking between therapist and client, and the subsequent establishment of a therapeutic alliance, will become evident quickly. This is supported both by clinical observations (e.g., "The impression patient and therapist make on each other in their first encounter may crucially affect the subsequent course of therapy [Frank, 1978, p. 31].") and by controlled studies. For example, Saltzman, Luetgert, Roth, Creaser, and Howard (1976), in a study of long-term individual therapy, found that the strongest discriminator between dropouts versus remainers was measurements made during the third session of therapy. Similarly, measurements made by Ford (1978) over eight sessions of time-limited behavior therapy suggested that early in therapy a good therapist–therapy versus bad therapist–therapy judgment was made, which served as the basis for subsequent client continuation or dropout from therapy. In both of these studies, clients who persevered in treatment were those who felt they were liked and respected by the therapist.[3]

---

[3] Also, in studies showing a relationship between client perceptions of therapists and therapy outcome, the majority of the client ratings were obtained between the second and sixth sessions of therapy (see Gurman, 1977).

   With regard to the mechanism of self-esteem enhancement, I have posited that self-esteem is largely derived from social interaction (see Wills & Langner, 1980), and the evidence suggests that significant improvement in self-esteem derives from an interpersonal relationship in which the client perceives that he or she is accepted, respected, and liked by the other person. This aspect is in fact the major dimension in clients' perceptions of therapists (e.g., Gurman, 1977; Lambert, DeJulio, & Stein, 1978). Clinical writing from many schools of therapy also has emphasized the importance of establishing a relationship in which the therapist is nonjudgmental and nonevaluative, accepting the client's statements and feelings (without going beyond the bounds of dis-criminating, rational judgment) and trying continually to convey to the client the understanding that he or she is esteemed, respected, and valued (see, e.g., Frank, 1976; Strupp, 1976). A related, perhaps more subtle mechanism, is the simple fact that the client is taken seriously by the therapist. For clients who have a history of being rejected or ignored by other persons, the basic fact of having someone give serious attention to their thoughts, concerns, and problems may by itself have a significant impact on their feelings of self-worth.

Relationship Factors: Modeling

   Modeling has been called "the silent influence." Its operation is quiet, slow, and undramatic; yet modeling is one of the most general psychological processes. A large body of research with both children and adults has shown that people have a remarkable proclivity for modeling their behavior on the behavior of others, particularly others whom they perceive as likable or powerful (see, e.g., Bandura, 1969). Because modeling has been observed so consistently across many different types of human relationships, it would be surprising if this process were not an important factor in helping relationships as well. Yet little attention has been given to examining the ways in which clients may benefit by modeling the behavior or values of their therapists.
   Although the evidence on modeling is indirect, it is again suggestive that this is an important process in helping relationships. The evidence on clients' perceptions of therapists is instructive, for the studies show consistently, across several different types of therapy, a major dimension (sometimes termed a "good guy" factor) reflecting clients' perceptions that the therapist is a particularly admirable, mature, and competent person (e.g., Feifel & Eells, 1963; LaCrosse, 1977; Strupp *et al.*, 1969) whom they admire and would like to resemble. Another body of evidence shows consistently that clients tend, over the course of therapy, to adopt the attitudes and values of their therapist (for a review see Beutler, 1981). This evidence together strongly suggests that

clients in successful helping relationships tend to model themselves on the therapist.

The process of modeling may assume a particular importance with persons who have a history of troubled interpersonal relationships, which is the most important source of life stress (see Wills & Langner, 1980). In considering the etiology of such relationship problems one can (without wholeheartedly accepting Freudian notions about Oedipus conflict and the like) recognize that from the earliest years a child's main source of observation about interpersonal relationships is his or her own parents, and that parents may with significant frequency engage in derogatory criticism, destructive arguments, and general self-centeredness, rather than acceptance and support of other family members. A child who learns such behavior patterns and exhibits them with peers and elders may well go through adolescence and early adulthood generating a trail of hostility, rejection, and alienation from others (see, e.g., Hafner, Quast, & Shea, 1975; Kahle, Kulka, & Klingel, 1980) and being deprived of the opportunity ever to learn more constructive ways of dealing with people. If such a person becomes involved in a helping relationship in which he or she confronts someone who responds to life in a reasonable, noncritical, and mature manner, a fundamental relearning experience may begin, with great benefits ensuing. (There are limits to this, however. Persons with antisocial or psychopathic personality, who typically have a history of extremely negative family interactions and display general distrust of other people, are not very successful in psychotherapy; cf. A. K. Shapiro *et al.*, 1976.)

Having a positive approach to people is, of course, a quality that can be acquired without professional education, and it is likely that modeling of such qualities is a significant (and largely unobserved) source of therapeutic gain in informal helping relationships, if they are even construed as helping relationships at all. I have known some relatively unschooled people who I thought would make very effective therapists simply because they generally enjoyed life, had a positive outlook on most things, and did not get excessively bothered by everyday frustrations. Such an observation suggests more attention to the personal qualities of the therapist, such as personal security, general optimism, or frustration tolerance, as variables for further research. Several studies (Maskin, 1974; Selfridge & Vander Kolk, 1976) have in fact suggested that better-adjusted therapists are perceived by their clients as more effective.

The presentation so far has demonstrated the importance for therapeutic relationships of the therapist's (*a*) conveying liking and respect for the client, and (*b*) providing an example of a reasonably mature and admirable person for the client to model. The question that follows from this is whether these relationship skills are acquired only through professional training. The evidence suggests otherwise. Marked increases in interpersonal skills have been observed in brief training studies, leading Truax and Mitchell (1971) to note the possibility that "these skills are learned, either overtly or covertly, in early, formative interpersonal situations . . . and that focused training capitalizes on what may have been past incidental learning [p. 327]." This suggests that interpersonal skills are in large part acquired through ordinary social interaction and are possessed to much the same extent by a lay person with ample, positive social experience and by a professionally trained helper.[4,5]

Positive Expectation by Client and Therapist

One of the remarkable aspects of human psychology is the role of beliefs and expectations in therapeutic change. Persons who believe—for whatever reason—that they will improve or be cured tend to do just that, irrespective of whatever else is done to them. This process has been extensively studied in medical literature on placebo effects (e.g., A. K. Shapiro & Morris, 1978). This literature has shown that medical patients commonly experience significant, and sometimes dramatic, improvement even when given treatments that have no known medical value (but which patient or therapist believes will be effective); the magnitude of these effects is such that placebo controls are required aspects of medical research. That similarly powerful expectation effects may operate in psychotherapy has occurred to a number of investigators (e.g., Frank, 1978). It has been hypothesized that generating client expectations of improvement or relief from symptoms may be a crucial factor in therapeutic change, and Bandura (1977) has in fact proposed that a sense of self-efficacy is the necessary and sufficient condition for all therapeutic change.

It has generally been assumed that client expectations (that they will improve or recover) are implicated in the effects of general supportive psychotherapy, probably to an equivalent extent for any type of psychotherapy delivered by a credible professional who is convinced of the treatment's efficacy. The recent evidence indicates that expectation effects are also an important factor in behavior therapy. Even in the most specifically defined and carefully applied behavior therapy, such as systematic desensitization, client expectation effects have not been ruled out as the source of treatment effectiveness (Kazdin & Wilcoxon, 1976). (Although desensitization condi-

---

[4]This does not mean that these skills are immutable or that nothing is learned through professional training. For example, Pierce and Schauble (1970) found that clinical trainees whose supervisors functioned at high levels of interpersonal skills increased their own functioning significantly, whereas trainees with low-functioning supervisors did not change. A modeling explanation is suggested.

[5]A hypothesis following from this is that persons who in everyday life are able to form friendly relationships with a wide variety of persons will make better therapists.

tions are usually superior to placebo controls, the latter are regarded as less credible by clients.) As for other types of behavior therapy, the therapist–client relationship has been shown to have a significant effect on the outcome of systematic desensitization treatment (e.g., Morris & Suckerman, 1974a, 1974b) and there are grounds for believing that a major reason for clients' improvement in behavior therapy is that they become convinced that they can perform the target behavior. Clients' increased confidence probably derives to a significant extent from a supportive and encouraging relationship with the therapist.

In addition to clients' preexisting beliefs and conceptions of therapy, a major source of clients' expectations for improvement is probably the therapist. Studies of drug treatment in medical settings have shown that physicians readily communicate their beliefs about drug efficacy to patients (Frank, 1978), the effect being sufficiently powerful that double-blind procedures are a standard requirement for drug testing. How psychotherapists communicate treatment expectations to their clients has been shown by direct observations of behavior therapists at work:

> The therapist tells the patient at length about the power of the treatment method, pointing out that it has been successful with comparable patients and all but promising similar results for him too. The patient . . . is given a straightforward rationale for the way in which the specific treatment procedures will 'remove' his symptoms . . . . The explicit positive and authoritarian manner in which the therapist approaches the patients seems destined, if not designed, to establish the therapist as a powerful figure and turn the patient's hopes for success into concrete expectations [Klein, Dittman, Parloff, & Gill, 1969, p. 262].

The role of positive expectations in helping relationships seems particularly important in view of recent findings about the common elements of psychological disorders. Recent epidemiological findings (Dohrenwend, Shrout, Egri, & Mendelsohn, 1980) have shown that a syndrome termed *demoralization* is found in different types of disorders in both patient samples and general community samples. This syndrome, as originally proposed by Frank (1974), includes feelings of hopelessness, helplessness, depression, and the belief that things are going to get no better. The demoralization syndrome, which seems to represent the progenitor of both clinical psychological disorder and physical illness (e.g., Schmale, 1972), is the exact opposite of positive expectation, and it would seem that one of the major tasks in initial psychotherapy sessions is to convey to the patient a sense of hopefulness, a conviction that the therapy will help and that if the patient maintains commitment to the helping relationship, despite the costs and discomforts that may occur, improvement will follow. Indeed, current behavior therapists are advising clinicians to begin the therapeutic relationship with positive expectation inductions, providing encouragement and suggesting that the future will bring better things (cf. Ford, 1978; Meichenbaum & Genest, 1980).

Recognizing the role of expectation shifts in therapeutic change may account for one of the most perplexing findings on psychotherapy outcome. Smith *et al.* (1980) examined the relationship between therapy duration and outcome effect size, and found that there was no relationship whatsoever ($r = -.02$). For all practical purposes, the amount of demonstrable benefit derived from one session of therapy is equal to that derived from therapy lasting 10 sessions, 20 sessions, or more. This finding implies that whatever happens in therapy happens rapidly, and the suggestion is that sudden and marked changes in patients' expectations are an important factor in the initial sessions of therapy. This probably occurs through a confluence of events:

1. The client's own action in seeking help ends a period of indecision and demonstrates that he can do something.
2. The therapist's serious attention reassures the client that he is not crazy.
3. Acceptance for treatment by a credible and competent professional affords additional hope that the client will be better off in the future.
4. Warmth and acceptance by the therapist during the first treatment session provide the client with further encouragement and belief in his or her own potential.
5. As previously noted, the therapist may go to some lengths to explicitly emphasize the efficacy of the treatment procedure.

Although the intersect of conditions (1–5) no doubt represents the ideal beginning of therapy rather than the typical occurrence, in general one would predict that expectation effects would operate so as to produce rapid improvements in clients' subjective status quite early in the course of therapy, which in fact is what seems to be observed.

Mastery and Skill Learning

If a client were to gain increased self-esteem and more positive expectations, but remain vocationally incompetent and socially inept, it seems unlikely that such a person would show long-term improvement in adjustment. The learning of specific skills, especially social and interpersonal skills, may be a process that insures the maintenance of therapeutic gain. Such a phenomenon is suggested by Ford's (1978) study, which showed that therapeutic relationship factors predicted outcome measures at termination, but were not strongly related to follow-up measures obtained 2 months after therapy. Strupp and Hadley (1979) also have emphasized the need for long-term follow-up in studies comparing the effectiveness of professional and nonprofessional helpers.

Doubtless there is an interactive relation among increased self-esteem, greater efforts by the client at performing well in problematic situations, and consequent increase in feelings of confidence and mastery. Yet there is a suggestion that a therapist who is prepared to teach specific skills will be more effective. Hence a professionally trained therapist may have a specific advantage over lay helpers. For example, consider some of the interaction reported by Strupp (1980c, p. 833) between a client and a lay therapist, concerning a problematic discussion with the client's girl friend:

Therapist: "Had she gotten very angry at you? Did she say whether or not she displayed any inappropriate anger?"
Sam: "She didn't say. I don't think she did."
Therapist: "Did you tell her about your getting angry?"
Sam: "Yes."
Therapist: "Did you tell her about banging the wall? What did she say about that?"
Sam: "She said that was stupid." (laugh)
Therapist: "Would she care, do you think, if you went out with another girl this weekend?"
Sam: "I don't think so, I don't know. I doubt if she would."

The interaction continued in the same vein for some time. The therapist, rather than running the client through an elementary program on conflict resolution skills, continued the insight-oriented (and unproductive) questioning. Yet the lack of skill training is not limited to lay counselors, for consider the following interaction (Strupp, 1980b, p. 712) between a client and a professional therapist:

Patient: "I have a sour attitude toward life."
Therapist: "It can be changed."
Patient. "How can I have another other attitude?"
Therapist: "Change your behavior—that might change your attitude."
Patient: "So what do you want me to do, put on an act?"
Therapist: "At the moment, just look at yourself . . ."
Patient: (insistent) "This is the normal me."
Therapist: "I don't know what the 'real you' is."

Without denigrating the professional training received by other therapists, it can be noted that persons with behavior modification backgrounds usually have experience in skill training (e.g., assertiveness, dating skills, marital conflict resolution), and this may account for the finding that behavior therapies (broadly construed) are somewhat more effective than psychodynamic therapies (Smith *et al.*, 1980). It also follows that the more skills training a therapist has experience with, the more likely he or she is to be effective with a broad range of clients.

Feedback

People are not completely objective observers of their own behavior. Several different aspects of social perception and social interaction, for instance, create processes that influence people's perceptions of themselves. In particular, actor–observer differences in attributions create a tendency for persons to emphasize situational determinants of their own behavior (see Jones & Nisbett, 1971; Ross, 1977). Although this process has previously been investigated largely from the helper's standpoint (see Batson, O'Quin, & Pych, Chapter 4 in this volume; Wills, 1978), it applies with equal validity, and empirical support, to the client. Without falling back into notions that human behavior is governed by unconscious drives, it seems necessary to recognize that receiving information about oneself from an objective observer may be an important factor in providing people with useful information about their behavior to enable them to fit better with the demands—reasonable or unreasonable—of social living. Showing clients how their own behavior produces certain reactions by others and delineating consistent patterns of behavior that recur across different situations seem an essential element in guiding clients toward more effective social interaction.

Another aspect of the observation–feedback process is the simple fact of clearly defining the target behaviors for the client. One of the striking aspects of clinical work is the vague and trait-oriented terms in which clients typically describe their presenting problems. A therapist (professional or nonprofessional) may contribute significantly to alleviation of clients' difficulties merely by providing a clear description of the problem. This is just as true for behavior therapy as for other therapies; for example, Wilson and Evans (1977) have noted, "It is when the client has *no* clear goals, and has undertaken therapy out of diffuse personal dissatisfaction . . . that the influence of the therapist is likely to be most marked [pp. 546–547]."

In considering the cognitive change that occurs in psychotherapy, change in social comparison perspective also deserves more attention. In particular, research on adaptation level (Brickman & Campbell, 1971) has suggested that people do not evaluate their own well-being in absolute terms, but instead compare themselves with some reference standard. This process has been demonstrated consistently in field studies of satisfaction with income, material rewards, and general life circumstances (Cook, Crosby, & Hennigan, 1977), and the observed generality of this process suggests that it probably occurs in helping relationships as well. Receiving information from a credible authority to the effect that one is not crazy, or sick, and that one's adjustment and coping efforts are not really much worse than other peoples' may have a significant effect for enabling people to have a more realistic perspective on their own competence and to appreciate better the rewards of work, family, and daily living.

Self-Attribution of Change

People have a need to perceive themselves as freely choosing and determining their own behavior, originating their own actions, and remaining uninfluenced by other persons (see, e.g., Brehm & Brehm, 1981). Accordingly, a central element in a helping relationship is inducing the client to change while at the same time maintaining the client's belief that he or she (not the therapist) was responsible for the change. These two aspects of a helping relationship may seem paradoxical, but the process is no different than common occurrences in everyday life, such as the employee who manages to institute a change in an organization by convincing the boss that the change was his or her own idea. Recent studies in the behavioral medicine area have indicated that it is important for clients to attribute behavior change to their own efforts (e.g., Chambliss & Murray, 1979; Colletti & Kopel, 1979). This has also been demonstrated for psychotherapy (e.g., Liberman, 1978).

Managing this subtle and paradoxical aspect of the therapeutic relationship is undoubtedly a complex process, and clinical training may enable therapists to deal better with the almost hidden interplay of influence and resistance that occurs in the consulting room. I can well remember my initial shock and bafflement at hearing Jay Haley describe his methods of paradoxical therapy, but after listening to his procedural description and studying his classic book on psychotherapy (Haley, 1963), I felt better equipped to give consolation when listening to my colleagues in clinical training, who spent long hours bemoaning the fact that they would tell the clients exactly what they should do, but then the clients would not do it.[6]

In ongoing therapy relationships the management of influence and perceived freedom may proceed in stages, with the therapist being relatively noninfluential in the first session of therapy, becoming more structured and overtly directive in the middle stages, and fading out directiveness toward the end of therapy so as to shift perceived responsibility back to the client.[7] An interesting question, however, is whether professional training provides therapists with a significant advantage in therapeutic effectiveness by virtue of their improved ability to manage resistance. The research evidence suggests that it does not. In addition to the review by Durlak (1979), which found no overall difference between professionally trained helpers and untrained ones, a study by Strupp and Hadley (1979) found that professional therapists tended to achieve their successes primarily with highly motivated, non-resistant clients, whereas lay therapists tended to be moderately successful

[6]Strupp has observed cogently that a large part of clinical training may consist in teaching students what *not* to do (see Strupp, 1976, p. 98).

[7]There is evidence that this does occur. A quotation from a client illustrates: "When people solve a problem, they only solve it themselves [Strupp, 1980c, p. 837]." See also Chapter 9, by Lemkau, Bryant, and Brickman, in this volume.

irrespective of the patient's involvement in the relationship. This is another paradoxical finding about psychotherapy, but it may be explained by a hypothesis advanced previously (Wills, 1978) that a person's perception that he or she is participating in an influence relationship may, ipso facto, create resistance to the therapist's efforts. A final link in the argument is that clients perceive professional therapists as being specifically engaged in influence attempts, whereas clients may not perceive untrained therapists as having esoteric skills and powers and being influence oriented. Thus, professional therapists may be at a disadvantage from the outset because they tend to face clients who are more ambivalent and resistant, seeking, on the one hand, relief from their suffering, yet on the other hand resisting the therapist's efforts to influence the client toward a more productive life-style. It is tenable to suggest that this type of ambivalence and resistance is not as characteristic of relationships between lay therapists and the persons they work with.

Confronting Basic Problem Areas

One respect in which professional therapists may have a significant advantage is their ability to keep the therapeutic interaction focused on basic problem areas. Again, one does not have to accept Freudian notions of repression and unconscious processes to recognize that people have a tendency to deemphasize areas of their lives in which they are not functioning effectively and to avoid discussion about areas of fear or insecurity. This creates another paradoxical aspect of helping relationships, in that the areas a person is least likely to discuss are those in which change is most important, and accordingly, an important element in an effective helping relationship is whether the client really confronts and works through the areas of greatest anxiety and dysfunction.

On the face of the evidence, professionally trained therapists are better able to keep clients focused on basic problems, both because of their greater authority and credibility, and because of their sensitivity in recognizing the points at which the therapeutic interaction touches on a source of strong anxiety for the client. In reading the case studies presented by Strupp (1980a, 1980b, 1980c, 1980d) comparing interactions of professional and lay therapists, one is struck repeatedly by how the professionals gently, subtly kept the interaction focused on discussion and resolution of major problems, whereas the lay counselors tended to allow clients to avoid them. The following segment (Strupp, 1980c, p. 834) will serve as an example.

Therapist: (perhaps after 10 minutes of small talk) "Where do you stand as far as career goals? What does your Daddy think you ought to be doing?"
Sam: "His usual thing . . . accounting."

After one of these fairly brief and cryptic answers, Sam might turn toward accounting courses, instructors, and the like. Dr. H., being interested in the subject (as in most others), might then join the patient in the discussion, sharing information about university politics surrounding the teaching of these courses, etc. In this way, they might get diverted from the original topic. Often when Dr. H. did attempt to focus on therapy-related issues, he allowed the patient to stay at the surface, as illustrated by the following interchange:

Therapist: "Do you still feel you have trouble relating to people?"
Sam: (sounding fatigued) "At times. I think I've gotten better, I feel less depressed."
Therapist: "Glad to hear you are feeling better."

The therapist, encouraging superficiality (from a psychodynamic perspective) went on to say, "Just relax, be yourself, and go right on from there." He reassured Sam that "a lot of people have trouble meeting strangers."

An analysis of these interactions by independent raters in fact showed that professional therapists were significantly more likely to focus on important therapeutic issues, particularly on examination of patients' feelings (Gomes-Schwartz & Schwartz, 1978).

On a priori grounds it seems likely that enduring changes in anxiety, behavior, or social interaction will occur only if areas of major dysfunction are confronted. (This is not equivalent to the assertion that behavioral therapies must necessarily fail because they only treat the symptom and not the cause.) Further research is needed to provide long-term follow-up studies of therapy by professional and nonprofessional helpers, because this has been a significant omission in the available literature (Durlak, 1979; see also Strupp & Hadley, 1979). More research is also needed following the model used by Strupp (1980a, 1980b, 1980c, 1980d), comparing the specific interaction of therapists and clients and examining the mechanism through which the therapist identifies and pursues problem areas.[8] Again, it should be noted that the ability to keep interaction focused on important problems is equally important in behavior therapy as in other types of treatment. Wilson and Evans (1977) have noted that "the behavior therapist's ability to make the client feel at ease and talk about anxiety-provoking, embarrassing, or distressing material is critical [for successful treatment] [p. 547]."

Development of a World View

Over the course of a helping relationship, clients learn and develop a certain view of their own problems and of themselves as persons. That this occurs seems indisputable, as it has been alluded to frequently in clinical

[8]Note that the interpersonal relationship between helper and client may provide the leverage for keeping the client focused on problem areas, and thus may be an important factor in long-term change.

writing (e.g., Frank, 1976; Marmor, 1976), yet this remains one of the most vaguely described and least studied aspects of therapeutic relationships. A number of studies (reviewed by Beutler, 1981) show that the extent to which the client accepts the therapist's values over the course of therapy is related to outcome, but exactly how this occurs remains to be clarified. What conceptual frames of reference clients learn, how they integrate new information with their own preexisting world view, and how basic values and philosophies are communicated in clinical interaction is largely unknown at present. What views of problems (e.g., psychodynamic model, medical model, social learning model) are most productive for therapy is a largely unanswered question (for current research on this issue see Karuza, Zevon, Rabinowitz, & Brickman, Chapter 6 in this volume, and Lemkau, Bryant, & Brickman, Chapter 9 in this volume). But it may not matter greatly *what* world view is adopted. It may be that any coherent system that provides clients with clear rubrics for understanding their own behavior, and that of other persons, will introduce into their lives a greater degree of predictability and stability, with a consequent increase in their sense of well-being. Certainly this has been observed often enough in therapy. For example:

> We have frequently noticed occasions in our own [clinical] work in which a behavioral explanation of the origins of the problematic behavior (describing it in matter-of-fact rather than illness terms) and assurances that it can be altered, bring about a decrease in anxiety.... The strategy is...to provide clients with information which will produce a cognitive structure whereby they can organize their experiences in therapy [Wilson & Evans, 1977, p. 555].

Positing that all cognitive structures are equivalent is admittedly an extreme hypothesis, and it seems probable that some world views are, in some ways, more productive than others. Yet at this time there is no evidence to refute the general hypothesis. Definitely we need more attention to defining and measuring the conceptual frameworks that clients bring to psychotherapy, the mechanisms through which such frames of reference are modified or elaborated through participation in a helping relationship, and investigation of which frameworks are better for psychological well-being.

Qualities of the Client

Reading the clinical literature tends to convey to the reader the impression that certain qualities of the client (usually termed "motivation," "readiness," or "involvement" in therapy) are necessary for an effective therapeutic relationship. This may well be, and if so, such variables may represent an additional nonspecific factor in helping relationships. There are grounds for doubt about the conceptual status of this variable, however, for several reasons. One is that therapists' judgments about client motivation or client involvement in therapy are essentially identical with the therapist's personal liking versus disliking for the client (see, e.g., Elstein & VanPelt, 1968; Parsons & Parker, 1968; Strupp *et al.*, 1969; Wallach & Strupp, 1960), and accordingly, it is not at all clear whether these are different variables, or, if so, which is primary and which secondary. An additional issue about motivation is that clients' attitudes toward, and involvement in, therapy may be strongly affected by matters of timing and situational factors outside of therapy that may not be obvious to the therapist; thus, attributing motivational deficits to dispositional qualities of the client may represent another type of attributional error (see Wills, 1978). Because of these reservations, I regard the conceptual status of client motivation as an independent variable to be unclear at this time.

Discussion

In the preceding presentation I have discussed processes that probably represent the nonspecific factors that are shared by many different types of formal psychotherapies, and by informal helping relationships as well. It should be evident that these processes are by no means esoteric and mysterious, but in general are characteristics of any meaningful interpersonal relationship; given the nature of the processes, we might expect that any human being who was, say, in the upper quartile on maturity, personal security, and social skill would make a reasonably effective therapist. Indeed, the nonspecific factors presented here are not the kind of subject material usually taught in formal clinical training (cf. the findings of Elliott, Stiles, Shiffman, Barker, Burstein & Goodman, Chapter 15 in this volume), although, of course, such skills can undoubtedly be improved by modeling or simple trial-and-error learning.

In view of these nonspecific factors in helping, how do we account for empirical observations of the generally equivalent effectiveness of professional and nonprofessional helpers? As a preliminary step toward this question, I have summarized the processes in Table 17.1 with a rough coding of the expected effectiveness of the two types of helpers. The basis for these judgments is discussed briefly in the following sections.

Self-Esteem Enhancement

Although a professional therapist may contribute greater authority and credibility when conveying esteem-enhancing communications, nonprofessionals may derive a significant advantage from attributional aspects of the situation. It has been well established that statements made within the context of an assigned role, and/or under the inducement of external reward, have less credibility (e.g., Jones & Davis, 1965). This is exactly the attributional dilemma faced in formal psychotherapy, where it is not only the therapist's role, but also his or her job, to help the client. Thus, nonprofessional helpers, par-

Table 17.1
Comparison of Nonspecific Processes for Professional and Lay Helpers[a]

Process	Professional helpers		Lay helpers
Self-esteem enhancement			+
Modeling		Equal	
Positive expectation		Equal	
Skill learning	+[b]		
Feedback		Equal	
Self-attribution			++
Confronting basic problems	+		
World view	?		?

[a]+ = one group is superior; ++ = one group is markedly superior; ? = insufficient evidence for prediction.
[b]Qualified prediction.

ticularly in informal helping relationships, may have a significant advantage. An additional advantage of informal helping is that the client specifically chooses the helper, so that both credibility and liking are maximized.

Modeling

As previously noted, the process of modeling is a highly general one, and there is no reason to expect that persons will model a particularly admirable and likable nonprofessional any less than they would a professional.

Positive Expectation

Professionals may be quite effective at offering encouragement and support and raising the hopes of their clients. Yet there is no reason to expect that a reasonably astute and sympathetic nonprofessional cannot do this just as well. Equal effectiveness is predicted.

Skill Learning

Here, professional therapists may have a significant advantage if, in the first place, they conceive of psychotherapy as skill training at all and, in the second place, they have specific experience in skill training methods. Several considerations, however, qualify this prediction. One is that the skill deficits of clients may be in rather elementary areas, such as basic academic or social skills, so that remediation can be accomplished by persons without great sophistication. In fact, Durlak (1979) noted that the studies favoring nonprofessionals tended to be in exactly such areas. Also, in informal helping relationships much of the skill learning may take place in situ (e.g., at parties and social gatherings), where better learning would be expected. Thus, the prediction for this area is a qualified one.

Feedback

Because greater objectivity derives simply from being an uninvolved observer of a situation, it may not matter whether a professional or nonprofessional is doing the observing. Equal effectiveness is predicted.

Self-Attribution

In the preceding section it was noted that nonprofessionals may have a marked advantage in this area because of the strong forces of psychological reactance and resistance that are evoked by the context of a formal professional helping relationship. A significant advantage for nonprofessionals is predicted.

Confronting Basic Problems

The available evidence suggests that professional training may enable therapists to deal more effectively with clients in this respect. The prediction is somewhat qualified because this process may be more important on a long-term basis, and adequate follow-up studies are lacking. Also, in informal helping relationships the helper may deal with major problem situations as they arise, which would tend to enhance therapeutic effectiveness. Still, the available evidence suggests a superiority of professional helpers.

World View

Because so little is known about this process it is difficult to make a prediction. On a priori grounds there is no clear reason to expect either professionals or nonprofessionals to have an advantage in this area.

By summing the entries in Table 17.1, based on these admittedly rough predictions, the reader will see that an outcome of generally equal effectiveness results with, if anything, a slight favoring of nonprofessionals. This is exactly what the empirical evidence shows (Durlak, 1979). Although this demonstration does not decisively prove that the correct processes have been identified, it indicates at least that the present analysis is not seriously off the track.

Suggestions for Further Research

In this chapter I have delineated general psychological processes that apparently account for a major part of the psychological benefit produced by helping relationships. These processes operate irrespective of whether the therapist is professionally trained or not, and the basic nature of these processes is expected to be essentially the same, whatever the school of therapy employed. Doubtless there are specific domains of behavior for which some particular therapy will have more effect, but the general finding of comparable effectiveness for all psychotherapies studied suggests that these therapies derive their benefit largely from nonspecific factors. It is these factors that probably represent the essential basis for therapeutic change.

Because of the evident importance of nonspecific factors in helping, there is a need for further research on this domain of variables. As a general approach to this issue, a promising research strategy is to define or manipulate a particular nonspecific factor and then determine the effect of this variable on therapists' and clients' perceptions of outcome. To some extent this has been done for expectations of improvement in one type of behavior therapy (Kazdin & Wilcoxon, 1976), but the number of adequately designed studies is small, and the contribution of client expectations needs to be determined in other types of therapy. Observational studies of therapy sessions might show how therapists combat demoralization and generate positive expectations for improvement. Recognition that several nonspecific factors are involved in therapeutic relationships leads to the suggestion that outcome evaluations should be multidimensional, including not only global ratings of outcome but also assessments of the client's self-esteem, perception of self-efficacy, specific social skills, and general life values. Modeling processes need more detailed investigation, since past studies have usually obtained only a global rating of liking for the therapist; it would be informative to determine the dimensions of the client's impression of the therapist as a person, to measure the client's motivation to be more like the therapist, and to obtain client ratings of the relationship with the therapist in comparison with other past or current interpersonal relationships. Comparisons of professional and nonprofessional therapists on various nonspecific dimensions (e.g., relationship factors, skill training) would be most informative, and research on the extent of resistance by clients with professional and with nonprofessional helpers would clarify whether psychological reactance is differentially involved in various types of helping relationships. Similarly, clients' attributions about change could be compared for participants in formal and informal helping relationships, to determine whether there is any systematic difference in this domain. Naturalistic studies of how people acquire helping skills in everyday social interactions would be an interesting avenue of investigation. Observations of the type of feedback (categorized as positive versus negative, dispositional versus situational, problem description versus problem interpretation, and so on) that clients actually receive from various types of clinicians, together with measures of clients' reactions to and acceptance of various types of feedback, would provide more data about the operation of this process in helping. Finally, it would be particularly valuable to have some multivariate studies so that intercorrelations of different nonspecific factors could be determined and the relative independent contributions of different factors to therapeutic development and outcome could be compared. Such studies would require careful planning and measurement, but the yield from this type of research would probably be substantial.

Reference Note

1. Harris, D. E., & Lichtenstein, E. *The contribution of nonspecific social variables to a successful behavioral treatment of smoking.* Unpublished manuscript, University of Oregon, 1974.

References

Alexander, J. F., Barton, C., Schiavo, R. S., & Parsons, B. V. Systems-behavioral intervention with families of delinquents: Therapist characteristics, family behavior, and outcome. *Journal of Consulting and Clinical Psychology*, 1976, *44*, 656–664.

Baekeland, F., & Lundwall, L. Dropping out of treatment: A critical review. *Psychological Bulletin*, 1975, *82*, 738–783.

Bandura, A. *Principles of behavior modification.* New York: Holt, 1969.

Bandura, A. Self-efficacy: Toward a unifying theory of behavioral change. *Psychological Review*, 1977, *84*, 191–215.

Baumeister, R. F. A self-presentational view of social phenomena. *Psychological Bulletin*, 1982, *91*, 3–26.

Beutler, L. E. Convergence in counseling and psychotherapy: A current look. *Clinical Psychology Review*, 1981, *1*, 79–102.

Brehm, S. S., & Brehm, J. W. *Psychological reactance: A theory of freedom and control.* New York: Academic Press, 1981.

Brickman, P., & Campbell, D. T. Hedonic relativism and planning the good society. In M. H. Appley (Ed.), *Adaptation-level theory: A symposium.* New York: Academic Press, 1971.

Chambliss, C. A., & Murray, E. J. Efficacy attribution, locus of control, and weight loss. *Cognitive Therapy and Research*, 1979, *3*, 349–353.

Colletti, G., & Kopel, S. A. Maintaining behavior change: An investigation of three maintenance strategies and the relationship of self-attribution to the long-term reduction of cigarette smoking. *Journal of Consulting and Clinical Psychology*, 1979, *47*, 614–617.

Cook, T. D., Crosby, F., & Hennigan, K. M. The construct validity of relative deprivation. In J. M. Suls & R. L. Miller (Eds.), *Social comparison processes: Theoretical and empirical perspectives.* Washington, D.C.: Hemisphere, 1977.

DeVoge, J. T., & Beck, S. The therapist–client relationship in behavior therapy. In M. Hersen, R. M. Eisler, & P. M. Miller (Eds.), *Progress in behavior modification* (Vol. 6). New York: Academic Press, 1978.

Dohrenwend, B. P., Shrout, P. E., Egri, G., & Mendelsohn, F. S. Nonspecific psychological distress and other dimensions of psychopathology: Measures for use in the general population. *Archives of General Psychiatry*, 1980, *37*, 1229–1236.

Durlak, J. A. Comparative effectiveness of paraprofessional and professional helpers. *Psychological Bulletin*, 1979, *86*, 80–92.

Durlak, J. A. Evaluating comparative studies of paraprofessional and professional helpers: A reply to Nietzel and Fisher. *Psychological Bulletin*, 1981, *89*, 566–569.

Elstein, A. S., & VanPelt, J. D. Structure of staff perceptions of psychiatric patients. *Journal of Consulting and Clinical Psychology*, 1968, *32*, 550–559.

Feifel, H., & Eells, J. Patients and therapists assess the same psychotherapy. *Journal of Consulting Psychology*, 1963, *27*, 310–318.

Ford, J. D. Therapeutic relationship in behavior therapy: An empirical analysis. *Journal of Consulting and Clinical Psychology*, 1978, *46*, 1302–1314.

Frank, J. D. *Persuasion and healing* (Rev. ed.). New York: Schocken, 1974.

Frank, J. D. Restoration of morale and behavior change. In A. Burton (Ed.), *What makes behavior change possible?* New York: Brunner/Mazel, 1976.

Frank, J. D. Expectation and the therapeutic outcome—The placebo effect and the role induction interview. In J. D. Frank, R. Hoehn-Saric, S. D. Imber, B. L. Liberman, & A. R. Stone, *Effective ingredients of successful psychotherapy*. New York: Brunner/Mazel, 1978.

Garfield, S. L., & Affleck, D. C. Therapists' judgments concerning patients considered for psychotherapy. *Journal of Consulting Psychology*, 1961, *25*, 505–509.

Gomes-Schwartz, B., & Schwartz, J. M. Psychotherapy process variables distinguishing the "inherently helpful" person from the professional psychotherapist. *Journal of Consulting and Clinical Psychology*, 1978, *46*, 196–197.

Greenwald, A. G. The totalitarian ego: Fabrication and revision of personal history. *American Psychologist*, 1980, *35*, 603–618.

Gurman, A. S. The patient's perception of the therapeutic relationship. In A. S. Gurman & A. M. Razin (Eds.), *Effective psychotherapy: A handbook of research*. New York: Pergamon, 1977.

Hafner, A. J., Quast, W., & Shea, M. J. The adult adjustment of one thousand psychiatric and pediatric patients: Initial findings from a twenty-five year follow-up. In R. D. Wirt, G. Winokur, & M. Roff (Eds.), *Life history research in psychopathology* (Vol. 4). Minneapolis: Univ. of Minnesota Press, 1975.

Haley, J. *Strategies of psychotherapy*. New York: Grune & Stratton, 1963.

Howard, K. I., Orlinsky, D. E., & Perilstein, J. Contribution of therapists to patients' experiences in psychotherapy: A components of variance model for analyzing process data. *Journal of Consulting and Clinical Psychology*, 1976, *44*, 520–526.

Jacobson, N. S., & Margolin, G. *Marital therapy: Strategies based on social learning and behavior exchange principles*. New York: Brunner/Mazel, 1979.

Jones, E. E., & Davis, K. E. From acts to dispositions: The attribution process in person perception. In L. Berkowitz (Ed.), *Advances in experimental social psychology* (Vol. 2). New York: Academic Press, 1965.

Jones, E. E., & Nisbett, R. E. The actor and the observer: Divergent perceptions of the causes of behavior. In E. E. Jones, D. E. Kanouse, H. H. Kelley, R. E. Nisbett, S. Valins, & B. Weiner (Eds.), *Attribution: Perceiving the causes of behavior*. Morristown, N.J.: General Learning Press, 1971.

Kahle, L. R., Kulka, R. A., & Klingel, D. M. Low adolescent self-esteem leads to multiple interpersonal problems: A test of social-adaptation theory. *Journal of Personality and Social Psychology*, 1980, *39*, 496–502.

Kazdin, A. E., & Wilcoxon, L. A. Systematic desensitization and nonspecific treatment effects: A methodological evaluation. *Psychological Bulletin*, 1976, *83*, 729–758.

Klein, M. H., Dittman, A. T., Parloff, M. B., & Gill, M. M. Behavior therapy: Observations and reflections. *Journal of Consulting and Clinical Psychology*, 1969, *33*, 259–266.

LaCrosse, M. B. Comparative perceptions of counselor behavior: A replication and extension. *Journal of Counseling Psychology*, 1977, *24*, 464–471.

Lambert, M. J., DeJulio, S. S., & Stein, D. M. Therapist interpersonal skills: Process, outcome, methodological considerations, and recommendations for future research. *Psychological Bulletin*, 1978, *85*, 467–489.

Liberman, B. L. The role of mastery in psychotherapy: Maintenance of improvement and prescriptive change. In J. D. Frank, R. Hoehn-Saric, S. D. Imber, B. L. Liberman, & A. R. Stone, *Effective ingredients of successful psychotherapy*. New York: Brunner/Mazel, 1978.

Luborsky, L., Singer, B., & Luborsky, L. Comparative studies of psychotherapies: Is it true that "everyone has won and all must have prizes"? *Archives of General Psychiatry*, 1975, *32*, 995–1008.

Marmor, J. Common operational factors in diverse approaches to behavior change. In A. Burton (Ed.), *What makes behavior change possible?* New York: Brunner/Mazel, 1976.

Maskin, M. B. Differential impact of student counselors' self-concept on clients' perceptions of therapeutic effectiveness. *Psychological Reports*, 1974, *34*, 967–969.

Meichenbaum, D., & Genest, M. Cognitive behavior modification: An integration of cognitive and behavioral methods. In F. H. Kanfer & A. P. Goldstein (Eds.), *Helping people change: A textbook of methods* (2nd ed.). New York: Pergamon, 1980.

Mitchell, K. M., Bozarth, J. D., & Krauft, C. C. A reappraisal of the therapeutic effectiveness of accurate empathy, nonpossessive warmth, and genuineness. In A. S. Gurman & A. M. Razin (Eds.), *Effective psychotherapy: A handbook of research*. New York: Pergamon, 1977.

Morris, R. J., & Suckerman, K. R. The importance of the therapeutic relationship to systematic desensitization. *Journal of Consulting and Clinical Psychology*, 1974, *42*, 147. (a)

Morris, R. J., & Suckerman, K. R. Therapist warmth as a factor in automated systematic desensitization. *Journal of Consulting and Clinical Psychology*, 1974, *42*, 244–250. (b)

Nietzel, M. T., & Fisher, S. G. Effectiveness of professional and paraprofessional helpers: A comment on Durlak. *Psychological Bulletin*, 1981, *89*, 555–565.

Parsons, L. B., & Parker, G. V. D. Personal attitudes, clinical appraisals, and verbal behavior of trained and untrained therapists. *Journal of Consulting and Clinical Psychology*, 1968, *32*, 64–71.

Pierce, R. M., & Schauble, P. G. Graduate training of facilitative counselors: The effects of individual supervision. *Journal of Counseling Psychology*, 1970, *17*, 210–215.

Rosenzweig, S. P., & Folman, R. Patient and therapist variables affecting premature termination in group psychotherapy. *Psychotherapy: Theory, Research and Practice*, 1974, *11*, 76–79.

Ross, L. The intuitive psychologist and his shortcomings. In L. Berkowitz (Ed.), *Advances in experimental social psychology* (Vol. 10). New York: Academic Press, 1977.

Ryan, V. L., & Gizynski, M. N. Behavior therapy in retrospect: Patients' feelings about their behavior therapists. *Journal of Consulting and Clinical Psychology*, 1971, *37*, 1–9.

Saltzman, C., Leutgert, M. J., Roth, C. H., Creaser, J., & Howard, L. Formation of a therapeutic relationship: Experiences during the initial phase of psychotherapy as predictors of treatment duration and outcome. *Journal of Consulting and Clinical Psychology*, 1976, *44*, 546–555.

Schmale, A. Giving up as a final common pathway to changes in health. *Advances in Psychosomatic Medicine*, 1972, *8*, 20–40.

Selfridge, F. F., & Vander Kolk, C. Correlates of counselor self-actualization and client perceived facilitativeness. *Counselor Education and Supervision*, 1976, *16*, 189–194.

Shapiro, A. K. & Morris, L. A. Placebo effects in medical and psychological therapies. In S. L. Garfield & A. E. Bergin (Eds.), *Handbook of psychotherapy and behavior change* (2nd ed.). New York: Wiley, 1978.

Shapiro, A. K., Struening, E., Shapiro, E., & Barten, H. Prognostic correlates of psychotherapy in psychiatric outpatients. *American Journal of Psychiatry*, 1976, *133*, 802–808.

Shapiro, R. J. Therapist attitudes and premature termination in family and individual therapy. *Journal of Nervous and Mental Disease*, 1974, *159*, 101–107.

Sloane, R. B., Staples, F. R., Cristol, A. H., Yorkston, N. J., & Whipple, K. *Psychotherapy vs. behavior therapy*. Cambridge, Mass.: Harvard Univ. Press, 1975.

Smith, M. L., Glass, G. V., & Miller, T. I. *The benefits of psychotherapy*. Baltimore: Johns Hopkins Univ. Press, 1980.

Strupp, H. H. The nature of the therapeutic influence and its basic ingredients. In A. Burton (Ed.), *What makes behavior change possible?* New York: Brunner/Mazel, 1976.

Strupp, H. H. Success and failure in time-limited psychotherapy. A systematic comparison of two cases: Comparison 1. *Archives of General Psychiatry*, 1980, *37*, 595–603. (a)

Strupp, H. H. Success and failure in time-limited psychotherapy. A systematic comparison of two cases: Comparison 2. *Archives of General Psychiatry*, 1980, *37*, 708–716. (b)

Strupp, H. H. Success and failure in time-limited psychotherapy: With special reference to the performance of a lay counselor. *Archives of General Psychiatry*, 1980, *37*, 831–841. (c)

Strupp, H. H. Success and failure in time-limited psychotherapy. Further evidence: Comparison 4. *Archives of General Psychiatry*, 1980, *37*, 947–954. (d)

Strupp, H. H., Fox, R. E., & Lessler, K. *Patients view their psychotherapy*. Baltimore: Johns Hopkins Univ. Press, 1969.

Strupp, H. H., & Hadley, S. W. Specific vs. nonspecific factors in psychotherapy: A controlled study of outcome. *Archives of General Psychiatry*, 1979, *36*, 1125–1136.

Truax, C. B., & Mitchell, K. M. Research on certain therapist interpersonal skills in relation to process and outcome. In A. E. Bergin & S. L. Garfield (Eds.), *Handbook of psychotherapy and behavior change*. New York: Wiley, 1971.

Wallach, M. S., & Strupp, H. H. Psychotherapists' clinical judgments and attitudes towards patients. *Journal of Consulting Psychology*, 1960, *24*, 316–323.

Wegner, D. M., & Vallacher, R. R. (Eds.). *The self in social psychology*. New York: Oxford Univ. Press, 1980.

Wicklund, R. A. *Freedom and reactance*. Potomac, Md.: Erlbaum, 1974.

Wills, T. A. Perceptions of clients by professional helpers. *Psychological Bulletin*, 1978, *85*, 968–1000.

Wills, T. A. Downward comparison principles in social psychology. *Psychological Bulletin*, 1981, *90*, 245–271.

Wills, T. A., & Langner, T. S. Socioeconomic status and stress. In I. L. Kutash & L. B. Schlesinger (Eds.), *Handbook on stress and anxiety: Contemporary knowledge, theory, and treatment*. San Francisco: Jossey-Bass, 1980.

Wilson, G. T., & Evans, I. M. The therapist–client relationship in behavior therapy. In A. S. Gurman & A. M. Razin (Eds.), *Effective psychotherapy: A handbook of research*. New York: Pergamon, 1977.

chapter 18

Environmental Factors in Dependency among Nursing Home Residents: A Social Ecology Analysis

MARGRET M. BALTES

Introduction

This chapter has two parts. In the first, a behavioral research program on the social ecology associated with dependence in the elderly nursing home resident is presented. Specifically, operant–experimental research on behavioral modifiability and operant–observational research on the nature of the social ecology surrounding dependency in elderly persons are discussed. The author also alludes to how the findings of this research program blend with other current gerontological research that has variability, plasticity, or the ecological context of behavior as a focus.

In the second part, the discussion centers on the possible implications of the empirical findings described here for considerations of helping relationships, particularly as they relate to the social ecology of the nursing home. It is argued that there are multiple criteria that permit different interpretations depending upon whether, for example, individual–developmental or institutional perspectives are considered, or whether a biological decline model versus an interactive–developmental model of aging is posited.

Basic Processes in Helping Relationships

Research Program on Dependency

GOALS AND HYPOTHESES

Dependency in the elderly is a multifaceted concept and has been of long-standing interest in the aging literature. Only over the last few years, however, do we find systematic empirical efforts to include considerations of environmental factors in the understanding of dependency. For example, there is now relevant work on dependency as perceived lack of control (Langer & Rodin, 1976; Rodin & Langer, 1977; Schulz, 1976; Schulz & Hanusa, 1978), as an erroneous inference of incompetence (Langer, 1979; Langer & Benevento, 1978), as helplessness (Seligman, 1975), and as the outcome of social and physical contingencies. The research program conducted by the author and her colleagues (E. Barton, R. Burgess, S. Honn, and M. Orzech) belongs to this latter perspective.

The basic goal of my own research program was to investigate the possibility of dependency being not a necessary concomitant of aging, but rather contingent upon the presence of biological as well as environmental factors, or a combination of both. The aim was to focus on the analysis of environmental factors influencing dependency and independence in the elderly. Accordingly, two hypotheses were formulated: (1) Dependent behavior in the elderly can be modified (reversed) following a change in environmental conditions; and (2) dependent behavior of the elderly is maintained by naturally existing conditions in their ecology.

These two hypotheses were judged to require two distinct research paradigms. In order to test the modifiability hypothesis, an experimental research strategy appropriate for examining changes in dependent behaviors following an experimental intervention had to be used. For the study of the second ecological hypothesis, an observational research strategy was needed. Such a strategy should allow us to identify existing environmental conditions surrounding the occurrence of dependency and thereby possibly influencing the acquisition and maintenance of dependent behaviors in the elderly.

One methodological paradigm that can yield both experimental and observational information is the operant learning model (Baer, 1973; M. M. Baltes & Lerner, 1980). Furthermore, the operant paradigm appeared adequate as a theoretical model, since its core principles speak to the dynamic and reciprocal interrelationship between organism and the environment, and to the importance of environmental factors in the development and maintenance of behavior (Skinner, 1938). The possibility of utilizing the operant model for the description and explanation of aging processes has been discussed by several authors (e.g., M. M. Baltes & Barton, 1977, 1979; Hoyer, 1973, 1974; MacDonald, 1973; Patterson & Jackson, 1980a, 1980b). I do not see the operant paradigm as the only paradigm possible. However, I view it as a powerful one in developing an understanding of organism–environment interchanges in general, as well as social interactions in specific.

Systematic use of any methodological or theoretical paradigm, including the operant paradigm, has its influence on the definition of the phenomenon under study, in this case dependency. Dependency in our research, as well as in research by others using the operant paradigm, is defined by and limited to observable and overt behaviors. It may be legitimately criticized that we thereby buy accuracy at the cost of complexity in defining the term *dependency*. Furthermore, the use of an operant learning approach for the analysis of dependency favors a microanalytic treatment of the environment. In addition to this constraint of the operant approach, the present research program to date has focused on a particular ecological setting, namely the nursing home. I have chosen the nursing home as a research setting not only because I am interested in elderly nursing home residents per se, but also because the nursing home environment seems to provide a situation that contains an accumulation of dependency; thus, it might be a model for aging conditions in their extremity.

In any event, the use of the operant learning model in the analysis of dependence in the elderly seemed to be most adequate, particularly at the beginning of a research program with a focused interest on the role of environmental factors. It allows one to answer questions such as: How much modifiability is there? Under what environmental conditions do we find modifiability, or the lack of it? Which dependent behaviors are most effectively modified under what conditions? What are the environmental conditions necessary to redesign the aging process so as to prolong the onset of dependency or to avoid it altogether?

OPERANT–EXPERIMENTAL RESEARCH

The first hypothesis concerning modifiability of dependency seems to be supported by the operant–experimental findings by us and others (for reviews see M. M. Baltes & Barton, 1977, 1979; McClannahan, 1973; Patterson & Jackson, 1980b; Risley & Edwards, Note 1). Although the different studies had different foci, there were some major commonalities in design and approach: Subjects were mostly long-term nursing home residents who had no direct physical impairments that would completely prohibit the desired behaviors; target dependent behaviors had existed for a long time; a single-subject design was chosen; and change procedures consisted of reinforcement contingencies sometimes coupled with stimulus control procedures.

One example from our own work will suffice here as illustration (also discussed in M. M. Baltes & Zerbe, 1976). In this case the target dependent behavior to be changed was "not eating independently." The subject was a 79-year-old man whose overall dependency was due, in large part, to the effects of a stroke. However, he could move his arms and hands quite well. Stimulus control and reinforcement procedures were utilized to reestablish self-feeding behavior. The stimulus control procedure consisted of providing the man with eating utensils that he could grasp more easily and were thus more adequate tools for his somewhat stiff and crippled fingers. As reinforcement following any act of self-feeding (i.e., bringing food to the mouth and eating), continuous and immediate social praise was delivered by the man's wife, by other table companions, and by the experimenter. Figure 18.1 shows the experimental design used.

During baseline observations self-feeding occurred at a very low rate, whereas an increase in self-feeding could be observed after the introduction of the treatment phase. A decrease occurred, as expected, when baseline conditions were reverted to. Reintroduction of the treatment phase led again to an increase in self-feeding behavior, although the effect failed to stabilize. A posteriori examination suggested that a change in the reinforcement procedure, not controlled by the experimenter, had occurred: The wife was absent from the table because she had fallen sick. Discussions with the subject revealed that he not only missed his wife and her reinforcements, but that he also was worried about her sickness and afraid she might die. He indirectly asked for the treatment to be discontinued. Both environmental events, the experimental manipulation (treatment phases) and the uncontrolled manipulation by the extraexperimental ecology, show the impact of environmental factors upon behaviors.

This and a number of other experiments (for reviews see M. M. Baltes & Barton, 1977, 1979; Patterson & Jackson, 1980a, 1980b) have shown that aging behaviors, such as dependent behaviors, can be changed through both therapeutic (reinforcement) and prosthetic (stimulus control) environmental events. This conclusion concerning modifiability or plasticity of behaviors of the elderly is supported by most other experimental studies dealing not only with dependent behaviors, but also with a gamut of other behaviors, in elderly people. The only restriction is associated with direct biological or physical incapacitation. Even in these instances, however, compensatory effects or rehabilitation through prosthetic devices can be achieved.

Such early operant–experimental work would rarely be classified as "true" intervention since most effects vanished shortly after the experimenter left the setting. The reasons for this are manifold. Most commonly the discriminative stimuli and the reinforcing consequences used in treatment procedures were not inherent in the setting. Thus, the end of the experiment or the departure of the experimenter often reintroduced baseline conditions (in contrast, see an attempt to change staff behavior by Sperbeck & Whitbourne Krauss, 1981).

Despite these and other methodological problems, the findings strongly support the notion of a real potential for behavioral plasticity and optimization of functioning in old age and for the importance of both social and physical environmental factors influencing the level of functioning of the

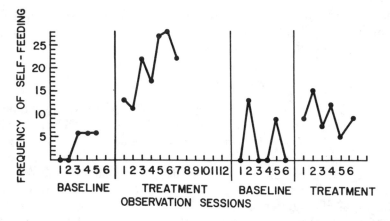

Figure 18.1. Single-subject reversal design showing frequency of self-feeding behavior in a 79-year-old nursing home resident.

elderly. The very fact that dependency is reversible suggests that environmental conditions at least codetermine the acquisition and maintenance of dependency in elderly nursing home residents. In philosophy of science terms, they are sufficient though not necessary conditions.

One last word about operant–experimental work is in order before turning to the operant–observational research. Operant–experimental work, in my opinion, should be continued in a much more rigorous fashion, perhaps in the laboratory, in order to establish taxonomies of reinforcers and discriminative stimuli: What is most effective under which conditions, with which behaviors and in which elderly people? We have very little systematic knowledge of the differential effectiveness of reinforcers in the elderly. We seem to be a little bit more fortunate when it comes to discriminative stimuli. Explorations and findings regarding the impact of the physical environment have shown great promise for designing prosthetic environments that optimize the elderly's functioning (Konzelik, 1976; McClannahan, 1973).

OPERANT–OBSERVATIONAL RESEARCH

This brings us to our second hypothesis: Dependent behaviors in the elderly are maintained by naturally existing environmental conditions in their ecology. As noted, operant–observational strategies, or the observations of naturally occurring behavior sequences, were warranted to test this hypothesis. Again, we restricted ourselves to elderly nursing home residents and their social ecology. Two observational strategies were used. First, in order to gain information about the daily behaviors of elderly nursing home residents and staff in their situational context, we performed a behavior mapping study.

Second, in order to focus on the social ecology, on the interactions between nursing home residents and their social partners, we designed several studies using an operant–observational strategy.

Behavior Mapping Study

Behavior mapping is a technique used in environmental psychology that has its roots in the familiar architect's floor plan (Ittelson, Rivlin, & Proshansky, 1970). Using this strategy elderly residents and staff in a nursing home were observed for two days, and their behaviors, location, and position were recorded across all times of the day. For details of the observation procedure the reader is referred to an extensive account of the study itself (M. M. Baltes, Barton, Orzech, & Lago, in press).

We devised a list of concrete behaviors, 41 resident and 29 staff behaviors, as a first attempt to cover all behavior instances that might occur in a nursing home setting. Any additional behaviors not on the list were to be added by the observers in situ. (In fact, no additions were judged to be necessary.) Table 18.1 shows an aggregation of all observed behaviors into a total of 18 behavior categories (11 for residents and 7 for staff). These categories were used in an analysis of the already collected data for ease in reporting.

Several aspects of the frequencies of behaviors observed and their environmental context are noteworthy. First, for residents we see a fair level of independent and socially engaged behaviors compared to a low level of dependent behaviors. Second, we see an abundance of relatively inactive behaviors (looking, sleeping). The high frequency of resident inactive behaviors corresponds to the most frequent location (the bedroom) and position (lying down) of residents.

Second, the frequencies of staff behaviors show socially engaged behaviors to be most prominent. More than half of these behaviors, however, entailed conversing with one another rather than with elderly residents. This is reflected in the staff's most frequent location, the hallway, which was rarely frequented by residents.

It is not the primary intention of this author to comment here on the desirability of the behavior–environment findings obtained. Yet it appears on the surface that the picture of the residents presented—one of inertia and little opportunity for social contact—cannot be the dominant objective of the staff and administrators. Nevertheless, certain administrative rules and regulations (such as the requirement to serve breakfast in bed for all residents and lunch and dinner in the bedroom for some) and certain architectural designs or lack thereof (such as one activity room on the ground level—difficult to reach for the second-floor residents—and no open seating arrangements in or off the hallway) contributed to creating rather than inhibiting inertia and isolation. A view emphasizing the role of inadvertent physical or administrative features would be consonant with positions such as Goffman's (1960) that accentuate

Table 18.1
Percentage of Behaviors in Resident and Staff Categories

Resident behavior category	Percentage	Staff behavior category	Percentage
Looking–watching	31	Social engagement	47
Sleeping	23	Administrative work	24
Social engagement	21	Assisting residents	16
Independence	11	Walking	10
Dependence	4	Hitting–screaming–	2
Work	1	restraining	
Stereotypic movements	5	Leisure	1
Talking to self	1	Personal maintenance	1
Screaming–crying	1		
Calling for help	1		
Other	1		

the effects of managerial goals as opposed to health or developmental goals for the residents of institutions.

Our main interest, however, was to illuminate the social ecology in terms of the interaction patterns between nursing home residents and their social partners (staff included). Specifically, we wanted to know how social partners respond or react to dependent and independent behaviors of the elderly. This objective is reflected in the following studies.

Sequential Observation Studies

To date, there are four available studies (M. M. Baltes, Burgess, & Stewart, 1980; Barton, Baltes, & Orzech, 1980; Lester & Baltes, 1978; M. M. Baltes, S. Honn, E. M. Barton, Orzech, & Lago, Note 2), all building upon one another, that attempt to analyze naturally occurring behavior sequences involving interaction between nursing home residents and their social partners.

The four studies had certain design characteristics in common: a nursing home population requiring intermediate or skilled nursing care; nursing home settings with a lower and middle social class population; sequential observations of interactions between target residents and their social partners; a behavior code focusing on overt, observable behaviors related to independent–dependent functioning; and repeated observations across days for each elderly participant. The data reported here were analyzed via Sackett's (1977) method of sequential lag analysis.[1] This method provides not only a representation of the probabilities of behavior sequences or patterns but also a statistical test indexing departures of observations from baseline expectations.

---

[1] I am aware of the criticism recently directed toward the significance testing of behavior sequences in the sequential lag program (Allison & Liker, 1982). The equation proposed by Sackett and used by us in the analyses described here produces conservative estimates of statistical significance.

The Sackett program is aimed at the identification of behavior sequences that show statistically significant deviations of the observed probability from the base probability. If such deviations occur, it is assumed that the occurrence of a criterion behavior or antecedent influences the occurrence of the consequent behavior, in either an inhibiting or a facilitating manner. Such a behavior sequence can be identified not only for events following each other immediately (Lag 1) but also for behavioral events 1, 2, 3, or more units removed from the antecedent event (Lag 2, Lag 3, etc.).

This is illustrated by Table 18.2. All base and conditional probabilities for all consequent behaviors for two lags are shown separately for each criterion behavior. Whether the occurrence of a criterion behavior has a significant effect on the consequent behaviors can easily be identified by comparing the conditional probability of that consequent event with its base or expected probability. Thus, for instance, you can see that the criterion behavior "dependent personal maintenance" of residents is followed most often by the consequent event "supportive of dependent personal maintenance" of social partners (conditional probability = .48, base probability = .03).

The results of these studies support and complement each other and yield to date the following picture. The most consistent and, for the present theme, important finding suggests the existence of discrepant social ecologies for dependent versus independent behaviors (see Figure 18.2). Specifically, we find a highly consistent and immediately supportive social environment for dependent behaviors related to personal maintenance, whereas independent behaviors in the context of self-care are not associated with observable responses by the social environment. For example, elderly residents not dressing themselves or making attempts to do so will most likely experience immediate help from social partners, who will dress the residents. In contrast, elderly residents dressing themselves will most likely continue to behave in an independent manner, but not receive any praise, encouragement, or attention of any kind from social partners. Accordingly, we can speak of a congruent relationship between residents and social partners regarding dependency, and not independence.

There are other independent behaviors of the elderly resident, however, such as writing a letter or assisting a fellow resident in walking (in short, independent, constructively engaged behaviors), for which we find some supportive reactions from the social ecology. However, this attention consists of inconsistent, irregular, or intermittent responses. Thus, even in these instances the naturally occurring social contingency does not have the same level of continuity and immediacy as is true for dependent behaviors and their social consequences.

This basic picture of discrepant interaction patterns related to dependent and independent functioning between elderly residents and their social ecology (support for dependent but absent or irregular support for independent functioning) appears fairly robust. For example, consideration of

Table 18.2

Base and Conditional Probabilities for Consequent Behaviors of Residents and Their Social Partners[a]

Criterion behavior	Code	Consequent behavior																			
		Lag 1										Lag 2									
		01	02	03	04	05	06	07	08	09	10	01	02	03	04	05	06	07	08	09	10
Behavior of residents																					
Independent, constructively engaged	01	*.50*	.07	.00	.06	.01	.23	.01	.02	.09	.02	*.64*	.10	.02	.10	.01	.07	.00	.01	.04	.01
Independent personal maintenance	02	.12	*.63*	.00	.06	.01	.05	.01	.02	.08	.01	.15	*.62*	.02	.10	.01	.05	.00	.01	.03	.01
Dependent personal maintenance	03	.08	.02	*.11*	.02	.02	.10	.05	.48	.08	.04	.13	.06	*.39*	.09	.01	.08	.03	*.12*	.07	.02
Nonengaged	04	.03	.02	.00	*.84*	.01	.01	.00	.01	.07	.01	.04	.03	.01	*.86*	.01	.01	.00	.01	.03	.01
Independent obstructively engaged	05	.05	.04	.01	.21	*.57*	.03	.01	.02	.07	.01	.06	.05	.02	.21	*.59*	.02	.01	.02	.03	.01
Behavior of social partners																					
Supportive of engagement	06	*.65*	.10	.03	.07	.01	.06	.01	.03	.03	.02	*.23*	.12	.03	.05	.01	*.38*	.02	.06	.06	.04
Supportive of independent personal maintenance	07	.13	*.48*	*.16*	.06	.01	.03	.04	.05	.01	.04	.12	.13	.08	.06	.01	.16	*.11*	*.25*	.05	.05
Supportive of dependent personal maintenance	08	.09	.04	*.65*	.03	.01	.06	.02	.05	.05	.01	.11	.03	*.15*	.04	.02	*.13*	.04	*.35*	.09	.04
No response	09	*.23*	*.16*	.02	*.44*	.03	.02	.00	.01	.06	.02	.19	*.16*	.02	*.41*	.03	.06	.01	.04	.06	.03
Leaving	10	*.24*	*.24*	.01	*.43*	.02	.01	.00	.01	.04	.02	*.20*	*.23*	.02	*.34*	.01	.08	.00	.01	*.11*	.01
Base probability		.19	.16	.03	.44	.03	.06	.01	.03	.06	.01	.19	.16	.03	.44	.03	.06	.01	.03	.06	.01

[a]Significantly increased conditional probabilities are italicized.

413

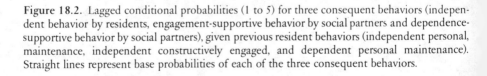

Figure 18.2. Lagged conditional probabilities (1 to 5) for three consequent behaviors (independent behavior by residents, engagement-supportive behavior by social partners and dependence-supportive behavior by social partners), given previous resident behaviors (independent personal, maintenance, independent constructively engaged, and dependent personal maintenance). Straight lines represent base probabilities of each of the three consequent behaviors.

other independent subject variables, such as length of institutionalization, health status, and sex of elderly residents, results in quantitative changes of level but does not alter the main interaction patterns. Furthermore, when sequential analyses are performed so that the antecedent behavior could not be followed by itself, the basic patterns are not altered: External support for dependency, no external support for independence related to personal maintenance, and intermittent external support for independence related to prosocial engagement remain the dominant findings.

One additional point is of interest here. It deals with the relationship of dependency, as defined in our research, to other behaviors that are often associated with dependency. In our behavior code we separated dependent behaviors related to personal maintenance from nonengagement (such as looking, sleeping, etc.). Not only do these behaviors show great differences in frequency; in contrast to dependent behaviors, nonengaged behaviors experience no external contingencies. This discrepancy has importance for the discussion of the equivalence of such terms as dependency, passivity, helplessness, and nonengagement. In other words, categories of various so-called dependent behaviors do not function as identical response or behavior classes in terms of their social consequences. Such a differentiation in terms of naturally existing learning contingencies has important implications for theory, method, and practice. In terms of social learning contingencies, dependency is not a unitary concept, a point that we will turn to again in the next section.

So far, data analysis of the observed resident–partner interactions has been straightforward but unidirectional. When the operant paradigm is applied to social episodes, however, each behavior event can be construed as being at the same time both the consequence of one behavior and the antecedent or discriminative stimulus of another. In the analyses reported, resident behavior has been our target or antecedent criterion behavior for which consequences were identified. But there is another side of the relationship between residents and their social ecology. What does our data show if staff behavior is treated as antecedent? In a further analysis an attempt was made to examine the behavioral flow subsequent to the behavior of social partners. When we use sequential lag analyses defining behaviors of social partners as antecedents, we find the most likely consequent event to be a congruent reaction by the residents. Accordingly, behavior of social partners that is supportive of elderly dependence is followed most often by "congruent" dependent behavior of residents. Similarly, behavior of social partners that is supportive of independence is followed by independent behavior of residents. Behaviors of social partners thus seem to function as strong discriminative stimuli for congruent behavior to be emitted by residents. Remember, however, that the reverse statement, that resident behaviors were strong discriminative stimuli for congruent behavior of social partners, held true only for dependent behavior of residents. In some sense then, there is beginning evidence that for the behaviors studied there might be more stimulus control from the social partners to the elderly resident than the reverse.

IMPLICATIONS FOR FORMULATIONS OF DEPENDENCY IN AGING

Dependency

The demonstration that dependent behaviors, even of chronic duration, are reversible suggests that dependency in the elderly can be the outcome of environmental conditions. Needless to say, such an environmental influence might come to bear more strongly with onsetting physical weaknesses or impairments. Accordingly, as mentioned earlier, environmental factors are surely among the sufficient conditions for the occurrence of dependency, though they are not the necessary ones, and likely operate in the context of other determining factors. A steep staircase, for instance, might only cause caution on the part of a well elderly person, whereas it might immobilize an elderly person with a heart condition.

Second, describing dependency as the function of existing social environmental factors should make us hesitate to use dependency, helplessness, lack of control, and nonengagement as synonyms. Learned helplessness (Seligman, 1975), for example, is the product of a lack, rather than the product of the presence of contingencies. Furthermore, dependency as defined here is not synonymous with perceived lack of control (Langer & Rodin, 1976; Rodin & Langer, 1977; Schulz, 1976) or the illusion of incompetence (Langer, 1979). The perception of lack of control by the elderly supposedly represents the reaction of old people to either their own physical or mental impairment or social biases or expectations by others. The question is not so much whether a cognitive interpretation of dependency is to be preferred over a behavioral one; rather, I want to argue that dependent behaviors may or may not be associated with the perception of lack of control.

It seems from the present research that dependent behaviors can have a clear instrumental function, namely, to gain external support, such as social contact. Thus, dependent behaviors would actually be the expression of gaining control over one's environment. This does not exclude the fact that some dependent behaviors can be the product of helplessness or the perception of lack of control. We have to be aware, however, that in the case of nursing home residents, dependence related to personal maintenance appears more often to be an instrumental act that yields control over the environment.

Independence

When independent behaviors of nursing home residents are considered, our findings provide as many new questions as answers to old questions. From a social–ecological point of view, there are at least three classes of independent behaviors: one related to personal maintenance or self-care, another involving prosocial, constructive, and engaged features, and a third referring to asocial, obstructive, and engaged behaviors. Since the third class of behaviors shows minimal frequency, I will discuss only the behavior patterns related to independent personal maintenance and constructive engagement.

Independent behaviors related to personal maintenance do not elicit any social responses; yet they are fairly frequent. We cannot observe any external reinforcements from either staff or other social agents. We are not able, in hindsight to analyze more closely the strings of independent behaviors related to personal maintenance. It may very well be that we are dealing with a chaining effect. In the operant terminology chaining means that each link (each behavior event in the chain) is a necessary discriminative stimulus for the subsequent behavior and/or a conditioned reinforcer for the preceding behavior. Such a chain of behaviors would explain why independent personal maintenance behaviors seem to be oblivious to observable external contingencies. In other words, an independent act, such as dressing oneself, might be set in motion by the independent act of getting out of bed in the morning and, in turn, set the occasion for eating breakfast. Future research will have to test this possibility.

In contrast, independent behaviors related to constructive engagement experience intermittent support and attention. Thus, intermittent supportive behaviors from social partners suffice to maintain a high degree of independent constructive engagement or prosocial behaviors of the elderly resident.

Aging versus Setting

One immediate question arising from the data concerns the interpretation of the observed interaction patterns as a setting effect or an aging effect. Are the interactional patterns that we observed more a function of the institutional setting (i.e., the nursing home in which they occurred) or of the fact that elderly persons were part of the interactional dynamics?

In earlier studies, setting and age were entangled and thus their effects were confounded. Based on the work of Goffman (1960) and more recent studies of the effect of institutionalization (Gottesman & Bourestom, 1974; Spasoff, Kraus, Beattie, Holden, Lawson, Rodenberg, & Woodstock, 1978; Lawton, Patniak, & Fulcomer, Note 3), one might argue that the findings are role-congruent with the setting. First, the old person lives in a nursing home because of some degree of loss of independence. Second, the role of the staff is to assist the residents in their daily life and activities. Third, each institutional system, including the nursing home, has to impose managerial rules in order to be able to exist. Rules and routines, however, have conforming effects and, in some cases, it is dependent behavior rather than independent behavior that allows for smooth operation without conflict. Explicitly or implicitly, an important goal of institutions is to manage in the administrative sense, rather than to provide for conditions under which human development (future healthy functioning) is optimized.

An aging effect, on the other hand, would suggest that elderly residents, either due to their behavioral dispositions or strategies or their stimulus characteristics as elderly persons for social partners, play a crucial role in the type of interactions observed. There is no definite answer to be gained from our data so far. To find empirical answers, we will need to design a longitudinal pre–post-institutionalization study plus comparative studies of elderly persons in community settings and children in institutional settings. For example, what happens to the social ecology when elderly persons move from a family setting to an institutional setting, or vice versa? Or, in regard to social consequences of dependent personal maintenance, do staff with young children (e.g., in an orphanage) exhibit patterns similar to those of staff with elderly residents in nursing homes?

Comparisons with Research from Other Helping Settings

Perhaps this is the place to attempt to build a bridge between the presented observational research and correlational data from studies analyzing the perception of clients by helping professionals, though the latter work considers institutions other than nursing homes and clients other than the elderly per se. I will make reference here to two variables out of many others that have been shown to be generally related to the perception of clients by helping professionals across settings, clients, and professions. The two variables, manageability, or the perception thereof, of clients and the personality characteristic of authoritarianism of professionals, seem to have particular relevance to our findings and their implications for helping relationships.

In his review, Wills (1978) discusses manageability as one of the key concepts in determining a "positive" or "negative" client in many studies. A positive client is described as one who is conforming, obedient, and deferential to staff. Furthermore, Wills stresses the fact that the outcome of many studies suggests a general negative attitude of helping professionals toward resistant clients and a more positive attitude toward cooperative or dependent clients. Caution is needed here, because of the multiplicity of definitions of dependency. Nevertheless, I want to argue that our observational data on behavior sequences between residents and their social partners are supportive of the construct of manageability.

As to the second variable, in many studies behaviors of helping professionals toward their clients have been described as authoritarian; restrictive and controlling behaviors are mentioned most. It is interesting to note that there is an inverse relationship between degree of authoritarianism and the amount of training of helping professionals. Thus, nurse's aides, for example, who in our studies have among the staff the most contact with the elderly resident, can be described on the average as rather restrictive and controlling. Accordingly, the dependent behavior of residents and the dependency-supportive behavior by staff are in agreement with the factors manageability of clients and authoritarianism of helping professionals. The two actors, residents and social partners, act in a role-congruent fashion. Thus, the data would speak for an institution effect rather than an aging effect. Further research as previously delineated is sorely needed in this area.

In conclusion, operant research on dependency in aging is consistent with the view that increased dependency in older nursing home residents is not solely regulated by biological conditions of the aging organism. First, as shown by operant–experimental work, dependency is modifiable. Second, as found through operant–observational work, dependency is maintained by naturally existing social contingencies in the environment of the elderly. Consequently, intraindividual variability is, indeed, paramount, and the role of environmental factors a necessary link in the understanding of behaviors of the elderly. This behavioral modifiability given different environmental influences has been termed behavioral plasticity.

Plasticity in Aging

Plasticity has become a household word in psychological gerontology. Nevertheless, it represents a major shift in the thinking of gerontologists (M. M. Baltes & P. B. Baltes, 1977, 1982, in press).

Variability in the sense of plasticity specifically refers to intraindividual changes, that is, to behavioral changes in an individual or individuals when exposed to differing conditions. Accordingly, the study of plasticity gives us insight into the range of functioning of an individual over time. Whereas traditionally gerontologists, like developmental psychologists, were essentially interested in universal increasing or decreasing relationships between chronological age and behaviors, now the focus has shifted to variability and plasticity. A host of studies, particularly in the areas of intellectual performance, memory, and learning, have demonstrated a substantial amount of interindividual differences and intraindividual change in performance (P. B. Baltes & S. L. Willis, 1981; Botwinick, 1977; Denney, 1979; Labouvie-Vief, 1976; Sterns & Sanders, 1980). Not only were these differences demonstrated, but their interrelationships with variables related to the situation, to the tasks, or to the subjects have been identified. An increasing concern with plasticity of functioning is evident also in the biological and medical literature (e.g., Fries, 1980; Platt, 1981).

Why is it important to study plasticity in gerontology and/or developmental psychology? It is essential, first of all, for theory construction. Knowledge about which behavior changes are plastic or variable and which ones are universal is rudimentary to a theory of aging. The study of plasticity allows us to learn about the many possible faces of aging given different conditions (M. M. Baltes & P. B. Baltes, 1982, in press; P. B. Baltes & Willis, 1982; Willis & Baltes, 1980). What we observe now might be only one of the possible ways of aging.

Second, the interest in plasticity leads to multimethod research endeavors termed *convergent operations* by McCall (1977) and *phases* by Baer (1973). These concepts refer to the combination of experimental and descriptive work both in laboratory and naturalistic settings. Together, they doubtlessly will yield a more complete picture of the etiology of aging behaviors. The research program on dependency described here is a work of this nature.

Third, the study of plasticity seems to have importance for social policies on a macrolevel and for help or helping relationships on a microlevel of the ecology of the elderly. Once we know about the diversity and plasticity among the groups of elderly, we will espouse policies geared toward the potential of the elderly, that is, toward optimization. As long as we focus on average processes, we tend to misinterpretations of the potential of older persons. I will come back to this issue in the next, concluding section of this chapter.

Implications for Helping Relationships

What are some implications of the experimental and observational data on dependency and independence in elderly nursing home residents for helping relationships, particularly as they occur in nursing home settings?

Helping relationships in institutional settings most likely have two objectives: to help the functioning of the resident and to help the functioning of the institution. Such a bifurcation of objectives in and of itself does not necessarily lead to conflicts. It easily can, however, particularly when the managerial functioning of the institution as a goal supersedes the present and future functioning of the elderly (Goffman, 1960, 1961; Kahana, 1973; Wack & Rodin, 1978). Not only can this be detrimental to individuals' possibility of development, it also can easily have a negative impact on the helping professionals in such institutions. Which goals will the professional identify with? The ensuing role conflict and its possible negative effects on the interactions between clients and professionals has been the object of many studies (for a review, see Wills, 1978) and is discussed in this volume by Crandall and Allen (see Chapter 19 in this volume) in detail.

For the present discussion let us assume for reasons of simplicity that the institutional and/or administrative philosophy is one that regards the functioning of the elderly resident as its prime goal. The major decision, then, concerns what functioning level of the elderly we strive for in terms of both present and future functioning.

To put this in a broader context, the question to be answered is: Do we envision development and, if so, what developmental goals do we envision for the elderly nursing home resident? Views on proper goals of aging involve combinatorial variables on several themes including the individual's beliefs, the attitudes and competencies of relevant professionals and other social partners, and the nature of existing sociopolitical conditions and societal values, as well as theoretical conceptions and knowledge of human development (for extensive discussion see Schneewind & Brandstädter, 1975; Wack & Rodin, 1978). Among these themes are obviously some in which the psychologist plays a critical role. Psychological researchers help to determine which theoretical considerations on the nature of human development and aging are proposed and how they are constructed. The psychologist can thereby help to build expectations held by professionals about the elderly (MacDonald, 1973).

The research presented here, as well as other work in the area of dependency, makes a strong argument for a theoretical model of aging that is defined by plasticity or modifiability and variability of aging processes (for detailed discussion see also M. M. Baltes & P. B. Baltes, 1982; P. B. Baltes & M. M. Baltes, 1980). Such variability and plasticity emphasizes the fact that individuals, their microenvironment, and society at large cannnot delegate "responsibility" for aging solely to a biological condition. On the contrary, humans are responsible for and have some control over what aging looks like and how it could be changed.

What is the consequence, then, of such a theoretical model compared to the traditional decline model for developmental goals and thus for helping relationships? It seems, first of all, that helping relationships need to be three-pronged: relationships geared toward correction and restoration, relationships aimed at maintenance, and relationships focused on enhancement and optimization (see also P. B. Baltes & Danish, 1979; Danish, Smyer, & Novak, 1980). Accordingly, in designing helping relationships, the developmental goal of self-actualization, for instance, discussed by Erikson (1959), by Havighurst (1972), and by Butler (1971) as being prominent and pertinent for the elderly, would have to be taken as seriously as the maintenance of a demented elderly person (Edwards, 1980). Helping relationships would have to work toward restoring, maintaining, and optimizing internal as well as external resources for the optimal functioning of the elderly. Correspondingly, helping relationships would create prosthetic, therapeutic, and/or enriching environments contingent upon the needs and status of the elderly.

These goals of prevention, enrichment, and rehabilitation apparently are not realized in the situations we studied, in which dependency-supportive behaviors or no response from staff and other social partners occurred so frequently. Dependency-supportive behaviors are contingent upon the beliefs of a deficit model of aging. As long as beliefs about deficits are predominant among staff members, the provision of custodial care for elderly residents by helping professionals will be the tendency. In this case, staff expectations of how the elderly can and are supposed to behave will be characterized by such concepts as dependency, adjustment to routines, and acceptance of the role of the old and the sick (MacDonald, 1973; Wack & Rodin, 1978).

As a second consequence of the notion of interindividual variability and intraindividual plasticity, helping relationships would have to be designed with the individual in mind, not an average target based on a group of elderly persons. Helping relationships would need to be tailored to each specific person–environment "package" rather than applied uniformly to elderly nursing home residents. Helping relationships would need to take into account the tremendous interindividual differences of the elderly, be they related to abilities, environmental and historical contexts, self-goals, or concurrent makeups of the elderly person.

Such demands will not fare well with helping professionals as long as the degree of manageability decides whether a client or patient is a "good" one or a "bad" one. Professionals who mainly play a controlling and restrictive role in dealing with clients are not likely to view helping relationships as geared toward interindividual and intraindividual differences. Such an attitude or role would also prohibit professionals from helping the client to develop self-control, the third and last implication to be mentioned.

It appears that a concern for individual liberty and humanitarianism would imply that helping relationships have to be geared toward self-control and the establishment of choices for the elderly person. Feeling in control or perceiving control over one's environment seems to gain more and more importance for the optimal functioning of the elderly (Langer, 1979; Langer & Benevento, 1978; Langer & Rodin, 1976; Ransen, 1981; Rodin & Langer, 1977; Schulz, 1976). If indeed, the recent experimental data by Avorn and Langer (Note 4) hold true (helping in the form of direct concrete assistance from social partners decreases the performance level, whereas helping in the form of encouragement or verbal suggestions increases the performance level of elderly nursing home residents), a strong argument can be made for helping relationships geared toward increasing feelings of control. In any case, it behooves us to create a data base that would provide information about the conditions under which aging individuals would function at high levels of independence and adequate control over their environments or, conversely, conditions under which aging individuals exhibit unnecessary decline in functioning. Whether such information is subsequently used by society at large, by helping professionals, and by institutions is a different matter.

Reference Notes

1. Risley, T. R., & Edwards, K. A. *Behavioral technology for nursing home care: Towards a system of nursing home organization and management.* Paper presented at the NOVA Behavioral Conference on Aging, Port St. Lucie, Fla., May 1978.
2. Baltes, M. M., Honn, S., Barton, E. M., Orzech, M. J., & Lago, D. *On the social ecology of dependence and independence in early nursing home residents: A replication and extension.* Manuscript submitted for publication, 1982.
3. Lawton, M. P., Patniak, B., & Fulcomer, M. *The ecology of the institutional setting.* Paper presented at the annual meeting of the Gerontological Society, New York, November 1976.
4. Avorn, J., & Langer, E. J. *Helping, helplessness, and the "incompetent" nursing home patient.* Unpublished manuscript, Harvard University, 1981.

References

Allison, P. D., & Liker, J. K. Analyzing sequential categorical data on diadic interaction: A comment on Gottman. *Psychological Bulletin*, 1982, *91*, 393–403.

Baer, D. M. The control of developmental processes: Why wait? In J. R. Nesselroade & H. W. Reese (Eds.), *Life-span developmental psychology: Methodological issues.* New York: Academic Press, 1973.

Baltes, M. M., & Baltes, P. B. The eco-psychological relativity and plasticity of psychological aging: Convergent perspectives of cohort effects and operant psychology. *Zeitschrift für Experimentelle und Angewandte Psychologie*, 1977, *24*, 179–197.

Baltes, M. M., & Baltes, P. B. Micro-analytical research on environmental factors and plasticity in psychological aging. In T. Field *et al.* (Eds.), *Review of human development.* New York: Wiley, 1982.

Baltes, M. M., & Barton, E. M. New approaches toward aging: A case for the operant model. *Educational Gerontology: An International Quarterly*, 1977, *2*, 383–405.

Baltes, M. M., & Barton, E. M. Behavioral analysis of aging: A review of the operant model and research. *International Journal of Behavioral Development*, 1979, *2*, 297–320.

Baltes, M. M. Barton, E. M., Orzech, M. J., & Lago, D. *The micro-ecology of residents and staff: Behavior mapping in a nursing home.* Appears in German translation in: *Zeitschrift für Gerontologie*, in press.

Baltes, M. M., Burgess, R. L., & Stewart, R. Independence and dependence in self-care behaviors in nursing home residents: An operant–observational study. *International Journal of Behavioral Development*, 1980, *3*, 489–500.

Baltes, M. M., & Lerner, R. M. Roles of the operant model and its methods in the life-span approach to human development. *Human Development*, 1980, *23*, 361–367.

Baltes, M. M., & Zerbe, M. B. Independence training in nursing home residents. *The Gerontologist*, 1976, *25*, 428–432.

Baltes, P. B., & Baltes, M. M. Plasticity and variability in psychological aging: Methodological and theoretical issues. In G. Gurski (Ed.), *Determining the effects of aging on the central nervous system.* Berlin: Schering, 1980.

Baltes, P. B., & Danish, S. J. Intervention in life-span development and aging: Issues and concepts. In R. R. Turner & H. W. Reese (Eds.), *Life-span developmental psychology: Intervention.* New York: Academic Press, 1979.

Baltes, P. B., & Willis, S. L. Enhancement (plasticity) of intellectual functioning in old age: Penn State's Adult Development and Enrichment Program (ADEPT). In F. I. M. Craik & S. E. Trehub (Eds.), *Aging and cognitive processes.* New York: Plenum, 1982.

Barton, E. M., Baltes, M. M., Orzech, M. J. On the etiology of dependence in older nursing home residents during morning care: The role of staff behavior. *Journal of Personality and Social Psychology*, 1980, *38*, 423–431.

Botwinick, J. Intellectual abilities. In J. E. Birren & K. W. Schaie (Eds.), *Handbook of the psychology of aging.* New York: Van Nostrand-Reinhold, 1977.

Butler, R. N. The life review. *Psychology Today*, 1971, *5*, 49–51.

Danish, S. J., Smyer, M. A., & Novak, D. A. Developmental intervention: Enhancing life-event processes. In P. B. Baltes & O. G. Brim, Jr. (Eds.), *Life-span development and behavior* (Vol. 3). New York: Academic Press, 1980.

Denney, N. W. Problem solving in later adulthood: Intervention research. In P. B. Baltes & O. G. Brim, Jr. (Eds.), *Life-span development and behavior* (Vol. 2). New York: Academic Press, 1979.

Edwards, K. A. Restoring functional behavior of senile elderly. In J. M. Ferguson & C. B. Taylor (Eds.), *The comprehensive handbook of behavioral medicine: Extended applications and issues* (Vol. 3). Jamaica, New York: SP Medical and Scientific Books, 1980.

Erikson, E. H. Identity and the life cycle. *Psychological Issues Monograph I*. New York: International Universities Press, 1959.

Fries, J. F. Aging, natural death, and the compression of morbidity. *New England Journal of Medicine*, 1980, *303*, 130–135.

Goffman, E. Characteristics of total institutions. In M. R. Stein, A. J. Violich, & D. M. White (Eds.), *Identity and anxiety: Survival of the person in mass society*. New York: Free Press, 1960.

Goffman, E. *Asylums: Essays on the social situation of mental patients and other inmates*. Chicago: Aldine, 1961.

Gottesman, L. E., & Bourestom, N. C. Why nursing homes do what they do. *The Gerontologist*, 1974, *14*, 501–506.

Havighurst, R. J. *Developmental tasks and education* (3rd ed.) New York: McKay, 1972.

Hoyer, W. J. Application of operant techniques to the modification of elderly behavior. *The Gerontologist*, 1973, *13*, 18–22.

Hoyer, W. J. Aging as intra-individual change. *Developmental Psychology*, 1974, *10*, 821–826.

Ittelson, W. H., Rivlin, L. G., & Proshansky, H. M. The use of behavioral maps in environmental psychology. In H. M. Proshansky, H. W. Ittelson, & L. S. Rivlin (Eds.), *Environmental psychology: Man and his physical setting*. New York: Holt, 1970.

Kahana, E. The humane treatment of old people in institutions. *The Gerontologist*, 1973, *13*, 282–289.

Konzelik, J. A. *Designing the open nursing home*. Stroudsburg, Pa.: Dowden, Hutchinson, & Ross, 1976.

Labouvie-Vief, G. Toward optimizing cognitive competence in later life. *Educational Gerontology: An International Quarterly*, 1976, *1*, 75–92.

Langer, E. J. The illusion of incompetence. In L. C. Perlmuter & R. A. Monty (Eds.), *Choice and perceived control*. Hillsdale, N.J.: Erlbaum, 1979.

Langer, E. J., & Benevento, A. Self-induced dependence. *Journal of Personality and Social Psychology*, 1978, *36*, 886–893.

Langer, E. J., & Rodin, J. The effects of choice and enhanced personal responsibility for the aged: A field experiment in an institutional setting. *Journal of Personality and Social Psychology*, 1976, *34*, 191–198.

Lester, P. B., & Baltes, M. M. Loss of independence in the elderly: The significance of environmental conditions. *Journal of Gerontological Nursing*, 1978, *4*, 23–27.

MacDonald, M. L. The forgotten Americans: A socio-psychological analysis of aging and nursing homes. *American Journal of Community Psychology*, 1973, *1*, 272–295.

McCall, R. B. Challenges to a science of developmental psychology. *Child Development*, 1977, *48*, 333–344.

McClannahan, L. B. Therapeutic and prosthetic living environments for nursing home residents. *The Gerontologist*, 1973, *13*, 424–429.

Patterson, R. J., & Jackson, G. M. Behavioral approaches to gerontology. In L. Michelson, M. Hersen, & S. Turner (Eds.), *Future perspectives in behavior therapy*, New York: Plenum, 1980. (a)

Patterson, R. L., & Jackson, G. M. Behavior modification with the elderly. In M. Hersen, R. M. Eisler, & P. Miller (Eds.), *Progress in behavior modification* (Vol. 7). New York: Academic Press, 1980. (b)

Platt, D. Das Defizitmodell des Alters aus biologisch-medizinischer Sicht. *Aktuelle Gerontologie*, 1981, *11*, 177–183.

Ransen, D. L. Long-term effects of two interventions with the aged: An ecological analysis. *Journal of Applied Developmental Psychology*, 1981, *2*, 13–27.

Rodin, J., & Langer, E. J. Long-term effects of a control-relevant intervention with the institutionalized aged. *Journal of Personality and Social Psychology*, 1977, *35*, 897–902.

Sackett, G. T. The lag sequential analysis of contingency and cyclicity in behavioral interaction research. In J. Osofsky (Ed.), *Handbook of infant development*. New York: Wiley, 1977.

Seligman, M. E. P. *Helplessness: On depression, development, and death.* San Francisco: Freeman 1975.

Schneewind, K. A., & Brandstädter, J. Psychology and the problem of optimal human development: II. Further elaboration of a programmatic developmental model. *Trierer Psychologische Berichte*, 1975, *2*(4), 1–33.

Schulz, R. The effects of control and predictability on the psychological and physical well-being of the institutionalized aged. *Journal of Personality and Social Psychology*, 1976, *33*, 563–573.

Schulz, R., & Hanusa, B. Long-term effects of control and predictability-enhancing interventions: Findings and ethical issues. *Journal of Personality and Social Psychology*, 1978, *36*, 1194–1201.

Skinner, B. F. *The behavior of organisms: An experimental approach.* New York: Appleton, 1938.

Spasoff, R. A., Kraus, A. S., Beattie, E. J., Holden, D. E. W., Lawson, J. S., Rodenberg, J., & Woodcock, S. M. A longitudinal study of the elderly residents of long-stay institutions: 1. Early response to institutional care. *The Gerontologist*, 1978, *18*, 281–292.

Sperbeck, D. J., & Whitbourne Krauss, S. Dependency in the institutional setting: A behavioral training program for geriatric staff. *The Gerontologist*, 1981, *21*, 268–275.

Sterns, H. L., & Sanders, R. E. Training and education of the elderly. In R. R. Turner & H. W. Reese (Eds.), *Life-span developmental psychology: Intervention.* New York: Academic Press, 1980.

Wack, J., & Rodin, J. Nursing homes for the aged: The human consequences of legislation-shaped environments. *Journal of Social Issues*, 1978, *34*(4), 7–21.

Willis, S. L., & Baltes, P. B. Intelligence in adulthood and aging: Contemporary issues. In L. Poon (Ed.), *Aging in the 1980s: Psychological issues.* Washington, D.C.: American Psychological Association, 1980.

Wills, T. A. Perception of clients by professional helpers. *Psychological Bulletin*, 1978, *85*, 968–1000.

PROCESSES IN STRESS
ON THE HELPER

A helping relationship has effects on the helper as well as on the recipient. The documented effects of professional helping experience include changes in general perceptions of clients, frustration with the helping role, and an increased level of perceived stress by the helper (Wills, 1978). These effects appear to be caused by structural and organizational factors in helping relationships. Although some professional helpers conduct therapy under near-ideal conditions, others provide help in conditions involving some combination of large case load, intense emotional interaction with clients, minimal resources to support the helping effort, and shifting or conflicting organizational demands. Research by the authors of the chapters in the following section is beginning to provide a sound conceptual and empirical basis for understanding the aspects of helping relationships that produce stress on the helper.

In Chapter 19, Crandall and Allen provide a detailed consideration of how organizational factors may affect the helper. Although a professional helper's primary focus is on therapeutic interaction with clients, in many settings the helper is also a member of an organization, and hence must respond to considerations such as role relationships, management objectives, institutional climate, and organizational demands (e.g., paperwork). This basic fact has two

427

important implications. One is that organizational factors may affect the helper–client relationship; as Crandall and Allen point out, organizations are integrated social systems, and a change in one part of the system has a way of producing effects on other parts. The authors provide a novel perspective on organizational aspects of helping by interpreting empirical findings in terms of *parallel-process* theory, which posits a reciprocal relationship between helper–organization interaction and helper–client interaction. A second implication of organizational factors is that the demands of the organization and the perspective of the client may not coincide. The helping resources provided by the organization may be insufficient to support the helper's efforts; the formal policies or regulations of the organization may be in some way inconsistent with the needs of the clients (cf. Baltes, Chapter 18 in this volume); the actual implementation of day-to-day procedures in a large organization may differ considerably from the formal organizational policy; the demands of the organization itself may be shifting or conflicting; and in some settings it has been observed that clients tend to have a different view of treatment than do the staff (e.g., Dimsdale, Klerman, & Shershow, 1979; Hornstra, Lubin, Lewis, & Willis, 1972; Polak, 1970; Zaslove, Ungerleider, & Fuller, 1966; Doherty & Liang, Note 1; cf. also Pelton, Chapter 5 in this volume). There has been relatively little research on how these various factors may affect the outcome of helping relationships, and the study of drug treatment agencies reported in the chapter provides a good example of how organizational research may be conducted in field settings. Crandall and Allen provide a number of valuable suggestions for further research on role structure, organizational climate, and client perceptions, and conclude with an interesting analysis of how therapists may interpret client behavior as a reflection of organizational structure.

In Chapter 20, Pines provides a wide-ranging discussion of the effects of stress on the helper. It has been observed in a number of studies that professional helpers may develop a syndrome involving loss of helping motivation, negative views of clients, and psychological and physical symptoms; this has aptly been termed the *burnout syndrome*. The research of Pines and colleagues has shown burnout to be a widely generalized phenomenon, affecting not only highly trained psychotherapists but also a variety of other human service professionals, including social workers, teachers, staff members in residential facilities, medical personnel, and workers in the criminal justice system. Factors that apparently contribute to burnout are a heavy case load, stressful client contact, feelings of restricted autonomy or significance in the professional role, a workload reflecting emphasis on organizational demands rather than direct helping efforts, and a perceived lack of change by clients, which is a generalized concern of professional helpers. A paradoxical finding in burnout studies is that persons with the strongest altruistic motivation, who are likely to be the most effective helpers, are the most susceptible to burnout; this finding has important implications for the helping professions because it suggests that in some settings there may be a disproportionate loss of the most talented professionals. (Burnout is related to personnel turnover rates.) Research by Pines and colleagues has provided an empirical basis for understanding how to prevent burnout among professional helpers. Interestingly, two promising avenues for prevention are to enable the helper to have a greater level of perceived control over his or her work (cf. Schorr & Rodin, Chapter 8 in this volume) and to obtain more social support from colleagues (cf. Moos & Mitchell, Chapter 10, Antonucci & Depner, Chapter 11 in this volume). Pines also suggests how work environments and professional education can be designed so as to achieve greater benefits for both helpers and clients.

Reference Note

1. Doherty, E. G., & Liang, J. *Helping relationships as perceived by psychiatrists and their inpatients over time*. Paper presented at the meeting of the Midwest Sociological Society, St. Louis, April 1976.

References

Dimsdale, J. E., Klerman, G., & Shershow, J. C. Conflict in treatment goals between patients and staff. *Social Psychiatry*, 1979, *14*, 1–4.

Hornstra, R. K., Lubin, B., Lewis, R. V., & Willis, B. S. Worlds apart: Patients and professionals. *Archives of General Psychiatry*, 1972, *27*, 553–557.

Polak, P. Patterns of discord: Goals of patients, therapists, and community members. *Archives of General Psychiatry*, 1970, *23*, 277–283.

Wills, T. A. Perceptions of clients by professional helpers. *Psychological Bulletin*, 1978, *85*, 968–1000.

Zaslove, M. O., Ungerleider, J. T., & Fuller, M. C. How psychiatric hospitalization helps: Patient views vs. staff views. *Journal of Nervous and Mental Disease*, 1966, *142*, 568–576.

chapter 19

The Organizational Context
of Helping Relationships

RICK CRANDALL
RICHARD D. ALLEN

Introduction

Our thesis in this chapter is that in order to fully understand the development of a therapeutic relationship one must pay attention to the organizational context within which the helping occurs. For example, consider what might transpire in a mental health service delivery agency that is experiencing a high client dropout rate. Various levels of the agency may recognize and respond to the problem in different ways. The high dropout rate might be identified by counselors who see a sudden drop in their caseloads. Since they may have seen their load as too high in the first place, counselors may not regard a decrease as a problem. From the administrative side, a high dropout rate is almost sure to be defined as a problem, since it normally translates into fewer dollars for the agency. Either counselors or administrators could be concerned about the dropout rate as a type of feedback from dissatisfied clients. They might analyze either individual clinical processes or overall agency structure in search of solutions.

According to traditional organizational theories, the agency administrators would make decisions about the dropout problem, including whether or not it was a problem. They would then communicate their concern and solutions

Basic Processes in Helping Relationships

down the managerial ladder to supervisors, and they in turn would transmit this message down to the counselors. This approach illustrates how the change desired by the administrators is communicated through the entire system. Traditional organizational approaches have typically viewed how those in power effect change in the system in which they work.

A different approach, which we discuss here, is to view the clients, counselors, and administrators as an interactive system. We outline a view of helping organizations that puts more emphasis on the line staff who are most intimately involved with the effects of agency policies and procedures. We also analyze how policies and procedures affect the interactional processes within the agency, and suggest how counselor–supervisor interactions can reflect the type of experiences the agency's clients have.

The purpose of this chapter is to show that is can be useful to look at helping relationships from an organizational perspective. By organizational perspective we mean the analysis of a helping setting as a human organization, subject to many of the same influences and problems as any business or service organization. Our discussion will deal with general processes that take place in most helping organizations. Research and thinking on helping relationships have usually been directed at client history or attitudes, therapeutic procedures, client–counselor interaction, and similar variables. Although each of these approaches can be valuable, it tends to focus attention on only one component of the treatment setting, overlooking the fact that the components of the helping setting are interactive and interdependent. Research on helping relationships has also tended to emphasize the unique aspects of the helping settings. This has obscured the fact that helping organizations are just that—organizations. The fact that even small therapeutic settings are organizations allows us to draw from the rich research traditions in general organizational research, providing a different perspective on helping organizations. In addition to reviewing work by others, we attempt to develop some theoretical and practical approaches that are applicable to both helping settings and other organizations.

SYSTEMS THEORY ANALYSIS OF ORGANIZATIONS

The most general approach to the analysis of organizations is probably open systems theory (Katz & Kahn, 1978). This approach has two strong assumptions: (1) that the parts of an organization are interrelated such that a change in one part may affect any other part, and (2) that the organization is influenced by its environment and must change and react accordingly.

Systems theory has been applied to many settings besides organizations. The concepts were originally developed in several fields, including biology. It sometimes helps to remember how a systems model applies by thinking of a living amoeba as a system: All its parts are interrelated—if one part moves, there is movement in other areas. An amoeba is also very sensitive to the environment; if you poke it, it reacts.

Another central part of systems theory is the concept of *throughput*. All organizations include the following steps in one form or another: (1) they take in input (material, people, etc.), (2) they process the input, and (3) they produce products that leave the system. In the example of a psychology clinic, the inputs are patients and the resources to do the job, the process is therapy, and the output is healthy ex-patients.

Our approach will be to view helping organizations as interactive social systems. We will focus on the interrelations among the people in a helping setting rather than on the transactions with the environment. We will also highlight a few ideas that are more commonly applied to general organizations than to helping settings. Much of the systems approach discussed here, as well as a research example discussed later, derives from years of research at the Institute of Behavioral Research at Texas Christian University. Other aspects of that work are discussed elsewhere (e.g., James, 1981; Sells, 1976).

Conceptual Framework for the Analysis of Helping Organizations

If you are in a counseling position in a helping organization, you tend to view everything as revolving around the provision of counseling services. From a systems theory perspective, you are partially right since the delivery of service is the "production work" of a helping system. However, organizations (like other living organisms) have a tendency to grow and defend themselves. This is generally coordinated by a managerial or administrative subsystem that is hierarchically above the production–helping subsystem. Sometimes the administrators are necessary to obtain funds for a clinic, and they may provide important functions to protect and support the delivery of services. Unfortunately, managers of helping units sometimes become separated from actual service delivery (i.e., full-time administrators) and develop a tendency to issue policy for the delivery of service, to give orders, and to show bureaucratic tendencies. When this happens, they tend to behave like administrators of any production-type company. Thus, traditional organizational issues concerning lines of authority, worker autonomy, and role definitions become important in many helping organizations.

ROLE DEFINITION

In the individual helping relationship, with one counselor and one client, authority and role definitions are clear. The helper or counselor is relatively autonomous. He or she both sets policy and carries it out. If the client does not like the approach, he or she goes elsewhere. However, once the helper becomes part of an organization new factors come into play. In some helping organizations, the administrators may have nothing to do with setting policy or procedures for the helping process itself, but they still influence counselors by demands for paperwork and work load, and through their influence on the overall organizational morale. In other cases, the administrators also have direct input to the counseling process. Such input can be constructive when supervisors act as consultants at the *request* of counselors or provide an experienced resource. However, this is not always the case. Often the supervisor plays an evaluative role or tries to guide counseling without actually being aware of all the details of a case. From an organizational perspective, then, the very existence of supervisors, managers, and administrators raises several issues.

In any organization, role definitions and responsibilities need to be made clear so that individuals will not infringe upon each other. For instance, therapeutic and organizational roles often conflict. The counselors are both helpers and disciplinarians for the clients. From an organizational perspective, however, the supportive helping role may conflict with the necessity of enforcing rules, imposing restraints, and not becoming personally involved. From a broader organizational perspective, the roles and interrelations of the helper and the administrator must be clearly defined; administrators can be a resource for the helper, or they can be an evaluator or meddler. Defining the areas of autonomy for the helper and authority for the administrator thus is especially important in a helping organization.

ORGANIZATIONAL DEMANDS

Other factors than can influence both treatment and helper satisfaction are organizational structures and demands. An organization that is involved with treatment places certain demands on all those functioning in the agency. For clients and counselors these demands have to do with the expected treatment outcomes. For example, in a correctional facility the desired treatment outcome is that inmates do not commit a crime when released from the facility. In order for the treatment agency to assist the client in meeting its demands, it employs counselors who provide various learning and therapeutic treatments that are designed to help the client meet the agency demands. Those who supervise the counselors have the demand of assisting the counselor to provide treatment that will enable the client to meet agency demands. Administrators have additional pressure to make the organization run smoothly and deal with outside forces.

The method employed by an agency to assist the client, counselor, and supervisory personnel in meeting the agency treatment demands is traditionally called the treatment modality. The treatment modality is essentially the structure provided by the agency to assist those associated with the agency to meet the *treatment demands* of the agency. In a correctional treatment facility, for example, behavior counseling techniques could be used to help inmates learn impulse control and evaluate the consequences of their behavior; this should assist the inmates in meeting the agency demands of not engaging in inappropriate or illegal behavior.

From a more complete systems analysis perspective we now see that the treatment structure of the agency will have several effects on the behavior of the counselors and others in the agency. The treatment structure will specify, either clearly or covertly, the degree of autonomy afforded the counselors in planning and implementing their therapeutic endeavors. The treatment structure will also place a number of restrictions and demands on the agency supervisors who will oversee the counselors. The treatment approach affects all those connected with an agency. In turn, those operating in the agency affect the treatment approach as well as each other.

PARALLEL PROCESS

In any hierarchical organization a given individual often fills two roles, supervisor and supervisee. The issues that arise for Person A as a supervisor can be identical to those of Person A's own supervisor. A traditional approach to helping organizations would not assume that how a counselor interacted with the client would be similar to or affect how the counselor interacted with the supervisor. However, a theory developed in psychiatric residence training termed *parallel process* suggests that the similarities between supervisor–counselor and counselor–client interactions will be particularly strong (Abroms, 1977; Ekstein & Wallenstein, 1958). In light of a general systems theory approach we feel that this theory can be applied somewhat more broadly to make predictions both in helping and nonhelping organizations.

In supervision, parallel process theory would state that the type of inter-actional process that occurs between the counselor in training and his client would be mirrored in the supervisory session. For example, if the client has been withholding information in the session, the counselor entering the supervision session will also be somewhat withholding, in part because he may not have much information to present, but also because the counselor may not feel comfortable with what went on and his defensiveness may come out in the form of reluctance to disclose freely. In supervision, it is advisable for the supervisor to become aware of not only the *content* of the counselor's presentation but also the *process*, as this may be indicative of the client's interactions during the session. This approach can also be used to suggest how an agency's clients may be dealing with the demands of the agency and their response to the structure provided. Counselors may frequently present material that indicates that they and their clients are frustrated with either organizational demands or structure. This could take the form of the counselor responding defensively to supervisor demands or being resistant to the structure being established by the supervisor. This may mean that the supervisor has been presented with some data indicating how the clients of an agency are responding to the demands and structure of the agency. This model is essentially a feedback model, in which the reactions of clients to the agency are assumed to be mirrored in their interactions in counseling, and this interaction then is mirrored in the supervision session. In a helping organization with several levels, the interactions at each level should affect the interactions with other levels. We will not have time here to discuss applications to nonhelping organizations. However, many of the conclusions developed here should apply in any organization.

ROLE CONFLICT

One of the more useful ideas for both helping organizations and for organizational research is to analyze the demands and support for various roles, sometimes conflicting, that can be carried out by a given individual in an organization. For many years a traditional area of organizational research concerned people's identification with either the organization itself or their broader professional group. Only recently was identification with a client group also considered (London & Howat, 1978). Clearly an individual in a helping organization can have varying degrees of loyalty to several groups, subgroups, or value systems, which may cause considerable role conflict.

There are probably four simple types of demands that can be present for a counselor in a helping organization, in addition to other types of identification the individual may have, such as with the profession in general. Two types of demands come from the helping organization. The first involves doing the formally defined job of helping clients using a particular type of approach. The second demand involves functioning as a member of the organization. In addition to dealing with political pressures and not rocking the boat, the most annoying thing for counselors usually is keeping up with a flood of paperwork to document what happens to the client. The paperwork relates to a more subtle demand in most organizations: to keep the head count of clients high. In some settings this can lead to support for client dependency. Thus, organizational demands for clinical results can conflict with subtler demands to ensure the survival of the organization by keeping clients in it.

The two types of demands that come from clients can also provide conflict for the counselor. Clients have a traditional interest in getting well, being released, etc. This is generally complementary to the organizational demand for results. Unfortunately, in day-to-day practice clients also often have a demand to "take it easy on me." This can involve an unwillingness to become involved in therapy, a resistance to the therapeutic modality encouraged by the agency, a resistance to organizational goals, fear, or simple laziness. It is the counselor's job to fight some of these client tendencies. However, the counselor must also identify with the clients and sometimes take their side against unreasonable demands from the organization. Here we have the simplest conflict for the counselor—between identifying with the organization or the client. The good counselor has to do both. From our current perspective this balance of identification determines much of the flow of influence between counselor, client, and the organization. Parallel process cases can be caused in part by the counselor identifying with the client without fully realizing it. In clinical practice these influences and conflicts need to be made explicit so that they can be dealt with in a more open and healthy manner.

Organizational Variables

Because helping organizations *are* organizations, almost every area of organizational research and theory might be applied in helping settings.[1] Some of the many areas of organizational functioning that are relevant to helping agencies are turnover, newcomer assimilation, employee morale, burnout, organizational politics, role conflict, communication, motivation, and leadership. Several of these are discussed in the following sections.

BURNOUT

Because *burnout* is discussed in detail by Pines (see Chapter 20 in this volume) we will use it only as a brief example here. Burnout refers to the case in which an employee loses interest in the job in a way that often leaves him or her apathetic. The concept is particularly appropriate in helping organizations since it can refer to a case in which the employee was very involved previously. The term is a good one. Sometimes the "fire" of work and inner enthusiasm burns hotly and out of control, leaving afterward only "ashes" psychologically.

Burnout is a good psychological example of processes in organizations. It relates to multiple concepts such as morale, worker expectations, integration into the job, job demands, and stress (e.g., Maslach, 1978). In a simple sense,

[1]Unfortunately, various organizational concepts have tended to become fads that are often applied inappropriately in helping organizations. A common example would be Management by Objectives (MBO). This can be a very useful approach, but as often applied it involves the imposition of goals by superiors on their subordinates. In the helping setting such a distortion of MBO would be particularly inappropriate. In any organization those affected by the goal must be committed to it in order to make it work. Counselors should normally be given much more autonomy in setting goals than the average "worker."

burnout is a reaction to high job stress, caused by things like excessively high job demands. Because burnout is a psychological phenomenon, it provides a good example of why it is valuable to measure worker–counselor attitudes and feelings about the job in great detail as discussed in the next section. With this information steps can be taken to avoid or deal with the burnout process.

PSYCHOLOGICAL CLIMATE

Perhaps the most complete way to understand workers' feelings, cognitions, and perceptions of their job is to measure "psychological climate." Psychological climate is defined as people's cognitive representations of their environment expressed in terms that reflect their psychological significance and meaning to the individual (e.g., James & Jones, 1974). In brief, psychological climate focuses on people's perceptions of their job. The types of psychological climate perceptions that have proved useful to measure in a variety of organizations fall into six general areas:

1. Role perceptions such as ambiguity and overload
2. Job perceptions such as challenge and autonomy
3. Perceptions of the leader such as support and influence
4. Work group perceptions such as cooperation and friendliness
5. Perceptions of positive organizational factors such as management concern and awareness
6. Perceptions of negative organizational factors such as politics and conflict

People's psychological climate perceptions are not expected to relate directly to objective reality. In fact, perceptions should relate more closely to people's behavior than would more objective measures because the perceptions reflect the processing and interpretation of objective events. This approach is covered more fully in work at the Institute of Behavioral Research at Texas Christian University by James and Jones (1974, 1976), Sells (1976), and others.

Past research on perceptions of organizations suggests several trends useful in the study of health delivery organizations:

1. The assessment of perceptions should emphasize factors that are most meaningful to the workers (for instance, their own roles, job responsibilities, peers, leaders, clients, and so forth).
2. The perceptions of people working in the same setting, even though it is essentially the same environment, will differ based on personal characteristics and interpretations; these differences in perceptions are important for understanding the unique viewpoint of each individual.
3. Workers in a helping setting will respond to organizational variables and initiatives as a function of the psychological meaning and importance of

these organizational factors to them as individuals. Since individuals will interpret and perceive how these organizational factors either help or hinder them in their work with clients, measuring these perceptions may provide information on how the counselor will evaluate the worth of the organization.

One way of integrating the many dimensions that can be measured for psychological climate perceptions is to determine how these perceptions relate to the demands and structure of the organization. This would involve an assessment to see if the demands and structure of the organization are congruent with the counselor's goals and treatment strategies. It would also involve finding out just how each counselor defines his or her role.

ROLE CHARACTERISTICS

Role characteristics that have an impact on the individual's perceptions of psychological climate include the variables of role conflict, role ambiguity, and overload. All of these issues are related to the demands and structure of the organization. An example of an organizational demand is a high caseload. Coupled with a structure requiring many contact hours and/or much paperwork, this would lead to perceptions of overload by counselors. Role conflicts tend to arise when counselors are not in agreement with the procedures (structure) established to help them assist their clients in meeting organizational demands. Role ambiguity is affected by the organizational structure and how it affects counselors in their attempts to meet organizational demands. Overload is also related to demands. If the organization establishes high demands and a great deal of structure, counselors may find that they do not have the resources, time, and energy to meet organizational demands. This in turn places counselors in the conflict position of attempting to satisfy certain organizational demands in a particular manner (structure) without having the means to do so, and has a negative impact on counselors' psychological climate perceptions.

OTHER FACTORS

Job characteristics such as challenge and autonomy also relate to the organization's demands and structure. Important aspects of job characteristics such as autonomy are influenced by the organization's demands on counselors and the structure that counselors attempt to use to assist the clients in meeting the demands. There are other factors that relate to the climate in an organization, such as leadership style and behavior, work group characteristics, and positive and negative organizational factors such as management concern and organizational politics. These variables are influenced by the organization's demands and structure as well as by the personality and management styles of those in the organization. Basically all of these variables are interdependent. If counselors are frustrated because the demands of the organization are too great and the structure is not helpful in assisting clients to meet organizational demands, then the counselors will, to some extent, express their frustrations in dealing with their co-workers, supervisors, and probably with their clients.

Research on Organizational Variables

We will briefly discuss research using organizational approaches to study treatment delivery. Many studies have collected perceptual data, the most common type being client ratings of counselors. These can be valuable in clarifying the relationship between the client and counselor but do not help clarify the overall organizational structure and style. Knowledge of the goals of clients (Dimsdale, Klerman, & Shershow, 1979) or the reactions of clients to counseling approaches (Obitz, 1975) could both provide data on how parallel process issues affect counselor–supervisor interactions.

A general acceptance of a systems-type organizational model is actually not uncommon in the health care delivery literature. However, it has seldom been actually used in management practice or research. Rand (1978) has discussed community mental health service delivery from an organizational perspective as well as the relevance of organizational development for such organizations. Spaniol (1975) discussed a model of program evaluation in rehabilitation settings that emphasized the importance of the total setting including the organizational system:

> One needs to look at the total rehabilitation system and all of its functions in order to have the perspective necessary to see where evaluation contributes to the system. It is not sufficient, for instance, to evaluate client and counselor characteristics extracted from the structure or management system within which they function [p. 1].

Olmstead (1973) discussed the relevance of studying organizational structure and climate for social welfare agencies. He covered many factors similar to those covered in our research, such as power and authority, communication, roles, leadership, and group relations. Glisson (1978) utilized a path-analytic approach and a general systems viewpoint to study the effects of organizational structure variables on technology routinization in many different social welfare organizations in the St. Louis area.

The interactive nature of the treatment setting has received extensive attention, particularly the fact the treatment outcomes depend on characteristics of some or all of the following: clients, counselor, therapeutic approach, and treatment organization. For instance, Thrasher and Smith (1973) discussed how patient roles could interact differently with different treatment settings, counselors, etc. Maslach (1978) discussed the importance of interaction and mutual influences between counselors and clients. Szapocznik and Ladner (1977) reviewed several articles that advocated an interactional model for treatment research and stated that it is a common assumption "that most therapies work better under some conditions and with certain types of patients than under others." Reed (1978) explicitly argued that treatment effectiveness depends on interactions of outcomes, clients, and components of the therapy process.

The approach in the health delivery area most similar to the one advocated here is probably that of Moos and his colleagues at the Stanford Veterans Administration Hospital. They have developed sets of instruments that focus on client perceptions of the treatment process and environment. These include perceptions of treatment and hospital environments rated by both clients and staff (Moos, 1974). One more recent study used a path model to measure several sets of variables that could affect alcohol treatment outcome. Their sets of client variables, treatment program variables, and client perceptions of the treatment environment variables predicted several outcome measures quite well (Cronkite & Moos, 1978).

Study of Drug Treatment Agencies

In this section we discuss a study that uses parts of the general systems approach described previously. The findings are interpreted in terms of general systems and parallel process concepts introduced earlier. This study was conducted by the Institute of Behavioral Research (IBR) at Texas Christian University. It built upon many years of research on both drug treatment and perceptions of organizations by Sells and James (e.g., James, 1981; Sells, 1976). Data were collected from over 60 drug treatment units that were part of 40 different helping organizations.[2]

The IBR study focused on the job perceptions of the counselors in drug treatment units. The units were from urban areas all over the United States. The average number of clients per unit was 126, with a range from 17 to 391. The average number of staff was 9.4, of whom about two-thirds were counselors. Units were selected that had heroin as a common drug for treatment. About half the units used methadone maintenance in treatment and half

---

[2]Extended reports of the study are available from the IBR in several publications (e.g., Crandall, Bruni, Hilton, James, & Sells, Note 1).

were drug free. Compared to all drug treatment programs reporting to the Client Oriented Data Acquisition Process (CODAP) system (most programs in the country, USDHEW, Note 2), the clients here were older (average about 30 years), had more prior treatment experience (68%), and were more likely to have heroin as the primary drug of abuse (71%).

The extensive results in the IBR study can be looked at in several ways. In keeping with our earlier discussion we will interpret some of the IBR results in a different framework from the original study in terms of the degree and type of demands placed on the client by both the counselor and agency.

Research at the IBR developed a classification of treatment approaches called *Change Oriented* and *Adaptive*. Change-oriented units place much higher demands on clients for change and provide more structure to help bring it about faster. Adaptive units place less demands on the client, with less structure, and try to help clients adapt gradually to a healthier life-style. The IBR study classified agencies as *High Demand*, those that expected their clients to be totally resocialized, or *Low Demand*, those that expected their clients only to modify their life-style somewhat. These two types of agencies were then also divided into two categories depending upon the type of treatment structure utilized (Methadone Maintenance or Drug Free). The overall results of the study suggested that there are relationships between the types of demands and agency structure and the types of counselor complaints and dissatisfaction.

CLIENT MOTIVATION

One type of unit studied was the low-demand–low-structure category. The type of agency in which this occurred was the drug-free, adaptive type of agency, where the expectation (demand) was that clients probably would not give up all usage of illicit drugs because they resided in an environment in which drug usage was prevalent. The focus of this type of agency, then, was to help clients to try to adapt to this type of environment and reduce their drug usage. This type of agency also provided low structure in that clients did not have mandatory therapy sessions and educational activities, nor did they have frequent urine tests or many sanctions that could be imposed for engaging in inappropriate behavior. In one sense it was up to the clients to establish treatment demands for themselves and also to utilize the loose agency structure to meet the treatment demands that they set. The results from the psychological climate study done with this type of agency were interesting in that the greatest source of dissatisfaction for the counselors was client motivation. Counselors perceived the clients as not involved to a great extent in treatment. There is a broad parallel between the lack of client motivation or involvement and the lack of demand and structure (involvement) by the agency itself.

CONFLICTING DEMANDS

In the other type of low-demand–low-structure agency, the demand on clients was again adaptive, that is to learn to reduce drug abuse while living in the same environment. The second characteristic of these agencies was the provision of methadone maintenance without accompanying structure. The agencies did not provide high structure in terms of organized treatment plans and were casual about requiring attendance in various treatment programs. The methadone maintenance doses in these organizations tended to be high (clients could be on maintenance over a long period of time with little demand that they change their pattern of usage). The results suggested that there was also low demand and low structure for the counselors. We infer this from the empirical finding that there were no relationships between counselors' perceptions of their jobs and measures that related to the quality of job performance. This absence of relationship between perceptions and performance has been found in other studies (e.g., James, Hater, Gent, & Bruni, 1978). It tends to occur because of conflicting or changing structure and demands, so that "correct" behavior becomes hard to determine. It can also occur when the job is very easy (e.g., low demand) and good performance is not rewarded differently from bad performance. Both of these were possibilities in the methadone maintenance adaptive programs. To look at this from a slightly different perspective, the counselors may have faced permanently conflicting demands in some of these agencies. The first was to reduce drug usage and otherwise cure clients. The second was to keep clients in the agency so that they would provide support for the agency. (Most public funding is done on "matrix" or head counts.) Since the goal of keeping clients in treatment through minimal demands is more easily achieved than curing them, the counselors may have chosen the logical approach. From a parallel process perspective, the counselors' ratings and their lack of relationship to other variables suggest that neither clients nor counselors hold treatment as a high priority in these situations.

ORGANIZATIONAL SUPPORT AND THERAPEUTIC PERFORMANCE

The study also dealt with agencies with high demands and high structure. One type of agency that had both was the drug-free–change-oriented agency. The goal in this type of agency was to eliminate substance abuse among its clients and to resocialize them so that they would no longer remain in the original environment. Besides having a high demand (abstinence from drug abuse), these agencies also had a great deal of structure, with mandatory attendance in counseling sessions and also mandatory attendance in resocializing treatment programs. In this type of agency, counselors' perceptions of job autonomy, leadership trust and support, psychological influence and work group cooperation were related significantly and positively to counselor efficiency, therapeutic performance, general satisfaction, and intention to remain in the job. Those measures that reflected agency support for the counselor in meeting high demands and using high structure were positively related to counselor satisfaction. That is, where the agency was perceived as providing support for meeting high demands and using a great deal of structure, there was more counselor satisfaction. This result generally confirms findings of earlier laboratory-based research that when clients' needs exceeded available resources and helpers were accountable for outcomes, helping was impaired (Adelberg & Batson, 1978).

The general results for counselor satisfaction described here may also apply to clients in high-demand situations with a great deal of structure. When the agency is flexible in helping clients to meet the demands, clients may have a better chance of succeeding. Part of an agency's flexibility can be provided by having individualized treatment plans for its clients that allow the counselor to tailor the treatment to meet the needs of a particular client. The negative aspects of this environment involve situations in which the counselors do not feel that they have enough support or enough autonomy to do their job. In an agency with high demands and a great deal of structure, if counselors do not have the flexibility and support to set reasonable goals, then they may become dissatisfied and tend to burn out. This may also occur with clients who are trying to meet high demands and structure but feel that the treatment agency wants too much from them or is not willing to take into account their individual needs.

The other type of high-demand–high-structure agency studied was the methadone maintenance, change-oriented agency. The demand in this type of agency was the eventual abstinence from all illicit drugs and complete resocialization so that clients could live and function in a drug-free community. This type of agency provided a great deal of structure in terms of therapy and resocialization programs and also provided a highly structured methadone maintenance program in which detoxification was considered one of the major goals of treatment. The results indicated that there were significant positive relationships between counselor climate perceptions and the availability of resources for counselors to use in helping their clients to reach agency demands. Negative aspects of the environment concerned the feelings of counselors that they could not meet the agency demands and that they were somewhat overwhelmed by them and by the lack of agency flexibility in helping them to meet the demands.

INTERPRETATIONS OF THE RESULTS

From the perspective taken here we can draw some general conclusions about how clients are affected by the agency. Our conclusions are based on our interpretation of the Methadone Maintenance versus Drug Free and Change Oriented versus Adaptive classifications in terms of our assumption of the central role played by the demands and structure provided by a helping organization. We believe that for both clients and counselors the type and strength of demands and the type of structure and support perceived has a major effect on clinical outcomes.

In low-demand–low-structure agencies, one key source of dissatisfaction among the counselors seemed to be the lack of client motivation. In terms of parallel process this suggests that we look at the degree to which the clients felt that they were committed to a realistic goal (demand) and the degree to which they felt that the agency structure was helpful to them in meeting the goal. The clients would translate their dissatisfaction with demands and structure into the interactional process with their counselor by not being very involved in the treatment process. This would then be reflected by counselors' ratings of dissatisfaction and low client motivation. It could also be reflected in the interaction between the counselors and supervisors. Of course, there could also be some self-selection by clients. People who did not want to quit using drugs could look for an undemanding program.

In high-demand–high-structure agencies the counselors were dissatisfied if they were unable to meet the high demands set by the agencies and to provide individual programming for their clients. A parallel process perspective would view the counselor–agency interactional process as mirroring the client–agency process. In a high-demand–high structure agency clients may have a difficult time meeting the demands and may feel the need for more individualized programming and help. Clients then reflect this resistance in counseling and counselors reflect it in interactions with their supervisors.

The detailed analysis of counselor perceptions provided by the IBR study is relatively unusual in the treatment organization field. We would suggest that this information can be of further value to the agency, which can also consider counselor satisfaction and perceptions as an indicator of the types of problems facing *clients* as they try to meet agency demands and try to use the agency structure to solve their problems. The parallel process perspective explains one way this may occur. This approach complements general systems ideas and organizational research that suggest that the counselors' loyalty may be torn between the agency and the clients as *different* interest groups (London & Howat, 1978). Such conflicts of interest add to counselors' role stress, which may then be reflected throughout the operational system and in counselors' perceptions and interactions with both clients and the agency. Other research suggests that such role conflict is a major problem in social welfare agencies (cf. Wills, 1978).

Application to Other Settings

In describing the previous research on drug treatment agencies we adopted a perspective that we feel is applicable to most helping organizations. To help make this generalization clearer we will provide an example based on our knowledge of clinical work in a correctional facility. In this setting it would be feasible to assess the *primary* and *secondary* goals of those working in the agency and then to determine if the goals held by different segments of the agency staff are congruent. Determining if the goals are congruent could be done by direct measurement or by observing the parallel process issues that arise between staff members. These would also provide an indication of how particular goal incongruences affect the inmate population.

PRIMARY AND SECONDARY GOALS

In a correction facility, the upper level administration would probably admit to having two definite sets of goals. The first is the rehabilitation of the inmates so that upon their release they would not commit antisocial acts in their community. The second goal would be to have a smoothly running correctional facility in which there would be a minimum of antisocial incidents (assaults upon other inmates and staff and attempted escapes). Depending upon how smoothly the facility is operating at any given time, the primary goal of the administration may change from rehabilitation to reducing current incidents of antisocial behavior. It might be noted that if the administrators of a facility were honest, they might admit that their primary goal would always be to run a smooth operation in which the number of antisocial incidents is low. The counseling staff may have the same two primary goals but may emphasize the goal of rehabilitating the clients since they may see this as the primary method for insuring that the agency will run smoothly.[3] The line staff in the agency (guards) would probably view maintaining a smoothly operating facility as their primary and most necessary goal and might or might not agree that the goal of rehabilitating the inmates is either feasible or desirable.

One manner in which these goals would come into conflict would be through the type of agency structure. The structure for change in a prison could be behavior modification and behavioral counseling. Let us say that a facility has a token economy and that the inmates' behavior is continuously monitored and reacted to by the guards, who use the token economy to reward appropriate behaviors, punish inappropriate behaviors, and to a great extent maintain control over the inmates.

Each of the three groups in the prison may see the clinical structure differently. The administration, having the two goals of rehabilitation and maintaining order, may view the behavior modification practices as being appropriate mechanisms for achieving both of these goals. The guards may see the behavioral structure as being helpful in maintaining their primary goal,

[3]Unfortunately, a review of research suggests that there are several factors that can make counselors see clients negatively, and, even in settings other than prison, counselors can become more concerned about manageability and less concerned about helping clients (Wills, 1978).

that of insuring order among the inmate population. The counseling staff may see behavior modification as primarily helping them to meet their primary goal of rehabilitating the inmates and also a useful system for providing them with feedback on inmate behavior. The counselors would probably also be interested in maintaining order, as it is reasonable to assume that few individuals enjoy working in an unstable environment.

CONFLICT OF ORGANIZATIONAL GOALS

A conflict of goals might arise if the counseling staff wanted to implement a program of decreasing reinforcement (fading) so that appropriate behaviors would receive intermittent reinforcement (the type of conditioning most resistant to extinction) and also to see how the inmates would operate with less control from the treatment staff. The guards may be very reluctant to give up their control and power over the inmate population, especially if they are concerned that this may result in the institution becoming less safe. The administration may also be reluctant to compromise the goals of maintaining a smoothly operating facility in order to provide for the rehabilitation of the prisoners. The notion of altering the behavioral systems being used may be interpreted by the guards and administration as fading control and by the counseling staff as fading reinforcement. The impact of having this type of goal incongruence may be that the guards may use the token economy inconsistently; that is, some guards may fade reinforcement and some may not, and the prisoners may then have a difficult time determining how the guards will respond to them at any given time. Since this will affect and establish guard–inmate conflicts, this type of conflict will be brought to the attention of the counselors in counseling sessions. The reaction of the counselors to this could be in terms of parallel process: to react to and come in conflict with institution policies and rules. The administration will experience this as the counselors expressing dissatisfaction, having a negative view of the psychological climate of the agency, and probably not complying with agency procedures and rules.

PARALLEL PROCESS ANALYSIS

If it becomes clear that there is dissatisfaction among the counseling staff with the rules of the agency, this can also suggest how the inmates are coming into conflict with the institution and its rules. Research has shown that clients often have quite a different view of the situation than do counselors (e.g., Dimsdale *et al.*, 1979). In assessing this, the administration may become aware that there is also incongruence between the goals maintained by various segments of the institution's staff. This incongruence reflects the utilization of the structure by different staff members in different ways. Therefore, efforts should be made to arrive at some degree of congruence and agreement between those working in the institution as to what the primary goals of the institution will be. There also should be an agreement on how each set of goals is going to fit in with different goals held by others working in the institution and how these goals will influence the utilization of the agency structure to meet the overall agency goals.

General Implications

There is no single way to apply an organizational perspective to management and research in a helping environment. However, a few suggestions can be made on the basis of present knowledge. No matter what the formal organizational structure is, the psychological emphasis should be on how the system actually works informally. It is important to determine how administrative interventions are perceived by those affected. In particular, emphasis should be placed on obtaining input from both counselors and clients.

We advocate a greater use of known organizational principles. However, helping organizations have some features that can set them apart from most other organizations. In particular they should be heavily service oriented and shallow hierarchically. That is, a high percentage of their employees should be involved in direct service delivery to clients. And no matter how large the organization, the administrative levels should never grow too far away from the front line, client contact function. Because client service is paramount, once counselors are trained, supervision should focus on counselor support and morale building rather than evaluation.

CLINICAL ISSUES

The issues of clarity of structure, counselor role definition, counselor autonomy, and client input are worthy of extra mention here. They are all important to the explicit clarification of how the client–counselor interaction will proceed within the organizational framework. We recommend that an extra effort be made to clarify expectations about the counselor and client roles. This should not be done in an authoritarian way. For counselors there should be an integration–training program when they join the organization. There should also be a continuing dialogue between management and counselors. Counselors should have a legitimate opportunity to influence the structure within which they work. Their areas of autonomy should be specified and protected. This approach will not only clarify roles but will improve morale and help prevent burnout. Counselors should be helped to take a similar approach with their clients.

For existing agencies of any size, one way to begin to implement some of the prior suggestions is to hold a series of discussions with counselors and clients on how to improve service. In order for this to be successful, management must be open to input. Questionnaires can also be developed *with the help of those who will answer it*. As in the IBR study described earlier, many scales are available to tap many aspects of counselor job perceptions and client viewpoints. Results should be fed back to the affected groups as well as analyzed by management and/or outside consultants.

The implication of parallel process for counselors is that they should become aware of how they are approaching their supervisor, what they want from their supervisor, and how they are feeling as supervisees. This is in part a function of how they are interacting with their clients and gives them information about the processes that their clients are going through. If their clients are showing consistent patterns, counselors can make the assumption that part of this is a response to agency goals and agency structure. If it is not a consistent pattern, the counselor can become better attuned to specific needs of a particular client and can deal with this in the context of the therapeutic relationship.

Supervisors can make similar inferences by attending closely to the behavior of counselors. For supervisors, this model provides a method for gaining insight into what transpires in the therapy session; with this increased understanding, supervisors can help their counselors or trainees to gain some insight into the dynamics of the therapeutic relationship. If supervisors note that there appears to be a consistent stance among their trainees or supervisees, then the supervisors can interpret this as a reflection of what clients are dealing with in terms of agency goals and structure, and they can make recommendations to modify programs and goals as needed.

The implications for the therapeutic process are fairly simple. The manner in which a client approaches the therapist, and approaches defining and dealing with problems, is a reflection of the basic manner in which that client deals with problems and people outside of the therapeutic situation. It is a reflection of the client's overall style and is something that the client needs to be made aware of in order to benefit from therapy.

ORGANIZATIONAL ISSUES

If the parallel process idea is applied to the area of organizational development, it can provide information that can be used in two ways. The first is in seeing if there are consistent counselor–client interactional processes. If so, this may reflect what is transpiring when clients attempt to meet the organizational goals. If there are consistent interactions that reflect clients' inability to meet therapist demands, then the clients may be in the position of being unable to meet agency demands. The second manner in which this can be used is in assessing the way that clients feel frustrated in utilizing, or being subjected to, agency structure. If there is a consistent pattern of clients being in conflict with the agency structure, then an appraisal should be done to determine if the various staff members in the agency are working toward the same goals. If not, there should be administrative interventions aimed at increasing congruence between staff goals so that clients are more effectively treated.

From a broader perspective, parallel process is one way of conceptualizing how relationships in one organizational dyad can affect other levels of the organizational system. It has been traditionally assumed that influence relationships follow formal organizational channels. For instance, it was assumed that leaders influenced subordinates. In fact, research now suggests that the "subordinate" has more influence on the leader than the leader has on the subordinate (James, 1981). The systems approach presented earlier provides a framework for the parallel process idea and extends it to suggest that client–counselor relationships will influence the whole organizational system, not just the supervisor in the case of counselor training. At the same time, the parallel process approach suggests an influence process that is not obvious from a more general systems approach. This is influence through style within linked dyads.

Summary

We have discussed a general approach to viewing interactions in helping organizations. An open systems model provided the general framework which encouraged us to consider the broad effects of any particular interaction as it ripples through the overall organization. Traditional organizational research focused our attention on issues such as the types of demands on, and amount of structure provided for, employees. The psychiatric training literature provided the idea of parallel process where client–counselor interactions can be mirrored in counselor–trainer interactions. We have used these approaches to provide an example of how viewing a treatment organization *as an organization* can be useful for those involved in service delivery. We also attempted to provide some suggestions which may apply to both general organizational research and to the management of helping organizations.

ACKNOWLEDGMENTS

Our thanks to Carolynn Crandall for typing the manuscript and to Thomas Ashby Wills for his comments on this chapter.

Reference Notes

1. Crandall, R., Bruni, J. R., Jr., Hilton, T. F., James, L. R., & Sells, S. B. *Perceived organizational characteristics of drug treatment units: Overview and preliminary results* (Report No. 79–18). Fort Worth, Tex.: Institute of Behavioral Research, Texas Christian University, 1979.
2. U.S. Department of Health, Education, and Welfare. *Data from the client oriented data acquisition process.* National Institute on Drug Abuse Statistical Series (Quarterly Report D-6). Rockville, Md: January–March, 1978.

References

Abroms, G. M. Supervision as metatherapy. In F. W. Kaslow & Associates (Eds.), *Supervision, consultation, and staff training in the helping professions.* San Francisco: Jossey-Bass, 1977.

Adelberg, S., & Batson, C. D. Accountability and helping: When needs exceed resources. *Journal of Personality and Social Psychology*, 1978, *36*, 343–350.

Cronkite, R. C., & Moos, R. H. Evaluating alcoholism treatment programs: An integrated approach. *Journal of Consulting and Clinical Psychology*, 1978, *46*, 1105–1119.

Dimsdale, J. E., Klerman, G., & Shershow, J. C. Conflict in treatment goals between patients and staff. *Social Psychiatry*, 1979, *14*, 1–4.

Ekstein, R., & Wallenstein, R. S. *The teaching and learning of psychotherapy.* New York: International Universities Press, 1958.

Glisson, C. A. Dependence of technological routinization on structural variables in human service organizations. *Administrative Science Quarterly*, 1978, *23*, 383–395.

James, L. R. A test for asymmetric relationships between two reciprocally related variables. *Multivariate Behavioral Research*, 1981, *16*, 63–82.

James, L. R. Hater, J. J., Gent, M. J., & Bruni, J. R. Psychological climate: Implications from cognitive social learning theory and interactional psychology. *Personnel Psychology*, 1978, *31*, 783–813.

James, L. R., & Jones, A. P. Organizational climate: A review of theory and research. *Psychological Bulletin*, 1974, *81*, 1096–1112.

James, L. R., & Jones, A. P. Organizational structure: A review of structural dimensions and their conceptual relationships with attitudes and behavior. *Organizational Behavior and Human Performance*, 1976, *16*, 74–113.

Katz, D., & Kahn, R. L. *The social psychology of organizations* (2nd ed.). New York: Wiley, 1978.

London, M., & Howat, G. The relationship between employee commitment and conflict resolution behavior. *Journal of Vocational Behavior*, 1978, *13*, 1–14.

Maslach, C. The client role in staff burn-out. *Journal of Social Issues*, 1978, *34*(4), 111–124.

Moos, R. H. *Evaluating treatment environments: A social ecological approach.* New York: Wiley, 1974.

Obitz, F. W. Alcoholics' perceptions of selected counseling techniques. *British Journal of Additions*, 1975, *70*, 187–191.

Olmstead, J. A. *Organizational structure and climate: Implications for agencies* (Working Paper No. 2). Washington, D.C.: Department of Health, Education and Welfare, 1973.

Rand, N. E. Organization development: A new modality for community mental health. *The American Journal of Community Psychology*, 1978, *6*, 157–170.

Reed, T. Outcome research on treatment and on the drug abuser: An exploration. *International Journal of the Addictions*, 1978, *13*, 149–171.

Sells, S. B. Organizational climate as a mediator of organizational performance. In E. I. Salkobitz

(Ed.), *Science, technology and the modern navy*. Arlington, Va.: Department of the Navy, Office of Naval Research, 1976.

Spaniol, L. A model for program evaluation in rehabilitation. In G. N. Wright & K. W. Reagles (Eds.), *Wisconsin studies in vocational rehabilitation* (Series 3, Monograph 19). Madison: University of Wisconsin, 1976.

Szapocznik, J., & Ladner, R. Factors related to successful retention in methadone maintenance: A review. *International Journal of the Addictions*, 1977, *12*, 1067–1086.

Thrasher, J. H., & Smith, H. L. Interactional contexts of psychiatric patients: Social roles and organizational implications. In J. J. Rossie & W. J. Filstead (Eds.), *The therapeutic community*. New York: Behavioral Publications, 1973.

Wills, T. A. Perceptions of clients by professional helpers. *Psychological Bulletin*, 1978, *85*, 968–1000.

chapter 20

Helpers' Motivation and the Burnout Syndrome

AYALA PINES

Introduction

As an example of how people may "burn out" in helping professions, consider the case of a probation officer. Elmar T. was born out of wedlock to an alcoholic mother and grew up in an inner-city slum. Because of his background he had great rapport with the juvenile delinquents on his case load. One of the things he liked most about them was their "street wisdom," which often was considered troublesome by other probation officers. Elmar developed an effective, behavioral program for motivating the truants on his case load to attend and perform well in school. His colleagues, who did not share his street background, readily admitted that he was more effective than they were with juvenile delinquents. They attributed his success to his understanding of their jargon and life-style, as well as to his ease in commanding an authoritative relationship with them. He himself attributed his success to his behavior modification skills, and to his "sensitivity to the tight line between being perceived as too weak or too controlling."

Unfortunately, Elmar discovered with time that unlike himself, many of the juveniles on his case load did not have the tenacity and long-term determination necessary to get out of the slum. While they were attending school

453

and performing well in their classes, they continued committing crimes on the streets. Thus, his basic assumption, that behavior modified at home and in school will ameliorate community behavior, was not supported. Elmar became disillusioned with the very basic premises of his work. He felt helpless to affect the lives of the youngsters on his case load and hopeless about their future, a bleak future he could see more clearly than any of his colleagues.

Elmar was also growing increasingly irritated with the bureaucratic aspects of his work. His program was effective in large part because it was simple: The youngsters received feedback from him in the form of relief from weekend public works duty, depending on their school performance that week. Once his program was adopted by the bureaucracy, however, it became complicated and cumbersome. Things that Elmar originally handled directly now required special forms and permissions. Some of the hostility that he felt the juveniles should have directed at the bureaucracy was unjustly directed toward him. He felt discouraged and resentful.

Elmar started drinking heavily, gained a lot of weight, withdrew from contact with his colleagues, and started cutting corners in his work. He would take the longest route possible to his field visits and stop to do his shopping on the way. A major crisis finally occurred when he did not show up for an important appointment he had with a juvenile and his parents because he had too much to drink over lunch and fell asleep. He knew he was in trouble and had to do something drastic. His decision was to start working part-time. It was not an easy decision, especially since he had doubts about his ability to manage financially. But since he had some money saved and was ready to lower his standard of living, he discovered that money created no problem. Since his "semiretirement" he has started long-distance running and participated in three marathons; he also started serious involvement with photography and liked to spend long hours in his darkroom. The time he spent in solitude enabled him to continue giving of himself emotionally when he was at work.

In Elmar's case a ghetto background, which was a major motivating force in his career choice, was also what enabled him to project himself into the situations of the juvenile delinquents on his case load and be exceptionally effective with them. Yet it was this projection of himself, and his faith in the basic premise that education provided a way out of the slum, that made him idealistic and thus particularly sensitive to discouragement when his helping efforts were not entirely successful. A similar relationship between career choice motivation and the burnout syndrome can be found in many case studies of burnout among helping professionals.

BURNOUT IN HELPING PROFESSIONS

Since the publication of the first articles on the subject of burnout (e.g., Freudenberger, 1974; Maslach, 1976; Maslach & Pines, 1977) the literature devoted to the syndrome has grown rapidly. The recent publication of five books on burnout in human services settings (Cherniss, 1980; Edelwich & Brodsky, 1980; Freudenberger, 1980; Pines & Aronson, 1981; Truch, 1980) indicates the importance of this process for the helping professions.

In our work on burnout (e.g., Kafry & Pines, 1980; Maslach & Pines, 1977; Pines, 1981; Pines & Aronson, 1980; Pines and Aronson [with Kafry] 1981; Pines & Kafry, 1981a, b, c; Pines & Maslach, 1978), we have observed human service professionals at work, collected extensive questionnaire data, and conducted personal interviews and workshops in the United States and abroad. The research has involved well over 5000 men and women: Americans, Canadians, Israelis, Australians, and Japanese. They represent a wide range of human services professionals: psychologists and psychiatrists, counselors, social workers, probation officers, and police officers, prison personnel; child care workers and teachers; medical and dental personnel; supervisors of various human service organizations; organizational development experts, and lawyers and politicians. In all these groups, we have found common aspects of the burnout phenomenon.

Based on our work, burnout is best defined as a state of physical, emotional, and mental exhaustion. It is marked by physical depletion and chronic fatigue, by feelings of hopelessness and helplessness, and by the development of negative self-concept and negative attitudes toward work, life, and other people. The negative self-concept is expressed in feelings of guilt, inadequacy, incompetence, and failure. While a similar cluster of reactions can be caused by any slow and gradual process of daily grinding, by any chronic stresses in the absence of challenge, significance and support (see Pines & Aronson, 1981, pp. 15–16), burnout is always caused by emotional stresses. It occurs as a result of intense involvement with people over long periods of time in situations that are emotionally demanding, which is characteristic of many helping professions. Burnout tends to hit hardest those persons who started out being the most idealistic and caring. As a result of burnout they start resenting their co-workers and their work and typically lose concern for their clients. Helpers who reach this state may come to treat their clients in detached and even dehumanized ways.

Some burned out professionals quit their current job and look for another one in the same field; others quit their field altogether and make a career change to a field that does not involve stressful work with people. Some professionals climb the administrative ladder as a way of avoiding direct client contact; others remain in their positions as "dead wood" doing just enough not to get fired. In all cases burnout represents a great loss for the individual, the organization, and society as a whole.

MEASURING HELPERS' BURNOUT

In our research, burnout was measured by a 21-item questionnaire representing three components: physical exhaustion (e.g., feeling weak, tired, rundown), emotional exhaustion (e.g., feeling depressed, trapped, hopeless), and mental exhaustion (e.g., self-perception of worthlessness, disillusionment, and resentment). Subjects were asked to indicate how often they had any of these experiences. Items were presented in random order and responded to on a 7-point frequency scale. The scale had the following anchors: 1 = never; 2 = once in a great while; 3 = rarely; 4 = sometimes; 5 = often; 6 = usually; 7 = always. The overall burnout score was the mean value of the response to the individual items. (An overall score of 4 was defined as a state of burnout.) Test–retest reliability of the measure was found to be .89 for a 1-month interval; .76 for a 2-month interval; and .66 for a 4-month interval. Internal consistency was assessed by the alpha coefficients for most samples studied; the values of the alpha coefficients ranged between .91 and .93. All correlations between the individual items and the composite score were statistically significant at the .001 level of significance in all the studies in which this scale was used. The overall mean value of burnout for all samples studied was 3.3. A factor analysis gave evidence supporting the notion that the questionnaire is assessing a single meaningful construct. Factor I, which accounted for 69% of the variance, had the highest loadings on feeling "burned out," "depressed," and "wiped out."

Construct validity of the burnout measure was examined by correlational analyses with several other theoretically relevant measures; for example, burnout was found to be negatively correlated with self-ratings of satisfaction from work, from life, and from oneself. In one study involving 322 human service professionals who participated in a burnout workshop in the San Francisco Bay Area, the following correlations between burnout and the three types of satisfaction were found: for satisfaction from work, $r = -.62, p < .001$; for satisfaction from life, $r = -.65, p < .001$; and for satisfaction from oneself, $r = .62, p < .001$. In all cases the highly significant correlations indicated that the more burned out the professionals were, the less satisfied they were with their work, their lives, and themselves.

Another consequence of burnout is job turnover. In a sample of 129 social service workers, burnout was strongly correlated with an intention to leave the job ($r = .58, p < .01$; Pines & Kafry, 1978). In a sample of 130 human service professionals who responded to the 20-item Hopelessness Questionnaire designed by Beck, Weissman, Lester, and Trenxler (1974); the correlation between hopelessness and burnout was .59 ($p < .001$). In a sample of 14 state residential facilities serving the developmentally disabled, "High Burnout Facilities" (HBF) had significantly higher turnover rates than "Low Burnout Facilities" (LBF): $t(12) = 3.00, p = .02$. The mean turnover rate for the HBFs was 48.8% compared with 17% for the LBFs. HBFs also had a significantly higher number of directors within the past 5 years than LBFs, $t(12) = 3.23, p = .01$. Mean tenure for a director in HBFs was 1 year and 10 months, compared with 4 years and 7 months in LBFs (Weinberg, Edwards, & Garove, 1979).

Burnout is also related to physical health problems. In a sample of 181 telephone operators (studied in collaboration with Jacob Golan; see Golan, Note 1) burnout was significantly correlated with poor physical health

($r = .46, p < .001$). In a study of 298 police officers (done in collaboration with Mimi Silbert; see note 2) burnout was correlated with such on-duty symptoms as headaches ($r = .32$, $p < .001$), loss of appetite ($r = .33$, $p < .001$), nervousness ($r = .38$, $p < .001$), backaches ($r = .20$, $p < .001$), and stomach aches ($r = .32$, $p < .001$). It was also significantly correlated with alcohol drinking ($r = .37$, $p < .002$).

GENERALITY OF THE BURNOUT PHENOMENON

Burnout was found to occur frequently and to a wide variety of people working in many of the human services. Table 20.1 presents means and standard deviations of the burnout scale for three rather different samples of human service professionals: teachers, police officers, and nurses.[1] For these three professions there are considerable differences in such basic characteristics as the ratio of men to women, job features, and job stress (for police officers physical danger is a major job stress, for teachers and nurses most of the time it is not a stress at all). Still, there is a great similarity in the reported experience of burnout. For example, for all three, police officers, teachers, and nurses, the symptom that contributed the highest mean to the composite burnout score was feeling tired ($\bar{X} = 4.2$ for police officers, $\bar{X} = 4.4$ for teachers, and $\bar{X} = 4.6$ for nurses). The third highest mean in all three samples was feeling physically exhausted (for police officers $\bar{X} = 3.9$, for teachers $\bar{X} = 3.8$, and for nurses $\bar{X} = 3.7$). For both teachers and nurses the second highest mean was emotional exhaustion ($\bar{X} = 3.9$ for teachers, $\bar{X} = 3.8$ for nurses). For police officers the second highest mean was feeling anxious ($\bar{X} = 4.0$), which no doubt reflects the stressful reality of their work environment.

The data in Table 20.1, together with findings from in-depth interviews and experiential workshops, indicate that burnout is experienced similarly in very different human service professions. We think that the causes of burnout are similar, because they are based in the conditions of helping relationships and the original motivation helpers had for their career choice.

Human service professionals share some motivations for their career choice with everyone who works. These include money, significance, autonomy, and social networks. Some motivations for their career choice are unique to human service professionals; these include working with people, helping meet people's needs, and making the world a better place to live in. And yet other motivations for a choice of a specific career are unique to the individual helper

[1]The sample of nurses ($N = 352$; 308 women and 44 men) was studied in collaboration with Mitzi Duxbury of the University of Minnesota as part of her national survey of turnover among nurses in intensive care units. The sample of police officers ($N = 267$; 316 men, 51 women) was studied in collaboration with Mimi Silbert as part of a survey of job stress in the San Francisco Police Department. The sample of 110 elementary school teachers was studied during professional inservice training in San Jose, California.

Table 20.1
Means and Standard Deviations of Individual Items in the Composite Burnout Score

Variable	Teachers (N = 110)		Police officers (N = 267)		Nurses (N = 352)	
	$\bar{X}$	SD	$\bar{X}$	SD	$\bar{X}$	SD
Tired	4.4	1.1	4.2	1.0	4.6	1.0
Depressed	3.4	1.2	3.0	1.2	3.5	1.0
Good day	3.0	1.1	2.8	1.0	3.1	0.9
Physical exhaustion	3.8	1.2	3.9	1.1	3.7	1.2
Emotional exhaustion	3.9	1.3	3.2	1.3	3.8	1.1
Happy	2.8	1.1	2.6	1.0	2.8	0.9
Wiped out	3.1	1.4	2.7	1.2	3.3	1.2
Burned out	3.2	1.5	2.7	1.3	3.0	1.3
Unhappy	3.0	1.2	3.0	1.1	3.2	1.0
Rundown	3.5	1.2	3.1	1.2	3.7	1.2
Trapped	3.2	1.7	2.4	1.4	2.7	1.4
Worthless	2.4	1.2	1.8	1.2	2.3	1.2
Weary	3.8	1.0	2.7	1.2	3.5	1.2
Troubled	3.4	1.1	2.7	1.2	3.2	1.1
Resentful	3.0	1.3	2.9	1.4	3.2	1.2
Weak	2.6	1.2	2.2	1.2	2.5	1.1
Hopeless	2.4	1.3	1.8	1.2	2.2	1.1
Rejected	2.6	1.2	1.9	1.2	2.4	1.1
Optimistic	3.2	1.4	3.4	1.4	3.2	1.0
Energetic	3.2	1.1	3.2	1.2	3.4	1.0
Anxious	3.6	1.2	4.0	1.4	3.6	1.1
Composite burnout score	3.2		2.9		3.2	

and often have to do with an influential person, a powerful event, or a special home background. As the following discussion will demonstrate frustrated motivation in any of these three categories is a common and powerful antecedent of burnout.

Universally Shared Work Motivations

MONEY AS A MOTIVATION

Everyone who works shares the hope or expectation of earning enough money to provide financial independence and a sense of security. Unfortunately, "enough money" is defined by comparison with a reference group similar to oneself. Martin Lipp (1977) noted that

The ideal income tends to remain elusively at ten to twenty percent above the current income, even at the very highest socioeconomic strata. Depending on income as the primary source of job satisfaction therefore tends to lead consistently to frustration: it's never enough. Paradoxically one's income becomes increasingly satisfying in inverse proportion to the importance attached to it. If you get pleasure from other aspects of your work, you are far more likely to be content with your income no matter how high or low it may be [p. 559].

In our own work it was repeatedly demonstrated, both in interviews and questionnaire research, that there is no direct relationship between burnout and satisfaction from pay. For example, in two studies (done in collaboration with Ditsa Kafry), one involving 205 San Francisco Bay Area professionals, the other involving 129 social service professionals, the correlation between burnout and satisfaction from pay was negligible ($r = .01$). There was also no correlation between satisfaction from pay and overall job satisfaction, liking of the job, and liking of the case load. The only significant correlation, found in the second study, was between pay and agency evaluation ($r = .26$).[2]

SIGNIFICANCE AS A MOTIVATION

Ernest Becker (1973) has argued that every person wants to feel significant: "He must desperately justify himself as an object of primary value in the universe; he must stand out, be a hero, make the biggest possible contribution to world life, show that he *counts* more than anything or anyone else [p. 4]." One of the primary motivations for people's work is achieving a sense of significance and purpose in their lives. Work provides an important function by structuring time in a meaningful way, but it also provides status and a sense of identity as a full-fledged member of society.

Even when a job is stressful or does not pay enough, if it provides the individual with a sense of meaning, he or she will not burn out. Professionals in the human services often report that in spite of the tremendous emotional stress involved in client contact, this is not what causes their burnout, because the same contact is also the most significant aspect of their work. Rather, it is the bureaucratic hassles, the senseless rules, and meaningless paperwork that cause burnout. "I like my field work" is a common statement made by welfare workers, social workers, and probation officers. "It is the reason why I chose this work in the first place. Going back to the office and having to waste long, desperately needed hours filling out dozens of forms that no one will ever read is what burns me out." David Harrison (1980) similarly found that burnout among protective service workers occurred in large part because the work lacked significance and opportunities for growth. As an example he reports

[2]All correlations reported are significant at or below the .05 level, unless otherwise noted.

that social workers often complained that their clerical responsibilities are overemphasized and their helper roles are underemphasized in statutory agencies.

Significance was repeatedly found in our studies to be a factor that reduced burnout. For example, in a sample of 277 professional women the correlation between burnout and work significance was −.23; in a sample of 205 professionals it was −.21. For all these professionals, feeling that their work was insignificant, that no matter how hard they tried they could not have an impact, was a powerful antecedent of burnout. Similar findings were reported by Barry Farber (Note 3), who studied the process and dimensions of burnout in 60 psychotherapists. He reported that most therapists (73.7%) cited "lack of therapeutic success" as the single most stressful aspect of their therapeutic work. In addition, 25% of the therapists in his sample admitted to occasionally feeling disillusioned with the therapeutic enterprise. Lack of therapeutic success often causes feelings of insignificance, disillusionment, helplessness, and burnout.

AUTONOMY AND GROWTH AS MOTIVATIONS

"There is in every organism, including man, an underlying flow of movement toward constructive fulfillment of its inherent possibilities, a natural tendency toward growth," wrote Carl Rogers (1961). Not every job provides opportunities for growth, and not all people expect to find opportunities for growth in their work environment. Yet for human service professionals job satisfaction often results from a feeling of psychological growth (Locke, 1976), whereas burnout, turnover, and low degrees of job satisfaction occur in large part because the work does not encourage or allow for the worker's psychological growth (Harrison, 1980). (In a sample of 724 human service professionals studied by Weinberg *et al.*, 1979, the correlation between burnout and self-actualization was −.30.) What most people expect of their work is to be able to do things their own way, to have control over their work environment, and to be paid enough to have independence and control over their lives outside of work. Thus, lack of control over one's work environment is a highly stressful experience. Studs Terkel in his book *Working* (1972) mentioned being oversupervised as a major source of stress in many occupational settings. Martin Seligman (1979) demonstrated how people develop learned helplessness and depression when they repeatedly undergo negative experiences over which they have no control. The exposure to uncontrollable events leads to motivational and affective debilitation.

In our work, frustration resulting from the lack of autonomy was found to be a common antecedent of burnout. In a study of 52 employees working within a large bureaucratic organization, the correlation between burnout symptoms and autonomy was −.35. In another study involving 205 professionals, the correlation was $-.28$; in a study of 273 professional women the correlation was $-.29$.

SOCIAL NETWORKS AS A MOTIVATION

Even when individuals are happily married, with a stable and supportive network of family and friends, work-related social contacts are still an important work motivation. All people share an explicit or implicit expectation that their co-workers will be exciting and friendly, will provide emotional support and professional challenge, will share one's view of the work and of the world in general, and will be fun to be with.

French and Kaplan (1973) demonstrated the positive relationship of work relations to both job satisfaction and the individual's general sense of well-being. Cary Cooper and Judi Marshall (1976) in their review of the literature relating to occupational sources of stress noted that a major source of stress at work is a poor relationship with one's boss, subordinates, and colleagues. Chris Argyris (1964) and Cary Cooper (1973) have both suggested that good relationships among members of a group are a central factor in individual and organizational health. And Myra Marx-Ferree (1976) pointed out that the work environment can be a clearinghouse of friendships and camaraderie. Friends make a job pleasurable, and social contacts are an important source of job satisfaction.

In a study involving 129 social service workers (Pines & Kafry, 1978), burnout was negatively correlated with work relations ($r = -.32$), social feedback ($r = -.36$), work sharing ($r = -.28$), and support ($r = -.29$). In another study involving 76 mental health workers (Pines & Maslach, 1978), it was found that when work relationships were good, staff members were more likely to express positive attitudes toward the institution as a whole ($r = .49$), to enjoy their work ($r = .38$), and to feel successful in it ($r = .31$). They also rated the institution more highly ($r = .41$), described their reasons for being in the mental health field as "self-fulfillment" ($r = .41$), had more "good days," and described the average schizophrenic patient in more positive terms. (All correlations in both studies are significant at $p < .001$.)

It is interesting to note when examining all the universally shared work motivation that stress literature has concentrated on the presence of negative conditions as a source of stress, and has largely ignored stress reactions that result from a lack of positive conditions. A study done in collaboration with Allen D. Kanner (1978) emphasized the importance of lack of positive conditions as a source of stress. The study demonstrated that lack of positive work features such as money, significance, growth, autonomy, and supportive social networks was significantly correlated with burnout. Also, the lack of positive work features was a source of stress independent of the presence of negative work features. Since these positive features are commonly shared motivations for work, not surprisingly their absence is a commonly shared antecedent of burnout for human service professionals.

Work Motivations Characterizing Human Service Professionals

The nature of occupational tasks acts as a screening device, attracting people with particular kinds of motivation and personality attributes. As Billingsley, Streshinsky, and Gurgin (1966) noted, most human service professionals are "essentially humanitarians. Their dominant approach is to help people in trouble [p. 53]." They tend to be "oriented more toward people than to things . . . and value themselves most through being sympathetic, understanding, unselfish and helpful to others [Registt, 1970, p. 11]." In almost every burnout workshop we have conducted (see Pines & Aronson, 1981, Appendix I), we found this to be true. When participants were asked why they chose their profession, their lists almost always included items such as, "I like people (or children, etc.)," "All my life people came to me for help," "I wanted to work with people," "I am a people's kind of person." Rosenberg (1964), who studied students aspiring for careers in the human services, likewise found that to them the ideal jobs "must permit [me] to work with people rather than things," and "give opportunities to be helpful to others." Kadushin (1974, pp. 701, 706) has termed this a *dedicatory ethic*, which elevates service motives so that the work is not seen as a job but as a calling.

CONDITIONS THAT FRUSTRATE HELPING MOTIVATION

Paradoxically, the desire to help troubled people may lead to frustration in real world helping conditions. Reid (1977) has noted:

> Throughout the professional socialization process the neophyte counselor is taught that the skills and the knowledge he is acquiring will have the direct effect of bringing about changes in the client's life. Case examples in the textbooks generally describe situations in which the helper successfully assists the client to resolve the issues with which he is struggling, because of the correct intervention at the proper time. Unfortunately, for a vast majority of the individuals and families who seek help the potential for success if often limited [p. 601].

The shock and disillusionment that occur when new helpers encounter real-world conditions have been described in several papers (e.g., Blau, 1960; Jacobs, 1968; Wasserman, 1970).

Another cause for unrealistic self-expectation is the "case load of one." Often part of the training for work in the helping professions involves working with one client. The young professional, often unfamiliar with typical conditions in helping agencies, invests everything he or she has, with a large dose of enthusiasm, and as a result manages to "do miracles." That case is forever after embedded in the helper's mind as an example of what he or she could do at the best. Unfortunately, one cannot give to 40, 50, or more service recipients what can be given to only one. Consequently, the self-induced ideal causes feelings of guilt and self-blame and becomes a powerful cause of burnout. There is indeed a good deal of evidence suggesting that changes in helpers' perceptions of their work occur primarily in the first years of actual clinical practice (see Wills, 1978).

CASE STUDY

I would like to present a case demonstrating the relationship between a work motivation that is shared by many human service professionals and the experience of burnout.

Carol, a special education teacher, always liked children, and for as long as she could remember thought about becoming a teacher. For 8 years she taught severely retarded primary school children. "I really like working with kids," says Carol, "and I liked the depth and close contact I had with the retarded kids. I was a combination parent–therapist–teacher." After 8 years she wanted a change and some new challenges, so when an opportunity came up to work with multiply handicapped children, Carol took it. In addition to being retarded, her new pupils had some other handicap and there were tremendous differences among the children in terms of their age, IQ, and combination of handicaps. At the beginning Carol was excited by these differences and challenged by the kids' problems. She had very high hopes: "These kids are extremely needy. When I started working in this class I thought I could attend to all these needs and have a real impact on their lives." In addition to her own hopes, there were the parents' expectations and needs as well as the administration's official objectives. "That was very scary for me, because I had all these objectives for the kids which were very hard to fulfill, given what was going on in the classroom."

"The room is dark, crowded, and noisy [there is another class taught by another teacher in the same classroom without dividers]. The physical environment is obnoxious. Toilet training is very difficult because there is no real toilet in the classroom, and there is no water to wash the kids' hands. The kids scream a lot when they need attention. There was never any relief from the stress, never time out. "I worked every day for 5½ solid hours. I felt like I couldn't breathe. Both my aide and I were constantly working. We hardly talked at all. There was always a crisis going on. It felt like a circus. I felt I could hardly keep up with things. And it was at that point when I was given another kid. That totally pushed me off. One day the bus driver pulled up and said, 'You are getting another kid tomorrow.' I had no say! The teachers very rarely have any say."

The hardest expectations were self-imposed, and Carol felt she was not fulfilling them. "While all the madness was going on in the classroom, I felt I should be able to keep up with it all, take care of the kids' physical, emotional and psychological needs and also have lessons and teach them. And I wasn't doing it. I wasn't fulfilling the objectives. It has been really horrible. It has been like a nightmare and I kept thinking maybe it is me. I thought I started to hate working with kids. They are too demanding. It is too hard to keep up with all their needs. I can't do it."

Carol started coming home from school totally exhausted, physically, emotionally and mentally. "I would walk in and collapse, sleeping 10 to 12 hr every night. I had a lot of back problems caused by tension. I felt depressed, trapped, and very inadequate. I felt scared. Teaching was something I loved and I was afraid that I would never love it again."

From Carol's case, and from hundreds of other cases we studied, it appears that frequently those very attributes that make some people choose work in the helping professions, and make them particularly qualified for the work, are also the attributes that make them more sensitive to the emotional pressures inherent in their work, and therefore more sensitive to the danger of burnout.

HELPERS' ATTRIBUTIONS ABOUT THEMSELVES

Any job in which a person tries to help other people involves special talents and abilities in relating to people. It can also involve high levels of emotional stress, depending on the particular demands of the job and the resources that are available to the professional (Maslach & Pines, 1977, 1979; Pines & Maslach, 1978, 1980). Since the most important instrument in the professional helper's work is the helper himself or herself, failure in a case may be regarded as a reflection on the helper's competence as a person (Kadushin, 1974). We found that professionals who utilize themselves as the helping instrument typically start out being very idealistic and caring helpers. Their idealism is often expressed in high work goals for themselves, for their service recipients, and for the organization. In a study (done in collaboration with Christina Maslach) involving 76 mental health workers it was found that the more personal rather than job-oriented the helpers' goals at work, the more they tended to appreciate opportunities for self-fulfillment at work ($r = -.25$), the more they tended to be involved with patients and the institution even after work hours ($r = -.55$), the less likely they were to "escape" patient contact by taking breaks ($r = .25$), and the more likely they were to utilize the support of colleagues in the form of consultations when having a difficulty with a patient ($r = -.27$). Unfortunately, it was discovered in the same study that the longer the helpers had worked with mental patients, the less conscious they were of their goals at work ($r = -.42$) and the less successful they felt in achieving goals ($r = -.42$). Feeling successful in achieving work goals was correlated with liking the job ($r = .28$), feeling successful with patients ($r = .26$), rating the institution positively ($r = .27$), and describing oneself very positively on several items of an Osgood Semantic Differential.

In a study done in collaboration with Steve Weinberg, Gary Edwards, and William Garove (1979) involving 724 employees of residential facilities serving the developmentally disabled, it was found that the major correlates of burnout were emotional overextension ($r = .42$), guilt ($r = .41$), overlap of stresses between life and work ($r = .41$), overload ($r = .39$), overcommitment ($r = .37$), conflicting demands ($r = .37$), administrative hassles ($r = .33$), decision-making difficulties ($r = .32$), and demand conflicts ($r = .30$). All these burnout correlates are directly related to the failure of meeting one's work goals. The result suggests that the more individuals value and attempt to meet their work ideals, the more likely is burnout. Thus, it is evident that although losing touch with one's goals is a symptom of burnout, having goals that are too high or unrealistic is a common pitfall of professional helpers and a powerful antecedent of burnout.

In summary, the desire to help, when blocked by real-world conditions or by clients' lack of success, may become a source of frustration. Moreover, to the extent that helpers are an important part of the helping process, they may feel personally responsible and incompetent when help does not succeed.

Work Motivations Unique to the Individual Helper

In addition to vulnerabilities, personal attributes, and humanitarian motives that they all share in common, people in the helping professions often have special empathy toward the particular group with which they chose to work. This empathy may be inspired by an influential person, their home background, or some special element in their personal history. The case of Elmar T., the probation officer, which was presented as an introduction to this chapter, is illustrative. In many cases of burnout one can find a similar relationship between the group helpers work with and some element in their background that consciously or unconsciously motivated their choice of a career in the helping professions. These personal histories, which make the professionals more empathetic, more caring, and often more effective (in great part because of that extra measure of empathy), also make them more likely to burn out.

A few examples of this double-edged relationship between helpers' motivation and the burnout syndrome can demonstrate the point. The following cases illustrate the fit of individual backgrounds to specific job choices, and the ironic relationship between that career choice and the burnout process.

A physiotherapist working in homes for the elderly, whose parents were killed in a Nazi concentration camp, chose his work because he felt committed to help old and lonely people, since he could never take care of his own parents. This empathy, which made him treat the elders under his care with great respect and affection, and made him their favorite, also made him experience great pain when witnessing the terrible conditions in some of the homes. Hardest of all was the thought that "This malnourished woman could have been my mother."

An office manager at a language school preparing foreign students for American colleges spent several years in Saudi Arabia. She knew firsthand how it felt to be a stranger in a new country, unfamiliar with the culture and its customs, and was very sympathetic to the difficulties of the Arab foreign students. Yet she had difficulty dealing with some of the cultural behaviors of the students. She was angered, in spite of her understanding, by students who refused to talk to a woman manager, and insisted on seeing "the real boss" (i.e., a man). When she told students that the tuition for a quarter in school was $400, she was furious with those who said, "I'll give you $200," even though she knew very well that the origin of the response was in the bargaining custom that was very acceptable in their culture. Actually, she felt that these cultural differences were more difficult for her to handle because of her particular sympathy with the foreign students.

A counselor working with sexually abused children who had herself been sexually abused; a recovered alcoholic treating alcoholics; a son of a deaf mother working in a school for the deaf and blind; an ex-prostitute working in the rehabilitation of victimized street prostitutes—all serve as examples of personal histories that motivated a certain career choice. Such personal histories intensify the helper's empathy and understanding of the client's perspective, but they also intensify the helper's pain and thus the likelihood of feeling discouraged. Psychoanalysts talk about therapist-related counter-transference as having a major role in the development of therapists' discouragement. Wile (1972) noted that

> A therapist is likely to feel unrealistically pessimistic about the therapeutic potential of patients who represent or remind them of unsatisfying aspects of his own life. This can happen in any of a number of different ways. The therapeutic relationship may recall or repeat occasions of deprivation and frustration in the therapist's past life. Certain patients may remind the therapist of a sibling, parent, friend, or perhaps even a previous patient, with whom he had had a mutually unsatisfying relationship. Or the patient may have problems similar to those that remain unresolved in the therapist's own life [p. 40].

Therapist-related countertransference is often viewed as a classical problem in the therapeutic relationship.

The sensitivities of human service professionals do not necessarily have to be seen as a problem. They can become a problem if not adequately dealt with, but they are also what makes certain professionals more caring, more idealistic, and more effective in their work. As noted earlier, it is the most idealistic and most caring professionals who burn out first. A sample of 111 teachers were asked to describe their level of idealism when they started working on a scale from 1 (not idealistic at all) to 7 (extremely idealistic). The mean initial idealism was $\bar{X} = 6.4$ ($SD = 1.6$). When asked to describe their current level of idealism on the same scale, the mean current idealism was $\bar{X} = 4.0$ ($SD = 1.5$). The loss of sensitive and highly motivated people may represent one of the highest costs of burnout, and it is clear that burnout has negative consequences both for professional helpers and for the recipients of their service.

Implications and Extensions

EFFECTS OF PROFESSIONAL EXPERIENCE ON THE HELPERS' PERCEPTIONS

One consequence of the burnout process is a change in helpers' perceptions of their clients and of their helping role. In a study investigating the characteristics of staff burnout in mental health settings (Pines & Maslach, 1978), it was found that the higher the educational level of staff members, the more the original reason for going into mental health work tended to be "self-fulfillment"; however, staff attitudes tended to become more negative with time. For example, staff attitudes toward patients changed negatively with time ($r = .24$). Highly educated staff members enter the mental health profession with high expectations but become more disappointed with time (compared to staff with less education) and increasingly come to view patients as weak ($r = .24$), apathetic ($r = .51$), and powerless ($r = .36$). They become pessimistic about the possible effect of their work and start to see little chance of curing patients ($r = -.25$.) They become increasingly tense ($r = .24$), introverted ($r = .27$), and distant ($r = .23$).

Similar results were found in a study investigating burnout in child care workers (Maslach & Pines, 1977). The higher the formal education received by the staff members (and the higher supposedly their expectation of the job) the more they came to dislike their job ($r = -.26$), to feel less successful in it ($r = -.33$), to feel that the worst things about the job were child related ($r = -.25$), to have more "bad days" ($r = .22$), to feel less conscious of goals ($r = -.23$), and to approve more of the use of tranquilizers to quiet children down ($r = .24$).

In both studies it was found that burnout often led helpers to focus on the negative aspects of the clients, to use derogatory language, and to withdraw both physically and emotionally from contact with clients. The process may therefore contribute to the negative tendency in helpers' perceptions that seems to occur during the first few years of professional helping experience (see Wills, 1978).

PREVENTION OF BURNOUT

Given the high cost of burnout in terms of turnover, tardiness, absenteeism, and poor delivery of services, organizations have a high stake in trying to prevent it. Unfortunately, some organizations try to do that by screening out those most likely to burn out, which is likely to cost them the loss of their best, most idealistic workers. Other organizations use the burnout process itself as a screening device (i.e., "let them burn out and quit; there are three people out there eagerly waiting for each position opened"). Instead of these negative ways of dealing with burnout, organizations should provide their staffs with such universally appreciated positive work features as adequate rewards, sense of significance, maximal autonomy, and good work relationships. In order to make helpers' humanitarian motivations an asset rather than a deficiency, it is crucial that they receive appropriate clinical education, on-the-job training, and ongoing support networks.

TRAINING

The clinical education received by helping professionals may build unrealistic expectations, and thus indirectly facilitates burnout. These expectations are encouraged by such things as textbook examples in which every intervention works, case loads of one, and the implicit assumption that the work itself will help the professional's own psychological growth.

In our workshops (see Pines & Aronson, 1981, Appendix I), we discovered that one of the best ways to help participants diagnose the burnout-causing stresses of their work is to ask them to write down their hopes and expectations when they chose their careers, as well as their goals in their current work. Often the elements that cause burnout most involve frustrated hopes and unfulfilled ambition. Jill Lésperance, a social worker, sees helpers as typically starting with unrealistic expectations, based on a romanticized picture of the helper's role, and a real lack of understanding of how people's troubles maintain a status quo in their lives. Because of these unrealistic expectations, they are more likely to burn out: "You feel powerless, useless, ineffective. It is very difficult to change family systems." In her own case, on-the-job training was very helpful.

> I always knew I was interested in people. I was touched by people's behavior and their motivation for behavior. During my training I realized how important it was to separate myself from the client, to realize when a button was pushed and deal with it so when a similar client came in another time it wouldn't happen. Through supervised role playing, videotaping and audiotaping of interviews I learned my role as a therapist. Through individual and group supervision I learned what parts of me were getting involved with the clients. I learned to recognize when I was overidentifying with clients or projecting myself on clients. The supervisory group challenged me: Why was I saying certain things and why didn't I say what I wanted.

> The resolution of my history was essential for me to be effective. You have to be accountable for your own behavior. It has to be conscious. You have to bring your beliefs into consciousness and awareness; that is what you are trying to do with others. You have got to be the role model. It is very important what you come with knowledge, experience, expectations—but it is much more important what you do with it. In my case the training and the ongoing active support groups, were crucial."

Kenneth E. Reid (1977), in his research on nonrational dynamics of the client–worker interaction, supports many of Lésperace's personal observations. In his article he noted that when the client and the worker come together in the helping relationship, both bring to that situation their total life experiences; personal baggage of values, prejudices, blind spots, weaknesses, and strengths; and a history of relating to others. According to Reid, it is the worker's humanness that "provides the ability to enter the client's life and assist him in the growth process. Similarly, it is this same humanness that may draw the worker into a destructive relationship with the person he is seeking to help [p. 601]." The process of professional training involves superimposing values, attitudes, methods, and skills upon this humanness. For example, the worker "is taught that he is to be nonjudgmental and not to force his personal values upon the client. He is encouraged to be objective and not to lose perspective by overidentifying or underidentifying with the client [p. 601]."

Although training can make professionals aware of the personal motivations they bring to their work, it is not enough. The evaluation of goals has to be continuous and an integral part of the helping process. One of the most effective ways for that process to take place is through support networks among colleagues.

SUPPORT NETWORKS AMONG COLLEAGUES

We have found repeatedly that burnout is reduced for individuals who have effective social networks or support systems at work (Maslach, & Pines, 1977, 1979, 1982; Pines & Kafry, 1978, 1981; Pines & Maslach, 1978, 1980). For example, the results of a study involving 531 preprofessional students, professionals, and postprofessionals between 17 and 87 years old indicated that the better the relations one had with co-workers, the less likely one was to experience burnout ($r = -.25$).

In another study involving 129 social service workers, five different features of a social support network were examined. They included social feedback, positive work relations, work sharing, support, and time out during periods of particular stress. All five were found to be associated with less likelihood of burnout (for social feedback, $r = -.36$; for work relations, $r = -.32$; for work sharing, $r = -.28$; for support, $r = -.29$; for time out, $r = -.27$). The multiple correlation was $R = .44$.

Social support networks at work serve a multitude of functions. When helpers encounter people in their work environment who fulfill these functions, they are protected from burnout and such support goes a long way toward reducing stress in their work. (For a detailed discussion of the functions of a social support system, see Pines & Aronson, 1981, pp. 124–132.) One of the important functions of any support system is listening. We all have occasions when we need someone who actively listens to us without giving advice or making judgments and who listens with understanding and sympathy. Another function is the sharing of social reality and the theoretical perspective in the work, as well as sharing in what is seen as important, what is unimportant, what is right and what is wrong, what is serious and what is funny. Technical appreciation is yet another function. It is important to receive technical appreciation and affirmation of competence for work well done, and it is important for the person providing this affirmation to be not only an expert in our field but also someone whose honesty and integrity we trust. Just as it is important to receive appreciation, it is important to be challenged at work. Challenge precludes the long-term risk of stagnation and boredom and assures continuous growth. Some of that growth can be psychological, with the helper being challenged to recognize personal motivations for work and learning to utilize them effectively in the helping process. In a study of 111 elementary school teachers the correlation between burnout and having technical support was $-.43$; between burnout and having technical challenge, $-.50$; and between burnout and sharing social reality, $-.43$.

One of the important ways in which an effective network of colleagues can support and challenge individual workers is by helping to develop and maintain the balance of "detached concern"; that is to say, the ability to be detached enough to be objective about the problem presented by the service recipient, yet concerned about the person presenting the problem. Harold Lief and Renee Fox (1963) coined the term *detached concern* for a stance in which the "empathetic physician is sufficiently detached or objective in his attitude toward the patient to exercise sound medical judgment and keep his equanimity, yet he also has enough concern for the patient to give him sensitive understanding care [p. 12]." Güggenbühl-Craig (1978) suggested that helping professionals lose their stance of detached concern when they are tempted to strive for power in the helping situation. He maintains that the root vulnerability of such a temptation is professionals' natural dread of encountering their own feelings of helplessness.

Maintaining a balance of detached concern requires a continuous struggle, a struggle that can be greatly eased by the help of sympathetic co-workers. Similarly, co-workers are best equipped to assist each other in making the important distinction between two categories of stressful work features: those that are under their control and can be modified to alleviate burnout and those that are an inherent part of the work reality and should be accepted as such. The two most common mistakes are giving up too early and hanging on too long.

It is also important for helpers to be aware of their long-term and short-term work goals and for those goals to be realistic ones for both the helpers and the recipients. Such goal setting is best done within a supportive and challenging network of colleagues. In our studies it was repeatedly demonstrated that burnout was less severe in those institutions that allowed staff to continuously develop new goals for themselves and their clients and to get feedback and support from co-workers.

CHANGING CONDITIONS IN THE HELPING ENVIRONMENT

Enlightened organizations can help prevent burnout by changing conditions in the helping environment, such as maintaining a manageable staff–client ratio, enabling flexibility in client selection, permitting time out, encouraging lateral job changes, and limiting involvement in stressful client contact.

Staff–Client Ratio

When case loads are exceedingly heavy, professionals who try not to compromise the quality of the care they provide can get extremely discouraged and frustrated. In one study (Maslach & Pines, 1977), for example, it was found that staff in child care centers with more children per adult liked their work less ($r = -.32$), rated their centers lower ($r = -.45$), felt less in control ($r = -.47$), and approved more of the use of tranquilizers ($r = .28$) and compulsory naps for children ($r = .34$). In another study (Pines & Maslach, 1978) it was similarly found that the larger the ratio of mental patients to staff, the more ready were staff members to quit their jobs if given the chance ($r = .46$), the more they tried to separate their work from the rest of their life ($r = .36$), and the more they viewed job conditions (rather than self-fulfillment or interaction with patients) as the best thing about their work ($r = .35$). Maintaining a manageable staff–client ratio enables helpers to provide the quality of care they feel their clients need, to do their best on the job, and to relate to their clients in a more complete and human way.

Flexibility in Client Selection

With their idiosyncratic motivations for choosing a career in the human services, professional helpers often have a corresponding set of strengths and weaknesses. Organizational flexibility that takes that fact into account in client assignment can change a source of stress into a source of strength for both the organization and the individual worker. For example, an Israeli anesthesiologist who had a "soft spot" for babies had great difficulty anesthetizing them in the operating room. For weeks following such an operation she would have nightmares in which she was haunted by dead babies with dilated pupils. Unfortunately, the hospital in which she worked had a strict rule concerning random assignment of patients to doctors and would not bend that rule. The stressful work with babies was the major cause of her burnout. As a result of her burnout crisis she had to leave work for a year. When she returned, the rule was still in effect: Employees were required to treat the patients to whom they were assigned. The organization would not change to accommodate her.

Lateral Job Changes

In every work setting there are certain well-recognized features that are more stressful than others. For example, in one social service agency 53 employees rated (on 7-point scales) the degrees of stress and satisfaction they received from various work activities. It was found that the most satisfying activities were providing technical guidance to other employees ($\bar{X} = 5.6$) and training other employees ($\bar{X} = 5.5$). The most stressful activity, by far, was providing information to the public ($\bar{X} = 5.5$). Not surprisingly, the most satisfying activities were negatively correlated with burnout ($r = -.27$ and $-.35$, respectively), and the most stressful activity was positively correlated with burnout ($r = .29$). In another study investigating burnout among mental health workers (Pines & Maslach, 1978), it was found that the more serious the mental condition of the clients (i.e., the higher the percentage of schizophrenics), the less staff members liked their work ($r = -.12$) and the less they were likely to view it as their ideal job ($r = -.35$).

When idealistic and highly motivated professionals take on a task that is known to be extremely demanding emotionally, it is best if that involvement is known to be time-limited from the start. In this way the professionals can throw themselves into the job, do their best, and then leave when the time is up, rather than leave as a result of burnout. Such lateral job changes may cut turnover rates in many highly stressful work environments.

Time Out

When helpers are under continuous emotional stress in their work, it is crucial for them to be able to withdraw temporarily from direct client contact when feeling strained and under pressure. In the child care study (Maslach & Pines, 1977), for example, it was found that when teachers could not take short breaks from "on the floor" work with children (to do such things as cleaning, food preparation, or paper work), they found themselves becoming increasingly impatient ($r = -.32$), strained ($r = -.29$), and irritable ($r = -.27$) at the end of the work day. In the mental health study (Pines & Maslach, 1978), it was found that staff who could afford to take time out from direct patient care (to prepare medication, etc.) felt they had more control during crisis situations ($r = .27$) and viewed patients as more capable ($r = .39$), reliable ($r = .26$), sane ($r = .34$), and understanding ($r = .29$), compared with staff who did not have such opportunities for voluntary withdrawal from stressful work. Time out gives the helper an emotional breather, an opportunity to restore a balance that may have been shaken by a stressful encounter or situation.

Stressful Client Contact

The number of hours professionals are involved in stressful client contact is frequently related in their sense of physical, emotional, and mental exhaustion. In the child care center (Maslach & Pines, 1977), for example, it was found that the more hours teachers worked on the floor, the more they were likely to experience a negative attitude change toward children ($r = -.28$). At the end of a working day they were likely to feel intolerant ($r = -.24$), moody ($r = -.22$), dissatisfied ($r = -.24$), and uncreative ($r = -.34$). Another revealing finding was the fact that on vacation days teachers tended to engage less often in child-related activities ($r = -.25$). Thus, it seems likely that organizations can help prevent burnout by limiting the involvement of their staff in particularly stressful client contact. The psychoanalyst Herbert Freudenberger (1975) described the common practices of double shifts and frequent overtime work as emotionally damaging practices that can result in entire organizations burning out.

SUGGESTIONS FOR FURTHER RESEARCH

Future research should explore the causal relationship between helpers' career motivations and the burnout syndrome. Such causal relationships can best be investigated via longitudinal studies in which helpers are followed from the time of their career choice through training, the reality shock of the first work experiences, the emotional stresses of the work, and eventually, for some, burnout. Such longitudinal studies can help differentiate between the effects of the three categories of helpers' motivation mentioned previously (i.e., those universal motivations that are shared by all those who work, those motivations that are shared by those who choose to work in the human services, and those idiosyncratic motivations unique to the individual helper) in terms of their effect first on career choice and eventually on burnout.

Studies are also needed to examine the relative effectiveness of various intervention strategies for reducing burnout tendencies. The ultimate goal of these interventions should be making the personal histories and motivations of human service professionals enhance their effectiveness as helpers without making them more susceptible to burnout.

ACKNOWLEDGMENTS

I would like to express my debt of gratitude to the following of my colleagues for their invaluable contributions to this chapter and to the whole of my work on burnout: Elliot Aronson, Mitzi Duxbury, Dalia Etzion, William E. Garove, Jacob Golan, Allen D. Kanner, Ditsa Kafry, Jill Lésperance, Christina Maslach, Mimi Silbert, Frank Tapia, Carol Wagner, and Steve Weinberg.

Reference Notes

1. Golan, J. *Attitudes, personal characteristics, and organizational factors and their relationship with absenteeism among telephone operators.* Unpublished M.Sc. thesis, School of Management, Tel Aviv University, Israel, 1979. In P. Belcastro (Ed.), Proceedings of the national conference on *professional burnout.* Southern Illinois University, Carbondale, Illinois.
2. Pines, A., & Silbert, M. Burnout of police officers. Manuscript submitted for publication, 1981.
3. Farber, B. A. *The process and dimension of burnout in psychotherapists.* Paper presented at the meeting of the American Psychological Association, Montreal, September 1980.

References

Argyris, C. *Integrating the individual and the organization.* New York: Wiley, 1964.

Beck, A. T., Weissman, A., Lester, D., & Trenxler, L. The measurement of pessimism: The Hopelessness Scale. *Journal of Consulting and Clinical Psychology*, 1974, *42*, 861–865.

Becker, E. *The denial of death.* New York: Free Press, 1973.

Billingsley, A., Streshinsky, N., & Gurgin, V. *Social work practice in child protective services.* Berkeley: University of California School of Social Welfare, 1966.

Blau, P. Orientation toward clients in a public welfare agency. *Administrative Science Quarterly*, 1960, *5*, 341–361.

Cherniss, C. *Staff burnout: Job stress in the human services.* Beverly Hills, Calif.: Sage, 1980.

Cooper, C. L. *Group training for individual and organizational development.* Basel: Karger, 1973.

Cooper, C. L., & Marshall, J. Occupational sources of stress: A review of the literature relating to coronary heart disease and mental ill health. *Journal of Occupational Psychology*, 1976, *49*, 11–28.

Edelwich, J., & Brodsky, A. *Burnout: Stages of disillusionment in the helping professions.* New York: Human Sciences Press, 1980.

French, J. R. P., & Kaplan, R. D. Organizational stress and individual stress. In A. J. Marrow (Ed.), *The failure of success.* New York: American Management Association, 1973.

Freudenberger, H. Staff burnout. *Journal of Social Issues, 1974, 30*(1), 159–164.

Freudenberger, H. The staff burnout syndrome in alternative institutions. *Psychotherapy: Theory, Research and Practice*, 1975, *12*, 73–82.

Freudenberger, H. *Burnout: The high cost of high achievement.* New York: Anchor Press/Doubleday, 1980.

Güggenbühl-Craig, A. *Power in the healing professions.* Dallas: Spring Publications, 1978.

Harrison, D. Role strain and burnout in child protective service workers. *Social Service Review*, 1980, *54*, 31–44.

Jacobs, G. Reification of the notion of subculture in public welfare. *Social Casework*, 1968, *49*, 527–534.

Kadushin, A. *Child welfare services.* New York: Macmillan, 1974.

Kafry, D., & Pines, A. The experience of tedium in life and work. *Human Relations*, 1980, *33*, 477–503.

Kanner, A., Kafry, D., & Pines, A. Conspicuous in its absence: The lack of positive conditions as source of stress. *Journal of Human Stress*, 1978, *4*(4), 33–39.

Lief, H. I., & Fox, R. C. Training for "detached concern" in medical students. In H. I. Lief, V. F. Lief, & N. R. Lief (Eds.), *The psychological basis of medical practice.* New York: Harper & Row, 1963.

Lipp, M. *Respectful treatments: The human side of medical care.* New York: Harper & Row, 1977.

Locke, E. A. The nature and causes of job satisfaction. In M. Dunnett (Ed.), *Handbook of industrial and organizational psychology.* Chicago: Rand McNally, 1976.

Maslach, C. Burned out. *Human Behavior*, September 1976, 16–22.

Maslach, C., & Pines, A. The burnout syndrome in day care settings. *Child Care Quarterly*, 1977, 6(2), 100–113.

Maslach, C., & Pines, A. "Burn out," the loss of human caring. In A. Pines & C. Maslach, *Experiencing social psychology*. New York: Random House, 1979. Pp. 245–252.

Marx-Ferree, M. The confused American housewife. *Psychology Today*, 1976, *10*, 76–80.

Pines, A. Burnout: A current problem in pediatrics. *Current Problems in Pediatrics*, 1981, *11*, 1–32.

Pines, A., & Aronson, E. *Burnout*. Schiller Park, Ill.: MTI Teleprograms, 1980.

Pines, A., & Aronson, E. (with Kafry, D.). *Burnout: From tedium to personal growth*. New York: Free Press, 1981.

Pines, A., & Aronson, E. Combatting burnout. *Children and Youth Services Review*, 1981.

Pines, A., & Kafry, D. Coping with burnout. In J. Jones (Ed.), *Selected readings in staff burnout*. Park Ridge, Ill.: London House Press, 1981. (a)

Pines, A., & Kafry, D. The experience of life tedium in three generations of professional women. *Sex Roles*, 1981, *7*, 117–134. (b)

Pines, A., & Kafry, D. Tedium in the life and work of professional women as compared with men. *Sex Roles*, 1981, *10*, 963–911. (c)

Pines, A., & Kafry, D. Occupational tedium in social service professionals. *Social Work*, 1978, *23*(6), 499–507.

Pines, A., & Maslach, C. Characteristics of staff burnout in mental health settings. *Hospital and Community Psychiatry*, 1978, *29*, 233–237.

Pines, A., & Maslach, C. Combatting staff burnout a in child care center. A case study. *Child Care Quarterly*, 1980, 9(1), 5–16.

Registt, W. *The occupational culture of the policeman and social workers*. Washington, D.C.: American Psychological Association, 1970.

Reid, K. E. Nonrational dynamics of the client–worker interaction. *Social Casework*, 1977, *58*, 600–606.

Rogers, C. R. *On becoming a person*. Boston: Houghton-Mifflin, 1961.

Seligman, M. *Helplessness: On depression, development, and death*. San Francisco: Freeman Press, 1979.

Terkel, S. *Working*. New York: Pocket Books, 1972.

Truch, S. *Teacher burnout and what to do about it*. New York: Academic Therapy Publications, 1980.

Wile, D. B. Negative countertransference and therapist discouragement. *International Journal of Psychoanalytic Psychotherapy*, 1972, *1*, 36–67.

Wasserman, H. Early careers of professional social workers in a public child welfare agency. *Social Work*, 1970, *15*(3), 93–101.

Weinberg, S., Edwards, G., & Garove, W. E. *Burnout among employees of residential facilities serving developmentally disabled persons*. Birmingham: University of Alabama, 1979.

Wills, T. A. Perceptions of clients by professional helpers. *Psychological Bulletin*, 1978, *85*, 968–1000.

PART VI

SUMMARY AND DISCUSSION

chapter 21

Directions for Research on Helping Relationships

THOMAS ASHBY WILLS

Introduction

What do we know about helping relationships? What more do we need to know? The chapters in this volume have addressed both of these questions. Basic research on clinical decision making has shown the advantage of formal decision procedures and also has shown various ways in which people may depart from optimal judgment procedures. Basic social-psychological processes seem to be relevant for professional helping relationships, and the evidence suggests that helper–client interactions are shaped by many of the same processes involved in general social interaction. Research on social networks has shown the substantial amount of helping resources available outside of professional helping relationships and has begun to clarify the specific aspects of help seeking in informal social settings. Knowledge of therapeutic relationships has been expanded considerably through recent research, and it is now evident that helping relationships involve some combination of facilitating processes (such as desire for personality feedback, convergence of helper and client belief systems, and interpersonal liking between helper and client) and inhibitory processes (such as threats to the client's self-esteem, reactance against influence, or limited communication).

479

Basic Processes in Helping Relationships

Finally, there is some evidence that a helper's orientation toward clients is influenced by the organizational context in which he or she works and that professional helping relationships involve several stressful elements, some of which derive from the altruistic motivations that led persons to enter the profession in the first place. Still there is more that needs to be known. In the following sections I review some commonalities in the contributors' work and discuss implications for further research on helping relationships.

Clinical Judgment

Decision making is a basic aspect of professional helping relationships, and the research reported in this volume has provided important findings about the process of clinical judgment. These findings raise a number of questions concerning how decisions are commonly made in clinical settings. One point that is not in question is whether formal decision procedures (based on a linear additive model) are effective; as Dawes has noted (see Chapter 3), superiority of formal decision procedures has been found in every study that has examined the issue. What is not known at this time is why formal procedures are not used more. Despite the compelling evidence in favor of formal decision procedures and the simplicity of such procedures, to the present day there is little indication that they are widely used, and the literature continues to show fundamental misconceptions of the nature of decision making, as in statements to the effect that "we're not dealing with a group but with an individual person" (e.g., Gabinet, 1981). Meehl's (1973) trenchant paper on case conferences remains the most thorough discussion of how clinical decisions are actually made, and there is no reason to believe that the errors Meehl noted are not continuing today. Indeed, a promising topic for research on clinical judgment is an investigation of the sources of resistance to formal decision procedures. What is it about such procedures that evoke antipathy? Is it because they are perceived to require more effort, or abstruse mathematical ability? Is it that formal decisions continue to be perceived as less effective, despite all the evidence to the contrary? Conversely, it would be informative to know what the perceived advantages of informal decision making are: whether it is perceived by clinicians as more humane, more sophisticated, requiring more "insight," or simply as involving less effort. It is possible that the apparent resistance to mathematical decision tools could be dissolved during clinical training by a brief seminar on how to use them and why they are effective; yet it is conceivable that there are strong sources of resistance to formal decision making, and if so, it would be important to know more about the nature of those sources.

One hypothesis that would be worth pursuing is based on the recognition that informal clinical judgments are usually made retrospectively. Interpretations of causality for problems are made after the problem has developed and the client has appeared in the consulting room; explanations for behavior are made after the behavior has occurred; predictions are rarely made on the basis of explicit criteria or their outcomes tabulated systematically. A considerable body of literature has examined the phenomenon of *hindsight effects* in human judgment (e.g., Fischhoff, 1980) and has shown a marked tendency for people to discount the influence of outcome knowledge on their judgments, believing that they would have seen in foresight what was only evident to them in retrospect. I would suggest that people may be resistant to adopting formal decision procedures because they are (unwittingly) reluctant to give up the advantage of making decisions on the basis of unstated criteria and then coming to terms with the outcome with the benefit of hindsight. Formal decision procedures may be more threatening in the sense that they require explicit statement of the decision criteria and make it possible to detect errors in judgment. Interestingly, one of the major objections by clinicians and academicians to formal decision procedures is that they make errors (see Dawes, 1979). The fact that the objectors seem unaware of the existence of error in informal judgments seems to me to be of profound importance and worthy of further investigation.

It is also clear from recent research that clinical judgments involve factors other than strictly clinical criteria. In addition to the various types of heuristic tendencies in probabilistic decision making discussed by Dawes, which have been little studied in actual clinical settings (although note progress in this direction by Arkes, 1981), it is evident that the clinician's personal liking for a client is an important factor in clinical decisions. As Fehrenbach and O'Leary have reported in Chapter 2, the variable of interpersonal liking is a basic aspect of decisions for intake, referral, and treatment. Their formulation of clinical judgment as a process of deciding about the client's treatability seems to fit the evidence fairly well. Further research on this issue will require multivariate designs to investigate the role of a client's (*a*) likability, (*b*) prognosis, (*c*) level of pathology, and (*d*) perceived manageability in the treatment setting. These variables have all been shown to be correlated in univariate studies, but a multivariate analysis, using techniques such as path analysis, would show the independent contribution of each variable.[1]

---

[1]The nature of these intercorrelations seems not to be widely appreciated. For example, Smith, Glass, and Miller (1980), in rating the similarity of helper and client, defined similarity in terms of "white, middle-class, well-educated, and mildly or moderately distressed clients [p. 62]." This produces a total confounding of social similarity with level of pathology, and makes any findings for this variable uninterpretable.

Processing of Clinical Information

It is equally important to pursue further research on the possibility that clinical training, professional helping experience, or simply occupying the role perspective of a therapist produces a dispositional bias in helpers' attributions about the nature of clients' problems. The available evidence, discussed by Batson, O'Quin, and Pych (Chapter 4) and Pelton (Chapter 5), suggests that attributional discrepancies may be more marked in social work settings (where situational factors are clearly an important component of clients' problems) than in the typical counseling or clinic setting. Yet again, methodological issues in the measurement of clients' attributions are important for interpreting the current evidence. For example, a study by House (Note 1) of 140 adult outpatient clients showed that rather than perceiving situational versus dispositional attributions as opposite ends of a single continuum, the clients actually perceived these as orthogonal factors, and in fact the absolute level of the ratings showed that clients perceived both situational and dispositional factors as important in causing their problems. Moreover, since studies of personality assessment have generally found Person × Situation interactions, rather than main effects, to be most important (see Jackson & Paunonen, 1980), it seems likely that people's attributions are responsive to this in some way, leading to the suggestion that there should be a careful assessment of possible interaction effects when measuring dispositional and situational attributions. Thus, further research will shed more light on this issue if multidimensional measures of clients' attributions are obtained.[2]

Research comparing helpers' and clients' attributions will need also to pay careful attention to methods of data analysis. An illustration is provided by reanalyses of data from the Rubenstein and Bloch (1978) study, the only one to date that has obtained helper and client judgments on a number of dimensions. These data admit of somewhat different conclusions depending on which analytic approach is pursued. The reanalysis by Pelton (Chapter 5) examined the overall distribution of attributions about intrapersonal problems and found a marked discrepancy between intrapersonal attributions by social workers (made for 78% of cases) and by clients (made by 42% of cases). A more precise analysis, however, is based on the frequencies of specific attributional combinations in worker–client dyads, examining the frequencies with which worker and client, respectively, make a specific type of attribution about a particular client. Because of the statistical problem of correlated

---

[2]A related issue, equally important although somewhat outside the scope of the present volume, is the relative contribution of personality factors and situational factors (particularly economic variables) in causing psychological distress. The current evidence in this area is ambiguous (see, e.g., Dooley & Catalano, 1980; Dooley, Catalano, Jackson, & Brownell, 1981), and examination of the role of situational factors for problems such as child abuse and marital conflict would be informative.

proportions, this type of analysis requires use of the McNemar test (Hays, 1973, pp. 740–742). My reanalysis using this test, based on the data in Table 2 of the Rubenstein and Bloch (1978) study, found that there was evidence of some disagreement between worker and client with respect to situational problems, $\chi^2(1) = 7.5, p < .01$, with workers more likely to see problems when the clients did not. Highly significant disagreements were found, however, for other types of attributions, with workers much more likely to perceive interpersonal problems, $\chi^2(1) = 19.1, p \ll .001$, and to perceive intrapersonal problems, $\chi^2(1) = 14.5, p \ll .001$. The reanalysis by Batson, O'Quin, and Pych (Chapter 4) focused on the overall frequency of agreement versus disagreement between worker and client. Examining the pooled frequencies of agreement and disagreement, they noted that these were not significantly different for intrapersonal problems compared with either situational or interpersonal problems. This analysis, however, does not consider the exact nature of the disagreement between worker and client. My reanalysis, using the data from Table 2 of Rubenstein and Bloch's (1978) study, examines the distribution of different types of disagreement between worker and client: (1) the case in which the worker perceives a problem but the client does not, and (2) the case in which the worker does not perceive a problem but the client does. This reanalysis indicates a marked discrepancy between worker and client judgments for intrapersonal problems; there were 19 cases of Type 1 disagreement and only one of Type 2 disagreement. Furthermore, the distribution of types of disagreement differed significantly across problem areas, with much more Type 1 disagreement for intrapersonal problems compared with situational problems (19:1 versus 145:101). The distribution of errors for situational problems was significantly different from the distribution for intrapersonal problems, $\chi^2(1) = 8.7, p < .01$, and the distribution for interpersonal problems, $\chi^2(1) = 7.2, p < .01$. Thus, one could draw somewhat different conclusions from such data, depending on which analytic approach was pursued. In my view the analysis of specific worker–client disagreement is the crucial issue, and I would recommend this analytic approach for further research. By this criterion, the Rubenstein and Bloch (1978) data do show evidence of attributional bias on the part of the therapists.

Another methodological issue that requires attention concerns the sampling of attribution data. Measures of attributions about problems obtained after clients have entered treatment are problematic for several reasons. For one thing, there is a marked self-selection bias in clinic samples, because only a minority of persons experiencing psychological distress ever seek professional treatment (see Wills, in press). The attributions made by persons who seek professional help for their problems may, and probably do, differ significantly from the attributions of persons who do not choose professional treatment, hence generalizations about attribution processes based on data from clinic samples may be premature. In addition, the phenomenon of therapist–client belief convergence in psychotherapy (Beutler, 1981) introduces an additional complication, since clients tend to adopt the attitudes and values of their therapists, hence data on clients' attributions obtained during the course of therapy may be influenced to a considerable extent by convergence effects. Thus, in order to obtain accurate and unbiased measures of the attributions that people make about their problems, it would seem desirable to study a reasonably large and representative sample of untreated persons.

An aspect of clinical information processing that needs much more attention is the issue of what information about clients is sampled in the first place. A specific questions concerns the extent to which helpers tend to sample strengths versus weaknesses of clients. As has previously been noted (Wills, 1978), there are several aspects of the professional helping role that may lead helpers to focus on clients' weaknesses, yet there has been little systematic research on information sampling by working clinicians. This process is not without implications for the therapeutic relationship. Two earlier studies investigating client-perceived helpfulness found that more effective therapists were those who focused on the clients' resources rather than on their pathology (Mitchell & Berenson, 1970; Mitchell & Hall, 1971), and Mitchell and Hall (1971) found that this difference between more- and less-effective therapists could be detected as early as the first half hour of the first therapy session. Moreover, the research of Snyder, Ingram, and Newburg (Chapter 13) has shown that a history of receiving negative personality feedback—and, by implication, the anticipation of receiving more negative feedback in the future—serves as a deterrent to help seeking. Thus, there is a need for further research on the beliefs that potential clients have concerning their anticipated evaluation by a professional helper, the actual behavior of clinicians in sampling positive versus negative aspects of clients' functioning during initial and subsequent interviews, and the relationship of this type of therapist behavior to therapeutic outcome.

Discrepancy between Helpers' and Clients' Perceptions

A discrepancy between helpers' and clients' perceptions has been found across several different areas of research. As Batson, O'Quin, and Pych (Chapter 4) and Pelton (Chapter 5) note, there are often substantial discrepancies between professionals' and laypersons' attributions about the nature of problems. Recent studies of psychotherapy outcome (e.g., Shapiro *et al.*, 1976) continue to find little relationship between clients' and therapists' judgments of the success of therapy. Perhaps most important, investigations of perceived helpfulness have shown little or no correlation between helpfulness as perceived by clients and as perceived by therapists (Elliott, Stiles, Shiffman, Barker, Burstein, & Goodman, Chapter 15; Gurman, 1977; Lambert, DeJulio,

& Stein, 1978). It is evident that when a helper and client participate in a therapeutic relationship they have remarkably different views of what is occurring in, and deriving from, the helping process. If anything, clients' perceptions tend to focus more on interpersonal aspects of the relationship, such as the respect and esteem that is conveyed to them by the therapist, whereas trained therapists seem to focus more on technical procedures or theoretical aspects of the progress of therapy. Most previous research has been conducted from the therapist's viewpoint, and the intriguing question for future research is: What is it that clients are perceiving? We need to know about the dimensions with which clients perceive helping and the way in which those perceptions articulate with those of the helper. Studies of helpers' perceptions show consistently that they perceive clients in terms of their treatability, success in therapy, or sometimes their manageability during treatment (Wills, 1978). Comparable studies of clients' perceptions of therapists would be valuable.

The importance of this issue is emphasized by the fact that clients' perceptions of the therapeutic relationship are at least as good, if not better, predictors than therapists' judgments. Studies from the "facilitative conditions" literature have found that client perceptions of helpfulness consistently correlate with independent measures of outcome, whereas measures of therapist behavior are not so related (Lambert *et al.*, 1978), and some of the work discussed in this volume (e.g., Pelton, Chapter 5) also suggests substantial validity for clients' perceptions. Although clients' perceptions are probably not immune to influences such as situational attribution tendencies or self-defensive biases, it is clear from all these considerations that measures of clients' perceptions should be an integral part of further research on helping relationships.

Structure of Clients' Belief Systems

Understanding of helping relationships will be further advanced by a detailed understanding of clients' belief systems. As DiNicola and DiMatteo (Chapter 14) and Schorr and Rodin (Chapter 8) have discussed, medical treatment is influenced to a considerable extent by patients' beliefs about treatment methods and alternative sources of treatment. Client beliefs are equally important in psychotherapy, where outcome is influenced by clients' expectations about treatment (discussed by Abramowitz, Berger, & Weary, Chapter 16; Wills, Chapter 17), their general world view (discussed by Lemkau, Bryant, & Brickman, Chapter 9), and their attributions about problems (Karuza, Zevon, Rabinowitz, & Brickman, Chapter 6; Fisher & Nadler, Chapter 7). Variables that need further study include clients' preferences for various types of treatment, the way in which clients' attributions shape their attitude toward therapy and their interaction with the therapist, and the manner in which client–therapist discrepancies in beliefs are dealt with over the course of therapy.

A comprehensive view of helping relationships also suggests that helping cannot be considered without an analysis of the help-seeking decision. Clients' decisions to seek professional help are clearly the end point of an extended process (see Wills, in press), and clients in the early phase of a helping relationship probably have a fairly clear view of why they sought treatment, of the availability or desirability of alternative coping resources, and of the way in which the help-seeking decision has affected their own view of themselves. Investigations of how various types of attributions about the nature of and solution to problems are related to help seeking would do much to clarify the selection process that guides some persons to professional helping agencies, some to informal helping resources, and others to various forms of self-help.

Rapid Development of Therapeutic Relationships

All of the work reported in this volume supports the proposition that therapeutic relationships develop quite rapidly. Fehrenbach and O'Leary (Chapter 2) found that therapists' perceptions of clients are essentially formed during the first contact, and a number of crucial client judgments, including the decision to continue or drop out from therapy, liking for the therapist, and expectation about the probable value of treatment, are largely formulated during the first two to three sessions of therapy (Wills, Chapter 17). This formulation suggests that further research should shift to intensive investigation of the early stages of relationship development to learn more about the determinants of clients' initial reactions to therapy and the rapid belief, expectation, and self-efficacy changes that probably occur during the first interview session and shortly thereafter. Perhaps it should be noted that this formulation construes helping more as an expectation change process than as a personality change process.

Previous research on psychotherapy has tended to focus on the outcome of therapy, and this is certainly a rational and reasonable approach to the investigation of helping. Yet it seems that we may ultimately learn more about helping by studying the early development of the helper–client relationship, focusing on the first few sessions of contact. Highly specific methodology (analogous to that used in studying fast chemical reactions) will be necessary to measure the information that helper and client exchange in the first interview, the momentary reactions that occur, the perceptions that crystallize in the midst of the ongoing interaction, and the shifts in expectation and attitude that occur within or by the end of the session. Analogue studies or process recall (similar to that employed by Elliott, Stiles, Shiffman, Barker,

Burstein, & Goodman, Chapter 15) may help to clarify how clients' perceptions of helpfulness are related to specific moments in the interaction, and continuous monitoring of therapist reactions may indicate the point at which a clear impression of liking versus disliking for the client is established. The yield from such studies will probably be a better understanding of the establishment of basic, enduring characteristics of the interpersonal relationship rather than momentary, transient reactions.

This perspective also suggests attempts to obtain empirical measures of what are posited to be systematic stages of therapy. Several contributors to this volume (Karuza, Zevon, Rabinowitz, & Brickman, Chapter 6; Schorr & Rodin, Chapter 8; Lemkau, Bryant, & Brickman, Chapter 9) have derived formulations of a helping relationship as an occurrence with definite stages that should be consistent across different helper–client dyads and/or types of therapy. At present, there is a need for research to quantify and test these formulations. Such studies would probably lead to a differentiated, developmental theory of helping relationships. This conception of helping is undoubtedly employed in practice by experienced clinicians, but has yet to be investigated through empirical research.

Interpersonal Liking

Another conclusion that emerges from recent work is that interpersonal liking between helper and client is not an epiphenomenon but a basic, and indeed crucial, aspect of a helping relationship. As Fehrenbach and O'Leary (Chapter 2) have shown, helpers' judgments about clients are strongly influenced by interpersonal attraction from the very first assessment session, and I have tried to show in detail (Chapter 17) how helper–client liking is related to therapeutic gain. Surprisingly, there has been little empirical attention to the determinants of liking in professional helping relationships, to the dimensionality of clients' liking for therapists—surely perceptions are more differentiated than a simple like–dislike reaction—and to the way in which clients' liking for professional versus nonprofessional helpers might differ. In addition, the area of professional training may benefit from the study of individual differences among therapists in the ability to establish a working relationship with a client. It seems that there are consistent differences in this ability (see Wills, Chapter 17), but further studies of the predictors of interpersonal skills are needed. It is not wildly implausible to predict that such skills are well established before a candidate enters clinical training (cf. Elliott, Stiles, Shiffman, Barker, Burstein, & Goodman, Chapter 15), and if so, more attention should be paid to research on selection of therapists. Again, it should be noted that the interpersonal skills involved in effective helping relationships may well be comparable, if not identical, to the social skills that are important for likability and respect in everyday social interaction. This is indeed suggested by the results of research on the helping functions of social networks (Moos & Mitchell, Chapter 10; Antonucci & Depner, Chapter 11).

Client Responsibility versus Dependency

The research reported in this volume has focused attention on the dimension of clients' perceived responsibility for problems. The work by Karuza, Zevon, Rabinowitz, and Brickman (Chapter 6) and Lemkau, Bryant, and Brickman (Chapter 9) has shown that it is productive to distinguish between responsibility for the problem and responsibility for the solution to the problem, and suggests that the latter dimension is the crucial one. This issue can be the basis for further research of several kinds, investigating the dimensionality of client-perceived responsibility, the nature of shifts in perceived responsibility over the course of therapy, the possible differences between clients' and therapists' perceptions of responsibility, and the relevance of attributional dimensions for matching of therapist and client. Research on this issue would probably best be combined with a comprehensive investigation of clients' perceived control and attributions about their behavior, for as Lemkau and colleagues, Schorr and Rodin, and DiNicola and DiMatteo have discussed (Chapters 9, 8, and 14, respectively), these variables may be of crucial importance for commitment to the therapeutic relationship and long-term maintenance of behavior change. It is known from studies using the Rotter internal–external locus of control scale that clients become significantly more internal over the course of therapy (see Strickland, 1978), but how this occurs has not been clarified, and it is not at all clear whether this effect is attributable to actions of the therapist or to cognitive changes that are largely client determined. It is striking also that this research has been conducted almost exclusively in settings in which the client has little or no choice over the type or conduct of therapy. The few studies that have actually offered clients a choice of treatment (Devine & Fernald, 1973; Gordon, 1976) have found that this variable improves outcome. Further studies examining the consequences of client choice of treatment or therapist for various dimensions (e.g., perceived responsibility for problem solution, perceived internality) seem a promising direction.

This issue assumes a particular importance on the research agenda because of recent findings about therapists' attitudes. The studies conducted by Fehrenbach and O'Leary (Chapter 2) in psychiatric settings, by Karuza and colleagues (Chapter 6) in social work settings, and by Baltes (Chapter 18) in gerontology setting, suggests that helpers may have somewhat positive attitudes toward client helplessness or dependency. The question is raised as to how the professional helping role is perceived by therapists, how expectations about responsibility are communicated in the context of an ongoing helping relationship, and how helpers respond to client dependency versus independence at various stages in the therapeutic relationship. Such studies would undoubtedly provide findings that would enable helpers to more effectively encourage client responsibility for problem solutions.

Convergence between Therapist and Client Belief Systems

The recent work has drawn attention to the importance of correspondence between therapist and client belief systems in helping relationships. This includes beliefs about the type of treatment (Schorr & Rodin, Chapter 8; DiNicola & DiMatteo, Chapter 14), and about general values and world view (Lemkau, Bryant & Brickman, Chapter 9; Abramowitz, Berger, & Weary, Chapter 16), beliefs that are relevant not only for the early stages of treatment but also for development of commitment to a therapeutic relationship. Understanding the structure of clients' belief systems and making client beliefs an explicit part of treatment planning seem to deserve more research. In addition, the general finding that therapist–client convergence in values is related to therapy outcome (Beutler, 1981) has profound implications for the study of helping relationships. Further studies are needed to determine the value dimensions for which convergence is most consistent, the relationship of helper–client liking to convergence effects, and the mechanism through which value convergence is related to outcome criteria such as self-esteem, self-efficacy, or client-perceived adjustment. It is evident that important cognitive changes take place during the process of helping, and it will be informative to have a more detailed understanding of how these occur.

Ambivalence about Receiving Help

The work reported here by several authors (Fisher & Nadler, Chapter 7; Lemkau, Bryant,& Brickman, Chapter 9; DePaulo, Chapter 12; and Snyder, Ingram,& Newburg, Chapter 13) provides a new perspective on helping relationships by delineating the ambivalence with which persons approach the helping process. Their work has shown that prospective help seekers consider the self-threatening aspects of receiving assistance as well as the possible benefits, and the ultimate decision to seek help is by no means a simple one. These authors have shown that a number of personality and situational variables affect the way in which helping is viewed by the client, and emphasize the nature of a helping relationship as a forum in which persons seek enhancement of self-esteem. It will be interesting to investigate how clients' beliefs about their problems are related to help-seeking decisions and reactions to help and to observe how therapists in various settings deal with the self-threatening aspects of the helping relationship. It would also be informative to pursue some of the paradoxical aspects of helping indicated by Fisher's work (Chapter 7) on the self-esteem variable, which showed that (*a*) clients with low self-esteem were more likely to respond positively to help, and (*b*) were not as threatened by receiving help, but that (*c*) aid that was not as self-threatening tended to elicit dependence on the helper. How this paradox is typically resolved in clinical settings with various types of clients is an issue with significant theoretical implications.

Dimensions of Helpfulness

One of the contributions of research on social support (discussed by Moos & Mitchell in Chapter 10 and Antonucci & Depner in Chapter 11) is a sharply defined model of the different functions of helping, which include self-enhancement, social affirmation, emotional support, companionship, cognitive guidance, and material assistance. This work suggests several ways to investigate in more detail the relative importance of different functions in professional helping relationships, perhaps using methods similar to those developed by Elliott and colleagues (see Chapter 15) to study client-perceived helpfulness. My own inclination is to view helping relationships in terms of a unitary helping process, and I think there are grounds for expecting self-esteem enhancement to be the major element of this process. Yet at the same time it seems necessary to recognize that people may seek help for a wide variety of different reasons and that the relevant function(s) of helping may differ considerably depending on the needs of individual clients at particular stages in the life cycle. Certainly this seems implied by the evidence on therapy duration and outcome (Smith, Glass, & Miller, 1980), showing that most clients improve significantly in just a few sessions; deep-seated personality change in a couple of hours seems unlikely, and the most probable explanation for this finding is that it includes a large proportion of clients who seek help for resolution of situational problems, for a brief moment of emotional support during crisis, or simply to assure themselves that they are not crazy. The literature on social support, although still developing, suggests that various functions of social support are relevant for clients with different types of problems (e.g., divorce versus alcoholism) and at different stages of the life cycle (e.g., job entry versus retirement). Use of this paradigm for research on helping seems likely to provide many useful findings on how to direct specific helping methods to particular types of persons.

Social Support and Therapy Outcome

The social support research is also quite informative in another respect, for it shows clearly the amount of help that is available—and used—apart from professional helping resources. The implications of this work for psychotherapy outcome research are straightforward, pointing to the necessity of including measurements of informal helping (from family, friends, physicians, ministers) in addition to that obtained from the professional therapist. Informal support may act to potentiate the effects of therapy, and accordingly, inclusion of extratherapy support measures may enable researchers to account for more of the variance in outcome. Another important methodological issue is the possibility of *interactions* between treatment method and informal help seeking. This is no idle speculation, for a recent study by Cross, Sheehan, and Khan (1980) showed that clients in a behavior therapy condition sought more extratherapy support than did clients in an insight-oriented therapy condition. (The authors speculated that the insight treatment had the effect of encouraging more independence by clients, and hence reduced dependence on outside help; unfortunately, there was no evidence to either confirm or disconfirm this suggestion.) Obviously, the existence of such interactions makes comparison of outcome for different treatment methods problematic unless measures of extratherapy support are obtained, and hence this procedure would seem a requirement for future outcome research.

Professional and Nonprofessional Helpers

Understanding of helping relationships will probably be advanced by detailed comparisons of professional and nonprofessional helpers. It is difficult to discard the belief that professionally trained therapists, who are carefully selected and trained over a period of years with a wide variety of clients, perform no differently in a helping situation than the average person off the street, but the current evidence has not supported this belief. I think there are some problems with the current literature, however. The available studies have largely focused on short-term outcome assessment, and long-term follow-up seems necessary to obtain an adequate test of the hypothesis of no difference between professionals and nonprofessionals. In addition, the outcome studies have typically been univariate, and it seems indicated for future research to assess a range of outcome variables in addition to global ratings of therapy success. In my discussion of nonspecific factors (Chapter 17) I have also suggested several ways in which professional helpers differ from nonprofessionals, and it would be informative to have more data on the self-esteem, self-attributions, and specific skills of clients in different types of helping relationships. It would be interesting to study the levels of perceived control among clients of professional and nonprofessional helpers, because clients of nonprofessionals may (*a*) be less intimidated by the expertise and authority of the helper, (*b*) be more willing to communicate any dissatisfaction with the therapeutic relationship, or (*c*) be more likely to attribute behavioral changes to themselves rather than to the influence of the therapist; all these considerations should lead to increased perception of control, and hence to better therapy outcome. Investigations of therapeutic interaction also seem worthwhile, including not only the therapist's focus on major problem areas (cf. Gomes-Schwartz & Schwartz, 1978) but also the client's perceptions of the helper as a person (with regard to competence, likability, values, and adjustment). I predict that such studies will show systematic differences between professionals and laypersons, although there will probably be many commonalities.

Influences from the Treatment Environment

A helping relationship does not occur in a vacuum, and the work of Crandall and Allen (Chapter 19) and Pines (Chapter 20) raises important issues for further research by showing how organizational and environmental factors may influence the helper, the helper–client interaction, or both. Professional helpers, like other employees of formal organizations, must respond to the obvious or subtle demands of their organization, and this influence may have significant effects on how therapeutic interaction is conducted. Considering the fact that many human service professionals work for local or state government agencies (with their formal bureaucratic struc-ture), the impact of organizational characteristics on the helper–client relation-ship probably is not trivial, yet this remains one of the least studied aspects of helping relationships. The research shows that helping motivation is not a constant force, maintained by some reservoir of altruistic drive, but is similar to other human motivations in that it can be strengthened or weakened by the environmental context in which the helper functions. As Crandall and Allen have noted, organizational demands are by no means wholly consistent, and serious role conflict decisions, in which professionals must reconcile judg-ments about client needs with the pressure of organizational demands, may be a frequent occurrence in some helping situations, producing a constant drain on the helper's energy. The research by Pines and colleagues has shown a number of ways in which long-term maintenance of helping motivation can be enhanced by factors in the treatment environment, and this topic seems a worthy avenue for further investigation.

Several aspects of the research discussed by Baltes (Chapter 18) and

Crandall and Allen (Chapter 19) also emphasize the fact that helping typically occurs within the context of an institution and that the requirements of the institution, as well as the needs of the client, may have a significant impact on the decisions that shape the day-to-day behavior of staff members. Previous research has indicated that professional helpers evidence a strong concern with clients' manageability—the extent to the client either fits smoothly into the institutional routine or presents difficulty in compliance with staff instructions and institutional regulations (see Wills, 1978). Moreover, the environmental and organizational perspective outlined by Baltes and Crandall and Allen draws attention to the possibility that institutional concerns (such as convenience to staff members) may shape decisions about patient care, rather than considerations of patient care shaping decisions about institutional matters. For example, an institutional regulation to serve breakfast in bed to all patients may make the management of meal service somewhat easier; yet the effect of such a policy on patients' dependency may not be optimal from the standpoint of helping. At present there is little research on how administrators and staff members make decisions about patient management. It would be informative to know more about the extent to which client-related and institution-related factors are involved in decisions about patient management, how basic patient management issues are viewed by staff members and patients, whether the organizational advantages of routinization of treatment are judged to result in a favorable cost–benefit trade-off when the overall effectiveness of treatment is summarized, and the extent to which staff members' actual behavior corresponds with institutional policy. This last issue is an important one, and there is no reason to expect a direct correspondence between formal policy and staff behavior on a day-to-day basis, especially for situations in which staff members face decisions about practices that make their job more convenient or enjoyable. The finding of Baltes and colleagues (see Chapter 18) that staff members spent more time talking to each other than to nursing home residents is relevant to this issue. It seems necessary to recognize that staff members' behavior is influenced by a number of factors, and there is a need for more research to delineate the nature of those factors and their relative effects in determining staff behavior toward patients.

Effects of Professional Experience on the Helper

Another topic needing further investigation concerns the effect of professional experience on the helper. The findings reported in this volume show lack of effects that might be expected, and also show some significant unexpected effects of professional experience. The studies by Elliott and colleagues (Chapter 15) have generally failed to find changes in helping communications over the course of clinical training, and although there is reason to believe that there are systematic differences between professional and nonprofessional helpers (Wills, Chapter 17), these remain to be demonstrated in replicated studies. Whether the skills applied by professional helpers are based on self-selection into the profession by "inherently helpful" persons, whether helping skills are developed in direct work with clients, or whether the skills used by helping professionals are simply a generalization of social skills learned in everyday life is an intriguing question and one that suggests several lines of research. In addition, the studies conducted by Fehrenbach and O'Leary (Chapter 2) and Pines (Chapter 20), consistent with other research on perceptions of clients, show that professional experience is associated with more negative perceptions of clients' personality characteristics and overall likability. How this occurs is largely unknown at present, and it would seem important for investigators to apply their research skills to identify the process or processes involved in this phenomenon. There is reason to expect that the major changes in helpers' perceptions of clients occur during the first year or two of direct contact with clients (Wills, 1978), and this would probably be the most fruitful period for investigation.

The Problem of Resistance

What I see as the largest gap in the current literature on helping relationships concerns the issue of client resistance. It is evident that there is a generalized concern among professional helpers with clients' manageability, resistance to influence, or lack of behavioral change (Wills, 1978), and the clinical literature is replete with practical suggestions about how to deal with client resistance (e.g., Wachtel, 1981). Yet we lack a basic theory of resistance, and I think that a sound theoretical formulation will probably be the key to advances in clinical applications. It seems unlikely that various types of client resistance (e.g., blocking, manipulativeness, lack of change, dropout from therapy) at different stages of treatment are a unitary phenomenon, but I think that the theoretical constructs proposed by the contributors to this volume may lead to a comprehensive formulation of resistance. Relevant constructs are psychological reactance (DiNicola & DiMatteo, Chapter 14), perceived control (Schorr & Rodin, Chapter 8), self-esteem maintenance (Fisher & Nadler, Chapter 7; DePaulo, Chapter 12), and cognitive factors such as beliefs about treatment or attributions about problems (Karuza, Zevon, Rabinowitz, & Brickman, Chapter 6; Lemkau, Bryant, & Brickman, Chapter 9). It is probably relevant to recognize, as Haley (1963) originally noted, that in the typical psychotherapy relationship there is a large imbalance of power and status (in favor of the therapist), and it is conceivable that a basic element in resistance is an effort by the client to deal with an unfavorable social comparison situation (cf. Wills, 1981). Whether this is an inherent and unavoidable aspect of any helping relationship, or a pattern of behavior evoked by particular methods of clinical practice, is a question to be examined. There should be careful attempts to distinguish between active resistance and simple lack of behavioral change, which seem conceptually distinct and may have different theoretical implications. Research on resistance would certainly benefit from basic studies of the prevalence and correlates of resistant behavior in psychotherapy relationships, comparable to the body of research that has been conducted in medical settings (DiNicola & DiMatteo, Chapter 14), and the possible role of situational, familial, and ecological factors would seem interesting to investigate. From a conceptual standpoint, it may well be that a better understanding of resistance will come about through a basic theoretical formulation of commitment, which almost by definition is the converse of resistance, and with a good theory of commitment (cf. Lemkau, Bryant, & Brickman, Chapter 9), new hypotheses about resistance may fall right out of the theory. Whatever approach is employed to study resistance, research in this area seems likely to advance our understanding of helping relationships considerably.

Reference Note

1. House, W. C. *Correlates of outpatients' attributions of their psychological problems.* Paper presented at the meeting of the American Psychological Association, Montreal, September 1980.

References

Arkes, H. R. Impediments to accurate clinical judgment and possible ways to minimize their impact. *Journal of Consulting and Clinical Psychology,* 1981, *49,* 323–330.

Beutler, L. E. Convergence in counseling and psychotherapy: A current look. *Clinical Psychology Review,* 1981, *1,* 79–102.

Cross, D. G. Sheehan, P. W., & Khan, J. A. Alternative advice and counsel in psychotherapy. *Journal of Consulting and Clinical Psychology,* 1980, *48,* 615–625.

Dawes, R. M. The robust beauty of improper linear models in decision making. *American Psychologist,* 1979, *34,* 571–582.

Devine, D. A., & Fernald, P. S. Outcome effects on receiving a preferred, randomly assigned, or nonpreferred therapy. *Journal of Consulting and Clinical Psychology,* 1973, *41,* 104–107.

Dooley, D., & Catalano, R. Economic change as a cause of behavioral disorder. *Psychological Bulletin,* 1980, *87,* 450–468.

Dooley, D., Catalano, R., Jackson, R., & Brownell, A. Economic, life, and symptom changes in a nonmetropolitan community. *Journal of Health and Social Behavior,* 1981, *22,* 144–154.

Fischhoff, B. For those condemned to study the past: Reflections on historical judgment. In R. A. Shweder & D. W. Fiske (Eds.), *New directions for methodology of behavioral science: Fallible judgment in behavioral research.* San Francisco: Jossey-Bass, 1980.

Gabinet, L. Comment on Jay Belsky. *American Psychologist,* 1981, *36,* 320–322.

Gomes-Schwartz, B., & Schwartz, J. M. Psychotherapy process variables distinguishing the "inherently helpful" person from the professional psychotherapist. *Journal of Consulting and Clinical Psychology,* 1978, *46,* 196–197.

Gordon, R. M. Effects of volunteering and responsibility on the perceived value and effectiveness of a clinical treatment. *Journal of Consulting and Clinical Psychology*, 1976, *44*, 799–801.

Gurman, A. S. The patient's perception of the therapeutic relationship. In A. S. Gurman & A. M. Razin (Eds.), *Effective psychotherapy: A handbook of research.* New York: Pergamon, 1977.

Haley, J. *Strategies of psychotherapy.* New York: Grune & Stratton, 1963.

Hayes, W. L. *Statistics for psychologists* (2nd ed.). New York: Holt, 1973.

Jackson, D. N., & Paunonen, S. V. Personality structure and assessment. In M. R. Rosenzweig & L. W. Porter (Eds.), *Annual review of psychology* (Vol. 31). Palo Alto, Calif.: Annual Reviews, Inc., 1980.

Lambert, M. J., DeJulio, S. S., & Stein, D. M. Therapist interpersonal skills: Process, outcome, methodological considerations, and recommendations for further research. *Psychological Bulletin*, 1978, *85*, 467–489.

Meehl, P. E. Why I do not attend case conferences. In P. E. Meehl (Ed.), *Psychodiagnosis: Selected papers.* Minneapolis: Univ. of Minnesota Press, 1973.

Mitchell, K. M., & Berenson, B. G. Differential use of confrontation by high and low facilitative therapists. *Journal of Nervous and Mental Disease*, 1970, *151*, 303–309.

Mitchell, K. M., & Hall, L. A. Frequency and type of confrontation over time within the first therapy interview. *Journal of Consulting and Clinical Psychology*, 1971, *37*, 437–442.

Rubenstein, H., & Bloch, M. H. Helping clients who are poor: Worker and client perceptions of problems, activities, and outcomes. *Social Service Review*, 1978, *52*, 69–84.

Shapiro, A. K., Struening, E., Shapiro, E., & Barten, H. Prognostic correlates of psychotherapy in psychiatric outpatients. *American Journal of Psychiatry*, 1976, *133*, 802–808.

Smith, M. L., Glass, G. V., & Miller, T. I. *The benefits of psychotherapy.* Baltimore: Johns Hopkins Univ. Press, 1980.

Strickland, B. R. Internal–external expectancies and health-related behaviors. *Journal of Consulting and Clinical Psychology*, 1978, *46*, 1192–1211.

Wachtel, P. (Ed.). *Resistance: Psychodynamic and behavioral approaches.* New York: Plenum, 1981.

Wills, T. A. Perceptions of clients by professional helpers. *Psychological Bulletin*, 1978, *85*, 968–1000.

Wills, T. A. Downward comparison principles in social psychology. *Psychological Bulletin*, 1981, *90*, 245–271.

Wills, T. A. Social comparison in coping and help-seeking. In B. M. DePaulo, A. Nadler, & J. D. Fisher (Eds.), *New directions in helping* (Vol. 2): *Help-seeking.* New York: Academic Press, in press.

Author Index

Subject Index